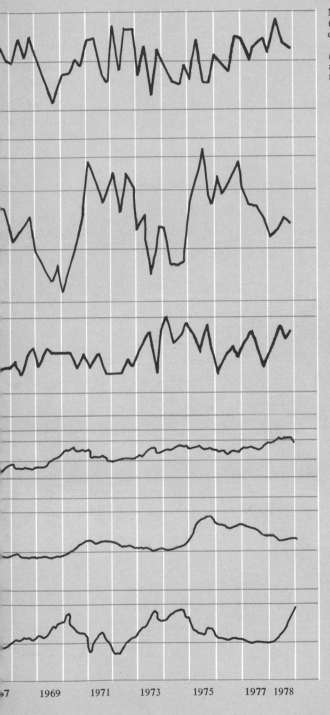

M1–B
(annual rate
of growth)

(3 months moving
average of monthly
rate of growth)

M2
(annual rate
of growth)

(3 months moving
average of monthly
rate of growth)

Consumer Price Index
(month-to-month
change)

Long Term
Interest Rates

Unemployment

Treasury Bill Rate

7   1969   1971   1973   1975   1977 1978

Money, Banking, and the Economy

Money, Banking, and the Economy

Thomas Mayer, *University of California, Davis*

James S. Duesenberry, *Harvard University*

Robert Z. Aliber, *University of Chicago*

W • W • NORTON & COMPANY
New York • London

W. W. Norton & Company, Inc. 500 Fifth Avenue, New York, N.Y. 10110
W. W. Norton & Company Ltd. 25 New Street Square, London EC4A 3NT

Library of Congress Cataloging in Publication Data
Mayer, Thomas.
  Money, banking, and the economy.
  Includes index.
    1. Money—United States. 2. Banks and banking—
United States. 3. Monetary policy—United States.
I. Duesenberry, James Stemble, 1918–   joint
author. II. Aliber, Robert Z., joint author.
III. Title.
HG540.M39 1981   332.1'0973 80–29109
ISBN 0-393-95121-9

2 3 4 5 6 7 8 9 0

Contents

Preface   x

PART ONE   The Financial Structure

1   Introduction   3

• Popular and Technical Definitions of Money   *4*   • The Functions of Money
5   • Specific Definition of Money   *11*   • Types of Money   *12*   • The
Cashless Society?   *14*   • Money and Near-Money   *16*   • Summary   *17*

2   The Financial System: An Overview   19

• The Role of Financial Institutions   *20*   • Portfolio Balance   *24*   • Government Supervision of Financial Institutions   *29*   • Summary   *33*

3   The Banking Industry   35

• A Sketch of Banking History   *35*   • Chartering and Examination   *40*
• Federal Reserve Membership   *43*   • Bank Capital   *44*   • Deposit Insurance   *48*   • Check Clearing   *55*   • Correspondence Banking   *58*   • Concentration in Banking   *58*   • Holding Companies   *64*   • International
Banking   *65*   • Social Regulation of Bank Loans   *66*   • Summary   *69*

4   The Banking Firm   72

• The Bank As Enterprise   *72*   • The Bank's Liabilities   *73*   • The Bank's
Assets   *81*   • Liability and Asset Management: Traditional and Current Approaches   *93*   • Bank Trust Departments   *98*   • Summary   *98*

5   Financial Intermediaries   101

• Thrift Institutions: A Profile   *101*   • Bank Competition and Regulation Q
116   • Insurance and Retirement Savings   *124*   • Mutual Funds   *128*
• Federal Credit Agencies   *129*   • Summary   *130*

6   Capital Markets   133

• Surpluses and Deficits   *133*   • Capital Markets: A Profile   *137*   • Short-
Term Security Markets   *138*   • Functions of the Short-Term Market   *140*
• Long-Term Markets   *145*   • Valuation in Long-Term Markets   *150*
• Specialization and Competition in Long-Term Capital Markets   *154*   • Term
Structure   *157*   • Valuing Wealth   *166*   • Summary   *170*

7   Central Banking   173

• The Central Bank: A Profile *173*   • The Formal Structure of the Federal Reserve System *177*   • The Informal Structure of the Federal Reserve System *184*   • Finances of the Federal Reserve System *188*   • Federal Reserve Independence *189*   • Summary *193*

8   A System in Flux   197

• Interest-Rate Ceilings *197*   • Interindustry Competition *205*   • Financial Reform: Problems and Difficulties *206*   • The 1980 Financial Reform *207*   • Competition in Banking *209*   • Modifying the Bank Regulatory Structure *210*   • Electronic Funds Transfer *212*   • Summary *213*

PART TWO   The Supply of Money

9   The Creation of Money   217

• Currency *217*   • Demand Deposits *218*   • Multiple Deposit Creation *220*   • Multiple Deposit Contraction *223*   • Leakages from the Deposit Creation Process *225*   • The Money Multipliers *228*   • Money-Supply Theory *230*   • The "New View" of Money Creation *231*   • The Stability of the Money Multiplier *233*   • Summary *236*

10   Bank Reserves and Related Measures   238

• Bank Reserves *238*   • The Reserve Base and Other Measures of Reserves *248*   • The Reserve Base, the Money Multiplier, and the Money Stock *250* • Summary *252*

11   The Measurement of Money   256

• Defining Money *256*   • The Vanishing Distinction between Demand and Savings Deposits *259*   • Credit Cards, Eurodollars, and Money Substitutes *264*   • Refining the Money Measurements *265*   • How Reliable Are the Data? *266*   • Summary *269*

PART THREE   Monetary Theory

12   Money, Interest, and Asset Prices   275

• The Meaning of Money *276*   • The Economic Impact of Money *277* • Transactions Demand for Money *279*   • Velocity of Money *282* • Transactions Demand and the Interest Rate *284*   • Money As an Investment *286*   • Total Demand for Money and the Interest Rate *290*   • Empirical Studies *291*   • Money Supply, Interest, and Income *294*   • Demand for Assets Versus Demand for Money *298*   • The Income-Expenditure Approach Versus the Monetarist Approach *303*   • Summary *304*

13   Income-Expenditure Theory   307

• The Structure of the National Income Accounts *308*   • Potential Output
313   • The Circular Flow of Income and Expenditures *314*   • Price Adjustments and Quantity Adjustments *317*   • Interest Rates and the Level of
Income and Expenditures *323*   • Prices and the Aggregate-Demand Curve
331   • Summary *337*

14   Investment and Consumption   341

• Determinants of Investment *341*   • Interest Rates and Investment: The
Investment-Demand Schedule *347*   • Residential Construction *351*   • Inventory Investment *356*   • Money, Wealth, and Consumption *357*   • Summary *363*

15   National Income   367

• Wealth and the *IS* Curve *367*   • The Equilibrium Price Level *371*   •
Short-Run Fluctuations in Output *374*   • Summary *378*

16   The Monetarist Approach   379

• The Quantity Theory—Basic Principles *380*   • Recent Developments of the
Quantity Theory *383*   • The Chicago Approach *384*   • Some Monetarist
Propositions *397*   • The Stability Issue *399*   • Summary *401*

17   Monetarism: Additional Models   404

• The St. Louis Approach *404*   • The Brunner-Meltzer Analysis *407*   •
The Real Balance Approach *409*   • Summary *417*

Appendix A   The St. Louis Model   418

Appendix B   More on the Brunner-Meltzer Model   421

18   The Monetarist-Keynesian Debate in Perspective   425

• Interest Elasticities in the *IS–LM* Model *427*   • Recent Models *428*
• Policy Differences *430*

PART FOUR   Inflation

19   Aggregate Supply, Aggregate Demand, and the
         Wage-Price Spiral   435

• Causes of Inflation *435*   • The Aggregate-Supply Curve *437*   • Real
Output, Employment, Prices, and Wages *442*   • Shifts in Aggregate Demand
454   • Money and Inflation *459*   • Interest Rates and Money Supply *460*
• Summary *461*

20   Inflation: The Recent Record   464

• How Inflationary Episodes Start: Five Cases *465* • Lessons of Recent Inflation *467* • Structural Shifts in the Phillips Curve *472* • Long-Term Structural Change *477* • Conflict between Full Employment and Price Stability *480* • Summary *481*

PART FIVE   Monetary Policy

21   The Goals of Monetary Policy   487

• The Goals *487* • Conflict among Goals *492* • What Should the Fed Do? *494* • Monetary Policy and Fiscal Policy *495* • Summary *497*

22   Tools of Monetary Policy   500

• Open-Market Operations *500* • The Discount Mechanism *504* • The Discount Rate *506* • Reserve-Requirement Changes *509* • Reserve Requirements: Some Controversies and Reform Proposals *510* • Are All Three Tools Needed? *514* • Selective Controls *514* • Moral Suasion *516* • Publicity and Advice *516* • Summary *517*

23   The Federal Reserve in the Money Market   520

• Target Variables *521* • Instruments *533* • Alternative Approaches *535* • Indicators *537* • The Federal Reserve's Policy Procedures *538* • Summary *543*

24   The Transmission of Monetary Policy   546

• Strength of Monetary Policy *546* • The Transmission Channels *548* • The Monetarist Transmission Process *549* • The Keynesian Approach *549* • International Trade Effects *559* • Expectational Effects *561* • Summary *562*

25   Monetary Policy and Resource Allocation   564

• Monetary Policy and Interest Rates *564* • The Criteria *566* • Consumption and Investment *568* • Residential Construction *568* • Impact on Governments *573* • Small and New Firms *574* • Impact on the Financial Market *575* • Income Distribution *577* • Credit Allocation *578* • Summary *580*

26   Can Countercyclical Monetary Policy Succeed?   583

• The Problem of Lags *584* • Rational Expectations *591* • Political Problems *598* • Summary *600*

27   The Record of Monetary Policy   603

• The Early Years   *603*   • Other Events in the 1920s   *607*   • The Great Depression   *608*   • Federal Reserve Policy   *611*   • War Finance and Interest-Rate Pegging   *618*   • The Mid- and Late-1950s   *621*   • The Last Two Decades   *622*   • How Much Has the Fed Learned?   *631*   • Summary   *632*

28   Alternative Monetary Policies   635

• Rules Versus Discretion   *635*   • The Monetarist Position   *640*   • The Countercyclical Policy Position   *642*   • The Easy-Money Position   *644*   • Summary   *645*

Part Five Appendix   Debt Management   648

PART SIX   International Money and Finance

29   The Evolution of the International Payments System   653

• The Gold Standard   *654*   • The Gold-Exchange Standard   *659*   • The Bretton Woods System   *661*   • The Switch to Floating Exchange Rates   *665*   • Summary   *667*

30   The Organization of the Foreign-Exchange Market   670

• The Market for Foreign Exchange   *672*   • The Relation between the Spot-Exchange and the Forward-Exchange Rates   *675*   • The Level of the Exchange Rate   *679*   • Central Bank Intervention in the Foreign-Exchange Market   *684*   • The Segmentation of National Money Markets   *686*   • The Balance-of-Payments Accounts   *687*   • Summary   *691*

31   International Banking and National Monetary Policies   694

• The Internationalization of Commercial Banking   *694*   • The Structure of International Banking   *697*   • The Growth of Offshore Banking   *700*   • The Monetary Implications of Offshore Deposits   *704*   • Reducing the Appeal of Offshore Banking   *706*   • Bank Regulation and Monetary Policy   *707*   • Summary   *708*

32   The Issues in International Finance   711

• Toward a New International Monetary System   *711*   • International Monetary Developments in the 1970s   *714*   • Optional Currency Areas and Monetary Unions   *716*   • The Choice between Floating and Pegged Exchange Rates *720*   • The System of Reserve Assets   *724*   • Gold As International Money *726*   • The Dollar and Other Fiat Assets   *727*   • The Role of International Monetary Institutions   *729*   • Summary   *730*

Index   733

Preface

There are many ways a money and banking text can be written, for the content of the course is limited principally by the hours available to teach it. We can perhaps best describe this book by explaining how we chose among the various alternatives for coverage and emphasis.

Our first decision was to offer the instructor the widest latitude in fitting the text to his or her preference. This brought us smack up against a critical question: how much space to allocate to institutional description as opposed to monetary theory and policy. Behind that question was our awareness of the "class struggle" that sometimes arises between instructors who prefer to stress theory and policy and a class that prefers to learn about bank management, capital markets, and the operations of the Federal Reserve. This conflict is less severe than it once was. With frequent shock waves of inflation rocking the financial structure, policy debates now focus sharply on the functioning of institutions as well as on the theories that influence the actions of monetary authorities. Thus, without skimping on strictly institutional material, we decided to go beyond merely describing the activities of banks, financial intermediaries, the central bank, and regulatory agencies to show the impact policy measures have on the financial sector.

The book, therefore, has taken the following shape. Parts One and Two, roughly the first third, deal with financial institutions, the creation of money and bank reserves, and the measurement of money. Part Three takes up monetary theory and is followed by a two-chapter part on inflation which, through its emphasis on aggregate supply, aggregate demand, and the wage-price spiral, provides a bridge to Part Five on monetary policy. As is customary, the text ends with a part on international money and finance, though for reasons we shall soon address, that part is more extensive than is usually the case.

Other considerations besides space governed the organization of the text. Recognizing that the financial system is experiencing such rapid change that what seems timely in the first years of the 1980s may be old-hat by mid-decade, we nonetheless decided to give full accounts of current policies and practices. Recent redefinitions of the monetary aggregates, the 1979 shift in Federal Reserve policy under Paul Volcker, and the March 1980 financial reform legislation all figure in the text. Most importantly, the economic and political factors underlying financial reforms including the problems of setting the right monetary targets and gauging lags are discussed at length, thus equipping the reader to understand new reforms as they occur. Our concern with the present is manifested not only in the policy sphere, but also in sections that cover aspects of the new banking technology such as electronic fund transfers and that elsewhere treat newer theories of economic behavior such as rational expectations.

Less an organizational problem and more a matter of controversy was how much monetarism to include in Part Four on monetary theory. Our solution has been to start with a Keynesian-neoclassical synthesis which makes allowance for many of the points monetarists have raised. This is followed by two chapters on the monetarist approach per se. The first sets forth the quantity theory as developed by Milton Friedman and the Chicago School. The second goes deeper into monetarism by taking up other theoretical models, including those of Don Patinkin and Brunner and Meltzer, and some empirical models including the forecasting model of the St. Louis branch of the Fed. This second chapter can be omitted without loss of continuity by instructors who want to devote less time to theory.

Having separate chapters on monetarism is, of course, not as desirable as presenting a generally accepted synthesis, but such a synthesis does not exist. We cannot pretend to students that economists agree on macroeconomics and monetary theory. But to reduce the anguish of this admission we start the theory section with a discussion of why economists disagree and end it by summing up the points at issue between monetarists and Keynesians.

A final comment on the distinctive features of our text. At one time international finance could be treated very briefly since it had little direct impact on domestic monetary institutions and policy. But this is no longer the case. The United States has become a much more open economy in recent years, and monetary policy is now influenced to a much larger extent by international considerations. Accordingly, after covering the evolution of the international payments system and operations of the foreign exchange market, we conclude with whole chapters on the structure of international banking and the most recent developments in the international monetary system.

The book is organized to permit flexible use in the classroom. In general, we have tried to write chapters so they are comprehensible to those who have omitted some of the earlier chapters. This was done at the cost of occasional recapitulation. Hence, it is possible to shift chapters around. For example, some instructors may want to take up the tools of monetary policy along with Part One, while others may want to shift the discussion of central banking from Part One into the discussion of monetary policy in Part Five. Others may want to take up monetary theory before the discussion of institutions in Part One.

Each instructor will, of course, have his or her own ideas about how much time to devote to the increasingly important topic of international finance. Beyond this, a short course stressing institutions rather than theory might well omit chapters 10 (to p. 248), 14, 16–18, 20, 21, 27, and 28, while a course that focuses on monetary policy might want to omit chapters 3, 6, 8, 10 (to p. 248), 17, and 20. By contrast, a course focusing on institutions could omit chapters 10 (to p. 248) 14, 17, 18, 20, 21, 27, and 28.

The allocation of various chapters among us was as follows: James S. Duesenberry took primary responsibility for Chapters 5, 6, 12–15, and 18 and Part Four on inflation; Robert Z. Aliber for Part Six on international finance; and Thomas Mayer for the other chapters. We are deeply indebted to a number of economists who read part or all of the manuscript and offered many helpful comments that sent us back to our desks to rewrite and to clarify. They are George Bentson, University of Rochester; William Brainard, Yale University; Karl Brunner, University of Rochester; Jonathan Eaton, Princeton University; Wilfred Ethier, University of Pennsylvania; Milton Friedman, Stanford University; Thomas Havrilesky, Duke University; Arnold Heggestad, University of Florida, Gainesville; Robert S. Holbrook, University of Michigan; David Laidler, University of Western Ontario; Edmund S. Phelps, Columbia University; James L. Pierce, University of California, Berkeley; William Poole, Brown University; and John Rutledge, Claremont Men's College.

We are also indebted to Steven Beckman of the University of California, Davis, for catching several errors and to our copy editor, Salena Rapp Kern, for not only spotting inconsistencies, but also coordinating our disparate writing styles. Donald S. Lamm at W. W. Norton did much more for this book than any author has a right to ask of an editor. Finally, we owe a debt to Marguerite Crown and to Ann Frischia for excellent secretarial services.

Davis, California   T.M.
Cambridge, Massachusetts   J.S.D.
Chicago, Illinois   R.Z.A.
November 1980

PART ONE

The Financial Structure

In Part One we shall do two things: lay the groundwork for the subsequent discussion and then look at financial institutions. Chapter 1 takes up the nature of money and how it functions. Chapter 2 looks at the role played in the U.S. economy by financial institutions, banks, savings and loan associations, etc., and explains how claims on them fit into people's portfolios, and why they are so extensively regulated.

The next four chapters look at private financial institutions in some detail. Commercial banks get two chapters, not only because they are so important, but also because most readers come into close contact with them. Other financial institutions are then discussed in chapter 5, while chapter 6 treats the money market and the capital market and begins the discussion of what determines interest rates. Chapter 7 then takes up the most important government financial institution, the Federal Reserve System. As will become apparent, the financial system is not working as well as it should, and over the years serious weaknesses have shown up. Hence, the last chapter in Part One looks at proposals for financial reform and at recently enacted reforms.

1

Introduction

It would certainly be an exaggeration to say that *all* our important economic problems are the result of malfunctions in the monetary system. But some of the most important ones are. Inflation is a monetary problem in the obvious sense that it means that our monetary unit, the dollar, is losing value. It is also a monetary problem in the much less obvious way: significant and sustained inflations have occurred only when the quantity of money has risen at a relatively fast rate. Hence, in one sense of the much abused term *cause,* one can say that major inflations are "caused" by a rapid rise in the money stock. Unemployment, while it has many nonmonetary aspects, is also closely connected with changes in the money supply. If the supply of money rises at a faster than expected rate, this lowers unemployment for some time, though not permanently, while a sharp decrease in the quantity of money usually increases unemployment for some time. While one may well argue about which one is cause and which is effect, every recession since 1908 has been associated with a decline in the growth rate of the money supply. And, as we shall show, the relative growth rates of the money supply in various countries are a major factor in determining their balance of payments positions and the exchange rates of their currencies.

Obviously, **monetary theory,** the theory that *deals with the relation between changes in the quantity of money, interest rates, and changes in money income,* is an important topic, and so is **monetary policy,** which is concerned with *how the quantity of money and interest rates should be managed.* This book deals with both of these topics.

But to understand how money and monetary policy affect the economy one must know something about banks and other financial institutions. This is so because banks create the dominant part of our money stock, and other financial institutions issue claims on themselves that in some respects are similar to money. And, of course, financial institutions are the main providers of credit. Beyond this, there is the fact that all of us have day-to-day dealings, whether as depositors or as borrowers, with financial institutions, and we should therefore know something about how they operate. For these reasons, chapters 2–8 of this book deal with financial institutions, particularly with banks. These chapters are descriptive rather than analytic because there exists no sufficiently specific theory that can

3

explain our financial system in adequate detail. Part Two of the book then deals primarily with how money is created. Part Three takes up monetary theory, Part Four inflation, and Part Five discusses monetary policy. Part Six then considers international finance, that is, how the monetary systems of various countries interact. But before getting at these things we shall take up in this chapter what money is and what it does.

Popular and Technical Definitions of Money

We have used the words *money* and *monetary* as though it were obvious what they mean, but this is far from the truth. Actually, a major reason why students often have difficulty in money and banking courses is that they forget that *money* has a very specific meaning in economics. By contrast, in normal conversation the term *money* is used to mean many different things. One of these is just currency, as in the phrase, "do you have any money with you?" But in modern economics, money is never defined solely as currency, because currency and checking deposits do the same thing: they pay for goods and services. In fact, only a small proportion of the dollar value of purchases, probably around one percent or so, is paid for with currency. Hence, if we were to define money as just currency we would have great difficulty in relating money to the bulk of all purchases that are made. And it is the very fact that money is related to total purchases that makes money interesting. Since currency and demand deposits do the same thing, and since we are interested in what money does, we must include demand deposits along with currency in the definition of money. One obvious objection to treating deposits as money just like currency is that one cannot make small payments, such as a bus fare, by check, and that even for larger payments checks are sometimes not accepted. This is perfectly true. But it is also true that if someone buying, say, $10 million of securities tried to pay by currency the deal would, in all probability, fall through. Besides, if we were to exclude checking deposits from the definition of money because checks are not accepted for small payments, we would also have to exclude some currency notes, such as $1,000 bills. In fact, it helps to think of money as essentially deposits, and of currency as the small change of the system. Although peasants like us use currency for a large proportion of our payments, this is not so for large transactors. This is brought out clearly in table 1.1. (Since this table is based on rather skimpy data, it provides three separate estimates for each figure.)

But while the popular definition of money as currency is too narrow to be useful in economics, there is also another popular definition of money that is too broad. This definition treats money as a synonym for wealth. Using a phrase such as "he has a lot of money," we mean to say that an individual is wealthy. If this particular usage were followed in economics, thus merging money with all other types of wealth, we would be ignoring the distinctive features of money. As will be shown later in

Table 1.1   Major Elements Is the U.S. Payments Mechanism, 1978

| | Percentage of transactions[a] | | | Percentage of combined dollar volume | | |
| | MOST | | | MOST | | |
	HIGH	REASONABLE	LOW	HIGH	REASONABLE	LOW
Cash	87.7	87.7	87.7	0.8	0.6	0.3
Checks	10.2	10.5	11.0	29.0	22.7	16.5
Credit Cards	2.0	1.8	1.3	0.4	0.2	0.1
Wire Transfer	b	b	b	69.8	76.5	83.1

a. Detail may not add due to rounding.
b. Less than one-tenth of 1 percent.
SOURCE: Ralph Kimball, "Wire Transfers and the Demand for Money," *New England Economic Review* (Federal Reserve Bank of Boston), March/April 1980, p. 8.

the book, it does make a difference whether wealth increases because the supply of money has increased or because, say, real-estate values have risen. But we cannot see this difference if we define money to be total wealth.

A third popular definition of money is to define it as income, by asking, for example, "how much money does he earn?" But defining money as income can be most confusing if we want to discuss, as we later will, whether changes in the money supply bring about equivalent changes in income. Moreover money is a *stock,* which means that it is a certain amount at any one moment in time, while income is a *flow* over time. If you are told that someone's income is, say, $5,000, you do not know whether he or she has a high or low income until you are told whether these $5,000 are income per year or per week. But if told that someone carries $3,000 of currency in his pocket, you do know that he has a large stock of currency.

Instead of defining money either so narrowly as just currency, or so broadly as to include all wealth, economists define money by its functions. Anything that functions as a medium of exchange or a standard of value or, according to many economists, as an extremely liquid store of wealth is considered money. But these functions of money need explaining.

The Functions of Money

So far we have defined money by listing the items that it includes. But this does not help us much in understanding what money really *is.* For such understanding it is better to define money as anything that fulfills certain functions. Money acts as (1) a medium of exchange, (2) a standard of value, and (3) a store of wealth. Anything that fulfills the first two of these functions is defined as money. (The third function is fulfilled by many other items besides money.) In discussing the functions of money we will deal with money as defined as currency and demand deposits.

Medium of Exchange

The medium of exchange function is an obvious one; we use money as an intermediary in exchange. Instead of paying each other with goods and services, we exchange goods and services for money, and then exchange this money for those goods and services we want to acquire. Such a round-about system of exchange is vastly superior to direct barter. It avoids the great disadvantage of barter, the need for a so-called double coincidence of wants. What this rather stuffy phrase means is that to effect barter we have to find someone who wants to obtain the goods and services we have to offer *and,* at the same time, can provide the goods and services we want to obtain in exchange.

In a primitive society with little division of labor, such a person may not be so hard to find, since only a few types of goods are being exchanged and much of the trading is ceremonial and governed by tradition. But in an advanced society with a myriad of commodities it is a different matter. A seller of steel who wishes to exchange it for, say, vanilla ice cream would have to look around a long time before finding someone who has extra vanilla ice cream and, at the same time, wants steel. By contrast, in an economy with money this exchange process is broken into two parts. The seller of steel first locates someone who wants steel and then someone who has ice cream to sell. It is much easier to locate two such people than to locate a person who just happens to combine both of these characteristics. Another problem with barter is the indivisibility of many goods. For example, a manufacturer of cars could hardly give a farmer, say, one three-thousandths of a car in exchange for a pound of butter.

The general idea that a developed economy could not function without a medium of exchange should be obvious, but let us analyze it a bit further. Such an analysis starts from the fact that resources can be used in three ways: to provide direct satisfaction, to produce other goods, and to search for information.[1] Simple, direct barter, such as swapping steel we produce for the ice cream we want, is a very costly system because it requires a lot of investment in obtaining information. We have to search, presumably a long time, until we find someone who both wants our goods and has the goods we want. A superior method is *indirect* barter. A producer of steel who wants to obtain ice cream may trade his steel, not directly for ice cream, but for, say, buckets. He does this because he knows that he is more likely to find an ice-cream producer who wants buckets than one who wants steel, while a bucket manufacturer is more likely to want steel. He could go even a step further and trade his steel, not for buckets, but for some item that he knows the bucket manufacturer wants more, say, aluminum for his new factory. Instead of a single trans-

---

[1] This discussion is based on Karl Brunner and Allan Meltzer, "The Uses of Money: Money in the Theory of an Exchange Economy," *American Economic Review* 61 (December 1971): 784–806.

action of steel against vanilla ice cream, the steelmaker may undertake a whole transaction chain.

The information needed for such a transaction chain is that the ice-cream producer wants buckets, the producer of buckets wants aluminum, and the producer of aluminum wants steel. The steel producer also needs information on the location of these people, and, last, but not least, information about the quality of aluminum, buckets, and ice cream so that he does not get stuck with any duds in this exchange process. Although all this information may well be less costly to acquire than discovering someone who has vanilla ice cream to trade and wants steel, it is still likely to be very costly and be a serious impediment to the division of labor.

But it is possible to economize on information costs by reducing the number of commodities used in transaction chains throughout the economy. The fewer they are, the less there has to be learned about the quality of the commodities used, as well as about the location and wants of various participants. With only a few goods used in various transaction chains, any given transactor is more likely to want the particular good one has to trade than would be the case if there are many goods used in transaction chains.

Fortunately a reduction in the number of goods used in transaction chains is likely to come about on its own accord. For trading purposes each good has particular information costs consisting of knowledge about who is willing to trade it, as well as knowledge about its quality. Such information costs differ for various goods, and the ones with the lowest information costs will be used for trading. As these goods are used more and more, participants in these transactions acquire more and more information about them, and this, in turn, further reduces the information costs of trading in these particular commodities as opposed to other ones. We have here an example of virtually unlimited economies of scale. Ultimately there is likely to be just one, or a handful, of goods that will be generally accepted in exchange. And they will be money.

For these reasons the invention of a medium of exchange ranks among man's greatest inventions. But even so, we do find barter used occasionally in a modern economy. One situation where barter may reappear to some extent is if the monetary system breaks down into a gigantic inflation, say with prices doubling every day. In this case money is such a poor store of value that even the very short period of time that necessarily must elapse between receiving and spending the money is too long to hold it, so that some, though certainly not all, transactions are conducted by barter.

A more common reason for barter is that prices are not allowed to adjust to equilibrium. There may be price control, and demand may substantially exceed supply at the controlled prices. In this case sellers may be reluctant to sell their goods for less money than they are worth, but they may be willing to exchange them for other goods since price controls usually do not apply to barter. A good example of this type of barter comes from the Allied occupation of Germany after World War II:

"Everybody knows that to get cement you must offer coal," said the city fathers of Stuttgart, and they bought liquor brewed in the surrounding countryside, shipped it to the French zone [of occupation] in exchange for cigarettes, shipped the cigarettes to a Ruhr mine and swapped them for coal, brought the coal back to a cement plant in Württemberg, and thus got the cement for reconstruction work.[2]

Another situation when barter is sometimes used is if there are laws setting a minimum price, or if sellers with market power keep their prices from falling when supply exceeds demand. For example, a country may set a minimum price for a basic commodity it exports, but then cannot sell all its output at that price. It may therefore barter this commodity with another country that is in the same fix, and neither country has to admit publicly that its commodity is not worth on the market all that it claims it is.

Apart from such special circumstances barter also occurs to a limited extent in more normal circumstances, for example, in trading in a car. Apparently barter arrangements have also become significant in countries with very high tax rates, such as Britain and Sweden, as a way of evading taxes.[3]

Standard of Value

The second function of money is to act as a standard of value, which simply means that we use money as a way of measuring values. We think of, and express, the values of goods and services in terms of money, so that money is the measuring rod of value the same way as a mile or kilometer is a measure of distance. Obviously, a modern economy requires continual comparisons of value; both producers and consumers have to compare the offers of numerous sellers, and this would be hard to do if different sellers denominated their prices in different goods; for example, if one store demands two pounds of butter for a pound of beef, and another store demands ten pencils for a pound of beef, which store has the lower price? And a similar problem would arise in deciding whether to buy, say, beef or fish, if the price of beef is expressed in terms of butter and the price of fish in terms of typewriter ribbons. To make rational decisions we would

[2] Horst Mendershausen, "Prices, Money and Distribution of Goods in Postwar Germany," *American Economic Review* 39 (June 1949): 656.

[3] There are also reports of "barter clubs" in the United States that allow members to swap goods and services. However, most of this activity involves the use of script as a medium of exchange, and dollars are, of course, used as a standard of value. Hence these transactions are not really barter transactions but are merely transactions in an informal currency. Presumably, a major advantage of these arrangements is that it facilitates income-tax evasion. But barter persists even if there is no tax advantage to it. As late as the early years of this century barter was used extensively in the more isolated areas of Wales, where there were close-knit communities, so that information costs were relatively low. See Marjorie Sykes," How to Live without Money," *The Countryman* 83 (Autumn 1978): 40–43.

have to know the ratios at which any one good exchanges for all the others.

Suppose that we have a very simple economy with only five commodities, A, B, C, D, and E. If there is no standard of value, and we want to know the exchange ratios of these five commodities in terms of each other, we have to learn ten different exchange ratios (A–B, A–C, A–D, A–E, B–C, B–D, B–E, C–D, C–E, D–E). But if we use one of these five commodities, say A, as our standard of value, we can express the prices of the other four goods in terms of it, and thus we have to learn only four exchange rates (A–B, A–C, A–D, A–E). In general, with N commodities, if there is no standard of value, we have to learn $(N-1)\frac{N}{2}$ exchange rates between them. (The first part of the expression is $N-1$ because the exchange rate of a commodity with itself is obviously unity, so that we have to discover the exchange rates of only $N-1$ commodities. For each of these commodities we have to know its exchange rate with every other one, so we have $(N-1)N$ exchange rates. But if we know the exchange rate of A with B we already know the exchange rate of B with A too, and for this reason we divide by 2.)

But if we use one of these commodities as the standard of value, there are only $N-1$ exchange ratios. (And if instead of using one of these commodities as money we had brought in a separate standard of value, we would have N exchange ratios.) Hence, a standard of value allows us to achieve an immense economizing of effort. Assume, for example, that someone is concerned with 201 items, hardly an outlandish number. Given a standard of value he or she has to ascertain only 200 prices in terms of this standard of value. But in the absence of a standard of value, he or she would be faced with 20,100 exchange ratios.

Unfortunately, as we all know, money as a standard of value may be inefficient because its value may be unstable. But this is another story, which we will take up later.

Store of Value

The final function of money is to serve as a store of value, that is, as a way of holding wealth. Although this function of money is no more important than the other ones, we will discuss it in more detail because it does bring out a number of important, and not quite so obvious, characteristics of money.

Money has several peculiarities as a store of wealth. One is that it has no, or only trivial, transaction costs. People who decide to hold any other asset as a store of wealth must take the money they receive as income and buy this asset. Later on, when they want to obtain goods or other assets in place of this asset they have to exchange it for money. Both of these transactions, from money into this asset and, later on, from this asset back into money, involve a cost. For example, suppose that someone saves $5,000 to buy a car next year and decides to put these $5,000 into common stock in the meantime. This person now has to take the time and trouble to decide which stock to buy, and to call a broker and pay a brokerage fee as well. Then, next year he or she has again to go to the trouble of calling the broker and paying another brokerage fee. In contrast, by holding these $5,000 as a demand deposit instead, both the brokerage costs and the implicit costs represented by the time and trouble required to buy the stock could have been avoided. This is a unique characteristic of money, and in this respect it is superior to all other assets.

A second characteristic of money as a store of value is that, quite obviously, its value in terms of money is fixed. This is important because debts are normally stated in money terms. Hence money has a fixed value in terms of debts and certain commitments, such as rental payments. Someone who wants an asset that will allow him or her to pay off a debt has a definite incentive to hold money. To be sure, money is not the only asset that has this convenient characteristic; a bond that matures when the debt is due has it too, but buying and selling a bond involves transactions costs.

The absence of significant transaction costs and the fixity of its value in terms of debts are the two basic characteristics of money as a store of wealth. Two other, but much less basic, characteristics are that the value of money fluctuates relative to goods and services, and that it usually has no explicit yield.[4] Hence, if someone wants an asset that will have stable purchasing power over goods and services rather than over debts, money is certainly not the ideal one. It may seem therefore that money is not as good a store of value as are assets whose money prices vary. While there is certainly some truth to this contention, it is subject to a major qualification. The prices of various assets and of goods and services do not fluctuate in unison. Hence, people who hold, say, common stocks or inventories of commodities may find that, despite the inflation, they are even worse off than they would have been had they held money instead. Certainly, despite the inflation since 1970, someone who bought seemingly sound Penn Central stock that year, just before the company went bankrupt, would have lost more purchasing power than someone who held money instead. And someone who buys diamonds as an inflation hedge faces not only the risk that the relative price of diamonds in terms of other goods will fall, but also the fact that the retail buyer of diamonds pays a price much above that at which he or she can resell them. Unfortunately, a good inflation hedge does not exist.

Interaction of the Functions of Money

In the United States a single monetary unit fulfills all three functions of money. A dollar bill, for example, is a medium of exchange and a store

---

[4] An explicit yield is a yield that is paid in money, and typically expressed as an interest rate. By contrast, an implicit yield consists of free services and convenience.

of value, while prices are stated in (abstract units) of dollars. But it is not always the case that all three functions of money are fulfilled by the same monetary unit. For example, in colonial America many merchants used the British pound as their standard of value in which they kept their books, but Spanish coins were a more common medium of exchange since there were more of them around. Similarly, in Britain, until recently, prices of certain high-status goods, for example, expensive clothes, were stated in terms of guineas, a guinea equaling one pound plus one shilling. But guineas were no longer in circulation and the customer paid for these goods with the medium of exchange, pounds and shillings.[5]

But usually the same unit performs all three functions of money. This is so because it would be inconvenient to have a different medium of exchange and standard of value. For example, suppose that the medium of exchange consists of silver coins, but that the standard of value in which prices are stated is a gold coin. Then at every purchase one would have to do a bit of mental arithmetic to calculate how many silver coins to give the merchant to meet the price set in terms of gold coins. And, as we just pointed out, as a store of value the advantage of money is precisely that it is the same unit as the medium of exchange (thus avoiding transactions costs) and as a standard of value (thus having a fixed value in terms of debts). And this requires that all three functions be fulfilled by the same monetary unit.

Specific Definition of Money

When it comes to defining money, not in a theoretical sense by pointing to its functions, but by specifying the particular (measurable) items that are included in it, some difficulties arise. Some economists emphasize the medium of exchange function, and hence include in money only those items that can be used as a medium of exchange, that is, currency and checking deposits. This is called M_1, or narrow money. Recently two variants of this definition of money have been distinguished. One called M-1A includes only checking deposits in commercial banks, while the other M-1B includes also deposits against which checks can be written in savings and loan associations and certain other institutions.

Some economists believe that whether checks can, or cannot, be

---

[5] The guinea was originally a gold coin while the pound was a silver coin. Dealing in gold rather than silver coinage indicates superior social status, hence the use of guineas for prices of prestige goods.

There is an extensive history to the use of different types of money by various social classes. The lower classes were sometimes paid in copper while the aristocracy dealt in gold. In ancient Greece, for example, the use of gold by the common people was prohibited at one time because gold could be used to bribe the gods, and this was not something the lower classes were supposed to do. Currently we still have one remnant of this tradition of "high" and "low" money—one should not leave pennies as part of the tip.

written against a deposit is not so important as long as depositors can quickly and costlessly take funds out of their deposits. They therefore define money in a broader way than M_1. One such way is to include all deposits in commercial banks, and not just demand deposits. This definition of money was called M_2. However, in 1980 the Federal Reserve defined a new measure of money, unfortunately also called *M-2*, which includes most savings and time deposits in commercial banks, savings and loan associations, mutual savings banks (which are institutions similar to savings and loan associations), and credit unions. We shall discuss this definition in detail in chapter 11.

At the time of this writing, one cannot be certain whether the new definitions will catch on, though this is likely. In any case the work of the economists whom we will be discussing in this book was done prior to 1980 using the traditional measures of money. Hence, when discussing their empirical findings we will use the traditional definitions of M_1 as currency and demand deposits, and M_2 as M_1 plus time and savings deposits in commercial banks.[6]

Types of Money

We now turn to a description of various types of money. **Full-bodied commodity money** is *money that has a value as a commodity fully equal to its value as a medium of exchange.* An obvious example is a gold coin with its value as gold, if sold on the gold market, equal to its face value. Such money involves the inconvenience of carrying around fairly heavy coins, because gold, being a soft metal, must be alloyed with other metals as well, thus raising the coin's weight. Besides, coins are subject to counterfeiting, clipping, and so on.[7] Hence, a more convenient money called **representative full-bodied money** was invented. It is *paper money that can be redeemed in full-bodied commodity money;* thus it is essentially a warehouse certificate for full-bodied money.

If *money does not itself have value as a commodity fully equal to its monetary value, and cannot be redeemed in such commodity money,* it is called **credit money.** All our current U.S. money is credit money. It con-

---

[6] Strictly speaking this definition is not quite correct; negotiable certificates of deposit, which we will define in chapter 3, of $100,000 and over are excluded.

[7] Clipping consists of filing off the edges of coins to obtain some of the metal. To prevent it coins were given serrated edges, and some of our coins still have these edges despite the fact that clipping would now hardly pay for itself. Another practice, sweating, consisted of heating coins over a fire and collecting drops from them. Still another way was to shake coins in a bag and collect the abraded scrapings. As far as counterfeiting is concerned, the traditional way to test whether a gold coin was genuine was to bite it, gold being a soft metal. This is hardly in accordance with our present-day ideas about hygiene. Private individuals, however, were not the only ones who debased the coinage by counterfeiting. Monarchs did it too on a large scale by calling in coins and issuing in exchange coins containing a smaller quantity of precious metal. This was a serious problem in the Middle Ages.

sists of currency issued by the government (that is, the U. S. Treasury and the twelve Federal Reserve banks) and deposits issued by commercial banks.

Currency is **legal tender.** This means that *it has to be accepted in payment of a debt unless the debt instrument itself specifically provides for another form of payment*, such as, for example, the delivery of commodities. But a deposit is not legal tender. A creditor does not have to accept a claim on it in the form of a check and can demand to be paid in currency instead. However, whether or not something is legal tender is *not* the criterion of whether it is money. As long as in actuality it is generally accepted in exchange, or used as a standard of value, we call it money.

Nature of Credit Money

What credit money, as opposed to commodity money, does is to economize on scarce resources. Instead of using gold or silver, items with a high cost of production, we use items with trivial production costs, entries on a bank's books, paper, or, in the case of coins, some base metals. For example, the cost of producing a currency note, be it a dollar bill or a thousand-dollar bill, is about two cents. Money is a token entitling the bearer to draw on the economy's goods and services, and what makes *us* willing to accept it is that *other people* are willing to accept it in exchange for their goods and services. It does not need to have any value as a commodity in its own right any more than the admission ticket to a concert has to be capable of producing music.

This point sometimes causes confusion. Some people feel uneasy with the idea that a certain item has value merely because other people think that it has value and are therefore willing to accept it. There *seems* to be something unreasonable, precarious, and circular about everyone treating something as valuable merely because other people consider it valuable. But actually there is nothing precarious about it—in so many of our actions we rely on other people acting in a predictable way. For example, the value of gold and silver depends upon the fact that other people consider these metals valuable, and not on any great technological superiority that gold and silver have over iron and coal.

This is not to foreclose the issue of whether or not full-bodied money, such as gold coins, or representative full-bodied money is preferable to credit money. While the quantity of a commodity money is governed by the availability of the commodity, the government controls the quantity of credit money. Opinions can reasonably differ on whether it is better to have the quantity of money controlled by accidents such as the discovery of new gold fields, or by governments.[8] Many economists believe that governments,

---

[8] Thus Huston McCulloch has responded to the argument that a commodity standard wastes resources with the following analogy: "A similar argument could be made for bicycle locks and chains. If metal locks could be replaced with symbolic paper locks, resources would be released that could be used productively elsewhere. As long as thieves honor paper locks as they would metal locks, your bike will be per-

unrestrained by a gold standard or some other rule, tend to increase the quantity of money too fast, which, as we shall see, results in inflation. They do this because in the short run raising the quantity of money rapidly has very pleasant results: unemployment falls and so does the interest rate.

Credit money requires considerable sophistication. People have to grasp the idea that something is valuable if other people will treat it as valuable, despite the fact that it has no value in direct use as a commodity. Not surprisingly, credit money is therefore a relatively recent innovation. While there had been episodes of credit money before, in 1930 most of the developed countries were on a gold standard, though credit money in the form of checks did circulate. In general, as one would expect, the evolution of money has been from concrete objects to abstract symbols, that is, from precious metals traded by weight, through coins made of precious metals, to paper money redeemable in precious coins, and to irredeemable paper money and bank deposits. But, as usual, evolution has not followed a straight line. For example, goldsmiths' deposits, which were essentially checks, were used as a means of payment in seventeenth-century England at a time when paper money was not yet acceptable.

The Cashless Society?

Has the evolution of money run its course, or will it go on? There is a widespread belief that not only will it continue, but that a substantial further step is close at hand. There is much concern now about the rapid growth in the volume of checks to be cleared each year, and the cost that this involves. Moreover, check clearing is a relatively slow and inconvenient process. But rapid advances in computer technology promise help. These innovations take many forms. One is automated clearinghouses that clear checks between banks cheaply. Another, more visible one, is the installation of automatic teller machines in many banks that allow customers to make withdrawals and deposits twenty-four hours a day without the intervention of a human teller. While such machines, though common in New York and some other cities, are still rare in some other areas, they will probably become more widespread. These machines need not be installed in the bank itself but can be installed, when the law permits, even in places like shopping centers, thus obviating the need for a branch bank. Moreover, similar machines can be installed at check-out counters in supermarkets and other stores, so that the customer can pay by having his or her account

fectly secure. Surely hardened steel and phosphor bronze shackles are evidence of irrationality on the part of those who insist on them" (*Money and Inflation* [New York: Academic Press, 1975], p. 78).

debited automatically. And not only banks, but also savings and loan associations can install such terminals.

One can allow one's imagination to roam beyond such relatively mundane devices and imagine a completely automated payments system. In such a system, income and virtually all other receipts would be credited automatically to a person's account by computer. When making purchases the buyer would rarely give the seller currency or a check but would offer an account number, which the seller would punch into a computer terminal. The payment would thus be automatically transferred to the seller's account. Recurrent payments, such as mortgage payments and utility bills, would be automatically subtracted from the payer's account, as, in fact, is already done in some cases.

However, there are still many difficulties needing to be solved before such a system can be established. In some experiments that have been undertaken the public has been less than enthusiastic about electronic payments, in part because such a system does not provide the choice of delaying paying bills when an account is low. It is probable that eventually we will move to a widespread electronic payments system, but we are not likely to do so soon. Note, however, that most large payments, that is, payments of many thousands of dollars, are already made by wire, that is, by telegraphic transfer, and not by check, to avoid delays in the mail. Throughout this book when we refer to transfer by checks we will also mean such wire transfers.

To see one problem with an electronic transfer system consider the following story. Some colonists in a new land were familiar with a monetary system, but had not brought any money with them. Being without a medium of exchange they could still benefit from their familiarity with money by using money as a unit of account. They bartered goods, but they expressed the values of the goods they brought to the market in terms of the standard of value. But, even with a unit of account, barter is cumbersome, so they decided to use a medium of exchange. Since they did not want to tie up valuable goods by using them as a medium of exchange they hit upon the idea of using a credit system. Each colonist was given a line of credit, and one of them served as a clerk who recorded all the transactions, crediting the account of the seller and debiting the account of the buyer. But although this was a great improvement over barter even this system was cumbersome; the clerk was kept very busy recording all the transactions and thought that recording very small transactions was a great nuisance. So he suggested that each colonist be given a piece of paper denoting small amounts to be credited to his or her account. They could then pass these pieces of paper to each other to make purchases. This would save a lot of bookkeeping. Only when one of the colonists accumulated more pieces of paper than needed would he or she turn them in to the clerk who would then credit his or her account. The colonists accepted this scheme and lived happily ever after. They had reinvented currency.

Money and Near-Money

The fact that the monetary system is evolving rather than static suggests that the distinction between money and "other things" is not clear-cut. At any particular time there may be some items that are just halfway in the process of becoming money. Moreover, as we discussed, some economists include time deposits in their definition of the money supply while others treat time deposits as an asset that is not money. Thus, the line of distinction between money and nonmoney is blurry. Where we want to draw this line depends, in part, on what our purpose is, what particular function of money we consider the most relevant for the problem at hand. For example, if we focus on the medium of exchange function, we want to define the money supply as just those items that generally function as a medium of exchange.

But suppose that we stress the store of value function instead. If so, we want to include in the definition of the money supply those assets that are extremely liquid, since it is its liquidity that differentiates money from other stores of value. The liquidity of an asset depends on (1) how easily it can be bought or sold, (2) the transaction cost of selling or buying it, and (3) how stable and predictable its price is. Narrow money, at one end of the scale, has perfect liquidity. Since it already is money there is no cost and trouble in selling it, that is, in turning it into money. And the price of a dollar is constant at one dollar. Towards the other end of the scale there are items like real estate, which may take quite some time to sell, involve a substantial brokerage cost, and may have to be sold at less than the anticipated price. We can rank all items by their liquidity, by their degree of *moneyness*.

The question now arises where along this spectrum of liquidity and moneyness one should draw the line between money and nonmoney. There is no point at which one can draw an obvious and clear-cut line. Regardless of how broadly or narrowly one defines money there are always some assets that, while excluded from the definition of money, are really very close to the borderline. Moneyness is a continuum. We therefore call *items that are excluded from the definition of money but are quite similar to some items that are included,* **near-moneys.** Obviously currency and demand deposits are money. But how about savings deposits in commercial banks? Some savings accounts can be transferred automatically by the bank into demand deposits and used to pay checks as they come in, but others can be withdrawn only by forfeiting some interest. But, if we decide to include savings deposits in commercial banks in the definition of money, how about deposits in savings and loan associations, in mutual savings banks, and in credit unions? And if one includes such deposits, how about extremely short-term government securities? Large firms with ready access to the money market can buy or sell them very quickly at a very low transaction cost, and their prices are very stable.

These near-moneys are items that are very liquid, but not *quite* as liquid as money. Admittedly, this is rather vague, and it is not clear exactly what items should be included. At one end of the spectrum, what items are included depends on the definition of money that is used. If one uses the M_1 definition, then savings deposits in commercial banks are obviously near-money. But if one defines money as M_2, then these savings deposits are money and not near-money. Deposits in mutual savings banks, in savings and loan associations, and in credit unions, as well as short-term government securities, and even short-term IOUs issued by very sound corporations, are then considered near-moneys. At the other end of the spectrum, where one draws the line between near-moneys and those assets that are too illiquid to be considered near-moneys is also arbitrary. While stock in corporations is definitely not a near-money, it is not clear whether, say, a government security that matures within one or two years should be considered a near-money.

Summary

This chapter started out with some definitions. It pointed out that demand deposits, and sometimes time deposits, are included in the definition of money, and warned against the common confusion of money with currency, with income, or with wealth. We then discussed the three functions of money: medium of exchange, standard of value, and store of wealth. A medium of exchange and standard of value are absolutely necessary for an efficient economy. As a store of value, narrow money has the characteristic of having virtually no transactions costs and possessing complete liquidity. In addition, its value in terms of debts denominated in money is fixed, although its value relative to commodities varies. Another characteristic of money is that it usually has no explicit yield. We then discussed why the three functions of money are usually performed by the same item.

We then looked at the types of money—full-bodied commodity money, representative full-bodied money, and credit money—and discussed why credit money has value. The last section of this chapter dealt with near-moneys.

QUESTIONS AND EXERCISES

1. Define: (a) currency, (b) money, (c) income, and (d) wealth. Distinguish between them.
2. Are your average money holdings greater than, roughly equal to, or less than your income, or is this a meaningless question?
3. Explain why demand deposits are included in the definition of money.
4. Explain how a medium of exchange economizes on effort. Do so also for a standard of value.
5. What characteristics distinguish money from other stores of wealth?

6. Explain the meaning of the following terms: (a) full-bodied commodity money, (b) representative commodity money, and (c) credit money. How do they differ?
7. Explain why credit money has value.
8. Discuss the meaning of the term near-moneys. What items are included?
9. Discuss what is meant by liquidity. How would you describe the liquidity of (a) corporate stock, (b) an expected inheritance, (c) a house, and (d) a deposit in a savings and loan association?
10. Rather cynically one may describe the exchange of gifts at Christmas as barter. Why do we use barter at that time instead of giving each other money when money is a so much better medium of exchange?

FURTHER READING

ALCHIAN, ARMEN. "Why Money?" *Journal of Money, Credit and Banking* 9 (February 1977), pt. 2, pp. 133–41. An excellent discussion of the medium of exchange role.

BRUNNER, KARL, and MELTZER, ALLAN. "The Uses of Money: Money in the Theory of an Exchange Economy." *American Economic Review* 61 (December 1971): 784–806. An excellent discussion of the medium of exchange function of money, but one that assumes some knowledge of economic theory.

MELITZ, JACQUES. *Primitive Money*. Reading, Mass.: Addison-Wesley, 1974. An interesting discussion of the anthropology of money.

———. "The Polanyi School of Anthropology on Money: An Economist's View." *American Anthropologist* 72 (October 1970): 1020–40. An interesting survey.

RADFORD, R. A. "The Economic Organization of a P.O.W. Camp." *Economica* 12 (November 1945): 189–201. A fascinating description of how "money" arose in a special situation.

2

The Financial System:
An Overview

In this book we will spend much time discussing how monetary policy operates, or, more generally, how changes in the money stock and interest rates change money income. Now, one person's expenditure is another person's income, so that for the whole economy, money income, or nominal income as it is frequently called, is equal to total expenditure, or aggregate demand, for goods and services.

But what determines total expenditures? One can approach this question in several ways. One way, which is usually stressed in introductory economics and in macroeconomics courses, is to make consumer expenditures a function primarily of household income and business expenditures a function of expected sales and the interest rate. While we will use this approach here, we will also use another approach. This is to look at people's portfolios of assets. We know from microeconomics that equilibrium requires that the marginal utility of a dollar spent on every commodity must be equal. And we can apply the same reasoning to all the assets (called a portfolio) that a person holds. In equilibrium the utility received at the margin from a dollar's worth of every asset must be equal, and it must equal the disutility of postponing consumption. Suppose that the disutility of postponing consumption for a year is greater than the utility of the interest that can be earned on an asset. Ignoring transactions costs, it is then rational to sell the asset and increase consumption. Conversely, if the utility of the interest that can be earned on a dollar of assets exceeds the disutility of postponing a dollar of consumption, then consumption should be cut.

Suppose now, to take a dramatic, though unrealistic, example, that a helicopter flies over a city and drops currency. The happy people now hold more currency, but since they were in equilibrium to start with, the marginal utility of a dollar of currency is less than the marginal utility of a dollar of other assets or consumption. Hence, they will try to buy other assets and raise consumption. As they raise consumption, aggregate demand obviously increases, and as they buy other physical assets such as houses or factories, aggregate demand rises, since someone now has an incentive to produce the additional assets that people want to buy.

19

But suppose they buy financial assets instead, say, by purchasing a corporate bond. In this case no immediate and direct demand for goods and services is generated, and we have to trace through a fairly complex chain of events to see how aggregate demand is affected.

Consider now another example. Suppose nobody drops money on people, but, for some reason, the attractiveness of some asset rises. If this asset is one that can be produced by the private sector, say, houses, aggregate demand increases. But suppose that this asset is money or government bonds. In this case, the public reduces its expenditures on goods and services in order to acquire more money or government bonds, and hence aggregate demand falls. Thus we can think of changes in aggregate demand as resulting from changes in the portfolio of assets (and debts, which are essentially negative assets).

We can therefore try to explain changes in real income and in prices by studying changes in the public's desired stock of assets and debts and changes in the supplies of various assets such as money. But to do this we first have to familiarize ourselves with the types of financial assets in people's portfolios. This we will do in this part of the book. The current chapter deals with three issues that form a background to our subsequent discussion of specific financial institutions: (1) the reason why financial institutions exist and the basic functions they perform, (2) the portfolio decisions of households and how the liabilities of financial institutions fit into their portfolios, and (3) the reasons for a very pervasive characteristic of financial institutions, extensive government supervision.

The Role of Financial Institutions

Private financial institutions, firms specializing in providing financial services (including insurance and real estate), play an important role in our economy. In 1978 they employed over 4 million people, and accounted for 14 percent of GNP. But what exactly is it that they do? They do not produce goods as manufacturing firms or farms do, nor do they transport and distribute goods. So why have them at all? One thing they do—and it is a very necessary activity—is to clear payments for other participants in the economy and thus facilitate the division of labor. For example, a bank clears checks and provides its customers with important bookkeeping services when it sends out monthly statements and cancelled checks. Other financial institutions, such as realty firms and stockbrokers, bring potential buyers and sellers of assets together.

But an important segment of the financial industry are the **financial intermediaries** who, while they may clear payments, do something else too. As their name implies, they *intermediate by obtaining the funds of savers in exchange for their own liabilities* (such as entries in a passbook), *and then, in turn, make loans to others.* They do not merely bring savers and ultimate borrowers together, but instead sell claims on *themselves* to their depositors and then buy claims on borrowers. Important examples of such financial intermediaries are savings and loan associations, mutual savings banks, and, to some extent, commercial banks.

Essentially, financial intermediaries buy and sell rights to future payments. For example, anyone opening an account in a savings and loan association gives it a current payment in exchange for its promise to make a payment to him or her in the future. And the savings and loan association then turns around and uses the current payment it received to make a loan, that is, to make a current payment to someone else, in return for that person's promise to make a payment to it in the future.

This activity of trading in current payments and promises for future payments is extraordinarily important. To see this, consider first the extreme case of an economy with no borrowing and lending at all. In such an economy people would still want to save and invest. Many people would want to defer income from the present to the future, either because they expect their income to dwindle as they get older, their needs to rise, or else because they hope to earn some yield on their savings. But many people would not be able to earn anything on their savings at all because they lack the opportunity to buy a physical asset that produces income, and they would not be able to lend to anyone who has this opportunity. At the same time, those who have the opportunity to acquire highly productive physical assets could do so only to the extent that they could cut back on their own consumption —and this hardly is the way to finance a steel mill! Obviously, such an economy would be very inefficient.

Now let us go to the opposite extreme and not only introduce borrowing and lending, but assume that these activities involve no information costs and no transaction costs. In this case there would be a great deal of borrowing and lending going on. Every household would save until its marginal loss from deferring consumption for one year is equal to the interest rate, and every investor would buy capital assets until the marginal yield on these assets would be equal to the interest rate. Moreover, at the margin, the productivity of a dollar newly invested in every kind of capital would have to be equal throughout the economy, for otherwise investors could gain by shifting funds (costlessly) between different sectors. Such an economy would therefore be using its capital very efficiently.

But, obviously, in the real world there are information costs and transaction costs. Potential lenders do not have costless knowledge of everyone who wants to borrow, nor do they know the interest each of these borrowers is willing to pay, or the soundness of the potential loans. It is costly for borrowers and lenders to learn of each other's existence, and then lenders have to undertake an often expensive investigation of the risk that the borrower will not be able—or willing—to repay. Moreover, there are transaction costs: loan contracts have to be drawn up, provisions for collateral may have to be made, and so on.

To visualize these problems, imagine that you decide to make a mortgage loan. You first have to locate a potential borrower, and then investigate his or her credit rating, as well as the current and probable future market value of the house. Then, if you decide to make the loan, you have to draw up a mortgage contract. Obviously all of this would be a time-consuming, and hence expensive, business, particularly if you try to do it right. And then, once you have made the mortgage loan, you would be holding a very illiquid asset, and hence may be in difficulty if you, yourself, suddenly need funds.

But fortunately these costs can be minimized the same way we minimize the costs of most other things. We do not raise and slaughter our own cattle to get meat, nor do we make our own furniture. We rely on the division of labor. And we do the same thing in finance. Most households do not make their own loans, or borrow significant sums directly from other households apart from relatives; instead they use financial intermediaries.

Advantages of Financial Intermediation

Under this system the lender and the ultimate borrower do not go to the trouble of seeking each other out, and since the lender does not take the ultimate borrower's IOU, he or she does not have to investigate the borrower's credit standing and the soundness of the loan. Instead, the lender gives his funds to, say, a savings and loan association, which, in turn, makes a mortgage loan. Now obviously every financial intermediary levies a charge —usually a fairly substantial charge—for its services. For example, a savings and loan association may pay 6 percent interest to its depositors, and lend their funds out at 9 percent interest. What makes it worthwhile for borrowers and lenders to pay this charge?

Minimize cost. We have already discussed one benefit of using a financial intermediary: it economizes on the information and transaction costs of borrowers and lenders. As a concrete example, consider a corporation that wants to borrow $10 million. Since there are few households able to make a $10-million loan, the corporation would have to scurry around and borrow, say, an average of $10,000 from a thousand households. Since these households would not know that this corporation wants to borrow from them, the corporation would have to seek them out by extensive advertising. And then it would have to convince them that it is a sound borrower. A financial intermediary, on the other hand, is set up to collect the funds of many small depositors. It does not have to let households know that it wants their funds every time a borrower approaches it for a loan. From past experience, and continual advertising, the public already knows that this intermediary, say, a savings and loan association, would like their funds. Moreover, since its deposits are insured, the public does not have to investigate the financial intermediary's credit standing. To be sure, the financial intermediary itself has to investigate the credit standing of the borrower, but a single investigation by an expert is much less costly than a thousand separate investigations by amateurs.

Long-term loans. A second advantage of financial intermediaries is that they make it possible for borrowers to obtain long-term loans even though the ultimate lenders are making only short-term loans. Much borrowing is done to acquire long-lived assets, such as houses or factories. And someone who borrows to buy assets that will pay for themselves only over a long period of time does not want to finance them with a short-term loan. For example, few families would want to finance the purchase of their homes by borrowing on a thirty-day promissory note, and face each month the problem of refinancing the loan. Obviously, the family would sleep more comfortably if it would finance its house with, say, a twenty-year mortgage. But now consider the same family in its role as lender. Would it want to make a twenty-year loan? Perhaps not, because it may want to have these funds available in case an emergency or some other need arises.

Here is where the financial intermediary comes in. A financial intermediary can make long-term, and therefore illiquid, loans to borrowers, and yet can provide its depositors with short-term deposits. Despite the fact that it has used depositors' funds to make long-term loans, a bank or a savings and loan association can tell the depositors that they can withdraw their deposits any time they want. If it has many individually small depositors whose decisions whether or not to withdraw their deposits are independent of each other, then it can predict quite well the probability distribution of deposit withdrawals on any day and hold small but sufficient reserves. Under normal conditions, the decision whether or not to withdraw a deposit depends largely on the particular circumstances of each depositor, for example, his or her decision to make a large purchase. Hence, one can, under normal conditions, assume that the decisions of various depositors are independent of each other, so that the law of large numbers applies. However, this fortunate state of affairs does not always hold. Suppose, for example, that the public becomes afraid that banks or other financial institutions will fail. It will then try to withdraw deposits on a massive scale. And the financial institutions will then not have sufficient liquid funds available to repay these deposits. Until 1934, when the federal government started to insure deposits, the United States suffered numerous financial panics in which many banks failed.

Liquidity. Since the claims on financial intermediaries are liquid they should be distinguished sharply from claims on other borrowers. Suppose you lend $1,000 to General Motors for ten years. In return you get a certificate called a bond that promises to pay you $90 per year and then return your $1,000 after ten years. Suppose, three years after you have bought this bond, you suddenly need your $1,000 back. General Motors will not pay off the bond for another seven years, and the only way you can get your $1,000 back before then is to sell the bond on the open market to some other investor. The price you will get depends on supply and demand, and may be significantly less—or more—than your original $1,000. By contrast, if you have a deposit in a savings and loan association, you can get your $1,000 back immediately, at any time, though, on some kinds of deposits, you lose some of the interest you have previously earned on it.

Risk pooling. Financial intermediaries also pool risks. Suppose there are a hundred loans to be made, and that it is reasonable to expect that ninety-nine of them will be repaid, while on one loan the creditor will not be repaid at all. Every lender is then afraid that he or she will be the unlucky one. But if the lenders pool their funds, then each lender will lose one percent of his or her loan and no more, thus avoiding the risk of a large loss in exchange for accepting a certain small loss. By pooling the funds of depositors, financial intermediaries reduce the riskiness of lending.

In summary then, indirect finance has three great advantages: it reduces the risk of lending; it makes loans more liquid than they otherwise would be; and it greatly reduces the information and transaction costs of lenders and borrowers.

Do these advantages mean that all finance takes place through financial intermediaries? Of course not. Since financial intermediaries charge a fee for their services, it is sometimes worthwhile for borrowers and lenders to deal directly. Beyond this, people who want to invest sometimes do not borrow at all, but reduce their own consumption to avoid the charges of a financial intermediary, or the costs of finding a willing lender on their own. This is likely to occur if the investment project is very risky, so that the potential borrower would have to pay a very high rate of interest to compensate the lender for the risk the lender sees in the project. The investor, say, the proverbial inventor of the better mousetrap, may well think that the risk is much less than lenders think it is, and hence does not want to pay the substantially higher interest rate the lenders require as compensation for assuming the risk.

Portfolio Balance

In the previous section we pointed out that financial intermediaries bridge the gap between the types of loans that borrowers want to obtain and that lenders want to make. We will now take this idea up in more detail by looking at the different characteristics of loans that borrowers and lenders prefer.

Most borrowers are not specialists in finance and do not want to pay the costs of acquiring a great deal of information. At the same time they are usually averse to taking risks. Both of these factors suggest that borrowers should try to limit the financial risks they take.

Avoiding Risk

How can they do this? Financial risks arise not only from holding financial assets that may decline in value, but also from having outstanding debts that may become due at a time when there are no readily available funds to pay them off. One way to avoid financial risk is therefore to **hedge,** that is, *to have one's assets and liabilities come due at the same time.* Suppose, for example, that you plan to buy an asset costing $10,000 that will yield $1,050 each year for ten years and then fall apart. If you finance it by borrowing $10,000 for ten years at a 5 percent interest rate, then the only risk you face is that the asset may not actually pay off as much as $1,050 a year for the ten years. But suppose you finance it by borrowing $10,000 for one year, and plan to obtain additional one-year loans in each of the following nine years. If so, you run an additional risk, because you may not be able to get a new loan at the end of each year, and hence may have to default on your previous loan as it becomes due, or else you may have to pay a much higher than anticipated interest rate on the new loans. Both of these contingencies can be avoided by taking out a loan with a maturity equal to the asset you buy with it.

Although such hedging reduces risk, borrowers will not always hedge because it may be too expensive to do so. For example, if the interest rate is, say, 6 percent on a five-year loan, and 7 percent on a ten-year loan, some borrowers will, rightly or wrongly, be tempted to take out a five-year loan, and accept the risk that they will have to pay a much higher interest rate after five years. But this does not mean that these borrowers do not *want* to hedge, any more than the fact that your buying a Volkswagen instead of a Rolls-Royce means that you prefer the ride of a Volkswagen to that of a Rolls-Royce.

A similar thing is true for lenders. The value to them of a security they purchase is, of course, a positive function of its yield but a negative function of its riskiness. Unfortunately for them there is usually a trade-off here; the higher the yield of a security the greater is its risk. This is the result of competition. If a security has little risk, the person who borrows by selling his or her IOU knows that he or she can sell it even if it pays only a low rate of interest.

So far we have used the term risk rather loosely. One type of risk is **default risk,** that is, the risk that the *borrower will simply not repay the loan,* either out of dishonesty or plain inability to do so. Another type of risk, called **purchasing-power risk,** is the risk that, due to an unexpectedly high inflation rate, the *future interest payments, and the principal of the loan when finally repaid, will have less purchasing power* than the lender anticipated at the time the loan was made. A similar risk is faced by borrowers. A borrower may cheerfully agree to pay, say, 9 percent interest, expecting that a 6 percent inflation rate will reduce the real value of the loan, so that he or she is actually paying only 3 percent. But inflation may be only 4 percent. A third type of risk is **interest rate risk,** that is the *risk that the market value of a security will fall because interest rates will rise.* We will discuss this further in a later chapter; here we just present the intuitive idea. Suppose that five years ago you bought a ten-year $1,000 bond carrying a 6 percent interest rate, and that the interest rate now obtainable on similar bonds that also have five years to go until they mature is 8 percent. Would anyone pay $1,000 for your bond? Surely not, because they could earn $80 per year by buying a new bond, and only $60 per year by buying your bond. Hence, to sell your bond you would have to reduce its price. But suppose the bond, instead of having five years to maturity, would mature in, say, ninety days; what would its price be then? It would still be less than $1,000 since the buyer would get 6 percent instead of 8 percent interest for ninety days; but since getting a lower interest rate for only ninety days does not involve much of a loss, the bond would sell for something close to $1,000. Hence, while holding any security with a fixed interest rate involves *some* interest-rate risk, the closer to maturity a security is, the lower is this risk. Of course, if interest rates fall you gain because your bond is worth more. But the fact that you may gain as well as lose does not mean that you are taking no risk.

Diversification

All three types of risk are relevant for deciding what assets to include in a portfolio, and what debts to have outstanding. But anyone holding more than one type of asset has to consider, not the risk of each asset taken by itself, but instead the totality of the risk on various assets and debts jointly. Suppose, for example, that someone has a $1,000 debt coming due five years from now; by holding a $1,000 government bond also due in five years, the risk can be eliminated completely on both the debt and the bond. Similarly, suppose someone holds stock in a company that is likely to gain from inflation, and stock in another company that is likely to lose from inflation. The riskiness of a portfolio that combines both of these stocks may be less than the riskiness of each stock taken separately. In other words, by holding in one's portfolio assets that are affected in opposite directions by a given future event, one can reduce the riskiness of one's portfolio, thus making it less risky in the aggregate than if each separate asset in it were taken separately. Hence a low-risk portfolio need not contain only assets that individually have little risk; sometimes one reduces the riskiness of a portfolio by adding some high-risk assets that offset the risks of other assets in it.

Buying assets with offsetting risks is one example of portfolio diversification. But one may want to diversify one's portfolio even if one cannot buy assets with offsetting risks. Suppose, for example, that you have the choice between an asset lasting one year with an expected 40 percent yield, but with a 20 percent chance that it will become completely worthless, or another asset that yields 5 percent, but is virtually riskless. Which asset should you buy? Obviously, this will depend upon your willingness to take risks. Most people are not willing to risk all their livelihood even for an exceptionally high expected rate of return, but many are willing to take a risk with a small proportion of their assets. Hence, they are willing to hold some proportion—often only a small proportion—of their portfolio in risky assets. They are thus diversifying their portfolios between high- and low-risk assets so that, while still having a chance for some spectacular gains, they avoid the risk of being wiped out completely. Most large portfolios are diversified, both by containing assets with offsetting risks, and also by containing some assets with small and some with large risks. And one of the major functions of a financial adviser is to tell people how they can diversify their porfolio efficiently.

To decide what assets to hold in a portfolio, one has to know the characteristics of selected assets. In table 2.1 we show the typical yields, liquidity, and risks on the following assets: money (defined as M_1), saving or time deposits in banks or savings and loan associations, government securities, corporate bonds and stocks, and capital held directly, such as an owned home or consumer durables. The first column shows a typical ranking of the monetary yield of these assets. This ranking, however, changes from time to time; sometimes deposits have a higher yield than short-term securities, and sometimes short-term securities have a higher yield than long-term securities. Similarly, the yield on stock (that is, the dividend plus capital gains and losses) fluctuates a great deal, and to the chagrin of stockholders it is sometimes negative. The next column shows the imputed yield (apart from liquidity) that an asset may have by providing free services, such as check clearing in the case of deposits, and shelter in the case of housing capital. The third column shows the asset's liquidity in the sense of the speed and ease with which it can be sold, and the lowness of the transaction costs of buying or selling it. The remaining three columns deal with the three types of risks. Interest-rate risk includes here not only the danger of actually selling an asset at a loss, but also the foregone opportunity cost if interest rates rise. For example, owners of bonds paying 6 percent may hold on to them when interest rates have risen to 9 percent, and thus avoid taking an explicit loss, but they still suffer a loss in the sense of foregone interest, because if they had not previously bought the 6 percent securities, they could now buy the 9 percent ones.

From table 2.1 one can see the role that various assets play in portfolios of households. Money is held for its yield in terms of convenience and for its liquidity. Although money is also safe—except for purchasing-power risk—it would be naïve to hold it primarily for this reason because in this respect it is dominated by time and savings deposits, which are not only safe but also pay interest. Savings and time deposits, as well as short-term government securities, are held primarily because of their high liquidity and safety, though their yield provides an additional motive for holding them. Long-term government securities often have a higher yield, but involve more interest rate risk than the previously discussed assets. Still, they, like savings and time deposits and short-term government securities, are often included in portfolios to provide safety in the sense of avoiding default risk. Corporate bonds are riskier since they have a default risk that varies depending on the particular bond. Corporate stock typically has a higher default risk than corporate bonds, but its yield has, on the average, been

Table 2.1   Characteristics of Selected Assets
(ranked with lowest yield, liquidity, or risk denoted by zero)

Asset	Typical monetary yield	Imputed yield from convenience	Imputed yield from liquidity	Default risk	Interest-rate risk	Purchasing-power risk
M_1	0	1	5	0	0	1
Insured savings and time deposits[a]	1 or 3[b]	0	3 or 4[b]	0	1–2[b]	1
Short-term government securities	2	0	4	0	1	1
Long-term government securities	3	0	3	0	2	1
Corporate bonds	4	0	2	1	2	1
Corporate stock	5	0	1	2	2	—[e]
Physical capital used by households	0	2	0	—[c]	—[d]	0

a. In commercial banks, mutual savings banks, and savings and loan associations. (NOW accounts are excluded.)

b. Depends on maturity of deposit.

c. No default risk per se, but risk that the capital equipment will not be as useful as anticipated.

d. Depends on its expected useful life.

e. Although corporate stock was for a long time considered an inflation hedge, recent evidence suggests that at least in the short run, it is even more vulnerable to inflation than many of the other assets listed.

higher than the yield on corporate bonds.[1] Capital owned directly has usually a high *imputed* yield such as providing the family with shelter, transportation, and so on, but it is very illiquid.

Another way to look at the seven types of assets listed in table 2.1 is to consider the types of institutions that issue them. The government issues part of the money stock, currency, and, of course, government securities. Banks issue the remainder of the money stock. Financial intermediaries issue saving and time deposits, and corporations issue corporate bonds and stock. With respect to default risk the safest assets are the obligations of the government and of financial intermediaries. It is simple to explain why the government's obligations are safe; since the government has the power to tax, and the power to create money, it can always pay off its debts. But what ensures the safety of the obligations of financial intermediaries. The answer is that the government insures them, and the related fact that it supervises them. We will take up the insurance systems in later chapters and now turn to the government's control over financial intermediaries.

Government Supervision of Financial Institutions

Financial intermediaries are very heavily regulated by both the federal and state governments. For example, one cannot just start a bank the way one can start another business. Instead, a prospective bank organizer must obtain special permission, called a charter, from either the federal or state authorities, and this permission is only sparingly given. It will not be given, for instance, if starting a new bank in the community would seriously weaken an existing bank. Thus already established banks are protected by the government from competition that could drive them out of business. Moreover, various government agencies supervise banks and financial intermediaries by inspecting the assets they hold and requiring them to get rid of risky ones. Furthermore, the government sets maximum interest rates that financial intermediaries can pay to limit the extent to which they can compete with each other.

While in many other industries the government prosecutes attempts to limit competition, in banking, as in some other regulated industries, the government imposes laws and regulations to reduce competition. Why is this? Essentially the answer is that an unregulated banking system would take too many risks. But this does not *necessarily* mean that government regulation is desirable, since it has its own disadvantages. As a general principle, the fact that the private market (or government regulation) suffers from some inefficiencies does not provide a sufficient case to replace it since the alternative might be worse.

---

[1] Strictly speaking, corporate stock does not have a default risk since the corporation is under no obligation to redeem it, but the term *default risk* can be stretched to include the risk that the stock's market value will fall.

Why would unregulated banks take too many risks? One explanation is *consumer ignorance*. For competition to work effectively the buyer must be able to evaluate the quality of the product with some degree of efficiency. Otherwise, various producers could succeed by offering a defective product at a low price. Now consumers can evaluate most products in either, or both, of two ways. One is through their own or friends' experience. They buy, say, a quart of milk advertised by a new dairy. If they like it they will continue to purchase it, and if they don't, not much is lost. The other way is by evaluating the product before purchase; for example, they may not buy a car that looks flimsy.

Unfortunately, neither of these two methods works well for deciding whether to buy the deposit services of a financial intermediary. The foremost characteristic a household looks for in a financial intermediary is that this institution be safe and not fail. But experience provides little help here. Once a bank has failed, depositors know that they should never have entrusted their funds to it, but by then it is too late—the damage is done.[2]

Similarly, the other method of evaluating a product, inspecting whether it is flimsy or not, does not work for financial intermediaries either. Very extensive effort and technical knowledge are required to evaluate the soundness of a bank or other financial intermediary. Just looking at the balance sheet won't do. For example, the potential depositor cannot tell whether the item listed as "loans" consists of loans made to sound or to risky borrowers.

And the financial intermediary has an incentive to buy assets that are too risky from the point of view of the depositor or the economy as a whole. This is so, not because it wants to fail, but because if it makes a risky loan all the additional interest the borrower pays because his loan is risky accrues to it. (The depositor, not knowing that the financial institution is taking these risks, does not ask for higher interest.) But the institution does not bear all the corresponding potential loss, since, in the absence of deposit insurance, the depositor stands to lose too. Thus, since the depositor bears part of the risk, the marginal cost of risk taking to both the financial institution and the depositor taken together exceeds the marginal cost of risk taking just to the institution. But in deciding how much risk to take, the financial institution sets the marginal revenue from taking risk equal to the marginal cost that risk imposed on it alone, so that it takes more risk than is justified when one considers the cost of taking the risk to both it and the depositors together.

Some mechanism is obviously needed to prevent financial intermediaries from taking too much risk. One possibility would be extensive con-

---

[2] Deposits are not the only example of large and infrequent expenditures on items whose technical soundness it is difficult to evaluate. This is so for houses, too. And here too we have government regulation (building codes) and inspection for safety and health defects that would not be obvious to the buyer. In the absence of such government regulations buyers would probably rely on private housing inspectors and on certificates by the builder. But the certificate of a failed bank would give a depositor little protection, and buildings are easier for a specialist to evaluate than are banks.

sumer information. Thus, in principle, depositors could subscribe to reports, written by accountants and financial analysts, that evaluate banks and other financial intermediaries. However, such reports may not be reliable enough and may be expensive, both in terms of purchase price and in terms of the time it takes to read and evaluate their competing (and presumably often differing) recommendations. In recent years large business firms that have deposits greatly exceeding the insurance limit have tried to evaluate the soundness of their banks. Vague rumors about these attempts suggest that they are far from reliable.

Another way to protect the depositor is to insure deposits. One possibility would be to have banks or other financial intermediaries insured by private insurance companies, but there would be the danger that if many large institutions failed, so would the insurance company. Bank failures cannot be predicted from actuarial tables the way deaths, or car accidents, are. However, the government is an institution that can always pay off its debts, and hence we have the government insure deposits.[3] But if the government insures deposits (up to $100,000), what protects the government against the danger of banks taking excessive risks? The answer is that the government prohibits financial institutions from buying certain risky assets, and inspects them to see that they obey these regulations.

A second, even more important reason, for government supervision of banking, is that *banks create the major part of our money supply*. Hence, a wave of bank failures could wipe out a significant proportion of the money stock. And this, in fact, happened in the Great Depression when M_1 fell by about one-quarter and M_2 by about one-third. In part three we will discuss how, and why, a reduction in the money stock causes real income and prices to fall. For now, we will merely assert that bank failures that would suddenly reduce the money stock, say, by 20 percent or more, would be a catastrophe. Thus the government has a strong incentive to prevent bank failures, and one way—though not the only one—is to prohibit banks from taking too many risks.

But how about government regulation of other financial intermediaries, such as savings and loan associations? Here the case is not as strong that a failure of, say, 20 percent of them would necessarily cause a major depression. But since it would mean a significant reduction in the public's liquid wealth, this too would *probably* result in a great shock to confidence, a substantial fall in aggregate demand, and a depression. Households that lost deposits would be reluctant to tie up their remaining funds in down payments for consumer durables and to take on additional debts. Builders, many of whom obtain loans to finance construction from savings and loan associations, would now have difficulty in getting such loans, and, in addition, many prospective home buyers would not get mortgages.

---

[3] Actually bank deposits are insured, not directly by the federal government per se, but by one of its agencies, the FDIC, which has accumulated only a limited insurance fund. But it is hard to conceive of a situation in which the U.S. Treasury would not come to the rescue of the FDIC if this were needed.

A third reason for government control over financial intermediaries is not so obvious and is much harder to defend. By controlling financial intermediaries the *government tries to subsidize residential construction and the building industry*. Savings and loan associations are limited in making business loans, or most types of consumer loans, so that they can make mortgage loans. By thus increasing the supply of mortgage loans the government tries to reduce the interest rate on them, and thereby to stimulate construction. Of course, this will not work in the long run since depositors will switch their funds out of savings and loan associations.[4] But in the short run this way of subsidizing residential construction has the great advantage of not showing up on the federal budget because no government expenditures are involved. Instead, the cost is paid by depositors in savings and loan associations, since, with these institutions not able to make some profitable business and consumer loans, their earnings, and hence their interest payments to depositors, are reduced. Since depositors in savings and loan associations have, on the average, a lower income than mortgage borrowers, this is regressive, but despite this, it is supported by many people on the (perhaps questionable) argument that one of our great national priorities should be to improve the quality of housing. Beyond this, the building industry has a great deal of political power so that that system is not likely to be changed.

A fourth reason for government control is to *limit great aggregations of economic power*. Hence banks are prohibited from starting branches in other states. If it were not for this regulation we might have some extremely large banks with branches from coast to coast. Given the size of the United States, and the absence of evidence for economies of scale (except for very small banks), it is unlikely that, in the absence of regulations, a few banks would dominate the banking business as they do in many countries. But probably some of our biggest banks would be even larger than they are now. And throughout American history there has been a great fear of both the aggregation of economic power and of the power that banks are supposed to have. Hence, it is not surprising that we prohibit banks from starting branches in other states, even though this reduces the competition that other banks face.

Do these four reasons for government regulations mean that the current heavy regulation of banks and other financial intermediaries is justified and not excessive? Not necessarily. While the authors believe that the first two reasons (the difficulty of evaluating the safety of financial institutions, and the need to prevent sharp declines in the stock of money and of near-moneys) justify some government regulations, we are much more skeptical about the other two reasons (subsidizing residential construction, and preventing the aggregation of economic power) though, of course, many respected economists disagree with us on both of these judgments.

[4] Moreover, although such subsidization raises the housing stock, once the additional housing has been built, construction activity returns to its previous level.

But even if one agrees that some controls over banks and other financial intermediaries are needed, this does not necessarily mean that our present level of controls is not excessive, and should not be reduced. For example, one way of reducing the role of government controls would be to allow private insurance companies to insure bank deposits up to a certain amount, with government insurance taking over beyond that point. Another, much more radical proposal, which we will discuss later on, would require banks to keep 100 percent reserves against their deposits. If this were done, the government would no longer have to supervise banks except to see that they keep all their required reserves. All in all, it is much easier to make a case for *some* government regulation of financial intermediaries than to decide just how much regulation is needed, and what form it should take. But more of this in chapter 8.

Summary

This chapter started by relating changes in decisions to spend to changes in either the supply of assets, or in the types of assets that people want to hold in their portfolios. It then looked at what financial intermediaries, the providers of many of our assets, do, and at why they exist. They improve the efficiency of the economy by reducing costs of borrowing and lending. And they can make illiquid long-term loans, and yet issue short-term claims on themselves. Not only do they create liquidity in this way, they also reduce risk. But since they do all this at a certain cost, not all finance goes through intermediation.

The next topic taken up is portfolio balance. By having assets and liabilities that have similar maturities, households and firms can reduce the interest rate risk to which they are exposed. In general, risk can be reduced by diversifying one's portfolio. To do this one has to know the various risk characteristics of different assets, and we discussed these characteristics of many assets. These risks, as well as the yields on assets, tell us why households hold certain assets.

Default risk on deposits is greatly reduced by government insurance and supervision. There are several reasons for this extensive government supervision and control, which work to substantially reduce competition. One is that otherwise depositors would generally lack the information needed to decide whether the institution is safe. And this gives depository institutions an incentive to take too much risk. A second reason is that large-scale failures of banks would bring about a major depression. And to a lesser degree this may be so for other depository institutions too. Another less convincing reason for government supervision is that the government tries in this way to channel additional funds into the mortgage market. A final reason is to curb the growth of great aggregations of economic power.

QUESTIONS AND EXERCISES

1. Explain why we have financial intermediaries.
2. Financial intermediaries hold relatively illiquid and somewhat risky assets and yet can issue very liquid and safe claims on themselves. Explain how they can do this magic. Can they do this without limit?
3. Which argument for government regulation of financial institutions do you find most convincing? Which least convincing? Give your reasons.
4. Suppose you had $100,000. How would you distribute your portfolio over various assets? Why?
5. Many households hold claims on financial intermediaries, and, at the same time, borrow from financial intermediaries. Why don't they "borrow" from themselves?
6. Suppose that you decide to set yourself up as a financial institution and issue $1,000 deposits to each of four customers. Suppose further that the probability of any one depositor demanding repayment of his or her deposit within the relevant period is 20 percent (and that the probabilities of various depositors demanding repayment are independent of each other). How much would you want to keep in reserves to meet potential depositor demand? (Hint: the answer involves more than just a simple number.)

FURTHER READING

BENSTON, GEORGE. "A Transactions Cost Approach to the Theory of Financial Intermediation." *Journal of Finance* 31 (May 1976): 215–32. A very thoughtful, elegant discussion, though a bit difficult at points.

GOLDSMITH, RAYMOND. *Financial Institutions.* New York: Random House, 1968. This is an excellent survey of the financial system.

GURLEY, JOHN, and SHAW, EDWARD. *Money in a Theory of Finance.* Washington, D.C.: Brookings Institution, 1960. An advanced, seminal treatise.

MOORE, BASIL. *An Introduction to the Theory of Finance.* New York: Free Press, 1968. Chapter two provides a very useful and thorough, yet brief, discussion of portfolio management.

SHAW, EDWARD. *Financial Deepening in Economic Development.* New York: Oxford University Press, 1973. An important discussion of the role of finance in less-developed countries.

3

The Banking
Industry

The previous chapter presented a bird's-eye view of financial institutions and their functions. This and the following chapter deal with our most prominent financial institutions, commercial banks. It would be nice at this point to define *commercial banks* or just *banks,* as we will call them. Unfortunately, the only accurate definition that can be given is the vacuous one that commercial banks are financial institutions that hold government charters as commercial banks. At one time commercial banks could be distinguished from savings banks by the fact that only commercial banks could issue checking deposits. But this is no longer the case.

Banks are our most important financial institutions as they create the bulk of our money stock and have such a wide range of activities; they are department stores of finance. We will therefore take up banking in considerable detail, both because the behavior of banks is relevant for monetary policy, and because, on a more personal level, all readers are likely to deal with banks as depositors, and perhaps as borrowers. In dealing with a bank it is obviously useful to be able to see things from the bank's point of view, and this requires some knowledge of how they operate.

The current chapter deals with the banking industry as a whole, and takes up the way banks are regulated, and how they interact with each other. The following chapter then looks at the individual bank as a profit-maximizing institution and at its assets and liabilities.

A Sketch of Banking History

Banking is an ancient business. There were banks already in ancient Babylon and the classical civilizations, particularly in Rome. But modern banking started in Renaissance Italy where bankers, apart from buying and selling foreign currencies, also took demand and time deposits. These demand deposits were usually transferred orally by the owner visiting the banker who sat behind his bench or table, though checks were not unknown. (Our term *bankruptcy* comes from the Italian custom of breaking

35

the bench of a banker who could not pay off his creditors.) The most famous of these Italian bankers were the Medici family, who for a time ruled Florence and made loans to princes and merchants both in Italy and in the rest of Europe.

In England banking grew out of the custom of goldsmiths, who took gold and silver from their customers for safekeeping. They then discovered that they could lend such coins out, keeping just a certain proportion as a reserve, since not all customers would come in for repayment at the same time. Moreover they gave their depositors interest-bearing receipts, which these depositors could pass on to other people, instead of paying with coins. Eventually, to make such transfers more convenient, the goldsmiths issued these receipts in round-number sums. Thus they became private banknotes; that is, notes in appearance more or less like our present currency notes, but repayable on demand by the banker in gold or silver.

In colonial America the first bank, in the modern sense of the term, was the Bank of North America, founded in 1782. (A contemporary bank, the First Pennsylvania Bank, can trace its ancestry back to this bank.) Subsequently, banking spread rapidly as the states chartered more and more banks, some of them owned by the state itself. Between 1781 and 1861 over twenty-five hundred banks were organized, but many of them were unsound; almost two-fifths of them had to close within ten years after they had opened.[1]

In 1791, at the urging of Alexander Hamilton, Congress temporarily chartered a national bank, the First Bank of the United States, located in Philadelphia, with the federal government owning part of it. This bank, which was much larger than the state-chartered banks, held deposits of the federal government and transferred funds for it to various parts of the country. It also tried to discipline the state-chartered banks that had issued too many banknotes, either by refusing to accept their notes in payment or by collecting a lot of them and presenting them to the unfortunate bank for redemption in gold all at once.

Not surprisingly, in 1811 when the charter of the First Bank of the United States came up in Congress for renewal, the state-chartered banks tried to kill it. Other arguments against it were that it was, in part, owned by foreigners, that the bank had dabbled in politics, doubts that the Constitution permitted Congress to charter a bank, and a belief that the bank had too much monopoly power. These arguments were effective. Congress did not renew the First Bank's charter. State banks, now being freed from the pressure to redeem their notes, became much more numerous, and as they issued more banknotes and demand deposits, they contributed to an inflation.

But in 1816 the Second Bank of the United States was chartered with the federal government owning one-fifth of the stock and appointing one-

---

[1] Benjamin Klebaner, *Commercial Banking in the United States: A History* (Hinsdale, Ill.: Dryden Press, 1974), p. 48.

fifth of the directors. Although it did a lot of good in curbing excessive expansion by state banks, its charter was allowed to expire in 1836. This occurred in good part because it was opposed by President Andrew Jackson who was concerned about the concentration of economic power in the Northeast and was an opponent of the bank's president, Nicholas Biddle.

The 1830s also saw another important change in banking. Until then states could charter banks only by a special act of the legislature. This led to much corruption, favoritism, and scandal. In 1837 Michigan led the way to a new system, called **free banking.** Under this system a *charter by the legislature was no longer needed;* anyone who met rather easy conditions could organize a bank and issue banknotes as well as take deposits, checks by this time having come into widespread usage. Although free banking avoided the scandals of the previous system, it developed its own problems. Many new banks were organized and issued their banknotes, and with so many different banknotes around, it was hard to differentiate between genuine and counterfeit notes, or even notes issued on nonexistent banks. Moreover, notes of certain banks, considered unsafe or located far away, circulated at less than full face value. Merchants had to look up the value of notes presented to them as payment in registers of banknotes that were issued periodically. Moreover a few—though not very many—banks, the so-called wildcat banks, located in out of the way places to make it hard to present their banknotes to them for redemption in coin. As a result some banknotes circulated well below their face value, and, in addition, bank failures were common. But, on the whole, the problems created by free banking were not so horrendous as is sometimes made out, and this system did provide the rapidly growing country with an expanding money stock.

But the confusion caused by so many different types of banknotes being in circulation, and the tendency of banks to issue more notes than they could redeem, as well as the need to finance the Civil War by opening up a new market for government bonds, led Congress to establish the National Banking System starting with the National Currency Act of 1863 (later amended and renamed the National Banking Act). The banknotes, issued by each of the national banks chartered by the federal government, were made uniform, and they were safe because each national bank had to deposit $100 of federal government bonds with the Comptroller of the Currency for each $90 of this new currency it issued. If a bank failed, the holders of its national banknotes were repaid by the Comptroller of the Currency out of the bonds the bank had deposited with him. State-chartered banks were effectively prevented from issuing banknotes by the imposition of an annual 10 percent tax on such notes. There was now a uniform and sound currency that, unlike the previous banknotes issued by state-chartered banks, was accepted at par (that is, at full value) throughout the country. Furthermore, funds could now be transferred all over the country at a cost that could not exceed the small cost of shipping banknotes, and was frequently less. But state banks, though they could no longer issue banknotes, did not disappear, as had been thought they would, because, with the rapidly growing use of checks, they could still provide a medium of exchange, demand deposits.

While the national banking system solved the problem of too many different types of banknotes circulating, and reduced the frequency of bank failures, it was far from perfect. Thus it did not provide an efficient system of check collection. A bank would send an out-of-town check deposited with it, usually not directly to the bank on which it was drawn, but to its correspondent bank, and the correspondent bank would frequently send it on to its correspondent bank, so that a check might pass through many banks, and take a long time before it was presented to the bank on which it was drawn.[2] If the check bounced either because it was fraudulent or because the depositor had insufficient funds, it would take a long time until this was discovered. The reason for this roundabout method of clearing was that, unless the check was presented by its correspondent bank, the bank on which a check was drawn would charge a fee for paying it to a bank in a different locality, a fee that allegedly covered the cost of shipping funds.

Another problem was that the reserve requirement (a certain proportion of a bank's deposits or banknotes must be kept in a specified safe form) was not very effective. Banks were reluctant to draw down their reserves, and some would rather close their doors than touch their reserves. Moreover, one bank might exhaust its reserves during a run while other banks still had all their reserves available. Furthermore, the way the reserve requirement was set was inefficient. National banks were divided into three classes: central reserve city banks (originally banks in New York, Chicago, and St. Louis), reserve city banks (originally banks in sixteen other large cities, but later forty-nine cities), and country banks (all national banks located elsewhere). Country banks had to keep a minimum of 6 percent of their deposits as currency in their own vaults, but could keep the remaining 9 percent of the 15 percent reserve requirement as deposits with their correspondent banks in reserve cities. And these reserve city banks could keep up to half *their* 25 percent reserve requirement as deposits with their central reserve city correspondents. The latter had to keep all of their 25 percent reserve requirement as vault cash. This system of reserve pyramiding, whereby the same dollar of currency could be counted as reserves three times if it were sent by a country bank to a reserve city bank, and sent by the reserve city bank to a central reserve city bank, led to trouble. When country banks needed additional currency, they would call in some of their reserves from the reserve city banks who, in turn, would call in reserves from the central reserve city banks. The central reserve city banks would then sometimes have to meet this

---

[2] Correspondent banks will be discussed later in this chapter. For the time being they can be thought of simply as banks that provided services such as check clearing for other banks associated with them.

demand by calling in their short-term loans to the money market and the stock market. As a result, interest rates would rise very sharply, and sometimes, if the country banks could not get the currency they needed, they would fail, and there would be a financial panic. Banks did, however, develop a device to ameliorate the impact of financial panics. They would jointly stop paying out currency to their depositors, and would pay instead in clearing house certificates, which were notes that could be used to make deposits, and hence would be accepted as payments in many cases, albeit often at a discount.

There was no central bank that could adjust the money supply to meet the need for money, and the money supply could therefore not expand along with the demand for money. Hence, there were frequent complaints about a "shortage" of money in the fall when the harvesting season raised the demand for money, and interest rates would rise. (Whether these complaints were justified, in the sense that the supply of money *should* expand along with the demand for it, is another matter, which we will take up in chapter 23.) A related complaint was that in a financial panic no additional currency was available to meet the increase in demand as the public, afraid of bank failures, tried to shift out of deposits, which were not secured like the banknotes by the Comptroller of the Currency, into currency. Bank failures were frequent, particularly among state banks, which, being less heavily regulated than national banks, had grown at a faster rate.

In 1907 the country suffered a very severe depression, which along with previous dissatisfaction with the National Banking System, resulted in the appointment of the National Monetary Commission. After exhaustive studies this commission recommended the establishment of a central banking system, our Federal Reserve System. But there was a great deal of opposition to the creation of a central bank out of fear that it would be run by bankers and lead to a banking cartel. It was not until 1913 that this opposition was overcome and the Federal Reserve Act was signed by President Woodrow Wilson.

We will discuss the Federal Reserve System in considerable detail in chapter 7. Here we will only note the ways in which this new system was intended to solve the problems that beset the National Banking System. Checks could now be cleared through the Federal Reserve System, instead of routing them through a whole chain of correspondent banks. Reserve pyramiding was abolished by requiring member banks to keep all their legal reserves as deposits with the Federal Reserve; subsequently banks were allowed to keep them also as currency in their vaults. The money supply was made more responsive to the demand for money by enabling banks to borrow from the Federal Reserve with certain constraints, and the Federal Reserve was charged with reducing seasonal fluctuations in interest rates. But the attempt to make banks safer failed miserably. There were many more bank failures in the period 1931–33 than at any other time.

Chartering and Examination

Our current banking system is heavily regulated. Government control over banks comes in several layers. Initially, there is chartering. One cannot just open a bank the way one opens an ordinary business. A prospective bank has to obtain a *charter, either from the federal government* as a **national bank,** or *from its state government* as a **state bank.**

Figure 3.1   The Structure of Bank Regulation

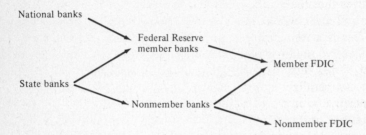

The structure of Bank Regulation

The second layer of government control is the Federal Reserve System. Although its main function is the conduct of monetary policy, its subsidiary function is to regulate banks. All national banks must, and state banks may, but need not, join the Federal Reserve System, becoming a **member bank**—this term *always refers to membership in the Federal Reserve System.* Third, there is the Federal Deposit Insurance Corporation (FDIC). All member banks *must* join the FDIC, thus becoming insured banks, while nonmember banks *may* join if they meet the FDIC's admission criteria. The resultant structure of government contacts is shown in figure 3.1. Table 3.1 shows the relative importance of the various types

Table 3.1   Distribution of Banks by Type
            June 1978

	Percent of all banks	*Percent of all bank deposits*
Uninsured Banks	2.2	2.1
Insured Banks	97.8	97.9
Member Banks	38.2	71.9
National Banks	31.4	54.6
State Banks	6.8	17.3
Nonmember Banks	61.8	28.1
All State Banks	68.6	45.4

SOURCE: *Federal Reserve Bulletin,* February 1980, p. A-17.

of banks. It shows that only one-third of all banks are national banks, but that, since on the average they are larger than state banks, they hold more than half of all deposits. Only 38.2 percent of all banks are member banks, but they hold 71.9 percent of all deposits. Practically all banks (97.8 percent), holding 97.9 percent of all deposits, are insured.

To obtain a charter a prospective bank applies for one either to the Comptroller of the Currency, an office of the U.S. Treasury Department, or to a state official called the superintendent of banks or a similar name. State requirements, which are generally looser than the requirements for a national bank, vary among states and apply only to state banks, and not to national banks located in the state.

A very important requirement for a national bank charter is that the government believes that there is a genuine public need for this new bank, and that its establishment would not take too much business away from existing banks. This is a remarkable requirement since it is so contrary to our general competitive philosophy of allowing efficient firms to force less efficient ones out of business. In banking (as in most regulated industries) we severely curb competition, on the grounds that if a bank fails and cannot repay its deposits, too much of the loss is borne by the FDIC and perhaps large depositors, rather than by the stockholders. However, many, though certainly not all, economists question this departure from the competitive norm, and believe that new banks should be allowed to enter the industry even if this weakens existing banks.

After a national bank has its charter and is in operation it still has many contacts with the Comptroller of the Currency or the state banking authority. One form of this contact is the **examination.** At least three times every two years, employees of the Comptroller of the Currency, called bank examiners, make *an unannounced visit to each national bank*. When examiners descend on a bank the junior examiners go to the tellers' cages and the vault to count the currency, while the senior examiners investigate the securities and the loan documents held by the bank.

Although preventing fraud is one of the purposes of bank examination, it is not the major one. The main emphasis is on seeing whether the bank is complying with various rules and regulations concerning its asset holdings, if it is carrying its assets on its books at a conservative value, and whether any securities held, and loans made, involve excessive risks. If a security is deemed too speculative the examiner can order the bank to sell it, and if repayment of a loan is doubtful the examiner can order the bank to write it off as a loss by deducting it from the bank's capital account. Since a bank is required to keep an acceptable minimum ratio of capital to deposits, the write-down of capital that results from writing off loan losses, or from selling low quality securities at a loss, may force it to raise more capital or curb the growth rate of its deposits. And even if a bank does not have to raise additional capital, the fact that it has to write off loans can hurt a bank by reducing the price of its stock. Obviously, since the quality of loans and securities is a matter of opinion, disputes between bank officers and bank examiners do arise. However, in some cases bank officers may welcome the advice of examiners who, as outsiders, may take a more objective view than do the bank's officers.[3]

The examiners may classify a bank as a "problem bank" if it has insufficient capital, or has made unwarranted loans to its officers, directors, or stockholders, has inefficient or possibly dishonest management, or has made an unusual amount of substandard loans. Such a problem bank will then be examined more frequently. Moreover, if the news that the bank has been classified as a problem bank leaks out, as has happened in the past, neither the bank's customers nor its stockholders are likely to react favorably.

However, it is easy to exaggerate the power of bank examiners, particularly in their dealings with a large bank. Large banks are very complex institutions, and it is difficult for examiners to acquire enough knowledge about the bank's affairs to be able to dispute successfully with the bank's officers and lawyers. A senior official of the office of the Comptroller of the Currency was once quoted as saying, "How can I tell David Rockefeller how to run his bank? I've never made more than $40,000 in my life." [4] Small banks, however, offer an easier target. All in all, a recent study discussing bank capital concluded:

> The lack of objective standards creates difficulties. Except when a bank is asking for a privilege, regulators can only urge or attempt to convince a bank that more capital is required. Arguments as to what is or is not adequate are difficult if not impossible to resolve. . . . The list of enforcement proceedings shows long delays when a bank decides not to cooperate. Examiners do find illegal and illogical actions, but they also miss many. In large banks they can be overwhelmed by details. . . .[5]

The Comptroller of the Currency and the state banking authorities are not the only ones who have a right to examine banks. The Federal Reserve too can examine its member banks, and the FDIC can examine all insured banks. However, to prevent unnecessary duplication, or even triplication, these banking agencies cooperate with each other. Thus for national banks the Federal Reserve usually accepts the examination reports of the Comptroller of the Currency and examines only its state member banks. And in some states the state banking authority relies on these Federal Reserve examination reports instead of making its own examinations. Similarly, while the FDIC has the right to examine all insured banks, it usually examines only nonmember banks, and uses Comptroller of the Currency or Federal Reserve examination reports for member banks.

---

[3] Since a bank examiner becomes familiar with the operating methods of many banks and obtains in this way a thorough knowledge of banking, some banks like to hire former bank examiners.

[4] *New York Times,* 22 December 1977, p. 49.

[5] Sherman Maisel et al., *Measuring Risk and the Adequacy of Capital in Commercial Banks* (National Bureau of Economic Research; Chicago: University of Chicago Press, in press). This extract is taken from a preliminary draft.

Federal Reserve Membership

As table 3.1 showed, 38 percent of all banks are Federal Reserve member banks, and these are mostly national banks. Few state banks, particularly the small ones, have joined the Federal Reserve System. (The Federal Reserve System, whose main task is conducting monetary policy, consists of a Board of Governors in Washington, D.C., and twelve regional Federal Reserve banks.) The most serious deterrent to Federal Reserve membership is that, as will be discussed in the next chapter, the Federal Reserve imposes a much more burdensome reserve requirement on its member banks than the states impose on nonmember banks. Since member banks are not paid interest on these reserves, joining the Federal Reserve requires banks to forgo some earnings. However, a new law passed in March 1980 will eventually eliminate this deterrent. Over an eight-year phasing-in period the new law will step by step impose the same reserve requirements on nonmember banks as on member banks. Other, but lesser, disadvantages of membership are that it subjects banks to examination by the Federal Reserve and that the Federal Reserve's regulations are probably more burdensome than state regulations.

What are the offsetting benefits? Until 1980 one benefit particularly important to small banks was that, under normal circumstances, only a member bank could borrow from the Federal Reserve. But since then nonmember banks too, as well as other depository institutions that keep reserves with the Fed, can borrow from it. For larger banks the main benefit of membership is that it allows them to attract the deposits of smaller banks in a correspondent relationship. Moreover, Federal Reserve membership confers prestige on a bank: it announces to the world that this bank is meeting more exacting minimum requirements than nonmember banks. For depositors whose deposits exceed the $100,000 insurance ceiling, this *may* be a consideration in choosing a bank.

When one compares the advantages and disadvantages of membership, it is not surprising that until 1980 (when the law was changed to impose the Fed's reserve requirements also on nonmember banks) Fed membership had fallen significantly. While in 1965 47 percent of all banks, holding 83 percent of all deposits, were members, by 1978 only 38 percent of all banks with 72 percent of all deposits were members, a trend that worried the Fed a great deal. But now that, after a phasing-in period, nonmember banks will have to hold the same reserves as member banks, the downward trend in membership may come to an end. Whether or not this will happen is hard to predict because what was previously the biggest benefit of membership, being able to borrow from the Fed, will now also be available to nonmember banks.

Bank Capital

We mentioned previously that banks have to meet a minimum capital requirement. The time has come to discuss bank equity capital in greater detail, since it presents a major problem for the banking industry and the bank regulatory agencies. **Bank equity capital** is the *stockholders' equity in the bank.* It is represented on the balance sheet mainly by outstanding stock, surplus, and retained earnings. In addition to equity capital, banks can count as part of their capital long-term funds they have obtained by selling bonds and notes.

The purpose of a capital requirement is to provide a cushion of safety both for depositors and for the FDIC. The reason why a large capital stock helps to make a bank safe for depositors and the FDIC is because capital, being only a residual claim, represents those funds that the bank can lose without endangering its ability to repay deposits. Suppose, for example, that a bank's capital is equal to 5 percent of its assets. Then even if, as a result of making unsound loans, it loses 5 percent of its assets, the depositors' funds are still covered; only the stockholders lose. But if this bank had had capital equal to only, say, 3 percent of its assets, the FDIC and perhaps large depositors would have suffered a loss. But with a 5 percent capital to assets ratio only the stockholders lose. And protection of stockholders is not a legitimate reason for bank regulation—stockholders are responsible for how they invest.

From the bank's point of view a certain cushion of equity capital is clearly desirable. It helps to protect the bank's stockholders against the danger of the bank failing and it reassures the bank's customers. Bank business borrowers, as well as large depositors, are reassured by a high capital ratio. Developing a borrowing relationship with a bank is time consuming, and a firm prefers not to borrow from a bank that is unlikely to be around next year. However, as with many activities, the marginal yield from adding capital declines after some point. Suppose, for example, that a bank already has a high stock of capital relative to its liabilities. The chance of its failing is already so low that adding even more capital does not influence its potential customers much.

At the same time, however, the more equity capital a bank has per dollar of assets, the greater is the number of dollars of capital over which the bank's earnings have to be spread. Assume, for example, that the bank earns a one percent profit on its total assets. If a bank's equity capital equals 10 percent of total assets, then this one percent earnings on assets represents a 10 percent yield to the bank's stockholders; on the other hand, if the bank has the same earnings, but only a 5 percent ratio of equity capital to total assets, then the stockholders earn 20 percent on their capital. For each bank there exists therefore an optimal ratio of capital to assets at which the marginal advantage of additional capital is just offset by its disadvantage.

But what constitutes an optimal capital stock—and hence the optimal amount of risk—from the bank's point of view is insufficient capital, and hence excessive risk, from the social viewpoint. If a bank would be the only one to lose if it fails, the social and private costs of risk taking would be the same. But this is not so. If a bank fails, the FDIC has to step in, often at a substantial cost, and rescue the insured deposits, and, in addition, depositors with accounts above the insurance ceiling may lose. More importantly, if a large bank fails, or many smaller banks fail almost simultaneously, the public may lose confidence in other banks, and try to withdraw deposits from them, thus causing them to fail. Quite apart from the losses and disruptions this could cause, it could also reduce the stock of money substantially and cause a recession.

When a bank decides how much risk it should accept it does not take these external costs of its potential failure into account, but selects a level of risk at which the marginal loss from risk taking is just equal to the marginal yield from taking this risk. Hence, it takes more risk than is socially optimal. This is why the government is justified in stepping in and limiting the amount of risk a bank is allowed to take.[6] It does this both by limiting the riskiness of the bank's loans and securities, and by requiring the bank to hold more capital than it would in the absence of regulations.[7]

The amount of capital a bank should have has to be related to some measure of the bank's size; clearly a bank with $1 million of assets does not need as much capital as a bank with $1 billion of assets. But a $10-billion bank does not have to have a thousand times as much capital as a $10-million bank. A large bank holds more diversified assets, and therefore its average losses each year can be predicted better. Second, fraud is a very frequent cause of bank failure. But a, say, $100-million fraud is extremely unlikely. Hence, a $10-billion bank with $500 million of capital is much less likely to be bankrupted by fraud than a $10-million bank with half a million dollars of capital.

One obvious measure of capital adequacy is to express capital as a percentage of total assets or deposits. But since the function of bank capital is to protect the bank against the losses it may suffer if some of its assets turn sour, or cannot be liquidated in time, a better measure of the adequacy of a bank's capital is to measure the bank's capital as a percentage of its risk assets, that is, those assets that involve some meaningful risk. Hence, one can exclude from the denominator of the capital ratio such assets as U.S. government securities and reserves with the Federal Reserve. A more sophisticated approach developed by the Federal Reserve System classifies bank assets into several different risk classes and then sets a different ratio of needed capital for each of these classes.

As figure 3.2 shows, the ratio of capital to risk assets has declined

---

[6] Alternatively, it could charge banks for the right to take more risk.

[7] See John Mingo, "Regulatory Influence on Bank Capital Investment," *Journal of Finance* 32 (June 1977): 1111–23.

Figure 3.2   Ratio of Capital to Total Assets and Risk Assets
              1935–75

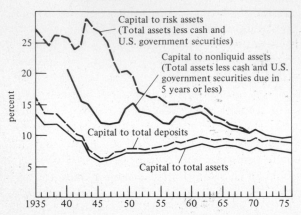

SOURCE: Emmanuel N. Roussakis, *Managing Commercial Bank Funds* (New York: Praeger, 1977), p. 13. Copyright © 1977 by Praeger Publishers, Inc. Reproduced by permission of Praeger Publishers.

since 1950, though this trend has come to an end or been reversed slightly in the last few years. The ratio of capital to total assets has not declined, however. The downward trend in the capital to risk asset ratio is presumably due to the fact that, with the FDIC insuring deposits starting in 1934, the public has become more willing to trust banks with a low capital to risk asset ratio, but it has taken the public some time to do so. The slight increase in the capital to risk asset ratios in recent years is probably due primarily to the shock effect of some large bank failures in the mid-1970s, which we will discuss in the following section. These figures are, of course, averages. As table 3.2 shows, the larger banks have a lower capital to assets ratio.

The federal regulatory authorities, the FDIC, the Federal Reserve, and the Comptroller of the Currency, are concerned about the low capital ratios of banks and have tried, without much success, to get the banks to raise them. This lack of success is due to several factors. One is that banks can maximize profits by having a low capital ratio. Thus, banks have been unwilling to sell additional equity on the argument that with bank stock selling at fairly low prices, a sale of additional equity would dilute the equity of the present owners. And while banks could obtain additional capital by plowing back earnings, banks argue that their current earnings are so low that they cannot obtain much capital this way except by reducing dividends, which would cause the price of their stock to fall.

A second factor explaining the regulators' lack of success in raising capital ratios is that they do not really have very much control over banks. If a particular bank has an unusually low capital ratio the regulators can discipline it, for example, by not allowing it to absorb another bank in a merger. But if all, or most, banks lower their capital ratios, more or less in

Table 3.2   Equity Capital as Percent of Total
Assets by Size of Bank
30 June 1977

Banks with total assets of (in millions of dollars):	Equity capital as percent of total assets
Less than 5.0	12.3
5.0–9.9	9.5
10.0–24.9	8.3
25.0–49.9	7.8
50.0–99.9	7.6
100.0–299.9	7.1
300.0–499.9	7.1
500.0–999.9	6.7
1000.0–4999.9	6.6
5000.0 and over	7.0
ALL BANKS	7.2

SOURCE: FDIC, *Assets and Liabilities: Commercial and Mutual Savings Banks,* 30 June 1977, table 9.

step, it is difficult for the regulators to punish any particular bank; it can argue that it is conducting itself in accord with standard banking practice. ("Grading on the curve" is not confined to the classroom!) This is so particularly since nobody really knows exactly what the socially desirable capital ratio is.

A third factor is that since the mid-1960s we have followed a monetary policy that has allowed bank deposits, and hence also bank assets, to rise at a very rapid rate. Hence, it would have required a very rapid rate of increase in bank capital to prevent the capital to deposit and capital to assets ratios from falling.

So far we have talked about bank capital as though it were obvious what bank capital is. But this is not the case. The great bulk of bank capital consists of equity capital, that is, capital belonging to the owners, that is, stockholders, but in recent years some large and medium-sized banks have also obtained capital by issuing debt securities, such as bonds. Bonds represent a claim on the bank, and hence are *not* equity capital. But banks, unlike firms in other industries, have been allowed to consider bonds as capital on the argument that these funds serve to protect the depositors, since in case of failure, the bondholders' claims are subordinated to the depositors' and the FDIC's claims. Yet, bonds are not fully capital because the bank is legally required to pay interest on them, whereas it can, if necessary, skip the dividend on its stock. Hence, some economists believe that one should count only equity capital in calculating the capital ratios. But, in any case, equity capital still accounts for all but 7 percent of bank capital, so that this is not a serious problem for many banks, at least not yet.

Deposit Insurance

In May 1974, the Franklin National Bank, previously the nation's twentieth largest bank with deposits close to $3 billion, faced a crisis. On 1 May
the Federal Reserve in denying Franklin's request to take over in a merger
another financial institution announced that the bank had overexpanded
and should retrench its operations. This triggered rumors about the bank's
safety and caused an outflow of funds, which forced the bank to borrow
heavily from the Federal Reserve. A few days afterwards Franklin announced that it could not pay its usual quarterly dividend (a most unusual
event for a large bank), and, also, that it had sizable foreign exchange
losses. These foreign exchange losses turned out to be but the tip of the
iceberg. In an attempt to expand too rapidly the bank had made a large
volume of unsound loans. As the bank's troubles became known large
depositors withdrew deposits, while many other banks refused to lend to it.
But Franklin was able to offset these deposit outflows by borrowing an un-
precedented $1.75 billion from the Federal Reserve.

At one time even this would not have sufficed because small depositors
would also have withdrawn their deposits. But small depositors did not do
so because they knew that all deposits were protected (up to $20,000 at
the time) by the FDIC. Had it not been for the FDIC, Franklin National
would have failed right away, and its failure *might* have triggered runs on
other banks, and hence a financial panic. But this did not happen, and
Franklin National was kept afloat until October 1974 when the FDIC
was able to merge it into another bank, the European-American Bank. A
possible financial crisis was therefore avoided, albeit at the cost of the
Federal Reserve, and hence ultimately taxpayers, having to subsidize an
inefficient commercial bank by giving it very large loans at below market
interest rates.

The FDIC commenced operations in 1934 as a government agency to
insure bank deposits in response to the massive bank failures that had
occurred between 1930 and 1933.[8] As pointed out before, all Federal Reserve member banks have to belong to the FDIC, and most nonmember
banks have joined too. All but 2 percent of all banks, which hold 2 percent
of all deposits, are members of the FDIC.[9] This almost universal membership is not surprising since membership in the FDIC gives a bank a great
competitive advantage over an uninsured bank in soliciting deposits. But

---

[8] Previously, some states had operated their own deposit insurance systems, but
most of them had ended in failure. For a description of these schemes see the mono-
graph by George Benston cited under Further Reading.

[9] The fact that insured banks are *members* of the FDIC is legalistic (but generally used) terminology. Insured banks do not control the FDIC. Its directors are
presidential appointees and the funds accumulated by the FDIC do not belong to its
members. Note, again, that the term *member bank* always refers to Federal Reserve
membership and not to FDIC membership.

FDIC membership is not a right. Before admitting a bank the FDIC evaluates its soundness by considering factors such as the adequacy of its capital, the quality of its management, and its future business prospects. Since competitive pressures make FDIC membership necessary for nearly every bank, the FDIC, in effect, has veto power over the formation of just about any new bank.

In return for an insurance premium paid by the banks, the FDIC insures deposits up to a certain amount, currently $100,000. If a depositor has several accounts in his or her own name in one bank, the total that is insured is still $100,000. But if an individual has several accounts under different names (for example, a personal account, a joint account with a business partner or a spouse), or if these accounts have different beneficiaries (as in the case of trust funds, for example), then each of these accounts is insured separately for $100,000. Similarly, if a person has accounts in his or her own name in several banks all of these accounts are insured. At present, nearly all accounts are fully insured, but the very few that are not include some very large accounts, so that only about 72 percent of the dollar value of deposits is insured.

But the existence of a $100,000 ceiling does not mean that in most bank failures depositors with larger accounts suffer losses. Thus in the period from 1934 to 1976 the FDIC paid out, or made available, 99.6 percent of all deposits in failing banks.[10] When a bank fails there are several possibilities. One is that the FDIC simply pays off all deposits only up to $100,000, and then reimburses itself to the extent possible by selling the bank's assets and collecting on its outstanding loans.[11] In this case there are, of course, losses to large depositors. But a second possibility—and it is the more common one—is that the FDIC merges the failing bank into a sound bank. (To induce a sound bank to marry the failing bank, the FDIC frequently has to buy some of the unsound assets of the failing bank at book value, or provide a dowry in some other way.) If so, all the deposits in the failed bank are taken over by the sound bank, and thus even deposits of over $100,000 are fully protected. A third, rather infrequently used, possibility is for the FDIC to make a loan to the bank so that it can survive.[12] Table 3.3 shows how frequently each method was used from 1964 to 1976, as well as the frequency and magnitude of bank

[10] Chayim Herzig-Marx, "Bank Failures," *Economic Perspectives* (Federal Reserve Bank of Chicago) 2 (March–April 1978): 28. In the period covered in this study the insurance ceiling was much lower than it is now.

[11] However, if you have an outstanding bank loan the FDIC will subtract the value of the loan from the size of your deposit, and pay out only the difference. This offset provision can reduce substantially the amount the FDIC has to pay out.

[12] In a very few cases where closing a bank would deprive a community of needed bank services, or lead to too much concentration in banking resources, the FDIC has temporarily opened its own bank, called a Deposit Insurance National Bank, which has then taken over the failed bank's deposits prior to either paying off deposits or merging the bank with a sound one, or else sold the stock of this bank to the public. Another possibility, though one rarely used, is for the FDIC to reorganize the bank.

Table 3.3 Frequency and Disposition of Bank Failures

YEAR	Number of failed banks		Deposits in failed banks (THOUSANDS)		Failure rate (per 10,000 banks)		Disposition of insured failed banks[a]	
	INSURED	NON-INSURED	INSURED	NON-INSURED	INSURED	NON-INSURED	DEPOSIT PAYOFF	PURCHASE AND ASSUMPTION[b]
YEARLY AVERAGE:								
1934–1943	39	10	$49,787	$4,134	28.8	66.2	24	15
1944–1953	3	1	8,914	650	2.2	17.7	0	3
1954–1963	3	2	8,868	967	2.1	42.6	2	1
YEARLY:								
1964	7	1	23,438	429	5.2	36.5	7	0
1965	5	4	43,861	1,395	3.7	152.1	3	2
1966	7	1	103,523	2,648	5.2	42.6	1	6
1967	4	0	10,878	0	3.0	0.0	4	0
1968	3	0	22,524	0	2.2	0.0	0	3
1969	9	0	40,134	0	6.7	0.0	4	5
1970	7	1	54,821	423	5.2	54.1	4	3
1971	6	2	132,152	0	4.4	0.0	5	1
1972	1	0	20,480	79,304	0.7	97.1	1	0
1973	6	0	971,296	0	4.3	0.0	3	3
1974	4	0	1,575,832	0	2.8	0.0	0	4
1975	13	1	339,574	1,004	9.0	38.3	3	10
1976	16	1	864,859	800	11.1	36.4	3	13

a. "Disposition of insured failed banks" and the number of insured failed banks do not agree because some insured failed banks subsequently reopened.

b. Includes opening of Deposit Insurance National Banks.

SOURCE: Based on Chayim Herzig-Marx, "Bank Failures," *Economic Perspectives* (Federal Reserve Bank of Chicago) 2 (March–April 1978):23.

failures. It includes those cases of de facto failure but, however, not de jure failure, in which a bank that is about to fail quickly merges on its own with another bank, thus avoiding failure.

Obviously, large depositors are better off if the FDIC uses the *merger route,* called **deposit assumption,** rather than paying off deposits just up to $100,000. Moreover, if a very large bank fails and the FDIC would pay off the small depositors, the losses experienced by large business depositors could have serious repercussions; some of them might fail and unemployment would increase. In addition, if there is some concern about the safety of other banks large depositors might start a run on these banks. Hence, there could well be a series of bank failures.

Since in the past the FDIC has used the merger route for large banks where there are many accounts over the insurance ceiling, the view has become prevalent that the FDIC, in effect, protects all deposits in large banks, or at least in, say, the twenty largest banks. But the law requires the FDIC to use whichever route is cheapest for it. But this may be hard to determine. And the FDIC has said that in one case, the failure of the San Diego National Bank in 1973, it has been close to paying off deposits and letting large depositors take their losses. Hence, it is not certain that it will always protect large deposits. But whether it will actually allow large depositors to lose in a case where this could cause serious disruptions and perhaps runs on other banks, or whether it will always conveniently determine that the merger route is cheaper, is something that only the future can tell.

In any case, in an indirect way the FDIC protects all depositors. If it were not for the existence of the FDIC, then during a financial crisis small depositors would run all banks that look shaky to them, and this could cause many banks to fail. Since banks hold only a small fraction of their deposits as currency in the bank, and since many of their assets cannot be liquidated immediately, any bank, regardless of how soundly managed it is, can be destroyed if too many of its depositors suddenly try to withdraw their deposits. By preventing small depositors from running a bank, the FDIC indirectly protects all deposits in banks that would otherwise be forced into bankruptcy by runs.

An obvious question that arises at this point is why the FDIC does not insure all bank deposits, why is there a $100,000 ceiling? The cost to the FDIC of covering all deposits would be trivial. The main argument against covering all deposits is that this would reduce some of the pressures towards safe management that are currently faced by banks. As long as there is a ceiling there are some depositors, presumably mainly business firms, who have an incentive to monitor a bank's operations and make sure that it is sound. To some extent, banks therefore compete for large deposits by following safe policies. But if all deposits were covered, then this pressure towards safe management would no longer exist.

In any case, some economists believe that even large depositors are not able to evaluate accurately the soundness of a bank, so that their monitoring is not an efficient way to control the risk taking of banks. Others believe that only very large depositors can monitor a bank effectively, so that the ceiling should be raised substantially. Another aspect of the ceiling is that if all bank deposits were fully insured, it would also be politically necessary to insure all savings and loan and mutual savings bank deposits fully. Banks could then object that this would help their competitors. Since banks have a greater reputation for safety, insuring large deposits in savings and loans as well as banks would reduce the comparative advantage that banks have now. Moreover, full insurance would reduce the competitive advantage that large banks have relative to small banks.

There would, of course, still be some other pressure toward safe management because stockholders stand to lose if their bank fails. In the period 1970 to 1976, when the insurance ceiling was lower than it is now (it was raised from $20,000 to $40,000 in 1974), stockholders bore 60 percent of the losses of insured bank failures, the FDIC 31 percent, other debtors 8 percent, and depositors 1 percent.[13]

Since the FDIC has to stand ready to pay out deposits in failed banks a question of obvious concern is the FDIC's ability to meet such claims. Its first line of defense consists of the insurance premiums (in 1977 one twenty-seventh of one percent of insured deposits) [14] it earns each year together with the interest it earns on its security holdings bought out of its previous earnings. These security holdings in 1977 constituted a fund of $8.6 billion, equal to about one percent of insured deposits. If these resources should ever become exhausted, the FDIC has a statutory right to borrow $3 billion from the U.S. Treasury. Beyond this there is the fact that the federal government could, and undoubtedly would, make additional loans available to the FDIC. Given the experience of catastrophic bank failures in the 1930s, it is almost impossible to imagine the federal government not stepping in to save bank depositors. Moreover, the very existence of deposit insurance makes it highly unlikely that there could actually occur the type of bank runs that would deplete the FDIC's resources.

So far the FDIC's loss experience since its beginnings in 1934—that is, only after the great wave of bank failures had subsided—has been very favorable. In most years the FDIC's actual losses have been less than $5 million and have amounted to less than 5 percent of its premium income.

Major reasons for this have been that banks are by nature rather conservative institutions and that bankers were confirmed in their conservative attitudes by their memories of the widespread bank failures of the 1930s. But in the 1960s a new breed of bankers, who were much more ready to live with risk, took charge of many banks. Moreover, banks had entered the postwar period with very liquid portfolios due to their large holdings of

[13] Bruce Summers, "Bank Capital Adequacy: Perspective and Prospects," *Economic Review* (Federal Reserve Bank of Richmond) 63 (July–August 1977): 30.

[14] The law fixes the premium at one-twelfth of one percent, but the FDIC refunds to the banks two-thirds of the amount by which the insurance premium exceeds its expenses.

government securities. In 1948 government securities accounted for 55 percent of total loans and investments, but by 1970 they were down to 13 percent. Hence, one possible explanation of the fact that there were so few bank failures in the postwar period until the 1970s is that, due to the memory of the 1930s and the banks' large holdings of government securities that resulted from World War II, this period was an exception to a general rule. This general rule is that a banking system that is not dominated by a few giant banks and in which banks keep only a fraction of their deposits as reserves is always liable to numerous bank failures. By 1970 the special circumstances of the postwar period had worn off, and the general rule reasserted itself again.

Whether it is this theory, or the existence of the FDIC, that accounted for the infrequency of bank failures until the 1970s is hard to say, but one thing is clear, and that is, as shown in figure 3.3, that in the 1970s bank

Figure 3.3   Frequency of Bank Failures
1934–77

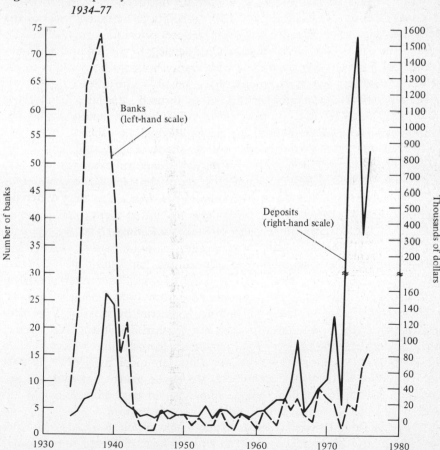

SOURCE: 1976 FDIC *Annual Report*, table 123.

failures became more frequent. And not only did bank failures become more frequent, but some very large banks failed. Until the 1970s nearly all bank failures, and potential failures, had occurred among small banks, and, as table 3.3 shows, there were not very many of them. From 1946 to 1970 the average bank that failed had deposits of about $14 million, while the largest bank to fail had only $40 million in deposits. But in 1972 a large Detroit bank, Bank of the Commonwealth, experienced heavy losses, and the FDIC had to provide it with funds to keep it alive. Then in 1973 there was the first insolvency of a billion dollar bank, the U.S. National Bank of San Diego, the rare case of a very large bank seriously damaged by self-dealing of its president. The following year there occurred the largest bank failure ever, the Franklin National Bank failure, already discussed. And, in 1975 and 1976, two other large banks turned belly up. In 1980 the First Pennsylvania, then the country's twenty-third largest bank, was in difficulty it had bought a large volume of long-term bonds that had declined in price as interest rates rose. The FDIC, along with some banks, made a loan to it to keep it alive.

Is this miniwave of large bank failures now over? No clear answer can be given. On the one hand, these bank failures shocked many banks into paying more attention to the safety of their loans. On the other hand, many banks still have on their books unsound loans they previously made to the mortgage market, and to firms chartering tankers. On a number of these loans repayment is now problematic. More recently, the large banks have made substantial loans to some less-developed countries, particularly Brazil, South Korea, Mexico, and Taiwan. There is much concern that a few of the less-developed countries will not be able to obtain sufficient dollars to repay these loans. However, even if the less-developed countries approach a situation in which they are unable to repay their loans the banks *may* still escape losses on these loans. The U.S. government may step in and make loans to these countries, which would allow them to repay their loans to the banks. The government, instead of the banks, would then be left with the uncollectible loans.

But these worries about bank failures should not be allowed to obscure the fact that *perhaps* we have too few bank failures. Failures of banks, as of other firms, fulfill a useful function: they weed out inefficient firms. It requires some failures to keep an industry efficient. Admittedly, bank failures are different from failures in most other industries since banks operate with such a high ratio of borrowed funds to their own capital. Hence, when a bank fails, its creditors as well as the FDIC may suffer a greater proportion of the losses than its stockholders. (Whether or not this happens depends on how badly the bank failed, as well as on its capital ratio.) Moreover, very extensive bank failures could cause a depression.

The fact that there have been so few bank failures suggests that bank supervision by the FDIC, as well as by the Federal Reserve, and other agencies, has not been an unmixed blessing. It has exacted a cost by limiting the venturesomeness of banks. The FDIC and other banking authorities have tended to discourage innovation and experimentation. Since they may be criticized when banks fail, it is in their interest to err on the side of safety.[15] But too much safety has its costs.

A possible solution to this problem would be to "sell" banks the right to take more risk. They would be allowed, if they so wanted, to make loans and buy securities the regulators consider too risky; and they could operate with a low capital ratio. This would reduce government control over banking, and allow banks to experiment. But would this not leave the FDIC "holding the bag"? Not necessarily; the FDIC would make its evaluation of the excess risk a bank is taking, and would then charge a higher insurance premium to make up for this greater risk. Not only would insuring risky banks (just like poor drivers) at a higher insurance premium allow those banks that want to to take more risk, but it would also give the FDIC a useful weapon in its arguments with banks. At present, there is really not very much the FDIC can do to a really large bank that is taking too much risk. In principle it could cancel the bank's insurance. But surely it will not do this since this might precipitate a run on this bank, or more realistically, force the Comptroller of the Currency, or the state authorities, to close it; and closing a major bank would disrupt industry and commerce. The FDIC has the power to ask a court to issue a cease-and-desist order against a misbehaving bank; but only the future will tell how effective this will be in the case of large banks with strong legal departments. But if the FDIC had the power to levy an extra insurance premium on a bank it could readily do this, and thus make the bank pay for the social cost of the additional risk it is taking.

However, the FDIC is unsympathetic to such a variable insurance premium system because it believes that it would be too difficult to decide what the premium should be; to which some academic economists reply that with a fixed premium the FDIC is implicitly assuming that all banks take the same amount of risk, and they believe that the FDIC can make a more accurate estimate than that.

Savings and loan associations are insured, not by the FDIC, but by the Federal Savings and Loan Insurance Corporation (FSLIC), which operates very much like the FDIC, with the same $100,000 insurance ceiling. Eighty-five percent of all savings and loan associations with 98.5 percent of all assets have joined the FSLIC. Credit unions are insured by the National Credit Union Administration (NCUA).

Check Clearing

We now turn from a serious, but episodic problem, to a minor, but continual one. Suppose that a check drawn on a San Francisco bank is deposited in a Boston bank. How is this check cleared, that is, presented for

---

[15] However, insurance has helped to stimulate competition in one important way. New banks, particularly small ones, would find it more difficult to get depositors if these depositors had to worry that they might lose if the bank failed.

payment? Since a vast number of checks, over 30 billion a year, have to be cleared, elaborate mechanisms for doing so have been developed. One mechanism is a **clearinghouse.** This is usually an *organization of local banks that meets every working day for a few hours.* Each bank appears at the clearinghouse, and presents the checks it has received that are drawn on the other banks belonging to the clearinghouse. The banks then offset their claims and liabilities against each other, and any bank with a favorable net balance receives payment. This is a much more efficient mechanism than having each bank send a messenger to every other bank demanding payments on the checks it has received drawn on that bank. With a clearinghouse each bank has to make only a single trip and has to settle only a single netted-out claim vis-à-vis all other banks.

For checks drawn on banks in other cities the clearing process is more complex. A large majority of small banks send the checks deposited with them to a larger member bank for clearing. Nonmember banks, as well as the other depository institutions that keep reserves with the Fed, have the right to clear checks directly through the Federal Reserve only under special conditions, otherwise they must send their out-of-town checks to a member bank, which in turn clears them through the Federal Reserve. (The Federal Reserve has established regional check-processing centers in certain areas, and nonmember banks in those areas may send checks directly to these centers for clearing.) But, in any case, it is usually more convenient for a nonmember bank to clear through a member bank rather than directly through the Federal Reserve.[16]

A larger bank usually sends its out-of-town checks directly to the Federal Reserve bank of its district, or to a Federal Reserve bank branch.[17] The Federal Reserve bank then credits the account of this bank and debits the account of the bank on which the check is drawn. But the depositing bank is not given immediate credit. Instead, its account is credited only after one or two days, depending upon the distance the check has to travel.[18] Suppose, for example, that a check drawn on the Chase Man-

---

[16] A few very small banks (less than half of one percent) are not permitted to clear checks through the Federal Reserve. These are banks that do not remit at par; that is, these banks do not pay the full value of the check, but deduct from the face value of the check a small service charge, which the recipient (and not the person who wrote the check) has to bear. This custom has been almost totally eliminated now, and less than a hundred banks do not remit at par.

[17] A few large banks can send checks directly to the Federal Reserve bank of the district of the bank on which the check is drawn. In an attempt to automate the clearing process the Federal Reserve has established some automated clearinghouses, which, instead of checks, receive computer tapes relating to regular payments, such as wage payments and social-security receipts, that are deposited in this way directly to the recipient's account, as well as receiving automatic payments made by depositors, such as mortgage payments.

[18] The fact that the bank receives credit for the check after a maximum of two days does *not* mean that it credits the customer's account after two days. The customer *may* have to wait up to ten days, so that, should the check be invalid, say, because of a lack of funds, the bank is protected. However, this waiting rule is frequently not enforced.

hattan Bank is deposited in the Bank of California. The Bank of California sends the check to the Federal Reserve Bank of San Francisco, which gives the Bank of California credit on its reserve account two days later, and sends the check on to the Federal Reserve Bank of New York, which in turn reduces the reserve account the Chase Manhattan Bank has with it. The two Federal Reserve banks then settle their accounts through the Interdistrict Settlement Fund at the Federal Reserve Board of Governors in Washington. Figure 3.4 illustrates the whole process.

Figure 3.4   Check Clearing between Federal Reserve Districts

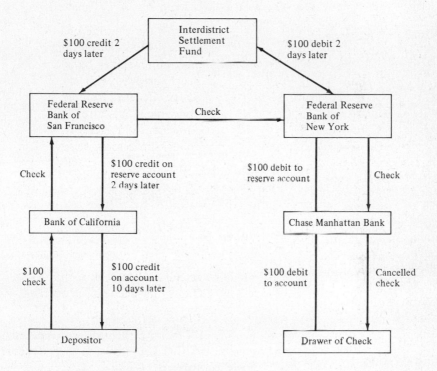

About 45 percent of all the checks that are written are cleared through the Federal Reserve System, which in 1976 cleared more than 12 *billion* items at a cost to it of $131.1 million. The rest are cleared either directly between the two banks, through a clearinghouse, through the correspondence system, or are cleared internally since they are deposited in the bank they are drawn on. In addition to clearing checks, the Federal Reserve also allows member banks and other depository institutions that keep reserves with it to use its telegraphic system to transfer funds, and most really large payments go that way instead of by check.

Some large depositors have developed a perfectly legal way of using delays in the clearing mechanism for their own benefit. They keep accounts in banks in remote locations where it takes an extra day or two until the checks are presented for payment. By slowing up their payments for a day or two they have additional funds to invest in the money market. Hence some banks proudly advertise how long it takes for checks drawn on them to clear. However, the Federal Reserve frowns on this.

Correspondence Banking

Apart from their links with governmental agencies such as the Federal Reserve and the FDIC, banks also have important links with each other. A correspondence system connects banks and eliminates many of the disadvantages that would otherwise follow from having so many small, isolated banks. Under this system country correspondent banks keep deposits, primarily demand deposits, with larger city correspondent banks, frequently with several of them. These deposits are by no means small, currently amounting to about 6 percent of all deposits.

The city banks pay for these deposits, not by paying interest, which insured banks are not allowed to pay on demand deposits, but by providing their country correspondent banks with many services. One important service is the clearing of checks in a more convenient way than the Federal Reserve System does, in part because they are frequently located closer to the country bank than is the nearest Federal Reserve bank or Federal Reserve branch bank. Moreover, correspondent banks do not require as much laborious sorting of checks as the Federal Reserve does, and unlike the Federal Reserve, frequently give the country bank immediate credit for the checks presented for clearing. In addition to clearing checks, city banks provide direct loans to country banks, and also participate with a country bank in making loans that are too large for the country bank to make on its own. Or, conversely, a country bank experiencing too little loan demand can participate in a profitable loan made by the city bank. The numerous other services that city correspondents provide to country correspondent banks include the sale or purchase of securities, access to the national money market, investment and general business advice, and buying or selling foreign exchange for its customers. In addition, the city bank sometimes makes personal loans to the officers of the country bank since regulations limit the amount a bank officer can borrow from his own bank. But it is illegal for a banker to place his bank's funds with a particular city correspondent merely to obtain personal benefits, and some suspicion that this might have occurred was a factor in forcing the resignation of Bert Lance, a former banker, as director of the Office of Management and Budget in 1977.

Concentration in Banking

There are close to fifteen thousand commercial banks in the United States. The ten largest banking organizations held only 18 percent of total domestic deposits in 1977, while the hundred largest held 45 percent.[19] Very few industries have that many firms and so little concentration, and one might therefore think that there is no "monopoly problem" in banking. Indeed, one might wonder whether the problem is not rather that there are too many banks, too many, that is, to reap economies of scale, and to be able to provide a sufficient range of services to bank customers. However, the empirical evidence does not show important economies of scale in banking. If they do exist they probably apply to small banks.

In any case, even if we do have too many small banks from the point of view of minimizing bank costs, this does not mean that we do not have a problem of insufficient banking competition as well. While large firms can borrow from banks anywhere in the country, small firms cannot do this. Being known only in their locality, they can borrow only from a local bank. It is simply not worthwhile for banks elsewhere to acquire the information needed to make them a loan. And within a firm's area there may be only one bank. In 13 percent of all rural counties in 1973 there was only a single bank. One way of measuring competition is to use an index—the Herfendahl index—that takes account of the number of firms and of their size distribution. A single large firm and, say, five tiny competitors offer less effective competition than, say, six firms of equal size. Using this index the average county had the equivalent of only 2.3 banks in 1973.[20] And several studies have found, not surprisingly, that the interest rate charged by banks tends to be at least somewhat higher if there is less competition.

On a national level there is, of course, much less concentration. Table 3.4 shows the size distribution of commercial banks, and table 3.5 lists the ten largest banks. These ten banks control about 40 percent of total bank assets, a much lower concentration ratio than is found in most industries.

As far as household depositors are concerned, they generally deal with banks in their own locality, and hence those living in some areas may have insufficient competitive alternatives. However, the existence of savings and loan associations and mutual savings banks does provide depositors with an important competitive alternative.

But an insufficient number of banks in a locality is not the only source of insufficient banking competition. As pointed out above, government regulators restrict the services that banks can provide by limiting innovations and experimentation in banking. Moreover, a Federal Reserve regulation for member banks (Regulation Q) and a similar FDIC regulation for insured nonmember banks set maximum interest rates that banks can pay

[19] The term *banking organization* includes holding companies, which sometimes control several banks. Norman Bowsher, "Have Multibank Holding Companies Affected Commercial Bank Performance?" *Review* (Federal Reserve Bank of St. Louis) 60 (April 1978): 9.

[20] Arnold Heggestad and John Mingo, "The Competitive Condition of the U.S. Banking Markets and the Impact of Structural Form," *Journal of Finance* 32 (June 1977): 655–56.

Table 3.4 Size Distribution of Insured Commercial Banks
             June 1977

Banks with total assets of (in millions of $):	*Percent of all commercial banks*	*Percent of all commercial bank assets*
Less than 5.0	9.9	0.5
5.0–9.9	18.9	1.9
10.0–24.9	34.5	7.9
25.0–49.9	19.2	9.2
50.0–99.9	9.6	9.2
100.0–299.9	5.1	11.5
300.0–499.9	1.1	5.7
500.0–999.9	7.4	7.1
1000.0–4999.9	7.5	19.1
5000.0 and over	.2	28.0
TOTAL	100.0	100.0

SOURCE: Based on FDIC, *Assets and Liabilities: Commercial and Mutual Savings Banks—30 June 1977*, table 9.

on deposits, and in this way reduce banking competition to the serious detriment of depositors. In addition, as in any other industry, there is the danger of collusion.

The issue of banking concentration has a long history. Many states have tried to prevent the growth of large banking firms by prohibiting branch banking. If a bank cannot have branches, its market area, and hence its size, is thereby limited. The extent to which banks are restricted in having branches varies from state to state. For example, Illinois banks are allowed to have only two branches, neither of which may be more than thirty-five hundred yards from the bank's head office. However, as the example of some very large Chicago banks illustrates, the virtual prohibition of branching is not an insuperable obstacle to a bank becoming one of the largest in the nation. In some states banks may have branches but only within the same county as their head office or in adjacent counties. In still other states they may have branches, but not in those counties where another bank has its head office. In 1976, as figure 3.5 shows, nineteen states allowed their banks to have branches all over the state, sixteen allowed banks to have branches within limited areas, and fifteen states prohibited branching. Furthermore, no bank may start branches in another state except in Maine, which allows out-of-state banks to enter. Apart from this a very few banks—for example the Bank of California—do have branches in more than one state. This is permitted because these branches were established before the law prohibited interstate branching. State branching regulations affect directly only state banks, but indirectly also national banks. The federal government has gone along with the states,

Table 3.5 The Nation's Ten Largest Banks
      31 December 1977

Banks	Assets (billions of dollars)	Shareholders' equity as percent of total assets	Foreign deposits as percent of total deposits
1. Bank of America (San Francisco)	82.0	3.3	40
2. Citicorp (New York)	77.1	3.7	66
3. Chase Manhattan (New York)	53.2	3.5	52
4. Manufacturers Hanover (New York)	35.8	3.6	34
5. J. P. Morgan (New York)	31.7	5.0	51
6. Chemical Bank (New York)	30.7	3.4	44
7. Continental Illinois (Chicago)	25.8	3.9	46
8. Bankers Trust (New York)	23.5	3.5	42
9. First Chicago (Chicago)	22.6	4.6	44
10. Western Bancorp (Los Angeles)	22.5	4.3	12

SOURCE: *Business Week*, 17 April 1978, p. 75.

and in each state national banks may branch only if state banks are allowed to.

However, there is now a definite trend towards allowing more branching, and even the restriction on interstate branching may sooner or later give way. And although banks are not allowed to open branches in other states, they can have so-called loan production offices in other states to help them make loans in these states. The large banks have them in many states. Similarly, banks may, and do, have so-called Edge Act subsidiaries in other states that finance international transactions. It is really only the gathering of demand deposits in other states that is prohibited. And even this prohibition may go sooner or later. To be ready for this, some banks have obtained finance companies in other states, in the hope that this will help them to gather deposits there and do other retail business if it becomes legal.

There is considerable doubt whether the limitations on branching can achieve their goal or are counterproductive. It is true that they limit monopoly and oligopoly in the sense of large aggregations of economic power. If it were not for restrictions on branch banking we would probably have

Figure 3.5 Types of Banking Systems
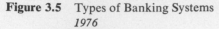
1976

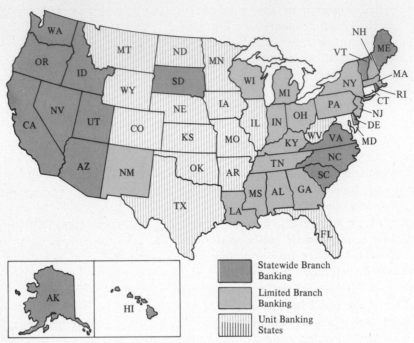

Statewide Branch Banking

Limited Branch Banking

Unit Banking States

more extremely large banks. In many European countries where branch banking is not restricted a few large banks dominate the scene; for example, in Britain four large banks hold the bulk of deposits. Given the size of the United States such extreme concentration is unlikely, particularly as the statistical evidence indicates that the costs of branching tend to offset any gains from economies of scale. Moreover, in California where there are very large branch systems, banks without branches—unit banks—are able to exist too. This suggests that banks without branches *can* compete with large branch systems. But still, if it were not for the restrictions on branching, we would have fewer banks, and some of our banks would be much larger than they are now.

Many economists believe that the limitations on branching, while serving to limit large aggregations of economic power, have also worked to preserve the monopoly or oligopoly positions of banks in small cities. In a number of localities the market is not large enough to support more than one bank, but it could support in addition to this bank also a branch of another bank; in these situations branching would reduce monopoly power. Moreover, in other industries, when a firm has a local monopoly it has to worry that if it sets its prices too high it will induce other firms to come into its market area. But, insofar as branching regulations prevent banks from entering another bank's market area, a local banking monopoly is more secure in exploiting its monopoly position. Hence, in the view of many economists, the limitation on branching has in many cases worked to preserve small business at the cost of *reducing* competition.[21] However, this view has been challenged on the argument that the empirical evidence shows that the easing of bank-branching laws in various states has not actually increased competition, since banks frequently enter new markets, not by starting new branches, but by merging with existing banks in these markets.[22]

In recent years there has been a wave of bank mergers. By merging banks have been able to enter areas where regulations would prevent them from starting a new branch. Mergers have also provided a way in which capital can flow more readily between regions. If a bank in a rapidly growing area merges with one in a more slowly growing locality, it can shift funds into the rapidly growing one. Moreover, many mergers have increased the efficiency of banking by allowing efficient banks to take over lethargic and badly managed ones. Such a device for eliminating mediocre management is badly needed because bank regulations have prevented efficient banks from entering, and driving inefficient banks out of business. In addition, mergers have allowed management to satisfy its preference for growth while allowing managers to diversify their assets. And for many small banks mergers have been a way in which the banker could sell out upon retirement and provide new management for the bank.

Mergers have led to much controversy and concern about their effects on competition. Clearly, if there are five banks in a city and they all merge, competition is eliminated. But it is much less clear that competition is reduced if banks in different cities merge. It would only reduce competition if, for at least some of the customers, the merging banks are potential competitors, that is, if the market areas of these banks overlap.

The law prohibits mergers that would "substantially" reduce competition, but this is a vague standard that has led to much litigation. Banks operate in many different markets—deposit markets, business loan markets, consumer loan markets, and so on—with some business customers being able to borrow anywhere in the nation and others not. It is therefore very hard to define the "market" a bank serves, and hence to determine if a merger would actually reduce competition. Moreover, the Department of Justice, which administers the antitrust laws, and the Federal Reserve have sometimes invoked the doctrine of potential competition by arguing that if a

[21] What is involved here is the distinction between the popular and the technical concerns about monopoly. On a popular level very large firms are often thought of as monopolists, while economists define monopoly much more in terms of the elasticity of the demand curve. More liberal branching regulations would result in larger banks, but would increase the elasticity of the demand curve for many banks. From the depositor's point of view the establishment of new branches means that he or she has more alternatives available, often at a more convenient location.

[22] For a survey of the empirical evidence see Stephen Rhoades, "Competitive Effects of Interstate Banking," *Federal Reserve Bulletin* 66 (January 1980): 1–8.

merger is prevented the frustrated acquirer will establish its own new branch, thus adding to competition. Obviously such an argument is hard to evaluate.

Holding Companies

A holding company is a corporation whose assets consist of a controlling stock ownership in one or more other corporations. This financial device is used in many industries. Traditionally it was used in banking to get around restrictive branching laws. In many states in which a bank is not allowed to have branches it can nevertheless form a holding company that holds a controlling stock interest in several banks, so that the bank has something akin to branches. And, while a bank itself cannot start a branch in another state, its holding company, subject to some restrictions, can control banks in several states.

But in the 1960s the holding-company device was used primarily in another way. There developed an explosion of one-bank holding companies. These holding companies hold the stock of only a single bank, but they also have subsidiaries in other industries. Banks themselves are prohibited from entering these other industries, but they can do so indirectly through the holding-company device. The law was then amended in 1970 to allow new bank holding companies to enter only certain industries that are related to banking. The Federal Reserve, which administers the Holding Company Act, both with regard to member and nonmember banks, was charged with drawing up a "laundry list" of activities closely related to banking that new bank holding companies could enter. They include operating a finance company, a factoring company, a company offering bookkeeping services such as preparing payrolls, or a credit-card company, and so on. These activities are considered "closely related" to banking.[23]

The ability to enter these other lines of business, some of which allow banks to use their facilities, such as computers and expertise, more fully is only one of the advantages of forming a holding company. A more important advantage for large banks is that holding companies can generate funds for the bank in ways the bank itself is not allowed to. For example, although a bank itself is not permitted to issue commercial paper, and thus borrow short-term funds in this way, a bank holding company can do so in its own name, and then give these funds to its bank.

It is therefore not surprising that nearly all of the country's largest

[23] To be "closely related" to banking an activity must meet at least one of the following criteria: (1) a significant number of banks have undertaken it for a number of years; (2) it involves taking deposits or lending; (3) it is complementary to banking services, for example, selling life insurance that extinguishes the borrower's debt to the bank in case of death; and (4) it is something in which banks have considerable expertise, for example, data processing.

banks are owned by holding companies, and that two-thirds of all commercial bank assets are in banks affiliated with a holding company. While the holding company legally owns the bank, de facto the holding company is an organization set up and dominated by the bank. The nonbank assets of the holding company are normally very small compared to the bank.

From the bank's point of view, holding companies have not been so successful. Their earnings record has been unimpressive. Moreover, they have increased risk; if one of the nonbank subsidiaries of a bank holding company is in danger of failing this reflects on the bank's reputation. Hence, banks have faced the temptation to prop up these subsidiaries by making additional loans to them, even if these loans are not justified by normal business practice. Although the law was drawn up in a way that tries to prevent this, there is still the danger that the failure of a nonbank subsidiary might cause a bank to fail. Fortunately, this danger is greatly reduced because in most cases the nonbank subsidiaries are very small relative to the bank. Some people have also been concerned that a bank might give loans on easier terms to firms that deal with the nonbank subsidiaries of its holding company, and hence these subsidiaries might have an unfair advantage. But it is far from clear that this is consistent with profit-maximizing behavior for the holding company.

International Banking

Since World War II American banking has become much more international; large American banks have established branches in many countries, particularly in Europe. In 1977 foreign assets accounted for 15 percent of the total assets of all insured banks. Some very large banks obtain more than half of their earnings from their foreign business, and as table 3.5 shows, eight of the ten largest banks have 40 percent or more of their deposits in foreign branches. London is, far and away, the most important domicile of American bank branches. This growth in the foreign activities of U.S. banks has given rise to the fear that the regulatory agencies cannot supervise these banks properly because foreign activities result in complexities unfamiliar to the bank examiners. (In any case, regardless of their foreign activities, the largest banks are such complicated institutions that their examination *may* not be very effective.) Moreover, suppose that the London branches of American banks become insolvent. As we will discuss in chapter 7, within the United States the Federal Reserve backstops the FDIC's protection of depositors. But it is far from clear whether the Federal Reserve, its British counterpart, the Bank of England, or anyone, is responsible for the problems of the London branches of American banks. Each might try to pass the buck to the other one.

Through their London branches, large American banks have been able to participate much more actively in the market for Eurodollars. **Euro-dollars** are *deposits denominated in dollars in foreign branches of U.S. banks, or in foreign banks*. Taking deposits in Eurodollars and borrowing Eurodollars has, at times, provided big American banks with a very convenient source of funds not subject to the Federal Reserve's usual reserve requirements. And they are able to make loans in Eurodollars too. In addition to dealing in Eurodollars, foreign branches allow banks to better serve their large corporate customers who themselves have branches in foreign countries. The rapid rise in Eurodollar deposits reflects, in part, the great internationalization of finance in recent years and also the very limited extent to which European banks, and European branches of American banks, are regulated, as well as the impact of the large U.S. balance of payments deficits, which provided foreigners with dollars.

There has also been a great expansion of the activities of foreign banks in the U.S. In 1979 the over three hundred foreign banking institutions operating in the United States had assets of over $140 billion, which is about 10 percent of all U.S. banking assets. Foreign banks made over 13 percent of all loans to business. The great majority of these foreign banks are in New York, and, to a lesser extent, in California. By establishing branches in the United States foreign banks not only are entering a market that they find profitable, but also their American branches allow foreign banks to better serve their multinational customers who are active in the United States and their compatriots who want to invest in the U.S.

Until recently foreign banks faced less onerous regulations than domestic banks, and to a minor extent this is still true. For example, they were able to establish subsidiaries (which are more or less similar to branches) in more than one state. But in 1978 they lost this privilege, although they were allowed to keep established subsidiaries in several states. They are now required to keep reserves with the Federal Reserve. All of them may join the FDIC, and those that accept deposits of less than $100,000 *must* do so. In chapter 31 we will discuss other aspects of international banking.

Social Regulation of Bank Loans

Traditionally, the purpose of bank regulation has been to ensure the safety of the bank and to deal with the problem of economic concentration. But in recent years, another set of regulations, applicable to other lenders as well as banks, has been growing rapidly. These regulations try to protect consumers and prevent discrimination.

Among the oldest of these regulations are the usury laws that many states have passed. The idea behind them is, of course, that a too high rate of interest is unfair to borrowers, and that borrowers have to be protected, either because they are ignorant or poor, or because of insufficient competition among lenders. The permitted maximum interest rates vary among states, and there are often many exclusions; for example, the New York usury law exempts loans to corporations.

The main criticism of usury laws is, of course, that the lender has a choice: instead of making the loan at the ceiling rate, he can refrain from making it at all, and lend his funds where they are exempt from the usury laws, for example, out of state. And further, if the interest rate is held below equilibrium, lenders have to ration the available supply of loans among the applicants, and will do so by excluding the riskier applicants, which in effect means the poorer applicants. Thus, while usury laws might *perhaps* help borrowers in general, they hurt the really poor who then have to deal with loan sharks or do without loans.

A federal law tries to ensure that borrowers are given sufficient credit information, particularly about the interest rate they are paying. Before this legislation was passed, creditors stated interest rates in ways that made it hard to understand and compare them. For example, on consumer loans the interest cost was usually stated as a percent of the amount initially borrowed, despite the fact that the loan is amortized, so that roughly the average amount outstanding over the life of the loan is only half the amount initially borrowed. Hence, borrowers were told that the interest rate was, say, 6 percent, whereas the actual rate they were paying on the average outstanding amount of the loans was approximately 12 percent. However, the Truth-in-Lending Law has the disadvantage of creating costs for the lender, which are, of course, passed on to the borrower. And it is not clear that many borrowers pay much attention to the additional information they are now getting.

Another piece of legislation deals with creditor rights. Suppose someone buys a defective item on credit and the merchant sells the buyer's IOU to a bank. In the past the buyer was legally obligated to make payment to the bank on this IOU regardless of the defect in the merchandise. This is no longer the case. Furthermore, in response to frequent complaints that minorities, women, and relief recipients faced discrimination in obtaining credit, federal legislation now makes such discrimination illegal, and lenders have to keep records on why they turned down loan applicants.

Another piece of legislation, the Community Redevelopment Act of 1975, deals with the problem of redlining. This is defined as a lender or insurer drawing a literal or figurative line around a certain neighborhood on a city map, and refusing to make any loans to households or business firms, or to insure any property, within that area even if the applicant himself or herself is a good risk and the property is sound collateral for the loan. The neighborhoods that are said to be redlined are usually decaying inner city areas with a high proportion of minority residents. And opponents of redlining claim that a major reason why the area is decaying is the very fact that it is difficult or impossible to obtain the mortgage loans that would be needed to arrest the decay and rehabilitate the neighborhood. Such redlining is seen by many people as one more instance of racial discrimination, either directly, or indirectly, in the sense that racial discrimination has prevented residents in that area from having the income and employment records that lenders expect potential borrowers to have. Hence, redlining is often treated as a civil-rights issue.

The Community Reinvestment Act states that banks and other insured mortgage lenders have an obligation to meet the reasonable credit needs of their local low-income communities. They have to keep records on the volume of loans made in various neighborhoods. When they apply for permission to open branches or to merge with other institutions the regulatory agency is supposed to treat their performance in serving low-income neighborhoods as a factor in deciding on their applications.

This legislation is based on several arguments. One is that redlining is to a considerable extent just one more manifestation of racial discrimination, that it largely results from white upper-middle-class bankers considering minorities to be unworthy of credit. A second argument is that redlining is a manifestation of laziness; instead of evaluating the loan application on its own merits the lender, without spending any thought on it, simply turns it down because it comes from the wrong neighborhood. A third argument is that banks with branches in decaying neighborhoods drain funds out of these areas by gathering deposits there, and making loans elsewhere. Still another argument is that one of our most serious problems is the decay of the inner cities, and that much will have to be done to help them. And while the government provides various subsidies for the inner cities, financial institutions should also be required to do their part, even if this reduces their profits. Since financial institutions obtain extensive government benefits such as insurance, the restriction on new entrants into their markets, and the Regulation Q ceiling on deposit interest rates, they can reasonably be asked in turn to help the government in salvaging the inner cities.

Opponents of the Community Reinvestment Act and similar legislation raise a number of issues. Thus, they question whether redlining actually exists to any large extent, because if a bank were to pass up any sound loan it would be reducing its own profits. To be sure, they argue, banks and other lenders may use certain rules of thumb to cut down the cost of credit investigation, but the use of such rules is in the public interest because otherwise too many resources would be used in investigating credit applications. But, by being willing to pay a higher interest rate, potential borrowers in decaying areas can often induce lenders to do this extra work. Hence, they argue that much of what appears to be redlining is not really that at all. Rather, the reason why so few mortgage loans are made in decaying areas is that there are few sound applicants for mortgage credit there. Of course, in declining neighborhoods there are many people who want to borrow, but the loans they want are usually risky, and banks are supposed to avoid risky loans. Hence, the argument runs, requiring banks to make a certain proportion of their loans in decaying areas means imposing a tax on banks because these loans are risky, and banks will shift this tax onto their customers. Moreover, even if under ideal conditions it might be desirable to curb redlining by legislation, in actual practice such legislation is likely to be very inefficient, to lead to a lot of red tape, and to be evaded. For example, a bank with a branch in a low-income neighborhood might simply close that branch, so that this neighborhood would no longer be part of the area in which it is supposed to make loans.

One reason why this whole debate about redlining has arisen is that there are so few minority banks, despite some limited attempts by the federal government to foster them. They are hindered by the general poverty of the inner city, which results in their having an inordinate number of small —and hence costly—deposits, and by relatively high losses on business loans. These high loan losses are in large part due to the fact that minority banks try to make loans not only on the basis of economic soundness but also on the basis of social usefulness. There is therefore considerable debate about whether these minority banks can help to raise inner-city income significantly. But it has been suggested that they can do so indirectly by providing minorities with the economic leadership role that seems naturally to attach itself to bankers. Turning from minority banking to what is really majority banking, banks run by women and making a special effort to cater to women customers have been established in New York, San Francisco, and some other cities because of a belief that many other banks discriminate against women. Of course, these banks also accept the business of male customers.

Summary

The American banking system has had a checkered history. Chartering of banks by state legislatures, two temporary national banks, free banking, and the National Banking System have preceded our current system. At present, banks are heavily regulated, both by chartering and by examination. The Comptroller of the Currency as well as state banking authorities charter banks. National banks must, and state banks may, join the Federal Reserve System, and just about all banks have joined the FDIC. Bank failures, a major problem of our banking system prior to the establishment of the FDIC, are now relatively rare, and indeed one might argue that they are too infrequent.

One issue that has attracted much attention is whether banks have a sufficient ratio of capital to deposits. Banks have an incentive to keep a low capital ratio, while the regulatory agencies have an incentive to make banks keep a higher ratio. Nearly all banks are insured by the FDIC. Frequently, when a bank fails, the FDIC fully protects large depositors, as well as small ones, by merging the failing bank into another bank. Within a locality banks clear checks among themselves through a clearinghouse. For checks drawn on banks in other areas the Federal Reserve provides a clearing service.

Banks are linked into a correspondence system, which allows small banks to provide their customers with many of the services of large banks. This is needed because the banking industry is so widely dispersed, there being about fifteen thousand banks. This large number of banks results from the severe limitations on branch banking. In recent years there have been many bank mergers, and to gain more freedom of operation many banks have set up one-bank holding companies. Banking has also become much more internationalized with many foreign banks establishing U.S. branches, while large U.S. banks have expanded into foreign markets.

In recent years there has been a burgeoning of social regulations imposed on banks. In addition to the older state usury laws, which probably hurt the very people they were intended to protect, banks now have to provide detailed and easily understood information on the cost of credit, and they may not discriminate on the basis of race, sex, and so on. In addition, there is much debate about whether banks "redline" certain areas and what should be done about this if it occurs.

QUESTIONS AND EXERCISES

1. "Banking is so different from other industries, that limiting entry to protect existing banks from excessive competition is not only justified, but is needed." Discuss.
2. Look up the branching regulations of your state. Then write an essay either defending or criticizing these regulations.
3. Banking is much more heavily regulated than other industries. How can this be justified?
4. Discuss the following proposals to loosen up deposit insurance:
   a. Allowing banks to obtain insurance from private insurance companies instead of the FDIC.
   b. Insuring depositors instead of banks, and permitting depositors, who would pay for the insurance premium, to decide whether they want to buy this insurance;
   c. Insuring only the accounts of households, and not of businesses.
5. Describe the process by which checks are cleared.
6. Critically discuss:
   a. "Banks should be allowed to decide on their own how much capital they want; after all, they are the ones who lose if it turns out that they have insufficient capital."
   b. "Banks should be required to keep a capital to deposit ratio of at least 25 percent."
7. What do you think is the most serious *current* problem facing bank regulation? (Articles on current banking problems can be found frequently in *Business Week*.)

8. Write an essay either defending or criticizing:
   a. usury laws;
   b. regulations prohibiting redlining.

FURTHER READING

BENSTON, GEORGE. *Bank Examination. The Bulletin* (New York University Graduate School of Business Administration) nos. 89–90 (1973). A very thorough and scholarly discussion.

———. "Optimal Banking Structure." *Journal of Banking Research* 3 (Winter 1973): 220–37. An excellent survey of a voluminous literature.

———. "The Persistent Myth of Redlining." *Fortune,* 13 March 1978, pp. 66–69. An interesting challenge to the view that banks redline.

CHASE, SAMUEL, and MINGO, JOHN. "The Regulation of Bank Holding Companies." *Journal of Finance* 30 (May 1975): 281–92. A thoughtful survey of the problem.

HAVRILESKY, THOMAS, and BOORMAN, JOHN. *Current Perspectives in Banking.* Arlington Heights, Ill.: AHM Publishing Corp., 1976. An interesting collection of readings.

KLEBANER, BENJAMIN. *Commercial Banking in the United States: A History.* Hinsdale, Ill.: Dryden Press, 1974. A compact and useful source of information.

LAWRENCE, ROBERT, and TALLEY, SAMUEL. "An Assessment of Bank Holding Companies." *Federal Reserve Bulletin* 62 (January 1976): 15–21. A short, but authoritative assessment.

ROSENBLUM, HARVEY. "Bank Holding Companies: An Overview." *Business Conditions* (Federal Reserve Bank of Chicago), August 1973, pp. 3–13. A useful survey.

SCOTT, KENNETH, and MAYER, THOMAS. "Risk and Regulation in Banking: Some Proposals for Federal Deposit Insurance Reform." *Stanford Law Review* 23 (May 1971): 857–902. A discussion of issues in deposit insurance.

VARVEL, WALTER. "FDIC Policy Towards Bank Failures." *Economic Review* (Federal Reserve Bank of Richmond) 62 (September–October 1976): 3–12. An excellent description of how deposit insurance works.

4

The Banking Firm

In the previous chapter we discussed the structure of the banking industry, and the regulatory environment in which it operates. This chapter, by contrast, focuses on the bank as a firm, and sees how this bank firm operates to maximize its profits.

The Bank As Enterprise

Banks function in a special environment. Not only, as already discussed, are they much more heavily regulated than most other firms, but they also face a peculiar balance sheet situation. A large proportion of a bank's liabilities are very short term, in effect being payable on demand. On the other hand, a bank's assets are much longer term.

Banks might therefore seem to be very risky and unstable enterprises, liable to collapse at any moment. Fortunately, there is an offsetting circumstance: on a day-to-day basis, a bank can predict more or less closely the percent of deposits that will be withdrawn. This is so because it has many depositors, none of whom predominate. And normally depositors behave in an offsetting way—as some draw their deposits down, others build theirs up. The *net* change in a bank's deposits is therefore small relative to the gross volume of deposit inflows and outflows.

But the bank *must* be prepared to meet some net deposit outflows that may occasionally be much larger than it expects. If it were ever unable, even just temporarily, to pay out a demand deposit it would be closed down. Hence, banks have to watch their liquidity position very carefully and make sure that they have enough highly liquid assets or possibilities of borrowing, to meet unexpected deposit drains. This is expensive. An ideal asset is one that is highly liquid for the holder, very safe, and pays a high rate of return. But such assets do not exist due to competition among lenders. Banks, like others, have to balance at the margin three characteristics of assets: safety, liquidity, and yield. Since banks have such highly liquid liabilities, they place a relatively great emphasis on the liquidity of their assets. At the same time, banks cannot ignore yield. They must cover their costs, and beyond that want to make a profit.

Another important characteristic of banks is the existence of a long-term and multiproduct relationship between the bank and its most important customers, business firms. A firm generally uses many bank services. Not only does it keep deposits in a bank and borrow from this bank, but it also uses many important specialized services of the bank, such as payroll preparation. A firm generally uses the same bank (or banks) for all of these activities rather than borrowing from one bank, while keeping all its deposits in other banks. However, a large firm frequently has several banks, both because it finds it convenient to have a bank in the several cities in which it has substantial operations, and also so that when it wants to borrow it has a connection with a number of banks.

A final characteristic of the banking industry is that it is heterogeneous. It comprises very small banks (close to 10 percent of all banks have deposits of less than $5 million), which finance the activities in their small towns, as well as very large internationally oriented banks—eighteen banks have assets of more than $5 billion. Some of these large banks, the Bank of America is the prime example, have an extensive branch network, and hence finance small business as well as the world's major corporations. But other large banks, such as the Harris Trust Company of Chicago, for example, so-called wholesale banks, obtain most of their deposits from—and make most of their loans to—large corporations.

The Bank's Liabilities

A bank is a dealer in debts. It issues its own debts (mainly deposits) and it holds the debts of borrowers. Both types of debts are recorded on the bank's balance sheet, which is simply a double-entry statement of assets and liabilities. We can therefore study the banking business by looking at each item on the balance sheet of this dealer in debts. Table 4.1 shows a balance sheet for all U.S. banks in 1977, and we will discuss all items listed in it, starting with the liabilities side.

Demand Deposits and NOW Accounts

The first set of items listed are demand deposits. These are our familiar checking deposits. Since 1935 insured banks have been prohibited from paying interest explicitly on demand deposits (except on federal government deposits). But, in effect, banks do pay *imputed* interest on demand deposits by providing free, or below cost, services to holders of demand deposits. For example, banks clear at least a certain number (and often an unlimited number) of checks without charge for depositors who maintain a minimum balance in their accounts. Business firms have more opportunities for getting free or underpriced services from banks than do households because they use more of the bank's services. For example, banks prepare payrolls for firms and, in addition, firms holding large deposits can

Table 4.1   Assets and Liabilities, All Banks
           December 1977   Percent Distribution

Assets		*Liabilities*	
Cash, reserves with banks and collection items—Total	14.4	Demand deposits—Total	32.7
Currency and coin	1.2	Individuals, partnerships, and corporations	24.5
Reserves with Federal Reserve banks	2.5	Government	2.3
Deposits with banks	5.1	Domestic banks[a]	3.7
Cash items in process of collection	5.7	Foreign governments and banks	0.9
		Certified and officer's checks, letters of credit, traveler's checks, etc.	1.4
Securities—Total	22.2		
U.S. Treasury securities	8.2		
Securities of other U.S. government agencies and corporations	3.1	Time and savings deposits —Total	47.8
Obligation of states and subdivisions	9.7	Individuals, partnerships, and corporations: Savings deposits	18.4
Other securities	1.2	Other time deposits	22.6
Loans (Gross)—Total	53.7	Government	5.0
Commercial and industrial loans	17.6	Domestic banks[a]	0.7
Loans to farmers (excluding real estate loans)	2.2	Foreign governments and banks	1.2
Real-estate loans	15.2		
Loans to individuals	12.0	Miscellaneous liabilities— Total	12.2
Securities loans	1.5	Federal funds purchased and securities sold under repurchase agreements	7.4
Other loans	5.2		
Other assets—Total	9.6	Other liabilities for borrowed money	0.9
Customers liability on account of acceptances	1.1	Acceptances outstanding	1.1
Federal funds sold and securities purchased under repurchase agreements	4.6	Other liabilities	2.8
Bank premises, etc.	1.6	Capital account—Total	7.3
		Capital notes and debentures	0.5
Miscellaneous assets	2.4	Equity capital	6.8
TOTAL	100.0%	TOTAL	100.0%

a. Includes mutual savings banks.
SOURCE: FDIC, *Annual Report,* 1977, table 107.

probably borrow at a lower interest rate. Moreover, some banks have devised a scheme for their large business customers whereby the bank in effect pays them interest on their large demand deposits. The way this works is that at the end of the business day the bank looks at the firm's account. And if the account is above a certain minimum (designed to compensate the bank for the services it renders to the firm, such as check clearing) the bank automatically borrows from the firm or sells it a security under a repurchase agreement. This means that the bank agrees to buy the security back the next day at a fixed price with the firm earning interest for one day on this security. For business firms, particularly large ones, the prohibition of interest payments is therefore not really effective.

It is probably more effective for households who sometimes do not use all the free services to which they are entitled. But, on the whole, it is realistic to say that banks do pay interest on demand deposits. How much is hard to say, but one recent study argued rather persuasively that banks pass on to the demand depositors in free services about one-third to one-half of what the competitive equilibrium interest rate on demand deposits would be in the absence of the prohibition.[1]

Such a system of payment results in an inefficient allocation of resources, because, at the margin, the utility of these free services to the customer is likely to be less than their cost to the bank. For example, customers offered free check clearing have an incentive to write checks even if the utility of paying by check rather than by currency is only, say, 2 cents to them; but clearing this check may cost the bank 15 cents.

Nonetheless, interest payments on demand deposits were prohibited in part because of the questionable belief that if banks were to pay interest on demand deposits, the need for higher earnings to pay this interest would drive the banks to make high yielding but risky loans. In addition, there was also the fear that large city banks, by paying a higher rate of interest, would take deposits away from small banks.

But in March 1980 the law was changed. Banks are still not allowed to pay interest on demand deposits per se, but, starting in January 1981, they can offer (and competition will eventually force them to offer) so-called NOW accounts to households and nonprofit organizations. While these NOW accounts are legally not demand deposits, they function just like demand deposits, and hence are demand deposits in an economic sense.[2] Such deposits can also be offered by savings and loan associations and mutual savings banks, while credit unions are allowed to offer share draft accounts that function in the same way. These NOW accounts pay an interest rate, which until 1986 wll be subject to a ceiling set by a government committee.

Table 4.2 shows the distribution of demand deposits among various types of owners. It shows that households own 34 percent of all demand deposits. Table 4.3 classifies demand deposit accounts by size. It shows that in 1975 39 percent of demand deposits were held in large accounts, that is, in accounts of over $100,000. Among households some of these large depositors are presumably people who have just sold securities or other assets and are temporarily "parking" the proceeds in their demand deposits, but some are probably unsophisticated people who keep much of their wealth in a demand deposit because they distrust other types of assets.

[1] Richard Startz, "Implicit Interest on Demand Deposits," *Journal of Monetary Economics* 5 (October 1979): 515–34.

[2] Technically the depositor does not write a check on a NOW account, but writes a *negotiable order of withdrawal* (hence the name NOW). This way of avoiding the prohibition of interest payments on demand deposits was developed by clever lawyers for a Massachusetts mutual savings bank.

Table 4.2   Ownership of Demand
Deposits
June 1978

	Percent of gross demand deposits
Financial business	9.5
Nonfinancial business	50.8
Consumers	34.3
Foreign	0.9
Other	4.6
Total	100.0

SOURCE: *Federal Reserve Bulletin* 64 (October
1978): A-25.

Table 4.3   Size of Demand Deposit Accounts, Individuals, Partnerships,
and Corporations
June 1975

	Percent of all accounts	*Percent of dollar value of all accounts*
$40,000 or less	99.4	50.3
$40,001–100,000	.4	10.5
$100,001 or more	.2	39.2

SOURCE: FDIC, *Summary of Accounts and Deposits,* 1975.

Before leaving demand deposits there are two special types of checks
that may need explaining. One is a *certified check*. This is a check on
which the bank has guaranteed to make payment. This avoids the problem
that the drawer of the check may not have sufficient funds in the bank to
cover it. (The bank covers itself by subtracting the amount of the check
from the depositor's account right away.) Such a certified check is therefore
sure to be good unless it is forged or obtained by fraud, and it is accepted
in some situations when a personal check is not. An *officer's check,* often
called a cashiers' check, is similar. It is a check drawn on the bank itself,
which a depositor buys for a fee from the bank.

Time Deposits

In addition to demand deposits banks also issue savings and time deposits. The technical distinction between demand deposits on the one
hand, and savings and other time deposits on the other, is that the bank has
a legal right to demand at least thirty days' notice before the withdrawal of

a savings or time deposit. However, for savings deposits of households, unlike for other time deposits, banks do not enforce this right to thirty days' notice. Should a bank try to enforce this right even temporarily, it would probably experience a run of demand depositors with deposits in excess of $100,000 who would be afraid that the bank is about to fail.

The most common form of savings deposits is the passbook account, but savings accounts can also be evidenced by a written agreement between the depositor and the bank rather than by a passbook. One type of agreement consists of open accounts, which allow for additions at any time. Another type of deposit, certificates of deposits, usually abbreviated as CDs, is for a fixed sum. Although households can cash their certificates of deposits before the stated maturity date, Federal Reserve and FDIC regulations impose an interest penalty for this. This penalty also exists for fixed-maturity passbook accounts. But other passbook accounts have no fixed maturity and can be cashed in any time. Table 4.4 shows the ownership distribution and the size distribution of time deposits.

Table 4.4   Time Deposits
            April 1978

	Percent of total time and savings deposits
Savings Deposits	39.3
Issued to individuals, and nonprofit organizations	36.4
partnerships and organizations operated for profit	
(other than commercial banks)	1.9
all other	1.0
Other interest-bearing time deposits in denominations of:	
less than $100,000	30.1
more than $100,000	29.2
Other[a]	1.4
TOTAL	100.0

a. Includes retirement accounts.

SOURCE: "Survey of Time and Savings Deposits in Commercial Banks, April 1978," *Federal Reserve Bulletin* 64 (August 1978): 624.

Large depositors can purchase negotiable CDs, which are issued only by relatively well known banks. They are negotiable so that the purchaser can reclaim the funds prior to the maturity date of the CD by selling it on the money market. Then, at maturity, the bank pays off the CD to whoever is holding it at that time. Such negotiable CDs are purchased almost only by business and governments since the minimum denomination is $100,000 and the normal denomination is $1 million or more. Corporations find these negotiable CDs very useful. They are highly liquid assets since there is an active market in them. The maturity of negotiable

CDs is usually a year or less and is often set to suit the convenience of the particular purchaser. By contrast, the small nonnegotiable CDs bought by households usually have a longer maturity. The interest rate on negotiable CDs is competitive with those on other short-term securities.

The Federal Reserve's Regulation Q for member banks and a similar FDIC regulation for insured nonmember banks set ceilings on the interest rates banks can pay on time deposits. These ceilings vary positively with the maturity of the deposit, and are changed from time to time. The July 1979 ones are shown in Table 4.5. There is no interest ceiling on CDs above $100,000; interest rates on them are determined by the market. The ability to set the interest rates on large CDs at any level needed to attract funds means that large banks can always obtain funds if they are willing to pay the price. If the interest rate ceiling would apply to large CDs too, the big money-market banks, who have large interest-sensitive depositors, might face a financial crisis if interest rates on other securities rise above the interest rate ceiling. As will be discussed in chapter 8 these Regulation Q ceilings will now be phased out.

Miscellaneous Liabilities and Capital

In addition to their deposits, banks have a set of miscellaneous liabilities. One of these is purchased federal funds. Federal funds are *not* funds belonging to the federal government as the name might suggest. Instead, they are deposits usually held at the Federal Reserve and traded among themselves by banks and some other institutions. They have the characteristic that they are transferred immediately, with the Federal Reserve giving the receiving bank credit the same day. By contrast, a check takes at least a day to clear. An important component of federal funds are reserves of a bank that are borrowed by another bank. The lending bank wires the Federal Reserve bank and tells it to transfer some of its reserves to the borrowing bank's account. However, federal funds can also take other forms; for example, a city bank can borrow the correspondent balances a country bank keeps with it. Apart from banks a few other institutions, such as federal government agencies, savings and loan associations, and mutual savings banks, are active in this market.

As Table 4.6 shows, it is a very large market, and the big money-market banks use it at times, not just to obtain the funds to meet their reserve requirements, but also to obtain funds for additional lending. The total amount borrowed in recent years has been substantially more than the required reserves of these banks. Most loans are made on a one-day basis, and it is a way in which banks can quickly obtain more reserves, or lend excess funds. Many small banks enter this market—typically as lenders —through their city correspondent banks. The great majority of banks are active in this market. Although it is actually a market for loans, in the language of the money market, transactions in it are described as sales of federal funds and as purchases rather than as loans. The *interest rate*

Table 4.5 Maximum Interest Rates Payable on Time and Savings Deposits at Federally Insured Institutions

Percent per annum, rates shown effective 31 July 1979

Type and maturity of deposit	Commercial banks		Savings and loan associations and mutual savings banks	
	Percent	*Effective date*	*Percent*	*Effective date*
Savings	5¼	7/1/79	5½	7/1/79
Negotiable order of withdrawal (NOW) accounts	5	1/1/74	5	1/1/74
TIME ACCOUNTS				
Fixed-ceiling rates by maturity				
30–89 days	5	7/1/73	8	—
90 days to 1 year	5½	7/1/73	5¾	c
1 to 2 years	6	7/1/73	6½	c
2 to 2½ years	6			
2½ to 4 years	6½	7/1/73	6¾	c
4 to 6 years	7¼	11/1/73	7½	11/1/73
6 to 8 years	7½	12/23/74	7¾	12/23/74
8 years or more	7¾	6/1/78	8	6/1/78
Issued to governmental units (all maturities)	8	6/1/78	8	6/1/78
Individual retirement accounts and Keogh (H.R. 10) plans (3 years or more)	8	6/1/78	8	6/1/78
Special variable-ceiling rates by maturity				
6 months (money-market time deposits)	(a)	(a)	(a)	(a)
4 years or more	(b)	(b)	(b)	(b)

a. The ceiling rate for commercial banks is the discount rate on most recently issued 6-month U.S. Treasury bills. When this rate is below 9 percent, savings and loan associations and mutual savings banks may pay up to ¼ percent more. (This full differential comes into effect when the bill rate is 8¾ or less.)

b. Effective 1 July 1979, commercial banks, savings and loan associations, and mutual savings banks are authorized to offer variable-ceiling accounts with no required minimum denomination and with maturities of 4 years or more. The maximum rate for commercial banks is 1¼ percentage points below the yield on 4-year U.S. Treasury securities; the ceiling rate for thrift institutions is ¼ percentage point higher than that for commercial banks. In July, the ceiling was 7.60 percent at commercial banks and 7.85 percent at thrift institutions.

c. 1 July 1973 for mutual savings banks, 6 July 1973 for savings and loan associations.

Note: For details and qualifications, see the original source.

SOURCE: *Federal Reserve Bulletin* 65 (August 1979), table A-10.

that the selling bank charges is called the **federal funds rate,** and it is an important indicator of the balance of supply and demand in this money market. As we will see in chapter 23, it is used by the Federal Reserve in formulating monetary policy.

Table 4.6   Commercial Bank Participation in Market for Federal Funds and
              Repurchase Agreements
              June 1977

Banks with total assets of (in $ millions):	*Federal funds sold and securities purchased under repurchase agreements*[a] *as percent of:*		*Federal funds purchased and securities sold under repurchase agreements*[a] *as percent of:*	
	TOTAL ASSETS	EQUITY CAPITAL	TOTAL ASSETS	EQUITY CAPITAL
Less than 5.0	5.7	46.8	0.4	3.2
5.0–9.9	4.3	48.1	0.6	6.1
10.0–24.9	3.6	43.5	0.6	7.6
25.0–49.9	3.2	41.0	0.9	11.2
50.0–99.9	2.9	37.7	1.5	20.2
100.0–299.9	3.3	46.3	3.1	43.5
300.0–499.9	3.8	53.3	4.6	64.2
500.0–999.9	4.3	64.1	8.0	119.0
1000.0–4999.9	4.6	69.0	11.7	175.9
5000.0 and over	4.2	59.9	12.7	180.5

a. Repurchase agreements are arrangements under which the seller of a security is committed
to repurchase it at a certain date at a fixed price.
SOURCE: Based on FDIC, *Assets, Liabilities, 1977 Report of Income Commercial & Mutual
Savings Banks,* table 9.

The next item on the balance sheet is "other liabilities for borrowed
money." This catch-all item includes various borrowings by a bank; for
example, borrowings from its own holding company. In July 1980 the
Comptroller proposed a change in regulations that would not allow national
banks to count such borrowing as capital. At present we do not know
whether this proposed change will actually take place.

Another liability item is outstanding acceptances. Acceptances arise
in a rather complicated way. A firm selling to another firm on credit may
not know enough about the buyer to feel safe in accepting its promise
to pay. This is particularly likely to be the case with a foreign customer,
in part because it is more difficult to sue in a foreign court than in a court
in one's own country. But while the seller does not want to take the customer's IOU, he is willing to take the IOU of the customer's bank. Hence,
a financial instrument, called a banker's acceptance, was developed. To
explain it, let us back off and look first at a transaction *not* involving a
bank. The seller draws up an order to pay by a certain date on the buyer
and releases ownership of the merchandise to him or her when the *buyer
"accepts" the order to pay by writing "accepted" across it*. It is now a
trade acceptance and is legally binding. Alternatively, the buyer can make
an arrangement with his or her bank allowing the seller to draw the order to pay, not on the buyer, but on the buyer's bank. *When the bank*

writes *"accepted"* *on this order to pay,* it becomes a **banker's acceptance.** Since the bank is liable to make the payment on it, when it accepts an order to pay, it is listed on the bank's balance sheet as a liability. However, the bank is not making a loan to the buyer when it gives him or her a document, a letter of credit, stating that it will accept a draft drawn on the buyer. The buyer is supposed to make payment to the bank by the date the bank has to make its payment on the acceptance. The bank lends its name and reputation, not its funds, to the buyer who usually has to pay a small fee for this service. The seller, when he receives the banker's acceptance, need not hold it to maturity. Often he wants to obtain his funds right away, and will therefore sell the acceptance (at a discount from face value) in the money market. The buyer of such an acceptance, frequently another bank, obtains an extremely safe and liquid asset. The final item subsumed under miscellaneous liabilities includes items like bills the bank has not yet paid, accrued salary, and so on.

The next item is reserves on loans and securities. This is just an accounting entry rather than an actual liability the bank has to someone else. A bank can reasonably expect *some* losses on its loans. It therefore carries on its balance sheet a reserve account against which to charge these losses. Similarly, a bank will sometimes sell securities it owns at a loss, and it charges this loss too against this reserve account. This leaves the capital account, which we have already discussed in the previous chapter.

The Bank's Assets

Primary Reserves

The first three assets listed on the balance sheet in table 4.1 compose the bank's primary reserves. They are currency and coin in the bank (also called vault cash), reserves with the Federal Reserve, and demand deposits with domestic banks, that is, correspondent bank balances. These three items form the bank's first line of defense against a deposit or currency outflow. This high liquidity of primary reserves is obtained at a cost; banks do not earn explicit interest on their primary reserves, though they obtain a competitively determined volume of free services from their city correspondent banks.

The biggest item among the primary reserves is the required reserves of member banks. The Federal Reserve requires member banks to hold a certain proportion of their deposits as reserves. They can hold these reserves either as vault cash, or as deposits with the Federal Reserve, that is, as entries on the Federal Reserve's books. And most of them are kept as deposits with the Federal Reserve rather than as vault cash.

The main purpose of the reserve requirement is *not,* as may seem at first, to ensure the safety of the bank's deposits. After all, with a, say, 12 percent reserve requirement, depositors, or rather the FDIC, would be very badly off if a bank failed and all that was available to pay off deposits were the reserves. Instead, depositors are protected by the soundness of the bank's overall assets, and if necessary by the FDIC, while the reserve requirement has a very different function. As we will show subsequently, it limits the volume of deposits that banks can create, and thus helps to control the quantity of money, besides being, in effect, a way of taxing banks and their customers. The reason why the Federal Reserve's reserve requirement is a tax is that it requires member banks to hold with the Federal Reserve deposits that do not bear any interest, thus, in effect, making the Federal Reserve an interest-free loan. The implicit tax, consisting of the forgone interest on these reserves, is received ultimately by the U.S. Treasury since, at the margin, the Federal Reserve turns over all its earnings to the Treasury.

At present the reserve requirement system is hard to describe because it is currently in a transition process that will last until 1988. Until March 1980 only member banks had to meet the Fed's reserve requirements. For demand deposits the required reserve percentage was graduated so that it increased with the size of the bank's deposits. The main reason for this was to take it easy on small banks, which are able to leave the Federal Reserve System more easily than large banks can. For time deposits the reserve requirement depended not on the size of the bank, but on the maturity of the deposit. Since the purpose of the reserve requirement is to control the quantity of deposits, and hence of money, it is reasonable to impose higher reserve requirements on deposits with short maturities since such deposits have more "moneyness."

Member banks do not have to abide by these reserve ratios on a daily basis. Instead, their reserves are averaged over a seven-day period (ending on Wednesdays) and compared to their average deposits for the corresponding seven-day period two weeks earlier.

In addition to the reserve requirements against deposits, banks also have to keep reserves against certain other liabilities, such as increases above a base-period level in federal funds purchased from nonbanks, Eurodollar borrowings, and funds obtained through certain repurchase agreements. Nonmember banks, as well as other institutions with transactions accounts, need not keep these reserves directly with the Fed or as vault cash, but may keep them with member banks (and in the case of nonbanks with certain government institutions) that then pass them on to the Fed.

Under the old rules nonmember banks are immune from these reserve requirements, but have to meet instead the reserve requirements set by their states. These vary from state to state. For example, one state, Illinois, has no explicit reserve requirements at all. In general, the state requirements are less onerous than the Federal Reserve's, despite the fact that the percentages that are set are on the average similar. But they apply to different things. Member banks can count as reserves only two items: reserves with the Federal Reserve and vault cash. State banks, on the other hand, can also count as reserves their deposits with city correspondent banks, and in most states uncollected funds, that is, funds still in the clearing process. These uncollected funds are substantial, amounting to about half the average reserve requirement. In addition, almost half the states allow their banks to count some U.S. or state and local government securities as part of their reserves. Since member banks hold such securities, as well as deposits with city correspondents, on top of their required reserves the reserve requirement is much more burdensome for them. In addition, though admittedly it is conjectural, it is possible that, at least in some states, the reserve requirement is not rigorously enforced, and is checked, if at all, only a few times a year.

Thus member banks face a much more severe tax than nonmember banks, and not surprisingly many banks have left the Federal Reserve System. Also, not very surprisingly, the Fed, afraid that this would weaken its control over the stock of money, responded by begging Congress to change the law so that nonmember banks would have to meet the same reserve requirements as member banks. For a long time Congress refused. But in March 1980 it changed the law and set up a new reserve requirement system. This new system sets reserve requirements for transaction accounts, that is, checkable deposits not only in banks, but also in savings and loan associations, mutual savings banks, and credit unions as well as on any business time deposits in such institutions. This new system is being phased in slowly, over a four-year period for member banks and an eight-year period for nonmember banks.

As table 4.7 shows, the new system, like the old one, imposes lower

Table 4.7   New Reserve Requirements

	Initial rate[c] (in percent)	Range within which Fed can vary requirement[d] (in percent)
Normal Reserves:		
Transaction Accounts:		
On deposits of:		
Less than $25 million[a]	3	—[e]
$25 million and over[a]	12	8–14
Nonpersonal Time Deposits	3	0–9
Supplementary Reserves[b]	0	0–4

a. The $25 million breaking-point will be increased each year after 1981 to reflect 80 percent of the increase in total transactions in that year.

b. Imposition requires affirmative vote of five governors.

c. Although this is called the initial rate it will be phased in and reached only in 1984.

d. In extraordinary circumstances the Fed may for 180 days set reserve requirements outside this range.

e. Fed cannot vary this requirement except as indicated in note c.

reserve requirements for transaction accounts on small banks than on large ones. Without such protection for small country banks, it is doubtful that Congress would have agreed to extend the Fed's reserve requirement to nonmember banks. There will now be no reserve requirements for the time deposits of households; only those of business and nonprofit institutions will have a reserve requirement. But the Fed, if it wants to, can abolish the time deposit reserve requirement entirely by setting the rate at zero. Congress did not want to decide whether time deposits are money. The Fed was given substantial additional powers to deal with emergencies. It can, on the affirmative vote of five of the seven members of the Board of Governors, impose an additional reserve requirement of up to 4 percent if this is required for effective implementation of monetary policy.[3] Moreover, in extraordinary circumstances the Fed can for 180 days set the reserve requirement at any level it considers necessary.

The next item on the balance sheet, cash items in the process of collection, is also extremely liquid, representing as it does checks and similar instruments that have just been deposited in the bank and that the bank has sent on for clearing. However, a bank does not count these cash items in the process of collection as part of its primary reserves (though in many states nonmember banks can count them as part of their legal reserves) because it knows that they are approximately offset by checks drawn by its own depositors on it that are currently in transit and will have to be paid.

Securities and Loans

Beyond its primary reserves a bank holds mainly *loans and securities*. These two items are known as **earning assets.** One part of these earning assets compose its **secondary reserves.** These are *assets that are not quite as liquid and safe as primary reserves, but still are very liquid*. They therefore provide the bank with a second line of defense if its primary reserves are insufficient. Secondary reserves have one great advantage over primary reserves; they earn a modest income for the bank. They are therefore included, along with other securities and loans, in the earning assets. However, their yield is less than that on less liquid and less safe assets.

It is not possible to identify secondary reserves on a bank's balance sheet, since the items constituting the secondary reserves are classified together with other items. One item included in secondary reserves is short-term government securities. Other secondary reserve assets are bankers acceptances, commercial paper—short-term promissory notes issued by large and very sound corporations—and call loans—loans mainly to brokers and security dealers on which the bank can demand repayment in a day.

Banks do not put all their available funds other than primary and

---

[3] However, it then has to pay interest on these additional reserves at the average rate which it earns on the securities it holds.

secondary reserves into loans; they hold fixed income securities too. These securities tend to be very safe in terms of repayment, but if interest rates have risen, a bank selling a bond with, say, 15 years to maturity can make a substantial loss on it. And if it holds the bond to maturity it is still making a loss in terms of opportunity costs. Bankers believe that a bank should place some of its funds into securities rather than into loans, that too high a ratio of loans to deposits is dangerous. Conventional ideas about the acceptable ratio of loans to deposits have varied over time, and they have increased along with the actually experienced loan to deposit ratio—an example of rules conforming to behavior. In 1979 the ratio was 81 percent; in 1948 when it was 29 percent, an 81 percent ratio would have been considered an outrage. Loans involve personal relationships between the banker and the borrower. Hence, they differ sharply from security purchases in which the bank buys securities usually from a dealer on the open market and does not know the borrower personally. Moreover, while a bank can sell a security again in the open market, there are few facilities for selling a loan, and the bank normally holds it until maturity.

Business loans. Commercial and industrial loans are the biggest component of total bank loans, accounting for 18 percent of the dollar volume of all loans in 1977. This heavy emphasis on commercial and industrial loans is not surprising since banks have a strong comparative advantage in making such loans. Retail banks, though not the large wholesale banks, make most of their loans to fairly small, local borrowers. Such loan applications require the evaluation of someone on the spot, as the local banker is. This gives banks a powerful advantage over large, distant lenders, such as insurance companies. Contrast, for example, the position of a bank and an insurance company in making a loan to a local grocery store and in buying a corporate bond. The bank knows much more about the local grocery store than the distant insurance company does and, hence, is in a much better position to decide whether to make it a loan. By contrast, the insurance company with its large staff of security analysts can reach a much more sophisticated decision about buying a corporate bond than can the typical bank.

An important characteristic of bank lending to business is credit rationing. A bank, unlike other firms, does not stand ready to provide as much of its product, loans, to a customer as he or she is willing to pay for. A seller of apples will normally be happy to provide the buyer with, say, ten times as much as he or she buys normally, but a bank will usually not be ready to make a borrower ten times the normal loan. Similarly, a bank will not make loans to just anyone who applies for one, even if he or she is willing to pay an interest rate high enough to offset the fact that this loan may be risky. Banks ration loans among applicants, both by turning away some loan customers and by limiting the size of loans to others. A major reason why banks, unlike sellers of apples, limit the amount of their product, the loans, they provide to each customer is surely that the bank, unlike the apple seller, takes a risk. It hands over its funds, and cannot be certain that it will get them back.

Credit rationing has both its defenders and its critics. The supporters point out that it is closely tied to an important function of banks. By granting loans to some customers, and not to others, banks play an important role in the allocation of resources. This is needed because firms may well be overly optimistic about their prospects. By scrutinizing loan requests, granting some, and denying others, the banker provides the economy with the services of a more or less objective outsider. The critics of credit rationing, on the other hand, point out that it allows banks to favor large depositors, and thereby to pay them implicit interest on demand deposits, over nondepositors or small depositors, who perhaps could use the capital more productively. Moreover, the critics argue, it gives bankers, particularly in small towns, a lot of arbitrary power, and it can be used as a weapon in forcing tie-in sales.

One factor that plays an important role in credit rationing is the existence of a customer relationship between the banker and the business borrower. Most of the business loans that banks make are to previous borrowers; business lending is a repeat business. Firms establish a customer relationship with a particular bank (or in the case of a large firm, with several banks) and, as long as the arrangement is mutually satisfactory, continue to both borrow from this bank and to keep deposits with it. This customer relationship comprises more than just a borrower-lender relationship; not only does the firm keep its deposit account with the bank it borrows from, but it also uses other services of the bank, such as the provision of foreign exchange, the making up of payrolls, etc. These services are often profitable and important for the bank. Large firms establish their customer relationships primarily with large and medium-sized banks, not only because these banks can provide these ancillary services, but also because national banks (and in many states, state banks) are allowed (with some exceptions) to lend to any one borrower an amount equal to no more than 10 percent of their capital.

This customer relationship implies that the bank has an obligation to take care of the reasonable credit needs of its existing customers. A bank is therefore not a completely free agent in making loans; it has to accommodate the reasonable demands for loans by its customers. To do this it may have to turn away other potential customers, even though these new customers would be willing to pay a higher interest rate than do existing customers. Similarly, it may have to ration loans among its existing customers rather than turning some of them down altogether. Or else, it may have to sell some of its securities, or obtain the funds needed for extra loans by obtaining more deposits through raising the interest rate it pays on large CDs.

This view of a bank as accommodating its customers may seem to conflict with the idea that banks are profit maximizers. But banks try to maximize long-term wealth, not merely the current month's profit. Meeting the loan demand of their customers, even if unprofitable in the short run, is profitable in the long run.

The existence of stable banking connections has one major advantage and also a major disadvantage. Its advantage is that it economizes on a scarce resource, information. Over the years a bank learns much about its customers. If these customers were to change banks frequently, this information would become worthless to the firm's old bank, and its new bank would have to spend resources to acquire this information. Hence, the banking industry would have higher costs. But, on the other hand, in a period of tight money, preexisting customer relationships lead to discrimination against new firms. At a time when banks have difficulty in meeting the loan demands of their existing customers, they are reluctant to take on new loan customers. Hence, even new firms with highly productive uses for capital may find it hard to obtain loans.

The maturity of bank loans varies widely. In the 1920s, banks made almost only short-term loans, that is, loans for less than a year, though some of these loans were renewed automatically, and hence were, in effect, long-term loans. But now banks make many **term loans,** loans *usually having a maturity of from one to five years,* and some are even for a longer term. A borrower can use these term loans to finance fixed investment. They are often amortized, that is, repaid in installments just like a consumer loan. On term loans the bank can protect itself by imposing certain restrictions on the borrower, such as limiting the amount of other debt that can be incurred.

Another way in which banks sometimes take care of the customer's need for fixed capital is to purchase capital equipment and lease it to the customer. Thus, banks own ships, airplanes, even cows. Such equipment leasing gives the bank the tax benefit of accelerated depreciation, while, if certain conditions are met, the leaser gains from the fact that his balance sheet does not show a debt, as it would had he borrowed from the bank to buy the item directly.

Instead of a term loan, a borrower may prefer to get frequent short-term loans. One way to do this is under a **line of credit.** This is an *arrangement whereby the bank agrees to make loans to a firm up to a certain amount, almost upon demand.* Lines of credit are usually established for a year and reviewed yearly. Under a firm line of credit the bank is more or less committed to make loans, and frequently charges a fee on the amount of the line that is *not* used, in addition to the interest on the amount that *is* used. As an alternative, a firm may obtain a revolving credit arrangement whereby it can borrow up to a certain amount, and then repay the loan at will without penalty. Later it can then borrow again up to the designated amount. A firm can also obtain a formal commitment from a bank to make it a loan in the future. For this it frequently has to pay a small fee. As table 4.8 shows, about half the dollar value of all loans is made under some form of loan commitment such as a line of credit or revolving credit.

Table 4.8 Commercial and Industrial Loans Made during 7–12 August 1978[a]

| | Size of loans (thousands of dollars) | | | | | | | | | |
| | SHORT-TERM LOANS | | | | | | LONG-TERM LOANS | | | |
	1– 24	25– 49	50– 99	100– 499	500– 999	1000 and over	1– 99	100– 499	500– 999	1000 and over
Percent of all loans	78.8	9.0	5.7	5.6	0.5	0.5	88.7	10.0	0.7	0.7
Percent of total dollar value of loans	14.6	7.8	8.9	26.4	7.4	35.0	20.7	25.1	7.0	47.2
Average size of loans (thousands of $)	7	33	60	182	617	2,597	15	160	662	4,523
Maturity (number of months)[b]	2.8	3.4	2.4	3.0	3.3	3.1	33.7	47.2	57.7	47.4
Percent of amount of loans:										
Made under commitment	15.2	21.0	27.5	31.2	58.5	54.9	25.0	35.7	50.6	71.2
Made with floating rate	32.0	36.6	46.5	43.2	57.4	60.1	30.1	62.3	55.1	84.3
Average interest rate (weighted average)	10.4	10.2	10.3	10.2	9.9	9.5	10.7	10.4	9.8	10.0

a. Excludes construction loans and land-development loans.
b. Average for loans weighted by their dollar amount.
SOURCE: *Federal Reserve Bulletin* 64 (November 1978) : A-26.

A bank frequently requires business borrowers who have a line of credit, and many who don't, to keep a compensating balance in the bank. This means that the firm may have to keep, say, 10 percent of its line of credit, or under other arrangements, say, 20 percent of its currently outstanding loans, as a demand deposit in the bank. Some banks require borrowers to keep such a minimum deposit at all times, while others require borrowers to keep their *average* balance at this level. The latter is a much less burdensome requirement since the borrower can then actually use the deposit at those times when the need for funds is greatest. A compensating balance requirement is not legally binding, but if the borrower does not adhere to it the bank may refuse him or her further loans, or may charge a higher interest rate on any subsequent loan. There is much variation in the compensating balance requirements of various banks. Some have rigid policies, while others merely consider the potential borrower's deposits as one factor in deciding on a loan request.

The compensating balance requirement raises the effective interest rate the borrower is paying. Suppose the bank makes a $100,000 loan at an 8 percent interest rate with a 20 percent minimum compensating balance requirement. The borrower can then use only $80,000 of that, but still pays 8 percent on $100,000, or $8,000, which is equivalent to 10 percent on the $80,000 actually used. But this example is applicable only to the case where the borrower obtains no benefit at all from holding the compensating balance. Suppose that, as a safeguard for emergencies or to obtain services from the bank, the borrower *wants* to keep an extra $20,000 in the demand deposit. If so, the compensating balance imposes no burden. In the more realistic intermediate case, however, where the utility of keeping an extra $20,000 in a demand deposit is less than the interest paid on the $20,000, the compensating balance requirement does impose a burden on the borrower.[4] Hence, bankers and borrowers frequently negotiate about the size of the required compensating balance.

Another requirement frequently imposed on a borrower is to provide the bank with collateral for the loan so that, in case it is not repaid, the bank can sell the collateral to pay it off. The collateral, which may consist of securities, inventory, and so on, often, though not always, exceeds the value of the loan to protect the bank in case its market value subsequently declines. Sometimes the bank may not require collateral as a condition for the loan but may offer the borrower a lower interest rate if he or she does provide collateral.

The interest rate charged on bank loans varies, of course, along with

---

[4] The compensating balance arrangement also imposes a burden on the bank since it has to keep reserves against the $100,000 deposit instead of just against the $80,000 the customer can actually use. There is therefore some dispute about why banks follow the compensating balance rule. One possible explanation is that by varying the compensating balance requirements both between customers and over time they can price discriminate.

open-market interest rates, though with a lag. Table 4.8 shows the interest rates charged on loans of various sizes in August 1978. It shows
that the larger the loan the lower the interest rate. This is not surprising
since the interest rate paid has to compensate the bank for the cost of making the loan, and the cost of making a $10 million loan is not a thousand
times as high as the cost of making a $10,000 loan. This does not mean
that the average borrower who obtains a small loan could lower his or her
interest rate by taking out a large loan; instead, a higher interest rate
would be paid because a large loan to a small firm is risky.

The *bellwether interest rate* is the **prime rate.** This rate was established in 1933 as a way of limiting interest rate competition among banks
by setting a uniform minimum rate that banks charged their soundest and
biggest borrowers. The large banks exercised price leadership and changed
the prime rate at infrequent intervals. In recent years, however, the prime-
rate system has changed in many ways. First, many more borrowers now
get the prime rate, and being able to borrow at the prime rate has become
a symbol of business success. Second, the prime rate now changes much
more frequently. For example, in the two years 1977 and 1978, the prime
rate charged by Morgan Guarantee (a large New York bank) changed
twenty-two times. In fact, one large bank, Citibank, has a floating prime
rate that is set at 1.25 percent above a certain commercial paper rate,
though Citibank does depart from this formula from time to time. Some
other large banks, while not using such a publicly announced formula, also
use the commercial paper rate as a guide, and still others use the Citibank
prime rate. As a result, it is no longer true that all banks charge the same
prime rate, though their prime rates are fairly similar. A bank keeping
its prime rate well below the prime rate of other banks for a long time would
face a serious problem. Its customers would switch their borrowing away
from other banks and to it. And due to the customer relationship the bank
would be under pressure to grant these loan requests. Hence, if other banks
raise their prime rate, a bank may have to go along to protect itself from
getting too many customers!

From time to time, particularly when loan demand is weak, especially
good customers can sometimes borrow at less than the prime rate, though
such arrangements are usually not publicized.[5] Loans to firms that do not
receive the prime rate are often scaled up from the prime rate. For example, the loan agreement may state that the interest rate will be half a
percent above the prime rate.

As table 4.8 shows, the interest rate charged is frequently a variable
rate, rather than a fixed rate; as the prime rate on newly contracted loans
changes, the rate on many previously made business loans changes along

---

[5] A few banks have established a special rate, below the prime rate, for loans to
certain small firms. At least to some extent this is a response to the public criticism
that banks charge too high a rate to small firms. It is hard to say how long this special
rate will last.

with it. Sometimes, however, the loan agreement contains a "cap" on how high the interest rate can rise.

Some banks specialize in the type of industry loans they make. This is the origin of the name of some banks, for example, the Chemical Bank, even though the bank may long ago have outgrown this specialization. Specialization allows a bank to take advantage of the knowledge it has developed over the years about a particular industry. On the other hand, it makes the bank's loan portfolio riskier because a downturn in this particular industry may then result in many of its loans all going into default at the same time. Moreover, if the particular industry is depressed the bank may have few customers for loans.

Some banks have only limited choice about specialization. For example, a small bank located in New York City at Broadway and Thirty-third Street will have most of its loan requests from firms connected with the garment trade and few loan requests from dealers in agricultural equipment. But to some extent banks can avoid this problem by participating in loans made by their correspondent banks to other industries. Another way is to establish branches in other areas. Large banks, of course, do not have this problem. They obtain their business from companies all over the world.

Other loans. Real-estate loans (that is, mortgage loans) on residential or nonresidential property are now almost as large a proportion of total bank loans as business loans. Residential mortgages may be insured or guaranteed by the Federal Housing Administration (FHA) or the Veterans Administration (VA). FHA and VA mortgages involve little risk for banks, but have the disadvantage that the maximum interest rate that the bank may charge is limited, though this ceiling can often be avoided by discounting the mortgage note using the points system in addition to charging interest. (Under the points system a customer will sign a promissory note, say, for $50,000 at a 9 percent interest rate. The bank gives the customer only, say, $48,000 for this $50,000 note, thus obtaining an additional $2,000 of interest.) Unfortunately, FHA and VA loans involve a lot of red tape. In addition, mortgage loans are long-term loans that can seriously reduce the bank's liquidity. But the actual maturity of mortgage loans is much less than their apparent maturity, since they are amortized (that is, repaid in installments) and, in addition, are frequently repaid when the house is sold. Moreover, a secondary market for mortgage loans, particularly FHA and VA loans, has developed on which banks can sell their mortgage loans.

Bank mortgage lending is countercyclical. Banks increase their mortgage loans when business activity is low and firms demand relatively few bank loans. Then, when business demand for loans picks up, banks cut back on their mortgage lending. This is so, in part, because banks do have a customer relationship with their business borrowers but not with households that want to take out mortgages. Another explanation focuses on the demand for mortgage loans instead of the supply, and argues that the demand for mortgage loans is more interest elastic than is the demand for business loans, so that demand for mortgage loans falls relative to business loan demand as interest rates rise during a business expansion.

Another major outlet for bank funds is consumer lending. Until the 1930s banks regarded lending to consumers as rather risky and not the sort of thing a commercial bank would want much to do with. But now consumer loans account for about 23 percent of total bank loans. One substantial advantage to banks of consumer loans is that they are very liquid. Since they are usually short term and amortized, their turnover is fairly rapid.

Most consumer loans are made for the purchase of durables, which then serve as collateral for the loan. Banks make consumer loans both directly and indirectly, the latter through dealers by financing loans originated by the dealer. The dealer, who receives a commission on such loan business, is required to put a small part of the loan into a fund to meet any losses from defaults on these loans.

However, banks also make general purpose loans to consumers. Among these are credit-card loans on which the bank receives not only interest from the borrower, but also a commission from the vendor. Some banks have set up an arrangement by which a credit-card holder can have his or her checking account credited (and the card debited) automatically if the balance in the checking account is insufficient to meet incoming checks. Other banks have set up similar arrangements for automatic loans to customers who do not have the bank's credit card. On the whole, our banks are moving towards the British overdraft system, under which the depositor can overdraw the account, with the bank treating the overdraft as a loan.

The interest rate charged on consumer loans is higher than on business loans. The reason for this is that the cost of making such loans is also high because these are relatively small and short-term loans. For example, if it costs a bank $50 to set up and take care of monthly payments on a $2,000 two-year loan, it must charge approximately 2.5 percent just to cover this cost. Nonetheless, banks usually charge a lower interest rate on their consumer loans than do other consumer lenders because they avoid the riskier loans that other lenders are more ready to make. Losses on consumer loans usually run between 0.75 and 1.25 percent of outstanding loan volume.

Banks also make loans for the purchase of securities. Such loans are made, not only to households, but also to security dealers and brokers who use them to finance the purchases of their customers, or their own security holdings. *Loans to security dealers and brokers are often made on a (renewable) one-day basis* (referred to as **call loans**) and are therefore extremely liquid for banks. As will be discussed in chapter 22, the Federal Reserve imposes a ceiling on the percent of the security's value that a bank or broker may lend. The purpose of this is not to protect the bank against too risky loans, but rather to limit "excessive" stock-market speculation.

Still another type of bank loan is the student loan. This loan is offered at a relatively low interest rate since it is subsidized by the federal government, which also guarantees repayment. This guarantee has had to be invoked much more frequently than was expected when the legislation authorizing it was passed.

Other Assets

Apart from the major assets discussed so far, the banks' balance sheet contains a number of minor assets as well. "Customer's liability on account of acceptances" is the counterpart of the acceptance item listed as a liability. When a bank accepts a draft for a customer the customer incurs a liability to the bank and this is an asset for the bank. Federal funds sold are, of course, an asset for the bank since they represent loans that the bank has made. An item joined with federal funds in the balance sheet, "securities purchased under repurchase agreements," is also an asset because these are securities that the bank currently holds. The penultimate item, "bank premises, etc.," is self-explanatory, and the final miscellaneous item includes a wide variety of minor assets.

Liability and Asset Management: Traditional and Current Approaches

Having explained the various assets and liabilities of banks, we can now discuss briefly how banks have changed the composition of their liabilities and assets over time.

The Changing Composition of Liabilities and Assets

Looking first at the asset side, American as well as British banks grew up with the tradition that banks should make only business loans. Consumers, particularly the spendthrift types who are likely to borrow, are unsound risks, and mortgage loans are risky too because they are long-term, and hence illiquid loans, and besides the real-estate market may collapse. American banks have frequently taken large losses on real-estate loans. Among business loans the traditional doctrine told banks that they should make only short-term self-liquidating loans.[6] Self-liquidating means that the loan is used in a way that generates the funds needed to repay it. For example, a loan to a merchant to buy inventory is self-liquidating; as he sells the goods he can use the proceeds to repay the loan. By contrast, a personal loan to buy a car is not self-liquidating; the borrower may have

---

[6] By contrast, the Continental banking tradition has banks making long-term loans to industry, buying stock in industry, and serving on the boards of directors of many companies.

sufficient income to repay it, but this income does not result from the loan itself. Well into the 1920s banks generally believed that it was their function to finance production rather than consumption or speculation; that is, to make only self-liquidating, nonspeculative loans. It was also widely believed at the time that if banks made only self-liquidating loans for production, rather than for speculation, the extension of bank credit would not be inflationary because the loan would be used to produce an equivalent amount of output, so that demand and supply would increase equally. (This is no longer accepted.) And by keeping these loans short term, say, ninety days or so, banks seemed to obtain liquidity, since many loans would be coming due all the time.

This doctrine, known as commercial loan theory, or real bills doctrine, did not survive the depression of the 1930s. During this depression relatively few sound firms wanted to borrow for activities consistent with this commercial loan theory, and besides, to everyone's surprise, it turned out that consumer loans had a better repayment record than did business loans. And banks did not have to rely so much on short-term business loans because the federal government's deficit provided them with a large supply of government securities they could buy instead. And this was so even more after the United States entered World War II. Whereas in 1928 banks held almost $3 of loans for every dollar of securities, by the end of the war the situation was just the reverse. Instead of relying on loan repayment for liquidity, banks now relied on the fact that they could sell their government securities immediately.

Table 4.9 shows how banks have changed the composition of their assets in recent years. Cash assets, that is, vault cash, reserves with the Federal Reserve, and deposits with other banks, have declined substantially as a proportion of total bank assets. This is due to several factors. One is that the Federal Reserve's reserve requirements have been cut substantially. Another is that banks have become more confident of being able to raise any additional funds they need (a confidence connected in part with the fading of the memories of the Great Depression) and hence have relied less on their stock of cash assets for liquidity. A third factor is that since interest rates have risen substantially in the postwar period it has become more and more expensive to hold idle cash. Government securities have declined too as a proportion of total bank assets as banks have found more profitable outlets for their funds. However, state and local government securities have become a more significant part, thanks to interest on them being exempted from federal income tax. Business loans have become a larger proportion of bank assets as firms have needed more bank loans to finance their expansion plans. Within the business loan category there has been a very substantial change; banks now make many longer term loans rather than mainly making short-term loans, as was the case before the war. Mortgage loans have risen substantially too, in part because of government insurance and guarantees of mortgage loans. Consumer loans and miscellaneous loans have been rising at an even faster rate than busi-

Table 4.9 Assets and Liabilities of Insured Commercial Banks
1950–1975   (Percentage Distribution)

	Assets					
	1950	1955	1960	1965	1970	1975
Cash assets	24	23	20	16	16	14
U.S. government and agency securities	37	29	24	17	13	12
State and local government securities	5	6	7	10	12	11
Other Securities	2	2	1	0	1	1
Business loans	13	16	17	19	19	18
Mortgage loans	8	10	11	13	13	14
Consumer loans	6	8	10	12	11	11
Other loans	4	5	8	10	11	13
Miscellaneous assets	1	1	2	3	4	6
TOTAL	100	100	100	100	100	100

	Liabilities					
	1950	1955	1960	1965	1970	1975
Demand deposits	70	68	61	49	43	34
Passbook savings deposits	17	18	22	25	17	17
Time deposits proper	5	6	7	11	19	22
Large negotiable CDs	0	0	0	4	5	9
Miscellaneous liabilities	2	1	2	3	9	11
Equity capital	6	7	8	8	7	7
TOTAL	100	100	100	100	100	100

SOURCE: William Silber, *Commercial Bank Liability Management* (Chicago, Ill.: Association of Reserve City Bankers, 1978), pp. 5, 6.

ness loans and mortgage loans as banks have developed more experience with such loans, and found them safe and profitable.

Bank liabilities have changed a great deal too. In the good old days before the Great Depression of the 1930s, the only families that held commercial bank deposits were middle- and upper-class ones. A textbook published in 1916 described the process of opening a bank account as follows:

There are so many ways in which a bank may be defrauded . . . that the officers must be very careful to whom they extend the privilege of opening an account. . . . One of the pleasantest ways to open an account with a bank is to be introduced by a depositor in good standing. . . . It is not always possible to arrange for a personal introduction. In such a case, a properly written letter addressed to an officer and signed by a depositor in good standing, or even by a mutual friend, will be of material assistance. . . . If it is impossible for a person to obtain either a personal or written introduction to the bank he had chosen, he may make application for the opening of an account without an introduction and have the assurance that such a procedure will not militate against him, if he presents his case properly.

> It is true that some banks will not, under any circumstances, open an account with a person unknown to them. In fact, it is good banking practice not to accept accounts from strangers. . . .[7]

This is a far cry from the way banks act now, chasing after depositors with singing commercials.

Table 4.9 also shows the ways bank liabilities have changed in the postwar period. Demand deposits accounted for 70 percent of all bank liabilities in 1950, but only for 34 percent by 1975. Since then they have fallen by another percentage point. This decline is surely due to the fact that interest rates on time deposits have risen substantially while no explicit interest may be paid on conventional demand deposits and until 1981 NOW accounts were available only in a few states. While passbook accounts have maintained their share of total liabilities, the share of small CDs has risen strongly; and large *negotiable* CDs, which were "invented" in 1961, accounted for close to 10 percent of all liabilities by 1975. Since then, miscellaneous liabilities have also risen rapidly. Bank capital has been a more or less constant proportion of total liabilities.

But one of the most important changes in bank behavior has been the rise of liability management, starting in 1961, to which we now turn.

Liability Management

The way in which banks have operated in the past was to treat most of their liabilities as more or less given from the outside. The traditional story is one of a banker who welcomes depositors coming to him but is not very active in soliciting deposits. He may advertise for depositors, or make loans to firms that promise to bring him their deposit business, but he does not go out and "buy" deposits the same way he buys assets. To a considerable extent, deposits "just happen." Most of the banker's energies are devoted to managing the asset side of his balance sheet, and he follows a rather passive policy with respect to the liabilities side.

This story is still a fair description of the way many small banks behave, but it is no longer true for large and medium-sized banks. During the early 1960s several things happened that made these banks active seekers after short-term funds. One was that business firms wanted to borrow more from these banks, and, as we saw, banks are obligated to meet the reasonable credit needs of their good customers; therefore banks were under pressure to obtain more funds. Second, as table 4.9 shows, by the early 1960s banks had run down their government securities substantially, and many of the government securities they did hold were pledged as collateral for public deposits or were held as needed secondary reserves.[8]

---

[7] Joseph F. Johnson, Howard M. Jefferson, and Franklin Escher, *Banking* (New York: Alexander Hamilton Institute, 1916), pp. 266–68.

[8] Many governments require banks holding their deposits to pledge specific government securities as collateral in case the bank fails. Deposit insurance covers only the first $100,000 of government deposits.

Hence, they could no longer meet a rise in the demand for loans by selling government securities as they had in the past. And large banks serving large corporations found it difficult to obtain additional funds the conventional way from their depositors because these corporations had learned various ways of economizing on their deposit holdings. Thus, these banks had to find new ways of acquiring funds. At the same time, by the 1960s the attitude of bankers had changed; many of those whose outlook toward risk had been shaped by the Great Depression had retired, and a new breed of more confident profit-oriented officers had taken charge. Moreover, in 1961 a new financial instrument, the large negotiable CD, was developed.

The large negotiable CD meant that banks could now issue a security that was similar to a Treasury bill in the sense that the owner does not have to hold it to maturity but can sell it at any time on the money market. This greatly broadened the market for large CDs. Large and medium-sized banks could now—at a price—obtain additional deposits whenever they wanted them by offering large CDs carrying a slightly higher rate of interest. In general, the rate a bank has to pay on its CDs depends on its size, both because large banks are better known and because the market believes that the FDIC is less likely to let a large bank fail with losses to depositors than a medium-sized bank.

And large CDs are not the only instrument of liability management. Another one is a repurchase agreement (RP); that is, an arrangement under which a bank "sells" some of its securities with a commitment to buy them back again, say, the next day, at a fixed price. In effect the "buyer" is making a loan to the bank. Another method of liability management is to have the bank's holding company sell commercial paper, or notes and debentures, and to make the funds thus obtained available to the bank. Still another way in which large banks obtain funds is to buy Eurodollars. An American bank can borrow, that is, "buy," such deposits from its own European branch or from other U.S. or foreign banks. In addition, banks can buy federal funds from other banks, or other participants in this market. And, as we will take up in chapter 7, member banks can borrow from the Federal Reserve.

Large banks can, and do, purchase a great volume of funds by these means. To cite an extreme example, in December 1976 the large banks that report weekly to the Federal Reserve had borrowed in these ways an amount equal to 25.7 percent of their total liabilities, while their corresponding lending in these markets equaled only 6.2 percent of their liabilities. Their *net* borrowings amounted to approximately three times their capital!

Small banks cannot play this game. Since they are not well enough known, and since they could only deal in small amounts, they would face prohibitive transactions costs in the large negotiable CD market and the Eurodollar market. However, through their correspondent banks, they can, and, as table 4.6 shows, do, enter the federal funds market, usually as sellers, and they can borrow from the Federal Reserve. In the long run they, as well as the large banks, can, of course, attract more small deposits by increasing their free services and sales promotion, and by opening new branches. But this does not provide them with funds quickly.

Bank Trust Departments

Our discussion of the banking business would not be complete without some reference to trust departments of banks. Since trust departments are not what makes banking important for monetary economics, we will discuss them only very briefly.

Bank trust departments control a very large amount of capital. In 1976 they held $489 billion, a sum equal to about one and a half times the narrow money stock (M_1). Only about one-quarter of all banks have trust departments and their holdings are highly concentrated. In 1976 just eighty banks held almost three-quarters of all bank trust funds.

Trust departments administer funds for wealthy households, estates, pension funds, and so on. For some trust funds the bank provides merely investment advice, but for much the greater part it has sole investment responsibility. Banks can, and do, invest these funds, unlike their own assets, in common stocks as well as in fixed-income securities.

There has been some concern about these trust activities of banks, and proposals have been made to take trust departments away from banks and to turn them into separate institutions. The main arguments for this are, first, that trust departments allow banks to accumulate great economic power, and second, that banks might not separate their trust and commercial banking activities as they are supposed to do. For example, a bank might use the information it obtains from a firm in the process of making it a loan to give it an unfair advantage over other stockholders. Thus, if the bank in its capacity as a lender hears of unfavorable developments ahead of other stockholders it might have its trust department sell this stock to the detriment of other stockholders. But banks are not supposed to do this, and whether this sort of thing actually occurs on a significant scale is a matter for debate.

Apart from personal trusts, the larger banks also handle trust matters for corporations. They administer corporate pension funds, send out interest and dividend payments on corporate bonds and stocks and register bond transfers. These activities can be a profitable part of the customer relationship for the bank.

Summary

In this chapter we discussed the functioning of the banking firm as a profit maximizer in a multiproduct market. Various products in its market are connected through the customer relationship it has with business firms. A central problem faced by the bank is that its assets are, on the whole, much less liquid than its liabilities.

We discussed each of the major types of bank liabilities: demand deposits, the various types of time deposits, and other liabilities. We then took up bank assets starting with primary and secondary reserves. This led into a discussion of required reserves both for member and nonmember banks. Beyond their primary and secondary reserves banks also hold securities for earnings and we discussed these. The main business of banks, however, on the asset side of their balance sheet, is making loans, and we looked at loans in some detail. We considered certain characteristics of business loans, the customer relationship, credit rationing, the maturity of loans, lines of credit, collateral, interest rates, and compensating balances. We then looked briefly at the historical development of bank assets and liabilities, and at how large, modern banks now manage their liabilities. We concluded with a very brief discussion of what might be called the "nonbanking" part of banks, their trust business.

QUESTIONS AND EXERCISES

1. Describe the way large banks manage their liabilities.
2. Describe the current system of reserve requirements for member and nonmember banks. Do you think it is proper and equitable?
3. Describe CDs, both negotiable and nonnegotiable ones.
4. Describe:
   a. bankers acceptances,
   b. cashier's check,
   c. federal funds,
   d. primary reserves.
5. Describe credit rationing. Why do banks do this?
6. Describe the customer relationship of banks. Is this desirable?
7. Describe the following characteristics of business loans:
   a. lines of credit,
   b. compensatory balances,
   c. collateral,
   d. the prime rate.
8. Suppose a banker tells you that in his twenty-five years as a loan officer he has never made a loan that went into default. Should you congratulate him for sound business judgment?
9. Describe the functions of bank trust departments.
10. "Capital requirements on banks should be lowered. If they have a smaller proportion of their funds tied up in capital they can make more loans." Discuss.

FURTHER READING

AMERICAN BANKERS ASSOCIATION. *The Commercial Banking Industry*. Englewood Cliffs, N.J.: Prentice-Hall, 1952. An authoritative, though somewhat dated, statement by the banking industry.

EHRLICH, EDNA. "The Functions and Investment Policies of Personal Trust Departments." *Monthly Review* (Federal Reserve Bank of New York) 54
(October 1972): 255–270. A detailed discussion of a survey of bank trust
departments.

FRIEDMAN, BENJAMIN. "Credit Rationing: A Review." *Board of Governors, Federal Reserve System, Staff Economy Study #72, 1972.* An excellent discussion of the large literature on credit rationing.

HAVRILESKY, THOMAS, and BOORMAN, JOHN. *Current Perspectives in Banking,*
Arlington Heights, Ill.: AHM Publishing Co., 1976. An interesting collection of readings.

HODGMAN, DONALD. *Commercial Bank Loan and Investment Policy.* Urbana, Ill.:
University of Illinois Press, 1963. An interesting argument that the deposit
business of banks takes precedence over their lending business.

JESSUP, PAUL. *Innovations in Bank Management.* New York: Holt, Rinehart and
Winston, 1969. A collection of papers presenting new ideas about banking.

LINDOW, WESLEY. *Inside the Money Market.* New York: Random House, 1972.
A fascinating discussion of liability management as seen by a banker.

ROBINSON, ROLAND. *The Management of Bank Funds.* New York: McGraw-Hill,
1962. An excellent text on how banks use their assets.

SILBER, WILLIAM L. *Commercial Bank Liability Management.* Chicago: Association of Reserve City Bankers, 1978. An interesting and detailed survey.

5

Financial Intermediaries

Most of us have a hard time saving, but when we do manage to save something we find that it is difficult to invest in an increasingly complex economy. A number of other institutions beside commercial banks serve to intermediate between savers and investors, and provide an alternative to direct finance. These institutions include mutual savings banks, savings and loan associations, credit unions, life insurance companies, and pension funds.

Most Americans depend on these financial intermediaries to do their investment for them. Some sacrifice of investment income is required to pay the cost of operating financial intermediaries, but most people, especially those of modest means, are willing to pay that price for the safety and convenience offered by the intermediaries. Wealthy individuals buy common stocks and may hold municipal bonds for tax-free income, but few American families hold common stocks, and even fewer hold tax-exempt bonds. Most families invest their savings in commercial banks and other intermediaries. Table 5.1 shows the distribution of household financial assets among the different kinds of directly held securities and financial intermediaries. Table 5.2 shows how the flow of household saving has been distributed among different kinds of securities and financial intermediaries.

In chapter 2 we discussed the rationale for the use of financial intermediaries. In this chapter we will review the development of several of the more important kinds of intermediaries. In addition to the ones mentioned above we will consider the role of consumer finance companies and of several important federal financial agencies.

Thrift Institutions: A Profile

The thrift institutions, mutual savings banks, savings and loan associations, and credit unions, provide the best and most important example of the functions of financial intermediaries outlined in chapter 2. As we indicated there, they reap economies of scale and the benefits of diversification, and create liquidity by pooling the assets of many individual savers.

101

Table 5.1   Household Balance Sheet
              31 December 1978   *(billions of dollars)*

Assets		*Liabilities*	
Demand deposits and currency	$ 218.9	Credit-market instruments	$1,164.3
		Home mortgages	734.4
Time and savings accounts	1,103.9	Other mortgages	27.9
At commercial banks	479.0	Installment consumer credit	275.6
At savings institutions	624.8	Other consumer credit	64.3
		Bank loans	22.7
Credit-market instruments	473.1	Other loans	39.3
U.S. government securities	172.9		
Treasury issues	139.5	Security credit	22.2
Savings bonds	80.7	Trade credit	13.2
Other treasury	58.8		
Agency issues	33.3	Deferred and unpaid life	
		insurance premiums	10.1
State and local obligations	89.4		
Corporate and foreign bonds	63.2		
Mortgages	106.0		
Open-market paper	30.8		
Money-market fund shares	10.8		
Corporate equities	791.9		
Investment company shares	43.8		
Other corporate equities	748.1		
Life-insurance reserves	188.6		
Pension-fund reserves	530.1		
Security credit	8.8		
Miscellaneous assets	59.0		
TOTAL: Financial Assets	$3,374.3	TOTAL: Liabilities	$1,209.7

SOURCE: Board of Governors of the Federal Reserve System, unpublished data.

Evolution of Thrift Institutions

Nowadays, commercial banks offer savings accounts and invest in mortgages and bonds in much the same way as the thrift institutions. It is not unreasonable to suppose that commercial banks could always have done so, obviating the need for specialized thrift institutions. But the financial arrangements we have now reflect the historical evolution of financial markets. Commercial banks arose mainly as note-issuing institutions, not as depositories. When they did develop demand deposits, they were generally concerned with business rather than with consumer accounts. On the lending side, banks originally concentrated on short-term business loans because their deposits and notes were payable on demand.

This left small savers with no satisfactory investment vehicle, while at the same time there was a strong demand for long-term funds, especially for mortgages. Mutual savings banks and savings and loan associations were developed to fill these needs. Nowadays they are regarded as rather similar institutions, but their origins were quite different.

Mutual savings banks in the United States were organized early in the nineteenth century to encourage saving among the growing artisan class in cities like Boston, Philadelphia, and New York. They were founded by groups of wealthy businessmen whose motives were partly philanthropic, but who also hoped to promote political stability by encouraging saving and property ownership for the working classes. The names of some of the earliest banks, like the Boston Five Cent Savings Bank and the Dime Savings Bank, show their interest in very small accounts. The incorporators subscribed the original capital, accepting a limited dividend. Mutual savings banks are controlled by self-perpetuating boards of trustees. All earnings, in excess of operating costs, are either paid out as interest to depositors or added to surplus as a cushion against losses.

Most of the mutual savings banks operate in New England and New York, with a very small number in other states. Many of the mutual savings banks are small, but several of the institutions in Boston and New York City measure their assets in billions of dollars. All of the mutual savings banks are state chartered and regulated by state banking commissioners. Under recent legislation, savings banks may now, if they wish, obtain federal charters and some have done so. They are permitted to invest in home mortgages and corporate bonds and make some installment loans. Partly by their own choice, and partly by regulation, they have been conservatively managed and have had few failures. Between 1930 and 1933 only ten mutual savings banks failed, while over nine thousand commercial banks and over five hundred savings and loan associations failed. The Massachusetts savings banks set up their own insurance fund in the nineteenth century so that most of them do not belong to the FDIC.

Savings and loan associations originated as self-help associations. A group of people who wanted to finance their own houses agreed to pool their savings. Each member received shares in proportion to his savings. When enough was accumulated to finance one home, a mortgage loan was made to a member selected by lot. With further accumulations another loan was made. With accumulating savings and repayments of mortgages, all the original members bought homes. When all the mortgages had been paid off the association was terminated. Later, of course, the association took in new members and operated on a continuing basis in much the same way as savings banks. They differ from savings banks, however, in several important respects.

First, many savings and loan associations are now organized as corporations rather than as mutual associations. There are only a few "stock" savings banks. Because of their origin, their investment powers are more limited. Savings and loans were restricted to mortgage loans and government securities until the law was changed in 1980.

The two thousand federally chartered savings and loans hold about

Table 5.2 Household Savings
(Billions of dollars; quarterly data at seasonally adjusted annual rates)

Year or quarter	Total	Increase in financial assets								Net investment in			Less: net increase in debt		
		Total	Currency and demand deposits	Savings accounts	Money-market fund shares	SECURITIES			Insurance and pension reserves	Nonfarm homes	Consumer durables	Noncorporate business assets	Mortgage debt on nonfarm homes	Consumer credit	Other debt
						Government securities	Corporate and foreign bonds	Corporate equities							
1946	24.4	18.8	5.6	6.3	—	-1.5	-0.9	1.1	5.3	3.6	6.1	2.1	3.6	3.1	-0.5
1947	20.2	13.2	.1	3.4	—	1.6	-.8	1.1	5.4	6.7	8.8	2.0	4.7	3.7	2.2
1948	24.5	9.1	-2.9	2.2	—	1.3	-.1	1.0	5.3	9.1	9.8	7.1	4.6	3.2	2.8
1949	21.3	9.9	-2.0	2.6	—	1.8	-.4	.7	5.6	8.4	10.9	2.0	4.4	3.2	2.2
1950	30.9	13.7	2.6	2.4	—	-.1	-.8	.7	6.9	11.8	14.9	7.0	6.7	4.8	5.0
1951	34.7	19.1	4.6	4.7	—	-.6	.2	1.8	6.3	11.7	11.3	4.4	6.6	1.6	3.6
1952	30.7	23.2	1.6	7.8	—	2.5	-.0	1.6	7.7	11.3	8.4	2.0	6.2	5.3	2.8
1953	31.6	22.8	1.0	8.1	—	2.5	-.1	1.0	7.9	12.3	9.4	.8	7.6	4.2	1.9
1954	27.7	22.2	2.2	9.1	—	1.0	-.9	.8	7.8	12.7	6.9	1.5	8.7	1.5	5.5
1955	33.4	28.0	1.2	8.6	—	5.8	.5	1.0	8.5	16.7	11.9	2.4	12.2	7.2	6.4
1956	36.7	30.2	1.8	9.4	—	3.9	1.1	2.0	9.5	15.6	8.7	.5	11.2	3.9	3.2
1957	35.8	28.6	-.4	11.9	—	2.3	.9	1.5	9.5	13.2	7.6	2.1	8.9	2.9	3.8
1958	33.4	31.6	3.8	13.9	—	-2.5	1.2	1.5	10.4	12.1	3.4	2.3	9.5	.5	6.0
1959	35.6	37.4	.8	11.1	—	10.1	.4	.6	11.9	15.9	6.9	3.4	12.8	8.0	7.2
1960	35.6	32.5	1.0	12.1	—	2.4	.7	-.5	11.5	14.3	6.7	3.1	11.7	4.4	4.8
1961	34.1	35.9	-.9	18.3	—	1.8	-.1	.3	12.1	12.0	4.1	3.3	12.2	2.5	6.5
1962	40.3	40.6	-1.2	26.1	—	1.8	-.5	-2.0	12.7	12.8	8.2	6.3	14.1	6.3	7.2
1963	45.2	47.3	4.2	26.3	—	1.2	.2	-2.6	13.9	13.4	11.8	8.5	16.2	8.9	10.6
1964	55.7	56.1	5.2	26.1	—	5.1	-.5	-.1	16.1	13.9	15.1	7.7	17.5	9.8	9.8

1965	63.8	59.0	7.5	27.8	—	3.9	.5	-2.1	16.9	13.4	20.2	11.2	17.0	10.6	12.6
1966	72.1	58.4	2.4	19.0	—	11.7	1.3	-.6	19.2	12.6	22.8	9.4	13.8	6.5	10.8
1967	77.6	70.4	9.9	35.3	—	-.7	3.9	-4.2	18.6	10.9	20.9	8.5	12.5	5.7	15.0
1968	82.2	76.2	11.1	31.1	—	5.7	4.3	-6.4	19.8	14.3	26.3	9.4	17.1	11.5	15.3
1969	73.7	64.5	-2.5	9.1	—	25.3	5.4	-3.6	21.5	14.2	26.2	11.4	18.5	10.8	13.3
1970	86.1	78.8	8.9	43.6	—	-7.3	9.5	-1.5	24.0	11.7	20.2	9.8	14.1	5.4	14.8
1971	98.7	103.0	12.2	67.8	—	-10.1	8.8	-5.1	27.5	18.8	26.2	13.5	26.4	14.7	21.8
1972	116.9	128.8	13.9	74.5	—	1.9	5.0	-5.6	29.4	26.0	35.1	17.7	41.5	19.8	29.5
1973	138.4	148.5	14.1	63.8	—	24.1	2.0	-6.7	33.0	28.2	41.1	20.3	47.1	26.0	26.5
1974	128.9	142.4	7.1	55.9	2.4	27.8	5.1	-2.2	36.3	23.1	28.6	2.8	35.4	9.9	22.7
1975	150.0	167.2	4.0	84.0	1.3	22.9	8.4	-3.6	43.5	20.8	26.6	.2	38.1	9.7	16.6
1976	164.6	208.1	14.9	109.3	0	12.0	5.8	-3.2	52.6	33.1	40.6	-1.0	61.3	25.6	29.2
1977	172.8	241.7	22.7	109.2	.2	18.3	-3.3	-6.1	65.4	48.1	50.9	5.9	93.2	40.6	40.0
1978	198.2	275.3	18.3	105.2	6.9	30.2	1.4	-6.2	77.9	59.2	57.5	6.9	103.8	50.6	46.2
1977:															
I	162.4	223.7	23.7	115.8	-.9	5.6	4.9	-11.0	56.9	39.8	50.8	3.4	77.5	30.7	47.0
II	166.5	236.8	31.1	103.5	-.1	13.1	-5.1	-3.5	60.0	45.7	49.8	7.7	93.5	42.5	37.6
III	189.7	263.8	25.5	120.6	.1	7.7	-4.7	-1.7	80.6	52.0	49.8	5.7	101.6	39.3	40.8
IV	172.7	242.6	10.4	96.9	1.7	46.9	-8.3	-8.3	63.8	54.9	53.1	6.7	100.2	49.7	34.7
1978:															
I	176.6	243.4	26.7	91.2	6.9	35.3	-8.9	-8.8	71.0	56.6	48.1	5.3	95.3	43.4	38.1
II	196.7	286.4	17.2	113.7	5.4	32.5	1.5	-.7	73.2	58.3	59.5	5.2	102.8	56.9	53.0
III	205.4	288.6	14.7	117.1	5.8	26.5	-1.0	-5.1	90.7	59.8	58.8	6.7	104.1	48.8	55.7
IV	214.2	282.9	14.7	98.8	9.6	27.1	3.0	-10.2	76.4	62.0	63.4	10.4	113.2	53.3	38.0
1979:															
I	170.5	248.8	-24.0	90.0	28.8	52.2	-1.0	-9.5	70.5	60.4	61.3	7.0	111.5	50.7	44.9
II	201.6	300.4	16.2	83.2	31.6	51.1	8.5	-13.1	85.1	58.5	52.5	6.7	117.4	44.7	54.5
III	194.1	281.8	17.7	108.5	33.1	-10.5	-1.4	-3.6	90.8	56.6	53.6	4.6	101.5	42.4	58.6

SOURCE: *Annual Report of the Council of Economic Advisers*, January 1980, p. 231.

60 percent of all deposits. The remainder is held by over three thousand state-chartered associations. While most associations are organized on a mutual basis, a few hundred relatively large incorporated associations, mainly in western states, hold 20 percent of deposits. Eighty-five percent of associations are insured by FSLIC, which is similar to FDIC. Most of the remaining deposits are insured by state-operated funds.

State-chartered associations are examined and supervised by state banking commissions. Federally chartered associations are supervised by the twelve regional Home Loan banks. The Home Loan Bank System was founded in the 1930s after the failure of a large number of savings and loan associations. Each regional bank is nominally owned by the federally chartered associations in its area, but their activities are controlled by the Federal Home Loan Bank Board, appointed by the president. The Federal Home Loan Bank Board sells securities on behalf of the twelve regional Federal Home Loan banks to finance loans to member associations. Thus the Home Loan Bank System provides its member associations with a "lender of last resort." However, the lending capacity of the system is more limited than in the case of the Federal Reserve. Ordinarily the Home Loan banks must charge borrowing associations a rate that covers its own borrowing costs. In emergencies the Home Loan Bank Board may borrow up to 5 billion dollars directly from the U.S. Treasury.

Investment Portfolios of Thrift Institutions

The thrift institutions have always invested heavily in home mortgages. Their concentration on mortgages reflects their comparative advantage over other investors in mortgage investment as well as legal restrictions. The thrift institutions have an advantage over other intermediaries in the mortgage field. The managers of local offices can readily keep up with changes in real-estate values, zoning laws, and tax changes in the immediate area. Thrift institutions also hope to attract deposit business from mortgage borrowers.

Because of legal restrictions, savings and loan investment portfolios consist mainly of real-estate loans, U.S. government securities, and cash, though under the new law this will change to some extent. Table 5.3 shows the aggregate balance sheet for U.S. savings and loan associations. Over 80 percent of savings and loan assets are invested in real-estate loans.

Savings and loans have specialized in mortgages on single-family homes, but they also lend to apartment developers and provide commercial mortgages for developers of shopping centers and other office and store buildings. Savings and loan associations make construction loans to builders. They advance funds as construction proceeds and are repaid when the building is sold. They also make mortgage "commitments" to builders, agreeing to make mortgage loans to the purchasers of homes in a tract development when the homes are completed and sold.

Table 5.3   Savings and Loan Associations' Balance Sheet
31 December 1978   (billions of dollars)

Assets		Liabilities	
Mortgages	$432.9	Saving shares	$431.1
Consumer credit	12.2		
		Credit-market instruments	54.3
Other assets	78.6	Corporate bonds	2.2
Demand deposits and currency	1.8	Mortgage loans in process	10.7
Time deposits	7.0	Bank loans	2.9
		FHLB advances	32.7
U.S. Treasury securities	.5.3		
U.S. government agency		Profit taxes payable	1.3
securities	28.4	Miscellaneous liabilities	13.8
State and local government			
securities	1.3		
Open-market paper	2.9		
Federal funds	9.0		
Miscellaneous assets	23.1		
TOTAL: Financial Assets	$523.8	TOTAL: Liabilities	$494.7

SOURCE: Board of Governors of the Federal Reserve System, unpublished data.

While the demand for mortgage credit is fairly steady, savings and loan associations have to adjust their policies to fluctuations in deposit inflows. When there is a temporary decline in deposit inflow they may borrow from the Federal Home Loan Bank (FHLB). However, in very tight money periods, they have had to ration their lending more severely. They may limit new commitments to deposit customers and builders with whom they have a continuing relationship. When their deposit inflow is large they repay the Federal Home Loan Bank and temporarily build up their holdings of government securities. In the longer run, of course, savings and loans adjust mortgage rates upward when they cannot meet demand for new commitments, and downward when they have surplus funds.

The investment activities of mutual savings banks are somewhat more complex because they have broader lending powers than the savings and loans. Mutual savings banks can buy corporate bonds and even some stocks and they have limited consumer-lending powers. Table 5.4 shows their balance sheet. Nonetheless, because they have a comparative advantage over insurance companies and pension funds in mortgage lending, mutual savings banks have placed about two-thirds of their funds in mortgages. Commercial mortgages make up about one-third of their mortgage portfolio. Since the savings banks are concentrated in states with relatively slow population growth, mutual savings banks often lend on mortgages in areas outside their home state.

Because they have the option of buying corporate bonds, mutual savings banks have an investment choice and are willing to shift funds into

Table 5.4   Mutual Savings Banks' Balance Sheet
              31 December 1978   (billions of dollars)

Assets		Liabilities	
Demand deposits and currency	$ 2.3	Savings deposits	$142.9
Time deposits	.6		
		Miscellaneous liabilities	5.0
Corporate equities	5.0		
Credit-market instruments	147.1		
U.S. Treasury securities	5.0		
U.S. government agency			
securities	13.5		
State and local obligations	3.4		
Corporate bonds	21.8		
Mortgages	95.0		
Consumer credit	3.8		
Commercial paper	1.8		
Miscellaneous assets	6.8		
TOTAL Financial Assets	$159.1	TOTAL Liabilities	$147.9

SOURCE: Board of Governors of the Federal Reserve System, unpublished data.

the bond market whenever bond yields rise relative to mortgage yields. As we shall see in the next chapter, their exercise of this choice is one of the links between bond and mortgage rates.

Together the thrift institutions hold about $500 billion in mortgages, nearly half of the total from all sources. Since they play such an important role in the mortgage market, any reduction in their lending activity affects the rate of residential construction. Because the home-building industry is large and politically powerful, the competitive problems of the thrift institutions have produced a good deal of political controversy and much legislation to assist the thrift institutions and to provide alternative sources of mortgage financing.

The Competition for the Consumers' Dollars

Savings deposits are the principal financial asset for many households and have for a long time absorbed a large proportion of total household savings. Nonetheless they do have to compete with other financial assets. Households with substantial financial assets have the option of buying corporate stock or bonds, municipal bonds, mortgages, or short-term liquid assets, such as Treasury bills. The composition of household portfolios changes appreciably with changes in the interest-rate differences between savings deposits and marketable securities.

Relatively wealthy households have most of their assets in common stock, municipal bonds, or real estate, since they seek tax-exempt interest returns, or capital gains, to avoid income taxes. However, they do hold substantial amounts of liquid assets. By doing so they can provide for temporary variations in income and expenditures without selling long-term assets. Sometimes they hold liquid assets after they have liquidated one investment and not made another. They can hold their liquid assets in savings deposits and will do so, at some sacrifice of interest earnings, because of the convenience of savings deposits. But from time to time there has been a sharp rise in short-term market rates, and people could earn 3 to 5 percent more on Treasury bills than on savings deposits. When that happened a good many people with savings accounts have bought Treasury bills. The resulting instability of the growth of savings deposits created uncertainty for the thrift institutions. And since the thrift institutions are major suppliers of mortgage funds it caused serious problems for the housing industry. Hence, the thrift institutions, as well as banks, were given the opportunity to issue six-month certificates of deposit that fluctuate with the Treasury bill rate. But having to pay this high interest rate hurt their earnings.

There is also active though less well publicized competition between savings deposits and other assets, especially long-term assets. Investors seeking a relatively safe asset usually find savings deposits more convenient than long-term government or corporate bonds or mortgages. When rates are steady, savings institutions are usually able to cover their costs while paying a deposit rate only 1 percent or so below the yield on long-term bonds. Most investors are willing to give up that much interest return to hold savings deposits. Mortgages may yield a little more but involve much more trouble and risk for the individual investor. During the fifties and early sixties, when savings and loan deposit rates were comparable to long-term bond yields, very few corporate bonds were sold to individuals.

In more recent years, however, savings deposit yields have fallen below those offered in corporate bonds and there has been a notable pickup in the volume of corporate bonds sold to individual households.

The competition between thrift institutions and open-market securities has been the most serious problem of the thrift institutions in recent years. Thrift institutions have been unable to increase deposit rates and meet competition from marketable securities. Their inability to do so arises in part from the nature of their investments, but the problem has been intensified by regulations limiting the maximum interest rates they can pay.

Growth of Thrift Deposits

Deposits at thrift institutions have grown rapidly since World War II, but at an uneven rate. From the end of World War II until the early 1960s, the thrift institutions increased their share of total consumer savings deposits from about 45 percent in 1945 to 62 percent in 1960. Their deposits continued to grow at over 10 percent per year until 1965, but the thrift institutions' share of deposits remained static. Since 1965 the thrift institutions' share of deposits has shown a modest decline but their deposits have tripled. However, the growth rate became very uneven after 1965. During 1965, thrift deposits grew by 13 billion dollars, deposit growth fell by almost 50 percent to $7 billion in 1966, rising again to $17 billion in 1967. These wide swings in the growth of deposits were repeated in later years. Thrift deposit growth declined sharply in 1969–70, and then recovered, only to collapse again in 1974–75. The erratic movement of the distribution of savings among competitive institutions is illustrated in figure 5.1.

Figure 5.1   Gains in Household Savings at Major Financial Institutions
        (Percentage Distribution)

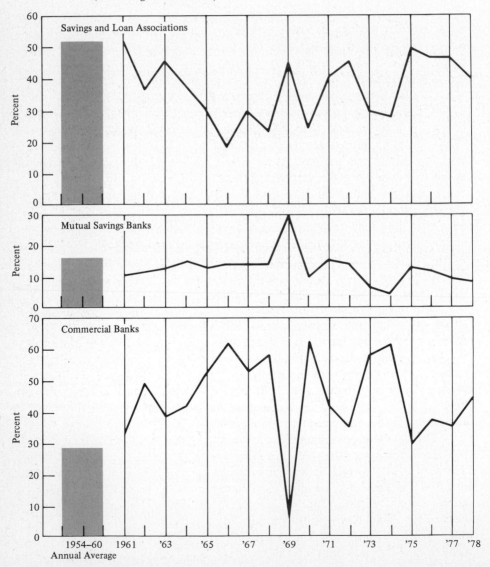

SOURCE: *Savings and Loan Fact Book,* 1979, p. 13.

The history of the growth of thrift deposits in the postwar period is dominated by two sets of factors: those relating to the competition between thrift institutions and commercial banks; and those relating to competition between savings deposits generally, and open-market securities, especially short-term ones.

To understand the changes in the competition between thrift institutions and commercial banks it is first necessary to examine the factors determining the rates offered on deposits in an unregulated market. We then have to take into account the influence of government regulation of deposit rates.

Setting Deposit Rates

In the past two decades financial institutions have been competing vigorously for savings deposits. Altogether more than fourteen thousand banks, six thousand savings and loans, and six hundred mutual savings banks with a total of nearly fifty thousand offices have sought to attract the savers' dollars.

In most urban areas there is vigorous competition among a number of institutions offering savings deposits. Consumers can choose among several banking offices located near home, place of work, or shopping center. When the rates offered are the same, consumers often choose one institution over another on the basis of locational convenience, hours of business, or because they like the clerks. Some households keep their savings account with the bank that gave them a mortgage loan. Commercial banks are generally supposed to have an advantage in attracting savings accounts because they offer "one-stop banking," enabling customers to keep a checking account and savings account in the same office. Many studies show that convenience is a dominant consideration. However, as we will discuss below, starting in 1981 thrift institutions will also be able to issue what are in effect demand deposits.

Customers are clearly responsive to interest-rate differentials as well as to locational and convenience factors. Changes in the rates paid by different institutions have a significant influence on their share of the local market for savings deposits. Figure 5.2 shows how commercial bank deposit rates have caught up with those offered by thrift institutions. The interest rates paid by both banks and thrift institutions, and hence the difference between them, is limited by Regulation Q. But in the following we will abstract from this and consider a free market.

The competition among different institutions in the same market tends to narrow the spread between the rate earned on assets and the rate paid depositors. The spread between the earnings on assets and rates paid to depositors at times may be more than enough to cover operating costs and a good return to capital. The high return to capital will then tend to create new competition. New institutions may be founded or existing institutions may open new branches. The result will be higher rates and greater convenience as the new entrants to local markets compete for deposits. At

Figure 5.2   Average Annual Yield on Savings at Major Financial Institutions

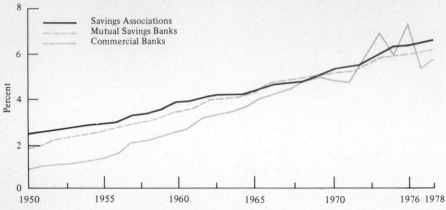

SOURCE: *Savings and Loan Fact Book,* 1979, p. 15.

the same time costs per dollar of deposits increase, with more offices per dollar of deposits. In the long run then, there is always a tendency for deposit rates to move with long-term security yields in a way that limits the spread between rates earned and rates paid.

When long-term interest rates fluctuate in a narrow range the result of competitive pressures is clearly determined and poses no problems. Some difficulties of adjustment arise when market rates show a rapid trend. These difficulties have been apparent in recent years when long-term rates have risen rapidly. To see how these problems arise we have to take a closer look at the rate-setting process.

Competition among banks is a little like competition among gas stations. The products offered are basically very similar but differentiated from one another by the convenience factors mentioned above. Because of those factors the elasticity of the supply of deposits to an individual bank or banking office is limited, especially in the short run. If one bank pays a little less than a rival, it will lose some customers but not all of them. In fact in a period of a year or two it will lose only a fraction of its business. On the other side if it raises its rate it will gain only a limited amount of deposits.

When long-term interest rates rise, each bank management will find it profitable to raise deposit rates to attract new deposits. Of course, they will wait for a while to see if the rate increase will persist. It is not good public relations to move rates up and down frequently. But, if the market rate increase is deemed permanent, deposit rates will tend to rise.

The general rule is that the rate should be raised to the point at which the marginal interest cost of obtaining a dollar of new deposits, plus increases in total operating cost per dollar of new deposits, just equals the net rate of return per dollar new investments.

But how much does it cost to get additional deposits? If the deposit rate is increased, additional interest must be paid on *all* savings deposits, old as well as new. The marginal cost in interest paid per dollar of new

Figure 5.3   Deposit-Rate Choice

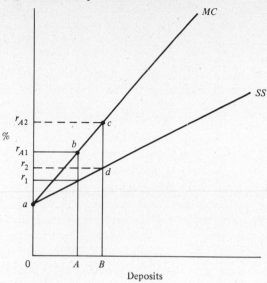

deposits may be much higher than the deposit rate itself. How much higher will depend on the elasticity of supply of deposits.

The elasticity of the supply of deposits to any institution will depend on a number of factors. The response of individual depositors to rate changes will depend on the size of their deposits and on the loss of convenience that may be involved in switching from one bank to another. In addition, elasticity of the supply of deposits to any one institution depends on how its competitors respond when it makes a rate change.

Effects of a Deposit-Rate Rise

Figure 5.3 shows the choice facing a typical thrift institution when a rise in the rate of return on new assets occurs. The horizontal axis shows the amount of the bank's deposits; interest rates are shown on the vertical axis. At the start our bank has deposits A, and pays interest rate r_1 on deposits. r_1 is also the rate paid by competing institutions. The line marked SS shows the increase in deposits the bank thinks it can get by raising its deposit rates, if all competing institutions keep their rates at r_1. The line MC shows the corresponding marginal cost of funds—the increment in interest costs per dollar of deposits gained. Additional operating costs of servicing new deposits are assumed to be zero. Marginal cost must be above the interest rate since the increased rate must be paid to old depositors as well as new ones. For example, suppose the bank initially paid 5 percent and had 100 million dollars of deposits. Its interest cost is 5 million dollars. Suppose it believed that it could attract 40 million dollars of new deposits by raising its rate ½ percent. At 5½ percent its interest costs would rise to 7.7 million dollars (5½ percent times 140 million dollars). Total interest costs would have to rise 2.7 million dollars to attract 40 million dollars of deposits. The increment in interest costs per dollar of new deposits is 6¾ percent $(2.7 \div 40 = .0675)$. It won't pay for the bank to raise its rate by ½ percent unless new assets will bring in at least 6¾ percent.

In figure 5.3 the initial earnings rate on assets is r_{A1}, just equal to marginal cost at the initial volume of deposits, so that marginal cost of funds just equals marginal revenue from deposits. If the interest rate on new assets rises to r_{A2}, it will pay the bank to raise its deposit rate until r_{A2} equals marginal cost at deposit volume B with the deposit rate read off the demand curve at r_2. That is not the end of the story, however. Other institutions will be in the same position and will raise their deposit rates too. The supply curve for our bank will shift upward.

The upward shift in the supply curve, and in the corresponding marginal cost of funds schedule, will lead to a further rise in rates. The second rise will be smaller than the first. After several "rounds" of competitive rate increases, rates will stop rising. The amount of deposit-rate increase induced by, say, a one percentage point rise in bond and mortgage rates will depend on a number of factors. It will obviously depend on the elasticity of deposit supply as perceived by savings and loan association or mutual savings bank managers. In markets with many small institutions the elasticity may appear high. The outcome will approach the purely competitive one, with deposit rates rising as fast as mortgage rates. In markets with only a few competitors each management will fear that any rate increase will be matched by its rivals. If individual institutions think they cannot increase their market share, they will expect to gain deposits only from commercial banks or by competing against marketable securities. They will be assuming a much lower supply elasticity than in the more competitive case.

The net change in profits of thrift institutions resulting from a rise in mortgage rates and the resulting rise in deposit rates will depend on the percentage gain in deposits. The amount of deposits gained by the thrift institutions from a deposit-rate increase will depend on what is happening elsewhere in the market.

For any single bank the net effect of a rise in mortgage rates depends on whether other market rates also rise, the rate responses of other thrift institutions, and the rate responses of commercial bank competitors. If only the mortgage rate increases and rival institutions keep their rates fixed, any single institution is bound to gain. It will raise interest costs just enough so that the added interest cost required to attract the last (marginal) additional dollar of deposits just balances the earnings on an additional dollar invested in new mortgages. It will increase profits on all the deposits gained up to the last one. The area $r_{A1}r_{A2}bc$ in figure 5.3 shows the net gain in profits.

In other cases the increase in deposits will be less and, in fact, it may turn out that thrift institutions can lose by a rise in mortgage rates. To take the extreme case, suppose that all market rates, not just the mortgage rate, increase and that commercial banks as well as thrift institutions are in active competition for deposits. All institutions will raise their rates, but cannot jointly induce households to switch from marketable securities to savings deposits unless they raise rates by *more* than the increase in mortgage and other market rates. And households are not likely to increase their total saving by very much either. The effect of rate increases by banks and thrift institutions will largely cancel out and they will be left with more or less the same deposits as at the start. They will, however, be paying more in interest to depositors.

The rise in interest cost would not matter so much if the total earnings of thrift institutions went up with earnings on new assets. Then they would get more earnings and pay more to depositors. Unfortunately, most of the earnings of thrift institutions come from old assets. Mortgage contracts run for a long time. The interest receipts of a savings and loan association come from mortgages written at various dates in the past. When mortgage rates go up, average recorded earnings of savings and loan associations rise only as old mortgages are paid off and new ones are written at the higher rates. This is a slow process. In chapter 8 we will describe a new form of mortgage that does not generate this problem. Some data on the relationship between average mortgage earnings and current mortgage rates are shown in figure 5.4. You can see that in a period of rising rates, thrift

Figure 5.4   Interest Rates Paid and Received by Savings and Loan Associations, and Income As a Percentage of the Value of Assets, 1955–73

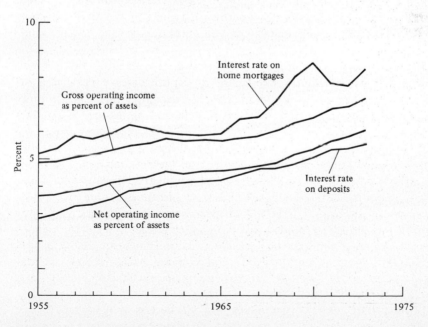

SOURCE: *Life Insurance Fact Book*, 1979, pp. 15, 39, 81, 88.

institution mortgage earnings average much less than current mortgage
rates. Because of the earnings lag, it is not only possible, but highly probable that a general unexpected rise in interest rates can reduce thrift institutions' net earnings and even turn them into net losses. Moreover, that
proposition is true even when each individual institution adjusts rates to
maximize net earnings under the circumstances facing it. Maximizing net
earnings may in fact mean minimizing net losses.

Bank Competition and Regulation Q

In the last section we noticed the effect of commercial bank competition
on the response of thrift deposits to increases in rates. Since 1933 the deposit rates paid by commercial banks have, in fact, been limited by the
Federal Reserve System. Acting under legislation passed in 1933, the Federal
Reserve Board issued **Regulation Q,** which *set the maximum, or ceiling,
interest rates that commercial banks may pay on time and savings deposits.*
Changes in the Q ceiling have had an important influence on the competitive position of commercial banks and thrift institutions.

History of Rate Competition

For the first decade after World War II the thrift institutions competed vigorously among themselves but were not much affected by competition from other commercial banks or marketable securities. In New
England the mutual savings banks had always dominated the saving market. In other areas, especially in rapidly growing ones like California and
Florida, demand for mortgages was strong. Savings and loans could readily
lend on mortgages at interest rates that enabled them to pay rates on
savings deposits well above those offered by commercial banks.

Commercial bank rates were held down by the Federal Reserve Regulation Q, and until 1957 most banks did not want to pay rates above those
permitted by the Regulation Q. In the absence of commercial bank competition, the thrift institutions grew rapidly, increasing their share of total
savings deposits from 45 percent in 1946 to 60 percent in 1957.

After the tight money period of 1955–57, the commercial banks began to seek new sources of funds. At their request, the deposit-rate ceiling
was moved up several times between 1957 and 1965. As banks raised their
rates, and went in for advertising and promotion of savings accounts, the
thrift institutions also raised their rates. In terms of the price-setting analysis
displayed in figure 5.3, the increase in commercial bank savings deposit
rates caused an upward shift in the deposit supply curve faced by thrift
institutions. However, the gap between thrift and commercial bank rates
narrowed and the commercial banks' share of the market stopped falling.
The rise in rates not only slowed the deposit growth of the thrift institutions but also ate into the net earnings available for additions to capital.

By 1965 the average net earnings of the savings and loans were reduced to less than ½ percent, and a few inefficiently managed associations were in the red. (See figure 5.4.)

Thus the thrift institutions, and especially the savings and loans, were in a poor position to deal with the impact of the Vietnam war boom. Faced with a slow growth in demand deposits, strong loan demand, and rising interest rates, commercial banks raised rates quickly after a rise in the deposit-rate ceiling in late 1965. Thrift institutions also raised rates but not so much.

At the same time a sharp rise in Treasury bill rates drew funds from all types of savings accounts into open-market securities. The commercial banks lost deposits to open-market securities but gained at the expense of thrift institutions while the latter lost both ways. Saving deposit inflows to commercial banks in 1966 were only slightly below the 1965 level while the flow to thrift institutions fell by almost 50 percent.

In the fall of 1966 the Federal Reserve Board *reduced* the Q ceiling on consumer savings deposits at commercial banks. At the same time, under new legislation, the Federal Deposit Insurance Corporation and the Federal Home Loan Bank Board were empowered to set deposit rates for federally regulated savings and loan associations and mutual savings banks. By agreement among the three regulatory agencies the ceiling rates for thrift institutions were set ½ percent above the maximum rates for commercial banks. The differential was justified by the banks' competitive advantage from one-stop banking. It has been since reduced to ¼ percent, but remains a sore point with commercial bankers. The use of the Q ceiling to suppress competition has been severely criticized. Some of the issues in the controversy are discussed below.

Once the Q ceiling stopped rising, and was applied to the thrift institutions, competition for savings deposits was limited to advertising, convenience branches, longer hours, and promotion gimmicks—"a free toaster with every new account."

With rate competition eliminated, the thrift institutions were able to maintain their share of the savings deposit market. Their share of consumer time and savings deposits has declined only slightly since 1966.

Open-Market Competition

The suppression of rate competition among the depository institutions did not eliminate all the competition faced by the thrift institutions. As noted above, they are also in competition with all types of open-market securities. Before 1965, the rates paid by thrift institutions were generally above or close to the rates paid on bonds. Thereafter, market rates on bonds rose much faster than thrift rates and households bought significant amounts of long-term corporate bonds.

A more serious problem arose from the wide fluctuation in the yields on short-term securities. A substantial proportion of time and savings deposits is normally held by households with large total assets. These families do not need immediate access to all their funds though they presumably want to keep them in a safe, liquid form. Moreover, they are knowledgeable about financial markets. In tight money periods the rates on Treasury bills rise well above those offered by banks and thrift institutions. During each tight money period since 1966 the *rise in short-term interest rates has drawn funds away from thrift institutions,* causing a sharp fall in the net inflow of thrift deposits. This process is called **disintermediation.** In ensuing easy money periods short-term rates fall and the interest-sensitive funds return to thrift institutions. This cycle of feast and famine causes concern about the stability of thrift institutions. They have not suffered significant net deposit losses and have not had to sell off their mortgage portfolio. But in each tight money period it appears that they *might* have to sell off mortgages or take losses, or even become insolvent.

A more immediate concern arises from the impact of variations in deposit flows to thrift institutions on the mortgage market. Many, though not all, economists believe that the decline in thrift deposits in 1966 led to severe rationing of mortgage credit and consequent reduction in residential construction. Housing starts in 1966 were 20 percent below 1965. Within the year they fell even more.

In 1969 short-term interest rates again rose sharply and savings deposits fell even more sharply than in 1966. The inflow to thrift institutions declined by one-third from 1968. Though this could have cut their mortgage lending by one-third, the resulting impact on the housing industry was cushioned by a very large expansion of mortgage lending by federal credit agencies described later in this chapter. Nonetheless, housing starts declined by 25 percent between the beginning of 1969 and the beginning of 1970. It should be noted that the activities of federal credit agencies may increase interest rates and draw more funds from thrift institutions. Figure 5.5 shows how savings and loan deposits were affected by the rise in Treasury bill rates in the even more severe credit crunch of 1973–74. Housing starts fell by more than 50 percent from their peak in 1973 to the trough in 1974, though other factors, for example, a large number of unsold condominium units as well as disintermediation, were responsible for the decline.

There is a clear association between tight money, rising interest rates, and reductions in housing construction. However, there is as usual some controversy as to the causal factors involved. Since houses last a long time, their value is more sensitive to change in interest rates than the values of other capital goods. One would therefore expect residential construction to be adversely affected by rising interest rates regardless of the channels through which mortgage credit flows. It is widely believed, however, that variations in the flow of funds to the thrift institutions cause a greater variation in residential construction than would be expected from the rise in mortgage interest rates as such. As already noted there is a good deal of evidence that mortgage lenders ration credit during periods of tight money and that the gap is not filled by other lenders. However, some econo-

Figure 5.5   Savings and Loan Deposits and Yield Differences

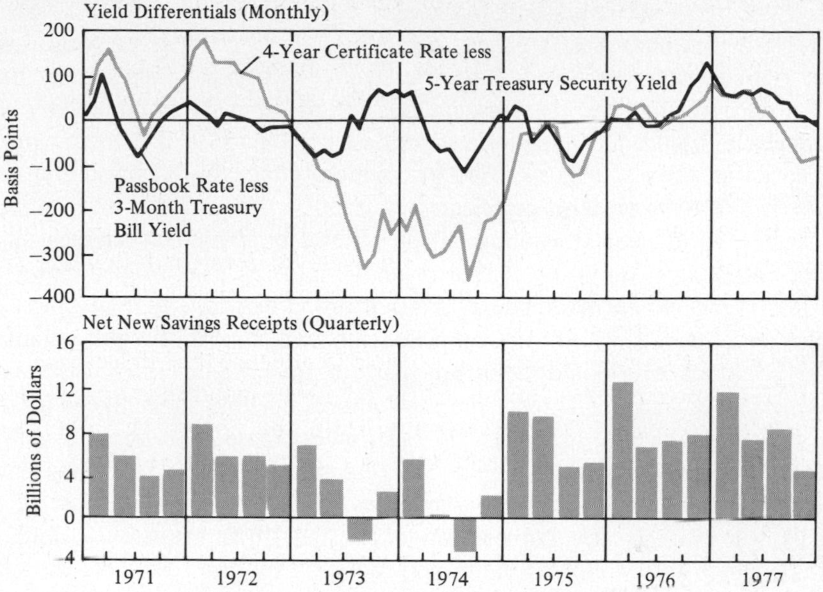

Yield Differentials (Monthly)

Net New Savings Receipts (Quarterly)

SOURCE: *Federal Home Loan Bank Board Journal* 11 (March 1978): 30.

mists do not find this evidence convincing and believe that the rise in mort-gage rates is sufficient to explain the decline in residential construction during tight money periods.

Each episode of tight money, outflows of interest-sensitive deposits from thrift institutions, mortgage credit rationing, and decline in housing construction creates political heat. The lobbies of the home builders and construction unions attack the Federal Reserve and demand remedial ac-tion. The expansion of federal lending agencies was one result of their pressure. Continued use of deposit-rate ceilings—though they do not solve the problem—is another. Threats to pass legislation requiring arbitrary allocation of credit to mortgage loans are another, though no legislation has been passed so far.

At times the special difficulties of the housing industry and the result-ing political response appear to have had an adverse affect on the Federal Reserve System's ability to pursue a monetary policy aimed at stabiliz-ing price-level and economic activity. This problem is discussed more fully in chapter 26.

Rates on Term Certificates

One further development should be noted before we come to a review of the acrimonious conflict over the use of deposit-rate ceilings. Before 1965, consumer time deposits mainly took the form of passbook savings accounts. Each time a customer makes a deposit or withdrawal an entry is recorded in the passbook and accrued interest is recorded and computed when the passbook is presented. Though a notice in front of the passbook states that the bank has the right to require advance notice of withdrawal, that right is never enforced. Customers may withdraw funds at any time.

When savings and loan associations found difficulty in competing with commercial banks and short-term securities in 1965–66 and faced a squeeze on earnings, they sought a device to compete effectively at minimum cost. They began to issue term certificates of deposit, running for three months to a year, at interest rates above those offered on passbook savings. Since those certificates cannot be cashed in until maturity, they slowed down deposit outflows when market rates rose. More important, perhaps, was the effect on cost. The certificates appealed most to depositors with relatively large accounts who could "lock up" part of their liquid assets for several months. These are, of course, precisely the depositors most likely to shift funds into marketable securities. By raising certificate rates above passbook rates the thrift institutions could compete for the most interest-sensitive funds without raising rates to passbook holders. The marginal cost of deposits was thus greatly reduced. In effect the thrift institutions, and the banks, which soon followed the same practice, used the certificate device as a means of discriminatory pricing. The effects are very similar to those of airline pricing practices. Price-sensitive travelers are attracted by cut-rate fares for 14–21 day excursions while business travelers, who have to go anyway, are not. The airline fills its seats by cutting fares to those most likely to respond, without losing revenue by a fare cut for those who would travel anyway.

When the general ceiling rates were imposed, higher ceilings were permitted on the term certificates. Since 1966 commercial bank passbook ceiling rates have been raised by only 1 percent, while much larger increases have been permitted on term certificates. Banks and thrift institutions now offer term certificates running as long as eight years with rates as high as 8 percent. (Those who wish to cash their certificates in advance have to pay a penalty.) In 1978 the thrift institutions were permitted to offer **short-term money-market certificates.**

The *six-month certificates carry interest rates linked to the Treasury bill rate.* Offered at a time of sharply rising interest rates, these certificates have been remarkably successful. In the spring of 1980 the volume of certificates outstanding at commercial banks and thrift institutions was $380 billion. This new instrument enabled the thrift institutions to hold funds which might otherwise have been shifted into Treasury bills. Nonetheless, the rise of short-term interest rates to nearly 20 percent in 1980 produced another collapse of homebuilding. In spite of the high rates paid on money-market certificates, the flow of funds to thrift institutions dried up as investors took advantage of even higher yields offered by money-market funds investing in commercial paper and commercial bank certificates of deposits. At the same time mortgage rates rose rapidly and housing starts declined sharply.

The imposition of ceilings has generated a great deal of controversy. Proponents of the ceilings have maintained that they were necessary to prevent widespread failure of financial institutions and to maintain the flow of mortgage funds for residential construction. Opponents of the ceiling argue that they have discriminated against the less wealthy households, led to inefficient resource allocation, and protected inefficient firms. Moreover, they have argued that protection of the mortgage market and residential construction is not an important social objective, that a relatively small rise in mortgage rates would provide a sufficient volume of mortgage funds, and that failure of a few financial institutions with insured deposits is not very costly to society. Finally, some have argued that the imposition of ceilings hurt rather than helped the thrift institutions by preventing them from setting profit-maximizing deposit rates.

Some of these issues relating to reform of the financial markets must be postponed to a discussion in chapter 8, but a few of the central questions may be raised here.

Effect of Ceilings on Net Earnings

As we noted earlier, the profit-maximizing deposit rate for any one institution depends on the rate that can be obtained on new assets. When mortgage rates rise, therefore, we expect that the profit-maximizing deposit rate for each institution will rise. That is the force that makes deposit rates follow security-market rates.

But what is true for each individual firm is not necessarily true for the group. The gain for any firm from raising deposits in response to a rise in mortgage and bond yields is obtained by raising its rate relative to its rivals. It thereby attracts deposits from them and earns the higher market rate on new assets. But if they all move together in response to the rise in market rates, their rate increases cancel out. They do not gain deposits from one another. Their gain in deposits results from attracting funds from the bond or other markets. The depository institutions therefore get only a small gain in deposits and only a small rise in earnings. But they have to pay higher rates on all deposits. The rise in mortgage and deposit rates therefore produces smaller rather than larger profits while depositors gain.

The imposition of ceiling rates checked competition for savings and enabled the thrift institutions to keep deposit rates below their average earnings on assets. In effect the imposition of ceilings protected thrift institution profits from competition just as a government-sponsored cartel would have done.

Ceilings and the Risk of Failures

Imposition of the ceilings undoubtedly raised thrift institution and commercial bank earnings over what they would have been under free-market conditions. In the case of the thrift institution the ceilings also prevented an absolute decline in net earnings. The general rise in market rates after 1965 produced only a gradual increase in thrift institution earnings. When the rise in market rates started, their earnings came from a portfolio of mortgages that had been negotiated at the rates in effect in the late 1950s and early 1960s. Earnings from those old mortgages did not rise when market rates rose. The thrift institutions benefited from the rise in market rates only as total deposits rose and old mortgages were repaid, which permitted new investment at higher rates. As figure 5.4 shows, average earnings lagged behind the market rates. The figure also shows that the net earnings of savings and loans in 1966 were only about ½ percent of deposits. A ½ percent increase in deposit rates in 1966 would have put the average association in the red.

In fact, of course, the earnings of associations varied widely. Some large, efficient associations had wide earnings margins while smaller or less efficient associations were already having problems before 1966.

Many associations could not have increased rates by even ½ percent in 1966 without incurring operating losses. In the absence of the ceilings those associations would have faced a dilemma. If they raised rates and showed operating losses their reputations would have suffered and they would have run the risk of heavy withdrawals. Moreover, their relatively small capital cushion would not last long in face of operating losses. On the other hand, if they did not raise rates, they would lose deposits to other institutions. To meet substantial deposit withdrawals, they would have to sell mortgages carrying rates below the current market rate. These mortgages would have to be sold at less than book value. The associations' capital would show a decline and eventually liquidation would be necessary.

Assessment of the problems of thrift institutions is made more difficult by the accounting conventions applied to their operations. An increase in interest rates reduces the capital value of the mortgages held by thrift institutions. However, those capital losses are not shown on the books unless the mortgages are actually sold. From an economic point of view, a thrift institution that has raised deposit rates as much as the increase in current mortgage rates is still earning a profit on its current operations since the spread between the earnings rate on the current value of its assets and the deposit rate is unchanged. However, because of the capital loss on old assets, its capital has been depleted or wiped out. In the latter case, it is technically insolvent, but its position is concealed by the convention of not recognizing capital losses on old mortgages unless they are actually sold.

These difficulties were certainly real but no one knows quite how serious they were. We do not know how far unrestrained rate competition would have gone, or whether insured depositors would worry about the payment of interest in excess of earnings, though it is hard to believe that uninsured depositors would not worry. We cannot therefore really tell how many failures would have occurred or what their consequences would have been.

Ceilings and the Mortgage Market

Interest-rate ceilings were imposed on the thrift institutions and the Regulation Q ceiling on commercial banks was reduced in 1966 in order to help the housing market as well as the thrift institutions, since thrifts channel a much larger proportion of their deposits into mortgages than do banks. It was assumed that the sharp decline in housing starts in 1966 reflected the decline in deposit flows to the thrift institutions, which invest heavily in mortgages. The ceilings were intended to help the mortgage market and residential construction by (1) limiting the growth of the commercial bank share of savings deposits, and (2) preventing a large number of failures of weak associations as a result of rate competition by commercial banks and strong savings and loan associations.

It does seem probable that the imposition of ceilings weakened the effectiveness of commercial bank competition for deposits so that thrift institutions retained a larger share of the market than they could have done under free competition. And, of course, it is hard to believe that a wave of failures would have improved the competitive position of the thrift institutions.

On the other hand the ceilings did not eliminate competition between thrift institutions and marketable securities. On the contrary, by limiting the response of the thrift institutions to rising market rates, the ceilings increased the spread between market rates and deposit rates and thereby increased substitutions of marketable securities for deposits in the portfolios of many investors.

As already noted the net effect on the flow of funds to the thrift institutions is problematical.

Costs of Ceilings

If the ceilings prevented some financial failures and helped the mortgage market even a little, why object to them? Opponents of the ceilings contend that the ceilings have been inequitable by discriminating against the less wealthy and sophisticated savers and have led to inefficiency.

The imposition of ceilings has created two kinds of discrimination. First, the more sophisticated and wealthy households have wider options than the less wealthy, less knowledgeable savers. When the spread between market rates and deposit rates is artificially widened, persons with large assets, who understand the opportunities available, can move out of deposit institutions. Less sophisticated persons and those with smaller assets either do not know about the market opportunity or find the amount of extra interest too small for the cost and inconvenience involved.

Second, as noted above, the ceiling-rate system has encouraged discriminatory pricing, through use of term certificates paying higher rates than passbook savings accounts. This device was invented before general deposit ceilings, but the administration of Regulation Q has encouraged the certificate development. It may, however, be argued that the stabilization effect of long-term certificates warrants the difference in rates paid.

As noted earlier the imposition of ceilings probably saved a number of relatively inefficient institutions from failure or merger into better managed institutions. In addition by increasing the margin between earnings on mortgages and the interest cost of additional deposits, the ceilings have encouraged both commercial banks and thrift institutions to open new branches, spend a lot on advertising, and engage in all sorts of give-away promotions.

The wisdom of imposing ceilings generally in 1966 can only be judged by speculating on what would have happened without them or what alternative measures might have been adopted. They may have made sense as a stopgap measure, but in view of their inefficiency and discriminatory effects, most economists feel that the ceilings should be removed.

After several years of congressional debate over a variety of proposals for eliminating the ceilings and improving the competitive position of the thrift institutions, legislation enacted in 1980 provides for gradual elimination of the ceiling over a six-year period. It provides broader lending powers for thrift institutions and permits banks and thrift institutions to offer interest-bearing checking accounts (NOW accounts). These measures and other financial reform issues are discussed in chapter 8.

Insurance and Retirement Savings

Household claims against life-insurance companies and pension funds are comparable in size to their holdings of time and savings deposits at commercial banks and thrift institutions. These institutions play a dominant role in the market for corporate bonds and have become increasingly important holders of common stock. Both kinds of institutions have grown in the postwar years, but pension-fund growth has been especially rapid.

Life Insurance

Life-insurance companies have been in operation for over two hundred years, but their growth and importance accelerated with urbanization and industrialization as people found themselves less able to rely on their children for support in their old age. Farmers and owners of small businesses have less need for life insurance because they can rely on their family farm or business to provide for dependents in case of the death of the principal earner. Moreover, they usually find it necessary to invest all their savings in the farm or business. Industrialization created a salaried middle class that could save and needed to provide for dependents. Life insurance is a way to provide for dependents but it usually also combines insurance with investment.

It is possible to buy life insurance without building up an asset. The holder of a term-insurance policy pays a premium just equal to the probability of death for his or her age group (plus sales and administrative costs). The insurance company with a large number of similar policies collects just enough in premiums to cover the death benefits to those who die in the current year plus its costs. The policyholders do not build up any claim, and the insurance company's assets are only a fraction of a year's premiums. However, term-insurance rates rise with age, and become painfully high just as the insured person begins to think seriously of the possibility of death.

Many people find a so-called ordinary-life, or level-premium, policy more attractive than term insurance. The holder of an ordinary-life policy pays a more expensive premium in early life than he or she would for a term premium. The insurance company invests the excess premiums and accumulates the earnings in a reserve account. The ordinary-life premium remains constant. It is calculated so that the total premiums paid plus earnings on reserves less expenses will always cover death benefits. In effect, holders of ordinary-life policies pay in advance for their insurance so that they will not have to face increasing term-insurance premiums. In the process they build up an investment in the life-insurance reserve. If a policyholder cancels his or her policy he or she is entitled to get back most of the reserve against the policy. The amount that can be returned to the individual is called the cash surrender value. Policyholders may also borrow against the reserve at a rate specified in the policy.

With rising population and income the amount of insurance in force has grown rapidly, life-insurance reserves grow annually at a rate of about 6 billion dollars.

Since life-insurance contracts run for many years and promise a fixed minimum rate of interest on reserves, life-insurance companies invest most of their insurance reserves in long-term assets. Since their investment income is not taxed at the regular corporate rate they invest only limited amounts in tax-exempt state and local securities. Their liabilities are fixed in dollar amount, so life-insurance reserves are not ordinarily invested in common stock. This is an example of the portfolio hedging we discussed in chapter 2. That leaves mortgages and corporate bonds as the principal investment outlet for life-insurance funds. At times life-insurance companies have invested substantial amounts in single-family home mortgages. In recent years, however, they have concentrated on commercial mortgages for relatively large offices, shopping centers, and apartment buildings, leaving the retail mortgage business to local thrift institutions and banks.

Pension Funds

The same forces of industrialization and urbanization that have generated the need for life insurance have also created the need for retirement saving. Increasing length of life and the widespread practice of mandatory retirement at age sixty-five have intensified the need for retirement funds.

The Social Security System, developed in the 1930s, provides a basic retirement income for nearly everyone, but many people wish additional retirement support. Anyone who wishes to can, of course, do his or her own saving and investment during working life and then retire on the income from his or her savings, gradually liquidate capital, or buy an annuity. However, there are tax advantages to saving through a pension fund. Many unions have negotiated for employer-funded pension plans and have been willing to take part of their wage increases in the form of pension contributions. Table 5.5 shows how rapidly pension funds have grown. Employer contributions to retirement funds approved by the Internal Revenue Service are treated as wage costs for tax purposes. Since employees pay no tax until benefits are received, they defer taxes by saving through a pension fund.

Employer-sponsored pension funds are administered by either a bank trust department or an insurance company. The contributions are invested by the fund manager mainly in corporate stock or bonds. Because the number of employees covered by pension funds has grown rapidly, and because wage rates have been rising, the contributions on behalf of current employees exceed the benefits paid to retired employees, and the assets of pension funds have been rising rapidly.

Other Forms of Insurance

Other insurance companies, principally marine, fire, and casualty companies, have much smaller financial assets than life-insurance companies; still the 60 billion dollars they hold is not negligible. Their sources of funds and investment patterns are quite different from those of the life-insurance companies. Marine, fire, and casualty companies offer fire, theft, and accident liability insurance to home owners, automobile owners, and to businesses. There is much more variation in their payments for losses than in the death-benefit payments of life-insurance companies. They have to have a substantial amount of capital obtained from sale of stock or plowed-back earnings. Their capital is invested in financial assets. In addition they collect premiums in advance and have the use of the policyholders' funds until losses are paid. (If premiums are collected at the start of the policy year and losses are evenly distributed they have the use of half a year's premiums.)

Marine, fire, and casualty companies have to keep part of their assets in liquid form, for example, in Treasury bills, commercial paper, or bank CDs, but the bulk of their funds are invested in long-term assets. Since they are fully taxed corporations these companies, like banks, prefer municipal bonds to corporate bonds. They also hold substantial amounts of corporate stock. Like the pension funds, they are prepared to switch from bonds to stock or vice versa in response to changes in yields. Marine, fire, and casualty companies are the only group of institutions whose portfolio choices provide a direct link between the yields on municipal bonds and anticipated yields on common stock.

Table 5.5 Growth of Private Pensions
Selected Years 1940–74

YEAR	Contributions				Benefits		
	NUMBER OF WORKERS COVERED (THOUSANDS)	AMOUNT OF PAYMENTS ($ MILLIONS)			NUMBER OF BENEFICIARIES (THOUSANDS)	AMOUNT OF PAYMENTS ($ MILLIONS)	RESERVES, END OF YEAR ($ BILLIONS)
		Total	Employer	Employee			
1940	4,100	310	180	130	160	140	2.4
1945	6,400	990	830	160	310	220	5.4
1950	9,800	2,080	1,750	330	450	370	12.1
1955	14,200	3,840	3,280	560	980	850	27.5
1960	18,700	5,490	4,710	780	1,780	1,720	52.0
1965	21,800	8,360	7,370	990	2,750	3,520	86.5
1970	26,100	14,000	12,580	1,420	4,740	7,360	137.1
1974	29,800	25,020	23,020	2,000	6,390	12,930	191.7

SOURCE: *New England Economic Review* (Federal Reserve Bank of Boston), March/April 1978, p. 7.

Mutual Funds

A good many people enjoy following the stock market, studying brokers' research reports, and making their own investment choices. They boast about the winners and keep quiet about the losers. Others, who want to invest in common stocks, because they hope for a better yield than they can get on fixed-income securities, find the task of investment management an onerous one. Wealthy people can afford to pay investment counsel and can buy a diversified portfolio of stocks without paying too much in brokerage charges. People with $10 or $20 thousand to invest in stocks cannot afford to pay too much for investment advice and find it difficult to get a diversified portfolio. The mutual funds solve their problem.

Common-stock mutual funds issue shares at, say, an initial price of $100 per share. They invest the proceeds, less a commission, in common stock. The value of the funds' shares fluctuates with the fortunes of the stocks held by the fund. The net asset value of a share is computed daily. After the initial offering the fund stands ready to sell new shares each day at the net asset value of existing shares or to redeem existing shares at the same price. When new sales exceed redemptions the fund buys additional stocks; when redemptions exceed new sales the fund must sell some of its holdings. The commission mentioned above is called a loading and usually runs about 4 percent. Most of the loading charge is used to pay commissions to brokers and other selling expenses. Many funds do not charge any loading. These no-load funds pay no sales commissions and spend little on advertising. Mutual funds are managed by professional money managers.

The investment managers get an annual fee, usually one-quarter percent to one-half percent of asset value. The remainder of dividends earned is paid to the holders of the fund's shares. If it pays out all dividends, the fund need not pay income taxes, but its shareholders must pay income tax on the dividends they receive. If the fund sells stock at a profit, it pays out a capital gains dividend, taxable to the fund's shareholders at capital gains rate.

Mutual funds provide a good example of the functions of intermediaries. Since they operate on a relatively large scale, they can provide professional investment management at relatively low cost per dollar invested. They can also manage and monitor a diversified portfolio to reduce risk at relatively low cost in management and brokerage charges.

A number of stock-market studies question the value of professional investment advice. There is no proof that any fund management can beat the market averages. However, few investors can buy all the stocks in Standard & Poors five-hundred-stock index, much less the fifteen hundred in the New York Stock Exchange Index. Whatever the merits of fund managements, they attract a continuing flow of funds from investors who want stocks but do not want to either throw darts or spend a lot of time and effort choosing investments.

There are a variety of types of funds. Some announce that they will invest for growth and capital gains. They do not say so but their shares involve a relatively high risk of loss as well as a chance of big gains. At the other end of the spectrum, balanced funds buy a variety of securities including bonds as well as stable dividend stocks and some growth stocks. In recent years some new types of funds appeared. In periods of high short-term interest rates money-market funds have burgeoned. These funds invest in Treasury bills, commercial paper, and bank CDs, seeking the highest short-term rates available.

They have worked out arrangements so that a bank will honor checks drawn against the funds. When the bank presents the check the fund liquidates assets and, of course, reduces the number of shares credited to the account of the person writing the check. There are also municipal bond funds, which provide a diversified portfolio of municipal bonds.

Though they have grown rapidly since World War II and have assets over 60 billion dollars, stock mutual funds still own only about 5 percent of all common stock. Nonetheless, they provide an opportunity for equity investment to a large number of people, who would otherwise find it difficult to participate in the equity market.

Federal Credit Agencies

The federal government sponsors a number of agencies that act as financial intermediaries. Altogether there are over seventy different agencies that borrow either in financial markets or from the Treasury and make loans for some special purpose. Their total outstanding loans amounted to $129 billion in 1978. These agencies lent $27 billion in 1978.

There are two types of rationale for the federal agencies. First, some agencies provide an outright subsidy to an activity considered desirable by the Congress. The Rural Electrification Administration provided 2-percent loans to rural cooperative electric utilities for many years. Second, many credit agencies were created because Congress was convinced that the private financial system was not working properly. The Farm Credit agencies (the twelve Banks for Cooperatives, the twelve Federal Intermediate Credit Banks, and twelve Federal Land Banks) were created in the 1930s when the farmers complained that they could not obtain sufficient credit from the small banks who served them. The Farm Credit agencies sell securities guaranteed by the Treasury and lend the proceeds to farmers through a complex network of local institutions. The farm borrowers pay interest rates that cover the interest on the guaranteed securities plus administrative costs. No outright subsidy is involved, but the farmers get the benefit of the superior credit standing of securities guaranteed by the U.S. Treasury. The Farm Credit agencies have over $40 billion of securities outstanding.

The most important federal credit agencies are those providing home mortgage credit. The Federal Home Loan Bank Board sells its own securities in the open market and lends the proceeds to twelve regional Federal Home Loan banks, which lend in turn to savings and loan associations, which finally make mortgage loans.

The Federal National Mortgage Association (FNMA) also sells securities in the open market and buys federally insured mortgages from banks and other lenders. FNMA makes commitments to buy mortgages from three to twelve months in the future, so that developers building a large number of houses can be assured that mortgage financing will be available when the houses are completed.

The FNMA and FHLBB serve as intermediaries in drawing funds from the general credit market into the mortgage market. They help to create a unified national mortgage market. They also provide a source of funds for mortgages that is independent of the growth of deposits at the thrift institutions. Their activities have greatly expanded since 1965 when the growth of deposits at thrift institutions began to fluctuate. The large increase in agency securities has provoked some controversy. Some security analysts argue that the increase in the volume of securities of federally sponsored agencies has an adverse effect on other security issuers. Others maintain that intermediation by government agencies serves to perfect the market and to provide low-cost pooling of risks.

Summary

This chapter started by discussing how thrift institutions are organized and how they developed. While (with one exception) mutual savings banks are state chartered, federally chartered savings and loan associations hold more than half the total assets of that industry. They are supervised by the Federal Home Loan Banks, which also make loans to them. The portfolios of savings and loan associations consist primarily of mortgage loans and construction loans. And while mutual savings banks have more diversified assets, mortgage loans do account for about two-thirds of their total assets. Between them, mutual savings banks and savings and loan associations account for nearly half of all outstanding mortgage loans.

Thrift institutions face competition for savings not only from each other, but also from commercial banks and from open-market securities, such as government bonds. As a result of this competition their savings flow has been very erratic. When open-market rates rose, thrift institutions could raise their deposit rates to hold onto their savings flows. But since the interest they earned on their previously made mortgages was fixed, they faced large potential losses. In 1966, to protect the thrift institutions, the federal government lowered the maximum interest rate banks could pay on savings and time deposits under Regulation Q, and imposed such interest-rate ceilings on thrift institutions too, albeit at a one-half of one percent higher rate. But this was only a partial solution because it did not prevent competition from higher yielding open-market securities, and hence thrift institutions lost deposits. As a result mortgage loans were much less available. There were periodic credit crunches, even though thrift institutions tried to protect themselves from disintermediation by issuing term certificates. Regulation Q led to much controversy. Some contend that without it there would have been massive failures of thrift institutions, and there is much controversy over whether Regulation Q actually helped the mortgage market. Among the disadvantages are discrimination against small savers, the protection of inefficient institutions, and periodic disintermediation.

We then looked at life-insurance companies and pension funds, as well as at other insurance companies. Pension funds have experienced rapid growth and like life-insurance companies can switch their investments readily between various types of assets. Mutual funds are a quite different type of intermediary: they allow small investors to indirectly hold a highly diversified portfolio. There are also a number of government financial intermediaries that borrow either on the open market or from the U.S. Treasury. These government financial intermediaries are particularly important in the residential mortgage market.

QUESTIONS AND EXERCISES

1. As net worth increases, the proportion of financial assets invested through financial intermediaries tends to decline. Why?
2. Financial intermediaries can invest in long-term assets, even though their deposits may be withdrawn without notice. Why is this possible? Are any risks involved?
3. Intermediation reduces the costs and risks of investment. Explain.
4. During the 1950s the share of time and savings deposits held in mutual savings banks and savings and loan associations increased; later on the share of time and savings deposits held in thrift institutions declined. Explain.
5. A decline in mortgage rates may sometimes increase the reported profits of savings and loan associations. Explain.
6. Regulation Q has tended to reduce the efficiency of financial institutions. Why?
7. Many economists believe that Regulation Q has encouraged policies that discriminate against the poorer depositors at banks and thrift institutions. Why?
8. A rapid increase in short-term interest rates can cause a sharp reduction in housing starts. Trace the connection between short-term interest rates and housing starts.
9. The growing use of term and group insurance reduces the amount of life-insurance reserves relative to the amount of insurance in force. Explain.
10. Life-insurance companies invest most of their resources in long-term assets. Why?
11. What is a mutual fund? Why do many small investors find them attractive?

FURTHER READING

ARCELSUS, and MELTZER, A. H. "The Markets for Housing and Housing Services." *Journal of Money, Credit and Banking* 5 (February 1973). A review of the evidence of the effects of rationing and other factors on the volume of residential construction.

BENSTON, GEORGE J. "Savings, Banking and the Public Interest." *Journal of Money, Credit and Banking* 4, no. 1, part 2 (February 1972). This long essay analyzes many of the issues relating to the regulation of savings banking.

BLOOM, MARSHALL, CROCKETT, JEAN, and FRIEND, IRWIN. *Mutual Funds and Other Institutional Investors.* New York: McGraw-Hill, 1970. A major study of the operation of mutual funds and the impact of institutional investors on the operation of the stock market.

FEDERAL RESERVE BANK OF BOSTON. *Housing and Monetary Policy.* Conference Series no. 4, Boston: 1970. This volume contains essays by economists, government officials, and officers of financial institutions on the effects of monetary policy and regulation of financial institutions on problems of residential construction.

————. *Policies for a More Competitive Financial System.* Conference Series no. 8, Boston: 1972. The essays in this volume evaluate a number of proposals for changes in the structure of the financial system and the regulation of financial intermediaries.

GURLEY, JOHN G., and SHAW, EDWARD S. *Money in a Theory of Finance.* Washington, D.C.: The Brookings Institution, 1960. A path-breaking, theoretical analysis of the role of financial intermediaries in the economic system.

MELTZER, ALLAN. "Credit Availability and Economic Decisions." *Journal of Finance* 29 (June 1974). This essay presents evidence indicating that rationing plays only a limited role in accounting for the instability of housing construction.

PROJECTOR, DOROTHY, and WEISS, GERTRUDE. *Survey of Financial Characteristics of Consumers.* Washington, D.C.: Board of Governors of the Federal Reserve System, 1966. Reports the results of one of the largest and most detailed surveys of the ownership of various financial assets.

TURE, NORMAN B. *The Future of Private Pension Plans.* Washington, D.C.: American Enterprise Institute for Public Policy Research, 1976. A review of the development of private pension plans and of issues in their regulation.

U.S. LEAGUE OF SAVINGS AND LOAN ASSOCIATIONS. *Savings and Loan Fact Book.* Chicago: 1977. This annually published volume contains a wealth of data on the operations of savings and loan associations, mortgage markets, and residential construction.

WELFLING, WELDON. *Mutual Savings Banks.* Cleveland: The Press of Case Western Reserve University, 1968. A history of savings banks together with an analysis of their operations and regulations.

6

Capital Markets

A growing, changing economy needs vast amounts of capital to take advantage of changing technology and to provide plant and equipment for a growing labor force. Much of the saving that is the ultimate source of the needed capital is done by households who do not own businesses and farms. They want to put their savings to work. Businesses and governments want to invest in physical capital but do not have the needed savings. In a large, complex economy a very elaborate set of arrangements is needed to bring savers and investors together. We noted in chapter 2 how financial intermediaries assist in that process, but they are only part of the system of capital markets. The function of the capital markets is to provide arrangements so that households, businesses, and governments that want to invest more than they save can bid for the funds of other spending units who have surplus funds.

There cannot, however, be a single pool of funds up for competitive bids. There have to be separate markets for long-term funds and short-term funds; some borrowers are well known, others have to establish their credit worthiness. Some loans involve collateral, some involve monthly payments or lots of bookkeeping. The markets for small loans are different from those involving large sums. The capital markets thus consist of a network of submarkets each dealing with a different type of loan or security. Nonetheless, these submarkets are closely linked so that interest-rate movements will draw funds from one market into another. Moreover, the pattern of financing demands is constantly changing. As the relative supplies of different kinds of securities change over the business cycle, interest rates must change in order to induce lenders to shift their pattern of security purchases and induce borrowers to change their methods of financing.

In this chapter we will examine the adaptation process in the markets for short-term assets, then in the markets for long-term securities, and finally look at the interaction between the two sets of markets. We will be mainly concerned with the way in which changes in interest differentials bring about an adjustment to changing supplies and demands for securities. In chapter 12 our concern will be the level of interest rates.

Surpluses and Deficits

Disputes over deficits in the federal government are familiar to almost everyone, especially in the last few years when deficits of over sixty billion dollars have been recorded. While we do not hear as much about deficits in other sectors of the economy, these deficits are often as large as those of the federal government. For purposes of financial analysis, a household or business has a **surplus** *when saving exceeds investment,* and a **deficit** *when investment exceeds saving.* While most households usually have a surplus, many will show deficits in years when they buy automobiles or houses. State and local governments seldom record deficits in their ordinary operations. The much publicized deficits of New York, Philadelphia, and Cleveland are exceptional. However, they often borrow for construction of schools and other public buildings so that many of them show deficits in their total operations. Businesses usually run deficits during booms. Of course, they are making profits then; but they are spending even more for investment than they are saving, so they have to borrow. Federal deficits usually occur during recessions, when tax revenues decline, while expenditures continue to rise, or during wars, when expenditures outrun taxes.

Since 1965 the federal government has reported a surplus in only one year. Businesses and state and local governments have shown deficits in every single year, while households in the aggregate have had surpluses every single year. It is important to note, however, that there is a lot of variation within these groups. Some businesses have surpluses even when there is a deficit for business as a whole, while many households have deficits even when there is a substantial surplus for the whole household sector.

When we add up all the surpluses and deficits for households, businesses, and governments, they will always just balance. You can see why if you remember that for the economy as a whole saving always has to equal investment. A surplus for each sector is defined as the excess of saving over investment for that sector (when the figure is negative we call it a deficit). When we add up the differences between saving and investment for all the sectors, that's exactly the same as taking the difference between total investment and total saving, and we know that that has to be zero.

But to bring total surpluses and deficits into balance, the financial markets have to match the supplies and demands for each separate kind of financial asset (from the point of view of a financial investor with a surplus) or liability (from the point of view of a borrower with a deficit). To understand the nature of that problem we must first make a quick examination of the methods used to finance particular kinds of expenditures. Figure 6.1 shows the distribution of amounts borrowed by major sectors of the economy.

Financing Deficits

Spending units with deficits do not always have to borrow. They may be able to finance a deficit for a particular month or year by using cash or selling financial assets accumulated in earlier periods when they had a surplus. In fact, large amounts of short-term deficits are financed in that

Figure 6.1   Major Nonfinancial Sectors: Net Funds Raised
Annually

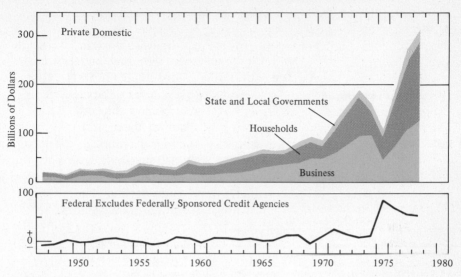

SOURCE: *Federal Reserve Chart Book*, 1979, p. 45.

way. In general, particular types of borrowing are not necessarily associated with particular expenditures, but special forms of financing are commonly used for purchases of durable goods and housing. A substantial proportion of automobiles and other durable goods purchases are financed with installment credit, provided either by banks or consumer finance companies. Gross extensions of consumer credit vary closely with durable goods sales. However, households are always making payments on outstanding debts. Almost all home purchases are at least partially financed with mortgages. The gross volume of mortgage loans is much larger than the amount of residential construction since new mortgages are often taken and old mortgages repaid when existing homes are sold. In addition home owners make regular monthly payments, thus reducing the total mortgage credit outstanding on their mortgages. For both reasons the net flow of mortgage credit is much smaller than the gross amount. The net increase in mortgage credit goes up and down with the amount of residential construction but the two do not exactly match.

Except for limited amounts of seasonal borrowing in anticipation of tax receipts, state and local governments do not—or at least are not supposed to—run deficits on their current operations. Most of their borrowing is directly connected to particular construction projects. They issue bonds to build schools, college dormitories, or water and sewer systems. Because of increasing population and strong popular demand for all kinds of public facilities, state and local debt has been growing rapidly ever since World War II.

As might be expected and as figure 6.2 shows, business financing is

Figure 6.2   Net Funds Raised by Nonfinancial Corporations
Annually, 1946–51; seasonally adjusted annual rates, quarterly, 1952–

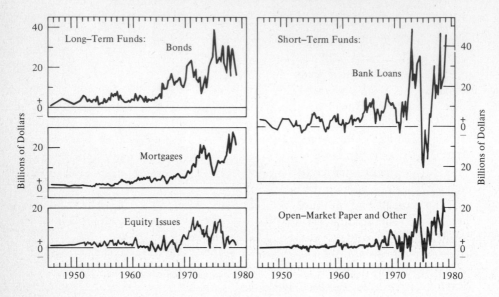

SOURCE: *Federal Reserve Chart Book,* 1979, p. 62.

more complex than government or household financing. Except in the case of office and store buildings, where mortgage financing is often used, business financing is not usually tied to particular expenditure projects. Businesses use a wide variety of sources of funds. Much of their investment is financed from their own retained earnings. But they may also sell new shares of stock, issue bonds, borrow from banks, or sell commercial paper. Moreover, corporations operate on both sides of the market, lending as well as borrowing. To provide for short-term fluctuations in receipts and expenditures they build up substantial holdings of demand deposits, bank CDs, and Treasury bills. One corporation may hold commercial paper issued by another. Moreover, corporations supply trade credit to smaller firms, that is, they ship their goods and allow the firm that is buying them, say, ninety days to make payment on them.

In choosing among alternative sources of finance, corporate treasurers have to balance a number of conflicting considerations. Other things equal, they would like to borrow as cheaply as possible, but they also want to arrange their financing so as to limit the risk of bankruptcy. Short-term borrowing is often cheaper than long-term debt. However, the firm that relies too heavily on short-term debt might have trouble if market interest rates rise rapidly, if lenders short of funds decide to ration credit more stringently, or if the firm's credit rating declines. Therefore, most firms want to finance only a small fraction of total assets with short-term debt. They also want to limit their total debt so as to limit the risk of bankruptcy in a depression. Moreover, even when bankruptcy is not an important concern, it is necessary to consider the effect of debt finance on the value of the stock. An increase in fixed interest charges will increase the variability of the corporation's net earnings and that may reduce the price of the stock.

Instead of borrowing, the corporation can obtain equity capital by retaining part of its earnings or issuing new shares. The tax law favors retention of earnings. The stockholders must pay income taxes on dividend receipts. If on the other hand, the corporation retains part of its earnings and reinvests them profitably, the corporation's earnings will increase. The increase in earnings will be reflected in the price of the stock. The stockholders will then obtain capital gains, which are taxed at lower rates, instead of dividends. Moreover, they can, if they wish, hold the shares for a long time, thus postponing tax payments. Because of the tax law, corporations seeking additional equity capital tend to rely much more heavily on retained earnings than on the issue of new shares.

Treasurers like to have a substantial amount of liquid assets on hand. By holding liquid assets they obtain flexibility to choose an advantageous time to borrow and avoid the risk of needing funds at a time when banks are cautious about expanding their loans. But to hold liquid assets they have to borrow in advance. It will usually cost more to borrow than the interest they receive on their liquid assets.

Most firms try to maintain a balance among sources of funds—equity from retained earnings and sale of shares, long-term debt, short-term debt. The mix they choose reflects the risks of the business and the relative costs of different kinds of financing. Firms with stable markets use more debt financing than cyclically sensitive businesses. Changes in the relative costs of different kinds of finance will cause shifts in the sources used and in the amount of liquid assets held.

In the short-run however, most firms adjust to the changing balance of receipts and expenditures by varying their holdings of liquid assets and their short-term debt. When they feel their short-term debt is too high and their liquid assets too low, they will issue bonds or sell stock. Thus their long-term financing will reflect their average deficit while liquid asset holdings and short-term debt respond to short-term changes in their position.

Capital Markets: A Profile

The process of transferring funds from households, businesses, and governments with surpluses to those with deficits involves far more than the collection and disbursement of funds. For each loan or security issue, lenders must evaluate the credit standing of borrowers; interest rates and terms of payment must be arranged. Moreover, since individual lenders frequently shift from a surplus position to a deficit position, or change their view about the prospective value of securities, there must be facilities for trading in existing securities. These processes are carried out through a variety of arrangements that bring borrowers and lenders together.

You can take a tour of a stock exchange, but most other financial

markets do not have physical identity. They exist in the form of organizations that buy and sell securities and well-established arrangements
for bringing buyers and sellers together. The market organization for each
type of transaction reflects the characteristics of the loans or securities
involved and the numbers of buyers and sellers involved in the market.
Security markets are usually classified as **primary markets,** *for new securities,* and **secondary markets,** *for trading in old securities.* They are also
divided between **open markets,** *where buyers and sellers compete in a kind
of auction market,* and **negotiated markets,** *where borrowers negotiate
terms with lenders directly.* Markets are also divided into short-term markets for bank loans, Treasury bills, and other short-term securities and
long-term markets for bonds, stocks, and mortgages. In the next section we
will consider the organization and functions of short-term markets giving
particular attention to the close linkages among the markets for different
types of short-term security. Then we will consider the long-term markets.

Short-Term Security Markets

In considering the organization of the short-term markets we have to discuss the markets for short-term Treasury securities, commercial paper, bank
certificates of deposit, federal funds, and bank loans. Figure 6.3 shows the
amounts of funds raised by the different kinds of short-term loans and
security issues.

Figure 6.3   Short-Term Borrowing
            Annually

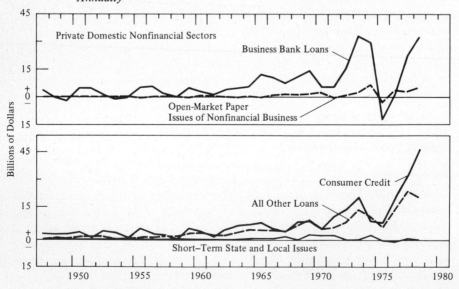

SOURCE: *Federal Reserve Chart Book,* 1979, p. 47.

U.S. Securities Market

The most important of the short-term security markets is the market in U.S. Treasury securities. Securities maturing in less than five years are generally considered to be short term. Treasury bills running for three months to a year are sold at weekly auctions through the Federal Reserve banks. Issues maturing in more than a year are often sold on a subscription basis. The Federal Reserve banks act as agents for the Treasury in handling subscriptions and receiving payments for bond issues. In principle anyone can subscribe for a new issue but most new bonds are sold to banks, government bond dealers, and other financial institutions. The Treasury announces the maturity and interest rate for a new issue and receives subscriptions. If the amount subscribed is less than the amount offered each subscriber gets the amount asked for. More commonly, the interest rate on the issue is set at a level that attracts an excess of subscribers. Securities then are usually distributed to subscribers on a fixed ratio between the total subscription and the amount of bonds offered.

The secondary market for U.S. Treasury securities involves a volume of transactions far larger than the activity of the stock exchanges. The volume of transactions in Treasury bills and other short-term Treasury securities can reach twenty billion dollars in a single day. Purchases and sales of existing government securities are usually made through government security dealers, some in banks, some affiliated with large brokerage houses. The dealers borrow from banks and buy an inventory of Treasury securities. At any time each dealer stands ready to offer to buy or sell government securities. Dealers make their profit from small spreads between their buying and selling prices. The dealer spread for transaction in Treasury bills is less than five hundred dollars for a million-dollar transaction. Usually they hold securities for only a brief time but because of the very large volume of activity their average inventory runs to above five billion dollars.

Commercial Paper

Commercial paper is one of the oldest forms of business financing in the United States, dating back to the 1830s. The securities called commercial paper are *promissory notes of well-known corporations* that, unlike the promissory notes given for bank loans, may be bought and sold. Although it is an old form of financing, it has played a relatively small role in the credit markets until recent years. Much of the commercial paper is issued by finance companies whose borrowing requirements have increased with the growth of consumer credit. Issuance of commercial paper by industrial corporations was stimulated by the financing problems of the tight money periods in 1966 and 1969 when some industrial corporations were unable to obtain bank credit.

Commercial paper is issued in two ways. Large issuers, particularly the "captive" finance companies of the automobile producers, such as the General Motors Acceptance Corporation, have salesmen to sell commercial paper directly to banks and corporations. Smaller issuers sell their commercial paper to dealers, who in turn sell it to banks and corporations. A number of the government bond dealers also act as dealers in commercial paper. There is also a resale or secondary market for commercial paper, and the dealers who participate in the issuance of new commercial paper buy "secondhand" commercial paper from banks and corporations and resell it to others.

Bank Certificates of Deposit

A third important component of the short-term securities markets is the market for **negotiable certificates of deposit** (CDs), the *transferable promissory notes issued by commercial banks*. These certificates are very similar to commercial paper except for the fact that they are issued by banks. Commercial banks generally sell their certificates of deposit directly without the assistance of dealers or brokers. A large proportion of their sales of certificates of deposits is made to their own customers, though large banks may also sell to others. Each bank sets the rate on its own issues of certificates of deposits each day. Since the market is highly competitive, it must match the rates offered by competing banks. Corporations, state and local governments, or banks that wish to resell certificates of deposit before the maturity date do so using the network of dealers who also serve the Treasury bill and commercial-paper markets.

The market for federal funds described in chapter 4 is also an important component of the short-term securities markets. Bank loans were discussed in chapter 4. We need only note here that the market for bank loans is linked to the open short-term securities markets in three ways: banks obtain funds for loans from the open market by selling CDs and buying federal funds; they supply funds to the market by buying short-term assets; and they finance dealers in securities.

Functions of the Short-Term Market

The short-term markets perform three important functions. First, these markets make it possible for businesses and governments to finance their short-term deficits and invest their short-term surpluses quickly and cheaply. Second, the short-term markets serve to integrate the banking system so that the deposits of individual banks can in effect be pooled in a national credit market. Third, much of the adjustment to cyclical and seasonal changes in surpluses and deficits of businesses, governments, and households is made through the short-term market.

Each day thousands of businesses find that their receipts exceed their payments, while others find themselves in the reverse position. They can of course build up their bank deposits when they are running a temporary surplus and draw them down when the balance of receipts and payments swings the other way. But since demand deposits yield no explicit interest, corporate treasurers prefer to invest temporary surpluses in interest-bearing securities that can be sold when they need cash. To do that, they need securities that are safe and readily salable at low cost. Treasury bills, commercial paper, and negotiable certificates of deposit meet these requirements very satisfactorily. By trading in the secondary markets for these securities, corporations in effect pool their surpluses and deficits so that they cancel out, without recourse to the banking system or to the sale of securities to the general public. State and local governments also participate in this pooling of surpluses and deficits. Because of the timing of tax receipts many governmental units have surplus funds for a period after collection of taxes. They invest their surplus funds in Treasury bills and other short-term securities and sell them later on when their budget shows a seasonal deficit. Corporations and state and local governments also finance one another by issuing securities that are bought by other corporations or state and local governments. As noted earlier, many corporations issue commercial paper that may be sold to another corporation. In the same way state and local governments issue short-term securities that may be sold to other governments or to corporations.

Corporations and state and local governments also finance one another indirectly using the commercial banking system as an intermediary. Businesses frequently borrow from banks to finance temporary deficits. The banks in turn obtain the funds by selling certificates of deposit to other corporations. The effect is the same as though one corporation had made a loan to another but the two corporations need never have any direct contact. The "lending corporation" obtains a lower rate of interest on the certificate of deposit that it buys than the bank obtains on the loan. The lending corporation, in effect, is paying the bank for its specialized services in evaluating the credit of the borrowing corporation and administering the loan.

The processes just outlined serve to cancel out many of the short-term surpluses and deficits of individual corporations and state and local governments. However, both corporations and state and local governments usually run a net deficit and must borrow funds from the household sector. While a few wealthy households may buy commercial paper directly or buy short-term securities of local governments, most of the net short-term financing of both businesses and governments is obtained from the banking system, even though households may in some sense be the ultimate suppliers of the funds. Corporations usually borrow from banks with which they have a well-established relationship and state and local governments usually borrow their short-term funds from local banks. However, loan demand at individual banks may not match the growth of deposits at those banks.

Short-term credit markets serve to pool the funds of all banks so that banks whose deposit growth is large relative to their loan demands may supply funds to other banks in the reverse position. This adjustment takes place in several different ways. Banks faced with particularly strong loan demand may sell Treasury bills or commercial paper that was purchased at an earlier time when they had surplus funds. These securities may be bought by another bank that has greater deposit growth than loan demand. And if they are bought instead by a household or corporation, the buyer pays for them by writing a check on his or her bank, so that the funds are transferred between banks in an indirect way. Large banks, with strong loan demand, issue certificates of deposit and these may be bought by smaller banks with temporary surplus funds. To serve their large customers, banks may arrange for other banks to "participate" or share in large loans. Finally, banks with surplus funds may sell federal funds to banks who need funds. This interchange of short-term assets creates a national pool of funds so that customers of one bank can gain access to funds supplied by depositors in other banks that may be in different parts of the country. In the business-cycle upswing when businesses are borrowing heavily, large city banks will have the heaviest loan demand and will draw funds from suburban banks whose deposits are growing faster than loan demand.

Households obviously play an important role in the short-term markets as suppliers of funds to commercial banks. They do not participate directly as borrowers in the open markets for short-term securities but they do obtain funds from the short-term market indirectly by borrowing funds from banks or finance companies. Households obtain large amounts of installment credit from banks and finance companies. Their demands for bank credit obviously compete with other demands for bank credit. In addition, finance companies obtain most of their funds either by borrowing from banks or by issuing their own commercial paper. Through banks and consumer finance companies, households are often important competitors for short-term funds.

The federal government is also an important participant in the short-term securities markets. The Treasury finances a large part of its deficits by sale of additional Treasury bills and other relatively short-term securities. In addition, the federal financing agencies such as the Federal Home Loan banks and Federal National Mortgage Association (FNMA) finance most of their operations by issue of short-term securities.

Balancing Cyclical Swings

As already noted, businesses finance cyclical variations in their deficits by increasing borrowing from banks and by reducing liquid asset accumulation when deficits increase. They reduce their borrowing and acquire liquid assets when deficits decline. The federal government also adjusts to changes in the size of its deficit by varying the increase in its short-term debt. At times these changes are offsetting; the government deficit may increase while business deficits decrease. Businesses then buy Treasury bills and borrow little from banks while the Treasury sells its securities to businesses and banks. At other times businesses have heavy deficits while the Treasury deficit is small. There are times, however, when both businesses and governments have large deficits while households have unusually large surpluses. Much of the household surplus will be reflected in commercial bank deposits, which will be channeled into business loans or acquisition of Treasury securities.

The swings in the deficits and surpluses of different sectors of the economy can be balanced off within the short-term security markets a good part of the time. At times however, there may be excess demand for short-term credit, which will have a significant effect on long-term mortgage and bond markets. We will discuss the interactions between long-term and short-term markets in the section on term structure. First, however, we need to discuss the operations of the short-term markets in more detail to see how the different submarkets are linked together.

Short-Term Interest-Rate Linkages

The markets for the different types of short-term credit are closely integrated. The interest rates in these markets move together because each class of market participants can choose to raise funds or supply funds in more than one way and can shift its asset portfolio or liability structure in response to changes in interest rates. A corporate treasurer needing funds to cover a short-term excess of payments over receipts can choose among selling the liquid assets (commercial paper, CDs, and Treasury bills) he holds, issuing new commercial paper, or borrowing from a bank.
payments over receipts can choose between selling the liquid assets (com-
Differences in interest rates and other costs involved in raising funds from alternative sources will be considered in making the choice. Corporate treasurers faced with a short-term excess of receipts over payments may acquire commercial paper, bank CDs, or Treasury bills, or fail to renew bank loans or commercial paper already outstanding.

If the interest rate on any one type of short-term credit tends to rise relative to other short-term rates, some treasurers will change their mode of adjustment to short-term cash-flow problems. A rise in Treasury bill rates relative to commercial-paper rates will cause some treasurers to sell commercial paper rather than Treasury bills, while those with surplus funds will buy Treasury bills rather than commercial paper. Thus the amount of Treasury bills demanded will rise and the amount supplied decrease while the reverse will be true for commercial paper. These adjustments will tend to hold the rates for different kinds of short-term credit together. Banks, of course, play a central role in these market adjustments since they deal in all forms of short-term credit and act as both borrowers and lenders. Small banks switch their liquid asset holdings between Treasury bills, commercial paper, CDs of large banks, and overnight federal fund loans to large banks in response to rate changes. The large banks price their loans to business in relation to the cost of raising short-term funds and, of course, try to obtain funds in the cheapest market.

Figure 6.4   Short-Term Interest Rates: Business Borrowing
          Prime rate, effective date of change; prime paper, quarterly averages

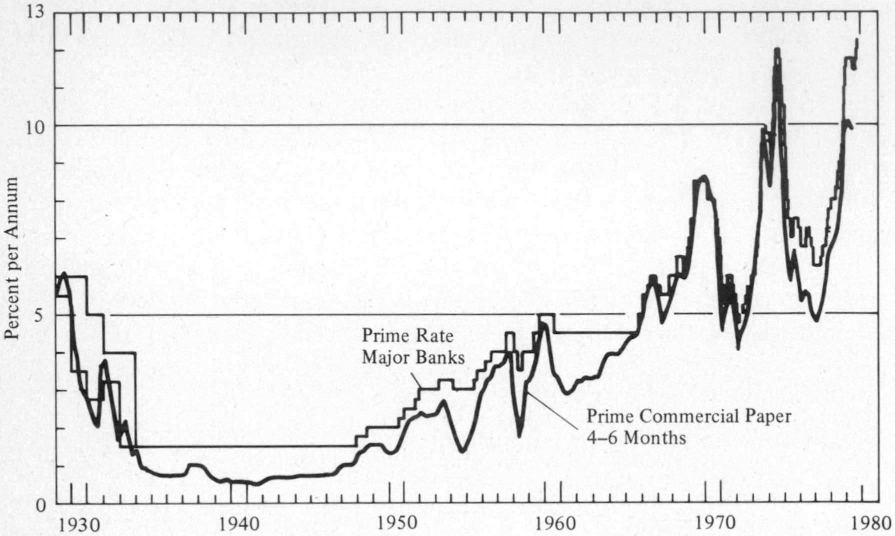

SOURCE: *Federal Reserve Chart Book*, 1979, p. 99.

Since the different types of short-term credit are such close substitutes for both banks and corporations it is hardly surprising that the interest rates involved move together. Figures 6.4 and 6.5 demonstrate this.

Indeed it may seem surprising that the structure of short-term interest rates varies as much as it does. Treasury bills, commercial paper, and bank CDs appear to be very similar instruments. They all run for short periods, can be sold before maturity, and are issued by borrowers with high credit ratings. From the standpoint of the buyers they differ in two respects: their risk, or more accurately the trouble of avoiding risk, and their marketability, the cost and speed with which they can be resold.

Treasury bills usually carry a slightly lower interest rate than other short-term securities because of their ready marketability. Because the outstanding volume is so large and because they are so widely held there is an active and continuous market for Treasury bills. Dealers are prepared to buy or sell Treasury bills in amounts as large as 50 million dollars on a moments notice at a very low charge. Other short-term securities can be sold in the secondary market, but it may take longer and cost more.

Treasury bills, of course, are regarded as completely riskless while there is always at least a bit of risk of repayment problems for commercial paper, even that issued by the largest and best-known corporations, or for the CDs of even the largest banks. Some banks and corporations buy commercial paper or CDs to earn a very slight differential in interest rate over the Treasury bill rate. Others are more risk averse and will prefer Treasury bills unless the rate spread is much larger.

The differential between the yields on Treasury and other securities may vary for two reasons. First, concern over risk varies; for example, after

Figure 6.5   Short-Term Interest Rates: Money Market
Discount rate, effective date of change; all others, quarterly averages

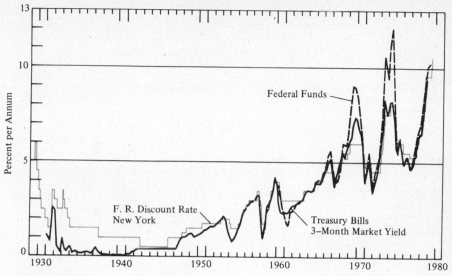

SOURCE: *Federal Reserve Chart Book,* 1979, p. 98.

Penn Central went bankrupt, many commercial-paper buyers became concerned over risk, and commercial-paper rates rose relative to Treasury bill rates. Second, the distribution of liquid asset holdings varies so that sometimes the more risk-averse asset buyers become relatively more important and the spread between bills and short-term securities widens. For example, at times foreign countries buy up a large amount of U.S. dollars to keep the dollar from falling relative to their own currencies. They tend to use these dollars to buy Treasury bills rather than CDs or commercial paper, and this has sometimes lowered—as in 1978 and 1979—the Treasury bill rate relative to other short-term rates. Thus, as a first approximation, all types of short-term credit can be regarded as nearly homogeneous substitutes with rates moving together in the major swings in credit conditions. But from day to day and week to week the special factors affecting different short-term credit markets can cause significant differences in the spreads among rates.

Long-Term Markets

The long-term capital markets provide financing for home buyers and for commercial building through the mortgage market. They finance schools, hospitals, and other public facilities through the municipal bond market. Corporations seeking permanent financing turn to the markets for corporate stock and bonds. Foreign corporations and governments also sell substantial amounts of securities in the U.S. long-term capital markets. Finally, the U.S. Treasury and various federal credit agencies sell long-

Figure 6.6 Long-Term Borrowing
               Annually

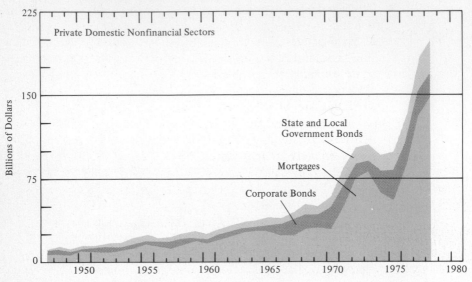

SOURCE: *Federal Reserve Chart Book,* 1979, p. 46.

term bonds and their securities are widely held and actively traded. Figure 6.6 shows the amounts of long-term funds raised in the capital markets.

The securities issued and traded in the long-term markets are far less homogeneous than short-term securities, and the markets in which they are issued and traded reflect the differences among long-term securities.

Bond Markets

Investment banking firms specialize in the issue of long-term corporate, municipal, and foreign bonds as well as common stock. A corporation proposing to sell securities arranges with an investment banking firm to underwrite the securities. The investment banking firm undertakes to buy the entire issue at an agreed-upon price. It then sells the issue piecemeal to life-insurance companies and pension funds in the case of foreign and corporate bonds, or to banks, marine, fire, and casualty companies, and wealthy individuals in the case of municipal bonds. If the issue is a large one, the investment banking firm may form an ad hoc group called a syndicate, joining with other investment banking firms and brokerage houses to share the risk. The syndicate tries to sell the bonds at a price a little above the buying price. If they have guessed the market correctly, they sell out the issue quickly and make money. When they misjudge the market they may have to sell part of the issue at a loss. To protect investors, the Securities and Exchange Commission (SEC) requires that a corporation provide much information when it sells a large bond issue. Providing this information and meeting all the required government regulations is expensive. Some corporations sell a whole bond issue directly to insurance companies or pension funds at a negotiated price. These sales are called private placements. By using this method the seller avoids paying the underwriter's profit and the cost of SEC registration for a public issue.

Competitive bidding is usually required by law for the bond issues of state and local governments and public utilities. Competition among investment banking firms and brokerage houses for these issues is very sharp. Sometimes the interest rates offered differ only in the fourth decimal place. Competitive bidding is, of course, inconsistent with private placements. Municipal-bond issues are usually sold in "strips." A twenty-year issue usually consists of twenty separate issues, a one-year issue, a two-year issue, and so on. Banks usually buy the shorter maturities.

The secondary markets for corporate and municipal bonds are limited. Most issues are held to maturity. There is some trading in old bonds on the New York Stock Exchange, and financial institutions sometimes trade bonds privately. Municipal bonds may be resold through brokers but the market is poorly organized because there are so many relatively small issues outstanding.

Because Congress has placed limits on the maximum interest rate payable on long-term bonds, the Treasury has been able to make only a few long-term issues in recent years. Nonetheless, there are large amounts of long-term U.S. Treasury securities outstanding. They are widely held and actively traded. The dealers who are so active in the short-term market also trade in long-term Treasury securities and the secondary market is better organized than the other bond markets.

The Stock Market

In the bond markets the volume of new issues is large relative to the amount of secondary trading. The reverse is true of the markets for common stocks. Daily trading on the stock exchanges can often exceed a billion dollars, while new common-stock issues run to only a few billion dollars per year. Indeed, in some years, the value of stock retirements (when companies buy back their own stock) has exceeded the value of new issues. The importance of the stock market cannot be judged by the volume of funds raised through stock issues. Though most corporations obtain equity capital by the retention of earnings, the opportunity to raise equity capital may be vitally important to a limited number of rapidly growing firms. Without the opportunity to sell equities they would have to sell out to some larger firm. The survival of independent, growing firms strengthens the competitive process.

Moreover, the stock market values the performance of managements and exerts pressure for efficiency and innovation. When a firm's management does not appear to be exploiting the opportunities available to it, the company's stock will be priced at a level that encourages a takeover bid by another firm.

Finally, the stock market provides capital indirectly. Stockholders are willing to forgo dividends so that firms can retain earnings and reinvest.

The stockholders hope that successful investment of retained earnings will produce higher earnings with increased dividends later on, and ultimately a higher price for the stock. They are prepared to forgo dividends in the hope of a capital gain. They would not be able to obtain capital gains without an active stock market. Moreover, active stock markets make it possible for investors to realize their capital gains at any time by selling some of their stock. If it were not for the fact that the stock markets permit investors to sell their stocks, many of them would not be so willing to hold as much stock as they now do.

New common-stock issues are usually sold through underwriters as in the case of bonds. Secondary trading in existing stocks is carried on through the New York Stock Exchange, the American Stock Exchange, and several regional exchanges. The shares of smaller unlisted corporations are traded through brokers in the so-called over-the-counter (OTC) market.

Residential Mortgage Markets

In many ways the residential mortgage market is the most complex of all the credit markets. It is by far the largest of the long-term credit markets. The annual net increase in mortgage debt exceeds 50 billion dollars in most years and the gross flow of mortgage credit is still larger, sometimes reaching 100 billion. The market for mortgages on single-family homes is almost necessarily a retail market in which millions of families arrange for mortgages with several thousand commercial banks, mutual savings banks, savings and loan associations, and other lenders. Although mortgage contracts are fairly well standardized, lenders must evaluate each property separately to be sure that its value exceeds the amount of the mortgage. Since foreclosures are expensive, lenders also want to know about the financial position of the borrower to assure themselves that the required payments will be made.

Most of the mortgage financing for purchase of existing homes is provided by local financial institutions—commercial banks, mutual savings banks, and savings and loans. Those institutions also provide the financing for single homes built for the owner or by small building firms. Mortgage financing for large tract developments and for apartment buildings can be obtained from a wider range of sources. Insurance companies provide mortgage credit for some large apartment projects. In the West and South, mortgage "banks" act as intermediaries between distant financial institutions and local builders of tract developments and apartments. These firms—not really banks at all—arrange mortgages on properties meeting the specifications of the lender, collect payments, and do all the legal work for a fee. Their operation has helped to make a national mortgage market.

Savings and loans, mutual savings banks, commercial banks, and, to a lesser extent, insurance companies provide most of the funds for home financing. However, the Federal Home Loan Bank Board (FHLBB) and the Federal National Mortgage Association (FNMA) also play an important role in the mortgage market. FHLBB sells bonds in a national security market and lends to savings and loan associations, which in turn, lend to local mortgage borrowers. FNMA, originally a federal agency and now a private corporation, also sells its securities in the national market and then buys mortgages from financial institutions.

Another federal agency, the Government National Mortgage Association (GNMA), guarantees securities backed by federally insured mortgages. These securities are issued by thrift institutions, which originate the underlying mortgages, and are sold to pension funds, insurance companies, and individual investors.

These institutions provide a source of mortgage funds not dependent on the flow of deposits to banks and thrift institutions. Thus, in spite of the local character of mortgage markets, funds may be drawn from any part of the country to any other area. After many years of evolution a unified national mortgage market has been developed.

In spite of the activities of the FNMA, FHLBB, and GNMA, the mortgage market remains heavily dependent on thrift institutions. In the previous chapter, we showed how fluctuations in short-term market interest rates lead to violent fluctuations in the flow of funds to the thrift institutions. Variation in the growth of thrift deposits causes variation in the supply of mortgage credit.

In a competitive auction market one might expect these changes in the supply and demand balance to be reflected in equally violent swings in mortgage rates. But in the credit crunches of 1966, 1969, and 1974, banks and thrift institutions did not raise rates fast enough to clear the market. They limited lending to their own area and often lent only to depositors or builders with whom they have had long-established connections. They also raised down payments and became more choosy about the credit standing of borrowers. At first glance, it may appear irrational for lenders to ration credit rather than to jack up interest rates rapidly. After all, they could increase earnings by pushing up rates and that would improve their ability to compete in the market for deposits. In fact, they do raise mortgage rates in the long run. But the rate adjustment process takes time. Each lender is in active competition with only a few others and no one wants to get too far ahead of the pack in raising rates. To do so would produce bad public relations and possible loss of deposit customers. It might break long-established relations with builders and real-estate agents (some of whom are favored in the rationing process). Each lender then, is prepared to raise rates a little, wait for others to react, and then move again. During the adjustment process the market price is out of equilibrium. Before interest rates have fully adjusted to the tight money period, the crunch is over. When deposits flow in rapidly, there may, for a time, be excess supplies of mortgage funds. Lenders follow the same cautious policy in moving rates down. It may be noted that quick rate increases in response to short supplies might also lead to quick cuts in surplus situations. What is lost in gradual upward adjustment of rates may be regained by gradual downward adjustments.

In the 1979–80 crunch the sharp rise in the rates on money-market certificates forced the thrift institutions to move mortgage rates up quickly. Since all institutions had the same problem they did not have to worry so much about keeping in step with their competitors. The sharp rise in mortgage rates reduced demand for housing and mortgages and brought demand into line with supply with much less rationing than in earlier credit crunches.

Valuation in Long-Term Markets

Long-term capital markets differ from the markets for shorter-term assets because of an important difference in the investment risks involved in the two markets. An investor who buys a short-term security has only to worry about the credit worthiness of the borrower. If the borrower remains solvent the lender will receive a fixed payment in a few months. Long-term lenders too have to worry about credit risk. In fact, they have to worry more because there is more time for a change in the borrower's fortunes before repayment is due. But long-term lenders have an additional risk. For one reason or another a long-term investor may want to sell the bonds before they mature. Even if the borrowers' credit standing remains good, the price of bonds can fall before they mature if the interest rates have risen since they were issued.

Valuing Bonds

For example, a $1,000 Treasury bond due in 1995 with a 3 percent annual interest payment sold for $830 in 1979. The fall in price was not due to a deterioration in the Treasury's credit standing but to the general rise in interest rates. In August 1979 new fifteen-year bonds with $1,000 maturity value could be sold at $1,000 with an annual interest payment of 9 percent. No one will pay one thousand dollars for a bond promising a twenty-five-dollar interest payment plus repayment of principal in twenty years when he or she can get an annual interest payment of ninety dollars and repayment of principal at the same date. Obviously, the old bonds with the low interest payment must sell for less than one thousand dollars. To find out how much less, we use the present-value approach to valuing contracts for future payments.

Start from the proposition that the promise—even if guaranteed—of one dollar in the future is always worth less than one dollar in hand now. The reason is that money in hand now can be invested at interest. If I invest one dollar now at 7 percent, I will have 1.07 dollars in a year. Conversely, if I want one dollar a year from now, I can invest $1/1.07 or $.934 and get one dollar in a year. If you promise one dollar in one year I will give you only 93¢ now for your promise, even if I have absolute faith in your honesty and ability to pay. $1/1.07 = $.934 is called the present value of one dollar discounted at 7 percent for one year. What about the value of one dollar to be paid in two years? One dollar invested for the first year produces $1.07; the whole $1.07 can be invested for the second year at 7 percent, and principal and interest at the end of the second year will be worth ($1.07)($1.07) or $1.145. To get one dollar in two years invest $1/1.145 or $.873. This is the present value of one dollar discounted at 7 percent for two years.

Following the same procedure the present value of one dollar discounted at 7 percent for twenty years is one dollar divided by 1.07^{20} or $.258. In general, the present value of one dollar discounted at any interest for any number of years is $1/((1+r)^n)$. Notice how small the present value has become when discounted for a period as long as twenty years. That is because the denominator in the calculations reflects the compounding of interest and grows rapidly as the time period increases. The curve marked 7 percent in figure 6.7 shows how present value declines with the increase in numbers of years of discounting. Of course, the rate of decline of present value also depends on the interest rate used. At 5 percent the numbers in the denominators of present-value calculations are always smaller (present value larger) than at 7 percent. The curve marked 5 percent in figure 6.7 illustrates the difference.

To value a bond we have to calculate separately the present value of

Figure 6.7   Present Value of One Dollar

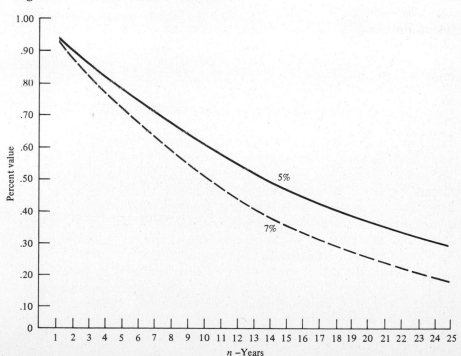

n –Years

each of the interest payments and the present value of the final repayment of interest and then add them up. Because the present value of payments due in the distant future is more sensitive to interest-rate changes than payments due in the relatively near future, the prices of long-term bonds will fluctuate much more in response to interest-rate changes than will the prices of shorter-term bonds.

Valuing Common Stocks

Bond valuations are based on more or less secure promises of future payment of interest and principal. Equity investors, on the other hand, often appear to show little concern for dividends. They seem to be a lot more interested in the prospective change in the price of the stock than in the current dividend. The day-to-day gyrations of the market are hard to understand. Commentators can always explain what happened yesterday but are not very good at predicting tomorrow. The only really safe prediction of stock-market behavior is the one made many years ago by J. P. Morgan. When asked what the market would do he said, "It will fluctuate." Nonetheless, the underlying basis of stock prices is the same as that of bond prices. The value of a stock depends upon the present value or the payments that the actual or prospective stockholders expect to receive

Lots of people buy stocks that have never paid a dividend. Small, growing companies may reinvest all their earnings. Investors expect that earnings will continue to grow and that eventually the company will start to pay dividends. Other companies have losses but are expected to "turn around" under new management or because they have a new product line. Some firms limp along barely surviving for years. The value placed on their stock may have the same explanation as Johnson's description of second marriages: "the triumph of hope over experience." But in most cases stock are valuable because there are good reasons for believing that they will pay dividends in the future. When everyone becomes convinced that there will never be any dividend payments, a stock becomes worthless.

The so-called investment value of a stock is the present value of the expected future dividends. One may imagine a company that is expected to pay a fixed dividend for an indefinite period. In that case the stock will be valued in the same way as a perpetual bond. A perpetual bond promises interest payments "forever" with no principal payment. The value of a perpetuity of one dollar discounted at 5 percent is twenty dollars. It takes a capital sum of twenty dollars to generate interest of one dollar per year. In the case of a stock we would expect discount rates to be relatively high because future dividend payments can never be certain.

A steady dividend is unusual in a growing economy. A typical company usually hopes to grow and increase its earnings over time by reinvesting part of its profits. Consider, for example, a company currently earning $2 per share after taxes and paying a one-dollar dividend. The company reinvests one dollar, and expects to earn 10 percent after taxes on its reinvested profits. Earnings will grow at 5 percent per year and, if the company always pays out half its earnings, dividends will also grow at 5 percent. We now have to value a growing stream of earnings. To do so, we apply the present-value method as in the case of bonds. The prospective stream of dividends is $1.05, $1.05², and so on, in successive years. Discounting this stream of dividends at r percent per year we have

$$\text{Present value} = \frac{1.05}{1 + r} + \left(\frac{1.05}{1 + r} \right)^2 + \cdots .$$

This is equivalent to present value $1.05/r - .05$. If, for example, r is 10 percent, present value is $1/(.10 - .05)$ or 20 times dividends or ten times earnings. The price-earnings ratio increases with the prospective growth rate and decreases with the discount rate applied to future earnings.

More complicated cases arise for companies expected to grow unusually rapidly for a time, and then settle down to a more ordinary rate of growth. There are tables that give present values for two-stage growth paths. They show that an expectation of unusually high earnings growth for a period of ten years or so will justify very high ratios of price to current earnings. That is the explanation of the high price-earnings ratio of "growth stocks" like IBM.

The theory of investment value has a perfectly sensible logic, but its application rests on a number of assumptions about the future. To calculate investment value one must assume a future earning stream and apply a discount rate. Any student of the stock market knows that earnings for next year are hard to predict, let alone the growth paths for earnings years ahead. The price of a stock can suddenly rise or fall in response to information leading to a revaluation of earnings prospects. Moreover, discount factors can change. They will be influenced by competing long-term bond yields, but they can be influenced even more by changes in confidence or lack of it about the future of the economy or of the particular company.

On the whole the stock market reacts quickly to new information relevant to the values of stocks. Many investors are ill-informed or inactive, but studies of stock-price movements show that the active, well informed investors cause prices to reflect any available information about the values of stocks. One might think that if a stock has been rising for some time, it is likely to continue to rise and is therefore a good buy. But this is not so. Investors have bid up its price to a level so high that the stock is just as likely to fall as to rise from then on. It is impossible to "beat the market" unless one has information that others lack or luck.

Inflation and Common-Stock Prices

It used to be thought that common stocks were a good hedge against inflation. An all-around rise in prices, wages, and other costs should raise dollar earnings in proportion to prices and leave the real value of earnings and stock prices unchanged. In fact, when inflation comes as a surprise, companies with outstanding long-term debt should gain. Earnings before interest should rise in proportion to prices and contract interest remains the same, so earnings after interest should increase relative to prices.

The response of stock prices to a fully anticipated, but not yet realized, inflation depends on the accompanying change in interest rates. Anticipated inflation will raise the projected growth of nominal earnings, but it will also raise interest rates. If the increase in interest rates exactly balances the anticipated increase in prices, the increase in the numerator in the present-value calculation is canceled out by the increase in the denominator. In general, we do expect interest rates to rise with anticipated inflation, but the change in interest rates need not be exactly the same as the change in the expected rate of price increase. In fact, as almost everyone knows by now, common stocks have been a poor hedge against inflation in the last decade. In the period of 1966–78, stock prices rose at an average annual rate of only 2.8 percent, while the consumers price index rose at a 6.2 percent rate. After taxes, corporate earnings have not kept up with prices. The tax system has worked against them. In calculating profits, many firms value the cost of materials drawn from inventory at the price they originally paid for them, rather than at the replacement costs. These corporations earn paper profits in the rise in the value of materials. The profits are not real since the materials drawn from inventory must be replaced at higher prices. Nonetheless, they have to pay taxes on those paper profits. In the same way depreciation on fixed capital is based on historical rather than replacement costs. Hence, the tax code does not allow firms to subtract from their taxable income a sufficient and realistic amount for depreciation. Their taxable income is therefore overstated, they have to pay more taxes, and this reduces the after-tax profits that are available for stockholders. In addition the stock market's evaluation of earnings has been adversely affected by investor fears that efforts to fight inflation will lead to a recession or price control.

Specialization and Competition in Long-Term Capital Markets

The markets for long-term debt are linked together but the different kinds of long-term debt are not such close substitutes as the short-term securities. Each type of long-term security has special features that make it more attractive to some groups of investors than others. The interest on municipal bonds is exempt from federal income taxes. Wealthy individuals and fully taxed corporations including banks will buy them at substantially lower yields than taxable corporate bonds. The tax advantage is much less significant to insurance companies, mutual savings banks, and savings and loan associations, which do not pay the regular corporate income-tax rate.

Mortgages are less attractive to most investors than corporate bonds because there are significant costs associated with acquiring and servicing them. The costs of collecting payments and making sure that taxes and insurance payments are kept up is considerably higher per dollar invested than the cost of managing a corporate bond portfolio. In addition, the lenders cannot invest safely without acquiring considerable expertise in the local real-estate market involved. Those negative considerations are more important to some investors than others. Savings and loan associations have to invest in mortgages because of restrictions on their investments. Savings and loan associations, mutual savings banks, and commercial banks with suburban branches can acquire and maintain information on residential markets more cheaply than other investors. Moreover, depository institutions expect to gain deposits by making mortgage loans to local customers. Thus, we find the savings and loan associations specializing in home mortgages, while mutual savings banks split their portfolios between home mortgages and corporate bonds. Commercial banks buy substantial amounts of home mortgages but put a larger share of their long-term investments into municipal bonds because of the tax advantages these yield to them. Life-insurance companies prefer corporate bonds and commercial mortgages on office buildings and shopping centers.

Institutional participation in the stock market is limited. Pension funds and marine, fire, and casualty companies together own about 15 percent of the common stocks. But most stocks are owned by individuals either directly or through mutual funds or bank trust departments. As noted earlier, corporate bonds are mainly held by life-insurance companies and mutual savings banks.

Since each type of lender specializes in a limited range of securities, the long-term market appears to be partially segmented into a number of separate compartments. The supply of funds to the different kinds of lenders follows a pattern unrelated to shifts in the offerings of different kinds of securities. If the long-term markets were completely separate from one another, supply and demand for each type of security would have to be balanced separately in each segment of the market. It would then be possible for interest rates in the different markets to move independently of one another.

In fact, however, the compartments in the security markets are far from watertight. Most lenders participate in more than one market. Their choices among the different securities help to link markets together directly. Insurance companies, for example, operate in both the commercial mortgage market and the corporate bond market. A rise in the supply of corporate bonds will first push up corporate bond yields and then induce insurance companies to buy more corporate bonds and less commercial mortgages. Commercial mortgage rates will then be pulled up, so that they move with the corporate bond yield. There are several of these competing portfolio pairs: corporate bonds versus home mortgages for savings banks, mortgages versus municipal bonds for commercial banks, common stocks versus corporate bonds for pension and endowment funds, and common stocks versus municipals for wealthy individuals.

In addition, all the markets are linked to the market for long-term

U.S. securities. Almost all institutional investors hold substantial amounts of longer-term U.S. securities. A rise in the yield of any one type of asset will cause lenders specializing in that asset to sell U.S. securities so as to buy the asset in question. The resulting rise in yields on U.S. securities will cause lenders specializing in other assets to try to sell them in order to buy U.S. securities. This shift will pull up the yields of those assets so that all the yields will move up together.

In spite of the specialization of financial institutions and the apparent segmentation of long-term security markets, the bond markets appear to function reasonably well. Yields on different types of securities do move together (see figure 6.8). The differences in yields appear on the whole

Figure 6.8   Long-Term Bond Yields
Quarterly averages

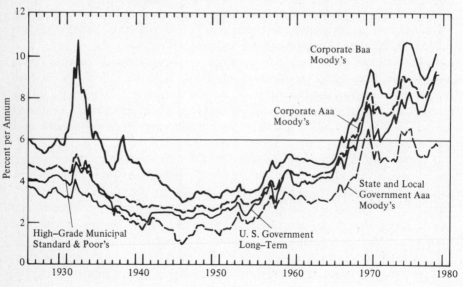

SOURCE: *Federal Reserve Chart Book,* 1979, p. 97.

to reflect differences in taxes, risk, and costs of placement and servicing of different kinds of securities in a fairly rational way. This reflects the fact that various markets can be tied together so long as a sufficient number of participants on the margin move readily from one market to another in response to interest-rate changes. As usual in economics, the action is at the margin.

However, the linkages among the long-term markets are not nearly so tight as in the short-term markets. The spread between municipal and corporate bond yields varies considerably because of the wide variation in commercial bank demand for municipals. When demand for bank loans is growing more rapidly than deposits, commercial banks often sharply reduce their purchases of municipal bonds. More bonds must be sold to individuals. That requires that one of two things happens: wealthy individuals in tax brackets above the 48 percent rate applicable to banks increase the proportion of municipal bonds in their portfolios, or individuals in lower tax brackets are induced to buy municipals. In either case, the yield of municipal bonds will have to rise sharply relative to the yields of other assets. When commercial banks have rapid deposit growth they will return to the municipal market and yields of state and local bonds will fall relative to others. The differential tax treatment of competing investors is ultimately responsible for the shifts in the relative yields of municipals.

As noted earlier, the mortgage market is the most glaring example of market failure in our capital markets. The variation in thrift institutions' demand for mortgages leads to imbalances in the supply and demand for mortgages. As noted in the last section these shifts in demand for mortgages are only partly reflected in interest-rate changes. These shifts often produce rationing rather than volatile fluctuations in interest rates.

You will notice that the two problem areas—the municipal and mortgage markets—are ones in which the long-term market is affected by activity in the short-term market. Variations in demand for short-term bank loans are responsible for variations in bank demand for municipal bonds. Variations in short-term interest rates are primarily responsible for variations in the flow of funds to thrift institutions and thereby for shifts in demand for mortgages. These are obvious cases, but there are other more pervasive links between the movements of short-term interest rates and those of long-term rates. This rather tricky and controversial subject is considered in the next section.

Term Structure

We have seen that the yields on different types of short-term securities all move together, though with some variations in the spreads among the rates on different short-term assets. We have also seen that rates on all the different kinds of long-term securities show similar patterns but with wider variations in the spreads among different rates. In both cases the rates are held together because security buyers are willing to substitute one kind of security for another in response to changes in the relative yields. Sellers will also change their methods of financing if one source of funds appears to be cheaper than another. The same thing applies to the relation between yields on short-term securities and yields on long-term securities. Figure 6.9 shows the rates on short-term commercial paper and the rates on long-term corporate bonds. If you examine it closely you will note that both rates usually move up and down at the same time; they show common trends, and the short rates move up and down much more than the long rates. The short rates in the period were usually below the long rates but occasionally short rates rose above the long rates.

Figure 6.9 shows rates for two kinds of securities: commercial paper maturing in six months and corporate bonds maturing in twenty years. At any one time there are securities available maturing at a variety of dates

Figure 6.9   Long- and Short-Term Interest Rates
Annually

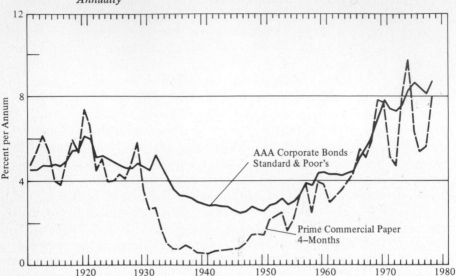

SOURCE: *Federal Reserve Chart Book,* 1979, p. 96.

from one day to thirty years or more ahead. Figure 6.10 shows actual yields
on Treasury securities for three different dates. The yield is shown on the
vertical axis. The horizontal axis shows the number of years to maturity.
The rising yield curve in the lowest line is typical of recession periods; the
falling yield curve at the top usually occurs during a boom. Changes in
yield curves reflect the investment decisions of investors in the financial
markets as well as the decisions of security issuers.

Though some investors, like insurance companies, tend to specialize in
shorter-term securities, they are not locked into any rigid investment pattern. An insurance company can put investment funds received from
premiums and from repayments of maturing bonds into short-term securities, if their yields appear sufficiently attractive. A bank will shift toward
longer-term securities if their yields look better than those on short-term
assets. In this respect long- and short-term securities are linked together
in the same way as different kinds of securities of the same maturity.

The linkage is a good deal more complex than in the case of competing securities of the same maturity. It involves two kinds of elements.
First, as in other cases in which investors specialize in certain kinds of
securities, the relative yield of long- and short-term securities may be influenced by the relative amounts of those securities outstanding, and by the
distribution of financial resources as between those institutions specializing
in long-term securities and those specializing in short-term ones. As we shall
see, there is some controversy over the importance of this consideration.

Second, yield curves are clearly influenced by expectations about the
future of interest rates. A buyer choosing between Treasury bills and com-

Figure 6.10   Yields of Treasury Securities, Based on Closing Bid Quotations

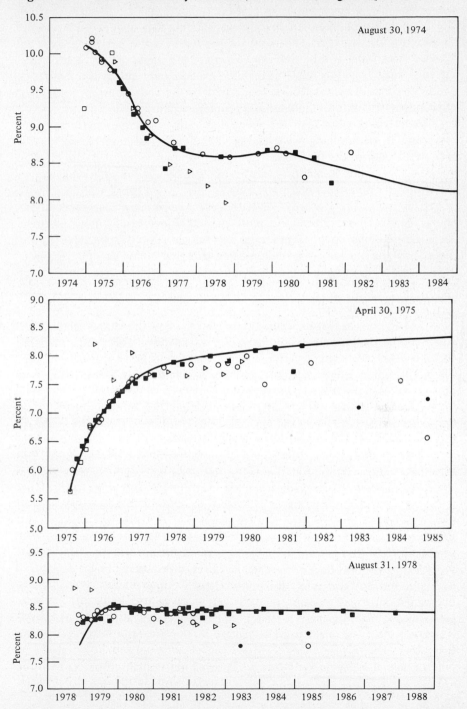

SOURCE: *U.S. Treasury Bulletin,* September 1974, p. 81; May 1973, p. 79; September 1978, p. 73.

mercial paper is choosing between two investments running for the same length of time. A buyer choosing between a bond and a one-year Treasury bill is choosing between an investment running for a year and another running for twenty years. To compare them he or she has to guess what future interest rates will be when the Treasury bill matures. The comparison depends very heavily on the investor's expectations about the future. It follows that yield curves will be influenced by the way investors form their expectations about future movements of interest rates.

Many economists take the view that only expectational factors are important in determining yield curves. In the next section we will show how yield curves are determined when only "permanent investors," who want to hold bonds to maturity, are in the market. In the following section we will show how the same approach applies to investors who may wish to sell bonds before maturity. In both cases we assume that expectations about the future are given. We must then consider briefly how investors form expectations about future rate movements. Finally, we have to examine how the maturity distribution of outstanding bonds and the resources of different kinds of financial institutions influence yield curves.

Permanent Investors

The importance of expectations in determining the shape of the yield curve can be shown by a simple example. An investor with funds available for two years can either purchase a one-year bond now and use the proceeds (including interest) to buy another one-year bond a year from now or he or she can purchase a two-year bond now.

To make a wise choice three things should be known: the yield on two-year bonds now; the yield on one-year bonds now; and the yield on the one-year bonds that will be available a year from now. The first two figures are found in the newspaper, but the third involves a guess, and this guess may be the crucial element in the decision. Suppose, for example, that one-year bonds now yield 4 percent, but our investor thinks that short-term interest rates are going to rise to 6 percent in the coming year. In that case one dollar invested in two successive one-year investments will produce $(1.04)(1.06)$ at the end of two years. (One dollar invested now produces $1.04 at 4 percent in one year, 1.04 dollars invested for the second year at 6 percent produces 1.04 times 1.06 dollars.) What yield is required to make a single two-year investment equally attractive? If the yield on two-year bonds is R percent per year the investor will have $\$(1+R)^2$ at the end of two years so $(1+R)^2$ must equal $(1.04)(1.06)$. In other words the two-year yield must be equal to the geometric average of the two expected one-year yields to make two-year bonds just as attractive as two successive one-year investments.[1] It turns out that $R = 5$ percent will be

---

[1] A geometric average is an average constructed by multiplying, instead of adding, the various numbers to be averaged, and then instead of dividing by the number of observations (n), taking the nth root. For example, the geometric average of 2 and 8 is $\sqrt{16} = 4$.

close to right. Exactly the same argument holds if we consider a three-year bond versus three successive one-year investments, or for that matter a twenty-year bond versus twenty successive one-year investments. In general, long-term securities are as attractive as short-term ones if the long-term yield equals the geometric average of the expected short-term yields over the whole life of the bond.

The following example will show how yield curves are related to the pattern of expected future interest rates. The economy is in a recession. The current rate on one-year securities is 4 percent, but investors foresee a vigorous recovery with rising rates. They expect the rate on one-year securities to rise to 5 percent in a year with a continued rise to 6 percent a year later and to 7 percent in another year at the peak of the boom. Thereafter, their foresight runs out, but investors expect that the boom will peter out and that thereafter rates on one-year securities will fluctuate between 5 percent and 7 percent with an average of 6 percent. Accordingly, the yield on a one-year security will be 4 percent, on a two-year security it will be about 4.5 percent. Yields will gradually rise toward 6 percent as the maturity increases.

Holding-Period Yields

The expectations theory outlined above assumes that investors intend to commit themselves for some considerable length of time. If they buy long-term securities they plan to hold them to maturity. If they buy short-term securities they plan to keep reinvesting in short-term securities. Some investors, like insurance companies, *do* plan to hold the securities they buy, but others may consider buying long-term securities even though they only want to hold them for a year. Or they may consider buying long-term securities to hold for a year and then reconsider whether to sell them or to continue holding them. Those investors are not directly interested in average yields over a long period. They are concerned with comparing the yield on one-year securities with the yield on long-term securities over a holding period of, say, a year.

If security prices stayed the same, the holding-period yield on a one-year investment would simply be the annual interest payment divided by the price. A bond paying six dollars per year and selling for one hundred dollars is said to have a "coupon" yield of 6 percent because a set of dated coupons each redeemable for six dollars is attached to the bond.

The one-year holding-period yield will exceed or fall short of the coupon yield by the percentage change in price during the year; for example, if the bond with the 6 percent coupon were purchased for ninety-five dollars at the start of the year and sold for ninety-seven dollars at the end, the holding-period yield would be 6.32 percent plus 2/95 or 8.42 percent. If it sold for ninety-three dollars, the holding-period yield would be 6.32 percent minus 2/95 or 4.22 percent.

Any investor who buys a bond maturing in more than one year wants to obtain a first-year holding-period yield at least equal to the yield on a one-year bond. That requirement is closely related to the requirement that the yield on a long-term bond should equal the geometric average of the expected short yield in future years. Go back now to our first example of a choice between a two-year bond and two successive one-year investments. We assumed there that the initial one-year rate was 4 percent, and the expected one-year rate a year hence 6 percent. The equivalent average yield for a two-year bond is approximately 5 percent. Suppose a two-year bond is issued at $100 with a five-dollar annual coupon interest payment. What will its price be a year hence? In the second year it must yield 6 percent, but it pays only a five-dollar coupon. Its price at the end of the first year, and start of the second year, must be ninety-nine dollars to produce a 6 percent holding-period yield—5 percent coupon yield, 1 percent gain in price from ninety-nine to maturity price of one hundred. For the first year the holding-period yield will be 4 percent—a 5 percent coupon yield less a 1 percent capital loss. In each period the holding-period yield equals the one-year yield. This kind of calculation can be extended to any number of years in the future.

Thus for any given set of expectations about future short-term yields, investors will accept the same bond yield whether they plan to hold the bond for one year or until maturity.

Expectations and Timing

The holding-period yield on a security is clearly the yield that is relevant to the decisions of a speculator considering whether to hold bonds for a short period, but it is also important to other investors. Speculators play a relatively small role in bond markets. The bond markets are dominated by issuers who will sooner or later need long-term financing, and by institutional buyers who normally invest most of their assets in long-term securities. However, the holding-period yield is relevant to the timing of bond issues and bond purchases. An insurance company may plan to keep most of its assets in long-term investments. Suppose that investment managers expect the holding-period yield on bonds to be lower than the current short-term yields. They can invest in short-term securities until the holding-period comparison becomes more favorable to bonds. In the same way, corporate treasurers may borrow short-term funds while planning to refinance by a bond issue. For example, a corporation buying a new factory has the option to finance it initially by issuing short-term security, and later on when those securities become due, to redeem them by issuing long-term bonds. The question is whether to bring out the issue now or wait until next year. If the holding-period yield on bonds is below the current short-term yield, now is the time to make the issue, otherwise it is better to wait.

The effect of these considerations is to move the holding-period yield for bonds toward equality with the current short-term yield. If everyone thinks the holding-period yield on bonds is below the current short-term yield, borrowers will tend to issue more bonds, investors will hold back on purchases, and bond prices will have to fall enough to raise the holding-period yield to equality with the short-term yield.

So far we have been concerned with the arithmetical relationship between yields and prices of long-term securities and expectations about future yields on short-term securities. In our examples we have supposed that we know what investors expect to happen. That provides only half a theory of yield curves. The other half of the explanation depends on the theory of how investors form their guesses about the future. Two kinds of considerations enter into the formation of expectations. First, investors may try to judge the future of interest rates from their past history. Second, investors try to understand the economy and use their information to deduce in a logical or "rational" way how interest rates will move in the future.

Many investors lack confidence in their ability to make a very accurate analysis of the future path of interest rates. Nonetheless, they have to make decisions and they may therefore be forced to assume that the future will be like the past. The simplest forecast of short-term interest rates is to assume that they will stay where they are. However, short-term interest rates jump around from day to day and week to week. Most investors will think that they can improve their forecast by using an average of rates for a few months back to iron out the random fluctuations. Moreover, they know that there are business fluctuations so that rates move up and down cyclically. They do not want to assume short-term rates will stay at the peak level or at the trough level. A more reasonable assumption is to suppose that future rates will tend to equal the average of past rates over three or four years. If current rates are above the average of the past few years investors then expect them to fall back to normal; if current rates are below the average of the past few years investors expect them to rise toward normal. If investors form their expectations in that way, long-term yields will show common cyclical fluctuations. But long rates will show cycles with a much smaller amplitude than short rates. Long and short rates will show similar trends since the "normal" rate is gradually adjusted upward in response to a rising trend in short rates.

Rational Expectations

Those Kiwi-fish expectations—the Kiwi fish swims backwards because it doesn't care where it's going, it only wants to know where it's been—would make sense for an investor who has no source of information except the past history of rates. In fact, of course, most investors try very hard to use all available sources of information. They make or buy forecasts of the economic outlook and try to anticipate changes in fiscal and monetary policy. Instead of basing their forecasts on mechanical or arithmetical projections based on the past history of rates they try to form rational expectations that take into account all the information available that might help them to forecast. The theory of rational expectations is still a matter of controversy and its implications have been fully worked out only for cases where investors are assumed to believe in a fairly simple model of the economic world.

However, it does have important implications that can help us to understand how security markets work. First, the rational-expectations theory implies that at any one time investors have already made full use of all the information available at the time. It is sometimes thought that information percolates through the market gradually. If something happens to increase the value of a security the "smart money" finds out first and acts to drive up prices, other investors catch on a little later and push prices up some more until the new information is fully reflected in security prices. That does not seem to happen. There is enough "smart money" so that all the price rise implied by any event occurs very quickly. In particular, if short rates rise, perhaps because the Federal Reserve has changed its monetary policy, or because business investment is picking up, and there is a reason for thinking that the new level of rates will persist, long-term yields will respond at once, not gradually as implied by the backward-looking approach outlined earlier. Second, the rational-expectations theory has important implications about the way security markets respond to policy actions. If the central bank follows any regular pattern in guiding short-term interest rates the market will take that pattern into account. Suppose, for example, that the Fed always pushes down short rates in a recession and gets them back up in recovery. When a recession occurs the market will act to bid up yields even before the Fed has done anything. But the extent of the rise in long-term yields will be limited by the expectations that short-term yields will be depressd for only a short time. The expected action of the Fed is built into the security prices. Some further implications of the rational-expectations approach are discussed later in chapter 26.

Inflation and Term Structure

The theory of rational expectations can be applied directly to the relationship between expectations of inflation and the structure of interest rates. We have yet to discuss the determination of the absolute level of short-term interest rates, but we are giving away no secrets by asserting that experience shows that a high rate of inflation is generally accompanied by high interest rates. It follows that when investors anticipate an acceleration in the rate of inflation, they expect that all interest rates will rise sooner or later. Investors may believe that inflation will accelerate for any of a variety of reasons, for example, an expansion of government expenditures or a rapid growth in the money supply. Whatever the reason they will respond by holding back on bond purchases until rates have risen to a level consistent with their expectations about inflation. If they are right, short-term rates will eventually rise, but at the moment of the change in expectations, long-term rates will rise relative to short-term rates.

Supply and Demand Factors

Expectations about future interest rates must play an important role in determining the term structure of interest rates. However, the expectations approach does not provide a complete theory of term structure except under some rather special conditions. The expectations approach provides a complete explanation if all buyers and sellers of securities have exactly the same expectations about future interest rates and the market participants hold their expectations with certainty or are indifferent to risk. In the latter case they seek to maximize the *expected* short-term holding-period yield on their portfolio and act in the same way as they would if they were certain of the outcome.

Given those two conditions the prices of bonds of any maturity must move in such a way as to equate their holding-period yields with current short-term yields. Moreover, the structure of yields will be the same regardless of the quantities of securities in the market. An increase in the volume of bonds outstanding and a corresponding decrease in the volume of short-term securities outstanding will have no effect on the pattern of yields.

What happens if the participants in the market disagree about the future of interest rates? At times there will be investors who expect short-term yields to rise rapidly in the near future while others expect them to rise slowly or not at all. The latter group will be willing to buy bonds at yields only a little above the current short-term yield. The first group will want a big spread before they will buy bonds. Now the relative quantities of long- and short-term bonds will matter. If the volume of bonds is small they can all be sold to the investors who think short-term rates will not rise much, and the bond yield will be only a little higher than the short yield. If there are more bonds and less shorts, some of the bonds will have to be sold to the group expecting more rapid short-term rate increases, and, to induce them to buy, bond yields must be higher relative to the short yield.

In practice there may be a continuous spectrum of opinion. Moderate changes in the distribution of outstanding securities will have some effect on yields but not a very large one.

A very similar argument applies to the willingness of investors to take risks and the degree of certainty of their expectations. To take one thing at a time, suppose that all investors agree on the expected levels of future short-term rates. Some, however, are quite sure of their judgment, while some think that the actual outcome might be well above or well below their best estimate of the future level of short-term rates. At the same time, some worry little about the risk in long-term investment, others will not take the risk unless the expected holding-period yield on bonds is well above the short-term yield.

In this case also the amounts of long-term and short-term securities outstanding will affect the spread between long- and short-term yields. If there are relatively few bonds they can be sold to buyers who think there is little risk or who don't mind taking a chance. The yield spread will come close to the one based on the pure expectations theory. With more bonds and less short-term securities, equilibrium bond prices must be lower and bond yields higher to induce bond purchases by those who are more uncertain about the future or more concerned about risk.

Differences of opinion about expected future interest rates, differences in uncertainty about the future, and different degrees of concern about risk all tend to make the spread between long- and short-term rates depend on the relative volumes of securities of different maturities outstanding.

Attitudes toward the risk involved in long-term investment are not just a matter of personal taste; they also reflect the nature of the investor's liabilities. Insurance companies, for example, have long-term liabilities promising a fixed interest rate on insurance reserves. They need not worry much about capital losses on bonds because they will not have to sell them. On the other hand if they hold short-term securities, rates might fall and they might not earn the contract interest. They will usually prefer to hold long-term securities when expected long-term yields equal short-term yields. Commercial banks on the other hand may have to liquidate securities if deposits decline or loan demand surges. They prefer shorts to longs at equal expected yields. Because of institutional differences in risk position the spreads between long- and short-term yields may depend on the distribution of assets among the different financial intermediaries as well as on the relative quantities of securities outstanding.

Valuing Wealth

The capital markets channel funds from surplus sectors of the economy to deficit sectors and allocate scarce capital resources among competing users. In the process the capital markets also determine the values of existing assets. When we consider the allocation function, we usually think in terms of the interest rates on different kinds of assets. But as our discussion of stock and bond valuation showed, a change in interest rates is the same thing as a change in the capital value of an asset offering a given stream of prospective returns. Thus, when events in the capital markets change interest rates on newly created financial assets, they also change the prices of all the old bonds and stocks in the market. Most people aren't much interested in resource allocation, but holders of stocks, bonds, and other assets are avidly interested in the effect of events in the capital market that change the prices of their assets.

From a less personal point of view, the prices of existing assets are important because the rate of investment expenditure is strongly influenced by the value of existing assets relative to the cost of producing new ones. Suppose, for example, that you could buy a firm that owns a particular type of factory for, say, 50 million dollars, while the cost of constructing such a factory is 55 million dollars. Obviously, instead of constructing this factory, you would buy the existing firm and its factory. Moreover, decisions to spend on consumption or to save are influenced by changes in wealth. We usually think that a family's wealth is mainly determined by its accumulated savings. However, the value of wealth can change in other ways besides accumulation from saving. In fact, the aggregate value of wealth—in real or money terms—is only indirectly related to the sum of past savings.

The bulk of the wealth of any market economy consists of claims direct or indirect against income-producing property: land, houses, offices, factories, and other equipment. The claims are stocks, corporate bonds, mortgages, and deeds to houses. Their aggregate value depends on the present value of the income they will produce as estimated by the securities markets. Thus the value of corporate securities depends in part on the judgments of security buyers about the future movements of corporate earnings. But the valuation of securities also depends on the interest rate used to discount future income. Thus a fall in interest rates, other things equal, should increase the present value of any given future stream of income. That conclusion applies not only to corporate securities but to farmlands, houses, and unincorporated businesses. Thus, if interest rates fall while prospective property income remains the same, total wealth should increase.

Wealth and Government Debt

Most of the national wealth consists of claims against private property, but the holders of state, local, and federal securities certainly think of them as part of their wealth whether they hold them directly or indirectly through intermediaries. However, it is difficult to estimate the net increase in wealth resulting from increases in government debt.

Consider the case of the debt of a suburban government. Suppose a town spends ten million dollars for a new high school and pays for it by issuing bonds. The bond buyers consider the bonds to be part of their wealth. But the interest on the bonds has to be paid for by raising real-estate taxes. Higher taxes tend to reduce property values so there may be a decrease in the wealth of the residents of the town offsetting the wealth of the bondholders. We say may be, because the new high school might increase the attractiveness of the town so that property values might be maintained in spite of the higher tax rate. To make it just a bit more complicated, it is also possible that the new high school will reduce property values in other towns. Thus, an increase in local government debt may change aggregate wealth by any amount from less than zero to an amount that is even greater than the increase in debt. The net effect cannot be predicted, but that kind of government debt does not pose any great problems in measuring the amount of wealth after the event. The net effect on wealth is all visible in the bonds themselves plus the value of the property affected directly or indirectly by property taxes and civic improvement.

A more serious problem arises when the interest on government debt is covered by income or sales taxes. When federal or state governments issue bonds, the bondholders have more assets. The public has an offsetting liability to pay more taxes of some sort but their tax liability is mixed up with all the other taxes and constitutes a relatively small part of the total tax burden. If the taxpayers are fully aware of their future tax liability and discount their future taxes at the same rate as the yield on the bonds, the implicit liability has the same value as the government bonds and there is no net increase in wealth from the bond issue per se. As in the case of the high school, prospective future income may be increased by the expenditures financed by government debt but in many cases, for example, in defense expenditure, government purchases financed by debt will not increase prospective future income.

However, it is not likely that taxpayers discount the future at the same yield as that paid on bonds. They are likely to discount uncertain future tax liabilities at a rate much higher than the yield on government bonds so that the issuance of debt causes a net increase of total nominal wealth.

Correspondingly, an increase or decrease in interest rates will cause a decrease or increase in the net wealth associated with government debt in the same way as in the case of private wealth.

Finally, in connection with government debt we have to take account of the power of the federal government to issue some interest-free debt in connection with its money-supply operations. When the government issues currency it is issuing interest-free debt. The currency is always someone's asset, but since no interest payment is required there is no offsetting tax liability. In fact the U.S. government does not issue much currency but the Federal Reserve does. Since the Federal Reserve holds one dollar of U.S. bonds for every dollar of currency issued and returns the interest received to the Treasury (after paying its own expenses), the effect of currency issues on the debt burden is the same as though the Treasury issued currency directly, and sold fewer interest-bearing bonds to the public. The Federal Reserve also acquires Treasury debt through open-market operations when it wants to increase bank reserves. Thus any increase in bank reserves through open-market operations gives the Treasury a free ride in the same way as an increase in demand for currency.

We noted earlier that an increase in interest-bearing government debt increases perceived wealth to the extent that the public "undervalues" the resulting increase in expected tax liability. We may suppose, for example, that because the taxpayers do not fully anticipate future debt service liabilities, or discounts them at a higher rate than the interest rate on government bonds, each dollar of additional debt adds, say, 55¢ to perceived wealth.

Now consider the effect of an open-market operation to increase bank reserves or to offset the reserve drain from increased currency demand. The open-market operation is in effect an exchange of non-interest-bearing for interest-bearing debt. After the open-market operation the public holds less interest-bearing debt and more non-interest-bearing debt. They hold the same amount of assets but their prospective tax liability is reduced and therefore their net wealth is greater. A dollar of non-interest-bearing debt adds one dollar to wealth. We assumed that one dollar of interest-bearing debt adds 55¢ to wealth. The open-market operation therefore increases net wealth by one dollar (increase in non-interest-bearing debt) less 55¢ (from the decrease in interest-bearing debt) for a net gain of 45¢.

Real Versus Nominal Wealth

So far we have discussed wealth in nominal terms, but it is the real value of wealth that counts. The real value of private wealth should be independent of the price level. If all wages and prices double the nominal value of property incomes from profits or rent should double and, given the interest rate, the nominal capital value of claims to profit and rent should also double. But since all other prices have doubled the purchasing power of those claims should remain unchanged. Individual debtors gain from a price level rise while creditors lose but those gains and losses cancel out.

The wealth associated with government debt and the money base, however, is stated in nominal terms and its real value is affected by changes in the price level. When the price level rises, the real value of the money supply declines and the moneyholders as a group are poorer. To be sure, for that part of the money supply that consists of bank deposits there is an offset since the banks who are the debtors for these deposits are better off as a result. (As creditors banks lose too, but those who borrowed from them gain.) However, for that part of the money supply that consists of currency everyone is poorer. Moreover, as prices rise the real value of government bond holdings is reduced, and so people feel poorer unless, as discussed before, they believe that their tax burden will now fall too. This change in real wealth resulting from this decline in the real value of currency and government debt is called the "real balance effect."

We have now noted a number of different ways in which wealth can change. Wealth based on private property can change in real value if either the expected future value of property income increases or the capital value of a given stream of prospective property income receipts changes. In the short run prospective future property income will change with business-cycle fluctuations. In the long run the accumulation of physical capital tends to increase expected real property incomes. The valuation of property incomes can change if the uncertainty of the outcome changes or if the interest rate falls.

Total real wealth can also be increased by the accumulation of government debt and by the exchange of interest-bearing for non-interest-bearing government debt through open-market operations, while the price level remains unchanged. Finally, a given stock of interest-bearing and non-interest-bearing government debt will decline in value if the price level rises.

It is important to recognize that the price-level factor and the other routes for changing wealth are not independent. The magic of wealth creation by increasing government debt or money supply is limited by the fact that too much of it may raise prices thereby causing a decline in the real value of wealth to offset the increase generated by deficits and open-market operations.

Summary

The capital markets perform the task of transferring very large amounts of funds from surplus spending units to deficit ones. On an annual basis over $200 billion of funds pass through the credit market. If we counted the short-term shifts in surplus and deficit positions of individual households, businesses, and governments the amount transferred would be far larger. These transfers involve credit evaluation, collection of monthly payments for mortgage and installment credit, and a good deal of legal work, so they are far from a routine matter. In order to perform the transfer function the markets have to operate in such a way as to match the kind of liabilities borrowers wish to issue with the kind of assets lenders wish to hold. They do this in two ways: 1) by intermediation: liabilities issued by borrowers are held by intermediaries who in turn issue a type of liability more attractive to the lenders; 2) the relative yields of different kinds of assets must adjust in such a way as to induce borrowers to issue the kind of liabilities lenders want, or to induce lenders to accept the kind of liabilities borrowers want to issue or both. For this to happen interest rates must be flexible and markets for different kinds of securities must be linked together so that all types of securities are competing with one another directly or indirectly. The test of performance is that intrinsically similar kinds of securities should pay similar, risk-adjusted interest rates regardless of their origin. On the whole, U.S. capital markets seem to meet that test. Credit markets are geographically unified so that interest rates are similar throughout the country. Institutional specialization does not create segmented or compartmentalized markets. However, the market for municipal bonds is significantly affected by the differential tax treatment of financial institutions.

On the whole the short-term markets are very well integrated, and so, with certain exceptions, are the long-term markets. The two sets of markets are also closely linked but the relationship between long- and short-term rates is heavily influenced by expectational considerations. There is also some evidence that the investment specialization of financial institutions does influence the relation between long- and short-term interest rates.

QUESTIONS AND EXERCISES

1. All short-term open-market interest rates tend to move up and down together. Why?
2. Treasury bill rates are almost always lower than commercial-paper rates. Explain.

3. Cite some reasons why spreads between Treasury bill and commercial-paper yields may vary from time to time.

4. Markets for short-term securities serve to link together all sectors of the capital market. Explain.

5. Since the volume of new equity issues is relatively small, the stock-market's role in the capital markets is really not very important in spite of the attention given to the stock market in the press. Comment.

6. Markets for bonds and mortgages are dominated by financial institutions. Each type of financial institution specializes in certain types of security, therefore, the long-term security markets operate in separate compartments that have little effect on one another. True or False? Explain your answer.

7. What is meant by a *yield curve*?

8. A falling yield curve usually indicates that investors expect bond yields to (a) rise or (b) fall. Choose one and explain.

9. The annual increase in the wealth held by Americans is equal to the annual net saving of businesses, households, and government during the year. True or False? Explain.

10. Does an increase in government debt increase wealth (a) always, (b) sometimes, or (c) never?

11. An open-market operation does not generate wealth. People just exchange bank deposits for government debt. Is this (a) always, (b) sometimes, or (c) never, true?

FURTHER READING

BAUMOL, WILLIAM J. *The Stock Market and Economic Efficiency.* Fordham University Press, 1965. This study reviews the theory and evidence of the efficiency of the stock market as a means of allocating capital among competing uses.

BOARD OF GOVERNORS OF THE FEDERAL RESERVE SYSTEM. *Joint Treasury–Federal Reserve Study of the U.S. Government Securities Market.* 1969. This is a summary of an exhaustive study of the operations of the market for U.S. government security.

DOUGALL, HERBERT E., and GAUMNITZ, JACK E. *Capital Markets and Institutions.* 3d ed. Englewood Cliffs, N.J.: Prentice-Hall, 1975. This short text describes each of the major capital markets and provides a wealth of detail on the volume of transactions and the decision-making process of the major participants.

FEDERAL RESERVE BANK OF BOSTON. *Financing State and Local Governments.* Conference Series No. 3, 1970. The papers in this volume discuss policy issues relating to the organization of the market for state and local securities and the role of tax-exemption in those markets.

FEDERAL RESERVE BANK OF BOSTON. *Issues in Federal Debt Management.* Conference Series No. 10, 1973. The papers in this volume discuss the number of policy issues relating to the organization of the market for U.S. Treasury securities and the possible effects of alternative and management policies by the Treasury.

FORTUNE, PETER. "Tax-Exemption of State and Local Interest Payments: An Economic Analysis of the Issues and an Alternative." *New England Economic Review,* Federal Reserve Bank of Boston, May/June 1973, pp. 3–20.

This paper proposes an alternative to tax-exemption of state and local security and analyzes its implications.

HURTLEY, EVELYN H. "The Commercial Paper Market." *Federal Reserve Bulletin* 63 (June 1977): 523–36. This article explains the organization of the commercial-paper market, reviews the history and outlines the factors accounting for differences in yields on commercial paper and other short-term instruments.

KUZNETS, S. SIMON. *Capital in the American Economy.* National Bureau of Economic Research, New York, 1961. Though out of date in some ways, this volume offers a broad perspective into the history of saving capital formation in the United States.

LIGHT, J. O., and WHITE, WILLIAM L. *The Financial System.* Homewood, Illinois: Richard D. Irwin, Inc., 1979. This volume discusses the organization of the capital markets in terms of the decision-making processes.

MELTON, WILLIAM C. "The Market for Large Negotiable CD's." *Quarterly Review,* Federal Reserve Bank of New York, Winter 1977–78, pp. 22–34. This paper gives a detailed description of the market for commercial bank certificates of deposit. It outlines the organization of the market for each of the major short-term securities.

7

Central Banking

In this chapter we will discuss our own central bank, the Federal Reserve System, in some detail, but before doing so, we have to look more generally at what central banks in developed noncommunist countries do.

The Central Bank: A Profile

Despite their name, central banks are not "banks" in the same sense as commercial banks. They are quite different institutions. Commercial banks try to invest their assets in ways that maximize their profits. By contrast, central banks are governmental, or quasi-governmental, institutions that are not concerned with maximizing their own profits, but with achieving certain goals for the entire economy such as the prevention of commercial bank failures, price-level stability, full employment, and so on. In other words, central banks, even if in a formal sense owned by private stockholders, carry out governmental functions, and are therefore part of the government.

Controlling the Money Supply

The reason why we need a central bank was put succinctly by the nineteenth-century British economist and financial journalist Walter Bagehot, when he wrote, "money will not manage itself." Each commercial bank, as it obtains reserves, expands its deposits. With no central bank, the growth rate of the money stock would depend upon what could be completely arbitrary factors that change bank reserves, and it may differ sharply from the rate that is necessary for the stable expansion of the economy and balance of payments equilibrium. To have the money stock grow at the proper rate someone has to see to it that bank reserves also grow at the proper rate. Nowadays this is the task of central banks.

Lender of Last Resort

A related reason for having a central bank is the need to guard against bank failures, particularly if there are many relatively small com-

173

mercial banks. This is not to say that central banks always did prevent wide-spread bank failures. The existence of the Federal Reserve did not prevent numerous failures of small banks in the 1920s, nor the three catastrophic waves of bank failures in the 1930s. Bank failures can have very serious consequences for the rest of the economy, and hence the public has a great stake in preventing them. In the United States we now rely in the first instance on deposit insurance to prevent banking panics with their runs on banks and the resulting widespread bank failures. But traditionally, in most developed countries, it has been the central bank that has guarded against bank failures. Its main tool for this is its ability to act as a lender of last resort. A lender of last resort is a lender who normally does not lend to the full extent of its resources. Instead, it normally keeps some of its resources uncommitted, and is therefore able to make loans at a time when other lenders do not have funds available.

Being a lender of last resort is not a profitable business for a commercial bank because it would have to keep substantial resources idle in normal times. The central bank, however, as we shall see, has the power to create the reserves it lends to banks in an emergency, and, besides, it is not a profit-maximizer.

Acting as a lender of last resort, and thereby preventing financial panics and large-scale bank failures, is an extremely important function of a central bank. It is easy to forget this for two reasons. One is that potential financial panics arise only very rarely, so that when one looks at the day-to-day activities of a central bank, its lender-of-last-resort function may seem not relevant and therefore unimportant. But one can say a similar thing about a fire extinguisher! The second reason is that we also have deposit insurance. But, as discussed in chapter 3, deposit insurance, while it insures most accounts, does not provide complete security for accounts over $100,000, and hence does not prevent panic withdrawals by large depositors. What does prevent such withdrawals is the belief of large depositors that the Federal Reserve is ready to act as a lender of last resort and provide any large solvent bank that faces a liquidity crisis with sufficient loans. Don't forget, therefore, that, although a central bank does not normally act as a lender of last resort, it must always stand ready to do so, even if it means that it must temporarily abandon other goals such as fighting inflation.

Origin of Central Banks

Central banks have developed in two ways. One is through a slow process of evolution, the prime example being the Bank of England, which started out as a commercial bank, but acquired over the years both the added powers and responsibilities that slowly turned it into a central bank. In this process of evolution it is hard to say when it ceased to be a commercial bank and became a central bank. In contrast to the Bank of England, many central banks did not just grow into central banks but were central banks right from the start. The leading example is the Federal Reserve System. Such a central bank is from the outset owned de facto by the government, although it may, like the Federal Reserve System, have private stockholders. But note that the question of private versus government ownership is a trivial detail. When a bank acts as a central bank, that is, determines its actions on the basis of the public interest rather than its stockholders' interest, it operates as a public institution even if the stockholders formally elect all of its chief officers.

Chore Functions

Acting as a lender of last resort and controlling the money supply are the main functions of a central bank. But the central bank also performs a number of other tasks, called chore functions. One set of these tasks consists of services it provides for commercial banks. Thus, it acts as a banker's bank, holding most of the reserves of commercial banks. In fact, these reserves consist mainly of entries on the books of the central bank, that is, of liabilities of the central bank to the commercial banks. To balance these liabilities the central bank typically holds as assets government securities, interest-bearing promissory notes of banks to which it has made loans, and gold, or claims to gold. Since the central bank holds reserves for commercial banks it frequently also clears checks for banks.

In addition to its services for commercial banks, a central bank provides many services to the government, both in controlling financial institutions and in acting as the government's banker. One group of services to the government arises directly out of the central bank's close relation with commercial banks. Thus the central bank typically administers certain government controls over commercial banks. For example, the Federal Reserve System controls bank mergers and examines member banks. In a number of countries the government has imposed controls (so-called exchange controls) over the purchase of foreign assets by its residents, and these controls are often administered by the central bank.

Central banks also function as a fiscal agent or bank of the government. The government keeps an account in the central bank, and writes its checks on this account. Similarly, the central banks often act as a selling agent for government securities. In a number of countries, in particular the less-developed countries, the central bank also makes loans to the government. And, in fact, a number of central banks—the Bank of England again is the prime example—originally started out as commercial banks that made loans to the government and got certain privileges in exchange. But having the central bank make loans to the government can turn out to be a bad practice because the central bank often cannot deny funds to the rest of the government. And when the government spends these borrowed funds they become additional reserves to commercial banks. Thus the central bank may find itself creating bank reserves, and indirectly, money, not because it believes that the increase in the money stock is good for the country, but because it has no choice. To prevent this, in the United States the Federal Reserve is allowed to lend to the Treasury directly only a trivial amount on a very short-term basis. However, what cannot be done openly can be, and is, done indirectly by using the public as an intermediary; the Treasury sells securities to the public, while the Federal Reserve buys the same amount of government securities from the public. The purpose of this is to prevent the rise in interest rates that would occur if the public were to hold more government securities.

Another chore function of a central bank is to issue currency. In many countries all the currency notes in circulation are issued, that is, placed into circulation, by the central bank, though sometimes the Treasury issues some currency notes as well. Since worn currency notes have to be withdrawn from circulation and new ones issued, this task is far from costless for the central bank. And the central bank also acts as an adviser to the government. Particularly in the area of international finance, governments rely strongly on the advice of their central banks. Many of the international financial contacts between governments are carried out through their central banks. And on a day-to-day basis many central banks buy and sell foreign currencies to keep exchange rates stable.

Other Aspects of Central Banking

Before leaving the topic of central banks per se, and turning to the Federal Reserve System, there are three more items to be discussed: the dealings of central banks with the general public, their relation to the rest of the government, and their ability to create reserves.

On the whole it is undesirable for a central bank to deal directly with the public. To do so would mean competing with commercial banks, thus creating a rivalry between commercial banks and the agency that is supposed to help them as well as to supervise them.

The relation of central banks to the rest of the government is complex. Although they are part of the government, they maintain a certain detachment from the rest of it. Thus their top executives usually do not change when the governing party loses an election, and they have much more independence from the administration than do such government agencies as the Treasury Department.

Finally, there is the central bank's ability to create reserves. Unless there is a law stating that the central bank must keep, say, 20 cents in gold for each dollar of its outstanding currency notes and deposits, it can create as many reserves for the commercial banks as it wants to. After all, these reserves consist, apart from currency, merely of entries on the central bank's books. Thus, the central bank can buy securities from the commercial banks, or make loans to them, simply by writing up their reserve accounts. The central bank does not have to pay out anything; it is just a matter of book entries. To illustrate the principle involved, suppose someone comes to you and says he would like to keep $100 with you. Suppose you therefore give him a $100 loan. You can do this simply by writing up his account with you even though you do not have the $100. And if you happen to be a central bank you do not have to worry that he will ever draw out these $100. If he does so, all that happens is that he gives a check for the $100 to someone (another banker) who uses this check simply to ask you to transfer the $100 to his account. But nobody actually asks you to hand over these $100.

All of this discussion of what central banks are and do has been a preliminary to the organization of the Federal Reserve System, the topic to which we now finally come.

The Formal Structure of the Federal Reserve System

The United States started a central bank only in 1913 when President Wilson signed the Federal Reserve Act. In 1907 an unusually severe financial panic with many bank failures had finally convinced enough people that a central bank was needed. Even then there was much opposition to it because of a fear that Wall Street would be able to use it as a tool to dominate Main Street. But the opposition to a central bank was eventually overcome as it became increasingly clear that a lender of last resort was needed. Moreover, other major faults of the national banking system, such as the inelasticity of the currency and the pyramiding of reserves, also suggested that the financial system stood in need of change. But, given the great concern that a central bank could lead to a powerful cartel of banks on the one hand, or to political control over banking on the other hand, a very careful and elaborate system of checks and balances was written into the Federal Reserve Act.

At its start, the Federal Reserve System was looked upon more as a cooperative enterprise of bankers, whose main function was to pool the previously dispersed reserves of banks, than as a government agency concerned with goals of full employment and price-level stability. But although its structure has changed less than its functions, the Federal Reserve System we have today is not the system that was originally set up in 1913. It has been changed both by major pieces of legislation, particularly the banking acts of 1933 and 1935, and by the slow evolution in modes of functioning that is a matter of internal organization and practice rather than of statutory change. The Federal Reserve Act of 1913 envisioned a highly decentralized system. Some people even saw the Fed not as a single central bank, but as twelve confederated regional central banks. But over the years the Federal Reserve has become more centralized. The twelve regional Federal Reserve banks, most of all the initially extremely powerful New York Bank, have lost power to the Board of Governors in Washington.

The major features of the Federal Reserve System, however, have not changed. It still consists of twelve Federal Reserve banks and the

Board of Governors. (The term Federal Reserve System as normally used does not include the member banks.)

The Federal Reserve Banks

The location of the twelve banks, and their branches, is shown in figure 7.1. The assets of various Federal Reserve banks are far from equal. More than half the assets are held by just three banks: New York, Chicago, and San Francisco, with the New York Bank alone accounting for almost one-quarter of all Federal Reserve assets. Apart from its size, the New York Bank is the "first among equals" because of its location, where it has direct contact with the country's main money market. Hence, it is this bank that carries out all the purchases and sales of securities on behalf of the whole Federal Reserve System. In addition, it is the Federal Reserve System's contact point in many, though not all, its dealings with foreign central banks and international institutions.

Each of these Federal Reserve banks is controlled by a board of nine part-time directors. Three of these directors, called class A directors, are elected by the member banks, and are bankers themselves. Member banks also elect three class B directors. These must be people experienced in industry, commerce, or agriculture, and may not be officers, employees, or stockholders of banks. In other words, the three class A directors are balanced by members of business groups that borrow from banks. To prevent domination by any particular size group of banks, member banks are divided into large, medium, and small banks, and each of these groups votes for one class A and one class B director. But actually, neither class A nor class B directors are "elected" in the proper sense of the term since there is usually only a single candidate for each election. Frequently the single candidate for the election as a class B director, and often also the candidate for the class A directorship, is someone suggested to the banks by the president of that Federal Reserve bank.

Finally, there are three class C directors. These are not elected by the member banks. They are appointed by the Board of Governors to embody the broader public interest beyond that of banks and their borrowers. One of these class C directors becomes the chairman of the board, and another the vice-chairman.

It is sometimes said that the member banks elect the majority of the Federal Reserve banks' directors, but this is misleading. When one takes account of the fact that in addition to the appointed class C directors, the president of the bank often de facto nominates the class B, and apparently in many cases even the class A, directors, it is more accurate to say that in actuality the Federal Reserve System selects the majority of the directors.

In describing the various classes of directors we were careful to avoid saying that any of the three classes "represents" a particular group, because all directors are supposed to represent the public interest rather than the narrow interests of bankers or borrowers. The public interest, however,

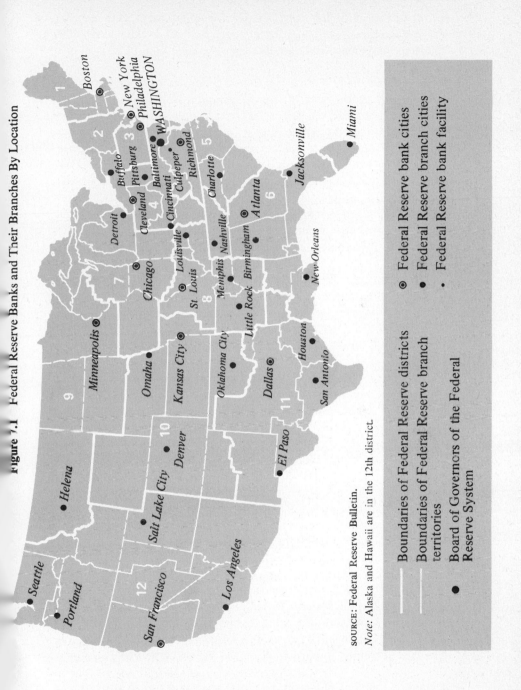

Figure 7.1   Federal Reserve Banks and Their Branches By Location

Boston
New York
Philadelphia
WASHINGTON
Buffalo
Pitsburg
Baltimore
Culpeper
Richmond
Charlotte
Jacksonville
Miami
Detroit
Cleveland
Cincinnati
Louisville
Nashville
Atlanta
Birmingham
Memphis
New Orleans
Chicago
St Louis
Little Rock
Houston
San Antonio
Minneapolis
Omaha
Kansas City
Oklahoma City
Dallas
Helena
Salt Lake City
Denver
El Paso
Seattle
Portland
San Francisco
Los Angeles

SOURCE: Federal Reserve Bulletin.

Note: Alaska and Hawaii are in the 12th district.

◉ Federal Reserve bank cities

● Federal Reserve branch cities

·   Federal Reserve bank facility

— Boundaries of Federal Reserve districts

    Boundaries of Federal Reserve branch
    territories

● Board of Governors of the Federal
    Reserve System

is like the proverbial elephant described by the blind men. One's social background, associations, and experience affect both the value judgments and the positive judgments that go into one's perception of the public interest.

There have been many complaints that the directors are selected only from "establishment types" and that until recently women and minority groups, as well as labor and consumers, were virtually unrepresented even among the class C directors. Part of this is due to the fact that the main function of the directors is not to make monetary policy, but rather to guide the bank's president in his administrative work of running the bank, a task in which those with business experience of their own have an obvious advantage. However, by participating in the selection of the bank's president, and also by informing him of their views on policy, which, however, he is free to ignore, the directors do have some influence on policy, so that the criticism that the directors are unrepresentative cannot be dismissed entirely.

The chief executive officer of each Federal Reserve bank is its president. He is chosen by the directors with the approval of the Board of Governors. In recent years he has frequently been someone initially suggested to the directors by the Board of Governors. Most of the recently appointed presidents, unlike most of the directors, have been professional economists.

The Federal Reserve banks perform many of the chore functions of the Federal Reserve System: examining member banks, passing on some bank-merger applications, clearing checks, withdrawing worn currency from circulation, and issuing new currency. But, in addition to these chore functions, the Federal Reserve banks have some policy functions too. Each Federal Reserve bank "sets" a **discount rate,** that is, *the rate the Federal Reserve charges on its loans to banks and other depository institutions that keep reserves with it.* But this rate has to be approved by the Board of Governors, and furthermore, the Board of Governors, by its power to approve or disapprove the existing discount rate, can force a Federal Reserve bank to change its current rate. Hence, the only real power the Federal Reserve banks have over the discount rate is the power to advise, and to delay a change in the discount rate for as long as two weeks.[1] However, each Federal Reserve bank administers its own discount window, that is, under general rules applicable to all Federal Reserve banks, it makes the particular decision when a bank or other depository institution in its district applies for a loan. A more important policy role of the Federal Reserve banks is, as will be described presently, to participate in the Federal Open Market Committee.

Still another function of the Federal Reserve banks is to provide the

---

[1] One can sometimes infer a particular Federal Reserve bank's attitude towards a discount-rate change by seeing whether the bank lags behind, or leads the parade, when the discount rate is changed. But, sometimes a lag may be merely a matter of administrative convenience.

Federal Reserve System with local contacts. Despite the vast amount of information that flows into Washington, statistical data become available only with some delay. However, by talking to local businessmen the Federal Reserve is able to obtain some indication of economic developments right away. Another important function of the Federal Reserve banks is to explain, and justify, Federal Reserve actions to the local business community, and thus to generate political support for the Federal Reserve System. This is an important, though informal, part of the directors' job. Finally, each Federal Reserve bank has a competent staff of economists who carry out research, not only on local conditions, but also on monetary policy and general economic problems.

The Board of Governors

At the apex of the Federal Reserve System is the Board of Governors (sometimes still called by its former name, "Federal Reserve Board") located in Washington, D.C. The seven governors are appointed by the president of the United States with the advice and consent of the Senate. They can be removed only for "cause," something that, so far, has never happened. They serve a fourteen-year term and cannot be reappointed after serving a full term, which is supposed to remove them from needing to seek the president's favor, or fearing his threats. When the Federal Reserve Act was revised in 1935, the term was raised from ten to fourteen years, probably to enhance the Fed's independence. If all the seven members were to serve their full terms, which are staggered, there would be only two vacancies on the Board every four years, so that within a single term a president could not dominate the Board. But the chairman's term, as chairman, though not as a Board member, is only four years so that each president can appoint his own chairman. These provisions are examples of the checks and balances built into the Federal Reserve System.

However, not all of them have worked well. Most Board members retire before their full fourteen-year term is up, sometimes because of age, and sometimes for financial reasons. Since 1960 the average actual length of service of a governor has been about five and a half years. Hence, usually more than two vacancies occur on the Board during any one presidential term. For example, there were four vacancies on the Board during President Carter's first three years in office. Moreover, when a member resigns from the Board the president can, if he wants to, appoint someone to the remaining years of the former member's term. This not only means that some governors have a less than fourteen-year term, but also that they are then eligible for reappointment to a full term of their own, and might therefore be tempted to favor the president's views.

Until the 1960s, most of the appointees to the Board had been bankers or other businessmen. But recently, the majority of the board members have been professional economists, some of whom had previously been staff economists in the Federal Reserve System.

The main function of the Board of Governors is to conduct monetary policy. It does so by buying or selling government securities, by changing reserve requirements, and the discount rate. These tools will be discussed in chapter 22. But here we want to mention another policy function of the Board. This is to act, through the chairman of the Board, as one of the main economic advisers to the president, and also to Congress. And members of the Board of Governors sometimes also act as U.S. representatives in negotiations with foreign central banks and governments. Beyond this, chairmen frequently press their views on fiscal policy and other economic issues in numerous statements to Congress and to the general public. The Board has a large and competent staff of economists to aid it in this work.

In addition to its macroeconomic policy functions the Board also has certain chore functions. For example, it passes on many bank-merger applications and decides the permissible lines of nonbank activity for bank holding companies. And it administers the laws that prohibit discrimination in the granting of credit and require the provision of truthful information about interest costs and credit terms. In these activities the Board of Governors' control extends beyond banking to credit in general. Closer to home it exercises some rather loose supervision over the Federal Reserve banks, which have to submit their budgets to the Board for approval.

The Federal Open Market Committee

The focal point for policymaking within the Federal Reserve System is the Federal Open Market Committee (FOMC), which meets nowadays about eight times a year and sometimes holds telephone conferences between meetings. This committee consists of the seven members of the Board of Governors and five presidents of the Federal Reserve banks.[2] The Federal Reserve banks rotate in these five slots on the FOMC except for the New York Bank, which has a permanent slot.[3] However, those Federal Reserve bank presidents who are not currently members of the FOMC are usually present at its meetings and participate in its discussion, though, of course, they do not vote. But since the FOMC tries to reach a consensus rather than just rely on a majority, their presence, even in a nonvoting capacity, gives all bank presidents some influence on the FOMC's decisions.

The FOMC's official function is to decide on **open-market operations,** that is, *Federal Reserve purchases and sales of securities.* For reasons to

[2] Although the law permits the first vice-president of a Federal Reserve bank to serve on the FOMC in place of its president, this is normally not done, except when a president is unable to attend a meeting.

[3] The permanent representation of the New York Bank is in large part explained by the great power this bank had in earlier years. In the early days of the Federal Reserve System it was far from clear whether the New York Bank or the Board was more powerful. Over the years the New York Bank has lost most of its power. At present, the best justification for its permanent membership on the FOMC is that its close contacts with the New York money market give it a special expertise.

be discussed in chapter 22, this is the Federal Reserve's most important tool of monetary policy. The FOMC does not carry out the security purchases or sales itself. Instead, it issues a directive telling the New York Federal Reserve Bank the open-market policy it should follow. The New York Federal Reserve Bank, being located in the country's predominant money market, then carries out the open-market operations for the accounts of all the Federal Reserve banks. But although the FOMC's power is limited to open-market operations, its informal mandate is much broader. It provides a forum for discussing the use of all the Federal Reserve's tools. Figure 7.2 summarizes the allocation of the Federal Reserve's tools among its various components.

Figure 7.2   Allocation of the Federal Reserve's Tools

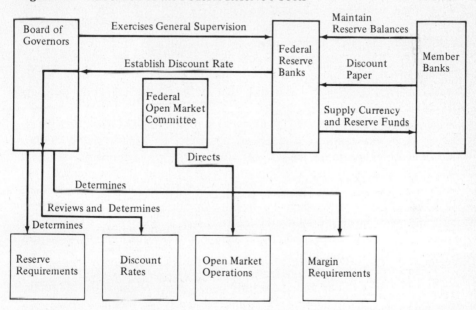

SOURCE: Adapted from Board of Governors Federal Reserve System, *The Federal Reserve System, Purposes and Functions* (Washington, D.C., 1974), p. 50.

There are some other Federal Reserve components, but they are *much* less important than the FOMC. One is the Federal Advisory Council, which consists of one commercial banker (usually a president of a large commercial bank) from each district. As the name implies, this committee advises the Board of Governors on banking and monetary problems, but that is all. Then there is the Conference of Federal Reserve Bank Presidents, which meets to discuss common problems, and there is a similar Conference of Federal Reserve Bank Chairmen. On a lower organizational level, committees consisting of economists from the staffs of the Board and the various banks meet to investigate particular research problems, such as changes in the demand for money.

The Informal Structure of the Federal Reserve System

Merely to know the formal, legal aspects of an organization is rarely sufficient, and the Fed, like any organization, has developed certain traditions
and other attributes that powerfully affect its operations. These informal
aspects are neither definite nor clear-cut. They involve the distribution of
power within the Federal Reserve, the constituency of the Federal Reserve,
and its behavior as a bureaucracy.

Distribution of Power within the Federal Reserve

The distribution of power over monetary policy within the Federal
Reserve System and among "outsiders," is, of course, a matter of judgment
rather than something that can be definitely and rigorously established.
However, based on his experience as a Federal Reserve governor, Sherman Maisel has given the estimate of the distribution of power shown in
Figure 7.3 with the length of the bars indicating the power of each group.
The importance of outside, relative to inside, power is not shown in this
chart because, as Maisel points out, this varies depending upon the particular issue involved.

However, there are two qualifications to figure 7.3. First, the distribution of power cannot be quantified precisely; as Maisel states, "Other
knowledgeable persons would certainly draw charts with different
weights." [4] For example, one former senior Federal Reserve official believes that the chairman has more power than figure 7.3 suggests. Second,
the distribution of power depends, in part, on the particular persons wield-
ing this power. Since the 1950s the Fed has had at least three strong-willed
chairmen. A more accommodative chairman in the future might wield less
power than figure 7.3 indicates.

The chairman's power is based on five sources. First, as the head of
the Board, his opinions and statements carry great weight with the public.
For example, Chairman Burns's strong advocacy of incomes policy apparently played an important role in the imposition of price controls in 1971.
And in 1977 his outspoken opposition to the proposed tax rebate was a
major factor in killing it. Second, a number of decisions do not even come
before the Board, but are taken by the chairman himself as the Board's
representative. For example, it is the chairman, and not the whole Board,
who meets with the president. Third, the chairman arranges the agenda
and exercises the leadership role at the Board's meetings. Fourth, the chairman maintains supervisory powers over the Board's staff members, who
therefore have a greater incentive to please him than other Board members.
Finally, the foregoing powers of the chairman give him an aura of authority,
which tends to induce other board members to vote the way he does.

---

[4] Sherman J. Maisel, *Managing the Dollar* (New York: W. W. Norton, 1973),
pp. 109–11.

Figure 7.3   Degree of Monetary Power
1965–1973

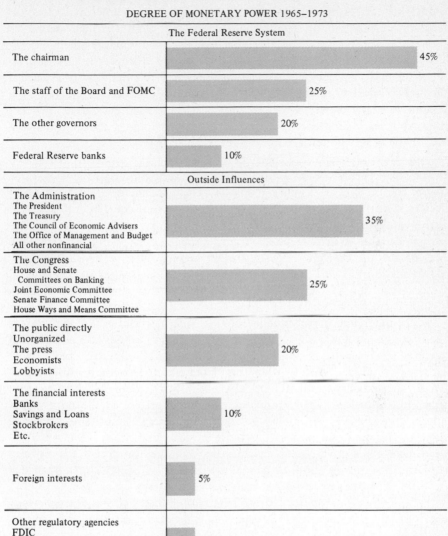

DEGREE OF MONETARY POWER 1965–1973

The Federal Reserve System	
The chairman	45%
The staff of the Board and FOMC	25%
The other governors	20%
Federal Reserve banks	10%

Outside Influences	
The Administration The President The Treasury The Council of Economic Advisers The Office of Management and Budget All other nonfinancial	35%
The Congress House and Senate Committees on Banking Joint Economic Committee Senate Finance Committee House Ways and Means Committee	25%
The public directly Unorganized The press Economists Lobbyists	20%
The financial interests Banks Savings and Loans Stockbrokers Etc.	10%
Foreign interests	5%
Other regulatory agencies FDIC Comptroller FHLBB SEC	5%

SOURCE: Sherman Maisel, *Managing the Dollar* (New York: W. W. Norton, 1973), p. 110.

The Federal Reserve's Constituency

To refer to the Federal Reserve's constituency is to use the term in a broader sense than when it is applied to a congressman's geographic constituency. A government agency tends to view itself as a spokesman for a particular group, and tries to represent this group's interests within the government. In return, the agency receives direct and indirect political support from its constituency. As former Secretary of the Treasury George Shultz put it: "Advocacy government is part of our unwritten constitution." [5] An example of this is the Department of Agriculture acting as spokesman for farmers and receiving support from congressmen elected from rural districts. The Department of Labor has a similar relationship to labor unions. This does not mean that these agencies necessarily disregard the public interest; rather the public interest is supposed to emerge as a consensus of the views of various groups as expressed by "their" government agencies. Admittedly, the view of the public interest that does emerge can too often be summarized as "more for me."

It seems plausible that the Federal Reserve views itself as having two major, and perhaps two minor, partly overlapping constituencies. One major constituency, obviously, consists of banks and the financial community. There is a great deal of populist criticism of the Federal Reserve, and its directors, for representing financial interests. For example, the late Wright Patman, a leading populist congressman, continually criticized the Fed because in his view it desired high interest rates to benefit bankers. But the authors doubt that this criticism is valid: historically the Federal Reserve has not advocated macroeconomic policies merely because they would benefit banks.[6]

The other major constituency of the Federal Reserve is composed of the fixed-income groups who stand to lose by inflation. Several government agencies (such as the Departments of Agriculture, Commerce, and Labor) represent producer groups while the Council of Economic Advisers is usually the spokesman for full-employment policies. Someone should represent those who lose when producers raise their prices, or the government adopts excessively expansionary policies. The Federal Reserve has assumed some of this task, at least in the sense of worrying more about inflation than most other government agencies do. Whether or not it has worried sufficiently about inflation, or has allowed itself to become an engine for inflation, is another issue that we must leave for later.

Two other, *but* minor, constituencies that the Federal Reserve *may* have are the press, particularly the financial press, and academic economists. With the Fed being in the news so much it obviously wants to get a favorable reception, both by the press and by academic economists, who, at times, have been sharply critical of it, both in their writings and in their testimony before Congress. But it is hard to say to what extent, if any, the Fed's policy has been influenced by its concern about the opinions of these two groups.

---

[5] "Reflections on Political Economy," *Journal of Finance* 29 (May 1974): 325.

[6] A better case could probably be made for the argument that in its regulatory activities the Fed tried to protect the competitive position of banks since it was concerned about the decline in membership.

The Federal Reserve as a Bureaucracy

Interest groups outside the Federal Reserve are not the only beneficiaries of the Federal Reserve's concern; to a considerable extent it probably also takes good care of its own institutional interests. The modern theory of bureaucracy argues that a government agency is not a Platonic philosopher-king, interested only in the public welfare. It is also concerned with its own survival and prestige, which it can easily rationalize as being indirectly a concern for the public welfare.

Assuming that the Federal Reserve is actually concerned with its own strength as an institution, how would one expect it, or any other central bank, to behave? First, it would, whenever possible, avoid conflicts with powerful people and institutions who could harm it. In practical terms this means that, for example, it would be tempted to follow expansionary policies that in the short run would meet Congress's and the administration's wish to keep interest rates down. Second, one would expect it to try to maintain its power and autonomy: to be unwilling, for example, to give up any of its policy tools, even those tools that are not very useful. Third, an organization that is trying to maintain its power and prestige is unlikely to admit that it made mistakes in the past, since to do so may suggest that it could conceivably be making mistakes currently too.

Fourth, a way for an organization to protect itself from criticism is to act myopically, that is, to pay a great deal of attention to the direct and immediate impact of its policies, and to pay too little attention to the longer run or less direct damage these policies may do. This is so because the organization is more likely to be blamed for those bad effects of its policies that are immediately visible and clearly its fault, than for those bad effects that could be the result of many other causes. For example, the Federal Reserve is blamed a great deal if financial markets are unstable and security prices fall sharply. But as far as inflation is concerned, the Fed can argue that this is the result of many factors, and not really its fault.

Finally, a central bank concerned with its own survival and prestige has an incentive not to commit itself publicly to precise and highly visible targets, because if it has clear-cut, readily observable targets it would face criticism if it misses them. Rather, it would focus either on targets that cannot be readily perceived by outsiders or that are simple to achieve even though they may be of little importance for the rest of the economy.[7] For example, if the Federal Reserve announces that it aims at a 3.5 percent growth rate of M_1 it is subject to criticism if the actual growth rate is only 3 percent. But if it announces that its target is "appropriate credit-market

---

[7] A central bank is not the only one who faces this temptation. A student who announces to her parents that her goal this semester is to get all As is taking a bigger risk of disappointing them than another student who announces that his goal is the much more difficult task of transforming himself into a thoughtful and perceptive person.

conditions," its policy is much harder to criticize since no one (including the Fed itself) knows what "appropriate credit-market conditions" really are. In any case, many central bankers tend to think of their job as an art that is practiced better by relying on the intuition of knowledgeable people than on rigorous analysis. For example, the preeminent central banker of the pre–World War II period, Sir Montague Norman, was once asked to state the reason for a decision he had made. He replied: "Reasons, Mr. Chairman? I don't have reasons. I have instincts." [8]

Do central banks in general, and the Federal Reserve specifically, really behave in this way? Some economists have argued that this is so, but the subject is still very much open to debate.

Some economists have criticized the Federal Reserve for trying to protect itself against criticism by not making enough information about its actions available to the public. While there may be much truth to this criticism, compared to foreign central banks, however, the Fed is a veritable chatterbox. In addition to occasional studies, the Board publishes each month the *Federal Reserve Bulletin,* which contains articles on current developments, a record of previous FOMC actions, detailed financial statistics, and so on. And the Federal Reserve banks issue without charge their own, usually monthly or quarterly, publications containing articles on banking and local economic conditions, and often on general issues of banking and monetary policy.

Finances of the Federal Reserve System

The outstanding stock of the Federal Reserve banks is owned by its member banks, who receive a fixed 6 percent dividend on this stock. The fact that the member banks own all the stock of the Federal Reserve banks is sometimes taken to mean that they own these Federal Reserve banks. But this is completely misleading. Ownership means two things: the right to appropriate all the net earnings, and the right to control the property. Member banks have no claim on the residual earnings of the Federal Reserve banks. They get their 6 percent dividend, de facto, regardless of the Fed's earnings, and they cannot cash in on the Fed's high earnings by selling their stock at a capital gain, since this stock cannot be sold on the market, but can only be sold back to the Fed itself at par. Similarly, they have little control over the Federal Reserve banks. To be sure, formally they elect the majority of the Federal Reserve bank directors, but as we pointed out earlier, the Federal Reserve bank presidents have much influence on this "election." Moreover, these directors are charged with functioning in the public interest, and not in the interests of the stockholders. In any case, the directors have little influence on monetary policy. For these reasons the private aspects of the Federal Reserve banks are not

[8] Quoted in Andrew Boyle, *Montague Norman* (London: Cassell, 1967), p. 327.

at all important; they are really fully public institutions, and not just "quasi-public" institutions as some writers have put it. Suppose, for example, that the law were changed to eliminate the election of directors by having class A and class B directors appointed by the Board, and that stock held by member banks was retired. It is hard to believe that these changes would have any effect at all on Federal Reserve policy.

The earnings of the Federal Reserve banks come primarily from their earnings on the securities they hold, and to a much smaller extent from interest on the loans they make. Under legislation passed in 1980 they will also earn income by charging financial institutions for the services they perform for them, such as clearing checks. But where do the funds that the Federal Reserve banks invest in these securities come from? The main source is the issuance of Federal Reserve notes. Suppose the Fed prints $1 million of Federal Reserve notes and ships them to a bank that asks for them. It then debits that bank's reserve account. If it wants to keep total bank reserves constant it then offsets this by buying $1 million of securities in the open market. Hence, on its books its liabilities for outstanding Federal Reserve notes are up by $1 million, but so are its government security holdings. Second, the Federal Reserve can buy securities in a way which is akin to deposit creation by the commercial banking system. It simply pays for the securities by giving banks credit on their reserve accounts. Similarly, when it makes loans to member banks it just writes up their reserve account.[9]

Out of the earnings on this capital the Federal Reserve banks pay their own expenses, as well as the expenses of the Board of Governors, and the dividends on member bank stock (which amounted to 0.8 percent of net earnings in 1977–79). After taking care of these expenses the Federal Reserve banks place a relatively small amount into their surplus accounts, but the great bulk of their net earnings (almost $6 billion in 1977, 98 percent of net earnings) was turned over to the U.S. Treasury. There is no law requiring the Federal Reserve to do this; it does so voluntarily, though if it did not, there would surely be a law requiring it.

Federal Reserve Independence

The Federal Reserve has a great deal of independence, much more than other government agencies. While the president of the United States with the advice and consent of the Senate appoints new governors as vacancies occur, and chooses his own chairman, once he has made these selections

---

[9] It may seem that when a member bank deposits reserves with its Federal Reserve bank the Fed obtains funds, which it can invest and hence earn interest on. But the total amount of currency and reserves is fixed. Assuming that there is no change in currency held by the public, then the only way one bank can obtain more reserves is for another bank's reserves to decline. Hence, there is no change in the total reserves, and hence in the earning assets, held by the Federal Reserve.

he does not officially have any more power over the Federal Reserve; in principle the Fed could ignore his wishes completely. To be sure, in a legalistic sense the Federal Reserve is a "creature of Congress," but Congress is neither set up to exercise day-to-day control over it, nor, under present legislation, has it the right to do so. Thus, while the Federal Reserve reports its targets for the growth rate of the money stock to Congress, in principle, it could ignore any congressional reactions to the targets it has chosen.

Extent of Independence

But, as usual, the formal situation as set forth in legislation is only part of the story. Actually, the president and Congress have considerable influence over the Fed. One source of the president's influence is moral suasion; the governors oppose the views of the one person elected by all the people only reluctantly; they go along if they feel they can do so without dereliction of duty. Second, the Federal Reserve is continually active in Congress, trying to obtain certain legislation, or trying to block legislation that would reduce its power or independence. It would like to have the support of the president in these legislative struggles, and hence has an incentive to keep on good terms with him. Third, the chairman wants the president's goodwill, so that when the president appoints a new governor, it will be someone the chairman prefers. Thus, one study found:

> The Federal Reserve shifted course in the fundamental sense easing or tightening significantly in 1953, 1961, 1969, 1971, 1974 and 1977. Except for 1971, these were years when the presidency also changed hands; and except for the changeover from President Kennedy to President Johnson, these were the only years when the presidency changed hands. Considering further that the thrust of monetary policy, which began to ease in 1961, eased significantly during Johnson's presidency from its first year (1964) it may be reasonably urged that the dominant guiding force behind monetary policy is the President. Congress plays only a "watchdog role." . . . The historical record shows that in each administration monetary policy fitted harmoniously with the President's economic and financial objectives and plans.[10]

Moreover, to ward off undesired legislation and to obtain the legislation it does want, the Federal Reserve probably bends at least to some extent to congressional pressures. However, to some extent the Fed's independence protects Congress from having to make hard choices. Some people think that Congress knows that it can take a politically popular stand in favor of low interest rates and rely on the Fed to play the role of the "heavy" nay-sayer.

In general, the Federal Reserve cannot take the continuation of its independence for granted. It is to some extent "a prisoner of its inde-

[10] Robert Weintraub, "Congressional Supervision of Monetary Policy," *Journal of Monetary Economics* 4 (April 1978): 349–50.

pendence." It may have to give in on some issues to prevent Congress from taking away some of its independence.

But the influence of the president and Congress should not be over-estimated; on some issues the Federal Reserve can mobilize an extraor-dinarily powerful lobby of bankers in each congressional district to pres-sure Congress into preserving the Fed's independence and freedom of action. Congressmen, by and large, doubt their ability to challenge the Federal Reserve, in part because the Fed claims to possess esoteric knowl-edge about monetary policy, and to safeguard us from explosive inflation. Moreover, there is usually little political benefit in challenging the Fed.

All in all, as Sherman Maisel has written,

> . . . independence is both ill-defined and circumscribed. . . . Although no legal method exists for the President to issue a directive to the System, its in-dependence in fact is not so great that it can use monetary policy as a club or threat to veto Administration action. The System's latitude for action is rather circumscribed. . . . In any showdown, no nonrepresentative group such as the Fed can or should be allowed to pursue its own goals in oppo-sition to those of the elected officials.[11]

The Case for Independence

There are several arguments on both sides of the independence issue. Supporters of independence argue that monetary policy, and hence the value of the dollar, is too important and too complex an issue to be left to the play of political forces. As a former chairman of the Board, William McChesney Martin, put it:

> An Independent Federal Reserve System is the primary bulwark of the free enterprise system and when it succumbs to the pressures of political expediency or the dictates of private interest, the ground work of sound money is undermined.[12]

In this view the political process is myopic: being overly concerned with the next election, it overplays the importance of short-term benefits, and hence is unwilling to make those hard and unpopular decisions—such as tolerating more unemployment in the short run—that are needed to obtain the long-run benefits of a stable price level. Moreover, politicians, if they can, are likely to use the central bank to finance increased government expenditures without raising taxes. In addition, pressure groups impart an inflationary bias to government policy. Furthermore, unless the Federal Reserve is independent it is likely to be under the de facto domination of the Treasury, and the Treasury, as the country's biggest borrower, is tempted to aim for low interest rates even when high interest rates are needed to curb inflation. Hence an independent central bank largely re-moved from political pressures is needed to ensure justice to creditors,

---

[11] Sherman Maisel, *Managing the Dollar*, pp. 24, 136.

[12] Quoted in A. Jerome Clifford, *The Independence of the Federal Reserve Sys-tem* (Philadelphia: University of Pennsylvania Press, 1965), p. 18.

and to others who lose from inflation. Anyone familiar with the case for a gold standard will probably see the similarity with the argument that the gold standard guards against unwise inflationary actions. The notions of central bank independence and of the gold standard have much in common.

Another variant of this argument puts it in terms of a "political business cycle." Before an election the government is tempted to adopt a very expansionary monetary policy, which results in lower interest rates and lower unemployment just before the election. The resulting inflation then occurs only after the election. At that point the government adopts restrictive policies, which it hopes the public will have forgotten by the time of the next election.

The Case against Independence

Critics of central bank independence reject these arguments. They believe that it is fundamentally undemocratic to say that elected officials should not be trusted to judge monetary policy. To be sure, monetary policy involves difficult decisions that need a long-run point of view, but the same thing is true of foreign policy or defense policy. Moreover, for better or worse, the public holds the president responsible for the economic conditions that result from *all* the policies followed during his administration. Hence, he should have control over monetary policy, one of the most important of these policies.

In addition, some economists maintain that the Fed has not used its independence well and therefore should be deprived of it. At times it has tolerated inflation, as in the late 1960s and 1970s, and in other years, the 1930s, for example, it has had a deflationary bias and allowed too much unemployment to develop. In addition, its independence has not really removed it from politics. Instead, it has had to become a political animal in order to defend both its actions and its independence. Moreover, its independence allows the Federal Reserve too much leeway to indulge in that characteristic weakness of a bureaucracy, continuous overemphasis of narrow, parochial interests, a charge that will be taken up in some detail in chapter 23.

Finally, monetary and fiscal policies should be integrated, and adequate integration cannot be achieved, the opponents of Federal Reserve independence claim, merely by a process of informal consultation. Rather it requires that the Federal Reserve be part of the administration. Giving the president control over the Federal Reserve need not necessarily weaken its influence, but might even strengthen it, because if it were part of the administration, the Fed's counsel would then be better heeded by the administration on many issues.

Possible Compromises

As is so often the case, these pro and con arguments give the misleading impression that the choice is between two irreconcilable extremes.

But this is not so. Even if the Federal Reserve were to lose its formal independence, and become a part of the administration, there would still be at least an attempt to keep it out of partisan politics. Those foreign central banks that are controlled by their administrations have much more autonomy than other government agencies, such as the Treasury. Moreover, as just pointed out, the independence that the Federal Reserve actually has in our present system is far from complete and is subject to both presidential and congressional influence.

On a more practical level, the more relevant debate does not deal with such "fundamental" issues as the Fed's complete independence, but focuses on proposals for relatively minor reductions in its independence. One issue that was recently debated in Congress concerned making the chairman's term of office coincide better with the president's so that each president could appoint his own chairman a year after he took office. And from time to time it is proposed that the ownership of Federal Reserve bank stock by the member banks be abolished as an anachronism. A much more important proposal is that the Federal Reserve be stripped of its bank supervisory functions, so that it could concentrate all its energies on monetary policy. Still other proposals would shorten the terms of the governors or eliminate the FOMC and shift its work to the Board of Governors. However, it is unlikely that any of these proposals—with the possible exception of a change in the chairman's term of office, will become law within the foreseeable future since the Federal Reserve is fighting them very strongly.

Summary

In this chapter we have discussed central banking in general, and the Federal Reserve System in particular. The first topic taken up was the nature of central banks, the reason why we have them, and how they differ from commercial banks. We also discussed how they developed, and their chore and policy functions, as well as their dealings with the general public, their relation to the rest of the government, and their ability to create reserves.

But the main topic of this chapter was not central banks in general, but the structure of the Federal Reserve System, which is summarized in figure 7.4. We therefore described the origin of the Federal Reserve System, and the initial opposition to it. We then described the organization of the Federal Reserve banks, their boards of directors, their presidents, and both their policy and chore functions. From there we went on to discuss the Board of Governors, its appointment and relation to the president, and its functions. This led to a discussion of the FOMC.

Having considered the formal structure of the Federal Reserve we then looked at its informal aspects, that is, the distribution of power within the Federal Reserve System, particularly the chairman's power and its

Figure 7.4   The Structure of the Federal Reserve System

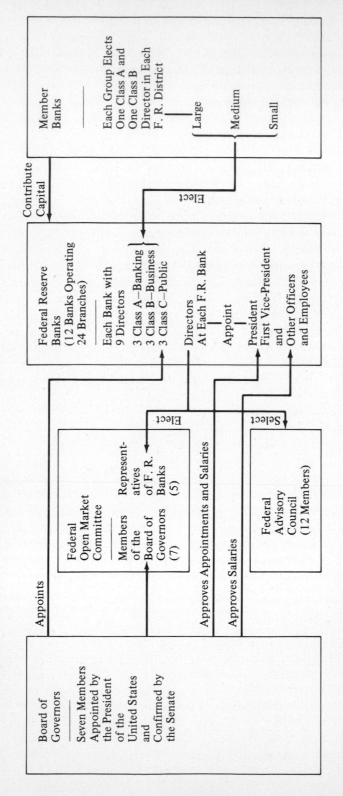

SOURCE: Board of Governors, Federal Reserve System, *The Federal Reserve System, Purposes and Functions*, (Washington, D.C., 1974), p. 18.

sources, the Federal Reserve's constituency, and the Federal Reserve as a bureaucracy that tries to enhance both its safety and power. We then returned to the more formal aspects of the Federal Reserve's organization by looking at its finances, and concluded by looking at the issue of Federal Reserve independence, the pro and con arguments, as well as at certain proposals for reducing its independence.

QUESTIONS AND EXERCISES

1. The term *central bank* is a misnomer; it is nothing like a bank. Discuss the extent to which this statement is true for the Federal Reserve System.
2. Why do countries have central banks?
3. What does the term *lender of last resort* mean?
4. Discuss the chore functions of the Federal Reserve.
5. What monetary policy functions are carried out by
   a. the Federal Reserve Banks,
   b. the Board of Governors,
   c. the FOMC?
6. Critically discuss: "The Federal Reserve banks have nothing at all to do with monetary policy; they only undertake the chore functions of the Federal Reserve system."
7. The Federal Reserve System is an example of a system of "checks and balances." Describe these checks and balances.
8. What does it mean to say that the Federal Reserve has constituencies? What are they?

FURTHER READING

ACHESON, KEITH, and CHANT, JOHN. "Bureaucratic Theory and the Choice of Central Bank Goals: The Case of the Bank of Canada." *Journal of Money, Credit and Banking* 5 (May 1973): 637–56. A pioneering application of bureaucratic theory to central bank behavior.

GALBRAITH, JOHN A. *The Economics of Banking Operations.* Montreal: McGill University Press, 1963. Chapter seven gives a useful and compact discussion of central banking.

KANE, EDWARD. "The Re-Politization of the Fed." *Journal of Financial and Quantitative Analysis* 9 (November 1974): 743–52. An important contribution to the debate about the Fed's independence.

MAISEL, SHERMAN. *Managing the Dollar.* New York: W. W. Norton, 1973. Provides important insights into Fed behavior by a former member of the Board of Governors.

MAYER, THOMAS. "The Structure and Operation of the Federal Reserve System: Some Needed Reforms." In U.S., Congress, House, Committee on Banking, Currency, and Housing, *Compendium of Papers Prepared for the Fine Study,* 94th Cong., 2d sess., 1976, 2: 669–726. A survey of the Fed's organization with proposals for changes.

TUFTE, EDWARD. *Political Control of the Economy*. Princeton: Princeton University Press, 1978. A discussion of the theory of the political business cycle by a political scientist.

WEINTRAUB, ROBERT. "Congressional Supervision of Monetary Policy." *Journal of Monetary Economics* 4 (April 1978): 341–63. An important discussion of the extent to which the Fed is actually independent.

8

A System in Flux

The picture of the U.S. financial structure presented in the previous chapters is hardly that of a system beyond improvement. Numerous problems have arisen, such as disintermediation at times of financial stringency. One reason for this is that financial evolution and new technological developments have had painful effects on some financial institutions. For example, in the 1970s as the world's capital markets became more integrated, more and more foreign banks invaded the U.S. market and hurt some U.S. banks. Another example is the development of electronic funds transfer (EFT) systems, which will increase competition between various types of financial institutions.

But a bigger factor creating the need for financial reform is that our present financial system was designed for a world of little or no inflation. Thus, the high nominal interest rate, which has resulted from inflation, is the underlying factor behind disintermediation and the imposition of Regulation Q.

Interest-Rate Ceilings

The place where the need for financial reform became most acute was the interest-rate ceiling on time deposits. As discussed in chapter 5, as interest rates rose sharply in 1966, many savings and loan associations would have incurred losses, and some would have failed, if they had tried to compete for deposits by offering the prevailing higher interest rates. Hence, in 1966, the government limited competition through Regulation Q by setting ceilings on the interest rates of depository institutions. This "stopgap" measure is still with us.

Disadvantages of Interest-Rate Ceilings

But Regulation Q has proved to be no real solution to the problem for several reasons, some of which were discussed already and will just be reviewed here. First, it could not be effective in the *long run* since there is profit to be made in finding ways around it. Thus, it has led to the development of money-market funds that pool relatively small deposits and buy money-market instruments, such as large CDs and commercial paper. So far these money-market funds are still fairly small because most depositors are not familiar with them, but as time proceeds more and more people will learn about them. Eventually, in this and other ways, Regulation Q would be "repealed" by the market. Second, as discussed in chapter 5, it leads to disintermediation when interest rates rise. Third, Regulation Q is inequitable because it prevents some savers from earning a competitive rate of return on their savings deposits while allowing others to do so. Fourth, Regulation Q creates inefficiencies because it transmutes price (that is, interest-rate) competition into product competition as various savings and loan associations, mutual savings banks, and commercial banks try to obtain more deposits by increased advertising, the opening of more branches, and the provision of various free services and gifts, all of which may have only limited value to the depositor.

Not only has Regulation Q limited the interest rate paid on time deposits, but banks have also been prohibited from paying interest on demand deposits, though in the 1970s depository institutions in New England, and in 1979 also in New York, were allowed to pay interest on de facto demand deposits under the label of NOW accounts. In 1978 banks everywhere were allowed to offer automatic transfer accounts, but the high service charge levied on these accounts severely limited their spread. The prohibition of interest payments on demand deposits discriminated against households with a relatively large proportion of their assets in demand deposits, and was probably regressive. Moreover, like Regulation Q, it led to inefficiencies as depositors, particularly households, were offered "free" services that have little value to them. Additional inefficiencies resulted from households going to the trouble of shifting funds between demand and time deposits to earn interest, or, with an automatic transfer system, from banks shifting funds between these accounts; surely a bit of wasted motion. Furthermore, the prohibition of interest payments on demand deposits has induced banks to pay imputed interest to large business depositors by taking care of their loan demands ahead of other customers in periods of tight money. This led to charges of discrimination against small business.

Disintermediation is by far the most dramatic side effect of the Regulation Q ceiling and the prohibition of interest payments on demand deposits, but another effect *may* be very important too: the distinction between money and other assets is being eroded. In the process of, de facto, repealing both the ceiling on time-deposit interest rates and the prohibition of interest payments on demand deposits, the market develops new financial instruments that legally are neither demand deposits nor time deposits, but function like such deposits as far as their economic impact is concerned. For example, many money-market funds allow their shareholders to write checks on their share accounts, though usually only for $500 and over. To some unknown extent these shares serve as money since some depositors think of their shares as means of payments, while for others they represent genuine savings. Such a fudging of the line between money and other assets complicates monetary policy. Suppose that the Federal Reserve wants the stock of money to grow at a 5 percent rate. Should it include the growth of these money-market funds in this figure?

Alternative Policies

There are several possible responses to the problems created by the ceiling on time-deposit interest rates and the prohibition of interest payments on demand deposits.

Repealing Regulation Q ceilings. One way is to take a free-market approach and simply to repeal the ceilings outright as unwarranted government interferences with the free market. But two factors militate against this. One is that nobody really knows how many thrift institutions would go bankrupt if the interest-rate ceiling were to be eliminated outright, and policymakers who have to bear the responsibility are less willing to find this out by trial and error than are some academic economists. Second, if banks are allowed to compete with thrift institutions by raising interest rates on time deposits and paying interest on demand deposits, then the thrift institutions would have fewer funds available to make mortgage loans. In particular, thrift institutions worry about giving up the benefit of having a one-quarter of one percent higher Regulation Q ceiling than do the commercial banks. And if thrift institutions make fewer mortgage loans, then residential construction *may* be cut back.

But actually, it is far from clear that residential construction will really be much worse off without Regulation Q than with it, since the repeal of Regulation Q will eliminate, or at least substantially reduce, the periodic waves of disintermediation that occur when interest rates rise. In addition, some economists argue that the availability of mortgage loans from thrift institutions has relatively little effect on the volume of residential construction in any case, since many potential borrowers who are denied mortgages can obtain funds in other ways, such as selling some of their securities. Similarly, those who do get mortgages, frequently use these funds to buy, in effect, other assets and not houses. Of course, they use the actual dollars they get from mortgage lenders to buy houses, but then they use their own funds that would otherwise have been used to buy houses to buy securities instead.[1]

However, some other economists, and the residential construction industry, believe that the elimination of Regulation Q could hurt the con-

[1] Professor Meltzer believes that in 1958 between one-quarter and one-third of the outstanding mortgage debt had thus been used indirectly to purchase stock. Allan Meltzer, "Credit Availability and Economic Decisions," in *Government Credit Allocation,* ed. Karl Brunner (San Francisco: Institute for Contemporary Studies, 1975), p. 132.

struction industry, which has as a result used its great political power to maintain Regulation Q.[2]

Lengthening liabilities and shortening assets. Another possibility is to get rid of the underlying problem that caused Regulation Q to be imposed before eliminating Regulation Q itself. Specifically, savings and loan associations have assets that are longer term than their liabilities, so that they are hurt severely if interest rates rise. One solution is therefore to lengthen their liabilities by shifting more liabilities out of passbook accounts into long-term certificates. But this has not happened. While passbook accounts have decreased as a percent of deposits, this has been more than offset by the rise in money market certificates and similar short term liabilities. But in the future depositors could be encouraged to shift more of their deposits into longer-term certificates by raising their interest rates relative to the passbook rate.

A related development is that thrift institutions are now obtaining more and more funds from sources other than regular deposits. Some large ones are issuing commercial paper and other securities, and a few are even selling large CDs in the Eurodollar market. Moreover, new financial institutions are developing that purchase mortgages from thrift institutions, and thus provide them with the wherewithal to make new ones. These new institutions finance themselves by borrowing on the money and capital markets.

Another possible way to solve the thrift institutions' problem is to work on the asset side of the balance sheet. The essence of the current problem is that as interest rates rise thrift institutions do not receive a higher rate on their outstanding mortgages. But this *need* not be so. Until the mid-1930s mortgage loans usually had a maturity of only something like five years. On maturity the borrower usually "repaid" the loan by taking out a new loan at whatever interest rate then prevailed. This system helped to protect the lender against interest-rate fluctuations, but the borrower had the trouble of taking out a new mortgage every few years and the worry about having to pay a higher interest rate.

A type of mortgage has been developed that is to some extent a return to this earlier system. This is a variable-interest-rate mortgage (VIM or VRM). It is a long-term mortgage, but the interest rate on it varies along with some other interest rate, such as the interest rate savings and loan associations pay on their deposits. Numerous protections for borrowers have been written into the law. Thus, federally chartered savings and loan associations may not raise the interest rate more than once a year, and not by more than half a percent per year, or more than 2.5 percent over

---

[2] The residential construction industry is so powerful, in part, because there are numerous contractors and thrift institutions in each congressional district. Moreover, the building unions, who, of course, support the industry's position, also have much political influence. In addition, as will be discussed in chapter 25, there is a widespread feeling that a higher level of residential construction is very important to the nation's welfare, so that many people who do not have an economic stake in residential construction oppose anything that might reduce residential construction.

the life of the mortgage. Moreover, loan customers have to be offered a choice of a traditional mortgage in place of the variable-rate one. In states allowing variable-rate mortgages, the state-chartered savings and loan associations must meet the requirements set by the state.

Despite these protections there is much opposition to such variable-rate mortgages. Opponents claim that they shift the risk of interest-rate fluctuations onto households who cannot predict what their mortgage costs will be in the future. However, this argument is weakened by the fact that sharp increases in interest rates are usually the result of inflation, and on the whole, household incomes, and hence ability to pay mortgage interest, rise along with inflation. Suppose that the interest rate increases by, say, 3 percent, because the inflation rate has risen by 3 percent too. In this case the variable-rate mortgage is keeping the *real* rate of interest constant. By contrast, with a conventional mortgage the real rate of interest would be falling.[3] But although the distinction between the nominal and the real interest rate therefore weakens the argument against variable-rate mortgages, it does not eliminate it completely. Once prices are *expected* to rise, the interest rate rises immediately, while prices and incomes rise only with a lag. Hence, potential home buyers face higher monthly payments before their incomes have actually risen, and before they can be certain that their incomes actually will rise.[4]

Consumerists also worry that some people may take out variable-rate mortgages without really understanding what it is they are getting into. Still another problem—and one that may actually be much more important— is that if variable-rate mortgages become widespread, a strong pressure group in favor of low interest rates will result.

Nonetheless, in April 1980 federally chartered savings and loan associations were given the right to make a type of mortgage loan that is quite similar to a variable-rate mortgage without having to offer fixed-rate mortgages as an alternative. These new mortgages are a partial return

---

[3] Actually, with a variable-rate mortgage, the *after tax* real rate of interest falls even if the interest rate rises as much as the inflation rate, because a borrower (who does not use the standard deduction on the income tax) can deduct his or her interest payment from taxable income, while the lender has to pay income taxes on what is in effect a return of capital. If prices rise by 3 percent, a 9 percent interest payment really represents a 3 percent return of capital and only a 6 percent interest income. But all 9 percent is taxed as income.

[4] In addition, a higher inflation rate means that the buyers are repaying their mortgages at a faster rate. Suppose, for example, that the inflation rate is 10 percent, that the nominal mortgage rate is 15 percent, and that a family takes out a 90 percent mortgage on a $100,000 home. At the end of the year the value of the house has risen to $110,000 so that, disregarding the repayment made on the mortgage during the year, the value of the mortgage is now equivalent to only 82 percent of the value of the house ($90,000 ÷ $110,000) compared to the previous 90 percent. The family has thus been forced by inflation to repay (through its 15 percent interest payments) 8 percent of the value of the house during this year. This may be a faster repayment schedule than the family wants. There exists another type of mortgage that avoids this problem by, in effect, raising the outstanding principal on the loan rather than the interest rate when prices increase. But this type of mortgage is complex, and so far has not caught on to the extent that the variable-rate mortgage has.

to the old system of fairly short-term mortgages. While the whole life of the mortgage may be, say, thirty years, the mortgage is renewable every three or five years. And although the renewal is quite automatic, it is renewed at an interest rate reflecting current market conditions with two limitations: the interest rate cannot rise by more than an average of a half a percentage point per year, and second, it cannot rise by more than five percentage points over the whole life of the mortgage. While this new rule affects only federally chartered savings and loan associations, state-chartered ones will surely be given the right to issue such mortgages too, because otherwise they might turn in their state charters and take out federal charters instead. This new ruling *may* therefore signal the virtual end of the traditional fixed-rate long-term mortgage.

The widespread of use of such mortgages, or of variable-rate mortgages is, however, not the only way the effective maturity of thrift institution assets can be reduced. Giving them the right to make consumer loans also reduces the average maturity of their assets.

Price discrimination. Another possible solution, or partial solution, is to make greater use of price discrimination. Not all depositors in thrift institutions are sensitive to interest-rate differentials; small savers have relatively limited opportunities to lend at higher rates on the open market. It is deposits of $10,000 and over—those large enough to buy the lowest denomination Treasury bill—that are most likely to leave thrift institutions as the interest rate on Treasury bills and other securities rises significantly above the Regulation Q ceiling. Hence, in addition to the price discrimination already discussed in chapter 5, in June 1978 mutual savings banks and savings and loan associations were allowed to offer six-months certificates, called money-market certificates, that paid one-quarter of one percent more than the Treasury bill rate. And in 1979 they were allowed to issue four-year certificates with an interest rate that fluctuates with the yield on four-year government bonds. Similar two-and-a-half-year certificates were also tried, but a "cap" was then imposed on their interest rate.[5] The money-market certificates were successful, at least initially, in protecting the residential construction industry from disintermediation. Figure 8.1 shows that in 1978 residential construction activity remained at a high level even though the Treasury bill rate rose more than one percent above the thrift institution passbook rate, while previously residential construction activity had declined sharply at such times. But by early 1980, thrift institutions were experiencing a drought of new funds, and either as a result of this, or of high interest rates, housing starts fell drastically.

The savings and loan industry has complained about having to pay such a higher interest rate on a substantial part of its deposits; by the end of March 1980 money-market certificates had risen to about 30 percent of total savings and loan deposits. (There were reports that some

---

[5] Commercial banks, however, could pay only the Treasury bill rate, while credit unions could pay half a percent above the bill rate.

Figure 8.1   New Privately Owned Housing Units Started

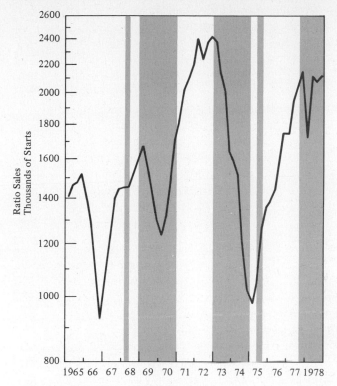

Shaded areas indicate periods when bond equivalent yield on three-month Treasury bills is greater than thrift institution passbook rates by a 100 or more basis points.

SOURCE: R. Alton Gilbert and Jean M. Lovati, "Disintermediation: An Old Disorder with a New Remedy," *Review* (Federal Reserve Bank of St. Louis) 61 (January 1979): 14.

savings and loan associations are investing these high-priced funds in large negotiable CDs, rather than using them to make mortgage loans.) Hence, in March 1979, the yield on money-market certificates was reduced by prohibiting the compounding of interest on them. This may seem minor, but it is not; for example, on a six-month certificate a 9.75 percent interest rate becomes about 10.25 percent with daily compounding. In addition, the interest-rate ceiling was lowered from one-quarter of one percent above the Treasury bill rate to just the Treasury bill rate whenever the Treasury bill rate exceeds 9 percent. But this led to a reduction of the inflow of funds into thrift institutions since there are some advantages to buying Treasury bills.[6]

[6] Treasury bills are sold on a discount basis. Hence, a Treasury bill rate of 10 percent represents a yield of *more* than 10 percent. For example, assume that the interest rate on a one-year Treasury bill is 10 percent. The buyer pays only $9,000 for a $10,000 Treasury bill since it is sold on a discount basis, so that he or she earns $1,000 on $9,000, an interest rate of 11 percent, not 10 percent. In addition, the interest received on Treasury bills is exempt from state and local income taxes.

Figure 8.2   Net Increase in Outstanding Mortgage Debt and Percent of
Net Increase Accounted for by Federally Sponsored Credit Agencies
1964–78

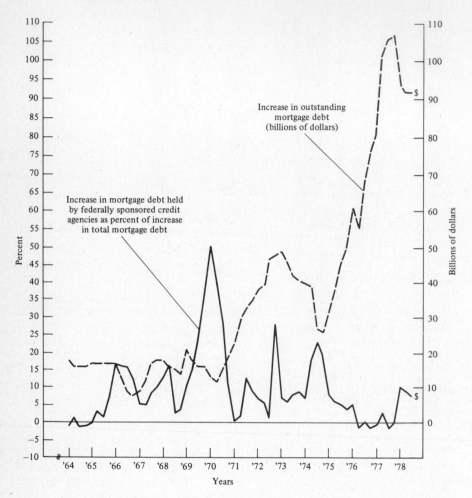

SOURCE: Unpublished data provided through the courtesy of the Board of Governors of the
Federal Reserve System.

As a last resort, another way of protecting the residential construction
industry is, despite its interference with private markets, for the federal
government to provide mortgage funds when rising interest rates draw
deposit funds away from thrift institutions. And, as figure 8.2 shows, it
has done this on a substantial scale to offset—in part—the disintermediation resulting from Regulation Q. For example, in the first quarter of 1970
federally sponsored credit agencies accounted for about half of the net
increase in outstanding mortgage debt.

In summary then, by the late 1970s the attempt to use Regulation Q to "solve" the problem of the thrift institutions' long-term assets and short-term liabilities was failing. Fortunately, the more fundamental solution of shortening thrift institution assets while lengthening their liabilities was making some headway. But it was too slow. Hence, as we shall discuss shortly, in 1980 a new law began to phase out the Regulation Q ceiling. But to explain this new law we must first discuss competition between types of financial institutions.

Interindustry Competition

As discussed in chapter 2, regulations impose barriers to competition between various types of financial institutions. Although commercial banks are allowed wide-ranging activities, savings and loan associations have been confined primarily to mortgage lending in the hope that this will raise the supply of mortgage funds. But this does not work in the long run because in the long run depositors can switch their deposits away from those financial institutions required to make less profitable loans (and hence providing a lower yield to depositors) into those institutions that can earn a higher rate of return. As a result there has been much discussion of eliminating the barriers that more or less tie thrift institutions to mortgages. As previously pointed out, permitting savings and loan associations to make consumer loans is a way to ameliorate their long-term assets/short-term liabilities problem.

Another way of giving thrift institutions greater scope is to allow them to issue demand deposits or NOW accounts. This obviously helps them to obtain a larger share of the deposit market.

Breaking down the barriers between banks and thrift institutions by allowing the latter to offer checkable deposits, and to diversify their assets out of mortgages has much to recommend it. First, there is the usual argument for letting the market decide what each firm will produce. If thrift institutions can earn more by making consumer loans and issuing demand deposits, then, in the absence of externalities, letting them do so improves resource allocation. Second, allowing thrift institutions to make consumer loans, and perhaps even business loans, and to issue demand deposits creates more competition for banks, and, as we saw in chapter 3, in many localities there are now too few banks for effective competition. Third, as already discussed, it ameliorates the long-term assets/short-term liabilities problem of thrift institutions.

This does not mean, however, that such a reform is *necessarily* a "good thing." Allowing savings and loan associations to make consumer loans probably reduces their mortgage lending. *If* one believes, as many people do, that there are significant externalities to housing, *and* that a decline in the volume of mortgage lending by thrift institutions would cause a substantial decrease in residential construction, then one may well oppose permitting them to make consumer loans. But if, at the same time, they are allowed to have NOW accounts, then the inflow of new deposits may well be large enough so that their mortgage lending would increase despite their making consumer loans.

Financial Reform: Problems and Difficulties

Over the years it became clear that minor tinkering with the financial structure would not solve the problem; basic reforms such as increasing interindustry competition or the phasing out of Regulation Q were needed. But reform was very slow in coming. One reason is that it is hard to get agreement on what needs changing; it is much easier to agree that *some* change is needed than to agree on exactly what this change should be. But the intellectual difficulties of financial reform are only part of the story. A much bigger obstacle is that any meaningful reforms take something away from some institutions and industries who won't "sit still" for this. And these industries, particularly the building industry savings and loan "complex," have great political power. Since there is no strong countervailing constituency for financial reform, it is unlikely that Congress will accept any reform plan that these institutions all oppose.[7] Imagine that a congressperson votes for a bill strongly opposed by both banks and savings and loan associations. There are probably several of these in his or her district, and their managers may now support the opposition candidate. And what countervailing support does the congressperson get in exchange? Will the general public be much influenced by his or her vote on a perhaps obscure piece of legislation dealing with an issue most voters think is too complex for them to understand? Moreover, many voters look upon bankers as being specially knowledgeable in this area, so that bankers' opposition is likely to cost a congressperson dearly.

What does help the cause of reform is that there are potential gainers as well as losers. For example, banks lose if thrift institutions are allowed to make consumer loans, but thrift institutions obviously gain. One might therefore expect that the political pressures from potential gainers and losers would more or less cancel out, and that the issue can be decided on its merits. But, for reasons that are not clear, this is usually not the way it works. Various types of financial institutions have enough power to keep others out of their turf, but not enough to invade the others' turf. *Perhaps* the explanation for this is an evolutionary one: that by now each type of institution already holds all the territory it could capture and defend

---

[7] Should one blame Congress for heeding the "special interests" and not the objective economists who propose reform? *Perhaps* not. Put yourself in the position of a congressperson who is told by an academic economist that a certain proposal would raise public welfare, and by a lobbyist that it would seriously hurt his industry. Public welfare should certainly be put in first place, but the economist talking about what would increase it may well be wrong. On the other hand, the lobbyist, though perhaps exaggerating, is not likely to be wrong in saying that his industry would be hurt since it is much easier to judge impacts on an industry than on the whole economy.

against intrusion. Or perhaps it is that fear of the new makes each industry fight harder to maintain its present turf than to capture a new one. Or perhaps congressional inertia is so strong that it takes *much* more powerful pressures to change laws than to maintain them on the books.

The obvious solution for such a situation where each pressure group can hold its own territory is to present a reform package that allows these groups to make trades. For example, savings and loan associations might "buy" from banks the right to have demand deposits and to make consumer loans by giving up their one-quarter percent higher Regulation Q ceiling.

Several such package solutions have been tried. In 1970, President Nixon appointed a commission (called the Hunt Commission after its chairman) consisting mainly of representatives of various financial institutions to recommend financial reform. The commission's proposals, which included the phasing out of the Regulation Q ceiling, consisted of extensive trade-offs. A revised version of the proposals was sent to Congress in 1973 but was rejected. In 1975 Congress attempted its own financial reform when the House Committee on Banking, Currency, and Housing came up with some trade-off proposals, again including the gradual elimination of the Regulation Q ceiling. But this attempt too failed.

All efforts at major financial reform appeared stymied, and it seemed that Donald Hester was right when he wrote:

> Historically, American monetary reforms have almost always been the result of unusually severe failures of the financial system or of war. The two early national banks surely facilitated war debt finance; and the National Banking Act was obviously a consequence of the Civil War. A series of sharp financial crises led to the founding of the Federal Reserve System, and most other major agencies regulating financial institutions emerged during the Depression. . . .
>
> The very pessimistic conclusion is that enlightened preventive maintenance of the financial mechanism is unlikely to occur. To be sure, legislation affecting financial institutions will be enacted, but it is likely to be the outcome of smoky cloakrooms and take the form of inadequately illuminated riders.[8]

The 1980 Financial Reform

But in March 1980 financial reform finally arrived. Why is hard to say. Probably a major factor was that if new legislation had not passed, credit unions would have lost their right to have what are de facto demand deposits, while savings and loan associations would have lost a powerful marketing tool, the right to have in various places, such as supermarkets, remote terminals that accept deposits and allow withdrawals. And banks would have lost the right to offer the automatic transfer services that shift funds automatically from the depositor's savings account into his or her

---

[8] Donald Hester, "Special Interests: The FINE Situation," *Journal of Money, Credit and Banking* 9 (November 1977): 653–55.

demand deposit to meet incoming checks. (All of these powers had been given under an interpretation of a previous law, but in 1979 the Supreme Court had ruled that this was not legal.) Only by agreeing to various reforms that the other institutions wanted could banks, savings and loan associations, and credit unions get new legislation that would ensure their rights to continue to offer these services. A related factor that may have been important is that groups that represent the depositors' interests, such as the Grey Panthers, put pressure on Congress to eliminate the Regulation Q ceiling.

In any case, Regulation Q was proving itself less and less effective in protecting thrift institutions. With depositors switching from other time deposits into money-market certificates, thrift institutions were paying approximately the market rate of interest on a rapidly growing share of their deposits. And had the government tried to "cap" the interest rate on money-market certificates, thrift institutions would have suffered a substantial outflow of funds. With the incentive of high interest rates on open-market securities, depositors were becoming more and more sophisticated and it became less and less feasible to exploit them.

Still another factor that may have played a role is that at the time the inflation rate was accelerating sharply, and Congress felt that it had to accept painful remedies, such as cutting cherished government programs. At such a time it was probably readier to overrule the banking industry, and give the Fed the control over nonmember bank reserve requirements that it claimed was needed for effective monetary control.

The new law is a complex compromise.[9] The thrift institutions will eventually lose the Regulation Q ceiling, and with it, of course, the one-quarter of one percent higher interest rates that banks dislike so much. The ceiling will not be eliminated right away, but will be phased out over a six-year period. The speed with which this is done is determined by a committee, the Depository Institutions Deregulation Committee, on which all the federal agencies that regulate banks, savings and loan associations, and credit unions are represented. This committee is given specific targets for the interest-rate ceiling over the next six years, but may depart from these targets if conditions require.[10]

In exchange, federally chartered thrift institutions are permitted to have NOW accounts. (State-chartered ones are sure to get the same right from their state authorities to preserve their competitive position.) In addition, they are given the right to maintain remote terminals.

On the asset side, federally chartered savings and loan associations (and soon surely state-chartered ones too) will have the right to invest up to 20 percent of their assets in consumer loans, commercial paper, and

---

[9] The name of the law is the Depository Institutions Deregulation and Monetary Control Act of 1980.

[10] The target is a one-quarter percentage point rise in the first eighteen months, another one-half percentage point in the next eighteen months, and a one-half percentage point rise in each of the following three years.

corporate debt securities. They are also permitted to provide credit cards and lines of credit and to offer trust services.[11] Moreover, geographic limitations on their mortgage loans are removed, as is the $75,000 limit on their mortgages, and in the case of residential real estate, the restriction to first mortgages.

In addition, there is a provision that benefits all federally insured financial institutions. This is that state usury-law ceilings on their first mortgage loans are eliminated unless the states reimpose these ceilings within three years.[12] Another provision protects these institutions for three years from low state usury law ceilings on commercial and industrial loans of over $25,000 by setting the maximum interest rate at 5 percent above the Fed's discount rate.

Other provisions of the law, and we cannot discuss all of them, provide a higher, permanent usury law ceiling for federally chartered credit unions who also, as already mentioned, are allowed to maintain their de facto checking accounts. Still another provision simplifies the truth-in-lending regulations. And federal deposit insurance ceilings are raised from $40,000 to $100,000. Last, but not least, as discussed in chapter 4, the Fed's reserve requirements are changed and are applied to nonmember banks as well as to the transaction (NOW) accounts and nonpersonal time deposits of thrift institutions. And while before only member banks could normally borrow from the Federal Reserve, now all of these institutions that keep reserves with it will be able to do so.

All in all, it is the most important piece of financial institutions legislation since at least the 1930s. But it still leaves some unresolved problems to which we now turn.

Competition in Banking

A number of economists would like to reform the banking industry by making it more competitive. Banking competition is now limited in several ways. The most obvious one is the restriction on entry, since someone wishing to open a new national bank (and in many states a state bank too) must show that there exists a "need" for a new bank, and that its establishment would not unduly weaken existing banks. Is this justified? Since depositors are generally protected by FDIC insurance, shouldn't banks be treated just like other firms, and subjected to the same process of weeding out of weak firms that cannot meet the competition? Of course, one can argue that there are larger unfavorable externalities from bank failures

[11] They are also given some more technical powers. In addition, federal mutual savings banks are given the right to make some business loans.

[12] If the states can override the federal override, why does the latter matter? The answer is that the state legislatures may want to raise their usury ceilings but may be afraid to do so because of adverse voter reaction. But there may be less voter reaction if they simply do not override the federal law.

than from failures in other industries, since banks have more debt per dollar of capital than do other firms. Hence, when a bank fails, it is the FDIC and certain creditors who sometimes lose more than the stockholders who deserve to lose when a firm fails. But does this justify *all* the protection from competition that banks are given?

Similarly, as discussed in chapter 3, another serious restraint on competition, the limitation on branching, has been defended as needed to prevent great aggregations of economic power.

But, all in all, protecting banks from new entrants and from branching by other banks seems difficult to justify, particularly since the government already gives banks other important privileges by restricting to them the right to issue demand deposits. And even though this special privilege has now been weakened substantially by the development of NOW accounts, only households and nonprofit organizations may hold NOW accounts. If there is effective competition among banks, the fact that only banks can issue demand deposits does not raise their profits because new entry, and the expansion of existing banks, forces them to pass the potential profits from money creation on to customers. But if the government limits entry into the industry, limits the expansion of existing banks by branching restrictions, and prohibits the payment of explicit interest on demand deposits, then banks may gain excess profits from their right to create money. The fact that bank charters are much sought after suggests that they do confer the right to garner a profit in excess of the competitive rate of return.

Modifying the Bank Regulatory Structure

Banks are regulated in a highly complex way that is often criticized as inefficient. In particular, banks are in the strange position of being able to choose their regulators. A bank can decide whether to operate under a federal or a state charter. For example, in 1979 when the New York State banking commissioner did not permit a large bank, the Marine Midland Bank, to merge into a foreign bank, the Hong Kong and Shanghai Banking Corp., the Marine Midland simply handed in its state charter and took out a national charter instead. Not only can a bank decide its chartering agency, but a state bank can also choose whether or not to be a member bank. If it wants to, a bank can therefore avoid being supervised by federal banking agencies, except for the FDIC, which practically every bank has to join. Giving banks the right to decide whether they want to abide by the stricter federal regulations, or by the generally more relaxed state regulations may seem strange; firms in other regulated industries are certainly not permitted to choose their regulatory agencies.[13]

Not only can banks choose their supervising agencies, they can play

---

[13] On the other hand, there is little evidence that banks have "captured" their federal regulatory agencies to the extent other regulated industries have.

one off against the other. Many economists believe that since the regulatory agencies do not want to lose banks from their supervision, they compete among themselves for banks, at least to some extent, by limiting the severity of their regulations. This "competition in laxity" has drawn much criticism from those who are concerned that banks are permitted to take too many risks. American history furnishes many examples of bank failures in which excess risk taking by some banks caused them to fail, which then induced depositors to run other banks, thus causing these banks to fail too. Some economists are worried that even now when FDIC insurance has eliminated the small depositors' incentive to run shaky banks, seriously disruptive bank failures could still occur.

But by no means do all economists agree that such alleged competition in laxity is bad. Many argue that it provides a useful counterweight to the inherent tendency of bank regulators to impose excessive regulation and to discourage risk taking too much. Bank regulators have an incentive to be too severe because they get blamed if they allow banks to do something that results in some bank failures. But they do *not* get blamed by the public if they prohibit something, say, a new type of loan, that would actually have been quite safe. If they prohibit it nobody ever finds out that it would have been safe. Insofar as this bias in the regulators' own reward and punishment system outweighs the bias that results from the pressures brought to bear by the banking industry, and from the regulators' tendency to be "nice" to their industry, regulations tend to be too severe, and some competition among regulating agencies is desirable. For example, NOW accounts would probably not have developed if all our financial intermediaries were regulated by a single government agency.

From time to time, bills are introduced in Congress to limit "competition in laxity" by abolishing one or more of the federal regulatory agencies, though most proposals would leave the state regulatory agencies untouched. Eliminating some of these agencies would also have the advantage of reducing the complexity and duplication of effort inherent in having several supervisory agencies. Former Federal Reserve Governor Sheehan has written: "Few who have not dealt with the problem personally can understand the complexity, inefficiency, overlapping responsibility and confusion which are involved in the hodge-podge of bank regulation as it has evolved in this country." [14]

The most radical proposal would eliminate state bank charters altogether and require all banks to take out a national charter. But this proposal has virtually no chance of becoming law in the foreseeable future. A more feasible reform—though even this is not likely to become law soon—would centralize *federal* bank supervision in a single government

---

[14] "1975—The Year for Federal Banking Regulation Reform," in U.S., Congress, Senate, Committee on Banking, Housing, and Urban Affairs, *Compendium on Major Issues in Bank Regulation*, 94th Cong., 1st sess., May 1975, p. 892. (For a contrary view, see the memorandum by Carter Golembe Associates reprinted in the same volume, p. 911.)

agency. But which one should this be? State banks would object to being supervised by the chartering agency for national banks, the Comptroller of the Currency. Similarly, nonmember banks would object to being regulated by the Federal Reserve. Moreover, enhanced regulatory duties might also distract the Federal Reserve from its primary duty of making monetary policy. In one way, the FDIC would be the logical choice as the sole regulating agency since it is the FDIC that has to pay out if banks fail. But this very fact may induce it to be overly cautious and to prohibit desirable risk taking. Hence, some economists have proposed vesting all federal bank regulation in an entirely new agency set up solely for this purpose. But, rightly or wrongly, others are afraid that the banks could "capture" such a single regulatory agency more easily than they can the present ones.

Not surprisingly, none of the present regulatory agencies wants to give up control over its banks. For example, the Federal Reserve argues that the information it obtains from bank examinations helps it in deciding on monetary policy. But some economists doubt this, and believe that the Fed could make better decisions about monetary policy if it had *less* contact with banks, since too much contact with banks *may* induce the Fed to give too much weight to their special concerns when making decisions about monetary policy.

Electronic Funds Transfer

The American financial system may also need reform because of changing technology. Eventually paper checks will be replaced in large part by a system of electronic funds transfer. One part of this system, point of sale terminals that allow customers to make deposits and withdraw currency in stores equipped with these terminals, has already eliminated some of the restrictions on branch banking, because such terminals allow depositors to do their banking right in the supermarket.

But the electronic transfer of funds is likely to bring about many other changes. Among these, Mark Flannery and Dwight Jaffee suggest, is an erosion of the distinction between demand and other deposits, since an EFT system will allow depositors to transfer funds immediately and almost effortlessly between demand deposits and time deposits in banks and thrift institutions. It will also reduce the distinction between banks and thrift institutions. This will result in a more competitive financial market, as well as in the development of long-term consumer loans and the spread of automatic overdraft systems. To get ready for electronic banking, Flannery and Jaffee suggest that all financial intermediaries should be allowed to hold the same assets, for example, thrift institutions should be permitted to make business loans and operate mutual funds.[15]

[15] Mark Flannery and Dwight Jaffee, *The Economic Implications of an Electronic Monetary Transfer System* (Lexington, Mass.: Lexington Books, 1973), p. 113.

Summary

In this chapter we considered a number of weaknesses of the financial structure and some solutions for them. The biggest factor behind the need for reform is that our financial structure was built for a world of little or no inflation. This is basic to the special problems of the thrift institutions that led to the imposition of Regulation Q. But Regulation Q has its own problems. It leads at times to disintermediation, it discriminates against some depositors, it causes waste by suppressing price competition, and it results in a fudging of the line between money and other liquid assets. We therefore looked at several alternative policies: the simple repeal of Regulation Q; getting thrift institutions into assets with shorter effective maturities, such as variable-interest-rate mortgages and consumer loans; lengthening the liabilities of thrift institutions; government intervention; and greater price discrimination by thrift institutions. We then considered the 1980 financial reforms that will phase out the Regulation Q ceiling, institute nationwide NOW accounts, and extend the Fed's reserve requirements to all banks.

But the 1980 reforms, important as they are, do not settle all disputed issues about regulating financial institutions. Hence we discussed regulations that limit competition in banking, that is, entry restrictions and branching restrictions. Turning to the way banks are supervised, we discussed the arguments for and against eliminating "competition in laxity" by ending the banks' ability to choose their regulatory agencies, and took up the question of what agency should supervise banks. We also looked briefly at some implications of electronic fund transfers.

QUESTIONS AND EXERCISES

1. State in your own words why inflation has created a need for financial reform.
2. Write an essay advocating the elimination of Regulation Q, and another essay advocating its retention.
3. Write an essay developing your suggestions for solving the problem of thrift institutions.
4. Do you favor the centralization of federal bank supervision? Why or why not?
5. What were the major aspects of the 1980 financial reform? What data would you look at to see if this legislation was successful?

FURTHER READING

BRUNNER, KARL, ed. "The President's Commission on Financial Structure and Regulation: A Symposium." *Journal of Money, Credit and Banking* 3 (February 1971): 1–34. A series of papers on the task facing the Hunt Commission.

FEDERAL RESERVE BANK OF BOSTON. *Policies for a More Competitive Financial System.* Boston: Federal Reserve Bank of Boston, 1972. A series of papers on a wide range of issues.

FLANNERY, MARK, and JAFFEE, DWIGHT. *The Economic Implications of an Electronic Monetary Transfer System.* Lexington, Mass.: Lexington Books, 1973. A detailed and thorough study.

MCNEILL, CHARLES, and RECHTER, DENISE. "The Depository Institutions Deregulation and Monetary Control Act of 1979." *Federal Reserve Bulletin* 66 (June 1980): 444–53. A useful summary of complex legislation.

MELTZER, ALLEN. "Major Issues in the Regulation of Financial Institutions." *Journal of Political Economy* 75 (August 1967): *Supplement* 482–501. A stimulating plea for greater reliance on free-market processes.

U.S. CONGRESS, HOUSE, COMMITTEE ON BANKING, CURRENCY, AND HOUSING. *Financial Institutions and the Nation's Economy, Compendium of Papers prepared for the FINE Study.* 94th Cong., 2d sess., 1976. A series of papers underlying the 1975 congressional reform effort.

U.S. CONGRESS, SENATE, COMMITTEE ON BANKING, HOUSING, AND URBAN AFFAIRS. *Compendium of Major Issues in Bank Regulations.* 94th cong., 1st sess., 1975. A large number of papers on many detailed aspects of bank regulation by economists, lawyers, and regulators.

PART TWO

||||||||||||||||||||||||||||||||||||||||||||||||||||||||||||||||||||||||||||||||||||||||||||||||||||||||||||||||||||||||||||

The Supply
of Money

The growth rate of the supply of money is a factor of great, perhaps overwhelming, importance in determining the course of a country's economy.
Over the long run it dominates the behavior of prices. Hence, we will spend
much time in this book discussing how the money stock is—or should be—
growing, and how this affects the economy. In this part we will take up how
money is created and measured. Part Three will then discuss the way in
which changes in the money supply affect income, while Part Five deals with
the Federal Reserve's policy with respect to the money stock and interest
rates.

Chapter 9 explains how banks can use their reserves to create deposits.
The following chapter discusses where banks get their reserves. Chapter 11
then takes up again the definition of money discussed in chapter 1, but this
time we can get much more specific. In this connection we also discuss the
difficulties that the Federal Reserve encounters in actually measuring the
money stock.

The material discussed in this section is less descriptive, and more
abstract, than that taken up in the previous section. Hence, it should require
less memorization, but more understanding of basic principles. Students
should avoid memorizing the arithmetic examples without understanding
what is really going on.

9

The Creation
of Money

In previous chapters when discussing banking we were primarily concerned with banks as private firms, for example, with the types of loans they make. But, for economists, what is even more important about banks is that they create deposits, that is, money. About three-quarters of our current money supply (*M-1*) consists of demand deposits. Since major changes in the quantity of money can generate substantial changes in unemployment, and in the long run determine the price level, there is every reason to take up deposit creation in considerable detail. We will first discuss it in terms of the traditional M_1 and M_2 definitions of money that include only deposits in commercial banks, and then subsequently relate it to the new definitions of money. But before we turn to that topic, we will discuss briefly the much easier topic of how the other component of our money stock, currency, is created.

Currency

The creation of currency is simple and straightforward. The U.S. Bureau of the Mint and the U.S. Bureau of Printing and Engraving, both agencies of the U.S. Treasury Department, buy various types of metal and paper and turn them into coins and paper money. How they do so interests counterfeiters, not economists. But the mere act of printing a currency note does not actually create money. We define money to include, not all the currency notes that have been printed, but only those held by the nonbank public, since notes that are printed but not held by the nonbank public do not affect aggregate demand. (The nonbank public is everyone in the economy besides the federal government and banks.) In principle, we should deduct from the total of outstanding currency those currency notes that are lost, destroyed, or sent abroad. Unfortunately, no reliable data on such currency losses are available, and hence cannot be subtracted. However, there is some evidence, from episodes when old currency issues were taken out of circulation, that currency losses are minor since nearly all the notes that had been issued were turned in; or perhaps the number of cleverly forged notes equals approximately the number of genuine notes that were lost or destroyed.

The way currency gets into the hands of the nonbank public is un-complicated: someone withdraws it from a bank. The bank then replenishes its currency supply by "buying" currency from a Federal Reserve bank, which debits the bank's account for this currency. The amount of currency in circulation therefore depends upon how much currency the public wants, given its total money holdings, that is, deposits plus currency. While it is getting a bit ahead of the story, note that our monetary policy never tries to control the supply of currency directly.[1] It operates by changing interest rates and the supply of money. It is entirely up to the public to determine what proportion of its money holdings it wants to hold as currency. The Federal Reserve and the Treasury then supply the banks with whatever currency they need to meet the demands of the public.[2]

Demand Deposits

Demand deposits are created by commercial banks every time a bank credits a customer's checking account. This is simple and obvious. But what is far from simple is that if a customer deposits a dollar of currency in a bank, the banking system as a whole can create several dollars of deposits. The main stumbling block in understanding this process of multiple deposit creation is that it gives the impression that something is created out of nothing. We shall try to avoid this confusion by showing first that deposits are not material objects.

The Nature of Deposits

What actually is a **deposit?** It is not a physical object like currency, but merely *a property right evidenced by an entry in the bank's books.* You cannot see a deposit, or hold it in your hand, any more than you can hold in your hand the right to a jury trial or someone's promise. This is confusing because when we speak of someone drawing a deposit out of the bank and receiving currency in exchange for the deposit, there cer-

[1] In some foreign countries, as well as in the Confederacy during the Civil War, a certain monetary policy that affects currency has been used. This is a so-called monetary reform when a highly inflated currency is called in and replaced by a new issue on a less than one-to-one basis. (Bank deposits are frozen and also converted into new deposits on a less than one-to-one basis.) In this way the quantity of money is reduced in one fell swoop. This was done, for example, after World War II in a number of European countries in which the quantity of money had been increased greatly during the German occupation.

[2] The exceptions to this are trivial or rare. One is a coin shortage when the mints cannot keep up with the unexpectedly high demand for certain coins. For example, in 1974 there was a shortage of pennies. Another exception was the closing of banks in 1933, to prevent further runs on them.

tainly is tangible currency being withdrawn. But when you "draw out your deposit" what you are actually doing is exchanging your right to receive payment from the bank in the future for a certain number of currency notes. When banks create deposits, they no more create something out of nothing than the Supreme Court does when it creates a new legal right. In neither case does what is created have any physical existence, and hence the law of conservation of matter and energy is not contradicted. It is important to keep this in mind because if you think of a deposit as a physical object like currency, the subsequent discussion of deposit creation becomes incomprehensible.

Two Special Cases

As one more preliminary to multiple deposit creation we will now take up two special cases in which it does *not* occur, and this will provide a hint as to why it does occur in more realistic situations.

One hundred percent reserves. The first special case is one in which the law in its awful majesty requires that the bank keep 100 percent reserves against its demand deposits. Consider what happens when a depositor brings $10,000 of currency to a bank to open an account. We can see this best by looking at a **T account,** *a condensed version of the bank's balance sheet,* which leaves out all previous entries, and shows just the ones we are currently considering. Such a T account now shows:

(1)

Assets		Liabilities	
currency	$10,000	demand deposit	$10,000

This bank is now in equilibrium; it has exactly the reserves that the law says it must hold against its deposit. Has there been multiple deposit creation? Certainly not. A $10,000 of deposits has been created against a $10,000 of currency reserves. This is a one-to-one ratio; there is nothing multiple about it. So this example demonstrates that one condition for multiple deposit creation is that the reserve ratio be less than 100 percent.

Loans in currency only. But does a reserve ratio of less than 100 percent *suffice* to give us multiple deposit creation? No, it does not. Consider another unrealistic case in which the required reserve ratio is only, say, 20 percent, but in which a borrower when he or she is granted a bank loan takes the proceeds entirely in the form of currency, and continues to hold this currency. In this case, since the required reserve ratio is less than 100 percent, the above T account does not represent an equilibrium for the bank. It can increase its profits by lending out $8,000 of the initial $10,000 deposit or by buying an $8,000 security, keeping the other $2,000 as a reserve against its deposits. Its T account now, after it has made a loan, looks as follows:

(2)

Assets		Liabilities	
currency	$2,000	demand deposit	$10,000
loan outstanding	$8,000		

This bank is now in equilibrium; it holds just the reserves it must hold against its deposit. But again, there has been no multiple deposit creation: the bank initially received $10,000 of currency, that is reserves, and $10,000 of deposits are outstanding, so that deposits have increased in a one-to-one ratio to reserves.

Multiple Deposit Creation

We now drop the peculiar assumption that a borrower, or seller of a security, holds the proceeds of a loan in the form of currency. This is most improbable because someone is not likely to borrow and pay interest unless he or she wants to use the money to make a purchase. And whomever he or she buys from is not likely to hold currency either, but will deposit the funds into a bank account. Since neither individuals nor corporations normally hoard currency, we can safely, as a first approximation, assume that all the proceeds of a sale will be deposited in a bank. (Later on an allowance will be made for the fact that this assumption is not *quite* correct.) We will now also assume that there is a 20 percent reserve requirement.

For reasons that will become clear later in this chapter, we simplify by assuming further that the public does not increase its time deposits and that banks use all their available reserves to make loans or to buy securities instead of holding some idle reserves.

How Multiple Deposit Creation Occurs

Consider now again a situation where someone deposits $10,000 of currency into a bank, which we shall call bank A. As in the previous case, this bank's T account now looks as follows:

BANK A

(3)

Assets		Liabilities	
currency	$10,000	demand deposits	$10,000

And, as before, since the bank has $8,000 more than the required 20 percent reserves, it increases its loans, and writes up the borrower's demand-deposit account by the amount of the loan. Its T account is:

BANK A

(4)	*Assets*		*Liabilities*	
	currency	$10,000	demand deposits	$18,000
	loan outstanding	$ 8,000		

It now sends the $10,000 of currency on to its Federal Reserve bank, so that its T account becomes:

BANK A

(5)	*Assets*		*Liabilities*	
	currency	0	demand deposits	$18,000
	loans outstanding	$ 8,000		
	reserves with F.R.	$10,000		

In the meantime the borrower does not sit on the $10,000 he or she has borrowed, but uses the funds to make a purchase. And the seller now deposits the $8,000 check received into his or her bank, bank B, which sends it to the Federal Reserve for clearing. After it clears, bank A's T account is:

BANK A

(6)	*Assets*		*Liabilities*	
	currency	0	demand deposits	$10,000
	loans outstanding	$8,000		
	reserves with F.R.	$2,000		

Its reserves, $2,000, are now just sufficient to cover the $10,000 deposit it has outstanding, so it is in equilibrium. However, bank B has now received $8,000 of deposits and reserves, which gives it the following T account:

BANK B

(7)	*Assets*		*Liabilities*	
	reserves with F.R.	$8,000	demand deposits	$8,000

But there is no reason why bank B should want to keep 100 percent reserves against the deposit. It needs to keep only $1,600 ($8,000 times 20 percent) reserves and can use the remainder, $6,400, to make a loan or buy a security. When the borrower, or seller of the security, spends the $6,400 the recipient deposits the check into his or her bank, bank C, which sends it to the Federal Reserve for clearing. As a result, bank B's T account becomes:

BANK B

(8)

Assets		Liabilities	
reserves with F.R.	$1,600	demand deposits	$8,000

Bank B is now in equilibrium, having just the $1,600 reserves it needs, and no more. But the story continues with bank C, which has received $6,400 of deposits and of reserves. It, too, will keep only 20 percent, that is, $1,280, as a reserve against the $6,400 deposit, and use $5,120 to buy a security or make a loan, which, by the now familiar process, will become a deposit in bank D, so that bank D can now lend out 80 percent of it, $4,096, which, in turn, will become a deposit in bank E, and that bank will again lend out, or buy a security with, 80 percent of this deposit.[3]

In this process, deposits are being created by every bank in the chain; we have deposits of $10,000 in bank A, $8,000 in bank B, $6,400 in bank C, $5,120 in bank D and $4,096 in bank E, and so on. In other words, we have here **multiple deposit creation;** *the initial deposit has called forth a series of subsequent deposits* in other banks. The two salient reasons why this occurs are, first, that no bank keeps a 100 percent reserve against its deposit and, second, while each bank loses an equivalent amount of reserves when it makes a loan or buys a security, it loses these reserves not to thin air, *but to another bank.* And this other bank then expands its loans or security holdings. In the previously discussed special cases, where banks kept 100 percent reserves, or where borrowers did not redeposit their loans into another bank, there was, as we saw, no multiple deposit creation.

The Demand-Deposit Multiplier

How much does the multiple deposit creation amount to? We have a series here that goes as follows: $10,000, $8,000, $6,400, $5,120, $4,096, and so on, each figure being 80 percent of the preceding one. (There is, of course, nothing special about the 20 percent reserve ratio we are assuming. It is just a number picked arbitrarily for the sake of the argument. Had a 50 percent reserve ratio been used, the sequence of deposits would have been $10,000, $5,000, $2,500, $1,250, . . .) Such a sequence forms a geometric progression

$$R[1 + \frac{1}{1-r} + (\frac{1}{1-r})^2 + (\frac{1}{1-r})^3 + \ldots], \qquad R[1 + (1-r) + (1-r)^2 +$$

and its sum is $\qquad\qquad\qquad\qquad\qquad (1-r)^3 + \ldots]$

$$D = \frac{1}{r} R$$

where D stands for deposits, r is the reserve ratio, and R is the initial increase in reserves that occurred when bank A obtained a $10,000 deposit of

---

[3] As an exercise, write out the T accounts for banks C, D, and E.

currency. With a 20 percent reserve ratio the total of deposit creation amounts to $\frac{1}{0.2}$ $10,000, that is $50,000.[4] Hence, we have here what is called a demand-deposit multiplier ($\frac{1}{r}$) of 5. In general, the **demand-deposit multiplier** is the *change in demand deposits that results from a change in reserves divided by this change in reserves*. (Do not confuse it with the Keynesian investment multiplier that relates a change in investment to the resulting change in income. Both use the same mathematical process, convergent geometric series, but they apply to very different things.)

Another way of explaining the creation of $50,000 of deposits is as follows. The process of a bank making a loan, losing reserves to another bank, and this bank making a loan, and so on, continues until all of the original $10,000 of extra reserves has become required reserves. (Strictly speaking, of course, the process never comes to a stop, but we can allow for this by rounding to the nearest dollar.) If the required reserve ratio is 20 percent, then when all of the $10,000 has become reserves, deposits must be equal to five times required reserves, that is, to $50,000.

The above example of the deposit multiplier is highly unrealistic. For example, we said bank B received $8,000 of reserves and deposits and then lent out exactly $6,400. Obviously, a bank is not likely to make a loan of just that amount. In actuality, banks do not look at particular receipts of reserves and deposits, and then try to lend out, or buy securities for, 80 percent of these particular receipts. Instead, banks have a continual inflow and outflow from a large number of transactions. Each morning a bank looks at the total inflow and outflow of reserves during the previous day, estimates the major changes likely to occur during the current day, and then decides whether it should expand or contract its loans and investments. Since the reserve requirement does not have to be met on a day-to-day basis, and since banks can acquire or dispose of unwanted reserves rapidly through the money market, there is no reason for banks to tie particular loans closely to particular reserve receipts. As a result, there can be a quite substantial delay between the acquisition of reserves and the full expansion of deposits. In fact, one study found that it takes about two years to complete the deposit creation process. But this is a rather controversial finding.

Multiple Deposit Contraction

Now let us consider the opposite case where reserves decrease because a customer withdraws $10,000 of currency from bank A. As in the previous case of deposit expansion, assume that initially bank A does not have any unneeded reserves, but to get some variation into our figures we will work

---

[4] Some readers may feel that if one adds up an infinite number of these geometrically decreasing terms the total *must* eventually exceed $50,000. We can only suggest that if you do not believe us, just try adding up a lot of terms.

with a reserve ratio of 25 percent instead of 20 percent. As bank A pays out the currency from its reserves (remember, vault cash is part of reserves), its T account looks as follows:

BANK A

(9)

Assets		*Liabilities*	
currency	−$10,000	demand deposits	−$10,000

But since the bank kept only $2,500 of reserves against this $10,000 deposit (the reserve ratio being 25 percent), it is short $7,500 of reserves and has to replenish its reserves by selling a security or calling in a loan for $7,500. When it does so, and the check for the security is credited to its Federal Reserve account, its T account becomes:

BANK A

(10)

Assets		*Liabilities*	
reserves		demand deposits	−$10,000
currency	−$10,000		
reserves with F.R.	$ 7,500		
loans and securities	−$ 7,500		

Bank A is now in equilibrium. It has had to pay $10,000 of currency out of its reserves, but has offset this reserve loss in two ways: by obtaining $7,500 of new reserves, and by reducing its required reserves by $2,500 due to the decline in its deposits.

But it has merely shifted part of its reserve shortage to another bank, because when it sold a security to a customer of bank B, it obtained for it a check drawn on bank B. As this check clears, bank B's T account becomes:

BANK B

(11)

Assets		*Liabilities*	
reserves with F.R.	−$7,500	demand deposits	−$7,500

Bank B kept $1,875 (= $7,500 × .25) against the $7,500 deposit, and it is now short $5,625 (= $7,500 − $1,875) of reserves. Hence, it too sells a security, or else calls in a loan, for $5,625. Its T account is:

BANK B

(12)

Assets		*Liabilities*	
reserves with F.R.	−$1,875	demand deposits	−$7,500
	(= −$7,500 + $5,625)		
loans and securities	−$5,625		

Bank B has therefore lost reserves equal to exactly 25 percent of its decline in deposits, and hence is no longer short of reserves. But when it obtained $5,625 by selling a security it received a check drawn on a deposit in bank C. As this check is cleared, bank C is short of reserves, its T account looking like this:

BANK C

(13)

Assets		Liabilities	
reserves with F.R.	−$5,625	demand deposits	−$5,625

Bank C does not have to worry about $1,406 ($= \$5,625 \times .25$) of this loss in its reserves because its deposits have fallen too. But it is still short $4,219 of reserves. So, suppose that it sells a security for $4,219 to a customer of bank D. It now has sufficient reserves again, but bank D is short $3,164 ($4,219 × .75) of reserves. So *it* sells a security, thus passing the problem on to bank E, and so on.

In this process, deposits are decreasing again in a geometrically declining sequence. They fell by $10,000 in bank A, by $7,500 in bank B, by $5,625 in bank C, and so on. Applying the formula for the sum of a declining geometric series again, we can see that deposits must fall by $4,000 or

$$\frac{1}{r} R = \frac{1}{.25} \$10,000.$$

Thus, multiple deposit contraction is just as possible as multiple deposit creation, and not surprisingly, on the mechanistic level we have worked on so far, the two are symmetrical. Any lack of appearance of symmetry is due to our using different reserve ratios in the two examples and showing in some cases the T accounts at different stages in the two processes.

Leakages from the Deposit Creation Process

The legal reserve requirement discussed so far is essentially a leakage from the demand-deposit creation process. It is a leakage because it reduces the volume of deposits that results from a dollar of additional reserves. Consider the extreme case where the reserve requirement is zero. Then, given all our other assumptions, the deposit multiplier would be infinity; a dollar deposited in one bank would lead to a continuous stream of additional one-dollar deposits in other banks.

But the legal reserve requirement is not the only leakage, as becomes apparent once we remove the assumptions made so far: that banks hold only the legally required minimum reserves, and that the public does not want to hold additional currency or time deposits as its demand deposits increase. We will discuss each of these assumptions in turn.

Excess reserves. As we saw in chapter 4, although banks do not earn anything directly on their excess reserve holdings, a profit-maximizing bank will frequently hold excess reserves to avoid either having to borrow from the Federal Reserve to buy deposits in the CD market, or else having to sell short-term securities. However, excess reserves are typically quite small. In the years 1977–79 they averaged only 0.6 percent of total reserves and in only one month of this period did they equal as much as 1.1 percent of total reserves.

How can we introduce excess reserves into the demand-deposit creation process? The simplest way is to think of them as functioning just like required reserves. Suppose a bank gets a $10,000 deposit and lends out only, say, 85 percent of it, holding 15 percent as reserves against this deposit. It does not matter for the deposit creation process whether all of these 15 percent are required reserves, or whether only, say, 14 percent are legally required and 1 percent are excess reserves that the bank wants to hold additionally. In either case, as the bank lends out $8,500, the next bank receives an $8,500 deposit. Hence, now that we allow banks to hold some legally excess reserves we write the demand-deposit multiplier, not just as $d = \frac{1}{r}$, but as $d = \frac{1}{r+e}$, where e is the *percent of each dollar of demand deposit that banks hold voluntarily* as **legally excess reserves.** If the required reserve ratio is 14 percent and banks hold 1 percent legally excess reserves, the deposit multiplier is $\frac{1}{.14 + .01}$ or 6.67.

What do we multiply these multipliers by to obtain total deposits; in other words, what is the multiplicand? If the only leakage is the required reserve ratio we use required reserves; for example, if required reserves are one-fifth of deposits and banks hold $1 billion of required reserves, then deposits are $5 billion. But once we introduce excess reserves we have to multiply the multiplier by total (the required plus excess) reserves. For example, if required plus excess reserves are one-third of deposits, so that the multiplier is 3, and required plus excess reserves are $1 billion, then deposits are $3 billion.

Demand deposits into currency. Next, we remove the assumption that the public does not want to hold any additional currency as its demand deposits increase during the multiple demand deposit creation process. This assumption is quite unrealistic, and was made only to simplify the examples of the deposit creation. In actuality, as the volume of demand deposits expands, and income rises along with it, people will want to exchange some of their additional deposits for currency.

Fortunately, this complication is easy to handle. Suppose that for each dollar of additional demand deposits that it holds the public wants to hold, say, 30 cents more currency. As far as demand-deposit creation is concerned, the 30 cents of currency that the banks have to pay out to the public for every dollar of new deposits are lost to the demand-deposit creation process just as much as are the 14 cents that, in this example, the banks have to keep with the Federal Reserve as required reserves. A bank receiving a $10,000 deposit keeps $1,400 as a legal reserve, $100 as a legally excess reserve, and pays out to the public \$3,000 as currency. Hence it can lend out, or spend on a security, only \$5,500, which then becomes a deposit in the next bank. So we can now write an extended formula for the demand deposit multiplier as

$$d = \frac{1}{r + e + k},$$

where k is the proportion of each dollar of demand deposits that the public withdraws as currency. In this example, we have

$$d = \frac{1}{.14 + .01 + .30} = 2.22.$$

Once currency is introduced as a leakage we must also introduce the fact that both bank reserves and currency are available to satisfy the need for reserves and currency holdings. Hence, the multiplicand is now no longer just R, but $R + C$ where C is volume of currency.[5]

Demand deposits into time deposits. But the shift out of demand deposits into currency is not the only shift that occurs. As someone's demand deposits increase, he or she will want to transfer some of the demand deposits into time deposits to earn additional interest. As discussed in chapter 2, every household and firm has an optimal portfolio, and if it gets more of one asset it will probably exchange some of it for other assets. So we have to make allowance for the fact that as the demand-deposit creation process proceeds there will be some shift out of demand deposits into time deposits.

It may seem that a term could simply be added for time deposits to the denominator of the multiplier formula, as was done in the case of legally excess reserves and currency. But this is not so. When a bank holds additional reserves, or a person withdraws additional currency, this sum is completely lost to the demand-deposit creation process; the next bank in the chain does not get any of it. But this is not so for a dollar shifted from a demand deposit into a time deposit. Here the dollar stays in the bank, and is therefore not completely lost to the demand-deposit expansion process. In fact, if banks did not keep reserves against time deposits, this shift would allow the demand-deposit creation process to go ahead unchanged. But there *are* reserve requirements against time deposits. Hence, when a customer shifts out of a demand deposit into a time deposit, the bank now has to take some reserves it could otherwise have used as reserves for demand deposits and use them as a reserve against the time deposit. Thus, what is lost to the demand-deposit creation process is not the whole amount shifted into time deposits, but only that amount times the reserve ratio against time deposits.

[5]Before we had $D = \frac{1}{r + e} R$, that is, $R = (r + e)D$. By definition $C = k'D$, where k' is the ratio of *total* currency holdings (including those of banks) to deposits. Adding the two yields, $R + C = (r + e)D + k'(D) = (r + e + k')D$, so that $D = \frac{1}{r + e + k'}$ $(R + C)$.

For example, consider a bank with a reserve requirement of 20 percent against demand deposits, and of 5 percent against time deposits. Initially it has no time deposits, so that ignoring all entries other than reserves and deposits, its T account looks as follows:

(14)

Assets		*Liabilities*	
reserves	$1,000	demand deposits	$5,000
(earning assets	$4,000)		

Now a customer shifts $1,000 from her demand deposit to a time deposit. The T account changes to:

(15)

Assets		*Liabilities*	
reserves against time deposits	$ 50	time deposits	$1,000
reserves against demand deposits	$ 800	demand deposits	$4,000
excess reserves	$ 150		
(earning assets	$4,000)		

Since the bank now has to keep $50 of its reserves against time deposits, it has only $950 available as reserves against its demand deposits, and so can have only $4,750 of demand deposits on its books, $250 less than before the shift into time deposits. However, it can increase its loans and investments now since it can lend out the time deposit too. When it does so it loses the additional reserves, and ends up with demand deposits of $4000.

To adjust the demand-deposit multiplier for the shift into time deposits, add to the denominator the leakage into time deposits per dollar of demand deposits times the legal reserve ratio against time deposits. So we now have

$$d = \frac{1}{r + e + k + t(r_t)},$$

where t is the proportion of demand deposits that are shifted into time deposits, and r_t is the reserve ratio (legal plus excess) held against time deposits. Suppose that t is 20 percent and r_t is 5 percent; the demand-deposit multiplier then is

$$d = \frac{1}{.14 + .01 + .30 + .2(.05)} = 2.17$$

This multiplier, 2.17, is much lower than 7.14, which is what the demand-deposit multiplier would have been if the required reserve ratio, 14 percent, had been the only leakage.

The Money Multipliers

We have discussed the demand-deposit multiplier at length, not because it is so important in and of itself, but because it allows us to calculate the money multipliers, and these money multipliers *are* very important.

Narrow money is defined as currency plus checking deposits, so that to get the narrow-money multiplier we only have to adjust the demand-deposit multiplier for the public's currency holdings. We can calculate the *nonbank public's* currency, K, by multiplying its demand-deposit holdings, D, by k ($K = kD$), since k has been defined as the ratio of currency to demand deposits. Now we know that demand deposits are

$$D = \frac{1}{r + e + k + tr_t} (R + C)$$

so that to get currency holdings, K, just multiply this expression by k, which gives

$$K = \frac{k}{r + e + k + tr_t} (R + C).$$

To get the total money stock now add this equation for currency to the equation for demand deposits,

$$D = \frac{1}{r + e + k + tr_t} (R + C)$$

so that the narrow-money stock is

$$K + D = \frac{1 + k}{r + e + k + tr_t} (R + C).[6]$$

To obtain the narrow-money multiplier, m_1, rather than the stock of narrow money, just omit the multiplicand $(R + C)$. The broad-money multiplier, m_2, can be obtained in a strictly analogous way; we just multiply demand deposits by t', the ratio of time deposits—other than large certificates of deposits—to demand deposits and add $\frac{t'}{r + e + k + tr_t} (R + C)$ to the narrow-money stock, thus getting

$$M_2 = \frac{1 + k + t'}{r + e + k + tr_t} (R + C).$$

The reason why t' rather than t appears in the numerator is that not all time deposits are included in the definition of M_2, large certificates of deposits are excluded.

The New Measures of the Money Stock

The money multipliers discussed so far, were formulated in terms of the traditional measures of money, M_1 and M_2, which count only currency and deposits in commercial banks. But, as will be discussed at length in chapter 11, in 1980 the Fed changed the ways in which it defines money. One of the new measures $M\text{-}1A$ is like the old M_1 except that it excludes deposits held by foreign banks and official institutions. The previous multiplier for M_1 can readily be adjusted to apply to $M\text{-}1A$ by excluding such foreign deposits, and adding to the denominator a term for leakage into such deposits, but since this leakage is very minor this is just a refinement.

[6] To simplify we are sloughing over the fact that the money stock as normally defined excludes government and interbank deposits. Hence, a more complicated version of the deposit multiplier adds terms for the leakages into government and interbank deposits.

Another measure of money is *M-1B,* which includes checkable deposits (such as NOW accounts) in savings and loan associations, mutual savings banks, and credit unions. This can be taken account of easily by simply extending the previous definition of deposits to include such deposits; hence in some of the examples previously given, bank B, for instance, might be a savings and loan association.

The new measure *M-2* is more troublesome. It includes savings and time deposits in banks and other depository institutions, except time deposits of $100,000 and over. This is taken care of easily by including such deposits in nonbank depository institutions in the term t' in the equation for M_2 given on page 229. But the new *M-2* also includes other items such as deposits in money-market funds and Eurodollar deposits. These have now to be included in our definition of deposits. Then there is *M-3,* which includes all time deposits regardless of size. To take account of this, t' in the equation for M_2 on page 229 must be replaced by t. In addition, since *M-3* includes term repurchase agreements, they must be included in the definition of *deposit* to get *M-3.*

In all of these cases where one redefines *deposits* one also has to change the required reserve ratio and all the other ratios, so that they are now the average ratios for all the items new as well as old, included in deposits.

Money-Supply Theory

We could end the story at this point and say that there is a fixed money multiplier determined by $r,$ $e,$ $k,$ $t,$ and r_t. One can take the average values of these coefficients and easily calculate the money multiplier. But this is a crude and mechanistic approach because it assumes that the values of these leakage coefficients are fixed. This is not so. The legal reserve requirements are set by the government, and changed from time to time, but the others depend on how the public wants to hold its assets. Since these decisions of the public are susceptible to economic analysis we need not take these leakage coefficients as "given," but can see how they change with economic conditions. This is important. As will be taken up in our discussion of monetary theory, there is a close correlation between changes in the money stock and in income. This raises the important question of which one is cause and which is effect. The extent to which the public's *demand* for money, which is influenced by the level of income, can bring about the desired change in the money stock is relevant for this question. Hence, we will now see what determines the size of the coefficients of the money multiplier and how stable they are.

The excess reserve ratio, *e,* that banks want to hold depends, on the one hand, on the interest rate that banks could earn by investing these excess reserves, and, on the other hand, on the benefits that banks expect to obtain from holding them. A profit-maximizing bank keeps excess reserves up to a point at which the interest forgone by holding these reserves idle minus the cost of investing them is just equal to what the bank thinks would be the cost to it of obtaining additional reserves if it runs short, times the probability that it will run short.

The public's desired currency ratio, k, depends in principle upon the interest rate paid by banks on demand deposits and NOWs, because this is the opportunity cost of holding currency rather than deposits, and on the interest rate paid on securities. If the yield on securities increases there is an incentive to switch to securities out of both deposits and currency. But it seems plausible that deposit holdings are more responsive to changes in security yields than are currency holdings, so that an increase in security yields raises the ratio of currency to deposits. The currency ratio also depends on income or wealth because these variables measure the extent to which people can afford to forgo earning interest on deposits or securities to obtain the convenience of holding currency, and on retail sales, the variable that measures the work to be done by currency.

The time-deposit ratio, t, depends on the interest rate on time deposits compared to the yield on demand deposits and on securities. Obviously, if banks raise the interest rate they pay on time deposits, while neither the yield on demand deposits nor on securities rises, the public will want to hold more time deposits. And the time-deposit ratio also depends on total wealth, since time deposits are one way of holding wealth.

Thus, income, wealth, and interest rates are factors determining e, k, and t, and hence the money multiplier. As income rises and interest rates increase, one would expect e to decline somewhat. But since it is already small to start with, this does not make very much difference. At the same time, with income and retail sales, as well as interest rates on securities, rising, k rises too. And with the rise in interest rates on time deposits lagging behind the rising yield on securities, one would expect t to fall.

Hence, the deposit multiplier is partly endogenous, that is, affected by the demand for money, so that even if the Federal Reserve keeps bank reserves constant, the stock of money tends to rise as income increases, and fall as income falls in other words, to behave procyclically. This approach to money creation, which makes the *money multiplier partially endogenous by allowing* e, k, *and* t *to vary,* is called **money-supply theory** to distinguish it from the mechanistic "textbook" approach that takes the money multiplier to be a constant.

The "New View" of Money Creation

Although money-supply theory is a substantial advance over the simple mechanistic approach, it has been challenged in recent years by a number of economists who believe that it does not go far enough. Their approach is called the New View, though by now there is nothing new about it. We will just sketch it briefly.

Adherents of the New View point out that there is something peculiar about the traditional view of money creation. It talks about the quantity of an economic good, deposits, solely from the point of view of what determines the supply, that is, the volume of deposits that banks can supply. But, surely, we know that as a general rule one should look at both supply *and* demand. Does the public's demand for deposits not matter at all? Does the public meekly accept whatever amount of deposits banks want to supply?

Moreover, do banks necessarily want to supply more deposits merely because they have more reserves available? Surely we would not accept an analysis that tells us that the quantity of steel sold is determined only by the supply of iron ore or steel scrap available to the steel companies.

If one treats banking like any other industry, one would have to conclude that the story told so far is at best seriously incomplete. It is no more complete than a rival story that asserts that the quantity of deposits in existence depends upon how much the public would like to hold, given the cost of holding deposits. The above discussion of deposit creation assumed implicitly that the public is always willing to hold any deposits the banking system creates. Couldn't one go to the opposite extreme, and assume instead that the banks are always able to create all the deposits that the public is willing to hold, so that the volume of outstanding deposits is determined by the demand for deposits? Suppose, for example, that the public wants to hold more demand deposits. Banks would then find that they can "sell" demand deposits to the public at a lower imputed yield, that is, at a lower cost, and would therefore expand their demand deposits.

But how would banks obtain the required reserves? To start with, since the public wants to hold more demand deposits, it will presumably deposit some of its currency holdings into banks and this raises bank reserves. Second, banks can increase their reserves by borrowing from the Federal Reserve. Moreover, the increased demand for total deposits can also be met by banks raising the (implicit or explicit) yield on time deposits, thus inducing some people to hold time deposits instead. While this drain into time deposits lowers M_1, it raises M_2 since the lower reserve requirement against time deposits means that banks can now have more total deposits outstanding than before. Hence, the New View argues, the supply of reserves is not as critical to the creation of money, particularly of M_2, as the traditional approach suggests.

Fortunately, the conflict between the two approaches is not quite as serious as may appear at first. Suppose that we start out with an equilibrium situation in which banks are producing their optimal volume of deposits, so that their marginal revenue from holding the public's deposits just equals the marginal cost of servicing these deposits. Now suppose that the Federal Reserve makes more reserves available to banks. One of the costs of servicing deposits is the forgone interest from holding reserves against these deposits. But with more reserves available, interest rates fall, and as a result the marginal cost of servicing deposits falls too. Marginal costs are now less than marginal revenue, so that banks expand their volume of deposits. Hence, critics of the New View believe that as the traditional view predicts when banks obtain additional reserves bank deposits increase.[7]

Moreover, these critics argue that although the traditional approach analyzes bank deposits in a way very different from that used for other goods, this does not necessarily mean that it is wrong. Deposits differ radically from other goods: an increase in their supply, after some time, raises the demand for them. It does so because, as will be shown subsequently, an increase in the money supply raises nominal income, that is, real income expressed in money terms. And the higher is nominal income, the greater is the demand for nominal money. Hence, when banks supply more deposits, after some time, the demand for deposits increases too, so that the yield on deposits does not necessarily have to rise to induce the public to hold more deposits.

In any case, money-supply theory is much less vulnerable to the New View's criticism than is the crude "textbook" multiplier, since it allows three leakage coefficients, e, k, and t, to be determined by economic conditions. For example, suppose that the demand function for deposits rises. This raises interest rates, and hence, changes e, k, and t. Money-supply theory therefore makes some room for the demand factor stressed by the New View, but gives it much less emphasis than the New View does. In a sense, it is a simplified version of the New View that gambles on the assumption that the leakage coefficients are stable enough so that we can avoid the full complexity (and it is a very great complexity) of the New View. If, in actuality, most of the observed changes in the money stock are due to changes in the volume of bank reserves, rather than in the money multiplier, then the relatively limited analysis of fluctuations in the money multiplier that money-supply theory gives us may be sufficient. This brings us to two related questions: first, how stable is the money multiplier, and, second, what proportion of the observed fluctuation in the money supply is due to changes in the volume of bank reserves, and what proportion is due to changes in the money multiplier? The first of these questions we can take up now; the second we defer until the next chapter, which takes up changes in bank reserves.

The Stability of the Money Multiplier

Figure 9.1 shows the money (M_1) multiplier for the adjusted base as well as the federal funds rate. Over the long run the two move in opposite di-

---

[7] Another way of explaining why banks expand deposits when their reserves increase is to say that the reserve requirement constrains banks to produce fewer deposits than the profit-maximizing condition of marginal revenue equals marginal costs requires. Hence, as they obtain additional reserves, they increase their deposits to get closer to this profit-maximizing level. However, this argument ignores that competition will drive banks to raise their imputed interest rate on demand deposits until for each bank marginal revenue from deposits equals marginal costs, so that they already are at the profit-maximizing point.

Figure 9.1 The Money Multiplier and the Interest Rate
1972–78

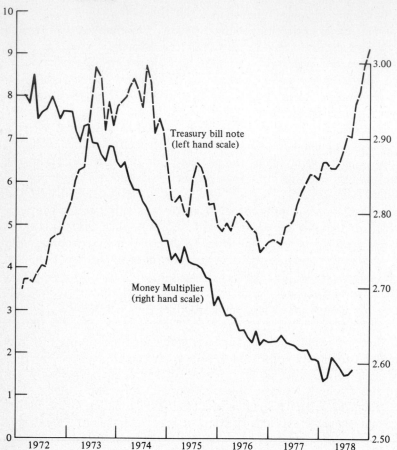

Note: Money multiplier is the M_1 multiplier applicable to the adjusted base, and includes one leakage that has not been discussed. This is the leakage into federal government deposits (which are excluded from the money supply). This leakage is quite minor, usually being less than 0.02. And it must be multiplied by the reserve requirement against demand deposits, so that its effect is trivial.

SOURCE: Unpublished data provided through the courtesy of the Federal Reserve Bank of Saint Louis; Board of Governors, Federal Reserve System, *Banking and Monetary Statistics, 1941–1975,* and *Annual Statistical Digest;* Council of Economic Advisers, *Economic Report of the President, 1979.*

rections, with the federal funds rate rising and the multiplier falling. For short-run movements there is little relation between them, so that this figure does not support the New View's argument that a rise in interest rates raises the money multiplier, and hence the money stock.

Figure 9.2 shows the leakages from the deposit creation process, and explains why the money multiplier has been falling. The main reason is the great rise in the currency ratio. Currency holdings now amount to an

Figure 9.2   Money-Multiplier Leakages
1972–78

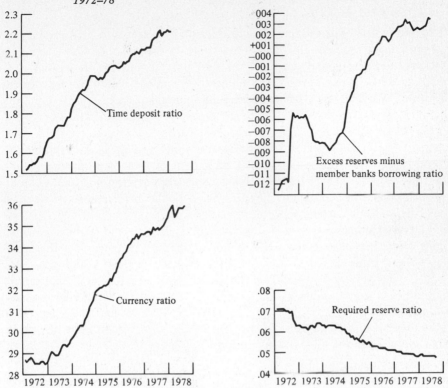

SOURCE: Unpublished data provided through the courtesy of the Federal Reserve Bank of Saint Louis; Board of Governors, Federal Reserve System, *Banking and Monetary Statistics, 1941–1975*, and *Annual Statistical Digest*; Council of Economic Advisers, *Economic Report of the President, 1979.*

amazing, and puzzling, $600 per adult.[8] The time-deposit ratio has also risen substantially, but this ratio has to be multiplied by the reserve requirement against time deposits, which is low. The reserve requirements against demand and time deposits have both been falling, while the excess reserve ratio has been small throughout the period.

[8] Some people have attributed the rise in the currency ratio to the rise in tax evasion and other crimes (which require the holding of untraceable currency rather than traceable deposits) and have used the rise in the currency ratio to calculate that illegal activities now amount to more than 10 percent of GNP. But this calculation is questionable. While currency has been rising relative to demand deposits it has not risen relative to demand plus time deposits. Someone who shifts funds into a time deposit out of demand deposits because interest rates on time deposits have risen may still want to hold the same amount of currency, but this shows up as a rise in the ratio of currency to demand deposits. Besides, currency held because of tax evasion, or because it was obtained in an illegal activity, is likely to circulate more slowly than other money, and hence to support a smaller amount of income.

Summary

The first topic of this chapter was the creation of currency, which turned out to present no problems. After that we took up the more complex topic of the creation of demand deposits. We first pointed out the basic fact that demand deposits are not physical objects, so that their multiple creation is feasible. We then took up two cases in which multiple deposit creation cannot occur: the case of 100 percent reserves and the case where the proceeds of a bank loan are not redeposited back into another bank. We then dropped these two unrealistic assumptions and gave an example of multiple deposit creation that results when someone deposits currency, tracing the process through several banks, and also determining the total of deposits that can be created. Next we took up the reverse case of deposit destruction when currency is withdrawn from banks.

The examples given so far dealt with a very simple, but unrealistic, case where the legal reserve requirement is the only leakage. We therefore introduced other leakages: into excess reserves, currency, and time deposits. These leakages greatly reduced the size of the demand-deposit multiplier. From this discussion of the demand-deposit multiplier we developed the money multiplier applicable to M_1 and M_2 and then discussed how they have to be adjusted to correspond to the new definitions of money that include deposits in thrift institutions.

Although so far the coefficients of the leakages were taken as constant, this is merely a simplifying assumption. We therefore looked at the factors that determine the leakage coefficients and saw that they make the money supply partially endogenous. This led to a discussion of the New View that stresses this endogeneity. We concluded with a discussion of how the money multiplier has behaved in recent years.

QUESTIONS AND EXERCISES

1. Carry out the example set out on pp. 220–222 through to bank G. Assume that bank G just holds the reserves it receives and does not make additional loans. On this assumption what is the deposit multiplier?
2. What happens in the example of deposit creation on p. 221 if the proceeds of the loan made by bank B are redeposited in bank B?
3. Set up an example of the deposit creation process using a 50 percent reserve ratio. Work it through for four banks.
4. Work out an example of deposit *contraction* using a 10 percent reserve ratio. Follow it through for six banks.
5. How would you answer a banker who claims that banks cannot create deposits, that they can lend out only the money deposited with them?
6. Carry the example of deposit contraction on pp. 223–225 forward and assume that bank F has excess reserves, and hence does not have to call a loan. What is the deposit multiplier now?

7. Can savings and loan associations create savings and loan deposits? Can banks create time deposits? Why or why not?
8. Suppose that we have an economy in which there is only a single bank, which has a reserve ratio of 20 percent. If someone deposits $1000 of currency in this bank, how much can this bank lend out?
9. Why do changes in income and wealth affect e, k, and t?
10. Explain the New View in your own words. How can adherents of the traditional view try to answer it?

FURTHER READING

BRUNNER, KARL. "The Role of Money and Monetary Policy." *Review* (Federal Reserve Bank of St. Louis) 50 (July 1968): 9–24. A strong criticism of the New View.

BURGER, ALBERT E. *Money Supply Process.* Belmont, Calif.: Wadsworth Publishing Co., 1971. Chapters 1–4 give an extremely thorough and detailed discussion of the deposit and money multipliers.

CACY, J. "Alternative Approaches to the Analysis of Financial Structure." *Monthly Review* (Federal Reserve Bank of Kansas City) 53 (March 1968). A good survey of the New View.

JOHANNES, JAMES, and RASCHE, ROBERT. "Predicting the Money Multiplier." *Journal of Monetary Economics* 5 (July 1979): 301–25. This article develops a way of predicting the money multiplier with a high degree of accuracy.

FEDERAL RESERVE BANK OF CHICAGO. *Modern Money Mechanism: Workbook.* Chicago: Federal Reserve Bank of Chicago, 1961, pp. 1–14. A very clear and lucid discussion of deposit creation.

PESEK, BORIS. "Monetary Theory in the Post-Robertsonian 'Alice in Wonderland' Era." *Journal of Economic Literature* 14 (September 1976): 867 ff. The latter part of this article is a forceful and stimulating criticism of the traditional view of deposit creation. For the traditionalist's response, see the debate in the *Journal of Economic Literature* 15 (September 1977): 908–27.

TETOM, JOHN, and LANG, RICHARD. "Automatic Transfers and the Money Supply Process." *Review* (Federal Reserve Bank of St. Louis) 61 (February 1979): 2–10. A discussion of how the money multipliers should be adjusted for the automatic transfer service, an issue passed over in this chapter.

TOBIN, JAMES. "Commercial Banks as Creators of 'Money.'" In *Banking and Monetary Studies,* edited by Deane Carson, pp. 408–19. Homewood, Ill.: Richard D. Irwin, 1963. A sharp critique of the traditional explanation of deposit creation.

10

Bank Reserves
and Related Measures

In the preceding chapter we discussed how the banking system can create deposits if a particular bank receives a deposit of currency, and hence an increase in its reserves. But a customer's deposit of currency is simply one of many factors that can increase bank reserves. And a moment's reflection should make it clear that any factor that provides additional reserves for the banking system can set off the multiple deposit creation process. In this chapter we will therefore first look at all of the factors that can increase or decrease bank reserves. We will then look at some other measures that are related to bank reserves. Then we consider the extent to which those changes in the money stock that do occur are due to changes in bank reserves, and to what extent they are due to changes in the money multiplier.

Bank Reserves

Any individual bank can obtain additional reserves, which for member banks consist only of vault cash and deposits with the Federal Reserve, by taking some reserves away from another bank. For example, a large bank can offer a slightly higher rate on its large CDs, and thereby induce depositors of other banks to shift their deposits to it, or a bank can sell a security to a depositor of another bank, and thus obtain reserves from that bank. But, obviously, the whole banking system cannot get reserves in this way. It can obtain additional reserves only from some entity outside of itself. These nonbank entities can be classified into the following: (1) the Federal Reserve, (2) the U.S. Treasury, (3) the U.S. nonbank public, and (4) foreigners.

The ways in which these entities change bank reserves is set out in a standardized accounting framework published by the Federal Reserve System every Friday, which the *Wall Street Journal* then carries on Monday in a section called "Federal Reserve data." Money-market analysts use this as one of their tools for assessing supply and demand in the money market. Table 10.1 is an example of this weekly statement. It is arranged so that the factors that increase bank reserves are listed first, followed by

Table 10.1   Weekly Published Federal Reserve Data—Member Bank
Reserve Changes
(Millons of dollars)

	Change from week ending:		
	JAN. 17 1979	JAN. 10 1979	JAN. 18 1978
Reserve bank credit:			
U.S. government securities:			
Bought outright	107,131	+ 2,394	+ 7,026
Held under repurchase agreement	—	—	− 377
Federal agency issues:			
Bought outright	7,892	—	− 112
Held under repurchase agreement	—	—	− 115
Acceptances—bought outright	—	—	—
Held under repurchase agreement	—	—	− 112
Member bank borrowings	792	+ 200	+ 401
Seasonal bank borrowings	105	+ 12	+ 78
Float	9,374	− 1,740	+ 3,880
Other Federal Reserve assets	4,386	− 126	+ 1,829
Total Reserve Bank credit	129,680	+ 741	+ 12,498
Gold stock	11,609	− 51	− 110
SDR certificates	1,300	—	+ 50
Treasury currency outstanding	11,864	+ 14	+ 472
Total	154,453	+ 704	+ 12,910
Currency in circulation	112,596	− 1,165	+ 10,460
Treasury cash holdings	250	+ 4	− 147
Treasury deposits with F.R. banks	3,302	+ 186	− 1,955
Foreign deposits with F.R. banks	277	− 64	− 28
Other deposits with F.R. banks	786	+ 76	+ 27
Other F.R. liabilities and capital	4,490	+ 73	+ 880
Total	121,701	− 890	+ 9,236

Note: A dash (—) denotes amounts less than $500,000.
SOURCE: *Wall Street Journal,* 19 January 1979, p. 20.

the factors that decrease them. Of course, the algebraic rule for multiplication of signs applics; a decrease in a factor of increase decreases bank reserves, while a decrease in a factor of decrease raises bank reserves.

However, not all of the reserves that are generated in this way are held by banks, some are held by thrift institutions as reserves against their transactions accounts and against their nonpersonal time deposits. Hence, while all of these reserves are available to support *M-3,* which includes all of these deposits, they are not all available to support *M-1* or *M-2.*

Factors That Increase Bank Reserves

The first of these items, U.S. government securities bought outright, is part of the Federal Reserve's open-market operations, and is undertaken by the Federal Reserve precisely for the sake of changing bank reserves.

(A negative entry for it means that the Federal Reserve has sold instead of bought securities, and thereby decreased bank reserves.) To see how a Federal Reserve purchase of securities raises bank reserves, consider first the case where the Fed buys these securities directly from a member bank. It pays for them by crediting the selling bank's reserve account, so that the bank's reserves go up automatically. The bank's and the Fed's T accounts now look as follows:

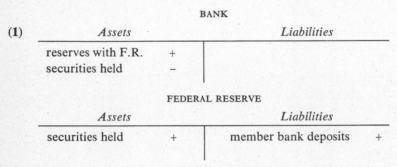

BANK

(1)

Assets		*Liabilities*
reserves with F.R.	+	
securities held	–	

FEDERAL RESERVE

Assets		*Liabilities*	
securities held	+	member bank deposits	+

Suppose that the Fed had bought these securities, not from a bank, but from General Motors. General Motors gets a check, which it deposits in its bank, and the bank clears the check by sending it to the Federal Reserve for credit. Its T account becomes:

(2)

Assets		*Liabilities*	
reserves with F.R.	+	demand deposits	+

In both of these cases the bank's reserve account goes up. The only difference is that in the second case demand deposits go up automatically, whereas in the first case, where the Fed bought the securities from a bank, deposits go up only when the bank uses the reserves to make a loan or to buy another security. (The Fed's balance sheet is the same in both cases.) Conversely, when the Fed sells a security to a nonbank, bank reserves fall, and the T account of the buyer's bank shows:

(3)

Assets		*Liabilities*	
reserves with F.R.	–	demand deposits	–

As will be discussed in chapter 22 when the Fed buys securities it frequently does not buy them in the everyday sense of buying, but buys them subject to a repurchase agreement. What this means is that the "purchase" is only temporary, and that the "seller" pledges himself to reverse this transaction by buying these securities back again at a fixed future date. But such a temporary purchase has exactly the same effect on bank reserves, and shows up exactly the same way in the T accounts, as does a permanent purchase.

In addition to buying and selling U.S. government securities, that is, securities issued by the U.S. Treasury, the Federal Reserve also deals in securities issued by certain U.S. government agencies, such as the Export-Import Bank and the U.S. Postal Service. Obviously, bank reserves and T accounts are affected the same way regardless of whether the Federal Reserve buys securities issued by the U.S. Treasury, or by another government agency, or buys ice-cream cones for that matter.

In chapter 4 we discussed banker's acceptances, the commitment of a bank to pay at a certain date a draft drawn on it. When a bank that holds such a banker's acceptance issued by another bank sells it to the Federal Reserve, the Fed credits its reserve account exactly the same way as if the bank had sold it a U.S. government security. And similarly if a nonbank sells to the Fed a banker's acceptance in its possession, the Fed pays with a check that, as in our second T account, becomes a deposit to the nonbank, and a reserve to the bank.

The next two items, member bank borrowings and seasonal bank borrowings, refer to the loans that member banks can obtain from their Federal Reserve banks. The Fed makes these loans by crediting the borrowing bank's reserve account, so that we have the following T account entries:

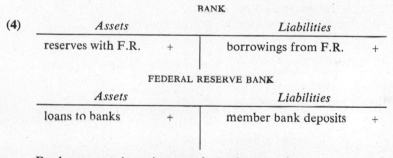

BANK

(4)

Assets	Liabilities
reserves with F.R. +	borrowings from F.R. +

FEDERAL RESERVE BANK

Assets	Liabilities
loans to banks +	member bank deposits +

Bank reserves have increased. And when the bank repays the loan the Fed will take the amount of the loan out of the bank's reserve account, so that the T account will show negative entries for all of these items, and the reserves will therefore disappear.

Float, the next item, works like a loan from the Federal Reserve. If the Federal Reserve were to give credit to a bank for a check it deposits exactly at the same time that it debits the account of the bank on which the check is drawn, then there would be no float. But, as previously discussed, the Federal Reserve credits the account of the depositing bank after one or two days, despite the fact that, due to transportation delays, and so on, it often takes longer than this before the check is debited against the account of the bank on which it is drawn. As a result of one bank's account having been credited for the check, while the other bank has not yet been debited, total bank reserves increase for a short time. Thus the T accounts of the bank that received the check, and the bank upon which the check was drawn, look as follows:

RECEIVING BANK

(5)

Assets	Liabilities
reserves with F.R. +	demand deposits +

DRAWER BANK

Assets	Liabilities
reserves with F.R. unchanged	demand deposits unchanged

For both banks together therefore reserves have temporarily increased. When the check finally is debited to the drawer bank, its reserve account is debited, and the increased reserves and deposits generated by float disappear. Since the volume of checks in the clearing process is extremely large, changes in float are usually quite substantial. However, currently (August 1980) the Fed is planning to reduce its float substantially, in part by extending the period until banks get credit for the checks they deposit.

Another factor raising bank reserves is an increase in other Federal Reserve assets. Whether the Federal Reserve buys paper clips, or a building, or pays an employee's salary, it does so by drawing a check on itself. When this check is deposited and cleared the Federal Reserve credits the reserve account of the bank that received it.[1] Here are the relevant T accounts when the seller has deposited his or her Federal Reserve check, and the check has cleared:

COMMERCIAL BANK

(6)

Assets	Liabilities
reserves with F.R. +	demand deposits +

FEDERAL RESERVE BANK

Assets	Liabilities
paper clips +	member bank deposits +

Then we come to various U.S. Treasury operations that change bank reserves. The first of these are changes in the U.S. gold stock. If the

---

[1] The biggest item among Federal Reserve purchases consists of foreign currencies it buys from other central banks in transactions intended to stabilize the foreign exchange market. These purchases do not, in the first instance, result in an increase of bank reserves. Instead, they show up twice in table 10.1, once as a factor of increase under other Federal Reserve assets and once as a factor of decrease under foreign deposits with the F.R. banks since the Federal Reserve credits the accounts of foreign central banks with the dollar equivalent of the currencies it buys from them. Later on, when the foreign central banks draw on these funds to buy, say, Treasury bills, foreign deposits with the Federal Reserve decrease, and bank reserves increase, as the sellers of the securities deposit the checks drawn on the Federal Reserve with their banks and the banks clear them.

Treasury buys gold, the Treasury's check eventually ends up in a bank, and bank deposits and reserves both increase.[2]

The next item, special drawing rights certificate account, we will defer for the moment, and turn instead to the following item, Treasury currency outstanding. Since currency is one way in which reserves can be held, an increase in outstanding currency—if held by a bank—means an increase in bank reserves. But how about the case where the increase in Treasury currency is held, not by a bank, but by the nonbank public? We will adjust for this in a moment by subtracting the public's currency holdings. Hence, an increase in Treasury currency held by the nonbank public is treated in this accounting framework in two separate steps: (1) as a factor increasing reserves (the increase in outstanding Treasury currency), and (2) as a factor decreasing reserves (the rise in the nonbank public's currency holdings).

Since we are adding Treasury currency in circulation, shouldn't we add Federal Reserve currency in circulation, too? The answer is that this has already been done indirectly by taking account of the factors that change the Federal Reserve's balance sheet, such as its loans to member banks. The proceeds of these loans can be taken either as an increase in reserves on the Federal Reserve's books or as currency. Hence, if the increases in Federal Reserve currency outstanding were added to the other items in table 10.1, the increase in Federal Reserve currency outstanding would be counted twice. But, we do not include the items changing the Treasury's balance sheet in table 10.1, and therefore we have to add in those Treasury items, such as an increase in outstanding Treasury currency, that change bank reserves.

Factors That Decrease Bank Reserves

This concludes the explanation of the items that increase bank reserves. Now let us look at the items that, if positive, take away reserves from banks. The first of these factors of decrease, currency in circulation, refers to the currency holdings of the nonbank public. Clearly, if the public withdraws currency from banks, bank reserves decrease. For example, when someone withdraws $1,000 out of a demand deposit, the following T account entries occur:

[2] Actually, the story is complex because the Treasury does not buy gold on the open market but buys only from other central banks. A foreign central bank is likely in the first instance to deposit the check into its account with the Federal Reserve so that initially bank reserves do not change. But this is taken care of in our accounting scheme in the following way. As will be discussed below, an increase in foreign deposits with the Federal Reserve is a factor of decrease, while, as just discussed, the Treasury gold purchase is a factor of increase. The two book entries that result from the Treasury's gold purchase therefore cancel out, so that our accounting system shows—as it should—that in the first instance bank reserves do not change. Later on when the foreign central bank spends the funds, and runs down its deposits with the Federal Reserve, then bank reserves and deposits do increase.

(7)

Assets		Liabilities	
vault cash	−$1000	demand deposits	−$1000

The following item in table 10.1 is Treasury cash holdings. The U.S. Treasury holds a certain amount of currency. Suppose that the Treasury now increases the amount of currency it holds in its vault. This currency must come from either the public's currency holdings, or out of the vault cash of banks. Insofar as it comes out of the banks' currency holdings, reserves have obviously decreased. But what if it comes from the currency held by the public? In this case there are two offsetting entries. One is an increase in Treasury cash holdings, which decreases reserves, and the other is a decrease in currency in circulation, which being a decrease in a factor of decrease, *increases* reserves, so that in this case our accounting framework rightly shows bank reserves as unchanged. Or put differently, suppose that the Treasury holds $2 million more currency, but that currency in circulation has fallen only by $1 million. The remaining $1 million must then have come out of the vault cash of banks.[3]

The next item is Treasury deposits with Federal Reserve banks. The Treasury deposits the checks it receives as taxes, at dates when major tax payments are due, and from sales of securities, initially into commercial banks. The Treasury does this to prevent what would otherwise be a devastating drain of bank reserves, which the Federal Reserve would have to offset. In general, large checks are automatically deposited into the so-called tax and loan accounts at the very banks on which they are drawn. But the government does not write checks on its balances with commercial banks. Instead, it writes them on its deposit with the Federal Reserve. And to replenish its account at the Federal Reserve, it issues *calls* on its deposits with commercial banks, and these banks then have to transfer funds to the Treasury's accounts at the Federal Reserve. As the banks do so, the Federal Reserve debits their reserve account—thus reducing bank reserves—and credits the Treasury's account. Here is the T account for a call:

BANK

(8)

Assets		Liabilities	
reserves with F.R.	−	demand deposits of U.S. Treasury	−

FEDERAL RESERVE BANK

Assets		Liabilities	
		member bank deposits	−
		U.S. Treasury deposits	+

[3] Treasury cash holdings include, apart from currency, also Treasury gold holdings against which it has not issued gold certificates to the Federal Reserve.

Occasionally, the Treasury has varied the size of its Federal Reserve account for the specific purpose of changing bank reserves, thus using its own monetary power to aid the Federal Reserve's monetary policy.

Now we are in a position to go back and look at the special drawing rights certificate account. **Special drawing rights (SDRs)** are a *form of international reserves created on the books of the International Monetary Fund (IMF) and used in transactions between nations.* When the IMF distributes additional special drawing rights, as it does from time to time, the Treasury, as a matter of government bookkeeping, treats its new SDRs as an asset, and adds their dollar equivalent to its account at the Federal Reserve. Thus, there is sometimes an increase in Treasury deposits at the Federal Reserve that does *not* result from the Treasury withdrawing deposits and reserves from commercial banks. Hence, if we are going to treat *every* increase in the Treasury's deposits at the Federal Reserve as though it means a decrease in bank reserves, we are subtracting too much, and therefore have to compensate for those increases that are due instead to the issue of special drawing rights. The way this is done is to add back in, as a factor of increase, the rise in the special drawing rights certificate account.

Foreign deposits with Federal Reserve banks is an item that arises because many foreign governments and central banks keep deposits with the Federal Reserve. Suppose a foreign central bank sells some U.S. Treasury bills it holds, and deposits the buyer's check in its account with the Federal Reserve. The Federal Reserve then debits some bank's account for this check. As the check clears it gives rise to the following T account entries:

BANK

(9)

Assets	Liabilities
reserves with F.R. –	demand deposits –

FEDERAL RESERVE BANK

Assets	Liabilities
	member bank deposits –
	foreign government deposits +

Other deposits with Federal Reserve banks is a catchall item that includes the clearing deposits that some nonmember banks carry with the Federal Reserve, deposits of international organizations, for example, the United Nations and the IMF, deposits of certain government corporations, such as the FDIC, and others. When a check drawn on a bank is deposited into any of these accounts, that bank's reserves are, of course, reduced.

The next item is Federal Reserve liabilities and capital. Suppose that a new member bank buys stock in the Federal Reserve, as all member banks are required to do, thus raising the Fed's capital. It pays for this stock by having the Federal Reserve debit its reserve account, so that total bank reserves decrease, the T account entries being:

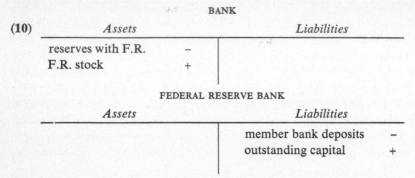

Other Federal Reserve liabilities are brought in to keep the books straight. Previously we treated all the increase in other Federal Reserve assets as though it meant an increase in bank reserves because the Federal Reserve pays for these assets. But insofar as these assets have not yet been paid for—so that Federal Reserve liabilities increase—bank reserves have actually not yet increased. Hence, having added too much to reserves by treating all Federal Reserve asset purchases as though they imply an increase in reserves, we must now compensate for this by subtracting the increase in Federal Reserve liabilities.

Having covered all the factors that supply or absorb bank reserves, the change in bank reserves can now be measured by subtracting the factors of decrease from the factors of increase.

Relative Importance of Factors Changing Bank Reserves

Obviously, not all of these factors are equally important. Which are the most important ones? There are two difficulties in answering this question. One is that the relative importance of various factors changes over time. For example, at a time when the Federal Reserve is trying to increase bank reserves at an unusually high rate, its security purchases will be unusually large relative to other factors, such as float.

The second complication relates to the time span considered. For some factors, such as Federal Reserve security purchases, the weekly changes tend to cumulate to some extent. For example, since the Fed tends to buy each week more securities than it sells, the net amount of reserves supplied by open-market operations over the span of a whole year is usually substantially bigger than the amount supplied in a particular week. But this is not so for certain other items, such as Treasury deposits with the Federal Reserve, where the positive entries in one week tend to be can-

Table 10.2   Relative Importance of Various Factors Determining Bank Reserves
1976–78

	Percent of absolute weekly change in reserves accounted for
FACTORS OF INCREASE	
Reserve Bank credit:	
U.S. government securities—	
Bought outright—system account	33.9
Held under repurchase agreements	24.5
Special Certificates	0.0
Federal agency obligations—	
Bought outright	2.1
Held under repurchase agreements	3.8
Acceptances—	
Bought outright	0.0
Held under repurchase agreements	4.5
Loans—	
Total member bank borrowing	8.3
Includes seasonal borrowing of:	.2
Other borrowing	0.0
Float	16.2
Other Federal Reserve assets	6.3
Total Reserve Bank credit	99.7
Gold Stock	0.0
Special Drawing Rights certificates account	0.0
Treasury currency outstanding	0.3
TOTAL	100.0
FACTORS OF DECREASE	
Currency in circulation	15.8
Treasury cash holdings	0.2
Treasury deposits with Federal Reserve banks	69.9
Foreign deposits with Federal Reserve banks	2.2
Other deposits with Federal Reserve banks	3.6
Other Federal Reserve liabilities and capital	8.3
TOTAL	100.0

SOURCE: Sample of Board of Governors, Federal Reserve System, releases H.4.a, July 1977–June 1978.

celled out by negative entries the following weeks. Hence, the relative importance of the factors increasing or decreasing reserves varies depending on the length of the time period considered.

But, keeping these qualifications in mind, we can look at table 10.2, which shows the relative importance of the various factors determining changes in bank reserves on a week-to-week basis. It shows absolute changes, that is, changes regardless of sign. For example, if the change in float was, say, +$150 million in one week, and –$100 million in the next week, this is treated as an average change of $125 million, not of $25 million.

Table 10.2 shows that Federal Reserve bank credit dominated the factors supplying reserves.[4] Almost two-thirds of the total of the reserves supplied during this period by the factors of increase was accounted for by Federal Reserve purchases of government and government-agency securities. Loans to member banks accounted for 8.5 percent. Float accounted for another 16.2 percent. The factors that decreased bank reserves were dominated by two items: Treasury deposits with the Federal Reserve and currency in circulation.

Thus the net change in bank reserves that occurred in 1976–78 was the result of many factors. Of these, Federal Reserve purchases of securities and, to some extent, borrowing by member banks (including seasonal loans) are directly under Federal Reserve control. The Fed has, of course, direct control over its security purchases, but it can control member bank borrowing only by changing the discount rate or by adopting a more (or less) permissive attitude towards banks that want to borrow.

The other factors, often called market factors or operating factors, are not controlled by the Fed. Does this mean that the Federal Reserve lacks effective control over bank reserves? Not really, because the Fed can, and does, forecast the reserve change that will result from market factors; and then, if it does not like this change, it could offset it by open-market purchases or sales of securities. Hence, the Fed could, if it wanted to, control bank reserves in this way. However, such control would not be perfect because the Fed's forecast of what the market factors will do to reserves is imprecise. The Fed's offsetting open-market operations could therefore be too large or too small, and, until it takes corrective action, bank reserves could differ from what it would like.

The Reserve Base and Other Measures of Reserves

Reserve base. Much of the discussion of monetary policy is phrased, not in terms of bank reserves, but using some related concept instead. The most important of these concepts is the reserve base, sometimes called the monetary base or just the base. One can think of the reserve base in terms of the accounting framework of "sources" and "uses." From the uses side, it consists of bank reserves and currency in circulation. From the sources side, it consists of all the factors determining bank reserves discussed in the previous section except currency in circulation. Since currency in circulation is included in the reserve base, an increase in it, although it decreases bank reserves, does not decrease the reserve base.

Adjusted base. A related concept is the adjusted base. Suppose that one wants to gauge whether monetary policy is restrictive or expansionary.

---

[4] Although the Federal Reserve Bank credit includes Federal Reserve purchases of government securities, such purchases are not credit in the usual sense of the word, which implies an obligation of the borrower to repay.

Just looking at the monetary base can give very misleading results if the Federal Reserve has changed reserve requirements. Even if the base has not expanded at all, monetary policy could still be expansionary if the reserve requirement ratio was reduced. Hence, it is useful for an analysis over time to adjust the base by adding to it the dollar equivalent of the change in the average required reserve ratio. The base thus adjusted for the change in reserve requirements is known as the extended base, or adjusted base, or net base.[5]

Unborrowed reserves. Banks are, at least to some extent, reluctant to borrow from the Federal Reserve. They may therefore be less willing to make loans and buy securities on the basis of a dollar of reserves they have borrowed from the Federal Reserve, so-called borrowed reserves, than on the basis of a dollar of reserves they own. Hence, it is useful to look, not only at the base, but also at the unborrowed base. To obtain this figure, all one has to do is to subtract from the base borrowings from the Fed.

To use this unborrowed base one has to adjust the money multiplier for bank borrowing since banks can obviously create more deposits if they can borrow some of the reserves for this. Hence, one has to subtract *b,* which is borrowing as a percent of deposits, from the denominator, thus getting

$$\frac{1}{r - b + e + k + rt_t}.$$

The easiest way to think of this is that banks meet part of their reserve requirement by borrowing, and hence have to keep from their owned reserves only a reserve requirements ratio of $r - b$.

Excess reserves. Another reserve measure consists of excess reserves, that is, reserves in excess of those that are legally required. This measure tells us the extent to which the banking system can, if it wants to, *expand* its loans and investments.

Free reserves. Still another base measure subtracts from excess reserves the amount that banks have borrowed from the Federal Reserve on the argument that before expanding their earning assets, that is, making loans and buying securities, banks will use their excess reserves to repay their borrowings from the Federal Reserve.[6] Hence, the extent to which banks are willing to expand earning assets is indicated by excess reserves minus borrowings from the Federal Reserve, a measure called free reserves. But such a mechanistic view of banks ignores the fact that if the discount rate, which is the cost of borrowing from the Fed, is low relative to other interest rates, a profit-maximizing bank will want to stay indebted to the Fed. Figure 10.1 summarizes all of these base measures.

---

[5] This base is adjusted also for those changes in the *average* reserve requirements that result from shifts of deposits between banks with different marginal reserve requirements and between different types of deposits.

[6] Actually, this statement is not quite correct as it stands. The amount borrowed by banks under their "seasonal borrowing privilege" (which will be discussed in chapter 22) is not subtracted since banks are not under great pressure to repay these loans.

Figure 10.1   Reserve Concepts

Measure	Definition
Reserve base, base, or monetary base	Currency plus bank reserves with the Federal Reserve
Adjusted base, extended base, or net base	Base adjusted for changes in reserve requirements
Unborrowed reserves	Base minus borrowings from Federal Reserve
Excess reserves	Total reserves minus required reserves
Free reserves	Excess reserves minus borrowing

The Reserve Base, the Money Multiplier, and the Money Stock

In this chapter we have discussed bank reserves and the reserve base, while the previous chapter dealt with the money multiplier. We can now bring these two together to see how they jointly determine their product, the money supply. The important question here is the extent to which changes in the money supply are due to variations in the money multiplier rather than to changes in the reserve base. This is an important issue because the Federal Reserve's relatively accurate control over the money stock comes primarily from its control over the extended base.

Unfortunately, one cannot give an unequivocal answer to the question of how much of the variation in the money stock is due to changes in the base and how much to changes in the money multiplier. It depends in large part on the time period considered. If the inquiry concerns the change in the money stock over a long period of time, say, ten years, the answer would be that most of the change is due to the base, while if a short period of time is considered, say, a month, this is not so. The reason for this difference is that the base is usually growing, so that over a decade its growth cumulates to a very substantial figure that accounts for most of the growth in the money supply. On the other hand, the money multiplier has much less of a consistent trend; it rises in one month, and declines in another, so that over a long period of time at least some of the variation in the money multiplier washes out. By contrast, over a very short period of time, say a month, the base grows very little. Hence, for short periods, changes in the money multiplier can more readily swamp changes in the base.

Figure 9.1 showed the recent behavior of the money multiplier. It illustrated that the money multiplier has been declining. This decline results mainly from a rise in the currency ratio and in the time-deposit ratio. Apart from this trendlike decline, the money multiplier seems fairly stable, but this stability can be deceptive. The Fed should know by how much the money stock *increases* if it raises the base by, say, $1 billion; in other words, it should know the *marginal* money multiplier as well as the average

Table 10.3 Frequency Distribution of the Percent of Quarterly Changes in the Money Stock Accounted for by Changes in the Monetary Base[a]

| | Number of cases | | Percent of cases | |
	M_1	M_2	M_1	M_2
Less than 50 percent[b]	0	3	0	7.5
50 percent and under 75 percent	3	11	7.5	27.5
75 percent and under 100 percent	7	13	17.5	32.5
100 percent and under 125 percent	7	10	17.5	25.0
125 percent and under 150 percent	10	2	25.0	5.0
150 percent and over	13	1	32.5	2.5
TOTAL	40	40	100 %	100 %

a. Percent changes in the money stock from February–May, May–August, August–November, and November–February, divided by the percent change in the base during the same period.
b. Includes negative cases, that is, cases where the money supply and the base changed in opposite directions.
SOURCE: Based on unpublished data provided through the courtesy of the St. Louis Federal Reserve Bank.

one, but figure 9.1 showed only that the average money multiplier is stable when adjusted for trend.

One way of measuring the stability of the marginal money multiplier is to ask what percentage of the change in the money stock is due to changes in the base, rather than in the money multiplier. Accordingly, table 10.3 shows the results of dividing the percentage change in the money stock over a three-month period by the corresponding percentage change in the base. (A figure of over 100 percent means that the money stock changed by a larger percentage than the base.)

In 90 percent of the cases the change in the base explains more than half of the change in the money stock during a three-month period. A figure of over 150 percent in table 10.3 should be interpreted as the change in the base explaining *less* than half of the change in the money stock, since it means that if one tries to predict the change in the money stock by assuming that it changes by the same percent as the base, one would be more than 50 percent off.

Table 10.4 investigates how well changes in the base can explain *year-to-year* changes in the money stock. It shows that changes in the base account for much of the change in the money stock.

The fact that over a three-month period in a number of cases changes in the base explain less of the change in the money stock than does the change in the money multiplier does not mean that the Fed's control over the money stock is weak. The Federal Reserve's control over the money stock does not require a *stable* numerical relationship between the base and the money stock, for example, it does not require that the money multiplier be 3.0. All it requires is a *predictable* relationship. If the Federal

Table 10.4　Year-to-Year Changes in the Money Stock and the Monetary Base
1967–68 to 1977–78

	Percentage change in:		*Change in M_1 as percent of change in base:*[a]
	M_1	BASE	
JUNE:			
1967–68	7.17	5.79	123.8
1968–69	6.33	6.56	96.5
1969–70	3.29	5.13	64.1
1970–71	7.55	8.23	91.7
1971–72	5.88	7.09	82.9
1972–73	8.69	8.90	97.6
1973–74	5.23	8.51	61.5
1974–75	4.93	8.66	56.9
1975–76	4.39	7.97	55.1
1976–77	7.00	7.64	91.6
1977–78	8.35	9.76	85.6

a. Changes in both M_1 and the base measured in percentage terms.

SOURCE: Based on unpublished data provided through the courtesy of the Federal Reserve Bank of St. Louis.

Reserve can predict how the money multiplier will vary, it can offset changes in it. For example, if the Federal Reserve wants the money stock to grow at a 4 percent rate, and knows that the money multiplier will decline by 2 percent, it can simply increase the base by 6 percent instead of 4 percent. Hence, the fact that the money multiplier has been declining sharply in recent years does not matter, since it is a fairly stable, and hence predictable, decline. However, this stability may be deceptive. The Fed has changed reserves in an attempt to stabilize interest rates. If the Fed had tried to maintain a given growth rate of the money stock instead, interest rates, and hence the money multiplier, would have varied more in the short run. By how much more is hard to say.

Summary

This chapter has dealt with the factors that change bank reserves, and explained why each of them did so. Here in table 10.5 is a list of these factors classified by the sector that is responsible for the changes, with a plus indicating that it is a factor of increase and a minus that it is a factor of decrease.

We then took up the relative importance of these factors. Several concepts related to bank reserves were then discussed: the base, the extended base, unborrowed reserves, excess reserves, and free reserves. The last section of the chapter dealt with the important issue of the extent to which

Table 10.5 Factors Changing Bank Reserves

Federal Reserve	U.S. Treasury	Nonbank public	Foreigners	Several sectors
+ U.S. government (and agency) securities bought	+ Gold purchases	− Currency in circulation	− Foreign deposits with Federal Reserve	− Other deposits with Federal Reserve
+ Acceptances bought	+ SDRs			− Other Federal Reserve liabilities and capital
+ Member bank borrowing	+ Treasury currency outstanding			
+ Float	− Treasury cash holdings			
+ Other Federal Reserve assets	− Treasury deposits with Federal Reserve			

changes in the money stock are due to changes in the money multiplier rather than to changes in reserves, and also took up the question of what this implies for the ability of the Federal Reserve to control the money stock.

QUESTIONS AND EXERCISES

1. Given the following data calculate the change in bank reserves:

		Change
1.	Federal Reserve security purchases (including repurchase agreements)	10
2.	Gold stock	−10
3.	Currency in circulation	5
4.	Acceptances bought by Federal Reserve	− 3
5.	Treasury currency	10
6.	Float	− 3
7.	Special Drawing Rights certificate account	10
8.	Other Federal Reserve liabilities and capital	1
9.	Other deposits with F.R. banks	− 1
10.	Other Federal Reserve assets	5
11.	Foreign deposits with F.R. banks	5
12.	Federal Reserve loans	20
13.	Treasury deposits with F.R. banks	− 5
14.	Treasury cash holdings	− 5

2. Take the data given in the previous example: (a) eliminate the figure shown for Federal Reserve security purchases, and (b) add the following:

15.	Member bank deposits at the Federal Reserve	− 3
16.	Currency held by banks	− 2
17.	Currency held by nonbank public	5

Now calculate Federal Reserve purchases of securities.

3. Take each of the items in question 1 and explain in your own words the effects of this item on bank reserves. Do not merely state whether its increase raises or lowers reserves, but explain why.

4. Evaluate the following statements:
   a. When the Treasury buys gold, the money stock increases because the country now has more gold.
   b. An increase in float increases the money stock because it means that there are more checks in transit, which, in turn, means that people are receiving more money. This increases the money stock.
   c. An increase in currency in circulation raises bank reserves because some of this currency will be deposited in banks.
   d. When Federal Reserve loans increase, bank reserves decline because by increasing the liabilities of banks to the Federal Reserve it reduces their *net* assets with the Federal Reserve.

5. Take each of the items in table 10.1 and set up, wherever relevant, the T accounts for commercial banks, the Federal Reserve, the Treasury, or the nonbank public.

6. Look at the factors supplying and absorbing bank reserves in last Monday's *Wall Street Journal*. Write a paragraph explaining in your own words what has happened.

7. Define and discuss the relation between: reserve base, extended base, high-powered money, free reserves, unborrowed reserves.

8. "The money stock depends upon the actions of the Federal Reserve, the Treasury, the commercial banks and the public." Explain this statement, pro-

viding examples of specific actions by each of them that change the money supply.

9. We stated that an increase in Treasury deposits with the Federal Reserve reduces bank reserves because these deposits are withdrawn from commercial banks. But what happens if the increase in Treasury deposits at the Federal Reserve results from: (a) the Treasury depositing surplus currency with the Federal Reserve, (b) the Federal Reserve providing Treasury currency to the Treasury, (c) the Treasury retiring some government securities held by the Federal Reserve?

FURTHER READING

BERGER, ALBERT. *The Money Supply Process.* Belmont, Calif.: Wadsworth Publishing Co., 1971. A very thorough and comprehensive survey of the factors that determine the money stock.

CAGAN, PHILLIP. *Determinants and Effects of Changes in the Stock of Money.* New York: Columbia University Press, 1965. A very detailed and scholarly analysis.

FEDERAL RESERVE BANK OF NEW YORK. *Glossary: Federal Reserve Statements.* New York: Federal Reserve Bank of New York, 1972. A useful explanation of various technical terms.

NICHOLS, DOROTHY (Federal Reserve Bank of Chicago). *Modern Money Mechanics.* Chicago: Federal Reserve Bank of Chicago, 1971. A simple and clear discussion of the factors changing bank reserves and of deposit creation.

11

The Measurement of Money

In chapter 1 we defined money in rather general terms, and this has sufficed so far. But before taking up monetary theory and policy in Parts Three and Four we have to consider additional aspects of the definition and measurement of the stock of money. This is important for monetary theory, since one of the leading monetary theories states that changes in nominal income can be explained primarily by changes in the stock of money. How is such a theory tested? Obviously, the data on past changes in nominal income and the money stock are studied. But to do this one needs a precise definition of money, so it is clear which data to turn to. In general, whenever we test a theory, we have to take some of the terms used in the theory, such as *money* and *income,* and find an empirically measurable analog or interpretation for them.

Similarly, for monetary policy we need to be able to measure, and hence define, money. It does little good to tell the Federal Reserve that it should increase the stock of money by, say, 6 percent, unless we can also tell it what particular measure of money we have in mind. Moreover, one of the major disputes in monetary policy, which will be discussed at length in chapter 23, is whether the Federal Reserve should use the money stock or the interest rate as the target for its policy. And one of the issues in this dispute is whether the Federal Reserve can measure the money stock accurately enough for it to be a workable target. After all, it makes little sense to aim at a target unless you know whether you have hit it, or how far away from it you are.

Defining Money

We will now take up the definition of *money* in some detail.

The A Priori and Empirical Approaches

There are two major approaches to defining the money stock. The first of these, called the **a priori approach,** is a rather philosophical one that *focuses on the nature of money*. It searches for ~~the characteristic that most distinguishes money from other things~~, and then defines money in terms of this characteristic. This is surely the way we usually define something.

To the question, ~~what is *the* distinguishing characteristic of money~~, there is a simple answer: it is its medium of exchange function. This is the function that is unique to money; nothing else is a general medium of exchange. By contrast, the store of value function is not unique to money; money shares this function with many other things, such as stocks and bonds. Hence, the a priori approach defines money as anything that is a generally accepted medium of exchange. The standard of value function is also unique to money, but this function is carried out by money in the abstract and not by a concrete unit. Thus it would be meaningless to ask, for example, by how much the quantity of the standard of value has changed last month. It would also be meaningless to ask whether the standard of value is M_1 or M_2. Hence, the standard of value function does not provide any guide to how we should define money for the purpose of testing its importance in determining nominal income, and it does not provide the Federal Reserve with any help in determining whether to use M_1 or M_2 as its target.

The a priori definition of money has the advantage of providing, at least on an abstract level, a fairly clear-cut differentiation between those items that are money and those that are not. Items that can normally be used to make payments, such as currency, demand deposits, and other transactions accounts such as NOW accounts, as well as traveler's checks, are money, while time deposits are *not*. Hence, this approach defines money as M_1 plus transactions accounts and traveler's checks.

While the a priori definition of money focuses on what is distinctive about money, that is, on its essence, the rival **empirical definition** *focuses instead on what makes the money stock important*. Money is important for policy for two reasons. One is that ~~changes in the money supply have a major, and numerous economists would say dominating, impact on nominal income~~. The second reason is that the Federal Reserve can control the supply of money. Since economists are largely concerned with giving policy advice, variables that the government can control are, obviously, more strategic to them than other variables, such as expectations, that may also have a powerful effect on nominal income, but cannot be controlled so easily.

The empirical definition of money therefore defines money, not by any inherent characteristics, but as that liquid asset, or collection of liquid assets, that (1) has the most predictable impact on nominal income, and (2) can be controlled by the Federal Reserve. In addition, supporters of the empirical definition of money prefer to use a variable for which we have data stretching over many years, so that we have more observations to test our theories by.

In practice, what measure of money does this amount to? Unfortunately, this question is simpler to pose than to answer. The last mentioned criterion, that data covering many years be available, points to an M_2 rather than an M_1 definition, since reliable data on M_1 are available only since 1915; before then the data did not make a *sharp* distinction between demand and time deposits. However, many economists believe the availability of data for the years prior to 1915 is not a significant argument for using an M_2 measure. They believe that our other data for these early years are not reliable in any case, and also that the economy has changed so much since then, that we can get little useful information from empirical tests using data from before 1915. To what extent this is actually the case is a much disputed issue.

In any case, a much more important criterion is which measure of the money stock yields the monetary variable that has the most predictable impact on nominal income. Some economists, Professor Friedman, for example, believe that this is M_2, while many other economists believe that this is M_1. It may seem that this is a question that could be answered simply by looking at the data. But this is not so for two reasons. First, data fitted to different periods, and to different functional relations between money and income, may show different results, and, second, the correlation between money and income that can be seen in the data reflects not only the effect that money has on income, but also the reserve effect that income has on the money supply. It is not easy to separate out from this the net effect of money on income. Moreover, at least for recent years, various definitions of money all show more or less equally good correlations with income.

And a minority of economists believe that the money stock should be defined more broadly than M_2. They prefer to include along with time deposits in commercial banks all deposits in thrift institutions, since to the depositor there is little difference between a time deposit in a commercial bank and a deposit in a thrift institution.

The final criterion is the extent to which the Federal Reserve can control the designated total. Here there is little difference between M_1 and M_2.

The Choice between Approaches

Which is better, the empirical or the a priori definition? Those who adhere to the a priori definition argue that the empirical definition is inadequate because it misses the essence of money and is subject to erratic shifts. Thus, the empirical definition of the money stock may define money as M_1 at one time and as M_2 at another time depending on which of these shows the closest correlation with income. This seems arbitrary to supporters of the a priori definition. Besides, the advocates of the empirical definition do not agree among themselves about which measure of the money stock is the best "handle" in controlling income. Supporters of the empirical definition such as Professor Friedman, on the other hand, see nothing wrong with the definition of money changing from time to time, and each of them believes that he or she has evidence that allows one to choose between M_1 and M_2.

Fortunately, this disagreement is unimportant. It is essentially a dispute about the ownership of the word *money,* and is not a disagreement about how the economy operates. Thus, one could accept the a priori definition of money as M_1, and yet if it turns out that M_2 has the more predictable effect on income, and is the more readily controllable total, one could think and talk mainly about M_2, using some word other than *money,* say *bread,* if one does not like to say M_2. On the other hand, one can go along with the empirical definition, and use the term *money* for, say, M_2, while being fully aware of the fact that the item that is the medium of exchange has a unique and interesting characteristic.

The Vanishing Distinction between Demand and Savings Deposits

As just pointed out, in the empirical approach the definition of the money stock may change as the economy changes. And in the 1970s important changes took place that have eroded the distinction between demand deposits and savings deposits. Thus, banks and thrift institutions were allowed to make preauthorized transfers for households from savings accounts; that is, a family could tell its bank or thrift institution to pay regular bills, such as utility and mortgage payments, each month directly out of its savings deposit. Under another arrangement depositors could transfer funds between their savings and demand deposits over the telephone. In 1978 banks and thrift institutions were allowed to offer arrangements under which they would transfer funds automatically from a household's savings deposit into its demand deposit to meet incoming checks, so that the household could keep its demand deposit balance at zero. And NOW accounts permitted households in New England (and since 1978 also in New York) to write what are in effect checks against their savings accounts at banks and thrift institutions. And in 1980 Congress passed a bill making such NOW accounts available nationwide.

All of these changes resulted in an erosion of the distinction between demand deposits and time deposits. This may seem to suggest that M_1 is losing its significance so that we should use the M_2 definition instead. However, things are more complicated. To start with, some of the institutional changes just reviewed tend to assimilate into demand deposits savings deposits, not just in commercial banks, but also in thrift institutions. Second, while savings deposits have thus become more liquid, another important component of M_2, time deposits, has become *less* liquid.[1] This is

---

[1] Recall that time deposits are deposits with a specific maturity, for example, one year, while savings deposits can, de facto, be withdrawn at any time.

due to the imposition in 1973 of interest penalties for early withdrawals of time deposits, and the substantial lengthening of the average maturity of these deposits. In addition, time deposits have risen relative to the more liquid savings deposits. Hence, it is far from clear that the solution lies in using M_2 in place of M_1. A much more basic change seemed called for; this is to recombine deposits into a new set of monetary aggregates. And in February 1980 the Federal Reserve responded.

New Measures of Money

The Fed's redefinition of the money measures reflects a development we saw already, the declining differentiation between thrift institutions and commercial banks. With many savings and loan associations, mutual savings banks, and credit unions now providing checkable deposits, such as NOW accounts, it makes little sense to include in money only demand deposits in commercial banks. Accordingly, the Federal Reserve now calls the traditional M_1, *M-1A* and introduced a new concept *M-1B* that includes checkable deposits in thrift institutions. (But it subtracts from both *M-1A* and *M-1B* the deposits of foreign commercial banks and government institutions. These are primarily clearing balances and do not affect expenditures on U.S. goods and services. The only reason that they were not previously subtracted from the old M_1 is that the Fed lacked data on them.)

Moreover, the Fed abandoned the traditional M_2 measure. In its new *M-2* it includes savings deposits and "small" time deposits, that is, time deposits of less than \$100,000 both in commercial banks and in thrift institutions. As Table 11.1 shows the new *M-2* also includes certain assets that are just as, or more, liquid than savings deposits. One of these is the overnight repurchase agreements of large corporations. As we explained in chapter 4, when a corporation buys a security from a bank late in the afternoon, and the bank pledges itself to buy it back when it opens for business the next morning, the corporation is not really relinquishing the use of its funds because it could not use them in any case while the bank is closed. Hence, the reductions in demand deposits that occur when corporations buy such securities are completely spurious, and the Fed adjusts for them by adding the value of these overnight repurchase agreements back into the money data. Instead of using repurchase agreements some firms put funds overnight into interest-bearing deposits at Caribbean branches of U.S. banks. These funds too are available the next morning and hence are counted in the new *M-2*. Most money-market mutual funds allow their customers to write checks of \$500 and over against their shares in these funds, and hence the Fed also includes these money-market fund shares in the new *M-2*. (In principle one might argue that they should be included in *M-1B* along with checkable deposits in banks and thrift institutions, but the data show that money-market shares are withdrawn about as frequently as are time and savings deposits.) Finally, there is a technical bookkeeping

Table 11.1   New Measures of Money and Liquid Assets

Aggregate	Component	Amount in billions of dollars (not seasonally adjusted) November 1979
M-1A		372.2
	Currency	106.6
	Demand deposits[a]	265.6
M-1B		387.9
	M-1A	372.2
	Other checkable deposits[b]	15.7
M-2		1510.0
	M-1B	387.9
	Overnight RPs issued by commercial banks	20.3
	Overnight Eurodollar deposits held by U.S. nonbank residents at Caribbean branches of U.S. banks	3.2
	Money-market mutual-fund shares	40.4
	Savings deposits at all depository institutions	420.0
	Small time deposits at all depository institutions[e]	640.8
	M-2 consolidation component[d]	−2.7
M-3		1759.1
	M-2	1510.0
	Large time deposits at all depository institutions[e]	219.5
	Term RPs issued by commercial banks	21.5
	Term RPs issued by savings and loan associations	8.2
L		2123.8
	M-3	1759.1
	Other Eurodollars of U.S. residents other than banks	34.5
	Bankers acceptances	27.6
	Commercial paper	97.1
	Savings bonds	80.0
	Liquid Treasury obligations	125.4

Note: Components of *M-2, M-3,* and *L* measures generally exclude amounts held by domestic depository institutions, foreign commercial banks and official institutions, the U.S. government (including the Federal Reserve), and money-market mutual funds. Exceptions are bankers acceptances and commercial paper for which data sources permit the removal only of amounts held by money-market mutual funds and, in the case of bankers acceptances, amounts held by accepting banks, the Federal Reserve, and the Federal Home Loan Bank System.

a. Net of demand deposits due to foreign commercial banks and official institutions.

b. Includes NOW, ATS, and credit-union share-draft balances and demand deposits at thrift institutions.

c. Time deposits issued in denominations of less than $100,000.

d. In order to avoid double counting of some deposits in *M-2,* those demand deposits owned by thrift institutions (a component of *M-1B*) that are estimated to be used for servicing their savings and small time deposit liabilities in *M-2* are removed.

e. Time deposits issued in denominations of $100,000 or more.

SOURCE: "The Redefinition of Monetary Aggregates," *Federal Reserve Bulletin* 66 (February 1980): 98.

adjustment called the *consolidation component*. Some demand deposits are held by banks and by thrift institutions to service their savings and small time deposits. To include in *M-2* both these demand deposits and the savings and time deposits that they support would be double counting. Hence, these demand deposits are subtracted from *M-2*.

The traditional measure M_3 adds to currency and deposits in com-

Table 11.2   Relation between New and Old Monetary Aggregates

Aggregate and Component	*Amount in billions of dollars (not seasonally adjusted)* *November 1979*
Old M₁	382.6
Less demand deposits of foreign commercial banks and official institutions	10.4
Equals: New M-1Aª	372.2
Plus other checkable deposits	15.7
Equals: New M-1B	387.9
Old M₂	945.3
Plus savings and time deposits at thrift institutions	664.2
Equals: Old M₃	1609.5
Plus overnight RPs and Eurodollars	23.4
Plus money-market mutual-fund shares	40.4
Plus demand deposits at mutual savings banksᵇ	1.0
Less large time deposits at all depository institutions in current *M-3*	151.2
Less demand deposits of foreign commercial banks and official institutions	10.4
Less consolidation componentᶜ	2.7
Equals: New M-2	1510.0
Plus large time deposits at all depository institutions	219.5
Plus term RPs at commercial banks and savings and loan institutions	29.8
Equals: New M-3	1759.1
Memo:	
Old M₂	945.3
Plus negotiable CDs at large commercial banks	95.9
Equals: Old M₄	1041.2
Old M₃	1609.5
Plus negotiable CDs at large commercial banks	95.9
Equals: Old M₅	1705.4

a. Also includes a very small amount of *M-1*-type balances at certain U.S. banking offices of foreign banks outside New York City that were not in the old M_1 measure.

b. Demand deposits at mutual savings banks were not included in any of the old monetary aggregates.

c. Consists of an estimate of demand deposits included in *M-1B* that are held by thrift institutions for use in servicing their savings and small time-deposits liabilities included in the new *M-2*.

SOURCE: "The Redefined Monetary Aggregates" *Federal Reserve Bulletin* 66 (February 1980): 99.

mercial banks deposits in thrift institutions. It therefore corresponds to some extent to the new *M-2*. The Fed's new *M-3* is different. It adds to the new *M-2* the large ($100,000 and over) time deposits of all depository institutions, as well as securities bought by corporations from banks and savings and loan associations under repurchase agreements for a longer period than just overnight.

Finally, there is an even broader measure of liquid assets called *L*, which includes the Eurodollar holdings of U.S. residents (but not of banks) as well as outstanding bankers acceptances, commercial paper, U.S. government savings bonds, and other liquid government securities. This new

Figure 11.1   Behavior of Various Measures of the Money Stock
1973–79

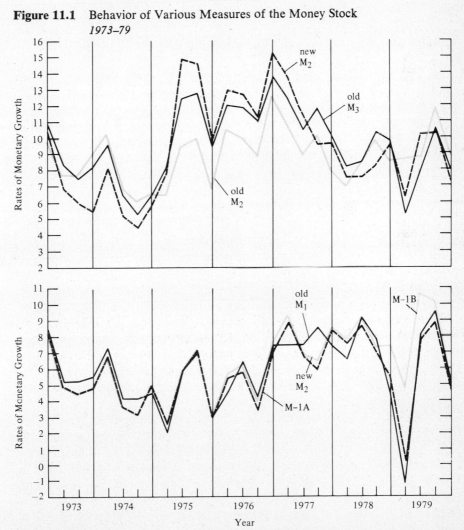

SOURCE: "The Redefined Monetary Aggregates," *Federal Reserve Bulletin* 66 (February 1980): 112–13.

measure, *L*, has no counterpart among the traditional measures of money, and it would be straining things to call it "money." For the other measures table 11.2 and figure 11.1 show how the new measures differ from the old ones.

Given the uncertainty about which of these various measures of the money stock to use, some economists have suggested using the adjusted monetary base instead. This is a total that has not been affected by any of the institutional changes, and it has a close relationship to income. Some economists are also angry at the Federal Reserve for changing its regulations in ways that break down the distinction between demand and savings deposits, and make money so hard to define. In their view the Fed is not so much a victim of institutional changes as the culprit.

Credit Cards, Eurodollars, and Money Substitutes

The Fed's proposed definitions are probably an improvement over the previous ones, but they still leave a serious problem. They exclude some items that function like money. In recent years, rising market interest rates and inflation have provided an incentive to reduce deposit holdings, and to develop new forms of "money" and money substitutes that pay an interest rate not controlled by Regulation Q. And the computer revolution, by greatly reducing the cost of paperwork, has contributed to this too. As a result, money substitutes, and forms of money that are not encompassed by the standard definitions of the money stock, have grown rapidly.

The most obvious example is credit cards. One can think of a credit-card line of credit as a substitute for holding money, or even as itself money. Lines of credit, such as those provided by credit cards, are like money in the sense of providing a widely, though not quite generally, accepted medium of exchange. (However, they differ from money in one important way: money is part of a person's wealth, but a line of credit is not; for example, wouldn't everyone rather receive a $1,000 check as a gift than have the ceiling on their credit-card credit raised by $1,000?) Moreover, in recent years many American banks have adopted a common practice of British banks, the extension of overdraft privileges. These banks allow certain customers to write checks in excess of their demand deposits, and these overdrafts are treated as automatic loans.

Another troublesome problem is created by Eurodollars, the dollar-denominated deposits in European banks and in European branches of American banks. (And there are also Asiadollars domiciled in Singapore.) The volume of Eurodollar deposits held by nonbanks was estimated in 1979 as about $120 billion, with about $22 billion of this owned by U.S. residents. It is uncertain what proportion of the Eurodollars of non-banks are held for the sake of making expenditures in the United States, but one rough estimate is that at the end of 1978 there were about $52 billion of Eurodollars that could reasonably have been considered part of the U.S. money stock defined as *M-3*.[2] However, this is only a very rough estimate, and economists are uncertain about how to integrate Eurodollars into their picture of the money supply. Many are uneasy about the current procedure of simply ignoring Eurodollars when looking at the growth rate of the U.S. money stock.

Something else that is creating concern is that some nonbank firms have started to issue liabilities that are more or less similar to bank deposits, and hence to money. Thus one large brokerage firm (Merrill Lynch Pierce Fenner & Smith) allows customers who have large accounts with it to use their accounts to transfer funds to others via a bank credit card or via checks written on a cooperating bank. At the same time, some large corporations are considering issuing short-term and intermediate-term securities in small denominations, say $100 or so, which would compete head-on with deposits in banks and thrift institutions. It is quite possible that some years from now the line that separates banks from other corporations will have eroded substantially. Under those circumstances, defining money could be quite a problem.

Refining the Money Measurements

So far we have discussed some broad issues in defining and measuring the money stock. It is about time that we looked at some more specific issues. It is easy to say that demand deposits should be counted as part of the money stock, but do we really want to include all types of demand deposits? No, we do not. We are interested in the size of the money stock, not because this is knowledge that ennobles a person's otherwise drab life, but only because changes in the money stock bring about changes in expenditures, and hence in nominal income. This suggests that we should include only those deposits that affect expenditures.

It follows that the deposits of the federal government should not be counted. Federal government expenditures are not influenced at all by the Treasury's money holdings. They are set by congressional authorization, and in some cases, for example in agricultural price support payments, by the behavior of the economy. The U.S. Treasury, unlike many households and firms, is never constrained in its expenditures by having insufficient money—it can always borrow more. And, similarly, high deposit holdings never cause it to increase its spending. For this reason U.S. government deposits—but not state and local government deposits—are excluded from the money supply.

Another item that is excluded is currency held by banks in their vaults. We exclude this because it too does not affect the bank's expendi-

[2] See Henry C. Wallich, "Why the Euromarket Needs Restraints," *Columbia Journal of World Business* 14 (Fall 1979): 18.

tures. And for the same reason interbank deposits are excluded too. In addition, we also exclude cash items in the process of collection, that is, checks, etc., currently in the process of clearing, on the, perhaps somewhat doubtful, assumption that those who wrote these checks have already deducted them from their outstanding balances. And what affects expenditures are the deposits that people *think* they have. These adjustments are not the only ones that are made to bank deposits to calculate the money stock. For example, deposits at certain corporations set up by banks to facilitate foreign trade have to be added in.

How Reliable Are the Data?

We now come to a painful topic. The data we often use on the growth rate of the money stock are very poor. The way we know this is that the initially published data are substantially revised later on. And since the revised data are presumably fairly accurate, it follows that the previously published data were highly inaccurate. This is illustrated by the third column of table 11.3, which shows the results of a revision made to the previously published 1977 money-stock data in March 1978. (And such revisions are made throughout a four-year period.) The mean absolute revision for 1977 was 1.8 percent for M_1 and 0.9 percent for M_2.[3] This is very high since even a 1 percent sustained change in the money growth rate is considered to be a significant change in monetary policy. Hence errors in estimating the money growth rate can give a very misleading picture. For example, in March 1978 the data showed a sharp retardation of the money growth rate for several months that some economists thought would lead to a recession. But when the data were revised shortly afterwards, this no longer seemed plausible.

    The unreliability of the data until several years afterwards when they have been completely revised has two major implications. First, one should not get upset about data showing that the money stock was growing at a highly undesirable rate for a short period of time. Over a period of, say, three or six months, errors tend to average out, but the weekly data on the growth of the money stock that are published in many newspapers are, in all probability, going to be revised substantially. When one adds to this the fact that the actual weekly growth rate of money fluctuates very erratically in any case, it follows that the publication of the weekly money-stock figures could constitutionally be banned under the Supreme Court criterion of being material without any redeeming social value.

---

[3] Another way of seeing how serious the errors are is to regress the actual change in M_1 on the first published estimate. If the preliminary estimates were completely correct, the correlation coefficient would be unity, and so would the regression coefficient. But a study for the period 1971–77 found, using seasonally adjusted data, a correlation coefficient of only 0.53 and a regression coefficient of 0.17! (Courtenay Stone and Jeffrey Olson, "Are the Preliminary Week-to-Week Fluctuations in M_1 Biased?" *Review* [Federal Reserve Bank of St. Louis] 60 [December 1978]: 19.)

Table 11.3   1978 Revision of Estimates of 1977 Money Growth Rates
(Percent growth rates over 2-month periods expressed at annual rates)

	Previous estimate	Revised estimate	Previous minus revised estimate	Old seasonals Revised estimate	Revised minus previous estimate
1977—M_1					
Jan.–Feb.	3.1	7.1	–4.0	4.4	–1.3
Feb.–March	3.1	6.5	–3.4	4.6	–1.5
March–April	12.4	10.8	1.6	13.9	–1.5
April–May	10.1	7.7	2.4	10.6	–0.5
May–June	2.6	4.3	–1.7	2.8	–0.2
June–July	11.4	9.5	1.9	11.5	–0.1
July–Aug.	12.1	9.1	3.0	11.7	0.4
Aug.–Sept.	6.6	7.5	–0.9	6.0	0.6
Sept.–Oct.	9.7	9.8	–0.1	9.1	0.6
Oct.–Nov.	5.3	5.6	–0.3	4.9	0.4
Nov.–Dec.	3.1	3.8	–0.7	3.0	–0.1
MEAN[a]			1.8		0.7
1977—M_2					
Jan.–Feb.	8.4	10.1	–1.7	8.9	–0.5
Feb.–March	7.9	9.4	–1.5	8.4	–0.5
March–April	11.1	10.2	0.9	11.6	–0.5
April–May	9.1	8.2	0.9	9.3	–0.2
May–June	6.4	7.3	–0.9	6.7	–0.3
June–July	12.4	11.3	1.1	12.8	–0.4
July–Aug.	11.6	10.6	1.0	11.7	–0.1
Aug.–Sept.	7.2	8.4	–1.2	7.3	–0.1
Sept.–Oct.	9.1	9.4	–0.3	9.1	0.0
Oct.–Nov.	7.4	7.6	–0.2	7.4	0.0
Nov.–Dec.	5.2	5.5	–0.3	5.2	0.0
MEAN[a]			0.9		0.2

Note: Data are seasonally adjusted.

a. Mean of absolute values, that is of values added regardless of signs.

SOURCE: Based on Richard Lang, "Benchmark Revisions of the Money Stock and Ranges of Money Stock Growth," *Review* (Federal Reserve Bank of St. Louis) 60 (June 1978): 17.

Second, the Federal Reserve has to make its current policy on the basis of its preliminary data. And since these data do not give a reliable indication of what the current monetary growth rate is, the Federal Reserve can hardly be expected to achieve the precise growth rate it desires.

Why are the data on the stock of money so bad? One reason is—or rather was—that until recently the Federal Reserve did not receive timely reports of deposits in nonmember banks. This is no longer a problem, since 1980 legislation allows the Federal Reserve to obtain such data through the FDIC whenever it wants them. And under the new reserve-requirements system that is being phased in the Fed will receive reports on their deposits directly from nonmember banks and thrift institutions.

A second reason is that there are a number of technical difficulties in estimating the money stock. For example, as pointed out above, cash items in the process of collection are deducted from the deposit total. But, actually, not all of them should be deducted since, for example, some of them relate to Eurodollar deposits that are not included in the money stock.

But the biggest source of errors is that the money-stock data, like most economic statistics, are adjusted for seasonal variations. For example, the demand for money always increases at Christmas time, and to reduce seasonal fluctuations in interest rates the Fed tries to adjust the supply of money for such seasonal variations in demand. To prevent these seasonal changes in supply from distorting the figures, the money stock for each month is divided by a seasonal adjustment factor that should cancel out these seasonal variations. If the seasonal pattern is constant, then this is a simple procedure that does not lead to significant errors. But the seasonal pattern is unstable; for example, in a year when the public feels prosperous its demand for money at Christmas may rise by more than it does in another year in which it feels pessimistic, and hence less generous. Obviously, such a variable seasonal pattern is hard to adjust for. This difficulty of adjusting the data for varying seasonal effects is the *major* reason why the preliminary money-stock data have to be revised so much. This can be seen in table 11.3 by comparing the revisions in the 1977 seasonally adjusted growth rates in the third column with the much smaller revisions shown in the fifth column that would have been made had the seasonal adjustment not been revised along with the underlying money figures.

If the errors in the money-stock figures were constant, for example, the money stock always being overstated by, say, $5 billion, these errors would not matter because they would not affect *relative* money *growth rates,* which is what we are concerned about when we try to predict changes in income. But, unfortunately, this is not the case. Thus, if the error in the seasonal adjustment factor is positive for one month, it must be negative for another month since over the whole year the seasonal adjustment factors cancel out.

One reason why the money growth figures are so bad is that small percentage errors in estimating the money *stock,* purely as a matter of arithmetic, can result in very large percentage errors in the estimate of how fast money has grown over a short period of time. For example, suppose that the actual money stock stood at $1,000 billion at the start of the month, and at $1,004 billion at the end of the month. This is a growth rate in annual terms of approximately 4.8 percent (0.4 percent times 12). But suppose that the money stock at the end of the month is estimated by mistake as $1,006 billion, an error of only 0.2 percent. The growth rate then appears to be about 7.2 percent instead of 4.8 percent. The shorter the period of time covered by the data, the greater is the error in the growth rate that results from a small mistake in estimating the stock at either the beginning or the end of the period.

The magnitude of the error in the monetary growth-rate estimates is brought out sharply by looking at the successive revisions of the M_1 growth rates for January, a month for which the seasonal adjustment is particularly troublesome. The growth rate for January 1972 was first published in 1972 as 3.7 percent. In the following five years it was revised successively to 1.0 percent, 1.5 percent, 3.1 percent, 8.2 percent, and 9.2 percent.[5] These are not trivial differences!

Summary

This chapter took up a necessary preliminary for discussing monetary theory and policy: the definition of money in a measurable way. There are two main approaches to this. The a priori approach emphasizes how money differs from other things, and hence focuses on the medium of exchange function of money. The other, empirical, approach is more policy-oriented. It selects that definition of the money stock that has the closest relationship to income and is readily controllable by the Federal Reserve. Adherents of this approach disagree among themselves whether this is M_1, M_2, or M_3. We pointed out that the dispute about the a priori versus the empirical definition of money is largely a dispute about the ownership of the term *money*. And the dispute about using M_1 or M_2 among the adherents of the empirical definition of money is being outdated by recent regulatory changes. Accordingly, the Federal Reserve in early 1980 redefined its measures of the money stock. It added a measure called *M-1B* that includes checking deposits in thrift institutions. Its new measure of *M-2* includes saving deposits and small time deposits in banks and in thrift institutions, deposits in money-market funds, and certain other readily available funds. Large time deposits and term repurchase agreements are now included along with *M-2* in *M-3*.

We then dealt with the more specific question of what deposits should be excluded from the money stock, and showed that government deposits, interbank deposits, and the vault cash of banks, as well as cash items in the process of collection, should be subtracted.

The final problem discussed in this chapter is the reliability of the early estimates of the money growth rate. We showed that these data are highly unreliable, and discussed the reasons for this. One is that small errors in estimating the level of the money stock translate into large errors in estimating its growth rate over a short period of time. A second reason involves such technicalities as the treatment of cash items in the process of collection, but the biggest reason is the inaccuracy of the seasonal adjustments.

[5] See Alfred Broaddus and Timothy Cook, "Some Factors Affecting Short-Run Growth Rates of the Money Supply," *Economic Review* (Federal Reserve Bank of Richmond) 63 (November–December 1977): 9.

QUESTIONS AND EXERCISES

1. Write an essay defending:
   a. the a priori approach to the definition of money.
   b. the empirical approach to the definition of money.
2. Describe a change in Federal Reserve or FDIC regulations that would induce you to make a change in the definition of money.
3. Look up recent data on the relative growth rates of *M-1A, M-1B, M-2, M-3.* Is there a significant divergence between them? If so, to what do you ascribe it?
4. Discuss why we exclude from *M-1A*:
   a. government deposits;
   b. cash items in the process of collection.
5. If you define money in terms of its medium of exchange function should you include in its measurement savings deposits subject to automatic transfers?

FURTHER READING

ADVISORY COMMITTEE ON MONETARY STATISTICS. *Improving the Monetary Aggregates.* Washington, D.C.: Board of Governors, Federal Reserve System, 1976. A storehouse of information on how the money data are constructed and on how they could be improved.

FRIEDMAN, MILTON, and SCHWARTZ, ANNA. *Monetary Statistics of the United States.* New York: Columbia University Press, 1970. Chapter three gives a cogent and powerful defense of the empirical approach to the definition of money.

LAIDLER, DAVID. "The Definition of Money: Theoretical and Empirical Problems." *Journal of Money, Credit and Banking* 1 (August 1969): 508–25. A very clear discussion that is easier than many of the other items cited here.

LAWLER, THOMAS. "Seasonal Adjustment of the Money Stock: Problems and Policy Implications." *Economic Review* (Federal Reserve Bank of Richmond) 63 (November–December 1977): 19–27. A thorough discussion of a technical issue.

SIMPSON, THOMAS. "The Redefinition of Monetary Aggregates." *Federal Reserve Bulletin* 66 (February 1980): 97–114. This is the Fed's statement of how it now defines money, and its reasons for adopting its definitions.

U.S., CONGRESS, HOUSE, SUBCOMMITTEE ON DOMESTIC MONETARY POLICY, COMMITTEE ON BANKING, FINANCE, AND URBAN AFFAIRS. *Measuring the Monetary Aggregates.* 96th Cong., 2d sess., February 1980. A useful compendium of economists' views.

YEAGER, LEYLAND B. "The Medium of Exchange." In *Monetary Theory,* edited by Robert Clower, pp. 37–60. Baltimore: Penguin Books, 1969. A rousing and subtle defense of the a priori approach to defining money.

PART THREE

‖‖

Monetary Theory

This Part deals with the factors that determine changes in nominal income with particular emphasis on the money supply. We will first take up the Keynesian theory and then the quantity theory and monetarist approach. As befits a book on money and banking we begin by discussing in chapter 12 the demand for money. In chapter 13 we then look at the interrelation of income and expenditures. The determinants of expenditures are then discussed in more detail in chapter 14. This leads to chapter 15, which pulls together the essentially Keynesian theory of income determination. But this is not the only theory that tries to explain national income. Hence, in chapters 16 and 17 we present the quantity theory and the monetarist approach. The following brief chapter is an epilogue that tries to clarify this debate.

The descriptive material taken up in Parts One and Two, while perhaps complex in the sense of involving much detail, has been straightforward in the sense that, except for the reform issues discussed in chapter 8, there is on the whole little disagreement among economists. The material in this Part is much more controversial, and before taking it up we must discuss how one goes about choosing between rival theories.

The Choice of Theories

To decide what theory or what collection of theories to accept we first have to know what it is we want from a theory. The seemingly obvious answer, "the truth," is so broad as to be almost meaningless. Instead, there are several different tasks that we want a theory to perform. One of these is to be a framework for organizing what we already know. Instead of memorizing a vast number of individual facts, we simply learn a theory that helps us to recall these facts at will. For example, the theory that highways are more crowded on weekends than on weekdays permits us to plan our trips without memorizing on what days the traffic is bad. In microeconomics we use marginal analysis for this purpose; instead of learning about the particular factors considered by each individual firm in deciding about its price, such as how a particular customer will react, we learn the generalization that a firm sets its price so that marginal revenue equals marginal cost.

Another function of a theory, one that is not so widely known, is to be a fruitful strategy for further research.[1] A theory is not a static entity that exists in unchanged form once it has escaped the great thinker's mind. Instead, if it is an important theory, it is a growing thing that is being continually revised. Hence, someone confronted with two theories might very reasonably prefer the one that at present is *less* accurate and reliable, if it is likely to be the more fruitful one in the sense of being more open to interesting developments. Thus a philosopher of science, R. G. A. Dolby, has written that a new theory "is likely to be received favorably by such young scientists if it appears simple, coherent and plausible. But the way in which the new approach generates promising prospects for further research is probably the most important factor of all." [2]

The third function of a theory is a familiar one: to predict future events, and to explain why past events occurred. Presumably, when people say that a theory should tell them "the truth," it is primarily this function of a theory that they have in mind.

Thus a theory has more than a single function. This raises the distinct possibility that instead of just selecting the best theory, in the sense of the theory that predicts most accurately, several theories may be useful, though they disagree on several points. And even within the confines of using a theory just to predict future events or explain past events, more than one theory may be helpful. For example, one theory may predict the effects of policy changes better than a second theory, while the second theory may forecast GNP more accurately. Similarly one theory may predict better for the short run, and the other theory for the long run. Thus the fact that at so many points in economics we have more than one theory is not really quite as bad as it looks.

But still it would be nice if economists were to agree more. Why don't they? One reason is that various economists place different degrees of emphasis on different problems, and, as just mentioned, for different problems different theories may be preferable. For example, the Keynesian theory has its *comparative* advantage in analyzing the short run, while the quantity theory of money has its *comparative* advantage in analyzing the long run. Those economists who are more interested in short-run problems are therefore more likely to be Keynesians than those who are interested primarily in

---

[1] For a discussion of this increasingly popular approach to scientific theories see Thomas Kuhn, *The Structure of Scientific Revolutions* (Chicago: University of Chicago Press, 1962).

[2] R. G. A. Dolby, "Sociology of Knowledge in Natural Science," *Science Studies* 1 (January 1971): 20.

the long run. Another reason why economists disagree (though it is probably a much less important reason than most people think) is differences in value judgments. Now, in principle, value judgments should not influence what we predict will happen. But this is not so even in the physical sciences.[3] Third, deciding which theory is the more convenient organizing principle is largely a matter of "scientific taste," and deciding which theory is likely to be more fruitful in the future involves much guesswork. Not surprisingly economists frequently disagree on such issues. Fourth, economists, unlike physical scientists, have a long tradition of trying to be helpful to policymakers by answering every important question, even if it means taking a guess. In recent years as pollution and similar problems have become important policy issues, physical scientists too have been forced to answer questions on which they have little information—and they also disagree frequently. Finally, but perhaps most importantly, while physical and biological scientists can settle many issues by laboratory experiments, in economics experiments are generally not possible. One would hardly recommend that the Federal Reserve adopt a policy that may cause a recession merely to find out if it actually does so. To be sure, economists can use statistical techniques (mainly regression analysis) to try to disentangle the effects that particular variables have had on the economy, but that is a very poor substitute for controlled experiments.[4]

What is a reasonable response to this disagreement? One obvious step is to see if it really is a disagreement on matters of substance, or if, as often happens, seeming disagreement is merely the result of different ways of expressing the same point. But suppose that there is genuine disagreement on points of substance between economists belonging to different schools.

[3] Consider, for example, the decision whether a certain chemical is a safe food additive. One cannot settle the question with certainty, but can only say that it is safe at a certain level of probability. Suppose that the additive, if actually bad for people, only gives them a slightly upset stomach. One may say that it is safe if the probability that it actually *is* safe is as high as 99 percent. But suppose that it can kill people; then a 99 percent probability that it is actually safe is not sufficient to call it safe. (See Richard Rudner, "The Scientist *Qua* Scientist Makes Value Judgments," *Philosophy of Science* 20 [January 1953]: 1–6.)

[4] One reason for this is that our data often lack a close correspondence to the variables that our theory tells us are important. For example, Keynesian theory places much importance on the marginal efficiency of investment, but there are no data that measure this variable, and hence we have to use some more or less imprecise proxies for it. Similarly, as we discussed in chapter 11, it is far from clear how one should measure the variable that the quantity theory calls "money." Another problem is that several theories can produce a close fit to past data, and it is hard to decide which one gives the best fit; this may well vary from period to period. Moreover, when we use these theories to predict into the future, neither one may perform well. This is so because information on the past could be used to formulate the theories, so that it is not surprising that they fit well to the past data. But when used to predict, where they do not have this advantage of having, so to speak, seen the "answers" to the examination ahead of time, they do not do as well. Another important reason is that when two variables show similar fluctuations, it is easier to say that they are related, than to determine which one is cause and which one is effect.

One response that is often reasonable is to take both views seriously. Suppose, for example, that one theory predicts that a certain action, say raising interest rates, will lead to a recession, while another theory claims that it will have little effect. Even if the Federal Reserve believes that the latter theory is more likely to be right, it may well decide not to raise interest rates. Or suppose that one group of economists believes that wage-price guidelines are needed to stop inflation, while another group believes that inflation will not end unless the budget is balanced. An administration that is eager to stop inflation quickly may well decide to "accept" both theories, despite their disagreement, and impose wage and price guidelines as well as balancing the budget. Finally, remember that economists are doing much research trying to resolve their disagreements. Over the decades at least some of these disagreements should be resolved. By studying several theories you put yourself in the position of being able to understand these resolutions as they occur.

12

Money, Interest, and Asset Prices

In previous chapters a lot of attention has been given to the determination of the supply of money. The beginning economics student soon learns that a discussion of supply is almost certain to be followed by an analysis of demand. Some economics students get to feel that the object of each course is to derive one curve that slopes upward and another that slopes down. The "answer," usually a price, is given where the curves cross. So that we don't disappoint you, this chapter covers the demand for money. Monetary theory is tricky, and the meaning of the price of money is not so obvious. Of course, the price of a dollar is always just one dollar, and that seems to end the price discussion. But you do often hear it said that the value of money has declined. In fact, people sometimes say today's dollar is really worth only 47¢ or some other figure. They mean that the value of money, or its purchasing power in terms of real goods and services, has declined relative to some other time. In that sense the price, or value, of money varies inversely with the general price level. We cannot measure the price or value of money absolutely because we are unable to combine all the different goods and services money can buy. But it does make sense to say that the value (price) of money goes down when the price level of goods goes up.

However, there is another kind of "price" for money. The interest rate is the rental price of money. When the interest rate is 5 percent you can rent, that is, borrow, $100 for one year for $5. Having to deal with two prices makes things more complicated. Of course, there are lots of similar cases. You can rent an apartment for so much per month. Or you can buy a similar condominium apartment outright. The rental price has a time dimension like an annual interest charge. The purchase price for the condominium is, say, $50,000, period—no time dimension is attached.

We will see, however, that there are interactions between the two prices. The price level or value of money does affect interest rates. On the other hand there is a feedback from interest rates to price-level movements. In this chapter we will be concerned with the way both kinds of prices affect the demand for money, that is, the amount people are willing to hold. We shall find, of course, that a lot of other factors are involved.

Our ultimate interest is not in the demand for money as such—it is with the process by which the demand for money is brought into balance with the supply of money provided by the central bank. Those processes exert an important influence on the determination of interest rates, asset prices, product prices, and outputs. That is why money is so important to the economy.

This chapter has two functions. On the one hand it can be regarded as a completion of our discussion of capital markets. After we have examined the factors determining demand for money, we will show how the processes that equate supply and demand for money serve to exert an important influence on the level of interest rates and asset prices. On the other hand the chapter will also serve as an introduction to the discussion in the following chapters of ways in which money can influence prices and the level of output for the economy as a whole.

The Meaning of Money

The "meaning of money" sounds a little like a title for a philosophical treatise. Our objectives here are more pedestrian. We just want to note three ways in which careless use of the term *money* can lead to confusion. First, we must distinguish between real and nominal quantities of money. Second, we must avoid confusion between money, wealth, and income. Third, we must note that the definition of money is a source of controversy and confusion.

Real versus nominal money. The fact that money only has meaning in relation to the prices of goods and services is the most fundamental proposition of monetary theory. The real quantities of physical assets—cars, houses, land, watches, and what-have-you—are invariant to changes in the level of prices. If all prices double there is no change in the number of cars or houses. Nor is there any change in their barter exchange values. When the price of my Volkswagen was $3,000 and the price of my house was $30,000 I could sell my house and buy ten Volkswagens. If Volkswagens go to $6,000 and the house to $60,000 I can still trade my house for ten VWs.

But if instead of a house I had $30,000 in the bank I would find that after the price level changed I could buy only five VWs instead of ten. At the doubled price level, $60,000 would have the same economic meaning to me as $30,000 at the original price level. Prices translate arbitrary units of money into real values in terms of goods and services.

Foreign travel is instructive in this respect. In Italy a good dinner may cost you 8,000 lire. A dinner check for 8,000 anything is a bit of a shock, but after a little arithmetic you find that 8,000 lire amounts to only $10. Italian restaurant prices run to big numbers in lire but so do all other Italian prices. Correspondingly Italians carry thousands of lire in their pockets and in their bank balances. Large quantities of money and high prices cancel each other out. For purposes of economic analysis we should be concerned not with the number of francs, pounds, pengös, or dollars in the money supply, but with the amount of goods and services the money supply will buy.

An example from recent experience at home may help. Between the recession trough in the second quarter of 1975 and the third quarter of 1977 the U.S. money supply measured in dollars rose by about 15 percent. But the price level also rose by about 15 percent, so that the real money supply, measured in terms of purchasing power over goods and services, did not rise at all. Since output was rising, the ratio of the real quantity of money to real output actually fell.

This brings us to a second proposition in monetary theory. The real quantity of money can be changed in two ways. First, the nominal quantity of money can change while prices are fixed. Second, prices can change while the nominal quantity of money remains fixed.

Money versus wealth and income. We noted in chapter 1 that while money may be part of wealth, it is not the same thing. Wealth can be held in many other forms.

A related question is whether increasing the aggregate money stock directly increases aggregate wealth. The answer from our discussion in chapter 6 is that the amount of nominal wealth created by an increase in money supply depends on how the increase in money comes about. The effect of an increase in money supply on real wealth also depends on whether the increment in money supply causes a change in the price level.

A third source of confusion arises from disagreements as to the best definition of the term *money*. We have discussed alternative definitions of money in a separate chapter. We will often use the term *money* in a general way when it is not necessary to be more precise. We will, however, try to point out how the response of demand for "money" to changes in interest, wealth, and income depends on which of the several definitions of money discussed in chapter 11 is used.

The Economic Impact of Money

The fact that money measures are only meaningful in terms of a price level has been known for a long time. Inflation is a very old phenomenon. The Greeks and Romans had plenty of experience with it, and certainly realized that a denarius didn't go as far in Nero's time as in the days of the Republic. In modern times discussion of the economic impact of money goes back to the seventeenth century when people were reacting to the effects of gold and silver imports from America. A little later there was raging controversy over trade policy. Mercantilist policy aimed at increasing exports of goods while restricting imports, with the difference paid in gold or silver. Proponents of mercantilism took it for granted that a country was better off if it had more gold and silver. Others argued that gold and silver do not produce anything and that too much of these metals only drives up prices.

Controversy centered on two alternative propositions, one holding that more money stimulates trade and the other that more money drives up prices. The money-stimulates-trade doctrine usually gained popularity in periods of depression. Its proponents assumed, at least implicitly, that prices were fixed and that there were unemployed resources. In that case, if more money led to more spending, it would also lead to more employment and output.

The more-money-raises-prices school assumed that prices were flexible and that production could not be increased in the short run. In that case, if an increased money supply induced more spending, prices would rise but not output or employment. Since the seventeenth and eighteenth centuries were periods of rising money supply and rising prices, this argument carried conviction. Nonetheless, the money-stimulates-trade doctrine reasserted its strength in the periodic depressions.

These disputes are of far more than historical interest. Modern monetary analysis is much more sophisticated and precise and has a stronger empirical base than the pamphlets of the seventeenth century. Nonetheless, there is still room for dispute. Indeed, criticism of Federal Reserve policy is the economist's favorite indoor sport. The central issue in the critique is the conflict between the desire for more rapid growth of money supply to stimulate trade—that is, to increase employment and output— and the fear that rapid money supply growth will accelerate inflation.

In this and the next seven chapters we will work to synthesize the true insights underlying both those slogans. We will find that under some circumstances more money does stimulate trade. In some circumstances it just drives up prices, and sometimes it first stimulates trade and then drives up prices. Meanwhile, we have to proceed step by step and avoid slogans.

When the moral philosophers and pamphleteers of the seventeenth and eighteenth centuries tried to work out the consequences of an increased money supply, they found it necessary, first of all, to develop a theory of what people would do with more money—hoard it, spend it, or lend it.

The Demand for Money

In their search for understanding of the impact of changes in money supply on economic activity and prices, seventeenth-century writers recognized that the key to the puzzle lay in the demand for money. Why do people hold money in the first place? It does not make an obvious contribution to the production process. Nor does it, except in the hands of misers, give the kind of satisfaction that ordinary goods and services provide.

On examination, though, it appears that money does contribute to productive efficiency and it does provide utility to its owner just as any durable good does. In chapter 1 we discussed the superior efficiency of a money economy over a barter economy. There we considered the social efficiency of a money economy. But each individual household or firm gets a return from holding money. Part of the return is associated with the medium of exchange or transactions function of money. Another part of the return arises from the safety and convenience of money as a form of wealth, a store of value. Next we will discuss the factors determining the amount of money held for transactions purposes. Then we will discuss the demand for money as an investment.

Transactions Demand for Money

When discussing the rationale for the use of money in exchange, we noted that the use of money makes it possible to split the exchange process into two parts. People sell goods or services for money at one time and then, at leisure, use the money to buy other goods and services. In the end, they have exchanged one set of goods and services for another. In the interval between transactions they are holding money. The ratio of the amount of money they hold to the annual value of transactions depends, in part, on the average length of the interval between the receipt of money from sale of goods and services and the payment of money for purchase of goods and services.

For households, the ratio of average money holdings to annual expenditure for goods and services will depend on how often the members of the household get paid. Consider the following simple case. A family receives a paycheck of $1,000 (we will neglect various tax and health insurance deductions) per month. They do not save anything, and spend the whole $1,000 each month, so they have a zero bank balance at the end of each month just before the next check arrives. They spend at a steady rate—$33.33 per day in a thirty-day month. When they receive each check they are holding $1,000. During the month their bank balance gradually declines to zero by the end of the month. It jumps to $1,000 on the first and the cycle repeats. The time pattern of the family's bank balance is shown in figure 12.1. On the average their balance is $500; half of one month's pay, or 1/24th of a year's income.

If the paycheck came weekly, the family's money holdings would

Figure 12.1   Time Pattern of Household Cash Balances

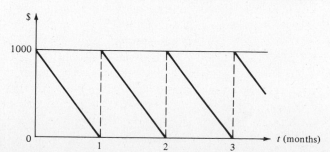

follow a similar pattern, but the average amount of money held would be only half a week's pay or 1/104th of a year's pay, only about a quarter as much as in the other case.

Of course, reality is a little more complicated. Nobody spends at a steady rate. People are likely to pay their rent on the first of the month, pay other bills around the tenth, and do their grocery shopping on Fridays. The important points, however, are that they do have to hold money because there is a time interval between receipt and expenditures, and that the average ratio of money held to expenditures depends on the structure of the payments system, which takes into account several factors such as the frequency of wage payments and whether goods and services are paid for at the time of purchase or charged and paid for monthly.

Very similar considerations apply to businesses. The paychecks that families receive usually come from businesses, and the money they pay for goods and services goes back to businesses. The same money can just pass back and forth between them. In a simple but unlikely example we may suppose that businesses accumulate money from sale of goods and services to households during the month and pay out all their receipts in wages and dividends at the end of the month. Their cash balances, shown in figure

Figure 12.2   Time Pattern of Business Cash Balances

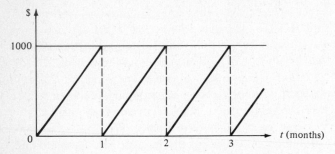

12.2, would follow a pattern the mirror image of the household one of figure 12.1.

If we consider a closed economy with no purchases from outside, with, say, one hundred families each earning $1,000 a month, the cash positions of households and businesses would look like figure 12.3. The total cash

Figure 12.3   Time Pattern of Total Cash Balances

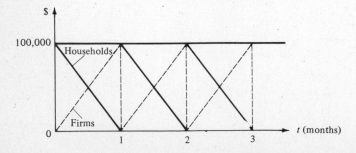

balance of the two combined is always $100,000; it is all in the hands of businesses at the end of the month, then all in the hands of households on the first. Then household money holdings gradually decline, business holdings gradually rise, until businesses again have it all at the end of the month. The GNP of this economy is $100,000 per month—1.2 million dollars per year. Total transactions are twice as much ($1.2 million annual wage payments, $1.2 million sales of goods and services). Combined money holdings of households and businesses are 1/12th of a year's GNP, 1/24th of a year's transactions.

Of course we have drastically oversimplified. Businesses have to make payments to one another as well as to labor. The timing of receipts and payments does not work out so neatly as in our example. Still, the amount of money held for transactions purposes does depend on the structure of the payments system. The amount of money required for a given real GNP at a given price level does depend on the organization of the payments system, especially on the frequency of payments.

That idea was recognized early in discussions of the demand for money. William Petty, the first economist who tried to measure the national income of England in the seventeenth century, described the "circle of payments" from household and business and back again. He wrote:

> . . . for the expense being forty millions, if the revolutions were in such short circles, viz., weekly as happens among poorer artisans and laborers who receive and pay every Saturday, then 40/52nd parts of one million of money would answer those ends. But if the circles be quarterly according to our custom of paying rent, and gathering taxes, then ten millions were requisite.[1]

The idea that the amount of nominal money people want to hold is simply a fixed proportion of total annual nominal expenditures or, alternatively, that the amount of money balances people want is proportional to total annual expenditures held sway for over three hundred years. The basic equation of exchange $M = kYP$ where M is money demand, Y is real output, P the price level, and k is the ratio of money holdings to total annual expenditure, or, in real terms, $M/P = kY$, was generally accepted. It was also agreed that k was mainly determined by the structure of the payments system. The equation could be reversed to read $PY = M/k$ Disputes raged, not over the value of k, but over the circumstances under which a rise in M would make output rise or make prices rise. Those problems will occupy us in the next eight chapters, but there is a lot more to be said about the demand for money.

Holding Precautionary Balances

The descriptions of household and business receipts and expenditure patterns summarized in figures 12.1 and 12.2 suggest a dull, repetitive life.

---

[1] Charles Henry Hull, ed., *Economic Writings of Sir William Petty* (London: Cambridge University Press, 1899), pp. 112–13.

Many individuals have a regular monthly pattern of wage and salary receipts and routine expenditures. They may also have dividend receipts quarterly, and royalties annually. On the payments side, income taxes have to
be paid quarterly, college tuition two or three times a year, and property
taxes annually. Those receipts and payments may be predictable but because they are large, people may give more care to the sums involved than
to their monthly salary checks and routine expenditures. Businesses, of
course, have all sorts of lumpy expenditures, for example, capital goods
purchases and dividend payments. They have irregular receipts from contract payments or from floating a bond issue.

Receipts and payments are not only irregular, they are often unpredictable. Households are often faced with large unexpected expenditures for
home or auto repairs. Their receipts vary because family members may
sometimes become unemployed, or at other times get a lot of overtime work.

Because their receipts and payments are lumpy, irregular, and partly
unpredictable, most households do not want to end the month with no
money, waiting for the postman to bring the check. If their assets are large
enough, they usually want to have some readily available liquid assets to
absorb the unevenness in the flow of receipts and payments, and they want
to avoid borrowing when things do go wrong. Businesses, of course, have
similar problems. Their sales vary unexpectedly, and they cannot predict
when major outlays for repairs may be necessary. They too usually want
to have a cushion of liquid assets so they don't have to rush to negotiate a
bank loan every time their cash flow predictions go wrong. Keynes labeled
funds held for these purposes precautionary balances. The fact that there are
irregular or lumpy receipts and payments, and some unpredictable ones,
does not destroy the basic idea of a close link between the level of aggregate
income and expenditure and the demand for money. The scale of irregular payments and of unusual receipts and expenditures varies with the
level of income. In a large population the timing of irregular receipts and
expenditures is smoothed out when taken together. Their existence does not
undermine the basis for the proposition that the structure of the payments
system strongly influences the ratio of aggregate money holdings to aggregate income and expenditure.

Velocity of Money

For some purposes it is convenient to ask how much money people want
to hold in relation to income and expenditure. But, especially when we are
asking how money affects expenditure, it is sometimes useful to ask how fast
money moves around the circle of payments from income to payments for
goods and services and back again to income. As D. H. Robertson put it,
we can think of "money sitting or money on the wing." We are unable to
measure how fast any individual dollar moved but we can ask how many
dollars worth of transactions per year are made with the average dollar. In

1978 approximately forty trillion dollars of transactions were made in the United States. The average money supply M_1 was $350 billion. The average dollar changed hands over one hundred times during the year. The *ratio of the annual volume of transactions to the stock of money* is called the **transactions velocity of money.**

A more commonly used concept is the income or circuit velocity of money. The number of times the average dollar goes around the circle from expenditure to income and back to income is the ratio of GNP to money stock. In 1979 GNP was $2,368.5 billion and the average money stock (M_1) was $382 billion, so the circuit velocity of money was six times per year.

Transactions velocity is always much higher than income velocity because total transactions include both income and expenditure payments and the expenditure payments include payments for intermediate goods as well as final products. GNP includes auto sales, but total transactions also include payments for coal to make steel, and payments for steel to make the cars. In addition, total transactions include transactions in financial assets and for sales of existing land and buildings. Nonetheless, the two move roughly together. We can rewrite the equation of exchange as $MV \equiv GNP$. The three-bar equality sign is used to indicate that the equation is an identity. It is always true because V is defined as $V = \frac{GNP}{M}$, which is just another arrangement of the equation of exchange. (The previously discussed equation, $M = kYP$, is also an identity.)

Since the equation is essentially a definition, it tells us nothing about the real world. But it does serve to remind us of some connections between money and other things that must always be true. In particular, any increase in M must be accompanied by either a decrease in V or an increase in output, prices, or both.

Actually velocity varies a good deal, as can be seen in figure 12.4. You can see that in 1945 the average dollar traveled the income circuit about

Figure 12.4   Income Velocity of Money in the U.S.
        1910–78

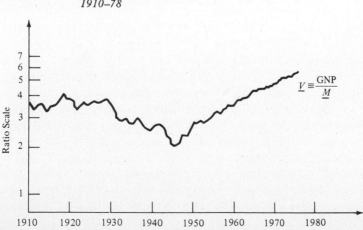

two times. In 1929 and 1965 the average dollar went around the income circuit nearly four times a year, and in 1979 the average dollar went around the circuit about six times a year.

Velocity also varies a good deal in the very short run. In fact quarter-to-quarter movements of velocity are closely associated with quarter-to-quarter movements of GNP.

There are many causes for variations in velocity. There have been important changes in institutional arrangements for making payments. There are some reasons for believing that there are economies of scale in the use of money so that although demand for money increases with the level of income and transactions, it does not increase proportionately. The short-run changes in velocity may simply reflect the fact that people do not adjust money holdings to short-run changes in income. Milton Friedman has argued that people adjust money holdings to "permanent income" that is, to the average expected income over the long run. In that case velocity will tend to rise whenever there is an unusually rapid rise in income not matched by a rise in money stock.

In addition, however, it appears that the demand for money at a given level of income also depends on the level of interest rates.

Transactions Demand and the Interest Rate

Our discussion of payment cycles, irregular receipts, and payments and precautionary balances shows that households and firms will often have money that they will not immediately disburse. They may expect to have funds idle for a day, for a week, several months, or in the case of precautionary balances, for an uncertain period. A major change in the theory of demand for money took place when it was fully recognized that there are alternatives to holding those funds in demand deposits or currency. It is usually possible to earn more interest by investing any cash not needed immediately and then disinvesting when it is needed. Whether investing is worthwhile depends on the kind of investments available, how much it costs to buy and sell them again, how much risk is involved, and what return they will pay. The length of time for which funds can be invested and the sum involved are also relevant.

In practice, households usually use time and savings deposits or certificates offered by banks and thrift institutions as alternatives to holding demand deposits. A few wealthy individuals may buy Treasury bills. Businesses usually use short-term marketable securities as alternatives to holding demand deposits. In chapter 6 we discussed the way corporate treasurers use short-term securities to get interest on temporarily idle funds. There we were mainly interested in their choice among alternative securities. Now we want to focus on their decisions as to whether to invest or not.

Treasurers of large corporations keep careful track of cash flows and project future receipts and outlays. That adds a good deal to overhead and would not be worthwhile if interest rates were not high enough to justify short-term investments. Suppose a treasurer finds that his cash-flow projection indicates that one million dollars can be invested for a week. If he invests in Treasury bills yielding 8 percent he will earn about $1,600 that week, more than enough to cover the dealer's spread, which will amount to $500. The transaction would obviously be less attractive at a lower interest rate. It would also be less worthwhile if only, say, $100,000 were involved, or if the funds were available for only, say, three days.

When interest rates are low, only firms with surplus funds that are either large, or available for a long time, will find it worthwhile to reduce demand-deposit holdings by making temporary investments in securities. As interest rates rise smaller amounts, or amounts available for shorter periods, can be profitably invested. Thus the proportion of liquid assets businesses hold in demand deposits will be relatively large when interest rates are low, and relatively small when they are high.

Notice that both payments and receipts of businesses get larger when GNP is larger. Their total liquid asset holdings are likely to grow in rough proportion to GNP. Thus at any given GNP their demand for money will be a downward sloping function of interest rates. But at a higher GNP they will hold more money and more securities at any given interest rate. In figure 12.5 the line marked Y_0 shows business demand for money at

Figure 12.5 Business Transactions Demand for Money

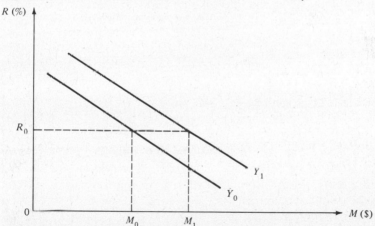

different interest rates with GNP = Y_0. The line y_1 shows their demand for money in relation to interest rates at the higher GNP, Y_1.

The situation for households is very similar in principle. Most households use bank or thrift institution accounts or certificates instead of short-term securities. This way they do not have to pay dealers' spreads to transfer funds into and out of savings accounts, but it does take time, trouble, and postage to shift funds back and forth. Just as in the case of businesses, the profitability of keeping temporarily available funds in interest-bearing form involves balancing interest earnings against the time, trouble, and cost of moving funds from one form to another. And, just as in the case of businesses, the amount of interest earned depends on the level of interest rates, the sum involved, and the time for which it can be invested.

When interest rates are high households may find it worthwhile to deposit part of their monthly checks into savings accounts and then withdraw later in the month. For example, if a family with a $2,000 monthly salary puts $1,000 in the savings bank at the start of the month and withdraws it in the middle, they earn interest on $1,000 for half a month. At 5 percent per year they get about $2.00 interest per month. Some families do that. Larger returns can be obtained by careful management of cash balances associated with lumpy or irregular receipts and payments.

Although the exact holding time is unpredictable, precautionary balances for a "rainy day" are likely to be investable for relatively long periods, so they can be attracted into savings accounts or deposit certificates at relatively low interest rates. Funds being accumulated for a one-time payment—real-estate taxes, or an annual insurance premium—may be on hand for several months, but whether it is worthwhile putting them into a savings account depends on the amount and the interest rate. The share going to savings accounts will clearly rise with interest rates. The same argument holds for the reverse case of a large receipt to be gradually spent. As in the case of businesses we can argue that total liquid assets of households will rise with GNP, and that the proportion held in demand-deposit form will increase as the interest rate falls. That leads to a household demand for money much like the one shown in figure 12.5.

Money As an Investment

In our discussion of transactions and precautionary demand, we regarded money as an asset held only because receipts and payments of individual households and firms are not perfectly synchronized, regular, or predictable. Those considerations are directly connected with the use of money as a medium of exchange. There are, however, other reasons for holding money that are more closely associated with the role of money as a store of value. In fact, until a couple of hundred years ago, money was far and away the most important financial asset. There were no common stocks or marketable bonds and no array of savings banks, insurance companies, and other financial institutions. Most people held their wealth in the form of land, houses, or unincorporated businesses. There were, of course, some mortgages, some trade debt. Lawyers and others often acted as intermediaries in arranging personal loans, often at high rates. There is always considerable uncertainty in the value of land, houses, and independent businesses. Any wealthy person who wanted to reduce the uncertainty in the value of his total portfolio found that the easiest way to do so was to hold part of his wealth in the form of money. Anyone who wanted to avoid the cares of owning physical assets or the risks and problems of making personal loans, directly or indirectly, found that money was a relatively attractive way of holding wealth.

The role of money as a financial asset held for investment, as opposed to transactions reasons, was recognized early in the game but it was not given a major role until the work of two famous economists, Alfred Marshall and A. C. Pigou, who successively held the chair of political economy at Cambridge University. The work of Marshall and Pigou not only recognized the importance of money as an asset in investment portfolios, but also treated decisions about money holding in that context as a matter of rational choice in the balancing of risk and return on an investment portfolio.

However, they did not carry that notion very far. When dealing with the theory of the relation between prices and money in the long run, they were content to use a summary formulation in which they assumed that aggregate wealth is proportional to aggregate income and that demand for money can be approximated as a fixed proportion of wealth, k_1, plus a fixed proportion, k_2, of income. On those assumptions, demand for money is given by $M = k_1 W + k_2 Y p$, where W is wealth and Y is real income and p prices. If the ratio of wealth to income is w, then W can be replaced by wY and the money demand equation can be rewritten as $M = k_1 w Y p + k_2 Y p$, or $M = (k_1 w + k_2) Y p$. In short $M = kYp$ where $k = (k_1 w + k_2)$.

This equation is called the **Cambridge Equation.** Since the velocity of money is defined as the ratio of Y to M, you can see that since $k = \frac{M}{YP}$, V is just the inverse of the Cambridge K.

Marshall particularly was interested in short-run business-cycle problems as well as in long-run price theory. In fact he was one of the greatest economists of all time and part of his greatness lay in his ability to deal realistically with most important economic problems. In explaining the depressions and financial panics of the nineteenth century, Marshall placed great emphasis on the variability of k. He attributed variations in k to fluctuations in business confidence. The resulting variation in the velocity of money caused corresponding variations in nominal money expenditures and therefore led to fluctuations in prices and output. Marshall's short-run business-cycle version of the Cambridge Equation did not make a great impact on monetary economics, and there were lots of competing cycle theories. But with the Great Depression of the 1930s another Cambridge economist, John Maynard Keynes, made use of Marshall's variable k approach. He adapted Marshall's approach to provide a central element in his explanation of the Great Depression. His argument was more systematic, but not necessarily better.

Keynes argued that people hold money as an asset (in addition to the amounts required for transactions and as precautionary balances in order to avoid or limit the risk associated with changes in interest rates and bond prices). He used an argument intended to explain the movement of money holdings and interest rates during the Great Depression. While

Keynes's depression model has been superseded by more general ones, his emphasis on the role of money as an asset that can be used to limit or dilute risk led to an important new development in monetary theory.

Liquidity Preference

Keynes's speculative or liquidity preference theory of demand for money emphasized the effects of investors' expectations of a change in interest rates. Indeed, one writer remarked that, according to Keynes's theory, "interest rates are what they are because they are expected to be different from what they are." Sometimes, of course, bond investors do have strong views on which way interest rates will go, but often they are uncertain. They know rates will change, but they can only guess the direction and timing of change. Anyone who buys bonds must accept some risk.

James Tobin of Yale generalized Keynes's approach by arguing that even when investors think it just as likely that interest rates will rise as fall, they will still want to hold a safe asset to reduce the risk on their total portfolio. The greater the proportion of wealth held in money, the lower the percentage change in the value of the total portfolio from a given percentage change in bond prices. Investors can then be regarded as trading-off risk for return by varying the proportion of the money and bonds in their portfolios. At any given interest rate the average return on their total portfolio increases as they shift toward progressively greater proportions of bonds and smaller proportions of money in their portfolio. But the risk they bear increases at the same time. As in any other commodity choice, investors will stop increasing the share of bonds in the portfolio when the additional reward from more bonds just balances the value they place on avoiding additional risk.

Different investors will have different views as to the risks involved at any one time, and they will also have different tastes for risk versus return. "Plungers" may borrow as much as they can to maximize return. Most investors, however, will place a progressively higher value on avoiding additional risks as they become more fully invested in risky assets. Most of them will decide to dilute the risk of their portfolio by holding some money. However, the reward they get for taking risks changes with interest rates. At high interest rates the bond-to-wealth ratio at which marginal risk aversion balances the return from additional bond holdings will be higher than at low rates. Conversely, the optimum money-to-wealth ratio will decline as interest rates rise. Tobin's argument thus leads to just the same conclusion that Keynes reached. Speculative demand for money will fall as interest rates rise and vice versa.

We can represent the speculative demand for money by plotting the amount of money demanded against the interest rate as in figure 12.6. The curve slopes downward because people want more money at lower interest rates than at higher ones.

Figure 12.6   Speculative Demand for Money

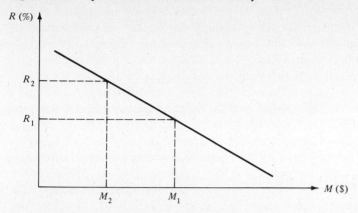

Assets and the Separation Theorem

In the argument just given we supposed that investors are choosing between just two assets, money and bonds. In fact, of course, there are lots of different bonds, and investors can also hold stock, real estate, and other risky assets.

The bonds versus money argument can be applied to any mix of assets. The investor's decision problem can be divided into two parts. The investor has first to choose the best mix of risky assets. He will want to get a mix of assets offering the best ratio of expected return to a measure of risk. To do that he will not buy just one asset. He can reduce the risk relative to expected return by diversification. Moreover, he can improve the return-risk ratio by buying assets whose prices move in opposite directions. For example, he can balance some *cyclical* stocks, whose prices fall in recessions, with some bonds, whose prices tend to rise in recessions when interest rates fall.

Having chosen the "best" portfolio of risky assets, the investor has a second decision. He has to decide what portion of his net worth should be invested in those assets and what portion held in money. The *proposition that the mix of risky assets can be chosen separately from the proportion of risky assets in the portfolio* is called the **separation theorem.**

The decision as to the share of money in the portfolio is exactly like the bonds or money choice described above. Investors who are risk adverse will hold a high proportion of assets in money and a low proportion in risky assets. Of course, the average return on the total portfolio will be low. That is the price of avoiding risk. Investors who are more willing to expose themselves to risk will invest a high proportion of net worth in risky assets and a low proportion in money. Accordingly, they can expect a higher return on the total portfolio in return for accepting greater risk.

A general rise in expected returns on risky assets (with no change in risk) will induce investors generally to hold less money and a fall in expected returns will increase demand for money. The Keynes-Tobin model of asset demand for money applies most directly when a single well-defined type of money is the only riskless asset. If no interest is paid on money holdings, the asset demand for money will tend to increase as the yield on risky assets declines, as in Figure 12.6. The R on the vertical axis must be interpreted as an index of the yield on risky assets. When interest is paid on money holdings the vertical axis should be interpreted as the differential between the yield on risky assets and the yield on money. That differential has been called the "market price of risk."

The Keynes-Tobin model cannot be applied literally because there are many kinds of "money" paying different interest rates and because there are other liquid assets not included in any definition of money. Nonetheless, the theory helps to explain why many people are prepared to accept relatively low yields on riskless assets. It also helps to provide the underlying logic for empirical studies of demand for money. Before considering empirical results we can use the theory to draw some general theoretical conclusions about the relation between interest-rate movements and demand for money. In doing so we must, of course, take account of transactions as well as asset demand for money.

Total Demand for Money and the Interest Rate

In general we expect that demand for all types of money will tend to increase with the level of income and the level of wealth. We also expect that, other things equal, an increase in the yield on risky assets relative to those offered on various types of deposits will reduce demand for money. The response of demand for particular monetary aggregates to change in the relative yields on different kinds of deposits and other liquid assets is more complex.

Demand for M-1A

Demand for currency and non-interest-bearing demand deposits is negatively related to the level of interest rates paid on all other liquid assets. As noted earlier, businesses tend to economize on demand deposits by more careful cash management and the use of Treasury bills and commercial paper when market interest rates rise. Households can economize on demand deposits by transferring funds into and out of savings accounts. Nowadays they can also use NOW accounts or other types of interest-bearing deposits against which checks may be drawn. Those deposits are included in M-$_{1B}$, which therefore tends to have a lower interest elasticity than M-$_{1A}$.

Demand for M-2 and M-3

The interest elasticity of M-2 is a little tricky because it is an amalgam of different components. The reaction of the demand deposit and currency component has just been noted. At the other end of the spectrum, money-market certificates pay interest rates linked to Treasury bill rates and demand for those certificates will not be adversely affected by increases in bill rates. Money-market certificates and funds may gain at the expense of savings accounts when short-term market rates rise, and lose when they fall. Those reactions will cancel out since both are in the *M-2* total. On the whole we expect that the time and saving components of *M-2* will have a much lower interest elasticity than *M-1*. Moreover, the development of money-market certificates serves to lower their elasticity with respect to market rates. Very similar observations apply to the thrift deposit components of *M-3*. *M-3* will, of course, show a positive elasticity with respect to differences in deposit rates offered by thrift institutions and commercial banks.

Income Versus Wealth

When we discussed the combined transactions and investment demand for money, we noted that transactions demand should be related to income, while investment demand should in principle be related to wealth. It can be argued, however, that the investment demand for money can be related to income. Wealth is the present value of property income, therefore the fundamental determinants of wealth are income and interest rate. We can think of relating demand for money directly to income and interest rate, skipping the intermediate wealth variable. (The interest rate does double duty, entering the picture as a determinant of wealth and as a determinant of the share of wealth held in money form.) However, that simplification is satisfactory only when there is a one-to-one correspondence between wealth and income at a given interest rate. In fact, of course, the value of wealth at a given interest rate and income can change for many reasons. The share of before-tax property income in GNP can vary. The tax law can change the ratio of after-tax income to GNP. Moreover, government debt is part of wealth for purposes of portfolio decisions regardless of our views about the perception of the negative wealth implied by future tax liabilities. Finally, part of the money supply may be wealth. In spite of those considerations it may be possible to use income instead of wealth as an approximation but that is an empirical issue.

Empirical Studies

Economists have worked hard at empirical testing of theories of demand for money and measurement of the response of money demand to changes in income, wealth, and interest rates. There are literally hundreds of studies of demand for money for the U.S. and other countries. As usual the results agree in some respects, disagree in others. We can report here only a few of the main conclusions and note some unsettled issues.

In a general way it can be said that empirical studies confirm the broad qualitative statements at the beginning of the last section. Money demand increases with income, and wealth decreases with asset return. That is true for both M_1 and M_2, for alternative measures of income, and for alternative measures of wealth.

The question whether income or wealth is more important is problematic mainly because they move together. We have to recall that two kinds of wealth are involved, human and nonhuman. Human wealth is usually measured as a moving average of actual past income. Most studies making the comparison show that money demand at a given date is more closely associated with a moving average of past income than with current income.

Measurement of the relative importance of nonhuman wealth and income is difficult because they both grow with similar trends. A number of studies using data for long periods have indicated that either income or wealth must be involved in the explanation of demand for money, and that if both are used together variations in wealth leave little for income to explain. On the other hand, one of the most thorough studies of postwar data, done by Stephen Goldfeld, concluded that income performs better than wealth in explaining money demand. He added, however, that short-run changes in wealth help to explain the data. Probably then, income and wealth play independent roles in determining demand for money, but it is difficult to disentangle their relative importance.

It also turns out to be difficult to separate the influence of the returns on different types of assets since they all move more or less together. Short-term and long-term interest rates move together in business cycles though short-term rates fluctuate over a wider range. On the whole they give equally good explanations of the demand for money. The reported demand elasticities are, of course, much higher for long-term rates than for short-term ones because the latter move so much more. The hypothesis that equity yields should be relevant is difficult to test because the prospective yield on equity cannot be readily measured. We can measure the dividend component, but the prospect for capital gain is in the eye of the beholder. Finally, recent studies in the U.S. indicate that the rates paid on time and savings deposits are an important factor in determining the demand for money.

Recent Instability in Money Demand

While empirical studies of demand for money agree as to broad qualitative conclusions about the direction and order of magnitude of the response of demand for money to changes in interest rates, income, and wealth, agreement is far from complete. Moreover, none of the empirical estimates have been wholly successful in predicting demand for money. Indeed, since 1975, they have all been notably unsuccessful.

Prior to 1975 short-run forecasts of demand for money showed substantial errors. However, an overprediction for one period of a few months was usually canceled out by an opposite error a few months later. There was clearly room for improvement, but the forecasters seemed to be on the right track. Since 1975, however, money-demand forecasters have been thrown into confusion. Forecasts of money demand have been too low by a wide margin. At first it was thought the prediction errors were an aberration, perhaps associated with the oil shock and the recession; however, the forecast errors persisted and have, indeed, grown larger.

In trying to explain what happened, economists have been reexamining the interest-rate measures used in their statistical equations in looking for new insights into the behavior underlying demand for money. Others have pointed to changes in regulations noted in chapter 11 that blur the distinction between demand and savings deposits.

Finally, new devices for economizing on money have been developed. Commercial banks have made new arrangements permitting corporate customers to reduce their holdings of demand deposits, while maintaining the availability of their funds for transactions purposes.[2]

Money-market mutual funds offer individuals an opportunity to obtain interest on a diversified portfolio of commercial paper and Treasury bills. The money-market mutuals have arranged with commercial banks to honor checks drawn on the fund's account, so that a fundholder collects interest while retaining the check-writing privilege. In effect, money-market mutual funds have become banks specializing in short-term money-market investment. They are a typical result of the constant effort to make a profit out of regulation.

Many economists believe that these developments are a reflection of the collision between a long sustained rise in interest rates on loans and marketable securities on the one hand, and regulation of deposit interest rates on the other. Demand for money might be much more stable if deposit institutions could pay competitive rates. Meanwhile, however, shifts in the money demand function pose serious problems for monetary policy. Some of these problems are discussed in chapter 24.

The Effect of Paying Interest on Demand Deposits

New legislation that permits both banks and thrift institutions to offer various forms of interest-bearing checking accounts will lead to continuing change in the relation between short-term interest rates and money demand.

Suppose, to take the extreme case, that all deposit interest rates maintained fixed differentials with a major short-term interest rate. In that case neither businesses nor households would have any incentive to switch be-

---

[2] A commercial bank sells Treasury bills to its corporate customers before the close of business each day and repurchases them in the morning. The customer collects interest at the federal funds rate, and has the use of its demand deposits in the daytime. Since deposits are measured for reserve purposes at the close of business, the corporation's deposit doesn't show in money supply figures. The bank doesn't have to hold reserves against the amount in question.

tween one type of deposit and another or between deposits and other liquid assets. Demand for money on any definition would become inelastic to short-term interest rates. Adjustment to a change in money supply would have to take place through changes in the prices of long-term assets and the influence of those changes on the level of income. Deposit rates are unlikely to become so completely responsive to market rates. Nonetheless, the new legislation permitting interest in checking accounts has important and uncertain implications.

Money Supply, Interest, and Income

So far we have been concerned with various partial aspects of the demand for money. The object of analyzing demand, however, is to enable us to understand the interaction among interest rates, money supply, and income. To get an overview of that interaction, we must neglect, but not forget, some of the complexities arising from the existence of a variety of money-like assets.

For simplicity first, assume that income and wealth move closely together so that income can be used as a proxy for both. Second, suppose that the only money is M_{-1A}, currency, and non-interest-bearing deposits. Third, assume that there is only one interest-bearing security. Under those circumstances, it is clear that the demand for money tends to rise with income and to fall as the interest rate rises.

The *LM* Curve

Those simplifications give us, as they should, a basis for a relatively simple theory of interest-rate determination. In figure 12.7 the curve marked Y_0 represents demand for money associated with some given income level Y_0. The vertical solid line $\overline{M}$ is the fixed money supply. Then the equilibrium interest rate is R_0. The dotted vertical line at M' corresponds to a larger

Figure 12.7 Determination of the Interest Rate

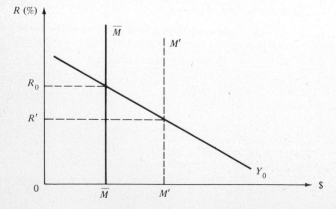

money supply. Demand and supply for money are equated at the lower interest rate R'. In general, when nominal income is fixed, a larger money supply reduces the short-term interest rate.

Figure 12.8 shows a set of money-demand curves, each corresponding

Figure 12.8   Effect of Changing Income on Equilibrium Interest Rate

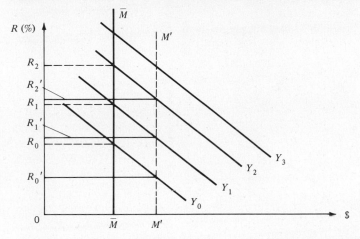

to a different level of nominal income. Y_0 is the lowest nominal income; Y_1 a higher one, and so on. The vertical line at $\overline{M}$ shows the money supply. M' as before shows a larger money supply. Ignore it for the moment.

You can see that $\overline{M}$ intersects Y_0 at R_0; it intersects Y_1 at a higher interest rate R_1, and so on. Clearly, when money supply is fixed the equilibrium interest rate rises as income rises.

Figure 12.9   The LM Curve

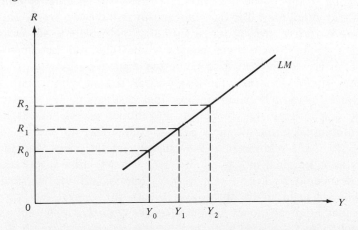

In figure 12.9 the information in figure 12.8 has been replotted with R on the vertical axis and Y on the horizontal axis. The upward sloping line LM is derived from the points R_0Y_0, R_1Y_1, and so forth, on figure 12.8. The

LM curve *shows the equilibrium interest rate for each level of nominal income and a given money supply.* It strongly emphasizes the fact that a rise in money income must be accompanied by a rising interest rate if money supply remains fixed. Notice that a change in money supply shifts the whole *LM* curve. We will make a great deal of use of the *LM* curve in the next three chapters. In figure 12.10 the solid line *LM* is the same as in figure

Figure 12.10   Increase in Money Supply Shifts the *LM* Curve

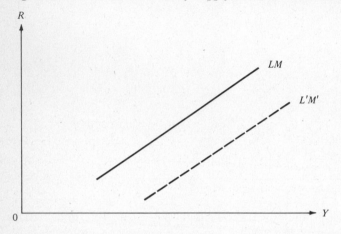

12.9. The lower dotted line *L'M'* is derived in the same way as *LM* from figure 12.8 using the larger money supply *M'* and plotting the alternative equilibrium points $R'_0 Y_0$, $R'_1 Y_1$, and so on.

Changing Price Levels

The discussion so far has been carried on in terms of nominal income and nominal money supplies, rather than in terms of real money supply and income. As long as prices stay constant this does not matter. But in a world of inflation nominal income can change a lot while real income remains the same. It is very important to make the distinction between real and nominal magnitudes. In fact, the analysis of the relation between money supply and inflation is based on just that distinction. We started this chapter by emphasizing that monetary magnitudes are significant in real rather than nominal terms. We now have to follow that up and try to adapt our analysis of the relation of money supply, interest rates, and income to one relating nominal money supply, real income, price level, and interest rates. We could have said real money supply, real income, and interest rate, but we want to be able to deal with the central fact that the Fed determines nominal money supply. The *New York Times* reports the market reaction to each week's change in nominal money supply. It never reports changes in real money supply. At least in the short run, prices are influenced by a variety of forces other than money, so that the Fed determines nominal money supply, while other things determine prices.

The two together determine the change in real money supply. In the long run, money supply may be a major determinant of price levels but that is not true from month to month.

With a little mathematics the whole *LM* analysis can be shown in real terms. The basic equation for the demand for money can be written

$$M = L(R)Y$$

where M is nominal money, R is interest rate, Y is nominal GNP, and P the price level. If we divide both sides by P we have

$$M/P = L(R)Y/P.$$

We can now derive the *LM* curve in real terms exactly as we did using figures 12.8, 12.9, and 12.10, replacing M with M/P and Y with Y/P. Notice that we can change the real money supply, either by changing nominal money supply, while prices remain constant, or by changing prices while nominal money supply remains constant. With a given nominal money supply, a rise in the price level reduces real money supply and shifts the whole *LM* curve to the left; while a lower price level shifts the whole curve to the right.

A graphical example may help clarify the mathematical equations.

Figure 12.11   Effect of Price-Level Change on Interest Rate

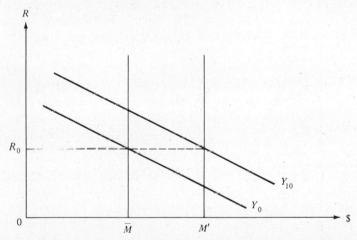

In figure 12.11 the solid line Y_0 is just the same as in figure 12.7. The vertical line $\overline{M}$ shows the initial nominal money supply. Now suppose the price level moves up 10 percent, while real income stays the same. Y_{10} shows the new money-demand curve. At each interest rate, people want to hold just 10 percent more money because with the same real income their nominal transactions are all inflated by 10 percent. M' is just 10 percent bigger than $\overline{M}$ so that M/P is unchanged by the price-level change, and (surprise) it intersects Y_{10} at the same interest rate R_0 as the intersection of $\overline{M}$ and Y_0. We get the same combination of interest rate and real income when we keep the real money supply constant. Alternatively, if money supply remained at $\overline{M}$ the real money supply would have fallen and, as figure 12.11 shows, the interest rate would have risen. You can see that if we plot an *LM* curve with real income on the horizontal axis, the *LM* curve corresponding to any given nominal money supply will be higher when the price level rises.

Demand for Assets Versus Demand for Money

Determining the interest rate or the level of asset prices by equating the supply and demand for money seems a little artificial. In fact, however, it is readily shown that that way of doing it is exactly the same as attacking the problem the other way around and considering the supply and demand for assets. However, it also turns out that a direct look at the supply and demand for assets reveals certain aspects of the problem that are concealed by the supply and demand for money approach. To see the relation between the two approaches in its simplest form, suppose that there are only two assets, money and bonds. To make things even simpler suppose there is no transaction demand. Total wealth in nominal terms is the stock of money plus the value of bonds. To take the easiest case suppose that there are *B* bonds, each a perpetuity paying one dollar per year forever. R is the interest rate, each bond is worth $1/R$ dollars, and the total stock of bonds is worth $B \times 1/R$, which increases as *R* falls. Total wealth is $W = M + B \times 1/R$.

Each investor wants to divide his or her wealth between money and bonds so as to hold a proportion $L(R)$ in bonds and the remainder $1 - L(R)$ in money. $L(R)$ will increase as the interest rate increases—investors want a high proportion of wealth in bonds when interest rates are high.

Thus the value of bonds demanded at any interest rate is

$$
\begin{aligned}
B/R &= L(R)W \\
&= L(R)(M + B/R) \\
B &= L(R)(MR + B) \\
&= RL(R)M \ L(R)B \\
B(1 - L(R)) &= RL(R)M \\
B &= \frac{RL(R)M}{1 - L(R)}
\end{aligned}
$$

The number of bonds demanded will rise as the interest rate rises (price of bonds falls). The numerator of the demand function rises with the interest rate and the denominator falls (since $1 - L(R)$ decreases with R because $L(R)$ increases).

The solid curve marked M_0 in figure 12.12 shows a demand curve for bonds with money supply *M*. The vertical line B_0 is the supply of bonds, and the equilibrium interest rate is R_0. The dotted curve marked

Figure 12.12   Changing Money Supply Affects Demand for Bonds

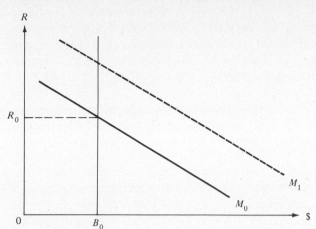

M_1 shows bond demand for a larger money supply M_1. You can see from the demand equation that more bonds will be demanded at every interest rate.

There are two ways in which money supply can increase. First, if more money is simply printed, the M in the demand equation above is increased and the demand curve for bonds shifts to the right, lowering the equilibrium interest rate. If the money is created by a banking-system purchase of existing bonds, then the supply of bonds is reduced while the demand increases, thus lowering the interest rate even more.

A similar argument can be applied to the many-asset case by reversing the application of the separation theorem used to show that a general rise in asset yields will reduce demand for money. That is analogous to the proposition that a rise in bond yields reduces demand for money. In the two-asset bond-money case we have just shown that equating supply and demand for money is equivalent to equating supply and demand for bonds because only one price is involved in a choice between two assets. In the same way we argue that if money is the riskless asset, an increase in money supply must raise the prices of risky assets generally in order to induce people to raise the ratio of money to risky assets in their portfolio.

However, that approach has important limitations. First, money is not the only riskless asset. Short-term securities and time deposits can serve to dilute risk as well as money. Second, while it is true that an increase in supply of money or other riskless assets tends to raise the price of risky assets, many other matters may be involved.

Accordingly, economists have developed a number of more pragmatic approaches for analysis of the links between money and the large number of assets and asset prices appearing in real markets. Three leading approaches to be discussed are the money-market and term-structure approach, the capital-market-model approach, and the three-assets approach developed by Brunner and Meltzer.

Money Market and Term Structure

The simplest approach is a two-step one. We first analyze the movements of short-term interest rates on the assumption that from week to week and month to month most of the activity in balancing supply and demand for money takes place in the market for Treasury bills, bank CDs, and commercial paper. This is called the money-market view of interest rates. Then we link all other interest rates and asset prices to short rates by taking account of the term structure consideration in chapter 6. We look at those steps one at a time.

The money-market view of short-term interest rates. We already noted that some economists think that demand for money is much more responsive to the yields on short-term securities and time deposits than to any other yields. They argue that investors seeking a hedge against risk will hold Treasury bills, time deposits, or other liquid assets rather than money because they get a better return. Money will be held mainly for transactions purposes, and transactions demand at a given level of income will be determined by yields on the other liquid assets that can be quickly and cheaply converted into money.

That argument leads to the use of a demand for money equation like the Goldfeld equation, which makes demand for money depend on GNP and time and savings deposit rates, which can be regarded as a constant in the short run. In that case all the work of equating supply and demand for money in the short run has to be done by changes in the short-term interest rates (including those on money-market certificates).

With a given time-deposit rate the demand for money can be represented by figure 12.13, with a quantity of money on the horizontal axis and the short-term interest rate on the vertical axis. In figure 12.14 the solid lines show an initial equilibrium for the income y_0 and money supply M_0. The dotted line Y_1 shows money demand for a high level of income a year later. The vertical dotted lines M_1 and M'_1 show alternative levels of

Figure 12.13   Demand for Money

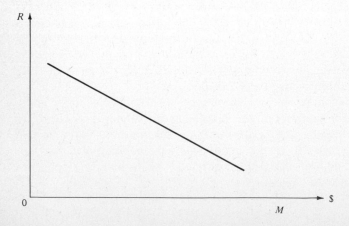

Figure 12.14 Equilibrium Interest Rate at Alternative Levels of Income
and Money Supply

money supply a year later. You can see that the movement of the short-
term interest rate can be regarded as the result of a race between growth of
income and growth of money supply. When money supply increases more
than enough to compensate for the increased money demand due to increased income the short-term interest rate falls. When money supply does
not grow so much the interest rate rises.

Generally nominal GNP rises from quarter to quarter with only an
occasional small decline in recessions. At the same time nominal money
supply almost always increases from quarter to quarter. However, quarter-
to-quarter percentage changes in both money supply and GNP vary widely
and the differences between them may vary even more so. It is the difference that counts.

In a recession nominal GNP tends to show little change, while money
supply increases, so that short-term rates fall. In booms, when GNP is
rising relatively rapidly there are two possibilities. Most of the time the Fed
more or less "accommodates" the boom, providing more money as GNP
increases. However, it does not usually go all the way. It increases money-
supply growth but not enough to prevent a gradual rise in interest rates.
Sometimes though, out of fear of inflation, the Fed holds down money-
supply growth and short-term interest rates rise rapidly. It is important to
recognize that the relation between income, demand for M_{1A}, and short-
term interest rates can be shifted by a variety of institutional changes discussed earlier. Such changes may either offset or accentuate the interest-rate
response to the relative growth rates of income and GNP.

Term and risk structure. If short-term interest rates can be analyzed in
terms of income movements and Federal Reserve action, it is possible that
other rates are determined by the factors considered in the discussion of
term structure in chapter 6. We suppose that long-term rates respond to
the actual movements of the short rate, and the expectations of future

short-rate movements, and we apply the term-structure theory. Bond buyers and sellers know what has happened to short rates, they guess what
will happen to GNP, they guess what the Fed will do to money supply,
and thereby guess what will happen to future short rates, and then decide
whether it is a good time to buy or sell bonds. Their decisions determine
the long-term bond prices and yields. The same argument applies to stock
but in that case investors also have to judge the implications of their GNP
forecasts for future corporate profits and dividends. In this elaborate guess-
ing game, expectations about inflation can play a central role. They may
influence bond and stock prices directly or indirectly.

Bond-market participants may guess the rate of inflation and use their
guess to deduce Federal Reserve policy. If they think that inflation will
accelerate they may conclude that the Fed will hold back on the money
supply and thereby raise short-term interest rates. That will lead to lower
bond prices and higher bond yields. But expectations of inflation may also
influence bond yields directly. Corporate treasurers will be more willing to
pay high rates to raise funds for capital goods purchases if they expect prices
to rise. Either way we can be pretty sure that expectations of accelerating
inflation will raise interest rates. We will return to that subject after the
discussion of inflation in later chapters.

The Capital-Market Model Approach

The money-market approach for short-term interest rates coupled with
the term-structure analysis of the relation between short rates and others is
a useful device. However, many economists think that it leaves out important aspects of the behavior of capital markets and financial intermediaries. They prefer to think of a system of linked capital markets,
which is built up by analysis of the portfolio decisions of households,
corporations, governments, and all the different kinds of intermediaries. In
this analysis the supply and demand for each type of asset (from the
buyer's point of view) or liability (from the issuer's point of view) is
derived from analysis of the decisions of each type of investor. The yield
on each type of asset must be the one that brings the supply and demand
for that asset into balance. All the markets are linked, however, because
the supply and demand curves depend on the yields of other assets. You
may regard the discussion of market interactions in chapter 6 as a crude
form of capital-market analysis with the addition that the short rate is
determined by the money-market approach. A number of very elaborate
statistical models of capital markets have been developed and some of them
are now used in large econometric models designed for forecasting.

The Brunner and Meltzer Approach

Another way of dealing with the multiple-asset problem has been
proposed by Brunner and Meltzer. They feel that the model of interest

rates based on bonds-money economy is too simple, not to say deceptive. They feel that the term-structure approach gives money too limited a role. On the other hand since they are interested in some general theoretical conclusions about income determination they feel that the detailed capital-market models place too much emphasis on the details of capital-market structure. In their view those details are important only in the very short run.

Brunner and Meltzer feel the most useful way to analyze capital markets is to split them into three pieces: the money market, the debt market, and the market for real capital. In their view expenditures for goods and services are given by the wealth embodied in the three types of assets, and the relative prices of those assets and of currently produced goods and services. We shall discuss their theory in more detail in chapter 17.

The Income-Expenditure Approach Versus the Monetarist Approach

Now that we have surveyed the development and empirical testing of theories of demand for money we have to return to the question of the use of those theories.

Many people are interested in demand for money because they are trying to predict the course of interest rates over the next few months and sort out the probable influence of Federal Reserve action on stock prices. The influence of money does not stop with its direct effect on securities markets. Everyone recognizes that changes in money supply exert an important influence on movements of aggregate output and prices. Indeed, so-called monetarist economists think of money as the dominant influence on nominal GNP and prices.

In dealing with those matters there are two basically different approaches. One, called the income-expenditure approach, begins by analyzing the factors causing households and businesses to vary their expenditures on goods and services. From that point of view changes in money supply are regarded as one factor, albeit an important one, influencing expenditures decisions. Moreover, money exerts its main influence indirectly through its influence on interest rates and asset prices. The game plan for income-expenditure analysis is to examine the determinants of expenditures on goods and services assuming a given level of interest rates and asset prices to find what income goes with each level of interest rates. The result is then coupled with the LM curve to find the equilibrium level of income for a given money supply. That equilibrium is one in which the income and interest rate on the LM curve are consistent with the interest rate and income from the first step. We will go into more detail on this in the next chapter.

The income-expenditure approach gives money a significant role in determining the rate of expenditure on goods and services, but it allows all sorts of other factors to do so too. Moreover, changes in money supply exert their influence only indirectly. A change in money supply first ripples through financial markets as people use money to bid up prices of financial assets. The resulting changes in interest rates and asset prices then exert their influence on consumption and investment decisions. The other approach is not necessarily inconsistent with the income-expenditure approach but it starts from the idea that money supply exerts a dominant influence on expenditures. Accordingly, analysis starts with the idea that an increase in money supply influences expenditures in many ways. One, but only one, of those links between money and expenditure is the effect of money on interest rates and asset prices. The monetarist approach is outlined in more detail in chapters 16 and 17.

In the next two chapters we deal with the Keynesian or income-expenditure approach. In doing so we first use a simple model whose monetary component is derived from the *LM* curve. In the following chapter we introduce some further effects of money. In chapters 16 and 17 we review monetarist analysis of expenditures. We then turn to the analysis of inflation. Finally we try to sum up the arguments and the agreements and disagreements of Keynesians and monetarists.

Summary

Money is an important asset in our economy, and changes in the supply of money play a major role in determining the prices of all other assets. The demand for money arises from the two main functions of money, as a store of value and as a medium of exchange. The demand for money as a medium of exchange stems from the fact that households and businesses must hold money during the intervals between the times when they receive payments from the sale of goods and services, and the times at which they make payments for goods and services. By taking time and trouble and using other liquid assets as substitutes for money, households and businesses can economize on the amount of money they hold. The extent to which it is worthwhile to economize in the use of money depends on the level of interest rates. Consequently, the transactions demand for money depends on the level of income and transactions, but it also depends on the level of interest rates.

The demand for money as an asset or a store of value stems from the fact that the nominal value of money is fixed so that money is a riskless asset, at least in nominal terms. The demand for money as an asset increases with total wealth, but the proportion of total wealth held in money form depends in part on the difference between the interest yields on money holdings and prospective yields on other assets. The asset demand for money may also depend on the public's views about the amount of risk involved in holding other assets. Empirical studies support the view that demand for money depends positively on the level of income and on the level of wealth, and negatively on the difference between the interest rate paid on money holdings and the interest rate on other assets. In equilibrium the available money supply must be held by someone. If we are given the rates paid on commercial-bank time deposits included in the money supply, we can show that the equilibrium interest rate is the one that equates the supply and demand for money. We can also show that for a given supply of money the equilibrium interest rate rises with the level of income. The curve showing the equilibrium interest rate for a given nominal money supply and a given nominal income is called an *LM* curve. We will make a lot of use of the *LM* curve in the following chapter.

QUESTIONS AND EXERCISES

1. Using diagrams like those in figure 12.10, show how the *LM* curve will shift in response to a reduction in money supply.
2. If more people received their paychecks monthly instead of weekly, the transactions demand for money would tend to increase. Explain.
3. An increase in savings-deposit rates tends to increase the velocity of *M-1*, but will have less effect on *M-2*. Explain.
4. Some people hold money to reduce the risk of change in the nominal value of their assets. Name some nonmoney assets that can serve the same purpose.
5. "Short-term interest rates are determined by the supply and demand for securities such as Treasury bills and commercial paper." "The Fed can influence short-term interest rates through its control of bank reserves and money supply." Are the two statements consistent? Explain how they can be reconciled.
6. Draw an *LM* curve with real income on the horizontal axis. How will the curve shift if the price level rises while nominal money supply remains fixed?

FURTHER READING

BAUMOL, W. "The Transactions Demand for Cash: An Inventory Theoretic Approach." *Quarterly Journal of Economics* 66 (November 1952): 545–56. This paper gives a formal exposition of the theory of transactions demand for money, emphasizing the trade-off between the cost in terms of interest forgone by holding an inventory of money and the benefit of reduction in the cost of making financial transactions.

BRUNNER, KARL, and MELTZER, ALLAN H. "Predicting Velocity: Implications for Theory and Policy." *Journal of Finance* 18 (May 1963): 319–54. An empirical study of the influence of interest rate, wealth, and income on the demand for money over a long period.

FRIEDMAN, MILTON. "The Demand for Money—Some Theoretical and Empirical Results." *Journal of Political Economy* 67 (June 1959): 327–51. An important exposition of Friedman's views on the demand for money, with tests of his views and competing ones.

FRIEDMAN, MILTON, and SCHWARTZ, ANNA J. *A Monetary History of the United States, 1867–1960*. Princeton, N.J.: National Bureau of Economic Research, 1963. This very large volume gives a detailed history of the causes of changes in the money supply over nearly a century, together with a detailed analysis of the response of the economy in each period.

GOLDFELD, STEPHEN M. "The Demand for Money Revisited." *Brookings Papers on Economic Activity,* 1973: 3, pp. 577–638. A statistical study of alternative formulations of the demand for money equation.

LAIDLER, DAVID. *The Demand for Money: Theories and Evidence*. 2d ed. New York: Dun-Donnelley, 1977. This book provides the most comprehensive view of the development of the theory of demand for money and the current state of the art. Summarizes a very large number of empirical studies.

PORTER, RICHARD, SIMPSON, THOMAS, and MAUSKOF, EILEEN. "Financial Innovation and Monetary Aggregates." *Brookings Papers on Economic Activity,* 1979: 1, pp. 213–29. This paper offers an explanation of an apparent downward shift in the demand for money in terms of changes in practices of banks' development of new substitutes for money.

TOBIN, JAMES. "The Interest Elasticity of Transaction Demand for Cash." *Review of Economics and Statistics* 38 (August 1956): 241–47. A classic exposition of the theory of the transactions demand for money.

———. "Liquidity Preference as Behavior Towards Risk." *Review of Economic Studies* 25 (February 1958): 65–86. This paper develops the theory of the demand for money as a means of avoiding the risk involved in holding other financial assets.

13

Income-Expenditure Theory

The development of the market-oriented industrial economies over the past three hundred years or so has been marked by a phenomenal but uneven growth in output. The output level of each decade has exceeded the level of the previous one, but there have also been significant fluctuations in output. Until the Second World War, major depressions marked by sharp price declines and widespread unemployment occurred every decade or so with a couple of minor recessions in between.

Those fluctuations in output, prices, and employment culminated in the Great Depression of the 1930s, a worldwide catastrophe that almost brought capitalism to an end and produced permanent changes in the structure and government policy of the market economies.

Even before the 1930s economists devoted a lot of effort to explaining fluctuations in output and prices. Neoclassical economics provided a basic framework for understanding the long-term growth process and the long-run adjustment of market economies to population growth, capital accumulation, and technological change. Short-run fluctuations were treated separately under the heading of "business cycles," but in spite of a good deal of effort, no theory of short-run output fluctuations was ever widely accepted.

In attempting to deal with short-run fluctuations in prices and output business-cycle theorists often resorted to play-by-play accounts. They recognized, for example, that business investment expenditures were more volatile than consumer expenditures and sought explanations for investment booms and slumps. At the same time they recognized that an investment boom would increase employment and income for consumers and lead to a rise in consumer expenditures. They tried to trace through the resulting cumulative process. Then they examined how the boom might be checked. For example, rapidly rising prices and output could push up interest rates, slow investment expenditures, and throw the whole process into reverse.

Much of their difficulty lay in the absence of adequate data on short-run movements of demand and in the lack of any systematic framework for the analysis of the interactions among the components of demand.

In seeking an explanation of the Great Depression of the 1930s, John Maynard Keynes made effective use of the income-expenditure approach. That approach emphasizes the fact that decisions to spend are strongly influenced by income or expected income. At the same time it asserts that "one person's expenditure is another's income." By contrast, the mainstream of classical theory had looked upon expenditures as being determined by the quantity of money. Keynes used national income accounts as a conceptual framework, together with a few bold generalizations about the response of consumers to changes in income, the response of interest-rate changes to changes in income and money supply, and the response of investment to changes in interest rates. With those elements he was able to give a systematic account of the factors controlling the total reaction of output to an initial change in investment or government expenditure. Keynes's work has been much criticized and elaborated in the last forty years, but it did get the analysis of short-run fluctuations in output off to a fresh start.

But Keynes had very little data to work with. The practical significance of his analysis was greatly increased by the publication, shortly after the appearance of the "General Theory of Employment, Interest, and Money," of the first set of comprehensive annual national accounts. These data, the fruit of many years of work by Simon Kuznets and the National Bureau of Economic Research, provided the basis for empirical measurement and testing of the relationships in Keynes's model and for its application to practical policy problems. Though many of Keynes's conclusions have been challenged or modified, the systematic analysis of interactions between income and expenditure in terms of national-income-account categories still forms the basis of most short-run forecasting and a great deal of policy analysis.

In this chapter we will first outline the structure of the national income accounts and then proceed to outline the main features of the Keynesian income-expenditure approach. In order to see the forest for the trees, we will concentrate on the simplest, most central features of the model. In the following two chapters we will consider a number of complications, especially those relating to the impact of monetary policy on changes in economic activity.

The Structure of the National Income Accounts

The national income accounts are based on a double-entry bookkeeping system for the nation. The central concept is the *measure of the aggregate value of the nation's output of goods and services*—**gross national product** or **GNP.** The idea is to measure and add up the output of all the nation's farms, factories, drugstores, doctors, universities, and so on.

In principle, it is simple to estimate the value of, say, coal, steel, and automobiles among other things produced in 1977. But does the sum of those values mean anything? It really cannot because the value of automobiles produced in any year includes the value of steel used in their manufacture. The value of steel produced includes the value of coal used to make it. Thus, in this example the coal is included three times and the steel twice.

A more useful way to measure output is to include only the "value added" for each production unit. **Value added** for a business firm is the *value of its total output less the value of materials and services purchased from other firms.* Thus, each firm's contribution to production is counted only once and the total is independent of the number of stages of production through which an intermediate product passes. Thus the U.S. GNP for any year, say 1977, is the sum of the value added during 1977 by each producing unit. The producing units include farms and business firms of all types. GNP also includes the value added by independent professionals such as lawyers, by nonprofit organizations like universities and churches, and by governments.

The value-added approach to measuring output not only solves the "double-counting" problem, but it also leads to a direct relation between the value of output and the incomes of factors of production. In fact, it turns out that if we keep the books balanced and follow the usual accounting conventions, the value of production in a year is identical with the total income of households, businesses, and governments.

Table 13.1 shows the calculation of profit for a hypothetical firm. Table 13.2 shows the same information arranged to show that value added by the firm is exactly equal to incomes paid to households and governments plus the profits of the firm. The latter are divided into dividends, corporate income taxes, and profits retained by the firm. Of course, that conclusion results from the definition of profits as a residual after everybody else has been paid.

Table 13.1   Income Statement of Typical Firm

Sales *Plus:*		$20,000
Inventory increase		1,000
Value of production		21,000
Less: Expenses		16,600
Purchased materials	$5,000	
Wages and salaries	10,000	
Interest payments	500	
Depreciation charges	1,100	
Profits		4,400
Less: State and local taxes		400
Profits before income taxes		4,000
Less: Corporate income taxes		1,800
Profits after income taxes		2,200
Less: Dividends		700
RETAINED EARNINGS		$1,500

Table 13.2   Income Statement of Typical Firm: An Alternative Presentation

Value added by firm		*Incomes paid by firm*		
Value of production	$21,000	Households		$11,200
Less: Purchased materials		Wages and salaries	$10,000	
from other firms	5,000	Interest payments	500	
		Dividends	700	
		State and local		
		governments		400
		Federal government		1,800
		Retained by firm		2,600
		Depreciation	1,100	
		Retained earnings	1,500	
VALUE ADDED	$16,000	TOTAL INCOME		$16,000

GNP As Final Product

There is another way to solve the double-counting problem. Instead of taking the value-added route, double counting can be eliminated by only counting production sold to final users. Thus, in the steel, coal, and automobile example we could just count the autos and not bother with the steel and coal. More generally, GNP can be regarded as the sum of the value of goods and services sold to consumers, capital goods such as machinery, factory, and office buildings sold to business, and goods and services sold to government. To these we would add residential construction, additions to inventories, and the excess of exports over imports. The latter item reflects the fact that some U.S. production is sold abroad, while some of the goods purchased by consumers and businesses are imported.

The total value of products sold for consumption, investment, or government purchase, plus exports minus imports has to be exactly equal to the sum of the value added by all producing units. In effect the value of any final product, for example, an automobile, can be built up from the value-added contributions of the auto dealer, the auto manufacturer, the suppliers of raw materials to the auto manufacturer, parts manufacturers, suppliers of raw materials to them, and so on. Those contributions include not only the physically identifiable elements of the final car but energy for heat, light, and power, and services of lawyers, insurance companies, advertising agents, and so on.

Double-Entry System

Gross national product regarded as the sum of the value-added contributions of all producing units can thus be readily broken down into classes of final products or into expenditures by different kinds of purchasers of final products. At the same time, the value-added contribution of each producing unit breaks down into income payments of different kinds—wages, rents, profits, taxes. Total GNP will therefore be equal to the sum of the national totals for the various income elements. Thus the national income accounts are a double-entry system in which the components of the product side—consumer expenditure, investment, government purchases, exports less imports—add up to GNP while the components of the income side—wages, profits, and so on—add to the same total.

We have seen that the total GNP is always distributed in income to households, businesses, and governments. That conclusion results directly from the definition of GNP and the definition of profits as the residual claim to value added for each production unit. Definitions, however, do not tell us anything about the relative size of the shares of GNP going to various sectors or about how those shares are likely to vary over the business cycle. In fact, the distribution process is fairly complicated for two reasons. First, the distribution takes place in two stages. The primary distribution divides the GNP between business gross profits (before depreciation) and household income, wages, salaries, rents, and interest, with a small share going directly to government in sales taxes. There are secondary distributions involving business payments of corporate income taxes to government out of profits, business payments of dividends to households, household payments of income taxes to government, and government payment of transfers (such as social security) to households. Second, the shares of income going to profits vary systematically over the cycle.

Initial Distribution of National Income

The primary distribution of GNP divides gross national income into three parts. First, government levies sales taxes and property taxes on business and these indirect business taxes are a first charge on output. Second, households receive wages and salaries, interest and rent from business. Third, what is left is the gross profit of business, which is divided into capital consumption allowances (more commonly called depreciation) and net profits.

The share of indirect taxes, mainly excise, sales, and property taxes in GNP, depends, of course, on governmental decisions in the setting of tax rates and the choice of commodities subject to tax. If tax rates were set and left alone, the share of GNP going to indirect taxes would, of course, depend on the sales volumes of the taxed commodities. In fact, however, state and local governments are constantly adjusting tax rates. The revenue from these taxes ultimately reflects the willingness of the public to pay taxes for government services and the resolution of political conflicts over the share of the tax burden paid by various groups. In fact, in the postwar period, the ratio of indirect taxes to GNP has varied in a fairly narrow range.

The share of corporate profits in GNP shows a rather complex pattern. From the late 1940s until the late 1960s, there was little trend in the ratio of gross corporate profits to GNP, but there were marked cyclical variations in the ratio. Corporate profits rose more than proportionately to GNP during booms and fell more than proportionately in slumps. Those changes in the share of corporate profits reflect the changes in labor productivity associated with short-run variations in capacity utilization. Prices seem to be adjusted to the trend of labor cost per unit of output, so that short-run variations in labor productivity and labor costs are reflected in profits. During the late 1960s and early 1970s, the share of corporate profits in GNP showed a downward trend, even after allowance for cyclical factors. There has been a good deal of dispute over the cause of the shift, but in recent years the share of corporate porfits has shown an upward trend.

Secondary Distribution of National Income

After the primary three-way split of gross national income, various redistributions occur. First, corporations allocate part of their gross profits to depreciation allowances in recognition of the fact that the plant and equipment used in the productive process is wearing out. Second, corporate net profits are divided among corporate income taxes, dividends, and retained earnings, for investment in the business. Third, there is an interchange between households and governments. Households pay income and social security taxes to governments. On the other hand, governments make transfer payments—social security, welfare, pensions, Medicaid—to households. *The net received by households from wages, salaries, rents, interest, dividends, and transfer payments, less taxes,* is called **disposable income.** We will make much use of that concept when we discuss the de-termination of consumer expenditures.

Real Versus Nominal GNP

The basic data for the national income accounts are measured in value terms. GNP measured by the final-product approach is obtained by adding up the value—price times quantity—of all the different kinds of output produced in the year. Thus the statement that the GNP in 1979 was 11 percent greater than in 1978 reflects both the changes in physical outputs and the changes in prices between the two years.

We need value data for many purposes, but changes in real output are even more important. Accordingly, we have a set of national income accounts in real or constant dollar terms. We can not measure real GNP directly as we can not add the output of apples, oranges, bicycles, and trucks. We combine the outputs of diverse goods and services by weight-ing them by their relative prices. Thus, we regard one $4,000 car as the equivalent of forty bicycles valued at $100 each. To get changes in the price level out of the picture we use the prices of a single base year for the value-weighting process. 1972 is the base year currently in use. In principle, we get the GNP in 1972 dollars for 1978 by multiplying the 1978 output of each product by its 1972 price and adding them up. We get the 1979 GNP measured in 1972 prices in the same way. When we compare the two constant dollar figures, the increase from 1978 to 1979 has been purged of the effects of inflation. The change reflects only changes in output since the same prices are used in each case.

In these days of persisting inflation there is a lot of difference between the movement of constant dollar GNP and the amounts of GNP in current value or nominal GNP, as shown in figure 13.1.

Figure 13.1   Gross National Product
Seasonally adjusted annual rates, quarterly

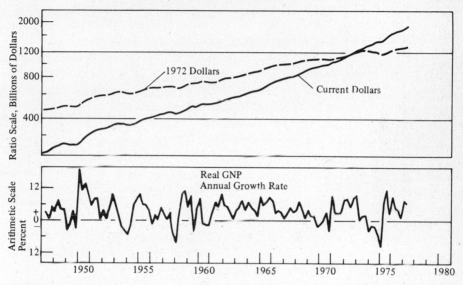

SOURCE: Board of Governors of the Federal Reserve System, *Historical Chart Book*, 1979, p. 12.

Potential Output

You can see from figure 13.1 that real GNP has been increasing for many years. In some periods its rate of growth is relatively high, in others real GNP grows slowly and occasionally actually declines a little, but the trend is distinctly upward. The upward trend of real GNP reflects the growth of our labor force, and the increased productivity from improved technology, better education, and a continuing increase in the stocks of all kinds of capital goods.

The upward trend of real GNP could not occur without a continuing increase in our capacity to produce, but it does not follow that the increase in real GNP for any one year is the same as the increase in capacity to produce. The rate of growth of real GNP is erratic while the capacity to produce output grows fairly steadily.

In the analysis of unemployment, capacity utilization, and of changes in prices and wages, it is useful to compare the actual constant dollar GNP with some measure of the aggregate output that could be produced in practice. The maximum theoretical GNP for a given labor input, say, an average workweek of forty hours for all of the labor force, would be produced if capital and labor resources were being used in the most efficient way. Resources are utilized with maximum efficiency if (1) it is not possible to produce more of one good without producing less of another, and (2) the amount of good A that must be given up to produce more of another good B just corresponds to the amount of A that consumers will give up to get another unit of B. In an unchanging world a competitive price system should produce just that result.

In practice we never achieve the most efficient utilization of our resources for two reasons. First, taxes, subsidies, regulations, and elements of monopoly prevent the price system from working perfectly. Second, prices have to be constantly adjusted to a moving target. In a world of change the accumulation of capital, changing technology, the growth of the labor force, and changes in its age distribution and educational level cause continual changes in the optimal distribution of resources. Moreover, individual workers are always entering and leaving the labor force, while firms frequently have to either lay off workers or expand employment. No price system can keep up with all those changes, so there are always some resources that are at least temporarily underutilized or used in relatively inefficient ways. There will be unemployment in some occupations while there are unfilled vacancies in others. There will be excess capacity in some industries while others are working overtime. In practice a certain amount of unemployment is inevitable. Even in World War II unemployment did not fall below one percent of the labor force and at that time there were widespread labor shortages and inflation in spite of the use of rationing and price and wage controls. A practical definition of an economy's "potential output" has to allow for a level of unemployment at which labor markets are in balance—a level at which upward pressures on prices in markets with excess demand are roughly in balance with downward pressures in markets with excess supply. For a number of years after the Second World War there was general agreement that labor markets would be roughly in balance at an unemployment rate of around 4 percent. More recently, economists have accepted the view that changes in the structure of the labor market require an unemployment target of 5 percent or even 6 percent. (That change will be discussed more fully in chapter 20.) Potential output changes from year to year, even with a given level of unemployment because of the growth of the labor force and its productivity.

The Circular Flow of Income and Expenditures

When we try to analyze the economic processes underlying the national income accounts data, it is useful to think of the national accounts as measuring a circular flow of expenditures for goods and services, and income payments for services used in production. The accounts should be thought of as measuring flows because all the national income data have a time dimension. The amount of water in a system of pipes is measured in gallons. But the rate of flow of water past a given point is measured in gallons *per minute*. In the same way gross national product and its components are measured in billions of dollars *per year*.

Figure 13.2 Circular Flow I

(1) □ Consumer expenditures
(2) □ Goods and services
(3) □ Wage payments
(4) □ Labor services

(a) □ Business
(b) □ Households

The simplest form of circular flow is shown in figure 13.2. In the diagram we assume that all income goes to households in wage payments, and that households spend all their income on consumption goods. The solid upper line shows the flow of consumer expenditures—payments from households to producing firms. The upper dotted line shows the flow of consumer goods from firms to households. The lower solid line shows the wage payments from firms to households, while the lower dotted line shows the flow of labor services from households to firms. The rates of flow of consumption expenditures and wage payments have to be equal, and, of course, both equal GNP. One measures the final product side of the accounts, the other the income side. In the continuing process we do not raise the chicken-egg question of whether the expenditures cause the production and income or vice versa.

Figure 13.3 shows a more realistic circular-flow picture. When we take account of investment and saving, the new diagram differs from the

Figure 13.3 Circular Flow II

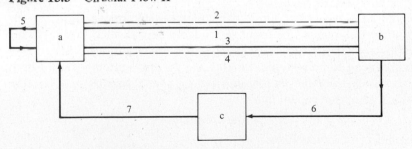

(1) Consumer expenditures
(2) Goods and services
(3) Wages, rent, interest dividends
(4) Labor services
(5) Capital goods purchases

(6) Household saving
(7) Business borrows

(a) Business
(b) Households
(c) Capital market

earlier one in three ways. First, we have shown a side flow of investment-expenditure payments from firms buying investment goods to those producing them. Second, households do not have to spend all their income on consumption. They may save and lend their savings to investing businesses through the capital market. Third, businesses can also save. The flow of payments from businesses to households is not equal to the whole GNP, but to GNP less depreciation and corporate retained earnings.

Figure 13.4   Circular Flow III

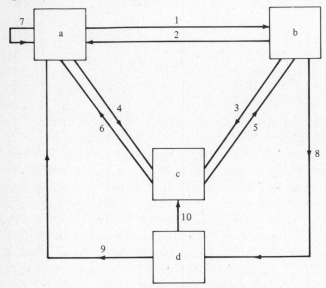

(a) Business	(5) Government wages and transfer payments
(b) Households	(6) Government purchases of goods and services
	(7) Capital goods purchases
(1) Wages, rent, interest	(8) Household saving
(2) Consumer expenditures	(9) Business borrowing
(3) Personal taxes	(10) Government borrowing
(4) Business taxes	

Figure 13.4 shows the additional complications arising from the introduction of government. Households and businesses make tax payments to government. Government purchases goods from business, and makes transfer payments to households. Finally, the government may run a deficit and draw funds from the capital market or run a surplus and lend to businesses through the capital market.

Equilibrium Circular Flow

In the real world the rate of flow of the various kinds of expenditures on goods and services is always changing, prices are changing, and income payments to various groups are always in flux. Moreover, it is clear that changes in any one part of the system will influence other parts. When the government canceled its support of the supersonic transport (SST), the reduction in government expenditures was felt in every part of Seattle. And since people in Seattle buy things made elsewhere the change was reflected in economic activity throughout the country. It is obvious that an attempt to trace step by step the way in which government expenditures, tax rates, or money supply affect the economy is certain to be a tedious and complicated process. Indeed, we are likely to get lost in the mass of detail, leave out some of the interactions, and get the wrong answer.

We can learn a lot and avoid some mistakes by asking a simpler question. We can ask under what conditions a circular-flow process will be in equilibrium in the sense that it keeps on repeating itself with the various flows in the system maintained at constant rates. To make sense out of that question, we have to assume some fixed characteristics of the economy with which we are dealing. At a minimum, we have to specify the labor force and capital stock of our economy and therefore its potential output measured in, say, 1972 dollars. Since we are going to be concerned with the effect of economic policy variables, we also specify the money supply, the real rate of government expenditures, and the tax rate and transfer payment formulas.

If a circular flow is to repeat itself, there must be a certain consistency between the given factors just mentioned and the rate of flow of GNP and its components. Moreover, there must be a certain consistency between the GNP and its constituent flows. First, the rates of household consumption and saving must be consistent with the rate of flow of GNP, the share going to households, and the tastes of consumers. Second, the rate of investment must be consistent with the prospective returns on investment and the interest rate. Third, producers have to sell their output. Total expenditures for goods and services must equal total production. Fourth, the amount of real money balances businesses and households want to hold must equal the amount available. You will recall from the last chapter that the demand for real money balances depends on real income and the interest rate. Fifth, the price level must be constant. The various elements in the circular flow can be measured either in money terms or in real, constant dollar terms. To have constant flows measured in both real and nominal terms the price level that links the two must be constant. Finally, the real flows must be consistent with the potential output of the economy. Real GNP cannot exceed potential output. It is physically possible for real GNP to fall short of potential output. However, it can be shown that a steady state equilibrium with output substantially below potential output is at least unusual, if not impossible.

Price Adjustments and Quantity Adjustments

We noted above that in an equilibrium steady state circular flow, production must equal expenditures. That condition is a little trickier than it sounds.

An examination of the national income accounts indicates that GNP measured from the production (value-added) point of view is always exactly equal to the total expenditures of households, business, and government. However, that identity holds only because the expenditure side includes investment in the form of additions to inventory. In a growing economy producers normally plan to increase their inventories each year. *Planned* inventory investment can be treated just like any other kind of investment demand. At times, however, firms may produce more or less than they sell because their sales fall short of expectations. Then they have unplanned additions to inventory and they will either change their output to match sales or change prices in the hope of adjusting sales to production, or do some of both. The condition for an equilibrium is that production matches expenditures for consumption, government purchases, fixed investment, and planned inventory investment. Unplanned inventory investment must be zero.

As already noted, firms can try to eliminate any difference between production and sales by a quantity adjustment (changing production and employment) or by a price adjustment. In a world of change, both kinds of adjustment are occurring all the time. But it will make our exposition easier if we first examine quantity adjustments, assuming that prices are fixed, and then turn to price adjustments.

In this section, the relations among real GNP, real investment, real government expenditures, and real consumption are analyzed. In particular, we will show how the responses of real consumption and real GNP to changes in real investment and government expenditures are influenced by the factors determining the share of GNP going to consumers and by the desires of consumers to save. That analysis gives us a limited insight into the impact of fiscal policy on the economy. It is important to remember, however, that the conclusions are only partial. To complete the analysis we must take account of monetary factors and allow for changes in the price level.

Goods-Market Equilibrium

The first requirement for a steady state circular flow is balance between the flow of production (GNP looked at from the production or value-added point of view) and the total that businesses, governments, and households want to spend on goods and services. The total of actual expenditures for consumption, investment, and government purchases is always equal to the value of production if we count inventory accumulation whether desired or not as part of expenditures. But clearly, firms will change their rate of production if they are accumulating unwanted inventories because they are unable to sell their output. Thus, if a steady rate of production is to be maintained, the sum of expenditures, government purchases, and investment in fixed capital plus any *planned* inventory investment must equal the value of production. That condition is not necessarily fulfilled.

In the simplest case, we could suppose that the real expenditures of households, businesses, and governments are just given arbitrarily. Then all the adjustment would be on the production side. In fact, however, real expenditures are likely to be influenced by real income. In particular consumer expenditures are strongly influenced by the level of disposable income. If that is so, then production is determined by expenditures while at the same time expenditures are at least partly determined by production. To analyze the implications of the mutual determination of expenditure and production, we make use of the concept of the consumption function.

The Consumption Function

Economists have long recognized that consumer expenditures are likely to respond to changes in income. Almost everyone finds it intuitively plausible that (other things equal) real consumption expenditures will be higher when real disposable income is high rather than when it is low. Keynes gave that notion a central role in his analysis of short-run changes in income and production. He labeled *the relation between real income and real consumption* the **consumption function.** According to Keynes, "the fundamental, psychological law, upon which we are entitled to depend with great confidence, both a priori from our knowledge of human nature and from the detailed facts of experience, is that men are disposed, as a rule and on the average, to increase their consumption as their income increases, but not by as much as the increase in their income."

Since Keynes's time, economists have devoted a lot of theoretical and empirical work to the analysis of consumption, and used much more complex formulations of the relation between income and consumption than the one embodied in Keynes's statement. We will discuss the consumption function in the next chapter, but for the purpose of showing how the income-consumption interaction works, a simple adaptation of Keynes's observation will suffice. A simple form of the consumption function is $C = AY + B$. C is real consumption, Y is real GNP. A indicates the increase in real consumption per dollar increase in real GNP. It reflects both the increase in real consumer expenditures per dollar of increase in real disposable income, and the increase in disposable income per dollar of income in GNP after allowing for the net increase in tax receipts less transfer payments and the increase in earnings retained by corporations per dollar increase in GNP. For example, if disposable income increases by 60 percent of any increase in GNP, while households spend 90 percent of any increase in disposable income, A would be .54. The constant B reflects all factors affecting consumer expenditures other than GNP. Thus, B includes consumption out of those transfer payments not related to GNP. In the next chapter, we will show that it also reflects such factors as the real wealth of households. For the moment, however, just take B as given.

The equation $C = AY + B$ is shown graphically in figure 13.5. The

Figure 13.5   The Consumption Function

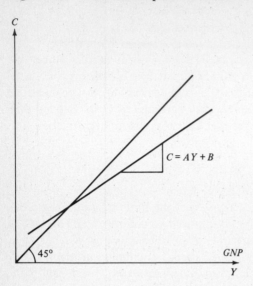

height of the line C at $Y = 0$ is B. A is the slope as shown in the little tri-angle. Figure 13.6 shows total expenditures by adding fixed rates of invest-ment and government expenditures to consumer expenditures at each level of GNP. $C + G$ represents consumption plus government expenditure, $C + I + G$ represents consumption plus government expenditures and invest-ment. Thus, the height of $C + I + G$ shows total desired expenditures at each GNP. GNP, on the other hand, is the rate of production.

Figure 13.6   Equilibrium of Production and Expenditure

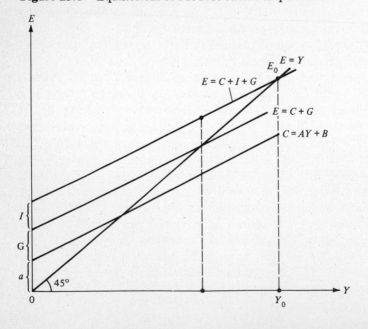

Figure 13.6 also includes a 45-degree line. All points on the 45-degree line satisfy the condition that total expenditures (measured vertically) equal total production (measured horizontally).

At point E_0 where the 45-degree line intersects the $C + I + G$ line both equilibrium conditions are satisfied. Consumers are spending the amount they want for the GNP, Y_0, while total expenditure equals production. Y_0 is the only GNP that satisfies both conditions. At any smaller GNP desired expenditure exceeds production. At any larger GNP production exceeds desired expenditure.

Changes in $I + G$: The Multiplier

Now let us consider what happens when $I + G$ changes. In figure 13.7, the line C is the same consumption function used before, and the solid line $C + I + G$ is the same as figure 13.6. The equilibrium position is at E. The dotted line marked $C + I' + G'$ represents total expenditures for a higher level of $I + G$. The new equilibrium is as E'. Notice that E' is above E by more than the increase in $I + G$. In fact the increase in equilibrium GNP is about twice the increase in $I + G$. That has to be so because the consumption function slopes upward. Each one-dollar increase in government and investment expenditures directly increases GNP by one dollar. Those expenditures increase disposable income. Households with more disposable income are induced to spend more on consumption. The total increase in GNP is a *multiple* of the initial increase generated by more government purchases or investment expenditures. With a little algebra the ratio of the increase in equilibrium GNP to the increase in government purchases or investment can be calculated.

There is a simple algebraic equivalent to our 45-degree line diagram. The equation of the $C + I + G$ line is given by adding $I + G$ to C so that

Figure 13.7   Changes in Equilibrium Income

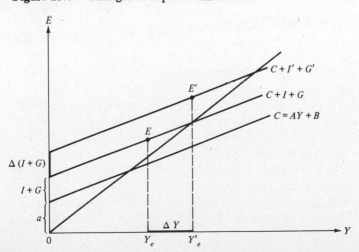

$C + I + G = AY + B + I + G$. The production-expenditure-equilibrium calculation is $C + I + G = Y$.

We have therefore that

$$Y = AY + B + I + G$$

or

$$Y - AY = B + I + G$$

or solving for Y

$$Y = (B + I + G) \frac{1}{1 - A}.$$

Thus the equilibrium GNP is equal to the sum of government expenditures, investment, and the part of consumer expenditures not affected by GNP—all *multiplied* by $\frac{1}{1-A}$. Since A is less than one, the multiplier must be greater than one. Any increase in I, G, or B will produce an increase in real GNP, which equals the initial change multiplied by $\frac{1}{1-A}$.

If A is close to one, the consumption line has a steep slope and the multiplier will be very large. If A is near zero, the consumption line is nearly flat, and the multiplier will be small. A is the income-consumption feedback coefficient.

Thus the size of the multiplier will depend on the way consumers divide increased disposable income between consumption and saving. The *ratio of increased consumption to increased disposable income* is called the **marginal propensity to consume** (MPC). The higher the MPC, the higher the multiplier.

The size of the multiplier will also depend on the share of additional income going to consumers. That will depend in part on the share of GNP going to profits, but it will also depend on the share going to indirect taxes and personal income taxes.

Fiscal Policy

The multiplier equation GNP $= (B + I + G) \cdot \frac{1}{1-A}$ can give some insight into the basic elements of fiscal policy. With fiscal policy the government can cause changes in GNP in three ways: by changing purchases of goods and services; by changing transfer payments; or by changing tax rates. First, an increase in the rate of government expenditures for goods and services changes G, and thereby changes GNP by G times the multiplier. Second, an increase in transfer payments can change either A or B. For example, an increase in social-security benefits can increase B in the multiplier equation because it makes disposable income higher at every level of GNP. On the other hand, an increase in unemployment benefits can reduce the disposable income changes by a smaller amount for each change in GNP. And third, by changing tax rates, governments can influence the size of the multiplier, since tax rates affect share of income going to consumers.

That is fiscal policy in one easy lesson. Unfortunately, there are all sorts of complications, so don't jump to any conclusions yet!

Interest Rates and the Level of Income and Expenditures

Investment and Interest Rates

Any change in the rate of investment will cause a change in equilibrium GNP by an amount equal to the multiplier times the initial change in investment. All sorts of things influence the level of investment, but the link between interest rates and investment deserves special attention in a book on money and banking. We will discuss the determinants of investment in detail in the next chapter, but at this point we will simply assert that other things equal, a rise in interest rates tends to lower the rate of investment. Figure 13.8 shows a hypothetical relationship between the

Figure 13.8   The Investment Function

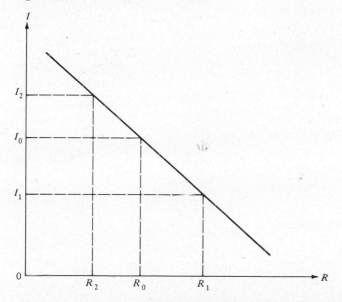

level of interest rates and the rate of investment. At interest rate R_0 we get investment rate I_0. At the higher rate R_1 we get lower investment I_1, and at the lower interest rate R_2 we get investment I_2.

The *IS* Curve

Now we want to link the level of interest rates to the level of GNP. That can be done very simply by transferring the hypothetical responses of investment to interest-rate levels shown in figure 13.8 to the 45-degree

Figure 13.9   Deriving the *IS* Curve I

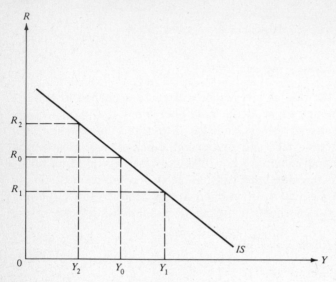

Figure 13.10   Deriving the *IS* Curve II

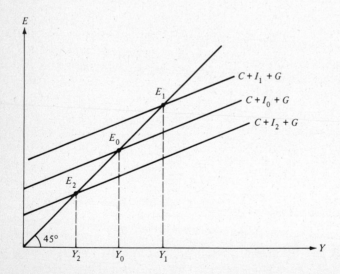

line diagram. In figure 13.10 we show three $C + I + G$ lines. The middle
one has investment I_0 corresponding to interest rate R_0, the lower one
has investment I_2 corresponding to interest rate R_2, the top one has investment I_1 corresponding to interest rate R_1. The level of government
expenditures and the consumption function are the same in all three cases.
You can see that as the interest rate moves up the equilibrium GNP moves
down and vice versa. The effect of a one percent change in interest rates

on GNP is the effect of the interest-rate change on the rate of investment times the multiplier.

If the equilibrium GNP corresponding to each level of interest rates is plotted we will get a downward sloping curve as in figure 13.9. Since the curve is for *equilibrium incomes where planned saving equals investment* it is called the **IS curve** (investment-saving equilibrium curve).

The *IS* curve can be represented algebraically by rewriting the multiplier equation with investment treated as a function of the interest rate instead of as a constant.

$$Y = [B + G + I(R)] \, \frac{1}{1-A}$$

I(R) is shorthand to indicate a relationship between the level of interest rates and the rate of investment like the one shown in figure 13.8.

The Position and Slope of the *IS* Curve

Each point on the *IS* curve represents an equilibrium level of income for the rate of investment corresponding to the indicated interest rate.

The position and slope of the curve will be affected by any of the fiscal policy actions discussed earlier. Thus an increase in real government expenditures will shift the curve outward by the amount of the expenditure increase times the multiplier $\frac{1}{1-A}$. A reduction in personal income tax rates will increase the multiplier. It will shift the curve outward because a larger multiplier applies to government expenditures and other elements not directly affected by the interest rate. It will also flatten the curve since a larger multiplier applies to investment, which increases as the interest rate falls.

The *IS* curve also summarizes the effect of changes in the interest rate on the level of income, taking multiplier effects into account. A fall in the interest rate first increases the rate of investment and then induces increases in consumption expenditure so that the total increase in GNP is a multiple of the increase in investment generated by the fall of interest rates.

Thus the slope of the *IS* curve depends on two factors: the slope of the investment function, which determines increases in investment resulting from the given fall in interest rates, and the size of the multiplier, which determines the ratio of the total GNP increase to the initial increase in investment.

IS and *LM* Curves

The *IS* curve is a device used to show how interest rates are related to GNP. Since the curve slopes down to the right, low interest rates are associated with high incomes. The curve is based on considerations relating to markets for goods and services and has nothing to do with financial markets.

We simply take the interest rate as given and look for a consistent level
of income and production.

But in the previous chapter we showed that the level of interest rates
(for a given money supply) depends on the level of income. We summarized the income–interest-rate relationship with the *LM* curve, which
showed that (given some real money supply) an increase in income is
associated with an increase in interest rates.

However, the *IS* curve relates low interest rates to high income, and
the *LM* curve relates high income to high interest rates. Do the two curves
contradict one another? No, this is another case of mutual or simultaneous
causation. Both the goods market and the money market have to be in
equilibrium at the same time. All interest-income combinations on the *IS*
curve are equilibrium positions for the goods markets but most of them are
not equilibrium positions for the money market. All interest-income combinations on the *LM* curve are equilibrium positions for the money market
but most of them are not equilibrium positions for the goods market. However, at a point where the curves cross both markets are in equilibrium.
Figure 13.11 shows the *IS* and *LM* curves together with the equilibrium
point at $R_0 Y_0$.

Figure 13.11   Equilibrium Income Determined by *IS–LM* Curves

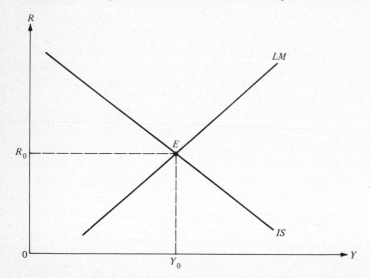

From your studies in other economics courses you will probably have
anticipated that this is leading up to the point where one curve will slope
down while the other slopes up, and the answer is where they cross.
However, it is important to remember that the two curves are devices for
summarizing a lot of information. The *IS* curve shows the net effect of a
change in interest rates on GNP. It takes into account both the direct response of investment to interest rates and the multiplier effect of changes
in investment on consumption expenditures. The *LM* curve condenses the

long story about financial markets, money substitutes, and demand for money in relation to income.

Together the two show that given the factors underlying the *IS* and *LM* curves, there is only one equilibrium set of rates of flow of real GNP and its components. The underlying variables are all in real terms. The equilibrium real GNP depends on a level of real government expenditures and transfer payments, real capital stock, and real money supply.

At every point on the *IS* curve, one of the conditions for circular-flow equilibrium is fulfilled: production equals expenditure at the indicated interest rate. At every point on the *LM* curve another condition for circular flow of equilibrium is satisfied: demand for money at the indicated interest rate and income equals supply of money. Both conditions are satisfied at the interest-rate–income combination at which the two curves intersect.

IS–LM curves and fiscal policy. We can get a better insight into the significance of the money-market equilibrium condition by reexamining our discussion of fiscal policy. You will recall that we ended our brief introduction to fiscal policy by noting that there were complications yet to be considered. The necessity of satisfying the money-market equilibrium condition is one of them. We can see how it comes into play by assuming a shift in the *IS* curve and following through the whole response assuming a fixed interest rate—ignoring the *LM* curve and then see how the reaction of the financial markets produces a reverse feedback offsetting part of the initial change.

Figure 13.12   Effect of Shift in *IS* Curve

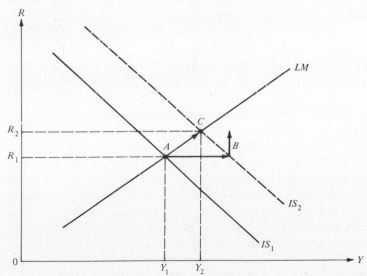

In figure 13.12 the solid curves IS_1LM_1 show an initial equilibrium $A - (R_1Y_1)$. Now suppose that an increase in government expenditures pushes the *IS* curve out as shown by the dotted line IS_2. The new equilibrium is at point $C - (R_2Y_2)$ but the economy does not automatically jump to this point. If the interest rate remains constant for a while the rise in government expenditures will raise GNP, and then generate a step-by-step multiplier process that would increase income to point B. That development however would throw the money market out of equilibrium.

The rise in income would increase demand for money for transactions purposes. Business firms would seek to sell securities and increase their cash holdings. Others would borrow from banks, which would in turn sell securities. Since by assumption the money supply is fixed, interest rates would have to rise to induce the public as a whole to get along with the same amount of money in spite of the rise in income. Some people would increase their money holdings but others would reduce them.

As interest rates rise, investment will be cut back, reducing incomes. Thus there will be a gradual rise in interest rates accompanied by falling investment and income. The movement is shown in figure 13.12 by the arrow along the *IS* curve. It will continue until the rise in interest rates and the fall in income have brought the money market back into balance. The whole system will be in a new equilibrium at C where the new *IS* curve crosses the *LM* curve.

In fact, of course, interest rates will start to move up as soon as government expenditures rise, so that investment will begin to fall before the multiplier response to government expenditure is completed. Simultaneous adjustment process is represented by the arrow from A to C showing the net effect of the increase in government expenditures offset by the decline in investment associated with rising interest rates.

The size of the total response to fiscal policy depends in part on the size of the ordinary (fixed interest rate) multiplier, but it also depends on the slopes of the *IS* and *LM* curves. In figure 13.12 the final equilibrium income at C is about halfway between the starting point at A and the simple fixed interest multiplier equilibrium at B. However, that result is an arbitrary by-product of the way the hypothetical *IS* and *LM* curves were drawn.

The actual outcome depends on the relative slopes of the *IS* and *LM* curves. Figures 13.13 (A) and (B) show two extreme cases. In figure 13.13 (A) the *IS* curves are steep, while the *LM* curve is very flat. Because the *LM* curve is very flat, a very small rise in interest rates is required to induce people to make a substantial reduction in the ratio of money holdings to income. So a big rise in income induces only a small increase in interest rates. With a very steep *IS* curve, the rise in interest rates cuts off only a small amount of investment. Thus, when a rise in government expenditures starts to push income up, the money-demand interest-rate feedback operates very weakly to limit the rise in income generated by increased government expenditures. Point C, the final equilibrium, is only a little to the left of point B, the simple multiplier equilibrium.

In figure 13.13 (B) the slopes are reversed. The *IS* curves are very responsive to interest rates, the *LM* curve is steep. In that case a small rise

Figure 13.13   How *IS* and *LM* Slopes Determine the Effect of Fiscal Policy

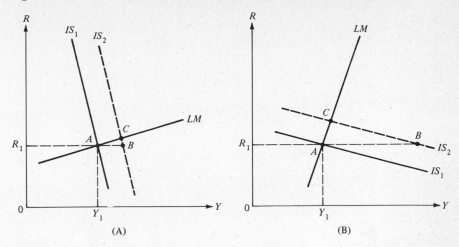

(A)   (B)

in income produces a large rise in interest rates because of the high *LM* slope. With a relatively flat *IS* curve, increased interest rates reduce investment a lot, thus offsetting the rise in government expenditure. In the figure, point *C* is far to the left of *B* and only a little to the right of *A*, showing that most of the effect of the rise in government expenditures has been "crowded out" by rising interest rates.

In general the effect of fiscal policy will be greater the lower the *LM* slope and the steeper the *IS* slope.

IS–LM curves and monetary policy. In the last example a change in fiscal policy was represented by a shift in the *IS* curve. In an analogous way a change in monetary policy can be represented by a shift in the *LM* curve. The *LM* curve shows the equilibrium interest rate associated with each level of income with a given money supply. As we showed in the last chapter, in the short run, which is what we are dealing with here, an increase in the money supply will reduce the interest rate at any given level of income. Alternatively a given interest rate will be consistent with a higher income when money supply increases. So an increase in *M* causes the *LM* curve to shift down to the right. In figure 13.14 the solid *IS* and *LM* curves are the same as in figure 13.12. The dotted curve *LM*₂ shows the effect of an increased money supply. The new equilibrium point is at γ where *IS*₁ and *LM*₂ cross, but as before it will take time for complete adjustment.

When the money supply increases no change in income has occurred, so the interest rates should drop quickly to keep the money market in equilibrium. With income the same, interest rates should drop to the level indicated by point β (old income on new *LM* curve). Then the lower interest rates should stimulate investment and raise income, but with the higher income, interest rates should rise again thus limiting the tendency for investment to rise. The new equilibrium is at γ, where the money market is in balance with a higher income, a lower interest rate, and a higher

Figure 13.14   Increased Money Supply Raises GNP

ratio of money to income than at the start. The interest rate is lower than at the start but higher than the one corresponding to β at the initial level of income.

The magnitude of the GNP change resulting from a given change in money supply depends on the relative *IS–LM* slopes. However, the effects of the slopes on the magnitudes of the income response to monetary changes are exactly opposite those in the fiscal policy case. Figures 13.15 (A) and (B) are analogous to figures 13.13 (A) and (B) but this time the *IS*

Figure 13.15   Effect of Monetary Policy

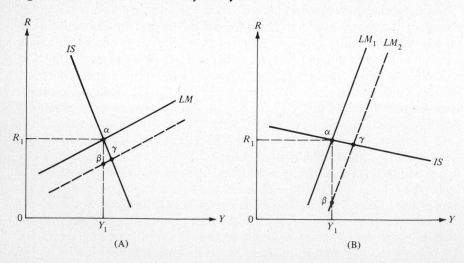

curves are fixed and the *LM* curves are shifted. In figure 13.15 (A) we show a steep *IS* curve and a flat *LM* curve. Figure 13.15 (B) shows the opposite case: steep *LM* curves, flat *IS* curve. The horizontal shift in the *LM* curves is the same in both cases on the assumption that a given increase in *M* permits equal increases in GNP at the initial interest rate.

You can readily see that in the first case monetary policy has relatively little impact since the increased money supply causes only a small initial reduction in interest rates, and the steep *IS* curve indicates a weak response of investment and income to interest-rate changes. In figure 13.15 (B) the increase in money supply has a powerful effect. The leftward shift in *LM* reduces interest rates a lot initially and investment responds strongly to lower interest rates. In general, monetary policy is more effective the more elastic the *IS* curve and the less elastic the *LM* curve, just the opposite of the fiscal policy case. Note, however, that this whole discussion assumes that prices are constant. As we will show in chapter 16, once prices are allowed to vary substantially, this result only holds in the short run.

A capsule summary of debates over monetary policy put forward by Professor James Tobin of Yale declares that there are three possible positions: "money does not matter; money matters; only money matters." Figure 13.15 (A) corresponds roughly to the first, figure 13.15 (B) corresponds roughly to the last, and figure 13.13, where both curves have significant but moderate slopes, corresponds to the middle position.

At this point you might expect us to cite some empirical evidence to give you some idea how to choose among those positions. We are going to wait until the next chapter for that for three reasons. First, the empirical evidence can not be examined without considering the theory of investment in more detail. Second, it turns out that there are reasons for expecting consumption as well as investment to respond to interest rates. Third, there are aspects of the response to changes in money supply that do not fit into the *IS–LM* model very neatly.

Before going on to those complications, however, we have to get price changes into the picture. In our discussion of the possible effects of changes in fiscal and monetary policy, we have so far assumed fixed prices. Consequently, movements of *IS* and *LM* curves, generated by monetary and fiscal policy, must be reflected in output changes. In the next section, we will see that when prices can vary, all or part of the impact of an initial change in fiscal or monetary policy may be translated into price instead of output change.

Prices and the Aggregate-Demand Curve

The level of prices must enter the picture because the price level influences the real money supply. We noted in the last chapter that the real money supply can change in two ways. First, the nominal money supply can

Figure 13.16   How the Price Level Affects Real Money Supply

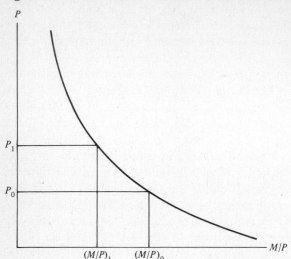

change while prices remain fixed. Second, prices can change while nominal money supply remains fixed. With a fixed money supply a fall in prices increases the real money supply and a rise in prices decreases the real money supply.

Figure 13.16 shows how alternative levels of real money supply can be generated by two alternative levels of nominal money supply and various price levels. Corresponding to each real money supply there is an *LM* curve. As the real money supply is increased the *LM* curve shifts downward to the right. Figure 13.17 shows an *IS* curve together with two *LM* curves corresponding to alternative price levels and real money supplies. There is an *LM* curve for each price level and a different intersection of *IS* and *LM* for each *LM* curve. As the price level declines the *LM*

Figure 13.17   Effect of Change in Real Money Supply

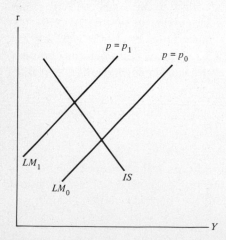

Figure 13.18   The Aggregate-Demand Curve

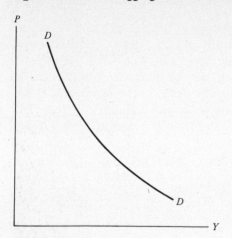

curve shifts down to the right and the equilibrium value of Y at the $IS-LM$ intersection moves to the right.

If we plot the equilibrium values of Y for alternative price levels, we get a downward sloping curve like DD in figure 13.18. DD is an aggregate-demand curve showing the relation between the price level and the quantity of output demanded.

Effects of Price Level Changes

The downward sloping aggregate-demand curve indicates that aggregate real demand will be greater, other things equal, when the price level is low than when it is high. It is important to stop and think why that should be so. Why should a lower price level lead to more aggregate real demand for goods and services? The answer is simple enough if you followed the argument up to this point. The aggregate-demand curve is drawn for a given nominal money supply. The real money supply corresponding to a given nominal money supply is greater when the price level is lower. The LM curve shifts to the right when the real money supply increases and the rightward shift in LM moves the equilibrium real output to the right.

Thus the effect of the real money change for a given drop in the price level depends on the slopes of the IS and LM curves in just the same way as the effect of a given nominal change in M with a fixed price level. So far we are leaving aside the effect that a drop in the price level has on consumption by changing wealth. When this is added in the next chapter, you will see another reason why the aggregate-demand curve slopes downward.

If the LM curve is steep and the IS curve is flat, a fall in the price level will cause a relatively large rise in real demand. In the opposite case, the price-level change will not have much impact.

Price Level and Potential Output

The only real circular-flow equilibrium in both money and real terms is one with constant prices and constant outputs. In terms of real GNP and output there is only one such equilibrium position. Real GNP has to equal potential output. Otherwise, there will be some tendency for prices to change. Correspondingly, there is only one price level for any set of real *IS* and *LM* curves that will be consistent with the condition that real GNP be equal to potential output. In figure 13.19 *DD* shows an aggregate-

Figure 13.19   The Equilibrium Price Level

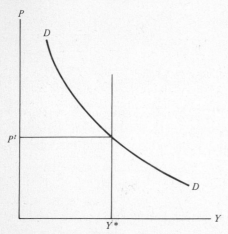

demand curve for given real government expenditures, tax rates, propensity to consume, and real capital stock and a given nominal money supply. Y^* is potential output. If actual real output is to equal Y^* the price level must be p^t, where the demand curve intersects the vertical line at Y^*.

In general, there is reason to believe that there is always some positive price level that would make aggregate real demand equal to potential output. We will discuss that issue more fully in the next chapter after we have taken account of some additional factors that help ensure that an equilibrium exists.

The real question is not whether any equilibrium exists, but whether we can "get there from here." Can prices be expected to adjust enough to keep real aggregate demand at potential output when potential output is growing, and the elements of *the real IS and LM curves* are changing? The record shows a mixed performance. Most of the time the U.S. and other market economies have achieved real outputs fairly close to, but not precisely at, potential output. The deviations consist of some relatively short-lived booms and slumps; a number of fairly deep and prolonged depressions; and some periods of excess demand and inflation.

The observed performance depends on how quickly actual prices adjust to changes in the equilibrium level. But unless prices are perfectly flexible, the outcome also depends on how much the aggregate demand shifts (in relation to potential output).

A play-by-play account of aggregate supply and demand analysis cannot be given; however we can provide some insight into the role of the price level in aggregate supply and demand analysis by considering some patterns of movement of aggregate-demand curves and the factors underlying them.

Perfectly Flexible Prices Versus Fixed Price Level

At one extreme it is possible to imagine that the price level is perfectly flexible in the sense that prices move continuously to equate aggregate demand with potential output no matter how the aggregate-demand curve shifts. In that case, changes in government expenditures and taxes and changes in the money supply as well as any events in the private sector affecting the aggregate-demand curve will be immediately translated into price changes while actual real output is always equal to potential output.

At the other extreme we can suppose that prices are rigidly fixed. If the price level remains permanently fixed, output is demand determined. Any shift in the aggregate-demand curve will be reflected in a change in real output up to the point of full capacity output. Thus, an increase or decrease in government expenditure or a change in taxes will shift the *IS* curve and the demand curve. An increase in *M* will shift the *LM* curve to the right, cause a shift in the aggregate-demand curve and an increase in output. As long as the intersection of the aggregate-demand curve with the fixed price line occurs to the left of Y^* it is physically possible, although economically unlikely, that prices can remain fixed. However, when the intersection is to the right of Y^* prices cannot remain fixed unless we have price control or rationing.

If we look at price-level movements over a long period, we do observe a good deal of fluctuation. At the same time there is a lot of variation in unemployment and capacity utilization. Clearly, neither of the extreme cases is realistic. Prices are not fixed, but they are not so flexible as to offset all shifts in aggregate demand.

Gradual Price Adjustment

Much of the observed behavior of outputs and prices can be explained if we assume that producers respond to short-run variations in aggregate demand, first by making quantity adjustments and then by making gradual price adjustments. When the aggregate-demand curve shifts upward, prices at first remain fixed, output rises. Then prices begin to rise, and if there is no further change in the aggregate-demand curve, prices rise until the system is back in equilibrium. In figure 13.20 we start with aggregate demand at $D_0 D_0$ and potential output at Y^*. The aggregate-demand curve shifts to $D_1 D_1$, prices remain fixed, and output rises to Y_1. Then prices begin

Figure 13.20   Price and Output Adjustment

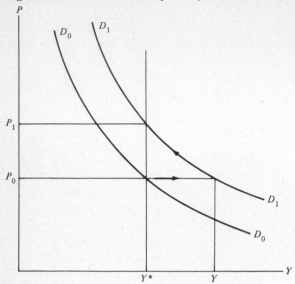

to rise and continue to do so until they reach P_1. At that point, real aggregate demand is back to Y^* and the system is again in full equilibrium. A similar story could be told for a downward shift of aggregate demand. A somewhat more realistic analysis takes account of the continuing growth of potential output. Potential output increases from year to year. Ordinarily, the aggregate-demand curve also shifts to the right as money supply and government expenditures increase. As a historical matter, investment demand at a given interest rate has on the average tended to grow with the scale of the economy. New, capital-intensive technologies have maintained the prospective return on investment in spite of continuing increases in capital per worker. But there is no reason why the rightward shift of the aggregate-demand curve should just keep pace with the growth of poential output from year to year.

Sometimes the aggregate-demand curve will shift rightward faster than potential output. If prices were perfectly flexible, output would grow with potential output. Prices would rise when aggregate-demand grew faster than potential output and fall or stop rising when the growth of aggregate demand fell behind the growth of potential output. In fact, however, prices do not adjust that quickly. A rapid growth of demand relative to potential output will cause output to rise as well as prices and a slowdown in the growth of aggregate demand will tend to cause prices to fall.

We shall discuss short-run price adjustment again in chapter 19 but the general conclusions we have just reached will hold so long as the race between aggregate demand and potential output is a fairly close one, with the movements of aggregate demand sometimes requiring a modest price increase and sometimes requiring a modest decline. The story will even work fairly well for a large "one-shot" rightward shift in aggregate demand. In a wartime inflation, for example, the aggregate-demand curve shifts sharply rightward under the combined impetus of an increase in real government expenditures (only partly offset by tax increases) and an increase in money supply as the government covers part of its deficit by creating new money. When the war is over, the government's real expenditures are reduced but the increase in money supply does not go away. In the end, the equilibrium price level is higher than at the start.

A gradual price-level-adjustment approach works as long as the adjustment of prices to any one change in the equilibrium price level is not affected by expectations of continuing price change. That will be so when shifts in aggregate demand relative to potential output are relatively small and when the gap between actual and potential output is sometimes positive and sometimes negative. It may be true in wartime cases if everyone expects that the inflationary pressure of the war will soon be over.

Sometimes, however, the aggregate-demand curve shifts outward faster than potential output and continues to shift outward by at least enough to compensate for the resulting rise in prices. That starts a continuing inflation period. When people expect inflation to continue, economic behavior changes in a number of important respects. We shall postpone those reactions to later chapters dealing with inflation. In those chapters, we will also discuss some factors influencing price change other than the gap between aggregate demand at the current price level and potential output. A realistic discussion of inflation can hardly omit the influence of supply shocks from changes in oil, food, and raw material prices.

Summary

The objective of income-expenditure analysis is to show how the expenditure decisions of households, businesses, and governments interact to simultaneously determine the equilibrium level of real and nominal GNP, the interest rate, and the price level. Income-expenditure analysis is based on the use of the national income accounts. The national income accounts provide a double-entry bookkeeping system for the nation. The expenditure side of the accounts shows the breakdown of final purchases into expenditures for consumption, different kinds of investment, and government expenditures. The total value of goods and services purchased during the year is called the gross national product (GNP). The income side of the accounts shows the breakdown of the incomes received by households, businesses, and governments. It can be shown that the total value of those incomes must exactly equal the total of GNP expenditures. Income-expenditure analysis proceeds toward the analysis of the overall equilibrium of the system by considering a series of subequilibriums. We first considered equilibrium in the goods market on the assumption that all prices are fixed and that interest rates are fixed. We then introduced the concept of a consumption function, which relates rate of expenditures for consumption to the disposable income of households, and then, taking account of the distribution of GNP, relates the level of consumption expenditures to the level of GNP. The level of production of goods and services is in equilibrium for a given rate of government expenditure and a given rate of investment; total production GNP equals the amount that households want to spend for consumption, plus the amount spent by businesses and governments. The equilibrium reflects the fact that GNP depends in part on the level of consumer expenditures, while consumer expenditures themselves depend on GNP. After deriving the basic equilibrium condition, we showed that the level of GNP will change by a multiple of any change in the sum of investment and government expenditures. We next introduced the concept of the investment-demand function, relating the rate of investment to the level of interest rates. We then showed that by combining the previous equilibrium analysis of GNP with the investment-demand curve, we could trace out a relationship between the level of interest rates and the equilibrium level of GNP. The curve showing the set of interest rate/GNP combinations, consistent with equilibrium in the goods market, is called the *IS* curve. Next, we introduced the *LM* curve derived in the previous chapter, and showed that given the factors underlying the *IS* curve and given the *LM* curve corresponding to some particular real money supply, there is only one combination of interest rate and GNP consistent with the *IS* equilibrium in the goods market and the *LM* equilibrium in the money market. Finally, we recalled that with a given nominal money supply, the real money supply varies with the price level. Consequently, for any given nominal money supply, there is a different *LM* curve for each price level. As we consider progressively lower price levels, we find that the *LM* curve shifts to the right. Accordingly, the intersection of a given *IS* curve with the *LM* curve occurs at progressively higher levels of real GNP as the price level falls. By plotting the *IS–LM* intersection, corresponding to a number of different price levels (keeping nominal money supply constant), we can derive an aggregate-demand curve. If we plot the price level on the vertical axis and real GNP on the horizontal axis, the curve slopes downward to the right. The intersection of the aggregate-demand curve with a vertical line at the potential output determines the equilibrium price level. The position of the aggregate-demand curve and, therefore, of the equilibrium price level can be shifted by changes in any of the factors underlying the *IS* curve—for example, government expenditures, taxes, or other factors—that might affect investment. It can also be shifted by changes in the nominal money supply.

QUESTIONS AND EXERCISES

1. Discuss the effect of each of the following on the *IS* curve: (a) an increase in the rate of government purchases of goods and services; (b) a reduction in personal income-tax rates; (c) an increase in Social-Security benefits.

2. An increase in the nominal money supply tends to shift the aggregate-demand curve to the right. Explain in terms of the *IS–LM* curve.

3. The size of the multiplier depends on the ratio of disposable income to GNP as well as on the propensity to save. List some of the factors that may influence the relations between disposable income and GNP.

4. The size of the multiplier affects the slope of the *IS* curve. Explain.

5. The aggregate-demand curve slopes downward to the right. Why? List some factors that influence the slope of the aggregate-demand curve.

6. If potential output rises while the aggregate-demand curve remains fixed, the equilibrium price level must fall. How does the reduction in price level lead to an increase in real output?

FURTHER READING

COUNCIL OF ECONOMIC ADVISERS. *Annual Report.* Government Printing Office, Washington, D.C. The first chapter of each council report usually contains an analysis of the causes of changes in GNP during the preceding year. The student will also find the tables at the end of the report a useful source of data on GNP and its components as well as on price changes and changes in employment and unemployment.

HICKS, JOHN R. "Mr. Keynes and the Classics: A Suggested Interpretation." *Econometrica* 5 (April 1937): 147–59. In this paper Professor Hicks introduced the *IS–LM* interpretation of Keynes's theory.

KEYNES, JOHN MAYNARD. *The General Theory of Employment Interest and Money.* New York: Harcourt Brace & Company, 1936. This important, but difficult to read and often paradoxical work has played a major role in shaping modern macroeconomics.

OKUN, ARTHUR M. "Potential Output: Its Measurement and Significance." Proceedings of the Business and Economic Statistics Section of the American Statistical Assn., 1962, pp. 98–104. This paper gives a detailed discussion of the concept of potential output, a methodology for measuring it, and major factors determining changes in potential output.

SAMUELSON, PAUL A. "The Simple Mathematics of Income Determination." In *Income, Employment and Public Policy,* by Lloyd A. Metzler et al., pp. 133–55. New York: W. W. Norton, 1948. A useful summary for those who are willing to follow some relatively elementary mathematics.

STEWART, KENNETH. "National Income Accounting and Economic Welfare." *Review* (Federal Reserve Bank of St. Louis) 56 (April 1974): 18–24. This paper discusses various criticisms of GNP as a measure of economic welfare and explains some important attempts to provide a better measure by adjusting GNP to take account of such considerations as the cost of pollution.

U.S., DEPARTMENT OF COMMERCE, OFFICE OF BUSINESS ECONOMICS. *Readings in Concepts and Methods of National Income Statistics.* Springfield, Va.: National Technical Information Service, 1976. These papers explain the structural framework of the GNP accounts in great detail and also how the department goes about measuring the GNP and its components from the statistical sources available.

U.S., DEPARTMENT OF COMMERCE, BUREAU OF ECONOMIC ANALYSIS. *The National Income and Product Accounts of the United States, 1929–74.* Washington, D.C.: Government Printing Office, 1976. This volume provides a set of tables for all components of GNP for the whole forty-five-year period.

————. *Survey of Current Business.* Washington, D.C.: Government Printing Office. Issued monthly. Each issue contains the national income data. The July issue provides more detailed tables.

14

Investment
and Consumption

The income-expenditure approach emphasizes the mutual determination of consumption, investment, GNP, interest rate, and price level. In our first survey of the income-expenditure approach, we used the simplest possible description of the reaction of consumption to disposable income and of investment to interest rates. In our concern to emphasize the big picture of the whole system, we had to neglect important aspects of the determination of investment and consumption expenditure.

In this chapter we will examine investment and consumption expenditures in much more detail.

Determinants of Investment

A growing economy must devote a substantial proportion of its total output to the production of capital goods—machinery and equipment, trucks, ships, planes, and railroad equipment, factories, office and store buildings. It must do so in order to take advantage of new technology and to provide plant and equipment for a growing labor force. Moreover, a growing population with rising income is prepared to pay for more and better housing requiring substantial expenditures on residential construction. Finally, as the economy grows, it requires increasing inventories of materials, work in process, and finished goods at each stage of the production and distribution process.

In the U.S. investment expenditures of all kinds have averaged around 15 percent of GNP in the years since World War II. In some rapidly growing countries, like Japan, the share of investment in GNP has been almost twice as high. Investment is only one of many factors responsible for Japan's high rate of growth, but it has certainly played an essential role in the growth process.

From a long-run point of view, capital formation is important to the growth of potential output, but variations in the rate of investment also play a major role in accounting for short-run variations in aggregate demand and output. Investment expenditures are much more volatile than consumption expenditures, so that in spite of their modest average share of total output, variations in the rate of investment account for a large proportion of the cyclical variations in the level and growth rate of aggregate output.

Plant and Equipment

In the U.S. business investment in plant and equipment accounts for two-thirds to three-quarters of total capital-formation expenditures. It includes the building of factories and their equipment as well as transportation and construction equipment and office and store buildings. These expenditures are made by thousands of business firms of all sorts, and their investment decisions involve a great variety of technical and market considerations. The paper work underlying a firm's decision to build a new plant, costing a couple of million dollars, may fill a book as large as this one. The work on a 100-million-dollar glass plant may fill a whole set of filing cases. The work behind an investment decision may involve an elaborate market analysis, as well as all sorts of engineering studies. In these days, of course, environmental-impact statements, health and safety regulations, and zoning conflicts generate more paper.

No simple statement can cover the complexity of all the decisions involved in the annual expenditure of a couple of hundred billion dollars on plant and equipment. In spite of their variety, when considered in detail, a few basic forces provide the motivation for most plant and equipment investment. Any investment expenditure is worth considering because it promises to bring in more revenue to the investor, or because it is expected to reduce future costs of some sort. Any firm's investment decision involves two parts: an evaluation of the amount and timing of the prospective additional revenues or reduced costs resulting from the investment; and a comparison of those revenues or cost savings with the costs of the capital goods involved. Since the prospective revenues or costs will occur in future years, while the investment expenditure is immediate, a comparison of the present value of future revenues with the initial capital costs is involved.

Sources of Investment Opportunity

Opportunities for firms to increase revenues (reduce costs) in the future by capital expenditures arise from a number of sources.

Maintenance costs. Anyone who owns a car knows that as mechanical equipment grows older, maintenance costs rise. At some point before the equipment becomes completely broken down, it will be worthwhile to examine whether the present value of maintenance and operating costs on the old equipment will exceed those for new similar equipment by enough to justify replacement.

Technological improvement of equipment and processes. Continuous technological progress has been one of the outstanding characteristics of market economies for the last three hundred years. When new technology moves from the laboratory and the pilot plant into practical use, it has to be embodied in new equipment. Firms will often find that the cost reduction available from the purchase of new equipment, embodying new technology, justifies replacing old equipment, even when replacement would not be justified on a maintenance cost basis.

New products. A great deal of investment is required for the production of new products. A substantial proportion of consumer expenditures today pays for products that did not exist thirty years ago. Black and white as well as color televisions, modern stereo equipment, instant cameras, and frozen foods are just a few examples.

Expanding output. In the long-run, aggregate demand must grow to keep pace with the growth of the labor force and with increases in productivity. Demand growth for old products, as well as new, can generate new opportunities for profitable investment.

As demand grows, existing firms find their plant fully utilized and may have to meet the demand by overtime, extra shifts, or by using obsolete equipment. At some point it will become profitable to build new capacity to avoid the extra cost involved. Alternatively, they can limit output and raise prices, but if they do so, new firms are likely to enter the industry. In either case the growth of demand generates opportunities for profitable investment. Because capital goods are durable, investment decisions must be based on expectations of demand conditions in the future. In fact, the observed growth of demand up to any date is important only to the extent that it helps to predict the level of demand in the future.

Although rising maintenance, technical change, new products, and aggregate-demand growth are separate forces generating investment opportunities, the potential return from any particular investment project may arise from the joint operation of more than one of those factors. For example, the cost saving from replacing old equipment may arise from both the high maintenance cost of the old equipment and the lower operating cost of new equipment embodying new technology.

Evaluating Investments

At any time thousands of firms are faced with opportunities to reduce cost or increase revenue by acquiring a new plant or equipment. They have to calculate whether the potential cost savings or added revenues are large enough to justify the capital outlay in question. As already noted, the investment decision involves comparison between capital outlay now and a stream of returns from reduced costs or increased revenues over a number of years in the future.

A firm facing a single investment opportunity can decide whether to accept or reject the investment by making a simple present-value calculation. Present value of the returns from the investment can be calculated in exactly the same way as in the bond- and stock-value calculations used in chapter 6.

$$\text{Present value} = \frac{R_1}{1 + r} + \frac{R_2}{(1 + r)^2} + \cdots \frac{R_n}{(1 + r)^n}$$

where r is the discount rate and $R_1, R_2 \ldots R_n$ are the net revenues or cost savings expected each year as a result of making the investment. If the cost of the initial investment is p_k, the project is worth doing if the present value is greater than p_k.

In practice the problem proves to be more difficult. The initial capital costs are fairly well known, but anyone who has had anything to do with a construction project knows that various unforeseen difficulties may raise costs above the initial estimates. The projected revenues or cost savings are even more uncertain. They are predicated on estimates of future sales, prices, and wages. Moreover, the new equipment may suddenly be made obsolete by new technological developments. New competing products may wipe out the market for the output. Firms making investment decisions may protect themselves against these contingencies by making conservative estimates of prospective revenues or cost savings. Alternatively, they may use their best estimates of the revenues and costs in computing the expected returns in the present-value equation. They can allow for risk by discounting future returns at a rate higher than the going interest rate. The higher discount rate has the effect of deflating distant prospective returns by more than the early ones, thus reflecting the greater uncertainty of estimates of conditions in the more distant future.

In many cases one design for an investment project is clearly better than any available alternative. In other cases, however, alternative types of equipment or building materials may be available, and it is necessary to choose between them. Each of the alternatives may pass a present-value test, but they are mutually exclusive—if one is accepted, the other will be rejected. In that case it is necessary to compute the present value of the difference between the costs and returns from the alternative designs.

For example, the firm may have to choose between cheap equipment with relatively short-service life or sharply rising maintenance costs and equipment that is more expensive but more durable. To choose between them, the firm needs to compute the difference in the present value of the two options.

An important variation on the mutually exclusive options problem is postponement. It often happens that a firm knows that sooner or later it will have to replace a piece of equipment or a plant, just as we all know that sooner or later we will have to replace the old car. A present-value calculation may show that it is worth building a new plant, but it may also turn out that the option of partial replacement or renovation to delay the construction of a complete new plant is still better.

The Effect of Tax Rates on Investment

Whenever investment falls relative to GNP or when the Congress becomes concerned about the need for more investment to raise the growth of productivity, proposals to change corporate income taxes in order to stimulate investment are heard. This is hardly surprising, because corporate tax rates can have a very important influence on investment returns and on the risks of investment. We can see how taxes affect investment by examining their effect on present-value comparisons.

As before, suppose we have to decide whether to purchase capital goods costing p_k. The investment is expected to generate a stream of before-tax returns R_1, R_2, . . . R_n. In the absence of taxes, we compute the present value of the project by discounting the prospective returns. Now, however, suppose that there is a 50 percent corporate income tax. If it applied to all returns, the present value of the prospective returns would be simply cut in half.

In fact, however, the tax does not apply to all the returns. The tax applies only to the return net of depreciation. You may have already noticed that the evaluation of investments by the present-value approach did not involve depreciation. If we evaluate investment by that approach, depreciation appears only as an accounting adjustment. But when corporate income taxes are accounted for, depreciation plays an important role in reducing the portion of total cash returns taken by taxes.

The after-tax return for any year is computed as follows:

gross return = R
depreciation = D
taxable income = $R - D$
tax = $t(R - D)$
after-tax return = $R - t(R - D)$, or $R - tR + tD$

Thus the present value of the return from investment depends on three elements: (1) the gross return; (2) the tax on the gross return; and (3) the reduction of taxes obtained by deduction of depreciation allowances.

If we like, we can think of the present value of depreciation as a reduction in the cost of the asset. It is the government's contribution to the cost of the asset, while the government also gets a part of the cash returns as they come. Notice that if the investing company has other taxable income, it gets the tax benefit of the depreciation allowance, even if the project is a failure and produces no revenue.

The present value of the tax deduction for depreciation allowances can be influenced by changes in tax regulations affecting the timing of depreciation allowances. Total depreciation can never exceed the original cost of the depreciating asset (unless it is resold), but the distribution of depreciation during the life of the asset can be changed. With simple "straight-line" depreciation, an equal amount of depreciation is allowed for tax purposes each year. The straight-line depreciation allowance for a $100,000 asset, lasting twenty years, is $5,000 per year. Other depreciation formulas allow firms to take more depreciation and reduce taxes more in the early years of the investment's life and correspondingly less in the late years. While the arithmetic sum of tax deductions under these formulas is the same as with straight-line depreciation, its present value is greater because the present value of a dollar saved in the early years is greater than the present value of a dollar saved a long time from now. Changes in the tax regulations, permitting faster depreciation in the early years of an investment's life, should encourage investment. Another device for encouraging investment is the investment tax credit. Under legislation passed in 1962, firms are permitted to deduct a percentage of the cost of new equipment from taxes at the time of purchase. In effect, the government pays part of the cost of new equipment. It is important to note that, under present law, depreciation allowances are based on the cost of plant and equipment at the time of acquisition. In an inflationary era, the tax savings from depreciation allowances do not rise with price level and after-tax revenues fall relative to before-tax revenues.

Inflation Expectations

The stream of prospective returns from an investment (the Rs in the present-value equation) involves both price and quantity elements. If the project is a labor-saving one, the return consists of a reduction in the number of hours of work employed for a given output, multiplied by the appropriate wage rate. If the project is intended to increase output, the return consists of the increased output multiplied by the difference between the price per unit of product and the unit cost of the labor and materials employed. In our discussion of the evaluation of investment projects, we implicitly assumed constant prices, but nowadays inflation is a fact of life, and expectations about future price changes are likely to play an important role in investment decisions.

The importance of inflation expectations is most obvious if we consider the choice between making an investment now or postponing for a year. Consider a case in which the interest rate is 4 percent, and prices are expected to be stable. A firm's management decides that it is just about a toss-up whether to build now or wait a year. Now consider the same choice when the management expects construction costs to rise by 7 percent in the next year. If the interest rate were still 4 percent, it would clearly be better to build now, since the investment required by the postponement alternative will be higher by 7 percent, while the build-now option is unchanged. In fact the build-now option would be preferable to delay at any interest rate up to 11 percent. At that rate the interest saved by postponement would just cancel the higher investment cost from a year's price rise, and the two plans would again be a toss-up. A more general approach involves systematic adjustment of the stream of prospective returns for expected inflation. Suppose that as before we have to compute the present value of an investment project in order to compare it with the cost of the capital goods involved. Suppose that, assuming fixed prices, the returns are expected to rise at i percent per year. Then, if we assume that the returns are collected at the end of the year, the expected return at the end of the first year is $R_1(1 + i)$; the return at the end of the second year is $R_2(1 + i)(1 + i) = R_2(1 + i)^2$, and so on.

The evaluation of the investment proposal now involves comparing the price of the capital good p_k (which remains unchanged) with the present value of the prospective returns, taking expected inflation into account. We now have

present value $= R_1(1 + i)/(1 + r) + R_2(1 + i)^2/(1 + r)^2 + \ldots R_n(1 + i)^n/(1 + r)^n$.

You can readily see that expected inflation offsets the effect of the interest rate on the discounted values of future returns. In fact the present-value formula can be rewritten as

present value $= R_1/(1 + r - i) + R_2/(1 + r - i)^2 \ldots$

Thus a one percent rise in the expected inflation rate has exactly the same effect on present value as a one percent reduction in the nominal interest rate. The present value of an investment depends on *the difference between nominal interest rate and the expected inflation rate*. This difference is called the **real rate of interest.** Notice two points. First, the real rate can be changed either by a change in the nominal rate with given inflation expectations, or by a change in inflation expectations with given nominal rate. Second, in times of inflation the nominal rate becomes a poor measure of the restrictive or expansive impact of monetary policy. Nominal interest rates usually rise during periods of inflation, but they sometimes lag behind inflation expectations so that the nominal rate may be rising while the real rate is falling.

Finally the above conclusions must be modified to take account of the adverse effect of the tax treatment of depreciation noted above.

Interest Rates and Investment: The Investment-Demand Schedule

So far we have been considering investment projects taken one at a time. We now want to consider the effects of interest rates on the aggregate rate of investment for the economy as a whole. To see how the level of interest rates affects investment, we can perform a hypothetical experiment. Suppose first that the going real interest rate on corporate bonds is 5 percent. Each of the many firms making investment decisions has its own views on the factors determining the prospective future revenues or cost savings from various investment options. They are faced with a certain set of prices for capital goods. Given all the relevant information, each firm will make a certain set of choices undertaking some projects now, choosing to postpone others, and rejecting others altogether. In the aggregate their decisions will lead to expenditure of, say, 200 billion dollars in a given year.

Now to make our hypothetical experiment, suppose that the corporate bond yield is 7 percent instead of 5 percent, while everything else remains the same. In what way will individual firm decisions and aggregate investment differ in the 7 percent case by comparison with the 5 percent case?

From our previous discussion it should be clear that the higher interest rate will lead to decisions generating a smaller amount of investment than the two hundred billion dollars of investment generated by the lower one. First, in simple one-option investment choices, there will be a certain set of projects in which the present value of prospective returns evaluated at 5 percent exceeds the required capital outlay by only a small margin. When the present-value calculation is made with a 7 percent discount rate, the present value of the returns will be smaller and in some cases will fall short of the required capital outlay.

Second, in the case of mutually exclusive alternatives the higher interest rate will reduce the benefits from expenditure on greater durability. The extra outlay for durability (or low maintenance cost in later years) remains the same, while a reduction in maintenance costs or deferral of replacement is deflated by a larger discount factor with the 7 percent rate than with the 5 percent rate. At the 7 percent rate, less durable alternatives with less initial outlay will be chosen, thus reducing total investment.

Third, the higher rate will favor postponement or renovations. Thus all things considered, the 7 percent rate will produce less investment (other things equal) than the 5 percent rate. Figure 14.1 shows the amount of investment at several rates. The dotted line shows what we might expect if we made a whole set of hypothetical experiments with rates ranging from 4 percent to 8 percent.

Figure 14.1   Investment-Demand Schedule

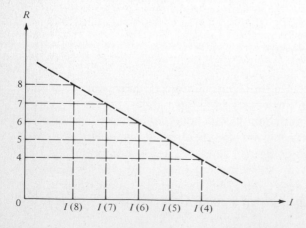

Shifts in Investment Demand

Each increase in the stock of capital as a result of investment tends to push the investment-demand schedule down. On the other hand increases in the expected level of output push the investment-demand schedule up. In a sense the net movement of the investment-demand schedule is the result of a continuing race between the growth of the capital stock and the actual and expected growth of output. In that race the capital stock maintains a somewhat steadier pace than expected output. Net additions to capital stock (measured as the excess of gross investment over depreciation allowance) vary from zero to 4 percent or so from year to year. The actual and expected growth of output appears to vary a good deal more than that and therefore accounts for much of the variation in investment demand.

The central role of the "race" between accumulation of capital through investment and the growth of output is confirmed by numerous empirical studies. Empirical studies indicate that variations in the ratio of output to capital stock account for much of the observed variation in the ratio of business fixed investment to GNP. Because the growth of the capital stock varies less than the growth of output, variations in the ratio of capital stock to output are most strongly influenced by the growth of output. Empirical studies show that a large part of the variation of investment can be explained by the average rate of growth of output over three- or four-year periods. *The link between the level of investment and the rate of growth of output* is called the **acceleration principle.** Investment tends to increase when output growth accelerates.

Of course, that is not the whole story. Changes in interest rates and taxes have a significant role in determining investment. Moreover, investment decisions will certainly be influenced by expectations about future movements of output. Business-management expectations about the economic outlook reflect their judgments about prospective changes in fiscal and monetary policy, as well as their views about the growth of potential output in the longer run. Management may believe that, because of or in spite of, government policy output will follow a path that stays close to potential output. In that case the effect of short-term variations in output growth will be limited. Investment will not be cut back drastically in a recession if an early recovery is expected. In a boom, management will be cautious about stepping up investment plans if it expects output to level off or decline in a short time. Nonetheless, many decisions about the timing of investment projects will be affected by judgments about the movement of demand over the next couple of years. That is why many business firms spend money for forecasts of GNP movements over the next year or two. Prospective changes in government policy always play an important role in those forecasts.

Shifts in investment demand are both a cause and a consequence of movements of aggregate demand. As we have just noted, variations in the growth of real output tend to cause variations in the rate of fixed investment. Thus, a rapid increase in aggregate demand will lead to an upward shift in investment demand, which will, in turn, contribute to the growth of demand. One is tempted at this point to envisage endless sequences of feedbacks from demand growth to investment and from investment to demand growth. In fact, however, that mutual interaction process is likely to be checked before it goes very far by rising interest rates. You can see why by using the *IS–LM* apparatus of chapter 13.

First, suppose that prices adjust slowly to any change in demand and that the nominal money supply is fixed. Accordingly the position of the *LM* curve is fixed. An upward shift in investment demand is represented as a shift in the *IS* curve. In figure 14.2 IS_0 is the original *IS* curve. IS_1

Figure 14.2   Effect of a Shift in Investment Demand on Equilibrium Income

is the new curve. Equilibrium output rises from $(Y/P)_0$ to $(Y/P)_1$, while equilibrium interest rate rises from R_0 to R_1. You will notice that the increase in equilibrium real output is only about half as large as the rightward shift of *IS* at a given interest rate. The actual result, however, depends on the slopes of *IS* and *LM*. You can see why, if you go back to the discussion of fiscal policy in chapter 13 (figures 13.13 (A) and (B)). The outcome of a shift in *IS* is the same, whether the shift is caused by fiscal policy, or investment demand.

Notice also that the impact of the shift in investment demand depends on what happens to money supply. In figure 14.2 we assumed a fixed nominal money supply. If the Fed wanted to, it could "accommodate" the increased investment demand by increasing nominal money supply, shifting *LM* to the right. On the other hand it could choke-off the investment demand by reducing nominal money supply, shifting *LM* to the left. You should also note that beliefs about what the Fed is likely to do will influence expectations about future demand.

Finally, we have to recognize that when the economy is near potential output, prices will rise when investment demand shifts up. We will
discuss the consequences of that alternative in chapter 19, when we consider inflation.

The conclusion then is that the acceleration-principle response of investment demand to fluctuations in output growth tends to accentuate those
fluctuations. The actual response of the system depends on how the money
supply changes, and on expectations about how it will change.

Residential Construction

The construction of new homes and apartment buildings accounts for
around one-fourth of the total capital outlays in the United States. Expenditures for additions and alterations have amounted to 15 billion dollars in recent years. In principle, the logic of investment in residential
construction is similar to the decision logic for any other investment project.
The same kind of choice between present capital outlays and future benefits is involved. But because it accounts for such a large volume of investment, the special characteristics of residential construction deserve more
attention. Moreover, the financing arrangements for residential building
make this type of investment particularly sensitive to changing financial
conditions.

We can first examine the organization of the industry and the calculations involved in deciding whether to build or buy apartment buildings
or homes, and then consider the significance of the special features of the
mortgage markets described in chapter 6.

Multifamily Buildings

Currently, around 25 percent of the two million housing units built
each year are in multifamily buildings and are rented or sold as condo-
miniums. Most of them are built by specialized developers who assemble
land, design the buildings, arrange for zoning-law changes, and obtain
building permits. Some developers operate their own buildings, but many
sell them to other investors upon completion.

Because apartment buildings last a long time, they are likely to be
sold several times before they are demolished. The valuation of existing
buildings makes a good starting place for an attempt to understand investment in residential construction.

Consider the problem of an investor who has a chance to buy an
existing apartment building. How much is it worth to him? As usual he has
to make a present-value calculation taking into account prospective rental
receipts, maintenance and operating costs, and real-estate taxes. If he
proposes to keep the building for a long time, he has to project the expected gross rents (allowing for vacancies) ahead for a number of years,

and do the same for various components of maintenance and operating costs and real-estate taxes. Even for the first few years, those projections must be subject to considerable error. Projections farther out are even more uncertain but less important because they are deflated by such a large discount factor.

His discount factor will have to be high enough to allow for the risk involved. His maximum offer for the building can be found by calculating at his discount rate the present value of the excess of the gross rental over maintenance, operating, and real-estate taxes each year for a number of years into the future. (We have neglected for the moment his federal income-tax problems, which involve depreciation allowances and possible capital gains if he sells the building.)

A developer considering a new building project can estimate the costs for constructing a certain type of building, add land-site costs, and his direct expense for architects, engineers, and legal costs of zoning changes and building permits. He can then compare those costs with 1) his own present-value calculation of net rental income if he plans to operate the building, or 2) the calculation of a prospective buyer, or 3) the sales price of similar, recently sold buildings. Those approaches are all essentially the same, and the value placed on the hypothetical new building always arises from calculating the present value of net rents.

Thus (land costs aside) the profitability of new construction for rental will depend on 1) the level of rents, 2) maintenance and operating costs, 3) real-estate taxes, all projected into the future, and 4) construction costs. The level of rents at any one time will depend in turn on the demand for apartments and the supply of existing apartments. The demand for apartments in any area will, of course, depend on the size and the composition of the population in the area. In actuality, rental-housing markets are very complex, since there are renters with different incomes and tastes, while buildings vary in quality, layout, and location. Moreover, there is an interaction between demand for rental housing and prices of single houses. Still, the basic forces at work can be grasped by considering a simple market for new or nearly new buildings, fixed rents on the old ones, and given prices for single houses.

The interaction between the supply and demand for rental units in a new building, capital values of those buildings, and the rate of new construction is illustrated in figure 14.3. Figure 14.3 (A) shows the supply and demand for rental units in relatively new buildings. In any short interval the number of existing units is given at N. The demand for rental units is represented by the line RR. Given the rents on old units, the number of households seeking to rent the new units increases as the rent level declines. As usual the equilibrium rent is determined at R_0 where the demand for new apartments equals the existing supply.

In figure 14.3 (B) the vertical axis is the capital value of an apartment unit at a rent corresponding to the one at the same height in figure

Figure 14.3   Determination of Residential Construction

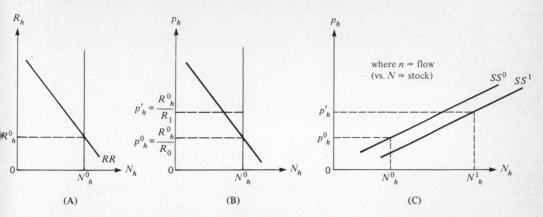

(A)   (B)   (C)

14.3 (A). p_h is equal to the present value of the net rent obtained from the gross rent at the same height in figure 14.3 (A), with present value calculated at some given interest rate. Thus figure 14.3 (B) shows the same supply and demand for rental units with rents converted into capital values. Finally, figure 14.3 (C) shows the supply of new units. Its rising slope reflects the tendency for construction costs to rise with increasing activity as well as the response of developers to the prospect of higher profits. The rate of new construction will be set at the point where the horizontal line representing the current present value of a new housing unit cuts the construction-supply curve.

The three linked diagrams reflect a number of factors that all interact to determine construction. In figure 14.3 (A) the equilibrium rental will tend to shift upward with rising population and income, factors that push up the rental-demand curve. Over time, however, as new units are built the vertical supply curve shifts leftward. That tends to depress rentals or to offset the effect of rising income and population. The middle diagram converts gross rentals into capital values. The conversion involves two kinds of elements. The capital value from given gross rentals will be reduced if operating costs, maintenance costs, or taxes rise. Second, for given values of those factors, the capital value of a given gross rent will rise if the interest rate falls and vice versa. The dotted line in figure 14.3 (B) shows the effect of a lower interest rate on capital values. Note that the new equilibrium value p'_h straight across to figure 14.3 (C) implies a rise in the rate of construction, if population and income rise steadily. While interest rates are constant, the rate of building should settle down to a level at which the rightward shift in the demand curve just balances the shift in supply, leaving prices constant.

The response of construction to changes in interest rate is seen in figure 14.4. Points A and B represent the points taken from figure 14.3 (C). More generally capital values of buildings will be lower at higher interest rates, and so will rates of construction.

Figure 14.4   Residential Construction in Relation to Interest Rates

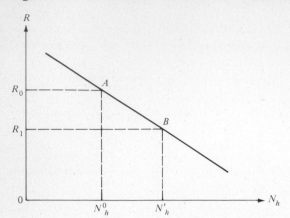

Single Houses

In its basic logic the single-house market is similar to the multifamily market. The similarity is somewhat concealed by the fact that most single houses are occupied by their owners, who do not pay an explicit rent. In effect, however, the homeowner is a building operator who rents to himself. We can think of a prospective homeowner as deciding that he is willing to pay a certain gross monthly rental for the house. Subtracting the taxes and operating costs (including whatever value he places on his own labor) he gets to the net rental income. The house is worth buying if the present value of the net rental income exceeds the asking price.

Thus the basic logic of the interaction between interest rates, rental values, capital values, and the rate of building of single homes is similar to the interaction outlined above for multifamily buildings.

Mortgage Markets and Residential Construction

The basic factors driving the demand for home building tend to move rather slowly and steadily. Population grows slowly at only 1 or 2 percent per year. The annual addition to the stock of houses is also a very small fraction of the existing stock. The growth of income varies a good deal from year to year, but most people consider their average income rather than their current income in choosing their housing accommodation. Taxes, maintenance costs, and construction costs vary but not enough to cause violent year-to-year shifts in the rate of building. Finally, nominal mortgage interest rates have risen over the years, but after allowance for inflationary expectations, the rise in real mortgage interest rates has been very small and so have the annual variations. One might expect therefore that expenditure on residential construction would show little cyclical fluctuation. Unfortunately for the home-building industry, the opposite is true.

Housing starts and residential construction expenditures vary more widely than any component of GNP except inventory investment. Moreover, the variations run counter to the cyclical variations in other types of expenditures. Since World War II housing booms have started during general recessions and faded during periods of general prosperity.

To some extent variations in the rate of home building reflect the influence of interest-rate changes. Nominal interest rates rise in booms and fall in recessions, and the long life of houses makes their value more sensitive to interest rates than other types of capital. However, the pattern of real interest-rate movements is less clear. Many economists believe the cyclical swings in home building reflect the peculiar problems of the mortgage markets discussed in chapter 6.

During business-cycle upswings, short-term interest rates rise relative to the rates offered by the mutual savings banks and savings and loan associations. The growth of deposits at those institutions slows as more sophisticated customers shift their funds to Treasury bills. Thus their withdrawals offset the continued growth of deposits of other investors. As a result the supply of mortgage funds is reduced. Mortgage lenders respond, of course, by raising rates, but they often do not raise them enough to balance supply and demand. Instead they restrict their lending by asking for higher down payments, raising the required ratio of income to mortgage payments, lending only to depositors and builders with whom they have established connections. More generally, when mortgage lenders are short of funds, the management instruction to loan officers is "when in doubt, turn it down."

Once a recession is underway, short-term interest rates usually decline and the whole process is reversed. The thrift institutions show large gains in deposits and soon begin to increase their mortgage commitments. After some lag, housing starts and construction expenditures begin to rise.

There is still considerable controversy among economists as to the mechanism involved. Some emphasize the effect of rising mortgage interest rates on the values of new houses and the consequent reduction in the rate of new building. They argue that it does not make much sense for lenders to ration loans when they could make more money by raising rates. Others emphasize the relative importance of rationing. They argue that lenders faced with a temporary tight money situation are willing to forgo a temporary rise in earnings in order to preserve their relationship with deposit customers and with builders who supply good quality mortgages over long periods.

For many purposes it does not matter whether rising mortgage rates as such or mortgage credit rationing is responsible for variations in residential construction. In either case the sensitivity of residential construction makes the *IS* curve more elastic to interest-rate change. The rationing issue becomes more significant when various proposals for changing the structure of mortgage markets are considered.

Inventory Investment

Inventory investment accounts on the average for only about one percent of GNP expenditures, but it is one of the most volatile components of GNP. Variations in the rate of inventory investment account for a significant part of the variation in the growth of demand and have played an important role in each recession since the Second World War.

Retailers and wholesalers carry inventories because their sales vary erratically, while it takes time to obtain merchandise from suppliers. If they do not have goods in stock when customers are ready to buy, they may lose a sale to a rival. In deciding how much inventory to carry, they have to balance the cost of storage and interest on their investment in inventories against the gain in sales from having goods on hand. It is not worth raising the average inventory if the probable gain in sales from holding it just balances the carrying cost. Actual inventory will vary around the target average precisely because sales do vary erratically.

Manufacturers carry inventories of finished goods in order to be able to fill orders promptly. In addition they hold inventories of finished goods to smooth production. Since it is costly to hire and dismiss labor for frequent variations in production, manufacturing firms try to maintain steady production rates while sales fluctuate. When sales increase, firms will let inventories decline for a while, then step up production by enough to rebuild inventories as well as to match the increased sales rate. The reverse will be true when sales decline.

Manufacturers also hold inventories of materials and components and work in process. They hold material inventories to ensure that production can continue in the face of delays or interruptions of supplies and because it is cheaper to transport and handle relatively large batches of materials. Work-in-process inventories are directly linked to the production process. They are relatively unimportant for simple, quickly produced items, but producers of complex capital goods like aircraft, ships, or generators have large inventories of partly finished product because each item takes weeks or months to complete.

Planned inventories tend to vary more or less proportionately with final product sales so that the rate of inventory investment tends to vary with the growth of the goods component of GNP. That produces an acceleration effect. The rate of inventory investment tends to rise when the rate of growth of goods output accelerates, thus temporarily giving an additional fillip to the growth of demand.

The target ratio of inventory to final sales may vary for a number of reasons. Work-in-process inventory will rise when new orders exceed shipments. As production increases in response to orders, the work in process in the pipeline rises. When finished product shipments catch up with orders, the flow of shipments out of the pipeline balances the flow in from new orders, and work-in-process inventories level off. When orders decline, shipments will be maintained for a while, but work in process will decline. Firms may also change their inventory targets in response to changing judgments about the availability and cost of materials and supplies. In an upswing, purchasing agents will increase orders if they fear that prices will rise or that suppliers will be unable to fill the orders promptly. Their efforts to protect themselves may increase the already high utilization of capacity and add to pressures on prices. Purchasing agents may trim inventory targets in a downswing for the opposite reason.

The factors noted above have caused significant variations in the rate of inventory investments, but the "big swings" in inventory investment seem to be connected with the problems of adjusting production to sales. Inventory accumulation is after all the difference between production and final product sales. A relatively small change in the gap between production and sales can result in significant unplanned inventory accumulation. A substantial adjustment of production may then be required if producers try to bring inventories back to normal in a short period. Figure 14.5 shows the course of the very large inventory swing in the 1965–67 period.

Figure 14.5   Total Gross National Product and Final Sales
1965–67

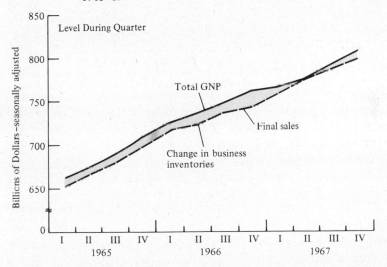

SOURCE: *Annual Report of the Council of Economic Advisers,* February 1968, p. 44.

Money, Wealth, and Consumption

In the previous chapter we introduced the notion of the consumption function and used the simplest possible relation between disposable income and consumption in order to see how the pieces of the income-expenditure model fit together. Now that we have worked out the whole model, we can consider a more complicated and realistic treatment of consumption. In particular, we want to show how changes in money supply influence consumption directly.

Consumer expenditures make up about 60 percent of total GNP. Even small variations in the ratio of consumption to disposable income can play an important role in the fluctuations of aggregate demand. On the average, American households save about 6½ percent of disposable income, and spend the balance on consumption, but, as figure 14.6 shows, the savings

Figure 14.6   Consumption and Disposable Income

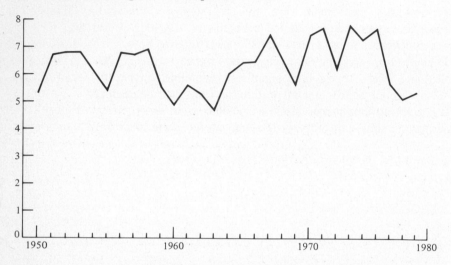

rate is sometimes as high as 8 percent and sometimes as low as 3 percent. A shift of a couple of percentage points in the ratio of consumption to disposable income, one way or the other, can make the difference between a boom year and a recession. Any realistic theory of income determination has to give some explanation of short-run variations in the savings rate. Moreover, crude empirical generalizations are always dangerous in economics. If we do not know why they hold, we do not know what kind of changes in circumstances will make them break down. In the case of personal saving, a simple empirical rule is dangerous because savings rates differ greatly from country to country. In Japan the personal savings rate is close to 25 percent of disposable income. In this section we are going to consider first some of the basic motivations for saving and their implications for the responses of consumers to changes in wealth. From that discussion we will be able to see why changes in money and wealth influence consumption expenditures.

The Life-Cycle Approach to Consumption and Saving

In our society there are only a few people who save because they have more income than they can use, or because they are misers, or because it is the right thing to do. Most people find that it is hard to save, and they only do so to achieve some definite purpose. They save for the down payment on a house, to start a small business, to prepare for future college expenses for their children, and very often to prepare for retirement. A relatively small number of people plan to leave estates for their children or to give bequests to charitable or educational institutions. You will notice that, except in the last case, the object of saving is to accumulate for a time and then to dissave when it is time for children to go to college or when retirement actually occurs. Because so many of the factors motivating saving have to do with the changes in circumstances that occur as people grow older, the saving theory built on those considerations is called the **life-cycle theory of saving.**

The central proposition of this theory is that *saving and dissaving occur because families do not receive income at the same time they wish to spend it*. To time the expenditure of limited resources efficiently, it is necessary to plan ahead and at some times spend less than current receipts, and at other times more. To do that properly, families have to guess the pattern of future income, anticipate special consumption problems like college expenses, choose a plan for consumption and saving for future years, and finally, carry out the first step in the plan in terms of current consumption and saving. That all sounds very difficult and it is. Most people have only a vague idea of how their income will change. They plan for college expenses, but most of today's parents did not anticipate current tuition rates.

Since people usually do not forecast their incomes correctly, they often have to go back to the drawing board to replan for the future. At each point in time it is necessary to plan anew how to distribute total planned resources over the remaining years of life. Those resources include expected future income receipts, and wealth currently on hand. Planning for the future is complicated because it is difficult to judge what the future will bring; yet the implications of an individual's views about his future prospects are fairly simple.

As a first approximation suppose a man wants to spend a constant amount per year in each of n remaining years of life. He starts with some initial wealth w and expects to receive a certain average income $\overline{Y}$ for the remainder of his life. His total lifetime resources are then $w + n\overline{Y}$. If he spends $\overline{C}$ per year and plans to leave no estate, his total consumption $n\overline{C}$ must equal total resources. That is, $n\overline{C} = w + n\overline{Y}$. Therefore $\overline{C} = \frac{w}{n} + \overline{Y}$. In most years his current income y will differ from his expected average income. His saving in any year will be $\overline{Y} - \overline{C}$ or $y - \overline{Y} - \frac{w}{n}$. In particular his preretirement income will be above average, and his postretirement income will be below average. Thus before retirement $y - \overline{Y}$ will be positive, and he will usually be a positive saver. After retirement $y - \overline{Y}$ will be negative and he will be dissaving by liquidating his accumulated wealth in order to finance consumption expenditures.

Those relatively simple considerations have some important implications for aggregate saving. First, notice that the lifetime saving of the individual who saves only for such things as retirement will be zero. He saves in one part of life and dissaves an equal amount at other times. Does that mean that the only net saving for the nation is accounted for by rich people who leave large estates? It would mean that if population and income were constant. In that case the positive saving of people of working age would be just canceled by the dissaving of retired people. In fact, of course, the growth of population implies net saving for the nation, even if no individual leaves anything behind. When population is rising, the number of people in each working-life-age group—for example, those between thirty and forty—is larger than the number in each retired-age group —say, sixty to seventy; so that the positive saving of those of working age outweighs the negative saving of those in retirement. That tendency is reinforced by the upward trend of per capita income. Young people today are anticipating a higher average lifetime income than did their predecessors thirty or forty years older, who are now entering retirement age. Correspondingly, those young people are saving for a higher retirement income than their parents have. The positive saving of the working-age group outweighs the negative saving of the retired group. Thus the life-cycle theory accounts for positive aggregate saving, even if no individual has any net saving over his whole life.

The life-cycle theory has another important implication. If each individual is seeking to accumulate assets for retirement, the amount he saves at any time will depend not only on his current and expected future income but also on the real value of the assets he owns. At any time, the past saving of the population is embodied in capital goods and houses. Thus the value of physical assets valued at cost will rise with accumulated saving. However, the real and nominal value of wealth can deviate from the sum of past savings.

The market value of wealth generally deviates from the cost of accumulated physical assets because prices, interest rates, and expectations of future profits and rents change all the time.

We noted in chapter 12 that the nominal value of wealth is equal to the present value of the property income from private assets, plus the net present value of interest-bearing government debt, plus the value of non-interest-bearing government debt (currency and bank reserves). The real value of government debt, whether interest bearing or not, will decline when prices rise or increase when prices fall. The real value of private property as a whole will not be directly affected by price change, though private debtors will gain from price increase while the creditors will lose.

Changes in interest rates will affect the value of all assets except non-interest-bearing government debts. A rise in interest rates obviously depresses bond prices. It is also apparent that stock prices are adversely affected by increasing interest rates. It also follows directly from present-value calculations that a rise in interest rates reduces the value of directly held physical assets. Of course, the interest rate relevant to the valuation of common stocks and physical assets is the real rather than the nominal interest rate.

The life-cycle theory indicates that consumer expenditures are likely to vary with wealth as well as with income, responding positively to both. Algebraically we can write $C = ay + bw$. Graphically we can represent the equation by showing consumption against income with a constant representing the value of wealth. Figure 14.7 shows two consumption lines: the

Figure 14.7   Effect of Wealth on Consumption

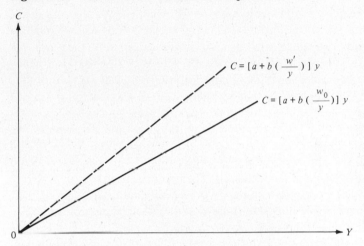

lower solid one corresponds to some particular level of the wealth-income ratio, while the higher dotted line shows the effect of an increase in wealth relative to income.

While the wealth associated with a given level of income can change for a variety of reasons, there are two reasons that play a particularly important role in monetary theory. First, a reduction of real interest rates tends to raise the real value of wealth relative to income, and therefore shifts the consumption line upward. That consideration makes consumption as well as investment responsive to the real interest rate. Second, a fall in the price level increases the value of real balances and therefore increases wealth and consumption. Thus the price level enters the picture in two ways: through the real balance effect just mentioned, or through a price change raising or lowering the real money supply and the resulting lower or higher interest rates. Finally, to the extent that money supply is increased by currency issues or increases in bank reserves, an increase in the money supply increases real balances even without a price-level change.

Limitations of the Life-Cycle Theory

The life-cycle approach provides a rationale for the savings behavior of many people. However, it has to be qualified in a number of ways.

In particular, it does not deal very well with the estate-building objectives of relatively high-income people. It may not apply well to a large number of relatively low-income families who have difficulty enough in making ends meet from month to month, without planning for the distant future.

The life-cycle hypothesis can, in principle, be extended to cover saving or estate-building purposes as well as for retirement. However, the assumptions required seem a little unrealistic. People planning for retirement usually have a fairly clear idea of the amount they will need to accumulate. People who hope to leave estates do not need to have a very precise objective. Very wealthy people may just spend what they want and leave an estate that is simply a residual. Middle-class people may save enough to provide for retirement with some cushion. If things go well, they will not need to liquidate all their assets before death. However, if they have heavy medical expenses or suffer losses from inflation, they will sell off their houses and other assets, leaving little behind them. Those considerations affect our view of the response of savings and consumption to changes in asset values. According to the life-cycle theory, capital gains and losses will have a direct effect on consumption. Households that suffer capital losses should reduce current consumption, planned consumption in retirement, and planned estate by the same percentage. It seems more probable that people with a rather imprecise estate-building objective will maintain most of their consumption objectives and let the estate take the blow. That consideration somewhat weakens the conclusion of the life-cycle theory.

There is also some doubt about the applicability of the life-cycle model to the lower end of the income and wealth scale. The chronic problem of poverty among the elderly indicates that a large number of people have difficulty carrying out a life-cycle plan. Private pension plans have tax advantages, and social security has proved advantageous to relatively low-income families. That may account for their popularity, but many people find pension plans and Social Security attractive as a means of getting the retirement problem off their hands. A high proportion of the population does almost all of its saving through pension funds, life insurance, and mortgage payments. They hold very little in liquid assets or stocks and bonds.

The result is that the behavior of half or more of the population may deviate from the life-cycle model in several respects. First, they may not save as much as would be expected from life-cycle considerations. Second, their consumption may be unaffected by changes in asset values. Third, their consumption will be directly linked to relatively short-term movements in income.

Short-Run Variations in Consumption

The life-cycle theory is intended to explain the trend of the average level of saving without giving much attention to short-run movements. In its unqualified form, the theory implies that households concerned with lifetime planning will not be much affected by short-run variations in disposable income. However, many households are forced to respond to short-run variations in disposable income, because their liquid asset holdings are small. Households who save mainly through pension funds, life insurance, and mortgage payments have to adjust their consumption expenditures when income declines. They can cushion the decline by drawing down whatever liquid assets they have and by borrowing, but many will also have to cut consumption expenditures. They will, of course, tend to increase expenditures when income rises again.

In adjusting to changes in income, most households find it is easier to reduce expenditures on durable goods than to reduce their payments for food, rent, or other nondurables and services. Making an old car last another year reduces their living standard only a little and can save a considerable amount in monthly automobile payments. Moreover, when unemployment rises, even households not directly affected may refrain from taking on new commitments for installment payments for fear that their incomes will fall. When disposable income is advancing rapidly many households will only gradually increase their expenditures on nondurables and services, but will use the slack in their budgets for installment payments on new durable goods. Variations in expenditures on consumer durables induced by changes in the growth of disposable income are accentuated by the resulting variations in the size of the stock of durable goods in the hands of consumers. In the recovery from a recession, purchases of autos and other durables will be increased as consumers make up for the purchases postponed during the recession. After a couple of years of rapid expansion, sales of durable goods may level off or decline because consumers have acquired large numbers of new cars and other durables during the upswing. Empirical studies show that sales of autos and other consumer durables vary much more than other consumer expenditures and contribute substantially to short-run fluctuations in aggregate demand.

Summary

Investment in plant and equipment, residential construction, and inventories makes up about 15 percent of total GNP, but accounts for a much larger fraction of fluctuations in the growth rate of GNP. Inventory investment, though accounting for only about one percent of total output on the average, accounts for a much larger proportion of fluctuations in output. In the long run inventory investment may be regarded as driven by the growth of output. In the short run, however, inventory investment reflects changes in the flow of orders for durable goods. It is often seriously disturbed by lags in the adjustment of production to final sales of goods. The demand for housing services tends to rise with increasing population and rising real per capita income. Continued outward shift in the demand for housing services is matched by a continued growth in the supply of housing from new construction. At any one moment, the equilibrium price of housing services will depend on the demand for housing services and the existing stock of houses. The price of houses will equal the discounted value of their rental services and will therefore be influenced by the interest rate. A fall in interest rates will raise the present value of houses and stimulate new construction, while a rise in interest rates will depress housing prices and reduce the rate of construction. However, much of the actual fluctuation in the rate of residential construction has resulted from the variation in the availability of mortgage credit as well as from variations in the interest rate.

Prospective profitability of investment in plant and equipment depends on the size and character of the existing stock of capital equipment, on technical change, and on expectations about the growth of demand in the future. It is also influenced by taxes and expectations about the prospects for future inflation. Finally, an investment is worth making if the present value of the prospective future returns exceeds the price of the capital goods involved in making the investment. The present value of the prospective stream of returns from an investment will vary with the interest rate. As in the case of housing, a rise in interest rates will reduce the present value of prospective returns and discourage investment, while a fall will increase the present value of prospective returns and stimulate investment.

Thus for both residential construction and plant and equipment, we may assert that, other things equal, there will be more investment at low interest rates than at high ones. Accordingly, there is a downward sloping demand curve for investment. However, it is important to bear in mind that the other-things-equal clause covers a large number of factors. Variations in the stock of capital goods and housing, changes in expectations about the growth of future income, changes in technology, and changes in tax rates may cause shifts in the investment demand function that are much more important than the movements along the investment demand curve caused by variations in interest rates after adjustment for inflation expectations.

In our discussion of the consumption function, we first outlined the life-cycle theory of consumption in which saving is explained in terms of the fact that the time profile of income receipts for households does not match the pattern of their expenditure needs. In particular, most households have to save in order to prepare for retirement. The theory implies first that households will be relatively insensitive to short-term variations in their disposable income. Second, it implies that their saving behavior can be influenced through changes in the market value of the assets that they hold. What counts is the real value of assets, so the saving of holders of money and other claims fixed in nominal value will be influenced by changes in the price level. Changes in interest rates will affect the valuation of all assets. Thus the aggregate rate of saving will be affected by changes in price levels and interest rates, as well as by changes in income.

The life-cycle theory is subject to two kinds of important qualifications. First, it may not apply well to very wealthy households. While they are small in number, they own a disproportionate part of total wealth. That consideration at least dilutes wealth effects emphasized in the life-cycle theory. Second, the theory may not hold very well for a large group of relatively low-income families who find it difficult to save. Their consumption behavior is likely to be much more responsive to short-run changes in disposable income than one would expect from a literal application of the life-cycle theory.

QUESTIONS AND EXERCISES

1. List some of the effects of tax policy on the prospective returns from investment in plant and equipment. Use present-value equations to illustrate your answers.
2. An increase in the rate of growth of output tends to raise the level of plant and equipment investment. Explain.
3. If business firms expect prices to rise each year, they will tend to invest more. Why?
4. A rise in interest rates can offset the effect of inflation expectations on investment. Illustrate using the present-value equation.
5. It is assumed that Social Security benefits will be permanently increased by 10 percent. How will personal savings be affected? Does it make any difference how the increased benefits are financed?
6. If lower birth rates cause the growth rate of U.S. population to decline, the personal savings rate is likely to fall. Why?
7. Would you expect the reduction in savings rates to occur at the same time as the decline in population growth?
8. Other things equal, a reduction in stock prices tends to increase the amount people want to save at a given level of income. Why?

FURTHER READING

ANDO, ALBERT and MODIGLIANI, FRANCO. "The 'Life Cycle' Hypothesis of Saving: Aggregate Implications and Tests." *American Economic Review* 53 (March 1963): 52–84. The basic exposition of the life-cycle hypothesis and its economic significance.

BOSWORTH, BARRY. "Analyzing Inventory Investment." *Brookings Papers on Economic Activity,* 1970:2, pp. 207–28. This paper offers a comprehensive explanation of the factors involved in short-run variations in inventory investment.

———. "The Stock Market and the Economy." *Brookings Papers on Economic Activity,* 1975:2, pp. 257–91. This paper reviews the evidence on the effect of fluctuations in stock prices on variations in consumer expenditures.

CLARK, PETER K. "Investment in the 1970s: Theory, Performance and Prediction," *Brookings Papers on Economic Activity,* 1979:1, pp. 73–114. A painstaking review of the performance of alternative theories of investment in the explanation and prediction of business-investment expenditures.

DUESENBERRY, JAMES. *Business Cycles and Economic Growth.* New York: McGraw-Hill, 1958. Chapters four and five provide a detailed analysis of the behavior of business firms in making investment decisions.

————. *Income, Saving and the Theory of Consumer Behavior.* Cambridge: Harvard University Press, 1952. Presents a theory of saving and consumption that stresses emulation.

EISNER, ROBERT. *Factors in Business Investment.* Cambridge, Mass.: Ballinger Publishing Co. (for the National Bureau of Economic Research), 1978. This volume provides tests of alternative theories of investment based on the records of a large sample of business corporations.

FRIEDMAN, MILTON. *A Theory of the Consumption Function.* Princeton, N.J.: Princeton University Press, 1957. This classic work presents Friedman's version of the consumption function together with a number of empirical tests of his and alternative hypotheses.

JORGENSON, D. W. "The Theory of Investment Behavior." In *Determinants of Investment Behavior,* edited by R. Ferber, pp. 129–56. New York: Columbia University Press, 1967. This article outlines the pure theory of investment decision and provides tests of a realistic empirical version of the theory.

KOPCKE, RICHARD W. "The Behavior of Investment Spending during the Recession and Recovery, 1973–76." *New England Economic Review* (Federal Reserve Bank of Boston), November/December 1977, pp. 5–41. This article tests the performance of alternative investment theories in light of the experience of the major business cycle of 1973–76.

MAYER, THOMAS. *Permanent Income, Wealth, and Consumption.* Berkeley: University of California Press, 1972. A review of alternative theories of consumption with an examination of evidence for and against each alternative.

MODIGLIANI, FRANCO. "Monetary Policy and Consumption." In *Consumer Spending and Monetary Policy: The Linkages,* pp. 9–97. Boston: Federal Reserve Bank of Boston, 1971. This essay presents the results of a large econometric model and shows how changes in monetary policy can influence consumption through their effects on income, interest rates, and wealth.

————. "The Life Cycle Hypothesis of Saving, the Demand for Wealth and the Supply of Capital," *Social Research* 33 (Summer 1966): 160–217. An excellent exposition of the life-cycle hypothesis.

15

National Income

Now that we have reviewed the determinants of investment and consumption in detail, it is time to reexamine our analysis of national income determination. Because so many factors are involved, it is not easy to keep track of all the pieces in the puzzle. In this chapter we will first show how we have to modify the *IS–LM* framework to take account of a more complex analysis of investment and consumption. The *IS–LM* framework will look much the same as in chapter 13, but you should now have a much richer understanding of the factors underlying the summary curves and of the reasons why they may shift. In particular, we will have to pay attention to the implications of the life-cycle theory for the way in which the *IS* curve responds to changes in interest rates and the price level. After reviewing the *IS–LM* framework, we will be in a position to summarize all of the factors involved in income determination, paying special attention to the channels in which monetary policy operates.

We then turn to the role of prices in the system, first attempting to summarize the factors determining the equilibrium price level and then examining what happens when there are departures from equilibrium, noting that sometimes price changes can cause destabilizing movements in output. Finally, we examine very briefly some of the causes of short-run variations in output.

Wealth and the *IS* Curve

In our discussion of the consumption function, we showed that an increase in wealth will tend to increase consumption for a given current income. We noted that wealth may increase for several reasons. Expectations of future property income may improve. The real interest rate may fall. The real net value of government debt and of currency and bank reserves may rise either because the nominal stock of those assets increases, while price level remains constant, or because the price level falls. We now have to show how those considerations can be represented in terms of the *IS* curve.

To see how wealth affects the *IS* curve, we can first consider the impact of a change in interest rate, holding government debt and money supply constant. Of course, the money supply has something to do with the

Figure 15.1   Interest Rate and Equilibrium Income

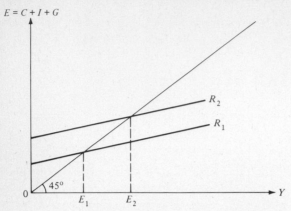

interest rates, but one thing at a time. Figure 15.1 shows the familiar 45-degree line diagram. The $C + I + G$ line marked R_1 shows total expenditures at each level of GNP when investment expenditure is the amount associated with interest rate R_1, and consumption reflects the wealth associated with interest rate R_1.

The line $C + I + G$ marked R_2 shows total expenditure when investment is based on the lower interest rate R_2 and consumption reflects the higher wealth associated with the lower interest rate R_2. The upward shift in the $C + I + G$ line reflects the response of wealth and consumption as well as investment to the lower interest rate. At the higher interest rate R_1, equilibrium income is at E_1—where $C + I + G$ (R_1) intersects the 45-degree line. At the lower interest rate, the equilibrium income is increased to E_2. Figure 15.2 shows two points on an *IS* curve derived from the data of figure 15.1. Point A at R_1Y_1 corresponds to E_1 in figure 15.1. Point B corresponds to E_2. The dotted line shows other points on the *IS* curve that could be derived by considering other interest rates.

Figure 15.2   The *IS* Curve

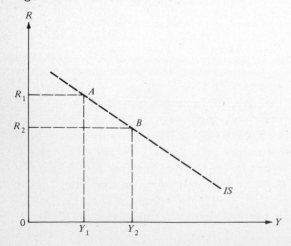

What happens to the *IS* curve when real wealth is increased by increasing government debt? The increase in real wealth will shift the consumption function outward and increase the equilibrium income. That will be true at any level of interest rate, so the result will be to shift the whole *IS* curve to the right as in figure 15.3. The same result will occur if the nominal amounts of government debt and money supply remain constant when the price level falls.

Figure 15.3 A Change in Wealth Shifts the *IS* Curve

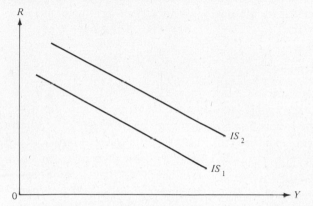

The theoretical role of wealth effects in the consumption function and thereby in the *IS* curve is generally accepted. Their empirical significance is a matter of considerable dispute. At one end of the spectrum, monetarists have attached great importance to wealth effects in general and real balance effects in particular.

Some economists impute considerable significance to wealth effects induced by changes in interest rates. However, their estimates of the quantitative significance of real balance effects suggest that they are not very important. Still others are impressed by limitations of the life-cycle theory. Moreover, they consider that changes in expectations of future profits are a much more important factor in the determination of wealth than changes in interest rates.

Shifts in the *IS* Curve

At this point it will be useful to summarize all the factors that can cause shifts in the *IS* curve. In addition to the shifts resulting from changes in the real value of outside money and the real net value of government debt noted above, a variety of other factors can cause shifts in the *IS* curve. Changes in the real value of government expenditures have a direct effect on the position of the curve. Changes in income tax rates affect the multiplier and, therefore, affect the curve. They change its slope because a different multiplier is applied to changes in investment induced by changing interest rates. Taxes affecting corporations can influence both consumption and investment. They can influence consumption because taxes paid by corporations affect the prices of stocks, thus changing household wealth. Corporate taxes, depreciation regulations, and the investment tax credit influence the prospective profitability of new investment projects. Events in the private sector can also cause important shifts in the *IS* curve. Prospective profitability of investment depends in part on the accumulated stock of capital goods in existence and also on business expectations about future demand conditions. Expectations of the growth of future income will also influence the savings decisions of households. Finally, of course, private investment can be influenced by the development of new products and new methods of production.

Channels of Monetary Policy

It may also be useful at this point to summarize the different ways in which changes in money supply influence expenditures. Aside from the real balance effects noted above, changes in money supply affect consumption and investment in three primary ways. First, by influencing interest rates, changes in money supply change the cost of capital for business investment and for investment in residential construction. Second, changes in interest rates may also affect the amount of rationing of mortgage credit, and thereby affect investment in residential construction. Third, changes in interest rates also affect the value of wealth in the form of stocks, bonds, and other property, and by doing so, influence consumption expenditures.

The Aggregate-Demand Curve and Price-Level Changes

The shift in the *IS* curve due to price-level change has an important effect on the aggregate-demand curve. In chapter 13 we derived an aggregate-demand curve showing increase in real income with lower prices. In that derivation, the link between price and real income depended entirely on the *LM* curve. The real money supply corresponding to a given nominal money supply increases as price level falls. The *LM* curve shifts down to the right, as the real money supply increases and intersects the *IS* curve at a higher level of real income.

We must now take account of the fact that, since a fall in the price level increases real wealth and consumption, the *IS* curve will shift to the right when the price level falls. The two effects reinforce one another, since each tends to flatten the aggregate-demand curve.

Moreover, the significance of the interest sensitivity of demand for money and of investment demand in determining the response of aggregate demand to price level is changed in a number of ways. First, through wealth effects a fall in interest rates can increase aggregate demand, even if investment demand is insensitive to interest rates.

Second, even if the demand for money is very interest elastic, producing a flat *LM* curve, an increase in real money supply and in the net value of government debt will shift the *IS* curve to the right when the price level falls.

The last point has a special theoretical importance. It ensures that the aggregate-demand curve will always intersect the potential output line at some positive price level, however low.

The Equilibrium Price Level

Now we will try to be more precise about the relation between the equilibrium price level and the factors underlying the *IS* and *LM* curves. The key to understanding the determination of the equilibrium price level is recognition of the fact that the price level determines the real value of nominal magnitudes affecting economic decisions. Thus the *LM* curve links real money supply, real income, and interest rate. The price level determines how much real money supply corresponds to a given nominal money supply. It is clear that if the nominal money supply is doubled and at the same time the price level is doubled, the position of the *LM* curve is unchanged. How about the *IS* curve? Some of the elements underlying the *IS* curve do not involve any nominal magnitudes. The investment function relates real investment to real interest rate. Its position is determined by real capital stock and expected real output. The investment function should be just the same at a higher or lower price level, but other relationships do involve nominal magnitudes. The consumption function is basically a relation between real consumer expenditure, real income, and real wealth. Some of the wealth is based on nominal holdings of money and government debt. Moreover, the *IS* curve is partly determined by government purchases, transfer payments, and taxes. Some of these fiscal policy factors are usually stated in nominal terms, for instance, cents-per-gallon gasoline taxes.

Income tax laws provide personal exemptions stated in dollar terms, and the tax rate rises with nominal income. Suppose we draw the *IS* curve with real income on the horizontal axis and with given values for all the nominal factors just mentioned and a given price level. The price level determines the real value of government purchases, wealth, and so on, and therefore determines the position of the *IS* curve.

Now reconsider the equilibrium price level. The solid lines in figure 15.4 show *IS* and *LM* curves for a given set of nominal magnitudes— money supply, government debt, government purchases, gasoline taxes, and other items—at a given price level P_0. The *IS* and *LM* curves intersect at E_0 to the left of the potential output line. The economy is at a partial equilibrium for less than full employment so that the price level is too high.

At a lower price level all the nominal magnitudes will have higher real values. The *LM* curve will shift rightward and so will the *IS* curve. At

Figure 15.4   Changes in Price Levels Shift *IS* and *LM* Curves

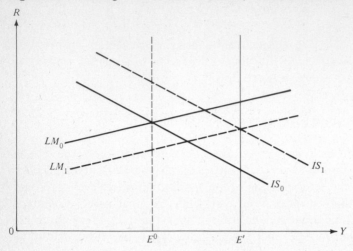

P_1 the two curves intersect at potential output. So P_1 is an equilibrium price level.

If we now double all these nominal magnitudes and at the same time double prices and wages, the real value of all the nominal magnitudes in the system will be unchanged, and the *IS* and *LM* curves will be unchanged, still intersecting at potential output. But notice that that result holds only when *all* nominal magnitudes are changed together. If, for example, the money supply is doubled but there is no change in government debt, transfer payments, and the other magnitudes, the equilibrium price level will not be twice as high.

Notice also that the position of the *IS* and *LM* curves can be shifted by other factors. The investment function can be shifted by technological factors or by the expected growth of output. The consumption function can be shifted by changes in age distribution or changes in the expected growth of income. To keep actual output at potential output, the equilibrium price level has to change to offset the upward or downward shift in the *IS* curve, resulting from shifts in the real as well as the nominal factors underlying the consumption function.

Changes in Prices Versus Differences in Price Level

In using the concept of an aggregate-demand curve and an equilibrium price level, it is important to remember that the aggregate-demand curve shows the effect on the demand for real output of the difference between one price level and another. The argument used to derive the aggregate-demand curve does not take account any effects of the process of changing prices on the behavior of consumers or investors. In figure 15.5, point *A* shows the aggregate demand for real output at a price level of 100 on the assumption that everyone is adapted to that price level, that prices are not

Figure 15.5   Aggregate-Demand Curve

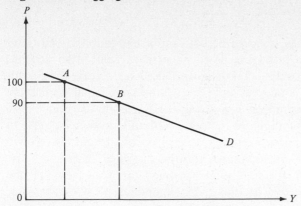

changing, and are not expected to change. Point *B* shows the corresponding amount of real output associated with a price level of 90 on the same assumptions. It cannot be assumed that real output will follow the path from *A* to *B* during a period in which prices are falling by 10 percent. If in fact the price-level change is very gradual, so that prices fall from 100 to 90 at 1 percent a year for a ten-year period, it might be reasonable to suppose that actual output would follow the path indicated by the aggregate-demand curve. If, however, a 10 percent price decline in one year were in question, the situation would be quite different. When prices move rapidly, either upward or downward, the process of change will in itself have effects not fully reflected in the derivation of the aggregate-demand curve. Rapid price changes will affect expectations about future prices and thereby influence the behavior of consumers and investors. Further complications arise from the existence of fixed price contracts. Creditors lose in unexpected inflations and gain in deflations. Conversely, debtors gain in inflations, lose—even go bankrupt—in deflations. The net response of consumers and investors to those redistributions is not reflected in the construction of the aggregate-demand curve. Thus, even perfect price flexibility does not guarantee that real GNP will always grow with potential output.

In fact, however, prices do not always adjust very rapidly. When the aggregate-demand curve shifts to the right faster than potential output, prices will rise but there is usually some increase in output. When the aggregate-demand curve does not grow as quickly as potential output, prices may decline but output will not keep pace with potential.

The historical record shows that over the long run, actual output has followed the trend of potential output. Prices, aggregate demand, and potential output have somehow been mutually adapted to one another. The adjustment has not been a one-sided one. Sometimes prices do all the work of bringing the actual price level to the equilibrium determined by potential output and a given aggregate-demand curve. At other times policy is changed to adapt the aggregate-demand curve to potential output and the existing price level.

Short-Run Fluctuations in Output

Over a very long period the trend of actual output has followed the trend
of potential output. In the short run, however, actual output often deviates
significantly from potential output. Those deviations occur because the growth
rate of aggregate demand is uneven, and prices do not move quickly enough
to cause the compensating movements along the aggregate-demand curve,
which would keep actual output at potential. In this section we give a
very brief outline of the major factors responsible for the uneven growth
of aggregate demand. Factors involved may be classified first into those
associated with changes in the supply and demand for money on the one
hand, and nonmonetary factors on the other. Nonmonetary factors, in turn,
can be divided into primary factors arising from changes in fiscal policy,
technology, and long-term expectations, which affect the investment-demand
function and the consumption function, and into further movements of
consumption and investment demand induced by prior changes in the rate
of growth of GNP. It is important to note that, while we may treat these
factors separately for expositional purposes, the monetary and nonmonetary
factors always interact so that the effect of a change in one factor depends
on what is happening to the others.

Monetary Instability

Changes in the equilibrium price level and therefore in either actual
prices or in output can arise if the nominal money supply moves erratically.
At times, of course, rapid movement of the money supply may offset
instability from other sources, but as noted above, a positive correlation
between changes in money supply and other sources of disturbance is a
frequent occurrence. Monetary instability may also be generated by erratic changes in the demand for money. It appears that there are frequent
month-to-month changes in demand for money of some significance. Most
of these changes "wash-out" fairly quickly before they can have much
effect on economic activity, but as we will see in our discussion of monetary
policy, their occurrence increases the difficulty of conducting monetary
policy. In the longer run, there are significant trends in the demand for
money. These trends arise from changes in the structure of the payments
system and in the availability and cost of switching into and out of substitutes for money, such as Treasury bills. Similarly, there are some instances,
particularly during the Great Depression, when the demand for money
function has shifted because of widespread fear of price declines and bankruptcies. Those shifts, of course, contributed to economic instability, but they
would not have occurred in the absence of rapid changes in prices and
economic activity generated from other sources.

"Real" Sources of Instability

Our analysis of the factors underlying the *IS* curve suggests that the primary sources of nonmonetary instability are likely to stem from changes in fiscal policy or from changes in the factors underlying investment demand.

Prior to the Great Depression, government outlays were rather small relative to GNP in peacetime, so that changes in fiscal policy during peacetime were seldom a substantial cause of economic instability. Many economists believe that rapid changes in government expenditures during and after wars, which have been only partially offset by tax increases, have played a major role in the history of business fluctuations. Since the Great Depression the scale of peacetime government expenditures has increased in most of the developed market economies and fiscal policy has therefore played a greater role. Nonetheless, the most important variations in fiscal policy have been associated with wars. The Second World War, the Korean War, and the Vietnam War were far and away the most important events in the history of economic instability in the last forty years. As our discussion of the record of monetary policy will show, money-supply changes during those episodes worked to intensify rather than to offset the instability generated by fiscal policy. Wars aside, frequent changes in federal expenditures and tax policy appear to play a substantial role in the short-run fluctuations in economic activity. These changes in fiscal policy have often been made with a view to offsetting instability generated elsewhere in the economy. However, the record of success in the timing of changes in fiscal policy for stabilization purposes has been a very mixed one.

The extent of the shift in aggregate demand generated by changes in fiscal policy depends in part on whether changes in money supply intensify or offset the change in fiscal policy. When money supply does not expand to accommodate an increase in government expenditure, the extent of the shift in aggregate demand depends, as noted earlier, on the slopes of the *IS* and *LM* curves and on the magnitude of real balance effects.

Rapid shifts in demand can and often have been generated by the private sector as well as by government. Changes in expectations about the profit prospects of major industries, such as railroads, have often caused sharp variations in investment demand. Investment demand has often also been affected by speculative booms in securities and land. Many economic historians have attributed much of the instability of the nineteenth century to the uneven pace of development of major new industries and to the erratic pace of development of frontier areas. The Florida land boom and the stock-market boom of the 1920s provide more recent examples of spectacular speculative booms. Changes in expectations may affect expenditures by consumers as well as investment outlays. For example, the sharp fall in automobile demand in 1974–75 is often attributed to the uncertainties arising from the acceleration of inflation at that time as well as to fears about the availability and price of gasoline. As in the case of fiscal policy, the change in aggregate demand resulting from shifts in investment demand or in the consumption function depends in part on monetary factors.

Induced Shifts in Demand

Any sustained change in the rate of growth of output, regardless of its origin, produces further repercussions throughout the economy. Changes in the growth of output can induce sharp changes in the rates of investment in plant and equipment, in inventories, and in expenditures for consumer durables.

An increase in the rate of growth of GNP, whether generated by government spending or an investment boom in some sector of the economy, can increase consumption spending through the multiplier, and the resulting improvement in capacity utilization can cause further increases in sectors not originally involved in the investment boom. When the original impetus weakens, the whole process can go into reverse.

Inventory cycles have played an important role in each recession since World War II. A rise in the rate of growth of income will tend to increase the rate of inventory investment, and that, in turn, will contribute to a further increase in the rate of growth of income. Exhaustion of the original impulse that set off the boom will not only slow down the growth of income directly, but will cause inventory investment to decline and might even cause an absolute drop in output. In that case producers will have excessive inventories, and they will for a time attempt to reduce them so that inventory investment becomes negative. That, of course, will make the situation even worse, causing a further decline in income and accentuating inventory problems. Because inventory investment is only a small part of the total, it will usually be possible to work off excess inventories. Nonetheless, the inventory mechanism can cause a fluctuation in output out of proportion to the original impulse that changed investment and the rate of growth of output.

Finally, variations in the rate of growth of GNP appear to cause disproportionate fluctuations in demand for automobiles and other consumer durables. Of course, all three processes interact with one another. Together they can cause much wider fluctuations in GNP growth than one would expect by taking them one at a time and adding their separate effects.

The complex processes just outlined cause continual variation in the rate of growth of output. We take for granted that there will be a boom every few years. There have been seven recessions since 1945. Since the Second World War, however, recessions have been relatively mild and brief. We have somehow avoided the major depressions that marked the economic history of the century and a half before the Second World War. In that period, peacetime fiscal policy was unimportant, and money supply was notably erratic. When recessions got underway, the feedbacks from investment to consumption, and back again, developed into a cumulative reduction in aggregate demand. During the process price reductions led to bankruptcies and contributed to the downswing. The historical causes of those booms and slumps are still a matter of controversy, but the history of that period clearly shows that price adjustments could not stabilize output. They may have compensated for gaps between the trend movement of aggregate demand and the trend growth of potential output, but the adjustment process was a very bumpy one. Our experience shows that the economic system cannot be regarded as a self-adjusting one. Many economists believe that some policy of managing aggregate demand is necessary.

Aggregate-Demand Policy

Fiscal and monetary policy exert a powerful influence for good or ill on movements of aggregate demand. Now that the Federal Reserve has control of the money supply, it must use it. It is making a decision whether it decides to keep money supply constant, change it by a formula, or use its own judgment as to the appropriate monetary growth rate. The president and Congress have to set tax rates and determine expenditure.

We no longer take a fatalistic attitude toward movements of aggregate demand. Most people agree that we should not cut federal expenditures sharply in a recession. An attempt to balance the decline in tax revenues that results from a decline in GNP will only make things worse. The federal deficit reached 70 billion dollars in 1975. Many economists believed that an attempt to close that gap by cutting federal expenditures would have created a major depression.

At the same time everyone agrees that if we cannot avoid wars altogether, we should at least avoid the gross error of fiscal and monetary policy that occurred during the Korean and Vietnam wars.

Beyond that, there is much less agreement as to the conduct of fiscal and monetary policy. Many economists believe that in principle, appropriate adjustments of fiscal policy could be used to offset any instability arising from the private sector, so as to keep output close to potential while maintaining price stability. In practice, that proves to be a difficult, not to say impossible, task. There is a considerable lag between a change in policy and its effect. It follows that active stabilization policies must be based on forecasts. Unfortunately, forecasters make lots of errors, so that complete stabilization is impossible. An overzealous policy of stabilization can do more harm than good. Fiscal and monetary managers who attempt a quick correction of every small actual or forecasted deviation from potential output may destabilize the economy. A biased policy of strong action to offset any threat of recession or to produce a quick recovery in the event one occurs may create inflationary pressures. Some economists argue that those errors can be avoided only by adopting some formula for the conduct of monetary and fiscal policy. Others, however, argue that no formula could do the job. They argue that no formula for monetary policy can take full account of trends in the demand for money; that no fiscal policy formula can take full account of the changing balance between investment demand and saving potential output. They argue that there is a golden mean between an overzealous policy and a formula policy. Monetary policy and fiscal policy are shifted gradually in response to changing economic conditions. There will be many relatively small policy errors, but it will be possible to avoid major errors that might occur from rigid adherence to some formula.

We will discuss those issues in detail in Part Five. It is clear, however, that one's views about the conduct of monetary policy depend very much upon one's views about how monetary policy effects the economy. Before going on to policy discussions, we have to consider the monetarist approach to the analysis of aggregate demand.

Summary

In this brief chapter we have tried to pull together the implications of a realistic theory of consumption and investment. We first showed how changes in interest rates and price levels can influence wealth and thereby influence consumption. Then we reviewed the derivation of the aggregate-supply curve and the determination of the equilibrium price level. We showed that in principle there always is a price level that will be consistent with the full use of the economy's potential output. However, we also showed that the process of changing prices can itself be a destabilizing force. The result is that actual output may often differ from potential output. We then turned to a discussion of the causes of short-run fluctuations in output and also discussed that once the growth of output was changed by any initial disturbance, from monetary policy, fiscal policy, or some source in the private sector, further shifts in investment and consumption demand were likely to occur.

QUESTIONS AND EXERCISES

1. List as many different causes of the shifts in the *IS* curve as you can.
2. Which ones reflect changes in monetary policy? Which ones reflect fiscal policy? Which ones reflect changes in the private sector?
3. Review the channels through which monetary policy affects the aggregate-demand curve. Give an example of each.
4. If prices were perfectly flexible all short-run shifts in aggregate demand would be reflected in prices, not in output. Explain.
5. Any initial shift in aggregate demand tends to induce further shifts in the same direction. Give some examples.

16

The Monetarist Approach

The theory we took up in the previous three chapters was a Keynesian theory. To be sure, it was not, by any means, the precise analysis presented by Lord Keynes in his great book, *The General Theory of Employment, Interest and Money*. Since 1936 when this book was published, economists working in the Keynesian tradition have modified it substantially, both as a result of their own theoretical and empirical research, and as a result of unfolding experience and changing economic circumstances. In doing so, they have accepted, at least in adumbrated form, many of the criticisms directed at Keynesian theory. For example, they now attach much more importance to changes in the quantity of money than they did in the 1940s. Hence, the theory so far discussed might with some justice be called a synthesis, rather than pure Keynesian theory.

But while this theory is probably the one more or less accepted by the majority of economists, it is by no means universally accepted. A rival approach, called the quantity theory of money, or monetarism, has garnered support from a growing number of economists. This is a "counterrevolution" in economic theory that has tried to return to many of the precepts that were accepted before the Keynesian revolution. But calling it a counterrevolution overdramatizes a bit. Actually, modern quantity theorists and monetarists do not by any means reject all of the Keynesian model; in fact, although they come up with very different conclusions about economic policy, they use important elements of Keynesian theory in doing so. Indeed, it has been argued—though this is an issue that we will not take up—that much of the so-called counterrevolution is merely trying to replace one brand of Keynesianism with another brand.[1] There is much less disagreement among economists than is apparent on the surface; on many issues the differences are matters of degree and emphasis. In the case of *moderate* Keynesians and *moderate* monetarists it is often difficult to tell the players without a scorecard.

This and the following chapter deal with this counterrevolution. We will discuss its basic, underlying idea first, and then turn to the work of Milton Friedman who is by far the best-known quantity theorist. In the

---

[1] See the articles by Milton Friedman and by Don Patinkin in *Friedman's Monetary Theory*, ed. Robert Gordon (Chicago: Aldine Publishing Co., 1974).

following chapter we will then take up the work of other quantity theorists and monetarists.

But before turning to the basic idea of the quantity theory, we have to discuss the relation of the terms *quantity theory* and *monetarism*. Unfortunately, the meaning of these terms is not standardized; while some economists prefer to call themselves quantity theorists, others who hold quite similar views prefer to call themselves monetarists. But these two terms should not really be used synonymously. Rather, we will use **quantity theory** to refer to *the twin propositions that changes in the money stock are the most important causes of changes in money income, and that changes in the money stock tend to bring about proportional changes in nominal income*. Monetarism will be used to denote the quantity theory *plus* some other propositions described in a later section of this chapter.

The Quantity Theory—Basic Principles

In chapter 12, we pointed out that the quantity theory of money has a long tradition in economics. The basic idea of the quantity theory—and its research strategy—is to analyze changes in aggregate demand by looking directly, not at consumption, investment, and government expenditures, but at the supply of, and demand for, money.

Equilibrium requires that everyone holds the quantity of money he or she wants to hold. Someone whose money holdings are not in equilibrium would simply increase them—by reducing expenditures or selling assets—or reduce them—by increasing net purchases—as the case may be.

As we discussed in chapter 12, desired nominal money holdings are a function of the price level, real income, real wealth, and the expected opportunity cost of holding money. One aspect of this functional relationship, the relation between the quantity of nominal money demanded and the price level, has an important and special characteristic. Suppose that prices double but that real income, real wealth, and real interest rates remain constant. What would one expect to happen to the *real* quantity of money demanded? The answer is nothing since the real values of the determinants of the demand for real money have not changed. But if the public wants to hold the same *real* quantity of money when prices double, it will have to hold twice as much *nominal* money; and similarly if prices fall by, say, 10 percent, it will want to hold 10 percent less nominal money. The demand for money therefore is strictly proportional to the price level. No such relationship necessarily holds for any of the other determinants of the demand for money.

To begin the examination of the quantity theory we temporarily introduce the simplification that only two assets exist, money and goods—and no securities. Suppose now that as a result of, say, Federal Reserve open-market operations and deposit creation by banks, the public initially holds more (real and nominal) money than it wants to at the prevailing level of prices, real incomes, real wealth, and the opportunity cost of holding money.

It is easy to predict what will happen. People will try to exchange the excess money for goods, and hence aggregate demand will increase. Conversely, if, perhaps due to Federal Reserve open-market sales, actual money balances are below desired levels, the public will try to accumulate more money by cutting back on its expenditures, and aggregate demand will fall. *Hence, we can determine what will happen to aggregate demand, and thus nominal income, simply by asking whether actual money holdings are above, equal to, or below desired money holdings.*

Although each person can reduce his or her money stock very easily by buying goods, this is not true for the whole economy. As one person gets rid of money by making a purchase, the seller's money holdings go up. How then can the public as a whole bring its money balances into equilibrium? The answer is that as people spend their excessive money balances, sellers face increased demand for their products, and hence raise their prices and their outputs so that nominal incomes increase. And as nominal incomes increase, so does the nominal amount of money people want to hold. Hence, as this process continues, a point is reached at which nominal money balances are no longer excessive. The economy is now back in equilibrium.

If we take the special case where real income is fixed, and only prices respond to the increased aggregate demand, we get a nice and simple result: prices have to rise in strict proportion to the excessive money balances. For example, if 10 percent more money is created than the public wants to hold at the existing price level, prices will rise by 10 percent. This is now a new equilibrium because the public is holding the same *real* quantity of money (M/P) as before. Hence, in this simple case where real income is fixed, and there are no securities, we readily get the traditional quantity theory result that prices vary in strict proportion to the quantity of money.

In the more complex case where real income is not taken as fixed, the story is different because there are now two factors that induce people to hold the previously excess money balances: the rise in prices and the rise in real income. Hence, in this case prices rise less than in proportion to the excessive money balances.

So far we have dealt only with an economy in which there are no securities, so that people could spend their excessive money balances only on goods. Now it is time to introduce interest-bearing securities. As in the previous case, people cannot eliminate excessive nominal money holdings from the economy merely by spending. The buyer gets rid of money, but the seller has it now. As before, the solution is that prices—including this time the prices of securities—rise. And rising security prices imply falling interest rates. So now several things happen. First, with falling interest rates it becomes more profitable for business firms to increase their investment expenditures, so that aggregate demand, and hence nominal income, increases. Second, as we discussed in chapter 14, the fall in interest rates increases consumption expenditures, so that nominal income rises for this reason too. Third, at any level of income the demand for money increases as interest rates fall. And fourth, if people expect that the increase in the money stock will raise prices they have an additional incentive to try to reduce their nominal money holdings, and to buy goods instead.[2]

With the interest rate having fallen, nominal income rises by less than it does if there are no securities, and the public can spend its excess money balances only on goods. This is so because the public now wants to hold more money at each level of nominal income. If the money stock increases by, say, 10 percent, nominal income may rise by, say, 7 percent, which—assuming for the sake of the example that the real income elasticity of demand for money is unity—makes the public want to hold only 7 percent more money. The other 3 percent are held because, with the interest rate having fallen, the public now wants to hold 3 percent more money for the reason that bonds are now less attractive to hold than they were previously when the interest rate was higher.

This can also be readily explained in terms of the Cambridge equation, $M = kPY_r$, of chapter 12, where M is the nominal stock of money, P the price level, Y_r real income, and k the proportion of nominal income (PY_r) that people want to hold as money. With the lower interest rate making it less costly to hold money, k increases, so that given M, PY_r is less than it would have been had the interest rate not fallen. Does this mean that the quantity-theory proposition that an increase in the money stock raises nominal income proportionately, applies only in a world without securities? Of course not; quantity theorists are not that naïve. As we will show later on, the 7 percent rise in nominal income in our example is not an equilibrium; eventually the interest rate will rise back to its previous level, and income will rise by the full 10 percent by which the money stock has increased.

The process just described shows how income is determined by the interaction between actual and desired money balances. No mention was made of the marginal propensity to consume and the marginal efficiency of investment. This is so, because once we know by how much people want to change their money holdings, we can derive *as a residual* how much they will spend, since any part of income not spent on commodities or securities must have been added to money holdings. Quantity theorists focus on the supply and demand for money (particularly on the supply of money) and derive aggregate demand in this way as a residual. Keynesians, on the other hand, follow a different research strategy. They put primary emphasis on the factors that make people and firms demand more or fewer goods either for consumption or investment, though they also take into account differences between the desired and actual money stocks. But this difference in research strategy is not the only difference between these two theories. They also disagree about certain empirical issues, such as the extent to which prices are flexible.

---

[2] In addition, as the price of securities rises, the transactions demand for money increases. On the other hand, the fall in the market value of wealth may induce the public to hold less money.

Recent Developments of the Quantity Theory

Although the quantity theory has a long history in economics, it fell into disrepute in the 1930s, in part because it seemed at the time that this theory could not explain the Great Depression, and partly because of the publication in 1936 of Keynes's theory. Although some economists continued to advocate the quantity theory, most economists, particularly the younger ones, became Keynesians, and treated the quantity theory as little more than ancient superstitition.

Only in the mid- and late-1950s did the quantity theory again become a serious rival to the Keynesian theory. There were several reasons for the revival of the quantity theory. One was that, contrary to the prediction of many Keynesians, upon the conclusion of World War II the American economy did not revert to the depressed conditions of the 1930s, but instead underwent inflation. Second, one seemingly great benefit of the Keynesian revolution had been its demonstration that by manipulating expenditures and taxes, the government could keep the economy close to full employment. But it turned out that there were serious political as well as economic difficulties in actually changing government expenditures and tax rates in these recommended ways, so that Keynesian theory appeared to be less useful than it had originally seemed. Third, the time was ripe for a change. Economists had expended much effort along Keynesian lines and were now ready for something new.[3]

But the resurgence of the quantity theory should not be attributed merely to impersonal historical events; surely it is also due to the fact that several extremely able economists wrote books and articles supporting this theory. Don Patinkin of Hebrew University restated the quantity theory in a rigorous way that avoids many of the crudities that infested earlier expositions. Milton Friedman, of the University of Chicago, and many of his former students provided a framework that allows one to test empirically the proposition that changes in the quantity of money dominate changes in income, and the tests they, as well as Clark Warburton, formerly of the FDIC, have performed provided statistical evidence that supports this theory. Moreover, Friedman and Anna Schwartz of the National Bureau of Economic Research argued in a lengthy study that the experience of the Great Depression should be interpreted as confirming the prediction of the quantity theory rather than that of the Keynesian theory. And two economists, Leonall Andersen and Jerry Jordan, then at the Federal Reserve Bank of St. Louis, presented data that they argued show that changes in the money supply have much more impact on nominal income than do changes in fiscal

[3] A major new theory opens up many exciting research opportunities because it raises questions that were previously ignored. After some time the more promising of these research opportunities have been exploited, and the profession is again in a receptive mood for a new theory.

policy. Since the 1960s, Karl Brunner of the University of Rochester and Allan Meltzer at Carnegie-Mellon University have jointly presented empirical evidence that the demand for money is stable in a way that supports the quantity theory and have built a new theoretical model that is in important ways more elaborate than the Keynesian model.

As a result of all of this work quantity theorists and monetarists are no longer a despised sect among economists. While they are probably a minority, they are a powerful minority. Moreover, many of the points made by monetarists have been accepted, at least in attenuated form, into the mainstream Keynesian model. But even so, as will become apparent as we proceed, the quantity theory and the Keynesian theory have quite different policy implications.

The monetarist "counterrevolution," unlike the Keynesian revolution, does not have a single Great Book as its source, and thus is much less of a unified whole than is Keynesian theory. In studying the quantity theory and monetarism in this and the following chapter we will therefore have to take up several distinct approaches.

The Chicago Approach

The best-known version of the monetarist approach is found in the work of Milton Friedman, a Nobel laureate, and of his former students at the University of Chicago. (Friedman is known to a much wider audience as a leading free-market advocate. While his views on monetary theory are consistent with a general free-market position, they do not require it. One can accept his views on monetary theory and policy without having to accept his general political views, and vice versa.) A major part of the work of Friedman and his students has centered on explaining the demand for money.[4] Recall the Cambridge equation, $M = kY_rP$. If, as Cambridge economists believed, k is stable, that is, if people want to hold in their money balances a constant fraction of their incomes, then we can predict how nominal income has to change when the money supply changes. But is k some stable number like, say, $\frac{1}{3}$? Surely not. In chapter 12, we saw that the real quantity of money demanded is a function of the interest rate. One can think of real money as being like any other commodity with the quantity that people want to hold depending on the cost of holding it, the costs of holding related commodities, on income or wealth, and on tastes.

Hence, Friedman's version of the quantity theory treats the quantity of money demanded (and thus k) not as a stable *number,* but as a

---

[4] See Milton Friedman, ed., *Studies in the Quantity Theory of Money* (Chicago: University of Chicago Press, 1956); and David Meiselman, ed., *Varieties of Monetary Experience* (Chicago: University of Chicago Press, 1970).

stable *function* of other variables.[5] If the demand for money is, in fact, a stable function of a few measurable variables, then, if the values of these variables are known, one can predict how much money will be demanded. Suppose that, as we assumed in drawing the *LM* curve, the demand for nominal money is a function of nominal income (Y_n) and the nominal interest rate (i), that is:

$$(1)\ M^d = f(\overset{+}{Y_n}, \overset{-}{i})$$

Since the empirical evidence suggests that supply and demand for money are fairly soon equilibrated by the money market, we can write:

$$(2)\ M^s = M^d = f(\overset{+}{Y_n}, \overset{-}{i});$$

or, more specifically

$$(3)\ M^s = M^d = a + b\overset{+}{Y_n} - \overset{-}{c}i,$$

where a, b and c are known constants. Now suppose that we also know i. In this case, *once we are told what will happen to the nominal money stock we know how nominal income must change to make equation (3) hold.* This is the approach of Friedman's refurbished quantity theory.

Keynesian theory teaches us that the factors that bring about changes in income are changes in the propensity to consume, the marginal efficiency of investment, liquidity preference, and the stock of money. What happens to all of these factors in Friedman's theory? One of them, the stock of money, is obviously included, and, in fact, plays the starring role. Another one, an autonomous change in the liquidity preference curve, is de-emphasized because of Friedman's belief that the money-demand function is stable.

The other two factors, changes in the propensity to consume and in the marginal efficiency of investment, enter Friedman's theory only indirectly. Suppose that households decide to raise their consumption, or firms their investment. In either case nominal income starts to rise. But equation (3) tells us that if the money supply is constant and income rises, then the interest rate must rise too. Put another way, if the public wants to spend more, it tries to get hold of more money to finance these increased expenditures. This increase in the demand for money raises the interest rate. This, in turn, reduces the Cambridge k, that is, it raises velocity. Thus, since changes in the propensity to consume and in the marginal efficiency of investment en-

[5] Another way in which Friedman has modified the traditional quantity theory is that he uses it primarily to determine nominal income rather than prices. The traditional quantity theory was a theory of the long run in which prices adapted to changes in the quantity of money while output was unaffected. Since Friedman wants to use it for the short run too, and further, since the Great Depression had demonstrated how inflexible downward prices can be, Friedman no longer makes it a theory of prices per se.

ter Friedman's theory indirectly, there is no substantive difference between the two theories on this formal abstract level.

The real disagreements relate to empirical issues. First, Friedman believes that the demand for money function is stable, while Keynesians believe that it varies more. In terms of equation (3) they believe that the coefficients *a, b,* and *c* vary at different times.

The second difference relates to the role of the rate of interest. Suppose that the quantity theorists are correct in saying that the money-demand function is stable, but contrary to their views suppose that the interest elasticity of demand for money is very high. (Alternatively, one could assume that the interest elasticity of investment and consumption is very low.) Assume also that prices are constant. If so, when the stock of money rises, the stable money-demand function, as the quantity theory claims, allows us to predict by how much income rises. *But,* contrary to the quantity theory, this rise in income is quite small instead of being strictly proportional to the rise in the money stock. Most of the increase in the money stock finds willing holders, not because nominal income has increased, but because the interest rate is lower.

And if a given change in the money stock generates only a relatively small change in income, this makes it at least somewhat more probable that the variations in the money stock that have actually occurred are not the main cause of the observed fluctuations in income.

Consequently, to maintain the quantity theory, Friedman must rely on one or more of the following three positions. One is that the interest elasticity of the demand for money is low. The second is that an increase in the supply of money does not lower the interest rate by much. (Insofar as the interest rate does not change much, the interest elasticity of demand for money has little room for play.) The third is that historically fluctuations in the money stock have been much greater than fluctuations in the chief Keynesian variable, investment. If the money stock has actually varied much more, then the fact that a significant part of the resulting variation in *kPT* has been absorbed by changes in *k* would still allow changes in the money stock to be responsible for most of the observed variation in *PT,* that is, in money income.

Friedman has taken all three of these approaches by examining empirically the relation between fluctuations in money and in income. First, his statistical analysis of the demand for money since 1869 has convinced him that most of the observed changes in the demand for money are the result of changes in permanent income, and that the interest rate plays only a small role in explaining the demand for money.[6] But this empirical analysis has been disputed by other economists who argue, from the same or similar data, that a decline in the interest rate *does* play a significant role

---

[6] He has sometimes been interpreted as saying that the interest elasticity of the demand for money is zero. But this is a misinterpretation. He estimates this elasticity at about −0.15. See Milton Friedman, *The Optimum Quantity of Money* (Chicago: Aldine Publishing Co., 1969), pp. 142–43n.

in making the public willing to hold additional money. And the evidence they have presented is persuasive. The second approach, which focuses on the way interest rates respond to changes in the money stock, needs more detailed discussion.

The Behavior of Interest Rates

Suppose one grants, even if only for the sake of argument, that the interest elasticity of demand for money is high, say 5. An increase in the quantity of money would still have a strictly proportional effect on nominal income, *if* it does not lower the interest rate. In (3) if i is constant, a change in M^s will have all of its impact on Y, regardless of the magnitude of c. Now Friedman agrees with other economists that the *initial* effect of a rise in the growth rate of the money stock is to lower the interest rate. It takes some time for income to rise and, in the meantime, the interest rate must fall by enough to make the public willing to hold all the additional money. But Friedman believes that although the nominal interest rate falls for a time when the quantity of money increases, it soon starts to rise again, and after about a year and a half is back to where it was initially.[7] What happens is that the fall in the expected real interest rate stimulates expenditures, and the resulting increase in nominal income then raises the interest rate again.[8] And as people realize that prices are rising they include an inflation premium in the nominal interest rate, so that it ultimately rises *above* its previous level.

Figure 16.1   Behavior of Interest Rates

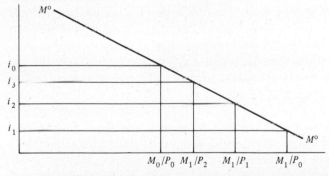

The return of the interest rate to its previous level is shown in figure 16.1. Suppose that the quantity of money is initially M_0/P_0 and the in-

---

[7] Milton Friedman, "The Role of Monetary Policy," *American Economic Review* 58 (March 1968): 1–17.

[8] Why the *expected real* rate? In deciding how much to invest firms are concerned about the real, rather than the nominal, rate. If prices rise at, say, a 5 percent rate, then an 8 percent nominal rate is no more burdensome than a 3 percent nominal rate would be at a time when prices are stable. But when making an investment decision, firms do not know how much prices will actually rise; all they can do is to form some expectation of the future inflation rate and subtract this from the nominal rate to obtain the expected real rate of interest.

terest rate is i_0. (Figure 16.1 takes real income as constant. It also makes no allowance for the addition of an inflation premium as people realize that prices will rise.) Since we start from an equilibrium in which prices are stable, this initial interest rate, i_0, is just high enough to maintain price stability. The nominal quantity of money now increases to M_1. Initially the *real* money supply becomes M_1/P_0, prices not yet having adjusted to the increase in the money supply. But at M_1/P_0 the interest rate is i_1, which is below the level required to keep prices stable. So prices now rise. As a result of this rise in prices, the *real* money stock now falls, first to M_1/P_1, which results in an interest rate of i_2, and then to M_1/P_2, so that the interest rate rises to i_3. But i_3 is still below i_0, so prices continue to rise. And they rise until the economy has returned to the initial real money stock and the initial interest rate, i_0, the interest rate that is just high enough to keep prices stable.

Thus Friedman believes that, except for a relatively brief transition period, it does not matter whether the interest elasticity of the demand for money is high or low. When the nominal stock of money increases, rising prices soon bring the *real* money stock, and hence the interest rate, back to the previous levels. Similarly, it does not matter, in principle, whether the interest elasticities of investment and consumption are high or low as long as they are not zero. If they were zero, then the fall in the interest rate would not result in any increase in expenditures, prices would not rise, and the interest rate would remain at i_1.

To see the Keynesian response to this, consider first a model in which prices are completely inflexible. As in Friedman's analysis, when the money stock increases the interest rate falls, and then starts to rise again. But now it cannot rise all the way back to its previous level. The only reason it rises is that real income is higher than before. But if the interest rate *were* to rise back to its previous level, then expenditures, and hence real income, would be *no* higher than before. Hence, to say that the interest rate returns *all the way* to its previous level would involve an inconsistency; it has to settle at some point like, say, i_3 in figure 16.1. And with the interest rate being below its previous level, k is greater than before, so that the rise in the money stock leads to a less than strictly proportional rise in income. (By contrast, if prices are completely flexible the interest rate can return to i_0 because no increase in real income, which would require a lower interest rate, is needed; with prices having risen in strict proportion to the increase in the money stock, so has the demand for money.)

Keynesians usually do not assume that prices are completely inflexible, but they do believe that prices adjust only slowly. This may seem strange, given the rapid rise of prices in recent years, but remember that we have to consider not only cases in which the money stock is increasing, but also cases in which it is decreasing. The latter requires falling prices to restore equilibrium, and prices are much stickier downwards than upwards. Hence, in Keynesian analysis when the quantity of money changes, it takes a long time for the interest rate to return to its previous level. Thus for a time span long enough to be relevant for the more interesting policy problems, say, five years, a rise in the money stock does lower the interest rate, and therefore raises k. As a result of this change in k, money income rises by less than the increase in the money stock.

An important point of disagreement between Friedman and the Keynesians is therefore the speed with which prices adjust. Who is right is an empirical question, but unfortunately the empirical evidence can be interpreted in two ways. While some statistical studies support Friedman's contention, others support the Keynesian case.[9]

In subsequent work Friedman has elaborated this analysis further.[10] For a time period long enough to be relevant for most of the important problems, he takes the *real* rate of interest as constant, and hence unaffected by changes in the quantity of money. If the supply of money is increased, nominal income rises, and the resulting expectations of a rise in prices cause the *nominal* interest rate to rise since borrowers and lenders add an inflation premium to the interest rate, thus keeping the expected real rate constant. This increase in the nominal interest rate in turn raises velocity. This may seem like a contradiction of the quantity theory since nominal income now rises *more* than strictly proportionately to the rise in the stock of money. But the sequence of events is that the previous increases in the money stock caused prices to rise, which raised the nominal interest rate, which, in turn, raised velocity. Hence, that part of the rise in nominal income that is not due directly to the increase in the money supply is due indirectly (via the increase in velocity) to a previous rise in the money stock. Thus the quantity-theory conclusion, that it is changes in the money stock that ultimately drive income, is vindicated.

Other Aspects of the Chicago Approach

Three additional aspects of the Chicago approach remain to be discussed. First, does it allow one to determine the impact of a change in the money stock on income in a precise way? Second, what is the *process* by which changes in the money stock bring about changes in nominal income? Third, what role does it leave for fiscal policy?

Predicting nominal income. Suppose that the money stock increases by 10 percent. Initially, the real interest rate falls, but when after some time it has returned to its previous level nominal income must have risen by just enough to make the public willing to hold 10 percent more money. How

[9] For example, the Federal Reserve's large econometric model has an increase in the quantity of money lowering interest rates for a long time. On the other hand, a study by Phillip Cagan and Arthur Gandolfi ("The Lag of Monetary Policy As Implied by the Time Pattern of Monetary Effects on Interest Rates," *American Economic Review* 59 [May 1969]:277–83) supports Friedman.

[10] Milton Friedman, *A Theoretical Framework for Monetary Analysis* (New York: National Bureau of Economic Research, Occasional Paper 112, 1971).

much of a rise in nominal income is this? And does it depend upon whether the rise in nominal income is a rise in real income or in prices?

Suppose, first, that *real* income is constant, so that all the increase in nominal income is the result of an increase in prices. If the public is fully aware of what is happening but does not expect any further price increases, it will want to hold the same real quantity of money as before. Hence, prices, and therefore nominal income, must rise by 10 percent too, so that M/P is back at its previous level.

Now drop the assumption that real income is constant, but assume instead that prices are constant. In this case the income elasticity of demand for real money (that is, the percentage change in the real quantity of money demanded per one percent change in real income) tells us by how much real income must rise to make the public willing to hold 10 percent more real money. If this income elasticity is 0.5, real income must rise by 20 percent (10%/0.5), but if it is 2.0, real income must rise only 5 percent. Only in the special case in which the income elasticity of demand for real money just happens to be unity would real income rise exactly in proportion to the increase in the money stock.

Finally, there is the in-between case in which both prices and real income rise. Assuming again that there is no money illusion, the rise in nominal income when the money supply increases by 10 percent depends on (1) the income elasticity of demand for real money and (2) the division of the rise in nominal income between prices and real income. Suppose, for example, that the income elasticity of demand for real money is 0.8 and that real income rises by 5 percent. This generates a 4 percent (5% × 0.8) rise in the demand for real money, and to absorb the remaining 6 percent of additional money, prices must rise by 6 percent. Thus, nominal income rises by 11 percent, despite the fact that the money stock rose by only 10 percent. By contrast, if the income elasticity of demand for real money is, say, 1.5, then the 5 percent rise in real income generates a 7.5 percent (5% × 1.5) increase in the demand for real money, so that prices have to rises by only 2.5 percent (10% – 7.5%) to absorb the 10 percent increase in the money stock. Hence, nominal income rises by 7.5 percent. Or, instead of having real income rise by 5 percent, assume that it rises by only 2 percent. If the income elasticity of demand for real money is again 0.8, then this raises the demand for money by 1.6 percent (2% × 0.8) and prices have to rise by 8.4 percent (10% – (2% × 0.8)) so that nominal income rises by 10.4 percent (8.4% + 2.0%). Hence, the strict quantity-theory result that the money stock and nominal income change strictly proportionately does not apply to the short run in which real income is variable, unless the income elasticity of demand for real money is unity. Moreover, to predict short-run changes in nominal income in the case in which the real income elasticity of demand for money differs substantially from unity, one has to know how much of the rise in nominal income represents a rise in prices and how much a rise in real income. Since sometimes this is not easy to predict, this weakens the quantity theory as well as other macroeconomic theories. However, this does not matter in the long run since then a rise in the money stock raises only prices and not real income.

The transmission mechanism. What is the mechanism, usually called the **transmission process,** by which money affects income? The simple Keynesian theory spells it out by saying that an *increase in the money supply lowers the interest rate, which raises the present value of future income streams, and hence makes investment more profitable.* In chapter 14 we described several other transmission channels, among them the effect on consumption. Friedman's explanation of the transmission process differs in three ways.

First, he does not refer to the interest rate, but instead says that when people hold excess money balances they raise their expenditures in an attempt to bring their money holdings into equilibrium. This difference between the Friedman and Keynesian approaches is not basic. In a formal sense, one can relate any point on a demand curve to either the price or the quantity axis, and no fundamental point of theory is involved in whether one says that the quantity of money has increased or that the interest rate has fallen.

The reason why Friedman talks in terms of the quantity of money rather than the interest rate is that the interest rate is hard to measure. To start with, there are many different interest rates, for example, interest rates on Treasury bills, consumer loans, long-term corporate bonds, bank loans, and so on. How can one combine all of these rates into something that corresponds to what in economic theory is called "the interest rate"? Moreover, insofar as credit is rationed, and not made available freely at the prevailing interest rate, the interest rate does not measure properly the cost and difficulty of borrowing. Beyond this, some important interest rates, such as the imputed rate firms charge themselves when they invest in capital equipment, are simply not known.

In addition, to predict expenditures one should look at neither the real nor the nominal interest rate, but at the *real interest rate people expect to pay* when they make expenditure decisions. Since all we can observe in the market are actual interest rates, to figure out what the *expected real* rate of interest is, one would have to know people's price expectations. But we do not know these.

Friedman believes that these problems in measuring the rate of interest are much more severe than the problems encountered in measuring the nominal money stock. Hence he describes the process as one of excess cash balances being spent, rather than as an increase in the money supply lowering the interest rate and thereby stimulating expenditures.

A second difference between *some* Keynesian versions of the transmission process and Friedman's version is that in the latter changes in the money supply affect not only investment but also consumption. Friedman does not try to determine which is the bigger effect. Since consumption is a much bigger total than investment, a change in the money stock *could* have the major part of its impact on income via consumption even if the interest elasticity of investment is much greater than the interest elasticity of consumption.

But while Keynes himself assumed that changes in the money stock would directly affect only investment and not consumption, many modern Keynesians believe that consumption is affected too. And in chapter 14, we described in some detail how this effect operates.

A third and related difference is that Friedman believes that changes in the money stock affect expenditures in so many and such complicated ways, that it is useless to try to find them all. Any attempt to do so would surely fail to find some of them, and would therefore underestimate the total effect that money has on income. Hence, instead of trying to set out an ambitious econometric model, Friedman (who, in any case, has less faith than most Keynesians in large econometric models) prefers to follow a different approach. This is to compare changes in the money supply and in nominal income over time without trying to trace through the particular channels by which money affects income. This has caused many other economists to criticize him for relying on a sort of "black box" where changes in the money stock are seen going in at one end and changes in income emerge at the other end, without the process that is at work being known. This point is often put by saying that Friedman is relying on a mere correlation of changes in money and in income, and that there are numerous examples in economics of correlations that do not prove that one variable is causing the other. For example, there is a correlation between the number of school teachers in a city and per capita alcohol consumption. On the other hand, Friedman believes that the empirical evidence—to be discussed below—shows that the correlation between money and prices is causal rather than spurious. Moreover, remember that economic theory tells us that when the supply of an item—for example, money—increases, its price—the purchasing power of money—falls.

Fiscal policy. Another difference between Friedman's theory and Keynesian theory concerns the role of fiscal policy. In a Keynesian model an increase in government expenditures (or any other outward shift of the *IS* curve) has several effects on income. It raises aggregate demand both directly and indirectly via the multiplier (and perhaps the accelerator), but it also tends to lower aggregate demand by raising the interest rate (as we move along the *LM* curve). Except in the extreme case of a completely vertical *LM* curve, the net effect of an increase in government expenditures or of a tax cut is to increase aggregate demand. In Friedman's analysis, however, while a rise in government expenditures could, in principle, raise aggregate demand (since k is falling as government borrowing pushes up interest rates), as an empirical matter government expenditures have virtually no effect on aggregate demand; they simply "crowd out" an equivalent amount of investment and consumption.[11] This does not mean that Friedman looks upon increases in government expenditures with equanimity. Far from it. First, on broad philosophical grounds, he opposes the growth in the public sector at the expense of the private sector, and, second, as an increase in government expenditures raises the interest rate there is often pressure on the Federal Reserve to increase the money supply at a faster rate in an (ultimately vain) attempt to lower the interest rate again. And these increases in the money supply can, of course, be inflationary.

The Behavior of Money and Income: Empirical Evidence

We have just said that Friedman's critics claim that his evidence consists of mere correlations. Just what are these correlations, and are they really "mere"? Figure 16.2, taken from a 1963 article by Friedman and

Figure 16.2   Moving Standard Deviation[a] of Annual Rates of Change in Money (1869–1958) and in Income (1871–1958)

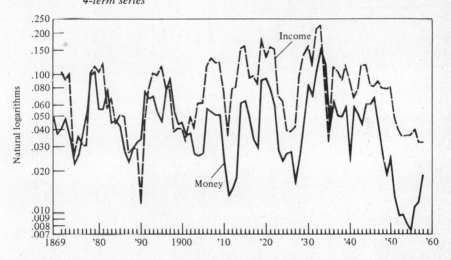

SOURCE: Milton Friedman and Anna Schwartz, "Money and Business Cycles," *Review of Economics and Statistics* 45 (February 1963): supplement, p. 41.

a. The figure charts moving standard deviations of money and income. This needs explaining. To calculate the standard deviation (which is a measure of the variation of a series), take the deviation of each observation from the mean and square it. Then divide the sum of these squared deviations by the number of observations minus one. Then take the square root of the result and this is the standard deviation. To get moving standard deviations calculate the standard deviation of several successive observations and attribute this figure to the middle year (or month) for the several observations. Then drop the first observation from the calculation and add a new one, and so on.

11 This crowding out does not occur right away, and hence an increase in government expenditure does raise nominal income for some time. In Friedman's analysis complete crowding out does not require a vertical *LM* curve because the rise in interest rates is supplemented by certain effects on wealth that also reduce consumption and investment.

Schwartz, shows a measure of the variation in the growth rate of the money stock (M_2) and nominal income from 1869 to 1958. These two series show an obvious correlation. This work has been corroborated and updated by Byron Higgins.[12] He calculated the ratio of the actual level of the money stock to what it would have been if it had grown over the last twelve months at the same rate as it was growing during the previous two years. This ratio, which he called the A/E (actual/extrapolated) ratio, is, of course, below unity if the money stock has grown at a lower rate during the past twelve months than during the previous two years. As figure 16.3 illustrates, this ratio always has fallen prior to a recession. And table 16.1 shows that—with one exception, 1966–67—every appreciable fall in this ratio has been followed by a recession.

Figure 16.3   A/E Ratios of Real and Nominal Money
              1952–78

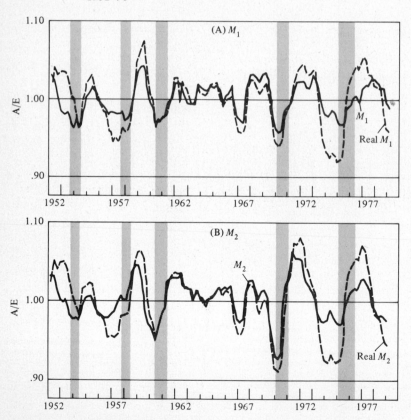

Note: Shaded areas indicate recessions.

SOURCE: Byron Higgins, "Monetary Growth and Business Cycles," *Economic Review* (Federal Reserve Bank of Kansas City) 64 (April 1979): 18–19.

[12] Byron Higgins, "Monetary Growth and Business Cycles," *Economic Review* (Federal Reserve Bank of Kansas City) 64 (April 1979): 12–23.

Table 16.1   Measures of the Degree of Monetary Deceleration

Periods of monetary deceleration	Minimum A/E ratios for:			
	M_1	M_2	Real M_1	Real M_2
1953–54[a]	.965	.979	.970	.984
1956–58[a]	.978	.980[b]	.984	.958
1960–61[a]	.965	.952	.966	.953
1962–63	.996	—[c]	.996	—[c]
1964	—	.999	—	.996
1965	.998	—[c]	.993	—[c]
1966–67	.971	.976	.960	.961
1969–70[a]	.960	.930	.940	.912
1973–75[a]	.968	.972	.923	.924
1976	.995	—[c]	—	—[c]

a. Monetary decelerations that were associated with a recession.

b. The period of deceleration in M_2 growth ended before the beginning of the recession in September 1957, and the minimum A/E ratio for M_2 occurred in June 1956. Because deceleration in the growth of all of the other monetary measures continued into the recession, however, it is reasonable to interpret the deceleration of M_2 growth in 1956 as being associated with the subsequent recession.

c. Minimum A/E ratios are reported only for monetary measures whose growth rates decelerated in the period.

SOURCE: Byron Higgins, "Monetary Growth and Business Cycles," *Economic Review* (Federal Reserve Bank of Kansas City) 64 (April 1979): 20.

Another way to illustrate the importance of money is to see how well changes in the money stock can explain changes in the consumer price index. Since money is not the only variable that affects prices (and Friedman never claimed that it is) an equation that tries to explain the percentage changes in the price index should include some other variables too. One such equation, developed by the staff of a congressional committee, uses the percentage change of the money stock two years earlier, the percentage changes in import prices, a special factor (a so-called dummy variable) to take account of the Korean War, and the previous year's percentage increase in the consumer price index. As figure 16.4 shows this equation gives a good explanation of past price changes, though as it subsequently turned out, and as is so often the case with regression analysis, its prediction for the future was not as good.

Does this high correlation between money and income mean that changes in the money growth rate cause changes in income, or should the correlation be interpreted the other way round, as changes in income causing changes in the money growth rate? In the latter case the correlation would certainly not be evidence supporting the quantity theory. Friedman and Schwartz support the hypothesis that causation runs from money to income in several ways. One is that they, as well as Phillip Cagan of Columbia University, have undertaken extensive historical studies of what factors

Figure 16.4   Consumer Price Index Year-to-Year Percent Change

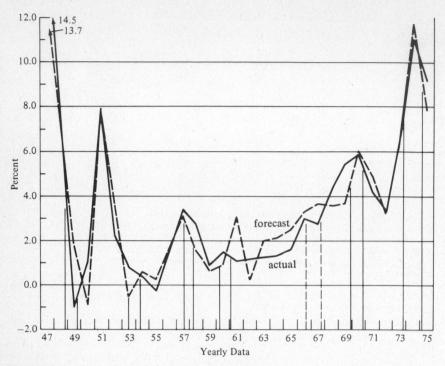

Note: Lines from the time axis delineate recession periods.

SOURCE: U.S., Congress, House, Committee on Banking, Finance, and Urban Affairs, Subcommittee on Domestic Monetary Policy, *The Impact of the Federal Reserve System's Monetary Policy on the Nation's Economy,* December 1976, p. 29.

caused the money stock to change. They concluded that in the severe recessions, such as the 1920–21 recession or the 1929–33 recession, the money stock fell for some specific reason other than a fall in income, such as widespread bank failures or a restrictive Federal Reserve policy. Hence, they argued, in these cases causation *must* have run from money to income since we know that what caused the decline in the money stock was something other than the drop in income. Similarly, large increases in the money stock can be explained by factors such as the development of new techniques for refining gold. For the minor business recessions, which are by far the more common ones, Friedman and Schwartz concede that the historical evidence is not nearly so clear-cut. (This incidentally allows one to develop a compromise between the Keynesian and Friedmanian theories, by saying that Keynesian theory can explain the usual minor recessions, but that really severe recessions are caused by a decline in the money growth rate.) [13]

---

[13] Friedman and Schwartz have also pointed to the fact that the peak in the growth rate of the money stock usually occurs prior to the peak in business cycles, but they consider this to be much less important evidence for their hypothesis that

Critics of the quantity theory have argued that the close correlation between money and income is not persuasive evidence for the quantity theory because, at least under modern conditions, a rise in income can bring about a rise in the money stock. To start with, as we saw in chapter 9, the money multiplier is not completely rigid, but increases to some extent when the interest rate does. And as income rises it pulls the interest rate up with it. Second, and much more importantly, as we shall see in Part Four, the Federal Reserve tends to increase bank reserves and hence the money supply at a faster rate when income is rising.

Some Monetarist Propositions

As stated at the start of this chapter there is more to monetarism than just the quantity theory. The authors believe that it is possible to isolate twelve major issues in the Keynesian-monetarist dispute.[14] Underlying the debate on these issues is a basic difference relating to the length of the horizon of one's analysis, and the speed with which the economy adapts. Keynesians accept many monetarist views as correct in the long run, but not in the shorter run that is relevant for economic policy.[15] Six of these differences relate to economic theory and will be discussed now; the remaining six relate to policy, and will be deferred until chapter 28.

The first and most basic of these six is the monetarist's belief in the quantity theory. The second is an hypothesis about the *way* in which changes in the money stock affect income, that is, the transmission process. We have already discussed Friedman's version of the transmission process, and in the next chapter we will look at the transmission process of two other prominent monetarists, Brunner and Meltzer.

Third, monetarists believe that the private sector of the economy is inherently stable; if only the government would not destabilize the economy by ill-considered policies, there would still be *some* fluctuations in income but we would have tolerable levels of unemployment and little inflation. Keynesians, on the other hand, by and large, believe that the private economy is inherently unstable, and that fiscal and monetary policies are therefore needed to stabilize it. This is obviously a very important issue and we will discuss it at some length in the next section.

---

causation runs from money to income than the just discussed historical evidence. In any case, as James Tobin ("Money and Income: Post Hoc, Ergo Propter Hoc," *Quarterly Journal of Economics* 84 [May 1970]: 301–17) has shown, this evidence is of doubtful value because one can develop a model in which income change is the cause and the change in the money growth rate the effect, and yet the money growth rate shows an earlier peak than does income. For a detailed presentation of the Friedman-Schwartz evidence see Milton Friedman, *The Optimum Quantity of Money* (Chicago: Aldine Publishing Co., 1969), ch. 10.

[14] For a further discussion of these issues see Thomas Mayer et al., *The Structure of Monetarism* (New York: W. W. Norton, 1978).

[15] Keynes made his famous statement, "in the long run we are all dead," as a response to the quantity theory. (*A Tract on Monetary Reform* [London: Macmillan, 1924], p. 80.

The next monetarist proposition is a subtle one relating to research strategy. It asserts that to determine nominal income one need look only at the factors changing aggregate demand as a whole, such as changes in the quantity of money, and can ignore the allocation of this demand among different sectors of the economy. By contrast, Keynesians determine aggregate demand by combining the demands in various sectors of the economy since they think of aggregate demand as being determined by the incentives to spend in these sectors. For example, both Keynesians and monetarists agree that when the money stock increases nominal income rises. In monetarist theory this occurs because the public raises its expenditures to bring its real money holdings back down to equilibrium. To determine what will happen to nominal income it is not necessary to go beyond this and ask what particular types of expenditures will increase; if some types of expenditures, for instance, the purchase of consumer durables, do not increase, others will increase even more to make up for this. By contrast, Keynesians reason that the rise in the money stock lowers interest rates, and they then investigate how expenditures in various sectors, such as in residential construction, respond to this fall in interest rates.

As a result, there is a fifth difference: while Keynesians generally like large-scale econometric models that describe various sectors of the economy in detail, monetarists prefer to use smaller, highly aggregated models, such as the St. Louis model described in the next chapter.

Finally, monetarists and Keynesians view the price level in a different way, with monetarists believing that prices are much more flexible—downward as well as upward—than Keynesians do. For example, suppose that the price of oil rises, say, by 20 percent. Keynesians tend to say that if oil accounts directly and indirectly as a raw material for, say, 10 percent of GNP, then this 20 percent rise in oil prices will raise the overall price level by two percent. Monetarists, on the other hand, say that, with the money stock held constant, much of the rise in the price of oil and oil products will be offset by declines in other prices (or, if an inflation is already going on, in the rate at which other prices are rising). If the price level were to rise by 2 percent, then the demand for nominal money would increase and exceed the supply, with the result that aggregate demand would fall, and hence prices would decline again.

These propositions are connected in many ways. Thus, one can readily see the quantity theory at work in the example of the rise in oil prices, and also in the monetarist proposition that one does not have to look at demands in various sectors of the economy to determine aggregate demand.[16] Similarly, viewing the private economy as basically stable fits in well with the hypothesis that the demand for money is stable. And if the private economy is stable, then there is less reason to bother about demand in particular sectors. Moreover, if one thinks of the price level as a single unit, so

[16] But one has to look at much more than aggregate demand to determine what will be the change in prices as opposed to changes in output.

that wage and price increases in one sector are offset by wage and price decreases (or a slowdown in the rate of increase) in other sectors along the lines of the above example of oil prices, then the economy is much less subject to cost-push inflation, and hence is stable in this sense. Furthermore, if one does not have to bother with allocative detail in various sectors, then why use a large econometric model? Thus these six monetarist propositions form an interconnected whole, though they are *not* so closely connected that to accept any one of them means that one *has* to accept the others as well.

The Stability Issue

An important issue on which Keynesians and monetarists disagree is the stability of a private enterprise economy, that is, its ability to avoid—without the help of government stabilization policies—substantial periods of extensive unemployment and severe inflations.[17] The Keynesian approach developed as a response to the unstable behavior of the economy. For nearly two hundred years before World War II, the progress of capitalist countries was periodically interrupted by panics, recessions, and depressions. The Great Depression of the 1930s was the last straw. Although monetarists attribute this and other severe depressions to sharp declines in the growth rate of the money stock, the Great Depression was widely interpreted as a result not of poor monetary arrangements but as an inherent fault in the capitalist system. Governments in all developed market economies became committed to interventionist policies aimed at preventing or limiting the erratic movements of production and employment that had caused so much waste and suffering in the past. Keynesian income-expenditure analysis provided a rationale for interventionist stabilization policy and a paradigm for the analysis of alternative stabilization policies.

Keynes's theory emphasized the instability of private investment and at the same time deprecated the notion that the private economy contained adjustment mechanisms that could offset the variations in income generated by variations in investment. Keynesians attributed the instability of investment to variations in the investment opportunities generated by new techniques and new products. They also supposed that those variations in investment were accentuated by speculation in security markets. Moreover, Keynes and his followers emphasized the tendency for swings in investment to feed on themselves. Increasing investment would increase consumption spending through the multiplier, and the resulting improvement in capacity utilization would cause further increases in investment in sectors not originally involved in the investment boom. When the original impetus weakens, the whole process could go into reverse. Much of the earlier business-cycle

---

[17] For an example of the Keynesian view, see Hyman Minsky, *John Maynard Keynes* (New York: Columbia University Press, 1975).

literature was based on similar arguments. Keynes and his followers could support their argument by pointing to the great stock-market boom of the late 1920s, to the Florida land boom of the early 1920s, to many cycles in land speculation, and to a succession of railroad booms in the 1900s.

In analyzing the sources of instability in an economic system, we have to make a distinction between primary causes of instability and the secondary responses of the system to those primary impulses. The oil shock of 1973–74 stands as a classic example of a primary shock or cause of instability. Multiplier response to a change in investment is a simple example of a secondary response.

Inventory cycles provide a more complex case. A rise in the rate of growth of income will tend to increase the rate of inventory investment, and that, in turn, will contribute to a further increase in the rate of growth of income. Exhaustion of the original impulse that sets off the boom not only slows down the growth of income directly but will cause inventory investment to decline and might even cause an absolute drop in output. In that case, producers will have excessive inventories, and will for a time attempt to reduce them so that inventory investment becomes negative. That, of course, will make the situation even worse, causing a further decline in income and accentuating inventory problems. Because inventory investment is only a small part of the total GNP, it will usually be possible to work off excess inventories. Nonetheless, the inventory mechanism can cause a fluctuation in output out of proportion to the original impulse that changed investment and the rate of growth of output.

Monetarists agree with Keynesians that all of these factors can, *in principle,* create economic fluctuations. However, monetarists argue that *as an empirical proposition* much the greater part of the income fluctuations we have actually experienced have been due to variations in the growth rate of the money stock. Second, monetarists put less emphasis than Keynesians on the *macroeconomic* effects of a given exogenous shock because they focus on the supply and demand for money, which works as an automatic stabilizer. Suppose, for example, that an innovation greatly raises investment in the airline industry. To the extent that these investment expenditures are not offset by declining investment in, say, the automobile industry, they tend to raise both output and prices. But as output and prices, and hence nominal income, rise, $k,$ the ratio of money to nominal income, falls. Ignoring changing interest rates for the moment, why should the public be willing to reduce its k? Since people are initially holding their desired ratio of money to nominal income, as nominal income rises, everyone will try to increase his or her money holdings. And they do this by cutting expenditures (or selling assets), so that the increase in output and prices in the industries producing the new capital goods for the airlines are offset by falling output or prices in other industries.

To be sure, the assumption that the public wants its k to remain constant is extreme and implausible because as the airlines invest more, the interest rate rises, and hence the public will want its k to fall. But monetarists believe that the interest elasticity of the demand for money is not very great, so that an investment boom lowers k only moderately. With the money stock constant and k falling only moderately, income rises only moderately. In monetarist analysis shocks, such as innovations, have much more effect on *relative* outputs and *relative* prices than they do on total output and the overall price level.

Third, while monetarists agree that the economy is subject to *some* shocks, they do not believe that these shocks (apart from those resulting from government policy) are as frequent and as big as many Keynesians claim. And the previously discussed secondary responses of consumption and investment need not be large either. One issue involved here is whether consumption depends mainly on income in the current year, or on income over a much longer period of time. If consumption is heavily dependent on income of previous years, then the marginal propensity to consume out of *current* income is relatively low, so that the multiplier is low too. Hence, changes in investment have relatively little effect on income. Similarly, if investment depends on the change in sales over several years, rather than in just one year, investment is stabler, because erratic swings in sales in any one year tend to offset each other.

The question whether a capitalist economy is stable or needs government intervention to avoid an unacceptable level of unemployment or inflation is obviously a very important one. Unfortunately, it is a question easier to pose than to answer. In the authors' view there is no convincing empirical evidence that would allow one to decide who is right. The following illustrates some of the problems encountered in trying to answer this question. One possible approach is to take an econometric model and put into it a stable monetary and fiscal policy in place of the policy actually followed, to see if the model then shows less fluctuation in income than was actually experienced. But, unfortunately, there is disagreement about what this shows. Another possible approach is to ask whether the economy has been more stable in the postwar years in which stabilization policy was used than before 1930 when it was not used. It turns out that it is more stable now, but monetarists can reply that this is due to the more erratic fluctuations in the money stock before 1930. A third approach is to ask whether in those countries in which the government does relatively little to stabilize income, income is actually stabler than it is in those countries that follow stronger stabilization policies. But the problem here is to determine the direction of causation. Certain countries may follow stronger stabilization policies precisely because they experience more income fluctuations.

Summary

This chapter has dealt with the quantity theory and monetarism. It first set out the basis of the quantity theory, which is a focus on equilibrium in the money market. If the money stock increases, then expenditures increase as the public runs down its excess money balances.

The Chicago approach to the quantity theory asserts that the demand for money is a stable function of a limited set of other variables, rather than being a stable number. It agrees with Keynesian theory that the demand for money has some interest elasticity, and shows that this is entirely consistent with the quantity theory. This is so, because if prices are fully flexible an increase in the money stock reduces the interest rate only temporarily. As the interest rate falls, expenditures increase, and hence prices and real income rise. This, in turn, causes the nominal quantity of money demanded to increase, until the expected real interest rate is again back at its previous equilibrium level, so that *k* is back at its previous equilibrium too.

We then discussed the magnitude of the rise in nominal income, and saw that this depends not only on the increase in the money stock, but also on the division of the rise in nominal income between prices and real incomes, as well as on the income elasticity of demand for real money. We then took up the transmission mechanism and discussed why Friedman formulates it in terms of changes in the money stock rather than in terms of changes in the interest rate, and why he does not spell it out in detail. We also discussed briefly Friedman's views on fiscal policy. After that we looked at the empirical evidence that shows a high correlation between changes in money and changes in income or prices, and discussed briefly whether this indicates that changes in money *cause* changes in nominal income.

We then turned to a broader set of ideas known as monetarism, and discussed six of its propositions. They are the validity of the quantity theory, a particular transmission process going from money to income, the stability of the private sector, the focus on aggregate demand as a whole rather than on its allocation between specific sectors of the economy, the focus on the price level as a unit, and a preference for small rather than large econometric models. These six propositions are interrelated. We then took one of these, the stability of the private sector, and discussed both the Keynesian and monetarist hypotheses about it.

QUESTIONS AND EXERCISES

1. Describe, in your own words, the *basic* idea behind the quantity theory.
2. If both the interest rate and real income are constant, and there is no money illusion, then a 10 percent rise in the money stock results in a 10 percent rise in nominal income. Discuss.
3. Show why a rise in the money stock would lead to a proportional increase in prices if (a) the demand for money is completely interest inelastic, or, alternatively, (b) if prices are flexible and the economy is at full employment.
4. "The disagreement between the Friedmanian theory and the Keynesian theory are not matters of economic theory, but are empirical issues." Discuss.
5. What are the main reasons why Friedman and the Keynesians come up with different answers?
6. Look up recent data on the money stock and on income. (They can be

found in the appendix of the *Economic Report of the President,* for example.) See if these data support Friedman's theory. Also calculate the Cambridge *k*. How stable has it been?

7. Germany experienced a hyperinflation after World War I. In November 1923 wholesale prices were one *billion* times what they had been sixteen months earlier. But in this period, the stock of money (as measured by the currency circulation of the central bank) was only (!) about twenty-one million times what it was sixteen months before. How can this be explained? Does it contradict the quantity theory?

FURTHER READING

BERMAN, PETER. *Inflation and the Money Supply in the United States.* Lexington, Ky.: Lexington Books, 1978. An interesting explanation of inflation based on changes in the money growth rate.

DAVIS, RICHARD. "The Role of the Money Supply in Business Cycles." *Monthly Review* (Federal Reserve Bank of New York) 50 (April 1968): 63–73. A powerful critique of the Friedman-Schwartz evidence for the quantity theory.

FRIEDMAN, MILTON. "Money." In *International Encyclopedia of the Social Sciences.* An excellent survey of monetary theory from a quantity theory standpoint.

———. "The Role of Monetary Policy." *American Economic Review* 58 (March 1968): 1–17. A powerful argument that changes in the money stock depress interest rates only temporarily, and that the Phillips curve is in real terms.

———. *Studies in the Quantity Theory of Money.* Chicago: University of Chicago Press, 1956. A classic statement of Friedman's view together with essays by his students providing empirical evidence. Chapter one is particularly useful.

FRIEDMAN, MILTON, and SCHWARTZ, ANNA. "Money and Business Cycles." *Review of Economics and Statistics* 45 (February 1963) supplement: 32–64. An important survey of the empirical evidence for the quantity theory.

GORDON, ROBERT J., ed. *Friedman's Monetary Theory.* Chicago: Aldine Publishing Co., 1974. This is the definitive statement of Friedman's monetary theory together with criticisms by eminent economists and Friedman's reply.

LAIDLER, DAVID. "Money and Money Income: An Essay on the Transmission Mechanism." *Journal of Monetary Economics* 4 (April 1978): 151–92. An excellent survey of one of the major disputes about the quantity theory.

MAYER, THOMAS, et al. *The Structure of Monetarism.* New York: W. W. Norton, 1978. A survey of, and debate about, the broader aspects of monetarism by both monetarist and nonmonetarist economists.

POOLE, WILLIAM. "The Relationship of Monetary Decelerations to Business Cycle Peaks: Another Look at the Evidence." *Journal of Finance* 30 (June 1975): 697–712. An update of the Friedman-Schwartz evidence.

SELDEN, RICHARD. "Monetarism." In *Modern Economic Thought,* edited by Sidney Weintraub, pp. 253–74. Philadelphia: University of Pennsylvania Press, 1976. A very useful survey.

17

Monetarism: Additional Models

In the previous chapter we discussed some issues that are basic to the quantity theory and to monetarism, and took up one major variant of this approach, the work of the Chicago School. In this chapter we consider the three other leading variants, the St. Louis model, the work of Karl Brunner and Allan Meltzer, and Don Patinkin's real balance effect.

The St. Louis Approach

It may seem that the way to settle the Keynesian-monetarist debate is to undertake the following empirical test. Let both Keynesians and monetarists select the variables that according to their theories explain income, and put them into so-called regression equations. (Regression analysis is a statistical technique that tries to show how one or more independent variables affect a dependent variable. For example, if consumption (C) is regressed on the money stock (M) the computer is told to find values for a and b in the equation $C = a + bM$, so that the square of the differences between the predicted and actual values for C are minimized.) We can then see which regression better explains past movements in income or better predicts future income. (However, in appendix A, which follows this chapter, we point out why such a test is likely to be far from conclusive.) Specifically, to have a test that is directly relevant to the question of what policy tools the government should use, let us see if income can be explained or predicted better by looking at fiscal policy or at monetary policy. Since Keynesian theory asserts that changes both in the deficit and in the money stock bring about changes in nominal income, a finding that fiscal policy, as well as monetary policy, does so supports Keynesian theory. But if the data show there is little, if any, correlation between the deficit (or any other fiscal variable) and changes in nominal income, while changes in the money stock have a powerful effect on income, then the quantity theory is vindicated and Keynesian theory is rejected.

This test was undertaken by two economists, then at the Federal Reserve Bank of St. Louis, Leonall Andersen and Jerry Jordan, who built on an earlier test by Milton Friedman and David Meiselman.[1] The variables they used to explain income were the narrow money stock (M_1), and the monetary base (currency plus reserves with the Federal Reserve) as well as *high employment* federal government receipts, expenditures, and deficits. These high employment fiscal variables need explaining. Suppose one compares actual federal government deficits with nominal income, and observes that there is no correlation between them. This would not necessarily mean that increases in the deficit have no effect on income. What *may* be going on is the following: when an increase in government expenditure and hence in the deficit occurs, it raises nominal income, as Keynesian theory predicts. However, remember it is also true that if for some reason, say, a decline in the marginal efficiency of investment, income falls, this fall in income reduces government tax receipts and thus results in an increase in the deficit. In the first case—an increase in government expenditures—there is a positive correlation between the deficit and nominal income, and in the second case—a drop in income—there is a negative correlation since the deficit increases whenever income drops. The net result may well be that the data that combine instances of both of these cases show very little, if any, correlation between the deficit and nominal income, even though, in the situation we have posited, an increase in the deficit *does* raise nominal income. To minimize this problem Andersen and Jordan used, not the *actual* figures on the government's expenditures and deficits, but estimates of what government receipts and deficits would have been at a *given* level of income that corresponds to high employment.

The results Andersen and Jordan obtained are dramatic. Changes in the nominal money stock, or in the monetary base, have powerful effects on nominal income, but the fiscal policy variables have no lasting effects on income. They raise income in the calendar quarter in which they increase, and in some equations, in the next calendar quarter too, but in the subsequent quarters they lower income, so that over a year, their *net* effect is close to zero. These results suggest that fiscal policy is not a useful stabilization tool. Monetary policy—that is, changing the quantity of money—on the other hand, is a much more powerful tool. In addition, monetary policy affects income quicker and to a more predictable extent than fiscal policy does, and for these reasons too monetary policy appears to be the better policy tool. A subsequent study by Michael Keran (then also at the St. Louis

[1] See Leonall Andersen and Jerry Jordan, "Monetary and Fiscal Actions: A Test of Their Relative Importance in Economic Stabilization," *Review* (Federal Reserve Bank of St. Louis) 50 (November 1968): 11–23; Milton Friedman and David Meiselman, "The Relative Stability of Monetary Velocity and the Investment Multiplier," in *Stabilization Policies*, ed. Commission on Money and Credit (Englewood Cliffs, N.J.: Prentice Hall, 1963), pp. 165–268. The latter concluded that changes in the nominal money stock explain much of the change in nominal income, but that changes in the Keynesian variables (business investment, the deficit, and net exports) had very little effect on income. Not surprisingly this study gave rise to a debate (much of it in the September 1965 *American Economic Review*) that dealt mainly with the way in which Friedman and Meiselman had defined the variables they used to test the Keynesian theory.

Federal Reserve) found similar results for several other countries. These results surprised most economists. They led to an extensive debate of which we will discuss only a few highlights.

One set of criticisms relates to the monetary variables used by Andersen and Jordan, that is, the money stock (M_1) in some regressions and the monetary base in others. For their analysis to be valid, causation should run from these monetary variables to income, but not from income back to these monetary variables. Otherwise the observed correlation between changes in nominal income and in nominal money could hardly be used as an argument that changes in the money stock *cause* changes in income. But does the correlation run almost only from money to income, and not from income to money? The critics of Andersen and Jordan point out that as income rises so does the interest rate, and when interest rates rise the Fed tends to increase the monetary base. Moreover, as we discussed in chapter 9, a rise in the interest rate tends to raise the money multiplier, though the Fed may offset this by reducing the supply of reserves. Hence these critics believe that the high correlation Andersen and Jordan found between changes in money and in nominal income does not confirm the quantity theory. Andersen and Jordan, however, believe that causation does run *primarily* from money to income. It may seem that this criticism focuses on the wrong thing because what is surprising about the Andersen-Jordan study is not that the monetary variables are powerful, but that the fiscal variables are so weak. However, since the monetary and fiscal variables are correlated in their data, these two results are connected. In their regressions, reducing the role that monetary variables play raises the importance of the fiscal variables.

Another criticism focuses on the fact that Andersen and Jordan used a very simple model with only a single equation instead of a large-scale econometric model. (But Andersen and Jordan consider this a virtue of their analysis, in part because they believe that large-scale econometric models are so complex that nobody knows what really goes on in them.) Accordingly, Franco Modigliani of M.I.T. and Albert Ando of the University of Pennsylvania did the following. They used the Federal Reserve's large-scale econometric model, which we will discuss in chapter 24, and fed into this model certain changes in the money stock and in government expenditures, and let the model estimate changes in nominal income. They then took these estimated changes in nominal income, and regressed them on the changes in the money stock and in government expenditures, which they had originally put into the model. They got results similar to the Andersen-Jordan ones; the money stock has a strong effect on income, while government expenditures do not.[2] But, although we do not know with certainty how the real-world economy (which is, of course, what Andersen and Jordan used for their original test) is constituted, we do know perfectly

---

[2] Franco Modigliani and Albert Ando, "Impacts of Fiscal Actions on Aggregate Income and the Monetarist Controversy: Theory and Evidence," in *Monetarism*, ed. Jerome Stein (Amsterdam: North Holland Press, 1976), pp. 17–42.

well how the Fed's econometric model is constructed. It is a more or less Keynesian model. And if the application of the Andersen-Jordan technique of regressing income on monetary and fiscal variables misleadingly yields monetarist results in a case where we *know* that a Keynesian "world" (the Fed's econometric model) generated the income data, then one should question the reliability of the Andersen-Jordan method when applied to real-world data. But the fact that Modigliani and Ando used actual government expenditures instead of the high employment government expenditures measure used by Andersen and Jordan weakens their argument.

The Andersen-Jordan study was originally intended primarily to compare the relative efficiency of monetary and fiscal policies. But if one knows what the money supply and fiscal policy will be, then one can also use it to predict income. Leonall Andersen and another economist at the St. Louis Fed, Keith Carson, have used it to construct a formal model of the economy, which is discussed in appendix A to this chapter.

The Brunner-Meltzer Analysis

When discussing Friedman's monetary theory we mentioned that (rightly or wrongly) he is often criticized for not sufficiently explaining *how* money affects income, and for relying on "mere correlations." And the same criticism has been made of the work of Andersen and Jordan. But this criticism is certainly not applicable to the work of two other leading monetarists, Karl Brunner and Allan Meltzer, to which we now turn. They have developed an extensive and complex analysis of the transmission process, in fact one that is so elaborate that we will just give a sketch of it here and then present a diagram in appendix B to this chapter.

Brunner and Meltzer reject the standard Keynesian transmission process, which is based on the *IS–LM* analysis discussed in chapter 13. In the *IS–LM* model an increase in the quantity of money operates by shifting the *LM* curve to the right, so that it intersects the *IS* curve at a point at which income is higher, and the interest rate lower than before (see figure 13.13). But, as we previously pointed out, the simple version of this model takes the price level as constant, and it is a great simplification also in other ways—a great oversimplification Brunner and Meltzer contend. (In our discussion in chapter 15, we adjusted the *IS–LM* analysis to make it applicable to the case in which prices change and also introduced wealth effects, in part because of the criticisms that Brunner and Meltzer have made of the simpler *IS–LM* analysis.) Thus, the *LM* curve is constructed by assuming that there are only two types of assets, money and bonds. But, surely, money and bonds are not the only assets that exist in our economy. An alternative way of holding wealth is to own capital goods, either directly, as in the case of houses and unincorporated businesses, or indirectly in the form of corporate stock. In the *IS–LM* model corporate stock and other ways of owning capital are subsumed under "bonds." This amounts to assuming that the expected yield on all types of capital is closely correlated with the yield on bonds, so that one can use the interest rate on bonds as a proxy measure for the yield on capital. If so, one can describe the demand for money with reference only to income (or wealth) and the interest rate on bonds. But Brunner and Meltzer refuse to grant the assumption that the yield on capital always stays in fixed proportion to the interest rate on bonds. Instead, in their model they explicitly introduce the expected yield on capital as well as the interest rate on bonds as determinants of the demand for money since holding corporate stock is an alternative to holding money, just as much as holding bonds or Treasury bills is.

Another simplification in the *IS–LM* model is that changes in the stocks of assets (other than money) are not taken into account, perhaps because the period considered is so short that stocks of assets do not vary by a significant percentage. But Brunner and Meltzer, building on some earlier work of Carl Christ of Johns Hopkins University, do not accept this simplification and introduce changes in asset stocks into their model. For example, suppose that government expenditures on goods and services increase. This raises aggregate demand directly as the government goes out and purchases these goods and services, and then there is the multiplier effect. But there is also a third, and less familiar effect. The government must finance the resulting deficit by selling securities to the public. The Federal Reserve can prevent this increase in the public's stock of securities by undertaking open-market purchases. But if it does so, bank reserves increase, and banks then create more money. Hence, the public's holdings of either money or bonds or both increase.

Consider first the case in which it is the money stock that increases. Microeconomics tells us that if the supply of any one item increases its *relative* price must fall to clear the market. But an increase in the supply of money cannot lower the price of money in dollar terms; a dollar always sells for a dollar. However, it can lower the *relative* price of money by raising the prices of all other items, that is, of consumer goods, capital goods, and bonds. As the prices of both consumer goods and of capital goods rise, it becomes more profitable to produce more of them, so that output now increases. And, similarly, the rise in bond prices makes it profitable for firms to issue more bonds and to buy capital goods with the proceeds of these bond sales. (Or, to express this in Keynesian terminology, the fall in the interest rate stimulates spending.) At first, all of this results in both output and prices rising. But output rises only as long as it is profitable to produce more because the price of output is high relative to the price of labor and other inputs needed to produce it. Once wages and other costs rise in proportion to the increase in output prices the additional production is no longer profitable, so that output now falls back to its previous equilibrium level. Thus, an increase in the money stock raises real income only temporarily, but prices, and hence nominal income, rise permanently.

Consider now the opposite case in which the government finances its rising expenditures by selling bonds to the public, instead of by letting the money stock increase. The increased supply of bonds lowers bond prices relative to the prices of other assets. The critical question is now what this fall in bond prices does to the demand for capital, and hence to investment. If one assumes (as the *IS–LM* model does implicitly) that bonds and capital are similar, and therefore good substitutes for each other, then as the public holds more bonds its demand for capital, both directly held and held in the form of corporate stock, is reduced. Hence stock prices, and prices of capital goods such as houses fall, and firms cut their investment. But Brunner and Meltzer (as well as some Keynesians, such as James Tobin) make the opposite assumption. In their view government bonds and capital are complements rather than substitutes. Hence, an increase in the supply of government bonds *raises* the demand for corporate stock and other types of capital as the public tries to sell its excess government bonds to buy corporate stock and physical capital instead. As a result, stock prices rise, so that corporations now have an incentive to issue more stock and build more plant and equipment. Investment and income therefore increase. Thus in the Brunner-Meltzer model, not only monetary policy, but also the size of the government deficit—fiscal policy—and the way it is financed can, at least in principle, have a powerful effect on income. This effect of fiscal policy is partly a direct effect through government purchases, partly a multiplier effect, and partly an effect via an increased stock of government bonds.

This role for fiscal policy has caused some economists to question whether the Brunner-Meltzer model is really monetarist and not Keynesian.[3] *In principle,* their model could even produce the old-fashioned and rigid Keynesian conclusion that fiscal policy has a powerful effect on income, while monetary policy is almost powerless. But Brunner and Meltzer believe that this is as it should be: a theory sets out various possibilities, and empirical tests then determine which of these possibilities corresponds to the real world. And Brunner and Meltzer have undertaken extensive empirical tests from which they conclude that the dominant impulse that drives nominal income is not fiscal policy, but changes in the nominal money stock. Since they have also shown that the Federal Reserve, if it wants to, can control the nominal money stock by varying bank reserves, they hold the Federal Reserve largely responsible for inflation and for fluctuations in real income. In appendix B we discuss their model further, showing by means of a diagram how the commodity market is equilibrated when government expenditures change.

The Real Balance Approach

Another approach to the quantity theory, called the real balance approach, has been developed by Don Patinkin of Hebrew University. This is a

---

[3] For example, see Rudiger Dornbusch, "Comments on Brunner and Meltzer," in *Monetarism,* ed. Jerome Stein (Amsterdam: North Holland, 1976), pp. 104–25. But see also Brunner and Meltzer's reply in the same volume, pp. 150–82.

more abstract approach than the ones considered so far, and is concerned primarily with establishing two theorems. Hence while Patinkin's model is certainly a quantity-theory model, one can accept it without accepting all, or many, of the monetarist propositions discussed in the previous chapter. The first of these theorems is that under certain specified conditions a change in the stock of money brings about a strictly proportional change in the price level, and the second is that Keynes was wrong when he claimed that there could be an equilibrium at less than full employment in an economy in which wages and prices are completely flexible. Patinkin does not deny that reestablishing full employment when, say, the marginal efficiency of investment falls, may *perhaps* take a much greater drop in wages than would be feasible; he is just concerned with showing that, in principle, falling wages and prices would bring about full employment.

Patinkin organized his analysis around the real balance effect. As a convenient, though hardly very realistic, expository device, suppose that a helicopter flies over a city and drops currency. The lucky inhabitants now find that they hold more money than they desire to hold, given their incomes, wealth, and the interest rate. The *marginal* utility of a dollar in cash balances is now less to them than the marginal utility of a dollar's worth of goods or securities; hence, they use this excess money to buy securities and physical assets. This basic idea of the real balance effect is obvious, and we have already discussed it at various points, but to understand it more fully, one must put it into a model that starts out with certain quite specific assumptions.

The Assumptions

The most dramatic assumption is that wages and prices are *completely* flexible so that as long as the supply of labor exceeds the demand for labor, wages continue to fall. Patinkin is not saying that this is the way labor actually behaves—he is merely trying to show what would happen if this assumption were to hold.

The second assumption is that people do not suffer from a "money illusion." This needs further explaining. Suppose that prices double and the real interest rate is constant, but that your income and wealth double also, so that you are as well off as before. Will you also double the *nominal* value of your expenditures, thus keeping your real expenditures constant? If you are fully aware of what has happened, and behave rationally, you will do so. Your propensity to consume depends on your real income, real wealth, and the real interest rate, and these variables are all unchanged. But it is certainly possible that you may not be fully aware that your real income and wealth are unchanged; for example, you may underestimate the rise in prices, and hence believe that your real income and wealth have risen. If so, you are said to suffer from a money illusion.

As prices rise or fall some redistribution of income takes place, and if gainers and losers have different marginal propensities to consume or to invest, aggregate demand is affected. But to simplify the analysis Patinkin assumes such redistribution effects do not occur. In addition, he assumes that as prices change people do not hold back or accelerate purchases in the expectation of further price changes. Purely for expository convenience, he also assumes that the government's budget is balanced. In addition to these assumptions, we will assume *temporarily* that there are no government bonds outstanding, and that all the money in existence is outside money, that is, currency.

The Model

We will aggregate all the numerous markets that exist in the economy into three. First, there is the commodity market in which a person's real expenditure on consumer goods (or a firm's expenditure on capital goods) is a function of real income, the interest rate, and wealth.

As we discussed briefly in chapter 6 people's wealth consists of three types of items. First, there are physical goods and direct claims on physical goods, such as corporate stock. Second, there are claims on other people, for example, corporate bonds and promissory notes. Third, there are claims on the government, such as currency and the reserves that member banks have with the Federal Reserve. What happens to these components of wealth as prices change? A *uniform* change in prices does not affect the real value of one's physical assets. If a house is worth, say, $100,000, and all prices double, the house is now worth $200,000, but its real value is unchanged. Similarly, for all people in the aggregate, the real value of their net security holdings is unchanged. Creditors experience a drop in real wealth because the IOUs that they hold are now worth less than before. But the reverse side of this is that debtors now are richer because debts they owe have fallen in value, so that the *net* effect of inflation on the value of private IOUs is zero. One can therefore say that unless there are government bonds outstanding, inflation reduces the *net* wealth of the public only by reducing the real value of its currency holdings and bank reserves, while the net value of all other forms of wealth is constant. Admittedly, on a less abstract and more realistic level one would have to take into account that inflation also reduces wealth by raising tax liabilities and by generating uncertainty.

As we saw in chapter 14, real consumption depends on real wealth as well as on real income. Thus, inflation, by reducing the value of currency and bonds and hence real wealth, reduces real consumption.

The second market is the labor market in which both the supply and demand for labor depend upon the real wage; the higher the real wage the greater is the supply of labor willing to work, but the smaller is the demand for labor. Third, there is the money market in which the interest rate depends on nominal income and upon the nominal money stock. The higher the nominal income is the greater the demand for money, and hence, the higher is the interest rate. And the greater the supply of money, the lower is the interest rate. These markets are shown in figure 17.1.

Figure 17.1   The Patinkin Model

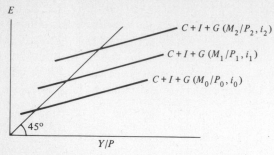

(A) The Commodity Market

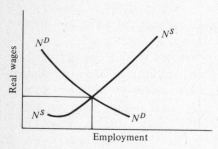

(B) The Labor Market

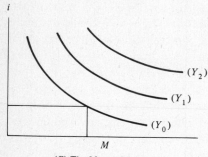

(C) The Money Market

The Workings of the Model

The variables that drive the Keynesian model are changes in (1) the quantity of money, (2) liquidity preference, that is, the demand for money, (3) investment (including government expenditures and exports), and (4) the marginal propensity to consume. An increase in the money stock usually raises real income since the economy is usually not at full employment, and also raises prices, but not proportionately to the rise in the money stock. An increase in liquidity preference lowers both real income and prices, while a rise in the marginal efficiency of investment or in the propensity to consume raises real income and prices. Do these things also happen in the Patinkin model?

Consider first what happens when the money stock increases; say, a

Figure 17.2   Equilibrium Conditions

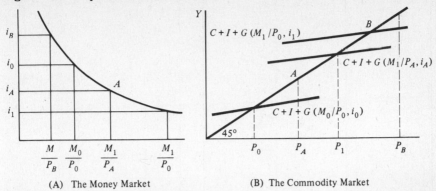

(A) The Money Market   (B) The Commodity Market

helicopter showers money on the population.[4] In figure 17.2 (A) the money market is initially in equilibrium at the interest rate i_0. The real money stock now rises suddenly to M_1/P_0 (prices not yet having adjusted) so that the interest rate falls to i_1. As a result of this fall in the interest rate, as well as due to the rise of wealth, the $C + I + G$ line in 17.2 (B) shifts upward to $C + I + G(M_1/P_0, i_1)$. Since real income is constant, due to our full-employment assumption, the horizontal axis of this 45° line diagram can be calculated in terms of prices instead of money income. And as prices rise from P_0 to P_1, this rise in prices feeds back into 17.2 (A) since it reduces the real money stock M/P. As M/P continues to fall, we eventually get back to the original real money stock M_0/P_0, so that the interest rate is again i_0. And the goods market of 17.2 (B) is also back in equilibrium at the price level P_1, where the new $C + I + G$ line intersects the 45-degree line.

By contrast, consider a point such as A in 17.2 (B). Prices have not yet fully adjusted, and the commodity market is not yet in equilibrium. The corresponding point A in 17.2 (A) shows that at this time M/P is still larger than in the previous equilibrium, so that the interest rate is below its equilibrium. Hence, in 17.2 (B) the upward pressure on prices from the wealth term in the consumption function is reinforced by the interest rate being below its equilibrium. For both of these reasons prices rise towards P_1. Similarly, suppose that prices were somehow to rise to point B in 17.2 (B), so that the money stock in (A) is M/P_B. The interest rate would now be above its equilibrium level and this, together with the fact that wealth has declined, would force prices down to P_1 again.

We have stated several times that the equilibrium point is one of full employment. The time has come to show that in this Patinkin model, full employment *is* the only possible equilibrium. Suppose that there is a drop in government expenditures, G, or in the propensity to consume, or in the

---

[4] How about the more realistic case in which the money stock increases because of Federal Reserve open-market purchases? The public gives up securities to the Fed, but since the money multiplier is about two, for each dollar of securities it relinquishes it gains about two dollars of money. Moreover, the rise in security prices due to the Fed's purchases also raises wealth.

Figure 17.3   The Real Balance Effect and Full Employment

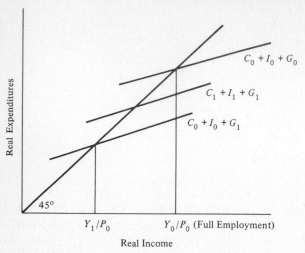

marginal efficiency of investment. In this model, as in the standard Keynesian model, the $C + I + G$ line in figure 17.3 (which, unlike figure 17.2, has real income on the horizontal axis) now shifts downward from $C_0 + I_0 + G_0$ to $C_0 + I_0 + G_1$, and excess inventories as well as unemployment start to appear. In a simple Keynesian model that has no real balance effect, or that takes prices as fixed, this is the end of the story; underemployment *can* be an equilibrium. But in the Patinkin model the fall in aggregate demand means that firms reduce their prices, and workers reduce their nominal wage demand. (With prices falling they can do so without suffering a decline in real wages.) And these wage and price declines will continue as long as firms have excess inventories they cannot sell, and workers are unemployed. (This is what the assumption of complete wage and price flexibility implies.) But as wages and prices fall two things happen. First, wealth increases and this pushes up consumption. Second, in the money market, the rise in the real money stock lowers the interest rate, and this too serves to raise expenditures. Thus the $C + I + G$ line shifts up. Suppose that it shifts to $C_1 + I_1 + G_1$. At this point there is still unemployment, so wages and prices continue to fall, and the $C + I + G$ curve continues to shift up. Only when it is back at the previous full-employment level do wages and prices stop falling. Hence the model has only one equilibrium position: full employment.

In this model in which wages and prices are completely flexible changes in government expenditures, the marginal efficiency of investment, exports, and the propensity to consume therefore have no effect on either real or nominal income. Real income is determined by the size of the labor force, the capital stock, and productivity, while nominal income depends on the quantity of money and on the desired ratio of money to nominal income, k.

What happens if k changes? In the Keynesian model an increase in liquidity preference raises the interest rate and results in unemployment. But this is not the equilibrium solution in the Patinkin model. As in the Keynesian model, initially the rise in the demand for money raises the interest rate, and thus lowers real expenditures, so that unsold inventories begin to appear and unemployment starts to occur. But when this happens wages and prices fall, so that the real quantity of money rises. Suppose that the initial change in liquidity preference was that the public wanted to hold 10 percent more real money. After wages and prices have fallen by 10 percent this additional demand for money is satisfied, and output is back at its full-employment level.

Thus, in the Patinkin model complete wage and price flexibility always generates full employment; unemployment can be only a temporary disequilibrium position that lasts only until wages and prices have adjusted. It follows from this that the only way anyone can claim that underemployment can be an equilibrium is to argue that wages and prices are not flexible.

The extent to which wages and prices are flexible in reality depends upon whether we are considering an increase or a decrease in the money stock since wages and prices are much stickier downward than upward. Moreover, it depends on the time span considered; prices obviously change more over a, say, ten-year period than over a one-month period. Another relevant consideration is whether the economy starts from a position of price stability or from inflation. If prices are rising, then the real balance effect can decrease wages and prices *relative* to what they otherwise would have been without requiring them to fall in dollar terms. In any case, as Patinkin well recognizes, the *practical* issue is not whether unemployment can be an equilibrium as the standard version of the 45-degree line diagram that is taught in introductory economics courses implies, but how *long* it takes for the market to eliminate serious unemployment. Suppose that there is only a small degree of wage and price flexibility, so that wages and prices fall only by at most, say, one percent per year. *Eventually,* if allowed to operate for long enough, even such a small degree of wage and price flexibility would reduce prices sufficiently to have a strong enough real balance effect to eliminate unemployment. But *if* it takes several decades to do so, one could hardly say that unemployment is unimportant since it represents only a "temporary" disequilibrium. Patinkin himself certainly does not argue that we should necessarily rely on the real balance effect to eliminate unemployment.

Inside Money, Outside Money, and Government Bonds

When we discussed the assumptions of the model we stated that we would remove two of these assumptions: that all money is outside money and that there are no government bonds. The time has come to deliver on this promise. Suppose that the stock of money is increased by 10 percent when there are government bonds outstanding. If so, a 10 percent rise in prices would no longer equilibrate our markets. The public now holds part of its wealth in government bonds that are denominated in dollar terms. Hence, if when the money stock rises by 10 percent, prices were to rise by 10 percent too, the public's real wealth would fall. As a result, real aggregate demand would fall too, and this would generate downward pressure on prices. Thus, if there are government bonds outstanding, prices must rise *less than proportionately* to the increase in the money stock. This means that the real money stock is now higher, and to make the public willing to hold this higher real money stock, interest rates must be lower.

Leaving government bonds aside, consider now what happens if there are both inside money and outside money, with each accounting for half the money stock. Inside money is money that is a claim on some member of the public, while outside money is a claim on the government. Thus a bank deposit is inside money, while a currency note is outside money. Hence, while an increase in real outside money raises the public's real wealth, an increase in inside money does not; the gains of those who hold inside money are matched by the losses of the banks that issued it.

Suppose that outside money increases by 20 percent, but that inside money is constant, so that the total money stock rises by 10 percent. If prices were to rise by a corresponding 10 percent this would *not* be an equilibrium. With nominal outside money rising by 20 percent, and prices only by 10 percent, net wealth increases. Hence, real consumption increases and prices rise. But, on the other hand, prices could not rise by the full 20 percent by which outside money has risen. If they did, the total real money stock would be less than it was originally, and hence interest rates would be higher. The resulting fall in aggregate demand would force prices down again. Hence, prices rise in this case by somewhere between 10 and 20 percent.

Conversely, suppose that inside money rises by 20 percent, but that outside money is constant, so that the total money stock again rises by 10 percent. This would result in a *less than* 10 percent increase in the price level. If the price level were to rise by 10 percent the interest rate would be unaffected since the real money stock would be constant. But the 10 percent rise in prices would reduce real wealth below its original level, so that real consumption would fall, and this decline in aggregate demand would then bring prices down again.

Thus, if both inside and outside money exist, then the result reached previously, that prices rise proportionately to the increase in the money stock, applies only in the special case in which both inside money and outside money rise in the same proportion.

These conclusions about what happens if there are government bonds or if both inside and outside money exist are controversial. As we discussed in chapter 6, some economists have argued that government bonds are not *net* wealth, because while they represent wealth to their owners, they are a liability of taxpayers. Hence when prices rise taxpayers in general feel richer because their outstanding liabilities are falling in value, and they increase their consumption by as much as bondholders cut theirs. If this is indeed the case, then the existence of government bonds does nothing to prevent prices rising in strict proportion to the stock of money. And other economists have argued that inside money is wealth just as much as outside money is, so that it does not matter which type of money is increased.

Summary

In this chapter we took up three monetarist approaches: the St. Louis approach, the Brunner-Meltzer approach, and the real balance approach. The St. Louis approach attempts to settle the Keynesian-monetarist dispute by looking at the relative importance of changes in fiscal policy and in monetary policy in explaining income. It found that fiscal-policy effects soon wash out, while changes in the money stock have a lasting effect. But this study has been criticized on the grounds that causation runs from income to money as well as from money to income, and that such a simple model cannot disentangle these interactions.

The Brunner-Meltzer analysis of the transmission process rejects the *IS–LM* approach as too simpleminded since it does not distinguish between capital and bonds, and ignores changes in stocks of assets. Brunner and Meltzer stress that if the government runs a deficit, the stocks of either money or bonds or both must increase. They show that both fiscal policy and monetary policy affect nominal income, but argue that the empirical evidence shows that changes in the money stock have much stronger effects than fiscal policy.

We then considered the real balance effect in an economy with completely flexible prices and wages. In this economy underemployment cannot be an equilibrium since falling wages and prices, by raising real balances, restore full employment. If all money is outside money, and there are no government bonds, then changes in the stock of money bring about strictly proportional changes in prices. But once one introduces government bonds into the analysis this result need not hold. Similarly, if there is inside as well as outside money, then (even in the absence of government bonds) prices change proportionately to the money stock only if both types of money change in the same proportion.

Appendix A

The St. Louis Model

This is a small model in which nominal income is "driven" primarily by changes in the money stock. Figure 17.4 shows its flowchart. The top line consists of the four exogenous variables—the variables whose values are determined outside the model and taken as given by the model. The first two of these, the money stock and high-employment government expenditures, we have already discussed.[5] The two new ones are potential output and previous changes in the price level.

The role of the previous price-change variable is to determine anticipated price changes, since in this model people form their expectations of future inflation by looking at past inflation rates. The *anticipated* price level is therefore an endogenous variable, and it, in turn, affects two other endogenous variables, the price level and the rate of interest. It affects the price level because in setting wages and prices for the period ahead, both firms and labor take account of the expected rate of inflation when they translate their desired real wages and prices into nominal wages and prices. And, as we explained in chapter 6, when prices are expected to rise interest rates rise too.

The other new exogenous variable, potential output, has two functions in this model. First, it affects demand pressures on prices since it measures the aggregate supply that is available to meet aggregate demand. Second, along with the level of aggregate demand, it determines the GNP gap, that is, the gap between potential (high-employment) output and actual output. And this gap, in turn, sets the unemployment rate.

In this model, changes in the money stock and changes in high-employment federal expenditures determine changes in total spending. And changes in total spending along with potential output affect demand pressures on commodity markets, and these demand pressures, along with anticipated inflation, determine the price level. The theory of inflation embodied in this model is that firms set prices to keep up with the expected rate of inflation adjusted for the extent to which demand for their own products is excessive or insufficient.

---

[5] Why are government expenditures given such a prominent role in this model despite the fact that their positive impact is offset by their negative impact after a short time? The reason is that in the Andersen-Jordan analysis, until it washes out, the effect of government expenditures is quite substantial.

Figure 17.4   Flow Chart of the St. Louis Model

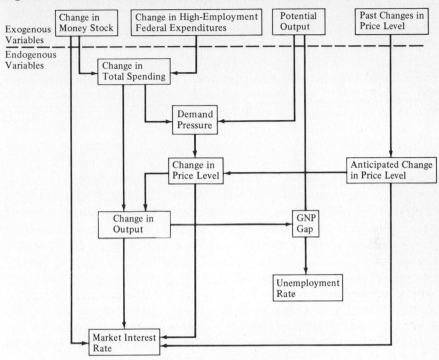

SOURCE: Leonall Andersen and Keith Carson, "A Monetarist Model for Economic Stabilization," *Review* (Federal Reserve Bank of St. Louis) 52 (April 1970): 10.

But prices are not the only variable that responds to changes in total spending, output does too. The change in output, in turn, affects the gap between high-employment GNP and actual GNP, and thus the unemployment rate. But since firms are willing to produce more if prices rise, the change in output depends not only on the change in total spending, but also on the change in the price level.

Finally, the market rate of interest is determined by four factors. Apart from the anticipated rate of price change already discussed, these are the actual change in prices and the change in output, as well as changes in the stock of money. The changes in output and in actual prices (in other words, changes in nominal income) affect the rate of interest by determining the demand for money. Juxtaposed to this change in the demand for money is the final determinant of the interest rate, the change in the supply of money.

This model differs in several ways from the usual Keynesian model, ways closely related to the characteristics of monetarism discussed in the last chapter. One of these ways is that in this model there is no way one can introduce changes in private demand, due to changes in, say, the marginal efficiency of investment or the propensity to consume. It therefore implies that private demand does not generate major fluctuations in the economy.

By contrast, in the Keynesian model such changes in private demand can show up in any of the numerous equations that describe private expenditures. Second, in this model aggregate demand is treated as a single unit, and not broken down into components such as plant and equipment expenditures and state and local government investment. Similarly, the output of this model consists only of aggregates, that is, real income, the price level, unemployment, and the interest rate, while Keynesian models generally break output down into several components.

Third, the price level is determined in the St. Louis model directly by the interaction of aggregate demand and potential output. By contrast, in Keynesian models aggregate demand often does not enter *directly* into price-determination equations. Instead, prices are taken as just a markup on standard labor costs and other costs. Aggregate demand does, however, enter *indirectly* since labor costs depend, via a Phillips curve, on the level of unemployment, and hence on aggregate demand. Price expectations enter these Keynesian models indirectly too, since their Phillips curve usually includes a term for the expected inflation rate. But these expectations, by and large, play a less important role in Keynesian models than they do in the St. Louis model.

Fourth, in the St. Louis model the interest rate does not help to determine any other variables, while in Keynesian models changes in the interest rate are a stepping stone in the transmission process by which monetary policy and other variables affect income.

How well has the St. Louis model predicted? The answer depends on whether one calls the glass half full or half empty. It has performed about as well—or badly—as some of the much bigger Keynesian models. And, while there are some small Keynesian models that have predicted better, others have predicted worse. Actually, in their original state most models predict fairly badly. To get a good prediction of income the owners of the models have to adjust, on the basis of their intuition and judgment, the raw predictions as they come out of the computer. For example, if a model has underpredicted GNP for the last three years by, say, $5 billion, one can simply add $5 billion to the model's forecast for next year. Much more sophisticated techniques for adjusting models are also available. But to evaluate the underlying theories one should compare the veracity of the models themselves, rather than the combination of the models plus the skill of their managers. Moreover, the predictive powers even of unadjusted econometric models would not provide much information on the validity of their underlying theories because models contain all sorts of devices that improve their predictions but are not part of their underlying theories. For example, using as one independent variable the past value of the variable to be predicted usually improves the prediction, but it provides little insight into the underlying mechanism at work. Hence, one should not choose between Keynesian and monetarist theories on the basis of how well the St. Louis model and Keynesian models forecast income.

Appendix B

░░

More on the Brunner-Meltzer Model

This appendix takes up the determination of equilibrium in the market for goods.[6] The complete Brunner-Meltzer model also contains markets for assets, but we omit these because of their complexity. Figure 17.5

Figure 17.5 The Goods Market

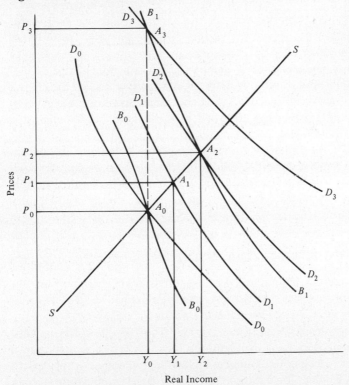

Real Income

[6] It is a condensed and simplified version of the description of the Brunner-Meltzer model given in Rudiger Dornbusch, "Comments on Brunner and Meltzer," in *Monetarism,* ed. Jerome Stein (Amsterdam: North Holland Publishing Co., 1976), pp. 104–25. Fairly similar models have also been constructed by Keynesian economists; see James Tobin and William Buiter, "Long Run Effects of Fiscal and Monetary Policy on Aggregate Demand," in ibid., pp. 273–309; and Alan Blinder and Robert Solow, "Does Fiscal Policy Matter?" *Journal of Public Economics* 2 (November 1973): 319–37.

shows the goods market. On the vertical axis is the price level, and on the horizontal axis real income. The *DD* curve measures aggregate demand. It slopes downward because a rise in prices reduces the real quantity of goods and services demanded. This is so, in part, because with the money stock fixed in nominal terms, a price increase lowers the real stock of money, and hence raises interest rates, and, also, because with income-tax exemptions and brackets being fixed in nominal terms, inflation pushes people into higher tax brackets, and hence lowers their real disposable income.

The aggregate supply curve, *SS,* shows the response of suppliers. With wages being assumed to lag behind prices, firms raise their output when prices rise, and for some time workers are willing to work more at higher nominal, but lower real wages.

The third line, the *BB* line, shows combinations of prices and real income levels at which the government budget is in balance. It slopes downward because both a rise in real income and a rise in prices tend to balance the budget. A rise in real income obviously raises tax revenues, and cuts government transfer payments that are related to unemployment, such as unemployment compensation. A rise in prices also raises government revenues since it pushes taxpayers into higher brackets. In addition, it also reduces real government expenditures by lowering the real value of government interest payments on the public debt. Since both a rise in real income and a rise in prices therefore help to eliminate a deficit, the higher is either one of these variables, the lower the other one must be to keep the government budget just at the point where there is neither a deficit nor a surplus.

In figure 17.5, the initial equilibrium is point A_0 where the output producers want to supply, shown by *SS,* is just equal to aggregate demand, shown by D_0D_0, so that the private sector is in equilibrium. Since at this point the government's budget just balances, the public sector is in equilibrium too. There is nothing in the nature of this analysis that requires the *BB* line to intersect at the same point as the *DD* and *SS* lines do, so that the government budget is just balanced at P_0Y_0. This multiple intersection is instead the necessary result of our decision to start with a situation of equilibrium. And on our simplifying assumption that the economy is not growing, equilibrium requires that the government's budget be just balanced so that it is neither emitting nor withdrawing bonds or money.

Now let government expenditures increase. The *BB* line shifts upward to B_1B_1, since with government expenditures having risen it would take a higher level of tax receipts—and hence higher real income or prices—to balance the budget again. In addition, the aggregate demand curve rises to D_1D_1 since an increase in government expenditures raises aggregate demand both directly and indirectly via the multiplier. The private sector now has a temporary equilibrium at A_1 where the aggregate supply curve and the new aggregate demand curve intersect.

But this is only a temporary equilibrium since the government is not in equilibrium, but is running a deficit. And as long as the deficit persists, the equilibrium of the private sector can only be a temporary one. This is so because the government has to finance the deficit by issuing either government securities, money, or a combination of the two. This is known as the *government budget constraint*. Whichever way it finances the deficit, the public's stock of money plus government securities must rise and the relative prices of goods, securities, and money must change. This change in relative prices in turn raises the public's expenditures. Hence, the DD line does not stay at D_1D_1, but continues to shift up as long as the government deficit persists. Ultimately, it gets to D_2D_2 at which point the deficit becomes zero, and the economy reaches a new equilibrium at a higher price level and output.

But even this equilibrium is not a permanent one, because in the full adjustment, workers obtain pay increases to offset fully the rise in prices. The increased output is then no longer profitable for firms and real income falls back to Y_0, and the increased government expenditure has raised only prices, but not output. This long-run SS curve is shown by the vertical dashed line A_0B_1. The new long-run equilibrium is at A_3. At this point prices have risen enough so that the budget is balanced, and they have risen this much because a rising stock of government securities or money has raised the aggregate demand curve to D_3D_3.[7]

QUESTIONS AND EXERCISES

1. Describe in your own words what Andersen and Jordan did and what they found. How convinced are you by this?
2. Describe the ways in which the Brunner-Meltzer model differs from Friedman's approach.
3. Discuss Brunner and Meltzer's criticism of the *IS–LM* model.
4. Show how the real balance effect operates to stop a wage-price spiral.
5. Describe the distinction between inside and outside money. Why is this distinction relevant?
6. Suppose that inside money (but not outside money) increases. What does this do to the equilibrium level of the interest rate?
7. (On appendix) Show how income reaches a new equilibrium if taxes are raised.
8. (On appendix) In what way does the St. Louis model exhibit the various characteristics of monetarism?

FURTHER READING

ANDERSEN, LEONALL, and CARSON, KEITH. "A Monetarist Model for Economic Stabilization." *Review* (Federal Reserve Bank of St. Louis) 52 (April 1970): 7–25. A detailed exposition if the St. Louis model.

[7] Our description of the movements to successive longer run equilibrium positions as occurring in a sequence is just a simplification. Actually, some movement towards long-run equilibrium starts to occur right away, but it just takes longer until the economy gets there.

ANDERSEN, LEONALL, and JORDAN, JERRY. "Monetary and Fiscal Actions: A Test of Their Relative Importance in Economic Stabilization." *Review* (Federal Reserve Bank of St. Louis) 50 (November 1968): 11–23. A classic.

DORNBUSCH, RUDIGER. "Comments on Brunner and Meltzer." In *Monetarism,* edited by Jerome Stein, pp. 104–25. Amsterdam: North Holland Publishing Co., 1976. Contains a remarkably clear exposition of the Brunner-Meltzer model.

NIEHANS, JÜRG. *The Theory of Money.* Baltimore: Johns Hopkins Press, 1978. An advanced treatise that incorporates recent developments.

PATINKIN, DON. *Money, Interest, and Prices.* 2d ed. New York: Harper and Row, 1965. This is an advanced treatise, but well worth reading.

PESEK, BORIS, and SAVING, THOMAS. *Money, Wealth and Economic Theory.* New York: Macmillan, 1967. An interesting argument that inside money is wealth too; therefore, the distinction between inside and outside money is irrelevant.

18

The Monetarist-Keynesian Debate in Perspective

It is sometimes difficult to get a clear view of the differences between monetarists and those who use the income-expenditure approach, because they appear to be using different languages to express their views. To compare their views, it is necessary to translate from one language to another with the danger that something will be lost in the translation.

In the income-expenditure approach, each component of the expenditure side of the national income accounts is "explained" in terms of other variables. Thus consumer expenditures are explained in terms of disposable income, wealth, and perhaps some other factors. Investment is supposed to vary with capacity utilization and interest rates. Price changes reflect changes in wages and in capacity utilization, but are also influenced by "exogenous" changes in food prices, taxes, and other factors. All of these linkages interact with one another in the complex system sketched out in chapters 13–15. In that kind of system, prices, output, and unemployment are strongly influenced by both monetary and fiscal policy, but they can be influenced by many other variables as well. Moreover, the structure of the system itself is subject to change without notice. The relations between unemployment and wage change can be influenced by changes in the strength of trade unions, by import competition, and by changes in regulation as well as by expectations of future government policy. Investment expenditures can be influenced by "speculation" about the rapid growth of new industries, by threats of war, and by confidence or lack of confidence in government policy.

The income-expenditure approach is built up from a great many pieces. Economists who use this approach have disagreements about the relative importance of the many variables entering the system. For example, some think that changes in wealth have a powerful influence on consumer expenditures. Others are skeptical about the effect of wealth. Statistical studies do not yield sufficiently precise results to resolve the controversy. The result is that there can be considerable differences in judgments about the effects of any proposed policy. What links Keynesians is not their conclusions but their basic way of approaching the analysis of the economy.

Much the same thing can be said of monetarists. They too have their differences, but they share a belief in the critical importance of variations in the rate of growth of money in the explanation of changes in prices and outputs. They tend to emphasize the existence of direct links between money on the one hand, and expenditures, prices, and output on the other, thus bypassing the complex causal chains appearing in Keynesian models. Some of the direct linkages relate prices and outputs to actual and expected changes in asset markets, particularly money markets. They give great weight to the role of stocks of assets in determining flows of expenditures so that, for example, they emphasize the link between stocks of wealth and flows of consumer expenditures. Moreover, monetarists tend to emphasize, more than Keynesians do, the importance of expectations, especially those connected with the rate of growth of the money stock. In addition, as already discussed in chapter 16, they consider that prices and wages are relatively flexible, that is, more flexible than Keynesians usually assume. And they also think of the private economy as relatively stable.

Finally, as mentioned in chapter 16, monetarists tend to have a longer time horizon than Keynesians. They are often concerned, for example, with the consequences of an increased rate of growth of money supply persisting over a period of years. Keynesians are more often concerned with short-run changes. Some misunderstandings arise from this source, because the short-run effect of a policy change may be quite different from its long-run effect.

At a very general theoretical level, Keynesians and monetarists often agree about the nature of the factors influencing prices, expenditures, and output. In summary paragraphs they often sound very similar. Unfortunately, the apparent agreement often amounts only to Robert Solow's summary of a student's progress in economics: In the elementary course he learns that everything depends on everything else. When he becomes a graduate student, he learns that everything depends on everything else in two ways.

For practical purposes, it is necessary to simplify things to some extent. Interactions considered to have minor effects must be neglected. The result is that Keynesians often neglect matters that monetarists consider important, and vice versa. In using different simplications, they often appear to be talking different languages.

In many ways, however, the monetarist description of the qualitative linkages between money and expenditures, prices and output does not sound so very different from the Keynesian approach. Milton Friedman's analysis of the demand for money is not fundamentally different from the Keynesian analysis. Patinkin's model of real balance effects can certainly be given a Keynesian interpretation. The Brunner-Meltzer model overlaps the Keynesian one in many ways—though containing its own special features. Up to a point one can think of Keynesians and monetarists as using a common model and differing about numerical magnitudes such as the interest elasticity of demand for money for the flexibility of prices. At one time, until the mid-1960s, the debate centered on the relative slopes of *IS* and *LM* curves, to which we now turn.

Interest Elasticities in the *IS–LM* Model

In any debate, it is always helpful to define the question in your own way. In the early stages of the Keynesian-monetarist debate, Keynesians treated monetarism as a special case of the Keynesian model. They argued that the quantity theory of nominal income would be correct if the demand for money were inelastic to interest rates, or if investment demand were highly elastic to interest rates. They then proceeded to make empirical arguments to show that neither was true. Monetarists were never very enthusiastic about that formulation of the issue, but they did debate some of the questions involved. The result of a long statistical wrangle and the accumulation of experience was to bring both positions together. The result of convergence, however, was not to produce agreement, but to shift the argument to new grounds.

Demand for Money

Many early Keynesians believed that (especially at the low rates prevailing after World War II) the interest elasticity of demand for money was almost infinite. Consequently, velocity would adjust to any change in GNP with very little change in interest rates. That view, of course, reflected the experience of the late thirties, World War II, and the early postwar years.

However, statistical studies covering longer periods as well as the experience of monetary restraint indicated that the interest elasticity of demand for money was not as high as some Keynesians had thought. On the other hand, those estimates were not so low as to justify a simple fixed-velocity quantity theory in which "only money matters." A moderate interest elasticity of demand for money leaves room for fiscal and other influences on the *IS* curve as well as for monetary influence through the *LM* curve shifts. Milton Friedman's permanent-income approach offered an alternative explanation. He showed that a model in which demand for money is made to depend on the trend of income could explain much of the cyclical variation in velocity. Later studies showed that even after taking the permanent-income effect into account, demand for money is generally still sensitive to interest rates. Nonetheless, Friedman's point was well taken, and most current formulations do use some average of past and current incomes as part of the explanation of demand for money.

Monetarists, including Friedman, as well as Keynesians, agree that demand for money is responsive to interest rates. On the other hand, they also agree that the short-run interest elasticity of demand for money is fairly low so that changes in the growth rate of money can have substantial effects on aggregate demand. There is still disagreement in this area, but it is no longer the basis for fundamental differences between monetarists and Keynesians.

Interest Elasticity of Expenditure

A somewhat similar convergence of views about the interest elasticity of expenditures has taken place. Early Keynesian expositions linked money to expenditure through the effect of money on interest rates and the effect of interest rates on investment. While that linkage played an important role in Keynes's exposition, his followers tended to argue that investment demand is very inelastic to interest rates. That argument provided another justification for a "money-doesn't-matter" position.

Again, a long series of statistical studies and accumulating experience showed that interest-rate variations can have significant effects on business investment. However, the difficulty of measuring the expected *real* interest rates makes precise measurement difficult.

The effect of interest-rate variations on residential constructions is well established, and in that case, nominal as well as real interest rates appear significant.

In addition the effects of interest rates extend to consumer expenditures through the influence of interest rates on wealth. Indeed, in a leading Keynesian econometric model, about half the total impact of monetary change results from the wealth effect.

As in the demand for money case, Keynesians have moved away from the "money-doesn't-matter" position. At the same time, interest elasticities are not so high as to provide any basis for an "only-money-matters" position. Again, there is room for disagreement about numbers, but the interest elasticity of expenditures is no longer a critical element in the division between Keynesians and monetarists.

Recent Models

As we discussed in the two preceding chapters, in the 1960s the Keynesian-monetarist debate drifted away from the issue of the slopes of the *IS* and *LM* curves. Milton Friedman argued that the slopes matter only for a relatively short time, because if the money stock is increased, the interest rate soon rises back to its previous level. On this issue of the behavior of the interest rate, there has so far been little convergence. Monetarists and Keynesians both can point to empirical studies that support their positions; regressions of the interest rate on changes in the money stock generally support the monetarists position, while econometric models tend to support the Keynesian position. And there is an extensive debate on the relative validity of simple regressions of one variable on another versus econometric models. This debate deals more with issues in econometrics than with issues of monetary theory.

Another important development in the debate has been the construction by Brunner and Meltzer of their model with its focus on changes in the relative prices of money, securities, and commodities (including capital), which was discussed in the previous chapter. While many Keynesians would dispute the practical relevance of this model, arguing that these relative price and wealth effects are unimportant in the short run, which is what they think matters for policy making, there has been some convergence, since some Keynesian economists have built models that are more or less similar to the Brunner-Meltzer model. All in all, among economists this debate is by no means as dogmatic as some newspaper reports suggest. Many economists take an intermediate position, and agree with monetarists on some issues and with Keynesians on others.

One important aspect of the debate, which we want to single out for further discussion, is whether in a three-asset model bonds are closer substitutes for money than for real capital or vice versa. If bonds are more like real capital than like money, an increased supply of bonds will depress the price of real assets. On the other hand, if bonds are more like money than like real capital, an increased stock of bonds will raise the price of real assets.

Why is that so important? Because government deficits financed without money creation have to generate bonds. If bond issues depress real capital prices, the expansive effect of deficit financing is blunted. If government bond issues raise the price of capital, the effect of deficit finance is enhanced.

Monetarists have emphasized this consideration much more than Keynesians. Many monetarists and some Keynesians consider government debt to be a relatively close substitute for real capital, which weakens the force of fiscal policy. Finally, some economists think that long-term debt is close to real capital, while short-term debt is close to money.

In spite of their disagreements, monetarists are linked together by their emphasis on the relevance of asset-market issues. At the one extreme an antifiscalist monetarist considers that (1) government debt is not wealth (in terms of its influence on consumption), and (2) government debt is a close substitute for real capital in asset portfolios. Those assumptions minimize the effect of fiscal policy. Other monetarists see more power in fiscal policy.

What makes them both monetarists is their emphasis on the asset-stock implications rather than the expenditure-flow aspects of fiscal policy. Their treatment of fiscal policy is parallel to their treatment of monetary policy. In both cases the influence of policy is from change in asset stocks (money, government bonds) to wealth and the relative prices existing and currently produced assets to spending on consumption and investment. In the same way, a change in tax rates is thought to influence spending not only through its effect on the deficit, but also through its effect on the value of assets and on the perceived present value of future aftertax earnings.

Policy Differences

The monetarist-Keynesian debate has gone on for a long time, and it has not become any simpler. Indeed, as interest in monetarism has increased, the number of monetarists has grown and they now disagree among themselves as much or more than the Keynesians do. However, monetarists tend to unite with one another in their disagreements with Keynesians about economic policy. In this section we will outline some basic differences between the Keynesian and monetarist approaches to the art of policy making, leaving a more detailed discussion until part five.

We can start with something everybody agrees about. At any one time there is a fairly well marked, practical limit to real GNP and a corresponding lower limit to unemployment. The corresponding unemployment rate is the natural rate or NAIRU (nonaccelerating inflation rate of unemployment). It is agreed that no policy can sustain an unemployment rate below the natural rate or NAIRU for long.

Does the opposite proposition hold? Can unemployment remain above NAIRU for a long time? Keynesians generally think so. Monetarists certainly recognize that disturbances from various sources (especially from rapid changes in the money growth rate) can cause unemployment to rise above the natural rate. However, they tend to believe that in the absence of new disturbances, price and wage adjustments will soon bring the system back to equilibrium.

It follows immediately that fiscal and monetary policy have only short-run effects on real output. Moreover, an activist policy is likely to do more harm than good. Managing monetary and fiscal policy to counter short-run shocks could help in principle, they say, but in practice, forecasting errors and politically motivated decisions will worsen rather than improve the economy's performance.

Keynesians, of course, are not nearly so sanguine about the self-adjusting capacity of the system. In their view, the balance between full-employment saving and investment is often disturbed. It needs to be corrected by shifts in monetary and fiscal policy. Moreover, they believe that the batting average of forecasters is good enough to permit policy actions to make the economy more rather than less stable and that policymakers can use these forecasts efficiently. Hence the dispute about policy involves much more than differing views about economic theory. It also involves differing views about the efficiency of the political process. A typical example of this difference is that Keynesians often point to sophisticated mathematical procedures by which the Fed could stabilize the economy, while monetarists point to blunders that the Fed has made in the past.

These days the big dispute is about inflation control. How can we keep the inflation rate from accelerating? Can we make it decelerate? Monetarists argue that we can prevent acceleration if we keep the growth of the money supply at a level equal to the existing rate of inflation, plus the growth of potential output, less the trend of velocity. If oil prices rise or if food prices are driven up by poor crops, there will be a temporary acceleration of inflation, a temporary rise of unemployment, but we will soon get back on the track. Those who think that fiscal policy has some power would also want to avoid any strong fiscal stimulus. A widespread monetarist prescription for deceleration of inflation is a gradual deceleration in money growth. Again some extra unemployment would occur, but it would be temporary.

Keynesians on the other hand find themselves in a dilemma. They think it will take a lot of unemployment for a long time to bring the inflation rate down. Moreover, price pressures from oil, food, and increased tax rates would have to be offset by even more unemployment. Many Keynesians think that we must live with a continuing inflation, or use guidelines or other interference in the wage and price-making process. These problems are discussed in chapters 19 and 20.

PART FOUR

Inflation

Inflation has been a chronic problem in almost all market economies in the years since World War II. The problem is hardly a new one. Reader's of Gibbon's *Decline and Fall of the Roman Empire* can find a lively account of the inflation problems of the Roman Empire and Emperor Diocletian's unsuccessful effort to enforce price control. Chinese history records inflation more than one thousand years ago. More recent examples include a period of inflation during the American Revolutionary War, when prices rose so much that the currency issued by the Continental Congress became virtually worthless. Both the Union and the Confederacy suffered from runaway inflation. During the U.S. Civil War, for example, a bag of groceries cost a basketful of Confederate currency, even before Appomattox. The German inflation that began with World War I is charged with destroying the savings of the German middle classes and helping to bring Hitler to power.

Viewed in purely economic terms, inflation tends to reduce economic efficiency. Everyone finds it harder to make price comparisons when prices are changing rapidly. It is more difficult to negotiate contracts for future deliveries and payments and to calculate the true return on investments in periods of rapid price change. Those costs would be much smaller if the rate of inflation could be fully anticipated but that is seldom possible. Unexpected changes in the rate of inflation cause arbitrary redistributions of income and wealth between debtors and creditors. Old people who depend on pensions in dollar amounts and on savings invested in bonds or mortgages are likely to be the big losers.

Inflation is a political as well as an economic problem. Widespread uncertainty about the future value of assets produces political as well as economic instability. Recent public opinion polls show fear of inflation to be of greater concern to the American public than unemployment, crime, pollution, or nuclear war.

The next two chapters provide a review of the major theoretical and empirical issues in the analysis of inflation. Chapter 19 contains a discussion of the theory of inflation. The occurrence of inflation is first interpreted in terms of aggregate supply and demand and changes in expectations. A different approach, somewhat more suitable for empirical analysis, is then used to explain what is popularly called the wage-price spiral.

Since we have already discussed aggregate demand, most of our attention is given to the supply side. Much of chapter 19 is devoted to discussion of theories of the response of wages and prices to changes in demand, and to further responses to changes in expectations of future price changes. The student has to remember, however, that changes in demand induced by changes in monetary and fiscal policy play a fundamental role in the causation of inflation. To bring that point home, the last part of chapter 19 contains some "scenarios" showing how prices will respond to several different sequences of changes in monetary and fiscal policy. Chapter 20 is more empirically oriented. The chapter begins with a history of inflation in the U.S. since World War II. The relative role of demand expansion and such "cost-push" factors as increases in the prices of raw materials, food, and fuel are then reviewed. The chapter also outlines some ways in which government actions directly affect cost and prices.

The remainder of the chapter is devoted to a detailed discussion of the operation of the labor markets and explanations of the simultaneous occurrence of increasing unemployment and more rapid inflation.

19

Aggregate Supply, Aggregate Demand, and the Wage-Price Spiral

Inflations have occurred in the history of many countries. Though, at times, inflations have been accompanied by rapid economic expansion and general prosperity, they have usually caused a good deal of social and political friction. For the last thirty years, and especially in the last fifteen, we have witnessed a continuing worldwide inflation. Though not so violent as in some earlier cases, it is a cause of deep concern in many countries. It is particularly vexing because its causes are not clear and it has proved difficult to find a cure less painful than the disease.

Causes of Inflation

Most of the inflations previous to World War II were associated with wars that had been financed with huge issues of paper money or, in earlier times, by recoining silver coins into silverplated copper ones, which made one silver coin into several "debased" ones. In those circumstances the occurrence of inflation was never very hard to explain. The government's expenditures and the induced expenditures of consumers whose incomes were increased created a demand for more goods than could be produced at the initial prices. Merchants, selling out their inventories, marked up prices; manufacturers, working at capacity, raised their prices and hired as much labor as they could get. Employers were ready to pay higher wages because increased output was profitable even at higher cost, and with help-wanted signs everywhere, they had to pay more. Everyone then had a higher income; and the government, having to pay more for military supplies, spent faster and printed money faster. "Too much money chasing too few goods" was a simple but adequate slogan for the typical wartime inflation.

Postwar Inflation

Since World War II inflation has been a chronic problem in market economies throughout the world. Inflation has occurred in peacetime as well as during wars, and in countries with budgetary surpluses as well as in those with chronic deficits. Worst of all inflation has continued during slumps as well as in booms. Inflation in depressed economies has been prevalent enough to get a name—"stagflation"—a stagnant economy suffering from inflation. Chronic and worldwide inflation is a new phenomenon harder to explain than the earlier inflations associated with wars, revolutions, or profligate monarchs. A new and complex phenomenon inevitably breeds controversy and there has been no lack of that. Books and articles purporting to explain inflation or to provide a remedy number in the thousands.

A little sampling of the literature will reveal two recurrent themes. Since prewar inflations were nearly all associated with excess demand it is not surprising to find a lot of attention given to the explanation and control of aggregate demand and especially to the conduct of monetary and fiscal policy. The other focus of attention is on the structure of markets in which prices and wages respond to changes in aggregate demand. This is a relatively new concern. In wars and other situations when demand in money terms is expanding far more rapidly than output, it seems obvious that prices must rise. But since World War II we have seldom experienced that kind of crude inflationary pressure, and inflation has continued in the face of rising unemployment and excess capacity. Clearly something more than the slogan, "too much money chasing too few goods," is required. Some people have tried to replace one simple explanation with another, such as placing the whole blame for inflation on trade-union pressure for wage increases or on greedy monopolists pushing up prices. The government can be blamed not only for errors in fiscal and monetary policy but for raising taxes, suppressing competition, and raising costs through regulatory requirements. All of these factors play a role in explaining inflation, but there is no simple market-structure explanation of the inflation problem.

In spite of all the controversy, economists have reached a very substantial measure of agreement on the broad outlines of the theory of inflation though they continue to disagree about the importance of many substantive points. The starting point is agreement on the proposition that the rate of inflation involves an *interaction* between aggregate demand and the structure of markets in which prices and wages are determined. With a given level of real GNP (relative to potential output) we can have more inflation with one kind of market structure than another—for example, tariffs and quotas may increase the inflationary response to a rise in real GNP. On the other hand the amount of inflation produced by any given market structure will depend on what happens to aggregate demand (in relation to potential output).

In previous chapters we showed that the equilibrium price level is determined by the intersection of the aggregate-demand curve and the potential output line. When the aggregate-demand curve shifts to the right faster than potential output, the equilibrium price level rises. During the transition the system is out of equilibrium. Prices are below equilibrium.

Output and employment may rise above the equilibrium level or, especially in wartime, there may be shortages of some products. We are accustomed from our experience of wartime inflation to associate inflation with low unemployment, high-capacity utilization, and "bottlenecks" or shortages.

During the past thirty years there have been times when inflation could be readily attributed to the pressure of demand on limited productive resources. But inflation has continued during periods when output was clearly below potential. The explanation of that kind of inflation lies in large measure in the characteristics of the supply curve. We will devote much of this chapter to discussion of the aggregate-supply curve.

Nonetheless, we have to remember that inflation always results from interaction between the supply curve and shifts in the aggregate-demand curve.

The position and slope of the aggregate demand curve depends on all the factors underlying the *IS–LM* analysis. These include "real factors" such as capital stock and technology and the long-term expectations of investors and consumers with respect to the growth of output. They also include "nominal" factors. Of these, the most important are nominal money stock, the nominal level of government expenditures, the nominally fixed elements in the tax system, for instance, the "brackets" in the income-tax schedule, and the outstanding debt. The aggregate-demand curve slopes downward to the right—lower price level, higher output—because the real value of the nominal magnitudes in the system increases with lower price levels. Both monetarists and Keynesians use the aggregate-demand apparatus. Monetarists emphasize the money supply as a major determinant of the position of the curve, while Keynesians give weight to other factors, but the demand-curve concept can be used by both.

For the moment, we can put their disputes aside and turn to an examination of the responses of prices and output to shifts in the aggregate-demand curve. For that purpose we can simply assume that the aggregate-demand curve shifts without pausing to ask why. When we have a clear picture of the response of prices and output to changes in aggregate demand, we can turn again to the controversy between monetarists and Keynesians.

The Aggregate-Supply Curve

Once we have an aggregate-demand curve sloping down to the right, it is very tempting to match it with an aggregate-supply curve sloping upward to the right. In fact, we will get to one, but we have to be very careful in doing so. The aggregate-demand curve slopes down to the right—lower price, higher output—because, as just noted, lower prices increase the real value of a given nominal money supply and of other nominal magnitudes.

There is no corresponding built-in nominal element in the aggregate-supply curve. We are accustomed to say that a rise in the price of a particular commodity will induce suppliers to produce and offer more of the product. That statement, however, is a shorthand one. We should say that a rise in the price of a commodity *relative* to other prices will increase the amount supplied. One way to raise the relative price of a commodity is to raise its price while other prices remain constant. But when we raise the general price level, we do not change the relative prices of commodities. They all move up together.

In the long run, with all prices in equilibrium relative to one another, one absolute price level generates the same output as another. Doubling all prices and wages leaves output unchanged. It is possible, however, to think of a short-run disequilibrium supply curve. It is only a short-run curve based on a given price history and, as we will see, it will shift with the passage of time, but it is helpful in understanding the inflationary process.

Disequilibrium Pricing

Change is the rule in modern market economies. Demand for individual products fluctuates for a variety of reasons: the weather, the seasons, fashion changes, the rise of new products, foreign competition. Some changes are persistent, others temporary. In the same way the balance of supply and demand in labor markets is in constant flux.

Prices change with shifts in demand but do not respond fully to temporary shifts. Product prices adjust slowly to shifts in demand for a variety of reasons. In some cases prices are fixed for a period by contract. In large firms there are administrative costs in deciding on new price schedules and publicizing them. In some industries a few firms control output and can operate jointly like a monopoly if they act together and limit price competition. To prevent "excessive" competition no firm changes a list price until it is clear that the others want to go along, though they may cheat by offering discounts without publicity. Prices will increase with a rise in demand and decline with a fall in demand but not as much or as fast as they would if firms regarded the demand shift as a permanent one. Prices do not rise enough to fully offset the demand increase so sales will have to rise. Some of the added sales will come from inventory and some firms will allow order books to rise, but generally when demand increases both output and price will rise.

A similar pattern appears in labor markets. Changes in output imply changes in employment, but employers will be slow to adjust wages to new labor-market conditions. Union contracts slow the adjustment of wages. When output rises, union employers will be able to get additional workers because they are already paying premium wages, but that will push the problem on to others. Most nonunion employers approach wage adjustment cautiously. Most large firms have a complex system of wage and salary administration. Jobs are classified into grades with established differentials. The wage levels and differentials are established on the basis of long-term judgments as to what wage levels are required to get the kinds of workers the firm wants. Each firm wants to maintain a certain position relative to its competitors in the labor market. In those circumstances many firms can make only marginal adjustments to temporary shifts in the labor-market conditions. When output and employment fall, firms can reduce their starting rates for new workers a little, and tighten up on granting merit increases, but those adjustments move average wages and costs only a little. When employment and output rise, there will be marginal changes the other way. To produce additional output firms will have to pay for overtime work, hire temporaries, or let some postponable work slide until the peak level passes.

Of course, many employers can make wage adjustments when labor-market conditions change but in general wages do not move enough to offset fluctuations in demand for labor. Employment and wages both tend to move up and down with demand in the short run.

Thus, we can envisage a short-run cyclical supply curve showing the price-output response to cyclical fluctuations in demand. In figure 19.1 the

Figure 19.1   Interaction of Shifting Aggregate-Demand and Aggregate-Supply Curves

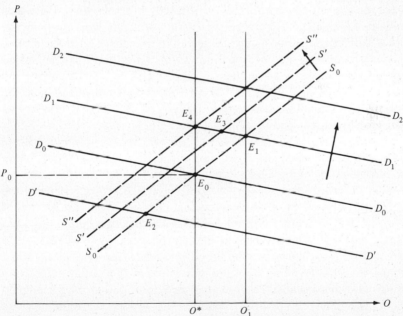

vertical line at O^* represents potential output and the curve D_0D_0 the average position of demand. It intersects O^* at P_0. P_0 is a price index, an average of prices, and we suppose that (with demand D_0D_0) relative prices are more or less in equilibrium. Some are a little above equilibrium, some below. Correspondingly some firms having vacancies get by with the use of overtime. Some workers are unemployed.

Now suppose that demand is shifting up and down. D_1D_1 shows the "peak of the boom" demand curve, $D'D'$ shows the "trough of the slump" demand curve. S_0S_0 is the short-run supply curve for the cyclical price-output response curve. It passes through the equilibrium point E_0 since the prices and outputs corresponding to P_0, O^* are the baseline from which price and output adjustments take place when demand shifts.

In a boom prices and output move up along S_0S_0 to E_1, then as demand shifts down they follow the short-run supply curve back down and at the trough of the slump reach E_2. If demand fluctuates up and down, price level fluctuates but does not show any trend. The fluctuations in demand lead to alternating mild inflation and deflation accompanied by fluctuations in employment and output.

Persisting Shifts in Demand

Now suppose that the boom has come to stay. Demand shifts upward to D_1D_1 and remains at the higher level. Will prices and output stay fixed at E_1? They will not because S_0S_0 is supposed to represent the response of prices to shifts in demands perceived as temporary. Once it appears that demand is not going to shift down, a new set of price adjustments will occur.

There are two reasons for further adjustment in prices. First, price and wage policies suitable for a temporary situation will not work well in the longer run. Administrative costs are large relative to the gain from a temporary price change but they are not important if the price can be raised and kept up. In concentrated industries, firms will be able to recognize their mutual interests in a price rise when they are all convinced that the rise in demand will continue. Trade-union contracts expire, and in addition nonunion employers will prefer to adjust their whole wage schedule rather than continue to operate with overtime, use temporaries, or get the work out while they are short-handed. Thus we can expect that as time passes there will be a further round of price and wage increases.

Second, the price response shown on the aggregate-supply curve is the response of each producer to the change in demand given the prices of all the others. But some of the price increases in the first round depicted in the S_0S_0 curve will increase costs to other producers. That will lead to a second round of price increases. In labor markets firms that made some wage adjustment will find that they did not improve their relative position as much as expected because other wages also rose. Those who made no adjustment find their competitive position has worsened. Workers who got a higher starting rate or a merit increase now find that the cost of living has risen and opportunities elsewhere have improved. Thus, to the extent that everyone finds actual prices higher than expected, a further round of price adjustment is required.

Thus if everyone regards the new price level as a permanent baseline, the whole short-run supply schedule $S'S'$ shifts upward and the new equilibrium price is at E_3 with higher price levels and somewhat lower outputs.

In time there should be a further reaction as all market participants respond to the second round of price increases and to the fact that they are still out of equilibrium. As long as output is above O^*, the level of vacancies, overtime work, and capacity utilization is still too high. Price and wage adjustments, which would have eliminated those problems for individual firms, fail to do so because their effect is canceled out by other price and wage increases. Prices will stop rising only when the short-run supply schedule shifts up enough so that it cuts the demand curve at E_4 where output is back to O^*.

The end result is the same as in the price flexibility case, but since the price adjustment process takes time, prices rise at a certain rate per year instead of in one jump. While they are adjusting, output is above normal.

We have argued that a one-shot persistent increase in demand would lead to a rise in output accompanied by a rise in prices, and then a further rise in prices over a period of time accompanied by a decline in output. Now suppose that the initial increase in demand occurred because the government wanted to achieve a higher level of output and a lower level of unemployment. Suppose it wants to keep output at O_1. It can do so, for a time at least, by making a further increase in aggregate demand. As the short-run supply curve shifts up from S_0S_0 to S_1S_1 an increase in money supply and government expenditure will shift demand up again to D_2D_2, so that output remains at O_1. This will, of course, make the supply curve shift up again since the movement of prices toward equilibrium has been offset by an upward movement in the equilibrium price level. However, that new upward shift in supply schedule can be offset by a further increase in demand. If the lags in the price-adjustment process remain the same as before and in particular if each price is adjusted on the expectation that prices will stay the same, it will be possible to maintain output at O_1 with some annual rate of inflation.

We should expect that the rate of inflation associated with any given output level will be higher as the difference between the actual output level, for example, O_1, and potential output, O^*, increases. In that case we can draw a curve showing the level of output in excess of O^* on the horizontal axis and the rate of inflation on the vertical axis. That curve shows the trade-off between output and employment on the one hand and rate of inflation on the other.

Before going on to consider the problems that arise when people come to expect continuing inflation, it is important to remember what is involved in maintaining a continuing inflation. If output is to be maintained at a fixed level above O^*, the aggregate-demand curve must be continually shifted upward. This can be done if nominal government expenditures, nominal money supply, and nominal outside money all grow at the rate of inflation. One might envisage other possibilities—perhaps a "stronger" fiscal expansion and a "weaker" monetary expansion—that could do the trick. However, we need not pursue the matter because the outcome will in fact be dominated by the expectational considerations discussed next.

Price Expectations

As usual, however, there are more complications. The notion that a particular rate of inflation will be associated with a given level of output depends upon the proposition that the price-wage responses of the system remain independent of the experienced rate of inflation. In fact, of course, that is not likely to be the case. The shifting supply-curve model used in the last section depended on 1) assuming that there are good reasons for avoiding price and wage adjustments that will have to be reversed and 2) that the price and wage adjustments that do occur will be based on the assumption that other prices remain fixed. An absolute price increase is expected to be a relative price increase because other prices are expected to be the same. But as soon as everyone expects that prices generally are going to keep rising at, say, 2 percent per year the whole game is changed. Firms have much less incentive to avoid price and wage increases because they do not expect them to be reversed. And anyone who feels that a relative price increase is profitable has to make a larger absolute increase to reach the same relative price target.

The result of that process will be to step up the rate of inflation from 2 percent per year to a higher figure. If, nonetheless, the government continues to engage in enough fiscal and monetary expansion to maintain the level of output at O_1^* everyone will come to expect continuance of the new higher rate of inflation and that will set the stage for a new acceleration.

Thus to maintain a level of output in excess of O^* the aggregate-demand curve must be shifted upward at a progressively more rapid rate. We will discuss the implications of that conclusion at the end of the chapter. First, however, we will look at the inflation process in a way that can be linked more directly to empirical work on inflation.

The use of aggregate-supply curves combines the wage-setting process in labor markets with the price-setting process in product markets. It is not very convenient for dealing with the special problems posed by fluctuations in raw material and farm prices. In empirical work on inflation, it is often convenient to analyze the forces leading to changes in wages, and then show how wages and other factors influence prices. In the following sections, we will outline the conclusions of that approach.

Real Output, Employment, Prices, and Wages

The determination of prices and wages in modern industrial economies is obviously a very complicated affair. Some industries more or less approximate the competitive model. Some look more like pure monopolies, many have characteristics of both models. Prices in some industries are regulated, for example, by public utility commissions; government enterprises produce quite a lot of output and have their own pricing procedures. Prices of agricultural products are influenced by fluctuations in weather as well as by government price-support programs. Sales and excise taxes, real-estate and corporate income taxes can influence prices. Finally, even in a relatively closed economy like the U.S. prices are influenced by foreign prices. Foreign prices are obviously important for imports like coffee, and prices charged by U.S. firms making steel, autos, and many other things are influenced by the prices offered by foreign competitors.

Labor markets are equally complicated. There are unions of varying strengths. Markets for unskilled labor appear to differ from those for lawyers, scientists, or business executives. Labor markets can be influenced by minimum wage legislation, unemployment compensation, and welfare payments.

In the face of all this complexity it is obviously difficult to find an overview. We can be pretty sure that most labor and products markets do not work like simple auction markets. But it is hard to know where to go from there.

In fact it turns out that a few relatively simple empirical generalizations will take us a long way although we have to beware of the oversimplification involved. Simplicity is what we want now, because we have to connect up some generalizations about wages and prices with other generalizations about demand, money, and prices in order to understand the whole picture. Once this picture is sketched out in this chapter, we can examine some more details, qualifications, and complications in chapter 20 without getting hopelessly lost.

Wages, Prices, and Unemployment

One of the most familiar and distressing phenomena of our era is the wage-price spiral. Everyone knows that big wage increases produce price increases and everyone knows that an increasing cost of living drives up wages. So business managements say we have a wage-price spiral—wage increases lead to price increases, which lead to wage increases, and so on. Labor leaders say it is the other way around, price increases lead to wage increases, wage increases lead to price increases, and so on. A great deal of rhetoric is wasted on the question of who started it. In fact, though wage-price or, if you prefer, price-wage spirals are a reality, they are much more complex than the "who-dunn-it" rhetoric suggests.

In the next two sections we will look briefly at the effect of wages on prices and then at the effect of prices on wages. Then we can look at the interaction process to try to understand wage-price spiral dynamics.

Prices and Labor Costs

In spite of all the complexities arising from variations in competitive structure and regulation, in practice prices of private nonfarm output produced in the U.S. are dominated by movements of labor costs. In a way this is not so surprising. Compensation of employees accounts for two-thirds of total costs. Moreover, in the long run, product prices must cover depreciation on the cost of capital goods. Capital-goods prices in turn are strongly influenced by labor costs. Even indirect business taxes are influenced by the wages of government employees, which move with the rest. There is obviously room for variation in the relation of prices to labor costs especially in the short run. There is even more room for short-run variation in that relationship in individual industries. But when we take them all together a lot of nonwage factors affecting individual industries come out in the wash. In the aggregate the trends of average prices for privately produced nonfarm products and the corresponding unit of labor costs are surprisingly close as shown in figure 19.2.

Figure 19.2   Unit Labor Costs and Deflator, Nonfarm Business

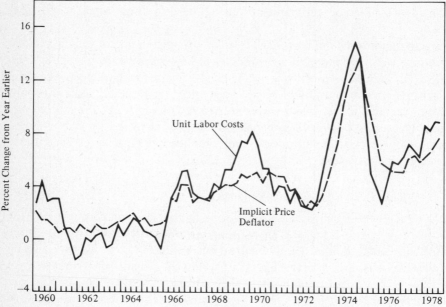

SOURCE: *Annual Report of the Council of Economic Advisers,* January 1979, p. 59.

Unit labor costs are defined as compensation of employees (wages plus fringe benefits) divided by output per hour. The corresponding measure of prices is the GNP deflator for the nonfarm private sector. It is not affected by prices of farm products or imported materials. From year to year or quarter to quarter, changes in the private nonfarm deflator and the corresponding unit labor cost are less closely correlated than in the long run.

Part of the deviation is explained by erratic and cyclical movements in productivity. Cyclically, when output rises fast and capacity utilization improves, productivity rises sharply. It increases slowly in slumps. Firms do not raise prices in slumps or lower them in booms. Their prices behave as though they were based on the trend of unit labor costs. There are some variations in profit margins in the short run, but statistical studies show that a good approximation of the nonfarm deflator is reached if it is supposed to move with the trend value of unit labor costs. The trend value has to be calculated so as to eliminate the ups and downs of productivity caused by fluctuations in output. In the U.S. the trend growth of productivity was about 2¾ percent per year from 1955 to 1966. Since then it appears to have slowed down to about 1 percent per year. We shall discuss some of the reasons for this slowdown in the next chapter.

A rough generalization about prices is to assert that the price level is proportional to unit labor costs so that $P = \frac{W}{OH} L$ where P is the private nonfarm deflator, W is compensation per hour, OH is the physical volume of output per hour, and L is a "markup" factor. Since percentage changes can be added if they are small, the average percentage change in price level equals the percentage change in wage, plus the percentage change in markup, less the percentage change in productivity. If we neglect the small changes in markup we can drop the last item so that changes in prices are related to changes in wages and the slowly changing productivity growth rate. In the short run the rate of change of wages will be the active cause of price change.

The consumer price index is more relevant than the nonfarm GNP deflator for some purposes. It is affected by farm prices and import prices. We will discuss that in the next chapter. Now however we must turn to wage determination.

Wage Determination

As in other markets the price of labor services is eventually a matter of supply and demand. We expect to find money wages rising relatively rapidly when demand for labor is high in relation to supply—that is, when unemployment is low and vacancies high. And we expect to find money wages rising slowly or even falling a little when demand for labor is low in relation to supply with unemployment high and vacancies low. Of course, that is only a crude generalization. With any given level of overall unemployment, demand for some particular types of labor will be strong relative to supply while other markets are in the reverse condition. Moreover, experience shows that some trade unions can get wage increases even in the face of heavy unemployment in their own occupation. Nonetheless, the record does show that, other things equal, wages increase faster when unemployment is low than when it is high. As we shall see, however, the other-things-equal clause covers a multitude of complexities.

The Phillips Curve

The empirical relationship between wage changes and the level of unemployment was reviewed by A. W. Phillips in 1958 using wage and unemployment data for the United Kingdom over a long period. He summarized his conclusion that wage changes are influenced by the level (not the change in level) of unemployment in figure 19.3. A relationship of that

Figure 19.3   The Original "Phillips Curve"
1861–1913

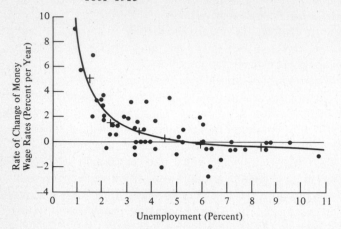

SOURCE: A. W. Phillips, "The Relationship between Unemployment and the Rate of Change of Money Wages in the United Kingdom, 1861–1957," *Economica* 25 (November 1958): 285.

Figure 19.4   Phillips Scatter Diagram for U.S.
1913–59

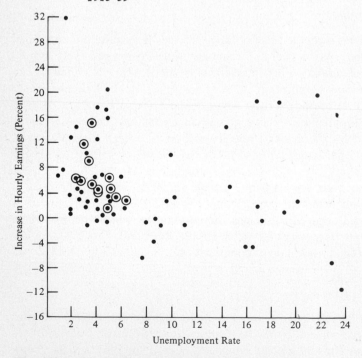

(The circled points are for recent years.)

SOURCE: Paul A. Samuelson and Robert Solow, "Analytic Aspects of Anti-Inflation Policy," *American Economic Review* 50 (May 1960): 188.

type with percentage wage changes on the vertical axis and the unemployment level on the horizontal has since been called a Phillips curve.

Figure 19.4 shows the relation between wage changes and unemployment in the U.S. for the period 1913–59. Though the relationship is far less clear than in the British case, American economists began to use the Phillips curve as a basic tool in the analysis of inflation.

From Wage Phillips Curve to Price Phillips Curve

We can turn the relationship of figure 19.4 into one linking unemployment with price changes by using the wage-price productivity relationship. Earlier we argued that roughly speaking the percentage change in prices equaled the difference between the percentage change in wage rates and the percentage change in productivity. The annual percentage change in prices is the percent change in money wages minus the annual percentage increase in output per hour. We can derive a price Phillips curve from the wage Phillips curve by just shifting the origin up by the annual growth in output per hour.

Figure 19.5   Wage and Price Phillips Curve

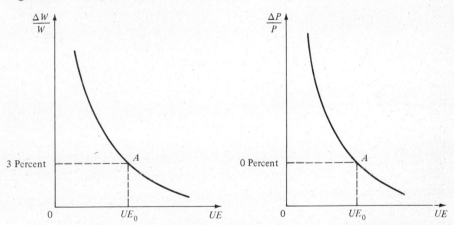

In figure 19.5 the left-hand panel is a wage Phillips curve and the right-hand panel is a price Phillips curve drawn on the assumption that the annual increase in productivity is 3 percent. It is exactly the same as the wage curve except that the vertical axis represents annual percentage increases in prices and the origin is moved up 3 percent. A horizontal line across the wage Phillips curve was drawn at a height of 3 percent.

At point A where the wage Phillips curve crosses the 3 percent line, wages are rising 3 percent per year, but since productivity is also rising 3 percent per year, prices are stable; so A is on the origin (zero price increase level) of the price Phillips curve. To the right of A, wages are still rising but prices are falling. To the left of A prices are rising 3 percent less than the rate of wage increase.

Figure 19.6   Shifts in the Phillips Curve

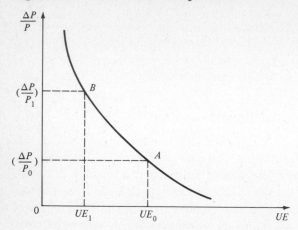

Acceptance of the Phillips curve approach led to the notion that public policymakers (and the public they serve) had a choice or "trade off" between a high rate of unemployment with a low rate of inflation—for example, point *A* on figure 19.6—or a low rate of unemployment and a high rate of inflation—for example, point *B* on figure 19.6. This gave opportunity for lots of philosophical discussion of the relative social cost of inflation and unemployment. Those issues are still alive but in a much more complicated form than in the Phillips curve discussion of twenty years ago.

Real Wages versus Money Wages

Experience in the late sixties showed that there was something fundamentally wrong with the simple Phillips curve approach. After 1966 the inflation rate increased, even when the level of unemployment showed little change or actually rose. Figure 19.7 shows the apparent shift in the Phillips curve of the U.S. since 1965.

The problem seemed to lie in the implicit assumption that the Phillips curve is invariant to the history of prices. Empirical studies of the process of wage change showed that the rate of increase in money wages in any one period is influenced by the past history of wage and price changes. They showed that after several years of inflation, the Phillips curve defined in nominal terms had shifted up. The rate of wage increase associated with a given level of unemployment was higher than before. Moreover, it appeared that a further rise in the rate of inflation resulted in another upward shift in the Phillips curve.

Employers are willing to raise money wages to improve or maintain their wage scale relative to the scale of wages offered by their competitors. They want to be able to recruit and retain workers with a certain level of skill and experience. Obviously, an employer's willingness to raise wages depends on the tightness of the labor market, but it also depends on what has

Figure 19.7   The U.S. Phillips Curve

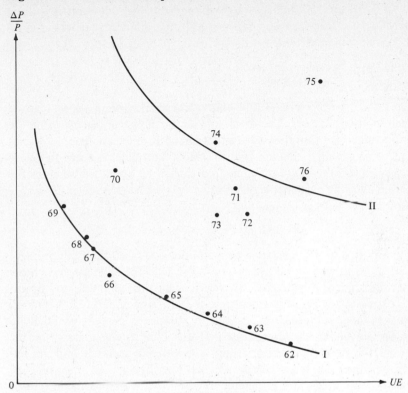

happened and what is expected to happen to other wages and prices. An employer will be more willing to push up wages if his competitor's prices have risen recently, or if he expects that they will rise. He will also have more recruiting problems if other firms have recently raised wages, or if he expects them to do so.

Trade unions, of course, want protection against expected price increases. They try to bargain for a wage increase large enough to cover expected price increases or for an "escalator" clause providing for automatic wage increases when prices rise. Trade-union leaders are often under pressure to keep up with gains of other unions in the same area or industry. Thus we expect that at any given level of unemployment, wages will tend to rise more rapidly if (1) wages have risen rapidly in the past, (2) wages are expected to rise rapidly in the future, (3) prices have risen rapidly in the past, or (4) they are expected to rise rapidly in the future. Notice that in both the wage-wage interaction and the price-wage interaction, firms and workers may be backward looking—making catch-up adjustments to past changes; or forward looking—getting the jump on what they expect to happen to wages and prices. Some economists think that attempts to catch-up with past wage and price movements are the most important part of the shifting Phillips curve. However, the most widely accepted view puts the emphasis on expectations of future inflation. Today's average wage change consists of two parts: the money-wage change that would result if no one expected the price level to rise, and the additional amount that would compensate for expected inflation.

Formation of Expectations

The rate of price increase that employers and workers expect can be influenced by many factors. The dominant factor, however, seems to be the actual price increases that they have experienced in the past. People do not just expect this month's inflation rate to persist but they do seem to act as though they expect the next year's inflation rate to be about the same as the average rate over the past couple of years.

Price Expectations and Shifting Phillips Curve

One way to adjust for inflation expectations is to shift the Phillips curve with changes in inflation expectations. In figure 19.8 the solid curve I shows a wage Phillips curve for a period when prices have been stable and no inflation is expected. At unemployment rate *A* both money and real wages are rising at 3 percent per year, just enough to balance 3 percent productivity when prices are stable. The dotted curve II is a Phillips curve drawn on the assumption that prices have been rising at 2 percent per year and are expected to continue doing so. The dotted curve is higher than the solid one by 2 percent at every level of unemployment. At unemployment rate *A* money wages are rising at 5 percent per year but *real* wages are rising at 3 percent just as on the solid curve.

The notion of a shifting Phillips curve together with the established

Figure 19.8   Changes in Inflation Expectations Shift the Phillips Curve

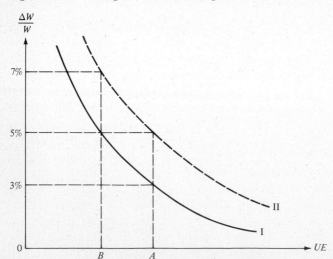

link between wage and price changes leads to the conclusion that any attempt to maintain a level of unemployment sufficiently low to start an inflation will lead to an indefinite increase in the rate of inflation. Suppose, for example, that starting from a period of price stability, with an initial Phillips curve like I, it is decided to expand demand and push the unemployment rate down to B. That produces a 5 percent rate of wage increase and a 2 percent inflation rate. But as everyone gets used to the 2 percent inflation rate the Phillips curve shifts up to II, wages rise at 7 percent, and inflation accelerates to 4 percent. After a while the higher rate of inflation will push the Phillips curve up and the rate of inflation will rise again. The sequence will repeat until unemployment rises again.

Moreover, raising the unemployment rate back to A will not stop the inflation. It will only stop it from rising. The inflation will continue indefinitely at whatever rate was built into people's expectations before the shift back to A.

Consider the effect of a rise in unemployment to A after the hypothetical events just outlined. Suppose that the last rise in the inflation rate from 2 percent to 4 percent is still regarded as temporary. Curve I based on expectations of 2 percent inflation is still relevant. When unemployment returns to A, the rate of wage increase will decline to 5 percent, and prices will rise at 2 percent per year. Expectations of 2 percent inflation will be confirmed by events. The inflation rate will continue at 2 percent as long as unemployment remains at A.

Notice that the unemployment rate A is the only one at which that can be true. At any unemployment rate below A, it will turn out that the actual rate of inflation exceeds the expected rate. Expectations will be adjusted upward, causing a further rise in the inflation rate. The reverse will be true for unemployment rates above A.

The unemployment rate A is a neutral one—where money-wage increases just balance productivity increases—but at that point the real wage increases permitted by productivity increases can be realized with any rate of inflation and money-wage increases that exceed the inflation rate by just the amount of productivity increase.

To reduce the inflation rate in the example it would be necessary to maintain a rate of unemployment higher than A. That would shift the Phillips curve down and slow the inflation. Ultimately unemployment could go back to the stable level A.

Milton Friedman called the unemployment rate corresponding to A "the natural rate of unemployment." Others who feel that high rates of unemployment are neither natural nor desirable have used the more neutral but more cumbersome term "nonaccelerating inflation rate of unemployment" or NAIRU.

The conclusion—contrary to the earlier Phillips curve trade-off view—is that no steady rate of inflation is possible if unemployment is below NAIRU. If prices have been stable in the past and the unemployment rate

Figure 19.9   Changes in Unemployment and a Shifting Phillips Curve

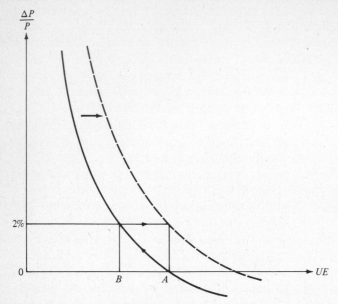

is held at *A* on figure 19.9 where the rate of price change is zero, then price stability will continue. If the unemployment rate is now pushed down to *B*, prices will start to rise—an initial trade-off of some price rise for a reduction in unemployment. However, if unemployment remains at *B*, the rate of inflation will rise again the next year, and again the year after. The trade-off for the reduction of unemployment from *A* to *B* is not a once-and-for-all rise in inflation rate from zero to 1 percent, but an indefinite succession of increases in the inflation rate until the level of unemployment is increased once more.

Another way to represent the response of the Phillips curve to changing prices is to build price expectations in from the beginning, using a relationship between unemployment on the one hand and expected real wages on the other.

According to this argument the dynamic price Phillips curve should look similar to the static one but with the vertical axis changed to read "actual minus expected inflation" as in figure 19.10.

The implications of that change are brought out clearly if we make the simplifying assumption that this year's expected inflation rate is the same as last year's actual inflation rate so that the vertical axis in figure 19.10 reads

$$(\tfrac{\Delta P}{P})_t - (\tfrac{\Delta P}{P})_{-1}.$$

UE* is where the dynamic Phillips curve crosses the origin, representing the natural rate of unemployment or NAIRU. At unemployment rates less than *UE**, for example, *UE***, inflation accelerates indefinitely at the rate indicated by the height of the dynamic Phillips curve. At unemployment rates greater than *UE**, the inflation rate decelerates. An empirical estimate of the dynamic Phillips curve is shown in figure 19.11.

Figure 19.10   A Dynamic Phillips Curve

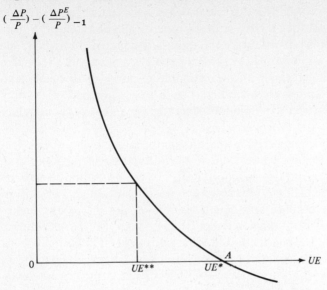

$$\left(\frac{\Delta P}{P}\right) - \left(\frac{\Delta P^E}{P}\right)_{-1}$$

Figure 19.11   Relation between the Unemployment Rate and the Change in Inflation
1953–74

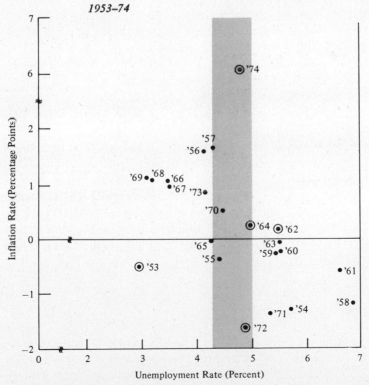

SOURCE: F. Modigliani and L. Papedemos, "Targets for Monetary Policy in the Coming Year," *Brookings Papers on Economic Activity*, 1975: 1, p. 148.

The dynamic Phillips curves shown in figures 19.10 and 19.11 are oversimplified in two respects. First, they neglect lags. In fact, considerable time is likely to elapse after a change in the rate of inflation before the adjustment of expectations about future inflation is completed. Moreover, the initial expectational response may vary with people's views about the causes of inflation and their perception of the probable response of monetary and fiscal policy. Their response to a one-time rise in energy or food prices may differ from their response to an inflation generated by a change in monetary and fiscal policy that is expected to persist.

Second, the models underlying the diagrams assume a literal one-for-one-response of the Phillips curve to increases in the rate of inflation. A 2 percent increase in the rate of inflation shifts the whole Phillips curve by *exactly* 2 percent. The reality is almost surely more complicated. The shift in the Phillips curve in response to inflation *may* be greater in the low unemployment range than in the high unemployment range. Moreover, the response *may* be different when the initial inflation is generated by tight labor markets than when it is generated by oil and food prices or changes in productivity. That *may* be so because wage changes reflect the product market as well as labor-market conditions.

It is apparent from the argument above that the rate of inflation tends to increase when aggregate demand grows fast enough to keep unemployment below NAIRU. The experience in the U.S. during the last fifteen years is consistent with the theoretical argument. The same theory appears to imply that the rate of inflation will decline if unemployment is kept below the critical NAIRU level. We are on much weaker grounds in making that assertion. Most recessions have been relatively brief and mild, and the response of wages and prices was not large. The 1975 recession was more severe than most, but it occurred after the oil crisis, which was itself inflationary.

Thus the recent empirical evidence on responses of wages to high levels of unemployment is not very strong. But for what it is worth, the evidence is consistent with the view that it may be harder to slow inflation than to speed it up. The deceleration in the rate of wage and price increase produced by raising unemployment to a level 1 percent above NAIRU may be substantially less than the acceleration produced by lowering unemployment to a level 1 percent below the NAIRU. The Phillips curve may flatten as unemployment increases.

Shifts in Aggregate Demand

So far in this chapter, we have emphasized supply problems and the reaction of prices to changes in demand and to the past history of price changes. In our discussion of the dynamics of aggregate supply and the Phillips curves, we simply assumed that demand is being manipulated to maintain some level of real GNP and unemployment. Now we have to return to the demand side of the picture to reexamine how the levels of real GNP and unemployment are affected by changes in prices.

We have already given the central message. In equilibrium terms a rightward shift in the aggregate-demand curve (starting from full equilibrium) first causes output to rise above potential. Prices then begin to rise and must continue to do so until movement along the aggregate-demand curve reduces output to its old level. With any fixed aggregate-demand curve, a rise in prices reduces the amount of aggregate goods and services demanded by reducing the real value of the nominal magnitudes underlying the aggregate-demand curve. A one-time shift in the aggregate-demand curve leads to a one-time rise in the price level. It will not produce a continuing inflation without a continuing rightward shift in the aggregate-demand curve. However, the adjustment process may not be a smooth one. In the next section we will examine the adjustment to a one-time rightward shift in aggregate demand in a little more detail.

A "One-Shot" Increase in Demand

A boom period with the aggregate-demand curve shifting rapidly to the right and outrunning the trend increase in potential output is a fairly common occurrence. Booms in private investment or in consumer durables often occur. Changes in fiscal policy, involving a rapid increase in government expenditures or a sharp reduction in tax rates, can readily occur. Shifts in the rate of growth of money supply can start or support a rapid increase in aggregate demand. Periods of rapid expansion, lasting for a couple of years, are not uncommon, and if at the start the economy is near its potential output, prices will rise for a time, but such events need not lead to continuing inflation. In fact they are unlikely to do so if there is no further increase in nominal government expenditures and nominal money supply after the initial demand shift.

If the economy is initially in equilibrium at UE^*, increased demand will first lead to increased output and reduced unemployment, but prices will also start to rise. In equilibrium, the level of output must be one at which prices do not tend to rise. That by hypothesis is the output corresponding to UE^*. The equilibrium price level must rise enough to crowd out enough expenditures to bring output back to potential. The crowding-out process has three elements: (1) higher prices mean lower real money supply and higher interest rates, thereby reducing investment and consumption (because higher interest rates reduce wealth); (2) higher prices reduce real money balances and thereby reduce consumption; (3) higher prices also reduce the real value of other nominal magnitudes—government debt, tax exemptions, and government expenditure will be reduced.

Dynamic adjustment. We can assert that the economy will not be in equilibrium until the price level has risen to its new equilibrium position and output is back to normal, but it does not follow that the adjustment will be a smooth one. If the rise in expenditure takes place very gradually, the adjustment might be smooth, but if there is a rapid increase in expenditure, the adjustment process may be rather bumpy. Three types of dynamic considerations have to be taken into account: those arising from expectations of rising prices; those arising from changes in the rate of growth of income; and credit-crunch problems.

Expectations. If prices rise for a while before monetary restraint takes hold, people may begin to project continued price increase. That will, of course, speed up the price rise. It will also imply that the expected real rate of interest rises less than the nominal rate. Indeed, the expected real rate may fall before it begins to rise again. That will stimulate demand and add to inflationary pressure.

Rate of change responses. The adjustment process implies some significant changes in the rate of growth of output. The initial impact of the increase in expenditures will accelerate the growth of output. Inflationary expectations may cause a further acceleration. If a higher rate of growth continues, it will tend to produce an acceleration-principle response in plant and equipment and inventory investment and in consumer durables purchases, pushing total demand up even further. Ultimately, however, rising prices working against a fixed money supply and other fixed nominal magnitudes will check the expansion. The rate of growth of output must fall in order to restore equilibrium. As it begins to do so, acceleration-principle effects may go in the reverse so that the boom ends in a recession instead of a smooth transition to the new equilibrium.

Credit crunch. The likelihood that the boom will end with a bang instead of a whimper is increased by the likelihood of a credit crunch. Monetary restraint in collision with expansionary fiscal policy (or any other nonmonetary source of expansion) is likely to produce sharply rising short-term interest rates. The result may be mortgage-market problems of the type described in chapter 6. There may also be bankruptcies or fears of bankruptcy for firms that have weak credit standing and heavy dependence on short-term financing.

The upshot is, first, that a rise in expenditures working against a fixed money supply will produce a rise in the equilibrium price level with the amount depending on the slopes of the *IS* and *LM* curves, and the importance of real money balance effects and the system's response to deflation of the real value of other fixed, nominal magnitudes. Second, it is quite likely that adjustment to the new equilibrium will cause some fluctuations in output.

Accommodating Inflation

In the case just outlined, the rise in prices was brought to a halt because rising prices deflated the value of real money supply, government expenditures, and other nominal magnitudes in the system. We assumed that nominal money supply did not grow (or did not grow any faster than potential output) while the government held fixed the dollar magnitudes in its budget in the face of rising prices.

Suppose, instead, that the government raises expenditures in pace with the rise in prices, so as to keep real expenditures intact. At the same time, suppose that the central bank allows the money supply to expand as fast as prices. (You may suppose that they do not want to be blamed for a credit crunch.) Then the automatic braking effect of the rise in prices is eliminated. The aggregate-demand curve keeps shifting upward; output is maintained at a level above potential output, and prices continue to rise.

In fact they not only continue to rise, they tend to rise faster and faster. The initial shift in aggregate demand produces a reduction in unemployment and leftward movement along the Phillips curve continues until prices rise at, say, 2 percent per year. But after a time, everyone gets used to inflationary conditions and the Phillips curve shifts upward by 2 percent. That causes a further increase in the rate of inflation.

If budget expenditures and money supply are adjusted upward to keep pace with the higher rate of inflation, unemployment will remain low, the Phillips curve will continue to shift upward, and the rate of inflation will continue to increase.

Sooner or later, of course, someone will call a halt. When the rate of inflation gets high enough, the public will support measures aimed at reducing the rate of inflation, or at least preventing any further increase in the rate of price increase.

Checking the upward spiral. Even the less ambitious objective of leveling off the inflation will not be easy. To prevent further acceleration in the rate of price increase, it will be necessary to do what should have been done in the first place. The rate of unemployment has to be raised to the NAIRU. The real money supply and the real value of government expenditure must be reduced enough to bring real GNP back to the potential output level. That will not be any easier than in the one-shot inflation case. The same credit-crunch problems and the same uneven adjustment to a change in the rate of growth of demand are likely to occur. The result is likely to be a recession with output falling below potential output.

An Equilibrium Inflation

In principle, at least, one can visualize an economy operating with an equilibrium rate of inflation. The level of real GNP would grow with potential output, the unemployment rate would be constant at NAIRU, and wages and prices would rise at a constant rate. To maintain the equilibrium, underlying factors, such as capital stock in relation to expected real output, would have to be constant. At the same time all of the nominal magnitudes in the system would grow steadily at a rate of growth equal to the rate of growth of potential output plus the rate of increase of prices. Maintenance of such a complete equilibrium over any long period is implausible. After all, there are hundreds of nominal magnitudes in the system. Government debt is not likely to maintain a fixed relationship to income, since the outstanding amount at any time is an inheritance from the past, unrelated to current demand conditions. Nonetheless, it is possible for an economy to maintain a fairly steady rate of inflation with expectations and the approximate growth rate of money supply and government expenditures adjusted to a continuing steady rate of inflation.

No one would assert that our economy has been in continuous equilibrium during the past few years. Nonetheless, it is true that we have maintained high rates of inflation by roughly adjusting many of the nominal magnitudes in the system to keep up with the cumulative rise in prices.

Notice that under these conditions, the inflation continues with no appearance of demand pressure. Real GNP equals potential output, unemployment is at the NAIRU. In contrast with the conditions ruling when the inflation rate is accelerating, the rise in prices cannot be attributed to high capacity utilization or labor shortages. The economy is just as much in balance as it would be with stable prices. Moreover, because prices and wages do not quickly respond to short-run fluctuations in demand, the inflation appears to be unconnected with demand movements, and it seems to continue inexorably.

Getting rid of inherited inflation. Once a situation approximating an equilibrium inflation has been established, it may be difficult to reach a new equilibrium with a substantially lower inflation rate. Experience strongly suggests that a brief, mild recession will not do the trick. In fact, experience and the logic of the Phillips curve argument indicate that to get a well-established rate of inflation down significantly, it will be necessary for unemployment to remain well above the NAIRU for several years.

To start the deceleration process, it would be necessary to break the equilibrium by holding down the growth of government expenditure and money supply in nominal terms and to let their real growth rates decline. The result would be to reduce real GNP and raise the unemployment rate. As usual the adjustment would not be a smooth one. It could not be accomplished without a sharp decline in output, a rise in unemployment followed by a partial recovery. That recession episode would reduce the rate of inflation but would not eliminate it. To make further progress, it would be necessary to manage monetary and fiscal policy to avoid a full recovery and keep unemployment above NAIRU. One would then hope to see a reversal of the accelerating price increase sequence, described earlier. The initial recession should first produce a reduction in the rate of inflation. That reduction should, after some lag, cause a downward shift in the Phillips curve, a further reduction in the inflation rate, and so on.

It appears, however, that the road back to price stability may be a long and bumpy one. Even the most optimistic estimates of the effect of unemployment on wage rates indicate that several years of high unemployment would be required for a return to full price stability unless expectations about inflation can be changed drastically. We will discuss the issues involved in evaluating those judgments in the next chapter.

Money and Inflation

So far our exposition of the causes of inflation has been neutral with respect to the issues dividing monetarists and Keynesians. The aggregate-demand approach can be used to summarize either *IS–LM* models or a monetarist model. In an extreme monetarist model, the position and slope of the aggregate-demand curve depends entirely on the stock of money, its expected growth rate, and the characteristics of the money-demand function. Those who use the income-expenditure approach include a much wider range of factors, without entirely neglecting money, in the determinants of the position and slope of the aggregate-demand curve. For theoretical purposes we can leave it at that without repeating the whole discussion of the previous five chapters. In practice, of course, policymakers have to form specific judgments as to the effect of monetary and fiscal actions and of events in the private sector, and the probable movements of nominal and real GNP in response to alternative combinations of monetary and fiscal policy. We will discuss the issues facing them in some detail in Part Five. Meanwhile, there is one other theoretical issue that divides monetarists and Keynesians.

Money and Expectations

Up till now money has been viewed as having an indirect influence on prices. Money supply influences aggregate demand, thereby influencing unemployment, and thereby influencing prices. Some monetarists accept that view, others argue that the growth of the money supply also influences wages and prices through its effect on expectations. They argue first that the equilibrium rate of inflation is determined by the rate of growth of the money supply. Moreover, they believe everyone knows that. Accordingly, if people are rational, they will form their expectations about future inflation by observing what is happening to the rate of growth of the money supply.

They argue that if the Federal Reserve were to make a firm commitment to the maintenance of a limited rate of growth of the money supply at, say, a rate of 4 percent, or to a gradual decrease in the rate of growth of the money supply, the public's expectational response would make it possible to bring down the rate of inflation without a long period of high unemployment. They argue that everyone would know that the Fed's commitment to limited monetary growth would ultimately bring the inflation to an end. The only uncertainty would be about the rate at which inflation would decelerate. Moreover, everyone would believe that if the rate of inflation did not decelerate rapidly, there would be a recession. Workers would tend to moderate their wage demands and employers would tend to resist demands for wage increases more strongly. There would, therefore, be some immediate deceleration in the rate of inflation. A little success on the inflation front would confirm the expectations of those involved in determining wages and prices and lead to further deceleration in the rate of inflation. Ultimately, the policy would work, and it would work much faster and with much less cost in terms of unemployment than one would expect from the use of the extended Phillips curve model.

Keynesians are generally skeptical of this scenario, though at least some of them recognize that expectations about monetary growth could make a significant contribution to the control of inflation. However, because they tend to give less weight to the objective, nonexpectational force of monetary factors, many Keynesians doubt the strength of the public's response. Moreover, they feel that as a practical matter the monetarists' proposal amounts to asking the Federal Reserve to play a game of chicken. The Federal Reserve is supposed to announce a policy that will only work if the public believes that the Fed is prepared to maintain its schedule of monetary growth, even in the face of a severe recession. Some Keynesians argue that the monetarists' expectational proposal might work, if the Fed could really establish the credibility of its intentions, but they do not believe that that is possible in the present American political situation. Some monetarists have pointed to the apparent success of a somewhat similar policy announced by the West German Bundesbank. The monetarists' opponents, however, point out that the German public is so much more concerned with inflation than the American public that the Bundesbank finds it much easier to establish the credibility of its announced policy. Some Keynesians, and monetarists as well, believe that if inflation in the U.S. continues to accelerate, the American public may finally become so annoyed that they too would be willing to accept the type of policy proposed by the "expectational monetarists," and that in those circumstances the policy might work. In general, however, Keynesians regard proposals of the type under discussion as very risky and potentially costly, while monetarists are more sanguine about the probable outcome or more fearful of the ultimate consequences of continuing inflation.

Interest Rates and Money Supply

In discussing the effects of monetary policy, we have noted changes in interest rates as we went along, but it may be useful to summarize the interest-rate implications of those cases. Then we can take account of the additional effects of inflationary expectations on interest rates. We have noted three kinds of factors influencing interest rates. First, shifts in the *IS* curve tend to push interest rates up or down just as in our analysis in chapter 13. Second, the first influence of a rise in money supply is to drive interest rates down, or if it accompanies any upward shift in *IS,* to moderate the rise in interest rates. But once inflation gets underway, it always tends to drive up interest rates by reducing the real value of any given nominal money supply. If nominal money-supply growth is increased to prevent a fall in real money supply, inflation is likely to accelerate. Unless the Fed is prepared to provide an ever-accelerating money growth, the acceleration of inflation will sooner or later drive interest rates up anyway. Ultimately, interest rates have to get to a level consistent with a GNP level at which inflation does not accelerate.

Real Versus Nominal Interest Rates

But that is not all. The expenditure decisions of households and firms are affected by expectations of future price increases. In fact, an expectation of a continuing 2 percent inflation has just the same effect as a 2 percent reduction in nominal interest rates. The real interest rate is 2 percent less than the nominal rate. In our *IS–LM* diagrams in chapter 16 (with nominal interest rates on the vertical axis) a rise in the expected rate of inflation causes a 2 percent upward shift in the *IS* curve. In a continuing inflation, the nominal interest rate required to keep inflation from accelerating must exceed the nominal rate required to keep inflation from getting started by just the rate of inflation.

The fact that accelerating inflation will ultimately push up nominal interest rates to offset the tendency for real interest rates to fall creates some paradoxical movements of interest rates. The *IS–LM* analysis makes it look as though increases in money supply will reduce nominal interest rates or prevent them from rising. But if those increases in money supply permit inflation to accelerate, then nominal interest rates will end up at a higher level than the one at which they started. Those observations are not just interesting implications of a theoretical model. They provide the basic explanation for the rise in interest rates since 1965. There has not been much change in real interest rates but the nominal interest rates have risen with the expected rate of inflation.

Summary

We have followed a long and tortuous path in this chapter. As a first approximation, prices rise when the aggregate-demand curve shifts to the right under the impact of a private sector boom, increasing government expenditure, increasing money supply, or any combination of those factors. Initially, prices and output rise together following the short-run supply curve. However, if the high level of demand persists, the supply curve will shift upward so that prices rise further and output falls back toward its equilibrium.

A continuing inflation will occur if money supply, government expenditure, and other nominal magnitudes are increased in pace with prices.

Moreover, after a time, expectations of continuing inflation will cause further shifts in the supply curve. Output cannot be maintained above the equilibrium level without a rising rate of inflation supported by progressively larger increases in money supply and government expenditures.

Essentially the same story can be told by the use of the Phillips curve. The wage Phillips curve summarizes the relation between the level of unemployment and the rate of change of wages. The price Phillips curve translates wage increases into price increases on the assumption that prices rise in proportion to unit labor costs (increases in wages, adjusted for the trend growth of productivity). Given the wage Phillips curve and the trend growth of productivity, there is some level of unemployment at which prices will remain stable.

If we start with an initial equilibrium, an increase in aggregate demand will first reduce unemployment, and cause wages to rise more than productivity so that prices rise. If demand grows fast enough in nominal terms to maintain the new lower level of unemployment, prices will continue to rise. Expectations of continuing inflation will shift the Phillips curve up. If aggregate demand is pushed up to maintain the low level of unemployment, price increases will accelerate.

Having worked through the theory of wage-price spirals, we then reviewed the effects of one-shot shifts in aggregate demand and of policies of accommodating inflation. We showed that it is possible to have a continuing equilibrium inflation, and noted the difficulties of getting rid of an inherited inflation.

Finally, we considered the possibility of a direct link between money growth and inflation expectations and reviewed the effects of inflation on interest rates.

QUESTIONS AND EXERCISES

1. Using aggregate-demand and supply curves, show how a rightward shift in aggregate demand will increase both prices and output.
2. If there is no further change in aggregate demand, will output remain at the new higher level?
3. List some of the events that can cause a shift in aggregate demand.
4. What actions by government would be required to maintain the level of output reached after the initial increase in demand?
5. Assume a given wage Phillips curve. How would the price Phillips curve be affected by a reduction in the rate of productivity growth?
6. "We can reduce unemployment if we are willing to tolerate a little more inflation." What evidence can be cited to support the quoted statement? Is the statement true? Why or why not?
7. A one-time increase in money supply or government expenditure can cause prices to rise for a time, but the rise in prices will in itself cause changes in output and employment that reduce the tendency for prices to rise. Explain.

8. "Inflation may continue in the face of high unemployment simply because everyone expects it to continue." Illustrate, using the shifting Phillips curve analysis.

FURTHER READING

FEDERAL RESERVE BANK OF BOSTON. *After the Phillips Curve*. Federal Reserve Bank of Boston Monetary Conference, 9 November 1978, Boston, Massachusetts. This volume contains a number of essays by leading economists on the most recent developments in inflation theory. The papers and discussions include a number of spirited debates between monetarists and Keynesians.

FRIEDMAN, MILTON. "The Role of Monetary Policy." *American Economic Review* 58 (March 1968). In this Presidential Address to the American Economic Association, Milton Friedman outlines his views on the theory of inflation and the effect of monetary policy on prices and economic activity.

————. "Nobel Lecture: Inflation and Unemployment." *Journal of Political Economy* 85 (May–June 1977): 451–72. In this paper Friedman restates his views in light of the experience of the decade since his Presidential Address.

GORDON, ROBERT J. "Recent Developments in the Theory of Inflation and Unemployment." *Journal of Monetary Economics* 2 (April 1976): 185–219. A well-organized summary and critique of competing theories of the inflationary process.

HUMPHREY, T. "Changing Views of the Phillips Curve." *Monthly Review* (Federal Reserve Bank of Richmond), July 1973. A very useful exposition of the development of the Phillips curve approach to wage determination. The student will find the graphical exposition particularly useful.

PHELPS, EDMUND S., et al., eds. *The Microeconomic Foundations of Employment and Inflation Theory*. New York: W. W. Norton, 1970. An interesting and influential study of the influence of inflationary expectations on the determination of wages and employment.

PHILLIPS, A. W. "The Relation between Unemployment and the Rate of Change of Money Wage Rates in the United Kingdom, 1861–1957." *Economica* 25 (November 1958): 283–99. The original "Phillips curve" study.

TOBIN, JAMES. "Inflation and Unemployment." *American Economic Review* 62 (March 1972). In this Presidential Address to the American Economic Association, Professor Tobin emphasizes the role of imperfect markets in explaining the simultaneous occurrence of inflation and unemployment.

20

Inflation:
The Recent Record

A man reputed to have very good judgment was asked how he acquired his wisdom. He replied, "You get good judgment from experience; you get experience from bad judgment." If economists understand inflation now, and that is not certain, it is because they have learned a lot from the experience of the last thirty years. Some of that experience reflects the bad judgment of economists.

The pattern of price changes since World War II seems to differ from that of earlier periods. All through the nineteenth century, prices rose in booms, in peace, as well as in war, but declined again in the ensuing recession. Since World War II prices have surged ahead in each boom, but have shown little or no decline in recessions. Up to 1961 the recessions at least served to check inflation if not to reverse it. But in the 1970–71 recession, inflation continued unabated. Currently, almost all countries have more inflation than they want.

The inflation experience since World War II seems different from that of earlier periods in two respects. First, the economic structure of the United States and many other countries as well seems to be more vulnerable to inflation than previously. Second, once inflation starts, it seems much more persistent.

In this chapter we are going to amplify the basic model developed in the last chapter, and use the amplified model to explain some of our experience and examine policies for dealing with our current problems.

We will begin with a brief review of five episodes of accelerating inflation, concentrating on the factors that got each surge of inflation under way. Then we will look more closely at the role of raw material and food prices, and note some of the ways in which the government has helped to raise costs and prices. Then we will look more closely at the rationale of the Phillips curve analysis of wage movements and see how changes in the structure of the labor market have tended to push the Phillips curve up, especially in the last decade. Finally, we will try to show how the material in this chapter can be used to modify the conclusions of the previous chapter and outline some alternative approaches to the control of inflation.

How Inflationary Episodes Start: Five Cases

Since World War II inflation has been a chronic disease in the United States and in many other countries as well. Five periods of accelerating inflation have been separated by intervals of relative price stability. By contrast with earlier periods, the consumer price index has seldom shown an absolute decline since World War II. Here we will give a very brief account of the history of inflation since the Second World War. In doing so, we will note some major changes in fiscal policy and in other factors affecting aggregate demand. In the following section we will give a summary account of major changes in monetary policy.

Postwar adjustment. Prices rose sharply after the elimination of World War II price controls. Between the end of 1945 and the end of 1948, consumer prices rose about 40 percent, then leveled off with the onset of the 1949 recession. Food prices rose rapidly with the end of wartime rationing and price controls, while trade unions negotiated very large wage settlements. Consumers flush with savings accumulated during the war provided a strong demand, while supplies were temporarily limited as producers switched from military to civilian production. But in a remarkably short time, by 1948, production caught up with demand and prices leveled off.

Korean War. The interval of price stability was a brief one. With the start of the Korean War in 1950, prices soared again under the impact of government demand and intense speculation in food products and raw materials as well as panic buying by consumers in anticipation of new wartime shortages. Sharp increases in income-tax rates checked the growth of demand, and food and raw material prices declined again. Their decline offset a continuing rise in labor costs. By 1952 the annual rise in consumer prices had been reduced to only 1 percent.

Midfifties. The rapid rise in prices after the end of price control in 1945 was more or less expected. It was regarded as the final part of the wartime inflation. And after the experience of World War II, no one was greatly surprised when a new war produced a new inflation. The reappearance of inflation in the midfifties, though very moderate by current standards, was more disconcerting, especially since there was no obvious excess demand. There was a rapid recovery from the 1954 recession. Overall, real GNP rose by more than 6 percent in 1955, led by an auto boom, a recovery of business investment, and a sharp rise in inventory investment. Although unemployment remained higher than in the Korean War period and overall capacity utilization was not unusually high, the boom was concentrated in the auto, steel, rubber, and related industries where strong unions predominated. According to a view widely accepted at the time, this concentrated boom enabled unions in those sectors to get large wage settlements. In any case, average wage increases did jump from around 3 percent per year between 1953 and 1955 to around 6 percent in 1956 and 1957. The resulting price rise was reinforced when food prices began to rise again in 1956. With the recessions of 1958 and 1960–61, the rate of price increase declined and prices remained relatively stable—rising about 1 percent per year until 1964.

Vietnam War. After several years of expansion in the early sixties the rate of growth of output accelerated in 1964 and rose for two years at an annual rate of 6 percent. The 1964 tax cut, expanding "Great Society" expenditure, the Vietnam War expansion, and an investment boom all served to step up the growth of demand. Some raw material prices had begun to rise as early as 1964 and food prices rose nearly 10 percent in 1965 but these events had only a minor effect compared to the wage acceleration that began in 1966. In this case the rise in wages was widespread and wages in unorganized industries rose earlier and for a time, faster than trade-union wages. The Vietnam boom continued through 1969 with inflation accelerating to a rate of 6 percent in terms of the consumer price index in 1969 and 4.9 percent in the GNP deflator. A recession starting at the end of 1969 seemed to retard inflation only a little. In 1971 a system of price controls was adopted. The consumer price index rose at only 3½ percent in 1971 and 1972 but whether that decline in the rate of inflation was due to price controls or the recession remains a matter of dispute.

1973 boom and oil crisis. In any case the slowdown in inflation was all too brief. In 1973 inflation came back with a vengeance. Everything happened at once. 1973 was a boom year not only in the U.S. but in all the industrialized countries. In large measure the boom reflected a general shift toward expansionary fiscal and monetary policy in response to the 1970–71 recession. This simultaneous expansion in many countries drove up prices of many raw materials. There were also shortages of processing capacity for many materials. However, the capacity shortages and rapid price increases reflected longer term developments in raw materials supplies as well as the worldwide boom.

At the same time crop failure in a number of countries, most notably in the Soviet Union, led to a spectacular increase in grain prices. The boom in demand played some role here, but the supply-side difficulties were clearly more important than the rise in demand.

Finally the boom coincided with the termination of price controls in the U.S. and many prices rose on that account.

At the end of 1973 the OPEC countries imposed an embargo, and then quadrupled the world price of oil.

All of these events raised the cost of living, and the rate of wage increases rose sharply in 1974 causing prices to rise more. During 1974 consumer prices rose by over 12 percent, while wholesale prices rose by more than 20 percent. A sharp recession in 1975 helped to reduce the rate of inflation. Recovery began in mid-1975 and continued until 1979. As unemployment fell from the very high levels of 1975, wage increases again accelerated and prices began to move up more rapidly. New increases in energy prices, a sharp rise in food prices, and the rise in the prices of imports as the exchange value of the dollar declined, drove the rate of inflation to 9 percent in 1978. The rate of price increase continued to rise during 1979. In early 1980, just before the start of a new recession, the GNP deflator rose at a 10 percent annual rate while the consumer price index rose at an annual rate of more than 15 percent, though it slowed later in the year.

Lessons of Recent Inflation

In many ways the actual course of inflation has conformed to the model outlined in chapter 19, but the history of inflation has reflected a number of factors not considered there. In this section we shall summarize a number of the major lessons from the experience of the postwar period. We deal first with the role of demand, then with cost-push factors, with wage-price spirals, and the persistence of inherited inflation. Finally, we note some changes in the structure of the economy, emphasizing the interaction between economic policy and the structure of the economy.

Role of Demand Expansion

Starting with the Korean War, each of the postwar inflation episodes has featured a rapid expansion of demand. In this respect the postwar inflations follow the pattern of centuries of inflation history. It may be possible to start an inflation without a surge of demand, but on the record it is not easy. There is no simple explanation for the demand shifts that marked the inflationary episodes described above. Fiscal policy played a dominant role in the Korean War inflation and in the last half of the 1960s. It was also important in causing the surge of demand in 1972–73, and it contributed significantly to the more moderate expansion following the 1975 recession. In each expansion, of course, consumer expenditures rose with increasing income, and private investment responded to a higher rate of growth of real GNP. In the expansion of the midfifties, a rapid growth in private investment and strong demand for consumer durables led the expansion. Strong consumer demand and a falling savings rate played a major role in the expansion following the 1975 recession.

The role of monetary policy in the inflationary episodes described above was a complex one. For much of the time the Fed's concern for interest-rate stability caused it to increase the money supply at just the time when other factors were tending to raise the growth of aggregate demand. On a few occasions, for example in 1966 and 1969, the Fed checked the growth of money supply in an effort to limit inflationary pressures. The record of monetary policy is discussed in detail in chapter 27.

As usual, opinions differ on the role of monetary policy in the recent inflation. Monetarists consider that the money-creation activities of the Fed supplied the major explanation for the shifts in aggregate demand during this period. Keynesians, on the other hand, think that most of those shifts were initiated elsewhere, but they too recognize that in the absence of the accommodating policy so often pursued by the Fed, the rapid shifts in demand that triggered the inflationary episodes described above would have been checked. Of course, they also emphasize that when the Fed did limit the growth of money supply (as in 1966, 1969, and 1974) the result was a credit crunch.

While periodic bursts of demand have played an important role at the outset of each inflationary episode, those outbursts certainly do not account for all of our inflation history. Our experience did not result from a continuing attempt to keep unemployment below the natural rate or NAIRU. Nor is it sufficient to suppose that occasional bursts of excess demand were followed by a policy of accommodating inherited inflation, though that is certainly part of the story.

We cannot explain postwar inflation without taking account of supply shocks and cost-push factors. Indeed, since 1970 unemployment has shown an upward trend. Even after allowance for some adverse developments in the labor market discussed below many economists believe that unemployment has been at or above NAIRU most of the time since 1970. The acceleration of inflation cannot be explained without reference to cost factors.

Nonetheless, demand policy played an important role because nominal money supply and government expenditure were raised enough to keep pace with rising prices. From an antiinflation point of view, demand policy in the seventies failed because demand was never held down long enough to eliminate the inflation inherited from the Vietnam expansion or to fully offset the effects of energy and other supply-side cost increases.

Finally, as we argue in a later section, the success of policy aimed at limiting unemployment may have tended to reduce the antiinflationary impact when it did occur.

Thus the experience of the postwar period confirms the role of demand in the initiation of bursts of inflation and in the maintenance of inherited inflation.

"Cost-Push" Factors in Inflation

In addition, several different types of supply or cost factors have influenced the course of inflation. First, rapid changes in raw materials, food, and fuel prices, partly generated by changes in demand, but partly due to events on the supply side, had a significant influence on price movements. Second, a variety of actions by government tended to increase the rate of inflation. Third, a decline in the rate of growth of productivity has helped to push up inflation in recent years.

Raw materials, food, and fuel. In three of the five postwar inflation episodes, rising prices for food, fuel, and raw materials played a major role in the initial stages of inflation. Even in the midfifties and the Vietnam inflation, food and raw material prices played some role.

The movements of raw material, food, and fuel prices depend on events on the supply side as well as on demand. Because demands for raw materials are inelastic, and because supplies become inelastic as capacity is approached, raw material prices fluctuate more strongly than others in response to shifts on demand. But the size of the price response to a given increase in demand can vary a good deal. Shifts in the supply curve due to weather conditions, strikes, revolutions, and long cycles in development of mineral resources all influence the price response. At some times, but not always, a surge of demand can drive up commodity prices enough to have a significant effect on consumer prices and thereby influence wages and other prices. Occasionally, supply shocks cause sharp increases in commodity prices, even in the face of weak demand.

How government raises costs. Prices are mainly set by market forces and must cover labor, raw material costs, and varying profit margins. But the prices consumers pay must also cover state, local, and a few federal excise taxes. In addition, housing costs reflect local real-estate taxes. Indirect business taxes paid by corporations have risen about as fast as other components of costs and have therefore had at least a small influence in pushing prices up. Indirect business taxes paid by the noncorporate sector (mainly real-estate taxes) have risen faster than GNP.

Employers' payments for social security (old age, survivors, disability, and health insurance) have soared with increased coverage, larger benefits, and the soaring cost of disability insurance and Medicare. The employers' tax rate has increased from 1 percent in 1948 to 6.1 percent, while the ceiling wage (highest wage on which the tax is paid) has increased faster than average wage levels. In addition many more employees are covered. Employees might regard the employer's payment as a pension contribution on their behalf and accordingly accept lower wage increases when the tax rate rises. In some cases that happens but it also appears that when tax rates rise total employment costs are pushed up and prices rise, thus speeding up the inflationary spiral.

Increasing costs for pollution control and the costs of meeting new health and safety regulations also show up in prices. Workers considering their real earnings do not appear willing to take lower real wages because jobs (not necessarily their own) are safer or because the products they buy cause less air or water pollution.

Medical costs make a significant contribution to inflation. Since 1964 they have risen twice as fast as the consumer price index. In considerable measure the rise results from the system of "third-party payment" through private health insurance, Medicaid, and Medicare. Though beneficial in many respects the health insurance system has been organized in such a way as to greatly reduce incentives to control costs in hospitals. At the same time it reduces the incentive for the patient and his doctor to use out-patient treatment and it encourages wasteful procedures. Government actions have fostered the system of third-party payments directly through Medicare and Medicaid and indirectly through the tax treatment of employer contributions to health insurance plans. These payments are treated as a deductible expense to the employer but are not taxed as income to the employee.

Finally, the government has made a notable contribution to inflation through tariffs, quotas, building codes, and some forms of price regulation. They have direct adverse effects on efficiency. In addition they reduce competitive pressures that could lead to increased productivity, lower costs, and reduced inflationary pressure.

Increases in indirect business taxes and reductions in productivity change the relation between the wage Phillips curve and the price Phillips curve. They raise the amount of price increase corresponding to any rate of nominal wage increase. The level of unemployment required to prevent inflation from accelerating shifts to the right by enough to compensate for the upward shift.

The productivity slowdown. Since 1973 the rate of growth of productivity has shown a marked decline. Output per hour has risen less than 1 percent per year. (See table 20.1.) Some of the decline can be explained by such factors as the expenditure of resources on pollution abatement and safety. A decline in the rate of capital formation has also played a role. Economists studying productivity have noted a number of other factors accounting for minor parts of the decline. However, much of the decline remains unexplained. Whatever the explanation, the productivity slowdown makes the

Table 20.1   Labor Productivity Growth
             1948–79   *(Percent change per year)*

Sector	1948 to 1955	1955 to 1965	1965 to 1973	1973 to 1978	1978 IV to 1979 IV[a]
Private business sector	2.5	2.4	1.6	0.8	–2.0
Nonfarm	2.4	2.5	1.6	.9	–2.2
Manufacturing	3.2	2.8	2.4	1.5	(b)
Nonmanufacturing	2.1	2.2	1.2	.5	(b)

a. Preliminary.
b. Not available.
Note: Data relate to output per hour for all employees.
SOURCE: *Annual Report of the Council of Economic Advisers,* February 1980, p. 85.

containment of inflation more difficult. For a given wage Phillips curve the price Phillips curve will be 2 percent higher at every level of unemployment with productivity growth at 1 percent per year instead of 3 percent per year.

Of course, the wage Phillips curve is not entirely independent of the growth of productivity, since employers are concerned about the effect of rising unit labor costs on profits and market position. Nonetheless, the productivity slowdown is a significant factor in the explanation of recent inflation.

Price-Wage Spirals

In chapter 19 we placed great emphasis on the proposition that the continuance of inflation for any considerable period causes shifts in the Phillips curve. Those shifts cause continued acceleration of inflation so long as unemployment remains below NAIRU. Moreover, those shifts account for the continuation of inflation even if unemployment goes back to but not below NAIRU. In a rough way that argument explains the acceleration of inflation in the late 1960s and its continuance into the early 1970s.

Persistent cost-push factors may also generate price-wage spirals, but it is not clear whether they work out in just the same way as in the case of inflations started by rapid demand expansion. As noted above a shift in the productivity trend raises the price Phillips curve in relation to the wage Phillips curve (see figure 19.5). The level of unemployment at which wage increases are balanced by price increases and prices are stable is now higher.

That, however, is only the first step. If unemployment were initially at NAIRU, it is now below it, and the inflation rate will start to rise just as though the initial cause of inflation had been a rise in demand.

One interpretation of actual events is to suppose that after 1973 unemployment rose enough to offset, partially but not completely, the effects of the reduction in productivity growth. A similar case could be made with respect to the trend of energy prices and taxes.

However, as noted in chapter 19, there are a variety of models of price-wage and wage-price spirals. In some of those models inflation will accelerate more rapidly when generated by demand factors than when started by cost-push factors. The full explanation of the events of the past few years is still controversial. Nonetheless, many economists believe that cost-push factors have played an important role in the inflation of the last few years.

Persistence

It has become commonplace to observe that inflations tend to persist once they have got underway. We have had significant inflation for many years. Moreover, inflation does not respond very readily to mild demand restraint. Indeed, the inflation rate and the unemployment rate both rose during the 1970s. The apparent paradox may be explained in part by the cost-push factors discussed above. Moreover, as we show in the next section, demographic and other changes in the structure of labor markets during the last two decades have raised the level of unemployment required to keep inflation from accelerating. But the statistical evidence suggests that even in the absence of those factors, a well-established inflation tends to persist in the face of slack demand. Many students of statistical Phillips curves assert that it will take many years of high unemployment to achieve a return to price stability. There is widespread though, of course, not universal agreement that inflation is now more resistant to the downward pressure of unemployment and excess capacity than it was before World War II.

Two kinds of structural change are cited to explain the apparent change. First, changes in the structure of labor and product markets may have reduced the downward flexibility of wages and prices. The increased strength of trade unions and the price "stabilizing" activities of government are often blamed. Second, the existence and partial success of policies aimed at averting deep depression and maintaining full employment weakens the economy's response to brief recessions. These explanations of the persistence of inflation are discussed later on.

Structural Shifts in the Phillips Curve

In the previous chapter we made use of the concepts of static and dynamic Phillips curves in the theoretical analysis of inflation. The Phillips curve is a helpful device for summarizing the response of wages to labor market conditions. The shape of the Phillips curve, however, depends on the underlying characteristics of the labor market.

We showed earlier how experience of inflation can shift the Phillips curve upward. That response is more or less built into the system. It does not take any changes in the structure of markets to make it occur. That kind of expectational shift in the static Phillips curve has to be sharply distinguished from historical events that change the response of wages to unemployment and price expectations. The difficulty of taming inflation and the coexistence of inflation and high unemployment has led to much discussion about the possibility that changes in the structure of the economy have shifted Phillips curves upward so that wages rise faster for any given level of unemployment and for any given set of inflation expectations. Attention has been given to three possible sources of Phillips curves shifts. First, some important demographic changes affecting unemployment have occurred, particularly since the midsixties. Second, it can be argued that government policies with respect to such matters as minimum wages, unemployment compensation, and welfare payments have affected the relation between wage increases and unemployment. Each of these matters involves controversial issues, and we can only touch on them here to avoid an oversimplified explanation of the inflation process. Third, it is possible that trade unions have an important influence on inflation. Since trade unions have been much stronger since World War II than in earlier prosperous periods and inflation has been more common since World War II than earlier, there is at least crude empirical support for that position.

Unemployment, Vacancies, and Wage Increases

To understand the significance of the change in the labor market noted above, we must ask why wages rise at all when there is unemployment. We can give a partial answer to this question by two considerations about the labor market.

First, the labor market is in constant flux. Workers are entering and leaving the labor market all the time. Something like 14 million people enter the labor market each year, while about 12 million leave for a net growth in labor force of 2 million each year. Every year workers quit their jobs to look for better ones. At the same time, individual firms or plants are constantly opening new jobs when demand for their product expands or laying off employees when demand contracts. It takes time for workers entering the labor force, quitting or losing a job, to find a new job, even if there were a job for every worker. The resulting unemployment is called *frictional* unemployment. A couple of million workers can be unemployed at the same time that a couple of million vacancies exist.

Second, workers are not a homogeneous group. We do not have a single labor market for a homogeneous commodity. We have thousands of overlapping submarkets defined by location, and the skills, education, and experience required for each occupational submarket. It is obviously possible to have shortages of labor in some markets and surpluses in others.

Thus for both reasons, there would be many unemployed workers, as well as many unfilled jobs, even if the total number of jobs available were just equal to the total number of workers in the labor market.

The rate of increase of money wages varies with the level of unemployment. Employers, faced with shortages of well-qualified workers, tend to raise wages to attract more of the kind of workers they want. But employers very seldom reduce money wages, even when faced with a surplus of qualified workers. Because of that asymmetry in the response of wages to labor shortages and surpluses, average money wages tend to rise at least a little when there are any submarkets with labor shortages. The average rises faster when unemployment is low because there are shortages in many submarkets. Average wages rise more slowly when unemployment is high and there are only a few shortages. In effect, the relative wage changes required to balance supply and demand in labor markets are accomplished by differential changes in absolute money wages rather than by increases in some wages and decreases in others. The process does produce relative wage changes and does help to direct labor into the areas and occupations where demand is expanding fastest. But because our economy is constantly changing, new imbalances in supplies and demands for labor are constantly being created, while relative wage changes eliminate older ones. The dynamic character of our economy together with the asymmetry in the response of wages to labor shortages and surpluses is a fundamental factor in explaining why money wages rise while there is still substantial unemployment.

Changing Composition of the Labor Force

The rate of wage change associated with a given level of unemployment can vary with the composition of the labor force. The composition of the labor force has changed in the past twenty years. The proportion of men over twenty-five in the labor force has decreased sharply while the proportion of women over twenty-five has increased and the share of younger men and women has increased even more rapidly. This marked shift in the composition of the labor force reflects an increasing tendency for women of all ages to go to work and to return to the labor force after marriage. It also reflects the very sharp rise in birth rates that began after World War II and continued until the mid-sixties. In addition labor-force participation rates for young men including those in school increased sharply. These changes have had significant effects on the relation between wage-rate changes and unemployment. Women and young people have always had higher unemployment rates than adult men mainly because they enter and leave the labor force much more frequently. Most men between twenty-five and sixty-five are in the labor force—working or seeking work—at all times.

By contrast, many women frequently enter and leave the labor force because of changing family responsibilities or because they have not committed themselves to a career. For many women there is a period of unemployment at each entry into the labor force. The result is a higher level of frictional unemployment in good times and bad. Young people—especially those who have not completed their education—also frequently enter and leave the labor force. They enter during vacations or when taking a "year out," and leave to return to school. Others seek part-time work while in school, but often leave the labor force because of the pressure of school work, or because their immediate needs have been satisfied.

Whatever the reasons for increased labor-force participation, the changes noted above have had significant effects on the composition of employment and unemployment. As noted earlier, a positive rate of unemployment is required to keep inflation from accelerating for four reasons: frictional unemployment due to the time required for persons entering the labor force to find a job even when suitable vacancies exist; frictional unemployment due to the time required for persons who have lost a job to find another even when vacancies in the same occupation or locality exist; temporary layoffs due to short-run production variations; mismatching or structural unemployment when workers in one area or skill group are unemployed while vacancies exist for other types of workers or in other areas.

The shifts in the composition of the labor force have relatively little effect on people who have lost jobs or are temporarily laid-off but significantly affect unemployment of people looking to enter the labor force or those affected by structural unemployment. An increase in the proportion of the labor force that frequently enters and leaves the labor force obviously increases the frictional unemployment due to entry and reentry. It may also have increased structural unemployment.

In 1956 unemployment was 4 percent and the labor market seemed reasonably well balanced. The unemployment rate for men over twenty-five was 3.1 percent and for women over twenty-five it was 4 percent. Suppose we use the 1956 unemployment rates for each age and sex group but weight them by the 1979 proposition of each group in the total labor force. The result is a rise in the overall unemployment rate by 1 percent. If we expected wages to rise faster than productivity at any employment rate less than 4 percent in 1956, we would now expect the same result at any unemployment rates below 5 percent.

Even that calculation may not reflect the whole increase in frictional unemployment. As participation rates for young people and women have increased, the amount of frictional unemployment per worker within these age and sex groups may have increased. A greater proportion of the young people in the labor force are still in school and have less attachment to regular employment than those who have left school. There are more women permanently in the labor force but the increase in participation rates for older women has necessarily increased the number of married women and correspondingly the amount of reentry friction.

Those considerations account in part for a moderate rise in unemployment among adult women relative to unemployment for adult men. The relative rate of unemployment for teenagers has nearly doubled. While this may reflect additional frictional problems it also may reflect a structural problem created by so large a shift in labor-force composition.

In view of the relatively slow growth of the adult male labor force, men have been in short supply in any period of rapid expansion. With relatively well educated women, often with previous work experience, available, employers have accepted women in previously all-male occupations—though wages for men were usually pushed up in the process. That substitution process has been much more difficult for the teenage population, for either part-time workers or drop-outs. These workers with few specific skills, little work experience, and a high turnover rate have not been attractive to employers seeking adult workers. Thus, employers have found it necessary, in periods of expansion to push up wages for adults, especially men, even though the overall unemployment rate was relatively high because of teenage unemployment.

Minimum Wages

The problem of youth unemployment has led to a reexamination of the minimum wage law. It could be argued that an excess supply of labor of any type should lead to a fall in wages. The fall in wages in turn should cause employers to substitute the type of labor in question for other labor and, at the same time, reduce the price of products using that type of labor, thereby increasing demand for those products and creating more employment for the group in question. An expansion of overall demand could then take up the slack in the other markets without any inflationary pressure. Finally, some workers willing to work at the minimum wage but unable to find work would drop out of the labor force if they knew they could only hope to be paid a substantially lower sum. That would improve the statistical unemployment figure, though not change reality.

There is a good deal of controversy over the significance of the minimum wage as a cause of youth unemployment. During the period of most rapid rise in teenage unemployment, the minimum wage fell relative to general wages but the proportion of employment covered increased. The net effect is uncertain. The law permits employers to apply for exemptions for trainees but the number of applications has not been large. That may, however, only reflect the paperwork involved and the fact that most teenage employment, in unskilled occupations, involves little training. Middle-class homeowners frequently complain that they cannot hire teenagers for odd jobs and yardwork unless they are willing to pay more than the minimum wage.

A reduction in the minimum wage for certain groups (relative to wages generally) could hardly hurt the teenage unemployment situation but may not be the panacea that some allege.

Unemployment Compensation and Welfare

Unemployment is most effective as a means of reducing wages or slowing increases when the unemployed have no alternatives but to take whatever work is available at the wage offered or starve. Whatever one thinks of the social-welfare implications of the Marie-Antoinette approach to unemployment, objectivity compels one to admit that programs that maintain the income of the unemployed do reduce the downward pressure of high unemployment on wages.

Unemployment compensation clearly reduces the pressure for displaced workers to accept employment that is substantially inferior in terms of wages, working conditions, fringe benefits, and job content relative to the job they have lost. For workers losing a job after six months or more of work, unemployment compensation will replace up to 50 percent of gross wages but, after allowing for tax differences and costs of transportation to work, the proportion of net wages lost by unemployment may be only 20–30 percent. For workers whose wives are employed the percentage loss in family income will be even smaller. For many workers then, the incentive to seek a new job may be relatively low so long as they are reasonably confident that they can return to their old jobs in a reasonable length of time. Thus workers on short layoffs (whether the recall date has been set or not) are not effectively in the labor force and available to fill other vacancies.

There have been no great changes in unemployment-compensation rates relative to wages in recent years, but coverage has been extended and during recessions the benefit period has been greatly extended. To the extent that the existence of unemployment compensation encourages workers to refrain from seeking work when laid-off temporarily or enables them to be more choosy about which jobs to accept, the Phillips curve is shifted upward. However, we cannot calculate the effect of changes in unemployment compensation on total unemployment by considering the particular workers involved.

Withdrawal or reduction of benefits may cause a particular well-qualified worker to seek and find work more quickly than he would have done while benefits were available. In many cases, however, he would simply displace another worker who would have got the job. What counts is that any extra inducement for workers—and particularly well-qualified ones— to fill vacancies more quickly can reduce the tendency for employers to make wage increases to recruit well-qualified workers. Then with the same unemployment rate we would have less inflation or with the same inflation rate less unemployment.

Welfare payments play a role similar to unemployment compensation and minimum wages. In some states payments to unemployed fathers (AFDC-UP) or state programs serve as an alternative form of unemployment compensation. Payments to women with dependent children have two effects. They enable men to remain unemployed, leaving their families to be supported by AFDC. They also enable women beneficiaries to remain at home rather than take low-wage jobs, thus reinforcing the effect of the minimum wage.

Whether any downward shift in the Phillips curve can be induced by changes in the welfare system is a complex matter. But it does seem likely that the downward pressure on wages exerted by unemployment is reduced by the existence of these programs.

All those changes shift both wage and price Phillips curves upward to the right, so that for any unemployment rate, wages and prices rise faster. As in the case of taxes and regulatory costs, the shift in Phillips curves implies that a higher rate of unemployment is required to keep inflation from accelerating.

Long-Term Structural Change

The changes discussed in the last section have occurred since the Second World War. Many economists believe that even more fundamental changes affecting price stability took place between 1929 and 1945. Of those changes, the rise of trade unions and the national commitment to full-employment policy may be the most important. The role of both of those changes is, however, very controversial.

Trade Unions and the Phillips Curve

Do trade unions raise the Phillips curve? The obvious answer seems to be yes because there appear to be cases when trade unions negotiate wage increases in circumstances when employees are having no difficulty recruiting or training labor and would be unlikely to raise wages without union pressure. In fact it is more complicated than that. Trade unions may raise some parts of the curve and lower others.

It is notable that trade-union wages tend to rise relative to other wages during periods of relatively high unemployment, for example, the early 1960s and the period between 1975 and 1977. It is also true that, at times anyway, trade-union wages are somewhat less responsive to boom conditions than those of the unorganized. That is partly due to the bargaining cycle. Unions with a three-year contract cannot get a wage increase until the contract expires, boom or no boom. In addition union wages may be less sensitive to demand conditions than others. Since union wages are relatively high, employers in organized industries have fewer recruiting problems in booms. And since the union members with the most political clout in the union are protected by seniority, the effect of unemployment on wage negotiations may be reduced.

On that approach we might suppose that there are separate union and nonunion static Phillips curves (that is, the curves appropriate when inflation expectations are absent). They might give us a picture like figure 20.1. Notice that if the rate of unemployment fluctuates around the point where

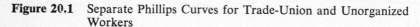

Figure 20.1 Separate Phillips Curves for Trade-Union and Unorganized Workers

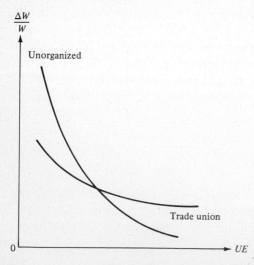

the curves cross there may be little secular change in relative wages. Relative wages of unions rise in the slumps and fall in the booms. However, that may not be the whole story. The union wage increases may be pulling up the nonunion ones. Unionists *may* get more than nonunionists when unemployment is high but in the absence of the union the unorganized might get no increase in money wages at all.

In that case unions reduce the inflation potential from an occasional boom but make it harder to get rid of inflation once it gets started. The latter influence may be strengthened when we consider responses to inflation expectations. Once inflation gets started unions may be better able to protect themselves from rising prices than unorganized workers and that may be especially so when unemployment is relatively high. Unions can, and do, negotiate escalator clauses that protect them from both expected and unexpected changes in the cost of living. Even when they do not have a formal escalator they can mobilize their members to get settlements that fully compensate for inflation. To the extent that this is true, and the current wide gap between union and nonunion settlements suggests that it is, the high-unemployment end of the Phillips curve will be shifted upward. Unions will make it harder to decelerate an inflation by raising unemployment. Finally, it may be noted that, at times anyway, unions may contribute significantly to wage increases in booms as well as in slumps. Many labor economists believe that the coincidence of the auto and capital goods boom of the midfifties with the timing of auto and steel settlements in 1955 and 1956 set off a round of large wage increases in durable goods industries. They believe that the expansion of employment in the boom would not have caused such big increases without strong unions. In the same way construction unions obtained very large wage increases during the construction boom of the late sixties. Had they not restricted entry into this highly paid employment, wages and construction costs might not have risen so much.

These observations are oversimplified and controversial. Some economists believe that these factors help to explain the chronic inflation of the postwar period while others believe that trade unions play only a very small role in inflation. In particular they may help to explain why prices, though rising in the booms as they have always done, have not declined; indeed they have continued to rise in the slumps. On the other hand, since trade-union strength has not generally been rising there is some difficulty in blaming trade unions for the increase in inflation rate or in the natural rate of unemployment that appears to have taken place in the last fifteen to twenty years.

The Effects of Stabilization Policy

At the end of the war, memories of the Great Depression of the 1930s were still vivid. The aggressive use of fiscal policy to maintain high employment, and especially to avoid a recurrence of major depressions, became the accepted basis of economic policy in all the industrial countries. By comparison with earlier times, that policy has been relatively successful. There have been no deep depressions, and recessions have been relatively brief and mild. Unfortunately, there are grounds for believing that the partial success of full-employment policy has made inflation control more difficult.

Policies aimed at maintaining full employment have direct and indirect effects on price stability. First, a commitment to full employment leads to accommodation of any established rate of inflation. We have simply been unwilling to suffer enough unemployment to eliminate inherited inflation.

In addition, however, a commitment to quick recovery from any recession weakens the effect of antiinflation measures when they are undertaken. In most markets, prices and wages are influenced by the expectations of buyers and sellers about future demand conditions as well as by the current state of demand. Firms faced with declining demand during a recession are under pressure to reduce prices and wages or at least to limit increases. The pressure is much less when they expect a quick recovery than it is when they fear worsening recession. The result is that successful pursuit of full employment may change the structure of the system so that a bigger dose of unemployment is required to achieve a given reduction in the rate of inflation.

Conflict between Full Employment and Price Stability

Ever since the end of World War II economic policy in all the developed market economies has been dominated by the conflict between the goal of full employment and the goal of price stability. The possible inflationary implications of a commitment to full employment were recognized in the early postwar years. It was thought then, however, that the conflict could be avoided by use of a "reasonable" definition of "full employment."

In the United States a 4 percent unemployment rate was widely accepted as a suitable target. It was supposed that an allowance of 4 percent for frictional unemployment and mismatching would be consistent with price stability. Because of the special circumstances of the postwar reconversion period in the late forties and the Korean War in the early fifties, the notion that 4 percent unemployment was consistent with price stability was not really tested until the midfifties. In fact, in 1956 and 1957 prices were rising at 3 percent per year, with unemployment around 4 percent. While that appeared a little discouraging, the speed of the 1955 expansion and its concentration on durable goods industries were cited as explanations. In addition, however, the inflationary potential of trade-union action and big business came in for a good deal of comment. In the early sixties unemployment remained at over 5 percent for several years, but prices still rose by 1–1½ percent per year, which suggested that very high rates of unemployment might be required to completely quell inflation. Since the 1960s demographic and other factors have been shifting price and wage Phillips curves upward. So much so that many economists now believe that

5½ percent to 6½ percent unemployment rates may be required to keep inflation from accelerating. Even higher rates would be required to bring inflation down significantly.

Full employment and price stability always lead the list of monetary policy goals, and conflict between those goals is likely to continue. Since the renewed acceleration of price increases in 1978–79, public concern about inflation has intensified but it does not follow that there is any less fear of unemployment. It is not at all clear that most people are willing to accept deep or prolonged depression as a means of getting back to price stability. The Fed has no clear mandate to give an unqualified priority either to price stability or to full employment.

It is sometimes said that the conflict should not exist because there is not a long-run trade-off between unemployment and inflation. That may be true in the long run in the sense that we are not able to keep unemployment below NAIRU without continuing acceleration of inflation. But we can have short-run acceleration of inflation. Moreover once we start with inherited inflation, we also have to face the option of keeping unemployment above NAIRU for several years in an effort to restore price stability. Even if there is agreement on the trade-off between the level of employment and the rate of change of inflation, it is not easy to reflect that agreement in terms of practical policy.

There is always dispute over just where the NAIRU is, and at any one time there is uncertainty and dispute over the policy appropriate to a given unemployment or GNP target. Finally, the system is subject to supply shocks, which will speed up the rate of inflation, unless offset by substantial unemployment. Thus makers of monetary and fiscal policy are always faced with conflicting goals. Even when they can agree on their objectives, they are often in dispute over the means of achieving the agreed-upon objective. Those complex issues are the main topic of Part Five.

Summary

Inflation has been a continuing problem since World War II. Periods of accelerating price increases have alternated with intervals of slower price rises, but there has been an upward trend in the rate of inflation. The history of inflation reflects an interaction between demand factors and a variety of other factors that directly influence costs and prices or indirectly affect the response of wages and prices to changes in demand. The latter factors include changes in raw material, food supply and energy prices as well as some cost-raising actions of the government. The response of wages to changes in the level of demand and unemployment reflect some long-standing imperfections in the labor market. In addition, changes in the composition of the labor force have increased the rate of unemployment consistent with price stability. Finally there is controversy over the role of trade unions, minimum wage policy, and unemployment compensation.

Disagreements over the role of changes in the labor markets and cost-push factors have intensified conflicts over the choice of targets for GNP and unemployment.

QUESTIONS AND EXERCISES

1. List some of the factors responsible for the rapid increase in demand in each of the inflationary episodes since World War II.
2. Raw material and food prices fluctuate more than most other prices. Why?
3. Trade-union wages appear to be less sensitive than nonunion wages to changes in the level of unemployment. Why may that be true? Is it always true?
4. Changes in the composition of the labor force have caused an upward shift in the Phillips curve. Explain. What other changes in labor-market conditions have exerted a similar influence?
5. Government has caused prices to rise by actions affecting production costs in competition as well as through its influence on aggregate demand. Give some examples.
6. "An increase in the cost of imported oil equal to 2 percent of GNP can add 2 percent to the inflation rate for an indefinite period." "Under appropriate aggregate-demand policy an increase in oil prices should result in a reduction in other prices and no inflation at all." What policies will make the first statement true? What policy is implied by the second statement?

FURTHER READING

FELDSTEIN, M. "The Importance of Temporary Layoffs: An Empirical Analysis," *Brookings Papers on Economic Activity* 1975:3, pp. 725–45. This article argues that many workers recorded as unemployed are not actively in the labor force or seeking work. It also argues that the unemployment-compensation system encourages workers on temporary layoff to remain out of the labor force.

————. "The Economics of the New Unemployment." *The Public Interest* 33 (Fall 1973): 3–42. Reviews the factors that have caused increasing unemployment in recent years.

FLANAGAN, R. J. "Wage Interdependence in Unionized Labor Markets," *Brookings Papers on Economic Activity* 1976:3, pp. 635–81. This paper examines the evidence for the hypothesis that large wages increases obtained by one trade union have a spillover effect on the wage increases obtained by other unions.

HICKS, SIR JOHN. *The Crisis in Keynesian Economics.* Part 3, pp. 59–85. New York: Basic Books, 1975. A thoughtful essay on the difficulties of maintaining "full employment" and stable prices.

PICOU, GLENN. "Labor Turnover: Another View of the Labor Market." *Monthly Review* (Federal Reserve Bank of Richmond) 58 (June 1973): 6–11. An examination of the role of labor turnover as a cause of employment.

SMITH, R. E.; VANSKI, J. E.; and HOLT, C. C. "Recession and the Employment of

Demographic Groups." *Brookings Papers on Economic Activity* 1974:3, pp. 737–60.

SOLOW, ROBERT M. "The Intelligent Citizen's Guide to Inflation." *The Public Interest* 38 (Winter 1975): 30–66.

————. "Macro-Policy and Full Employment." In *Jobs for Americans,* edited by Eli Ginzburg (Englewood Cliffs, N.J.: Prentice-Hall, 1976), pp. 37–58. These two papers provide an easy-to-read summary of the issues involved in dealing with the problems of unemployment and inflation.

VROMAN, WAYNE. "Worker Upgrading and the Business Cycle." *Brookings Papers on Economic Activity* 1977:1, pp. 229–52. This article gives evidence that employment opportunities for minorities are increased when demand expands rapidly.

PART FIVE

Monetary Policy

Having taken up monetary theory, we can now discuss monetary policy. With a small loss in accuracy we identify monetary policy with Federal Reserve policy, brushing aside the fact that the Treasury also has some very limited monetary policy powers. In the first chapter of this Part we therefore take up the Federal Reserve's goals, and in the following chapter we will look at the tools it has available to reach these goals. The subsequent chapter deals with how these tools operate in the money market, and the very controversial question of exactly how the Federal Reserve should use them. Chapter 24 then investigates how—and how strongly—monetary policy affects aggregate demand. In chapter 25 we then investigate how this impact of monetary policy is distributed over specific sectors of the economy. Chapter 26 then asks whether monetary policy can be used successfully to stabilize the economy, or whether it generates further instability. In chapter 27 we illustrate by specific historical examples some of the previously discussed points. The concluding chapter of this part then brings much of the material together by asking whether, given all the problems it has, countercyclical monetary policy is really desirable. An appendix discusses something in-between monetary and fiscal policy: debt management.

One warning is in order. Our discussion in Part Five relates entirely to the United States. In other countries monetary policy is very different both in its goals and techniques. In the less-developed countries the big issue in monetary policy is the extent to which the central bank should finance development projects by creating money, and what should be done about the resulting inflation. But even in other developed countries the goals of monetary policy differ. For example, in West Germany the clear priority of the central bank was to avoid inflation, while, at least until recently, in Britain it was to avoid unemployment.

Moreover, institutional differences provide countries with very different milieus for monetary policies. For example, in most countries, the government securities market is not large enough to allow the use of government securities in open-market operations; thus, in Switzerland, the central bank has to conduct its open-market operations by buying or selling foreign currencies. And, much more significantly, most countries are more "open" to foreign trade than the United States and have to take foreign-exchange rates and the balance of payments much more into account than the United States does. In addition, differences in the structure of the government influence the way monetary policy is used. Thus, in the United States monetary policy is treated as a much more flexible tool than fiscal policy because often—though by no means always—it takes a long time for Congress to pass bills that would change tax rates or government expenditures. In countries with a parliamentary system this can be done much more rapidly.

21

The Goals of Monetary Policy

Monetary policy shares the general goals of macroeconomic stabilization policy: high employment, price stability, exchange-rate stability, and a high rate of economic growth. But although monetary policy therefore has the same overall goals as fiscal policy it also has some specialized goals. These are interest-rate stability, an acceptable distribution of the burdens of restrictive monetary policy, and the prevention of large-scale bank failures and financial panics.

The Goals

We will first discuss these goals individually, and then take up the question of whether they are consistent in the sense that it is possible to meet all of them at the same time, or whether we have to sacrifice one to obtain another.

High employment. High employment is an obvious goal. Regardless of whether one focuses on the loss of output or on the human misery involved, practically everyone prefers high employment to large-scale unemployment. But an employment goal does raise serious issues.[1] One is its definition. Obviously, it does not mean zero percent unemployment. There is always some frictional unemployment that results from workers leaving one job to look for a better one, from new entrants to the labor force starting out as unemployed, and from a geographical or occupational mismatch of

[1] Some economists deplore the tendency to focus on the unemployment rate rather than the percentage of the total *population* that is employed. In recent years this ratio has been high and rising despite the fact that the unemployment rate has been high too, because a larger percentage of the population has entered the labor force. But, an efficient market should balance supply and demand so that at the prevailing price there is neither excess demand nor excess supply. Even if the proportion of the population employed is high, a high unemployment rate therefore indicates that the labor market is not functioning efficiently. However, since it is plausible that a rapid increase in the labor force will lead to a rise in the unemployment rate, the increased proportion of the population in the labor force should be taken into account in interpreting the unemployment figures.

workers and jobs. A certain level of unemployment is optimal for economic efficiency. By analogy consider the rental market in a city. If the vacancy rate for apartments were zero, then newcomers and those who want to change their housing, would be in great difficulty. Despite the *apparent* "waste" of having some empty apartments, this is not really a waste. Similarly, firms keep inventories to meet their customers' needs. These "idle" inventories may seem a great waste, but an economy without such inventories could not function efficiently. Unemployed workers are, to some extent, like idle inventories. Unfortunately, it is far from clear, even conceptually, how great the optimal level of frictional unemployment is.

And further, we do not have a good statistical measure of actual unemployment. Our unemployment data, which are gathered by monthly household surveys, are polluted in several ways. On the one hand, they understate the true extent of unemployment because they count only those people looking for work, thus leaving out those who have ceased to job-hunt because they believe that there is little chance of finding one. Second, part-time workers, who would prefer to work full time, are not counted as partially unemployed. On the other hand, if a male worker loses his job, his wife as well as he might then look for work so that the data count two people as unemployed, although the family is really looking for only one job. In addition, in some states people on welfare have to look for jobs, though presumably a number of them are not employable. Moreover, some people who work surreptitiously because they evade taxes, or are engaged in illegal activities, might classify themselves as unemployed. Beyond these statistical problems, the number of people actually unemployed also depends on the level and duration of unemployment-compensation payments. If these payments are high and obtainable for a long time, then workers have an incentive to look for good jobs rather than taking the first one that comes along. This is not necessarily bad. For example, if a skilled tool and die maker takes a job as a janitor when, with a few days more search he could have located a job in his trade, there is a clear loss in national income.

Thus, not only do we not know what the proper level of unemployment is, we also cannot accurately measure current unemployment. This means that it is sometimes difficult to decide whether unemployment is too high or too low. Obviously, this is not always the case. In the 1930s when frequently over a quarter of the nonfarm labor force was unemployed, there was little doubt the unemployment rate exceeded its desirable level, but this is much less clear if the unemployment rate is, say, 5 or even 6 percent. However, even a 5 percent level of unemployment may well be undesirable in the sense that with some better manpower programs, such as job training, and broader and better information on job vacancies, the appropriate level of frictional unemployment could be reduced.

So far we have talked about the optimal unemployment rate in terms of that level of unemployment that balances at the margin the loss from having idle labor, with the loss from not being able to find the workers needed to increase production. But probably a more relevant consideration is that a reduction in unemployment can generate inflation. As we discussed in chapter 19, there is a certain level of unemployment, sometimes called the natural rate, below which inflation takes off without limit. This consideration is actually a part of the conflict between goals, which we will discuss subsequently, but it is relevant here, because many economists define the proper level of unemployment, and hence by implication full employment, as the minimum level that is consistent with stable prices, or with an acceptable, or at least not accelerating, inflation rate.

Price stability. The next goal, price stability, may seem an obvious one, but actually it is far from obvious. Consider an economy in which prices have been rising at a rate of, say, 100 percent per year for the last fifty years, and everyone knows with certainty that the inflation rate will continue to be 100 percent. What damage does this inflation do? Clearly, it does not redistribute income because all wages and all contracts, as well as tax laws and accounting procedures, are adjusted for it. For example, if productivity is growing at a 2 percent rate, wages rise at a 102 percent rate each year, and the interest rate is, say, 103 percent instead of 3 percent. Such a fully anticipated inflation imposes only three types of losses. First, there is the bother and inconvenience of having to change price tags and catalogue prices frequently. Second, since prices cannot be changed continually, they will be out of equilibrium for the presumably short periods between price changes. Third, inflation creates an incentive to hold too little currency because currency holdings lose their real value without having the compensation of the higher nominal interest rate that other assets have. Hence, people are put to the inconvenience of continual trips to the banks to get currency. Yet, this seems a rather minor problem.

But the inflations we actually experience are not fully anticipated, and hence our economy is not fully indexed. Thus inflation raises tax payments. This can be criticized on equity grounds since some taxpayers are hit harder than others, as well as on the grounds that by taxing saving and corporate profits particularly hard it reduces the rate of capital formation.

In addition, it can be criticized for being a surreptitious way of increasing taxes. And since Congress is tempted to spend extra tax receipts, inflation in this way raises the size of the government sector relative to the private sector. But in the past Congress has, from time to time, cut tax rates enough to make up more or less for these automatic unlegislated tax increases. However, the government also gains because it is the largest debtor in the economy, and like all debtors experiences a reduction of the real burden of its debts as prices rise. All of this could, however, be avoided by indexing the tax system and government securities: for example, raising tax brackets and exemptions automatically by 10 percent if prices rose by 10 percent.

Apart from its effects on capital formation because of the tax system, inflation also misdirects investment because it makes it difficult to evaluate the profitability of firms, and it is the profitability of various firms and industries that should guide investment. Since in an inflationary period the recorded income of firms is distorted by an inadequate allowance for depreciation—and this distortion differs for different firms—the potential investor finds it harder to decide in which firm to invest. And in chapter 8 we saw how both conventional and variable-rate mortgages are inadequate credit arrangements in a period of substantial inflation, so that the share of residential construction in total investment is reduced.

But a much more obvious effect of unanticipated inflation is its impact on the distribution of income and wealth. Obviously, it hurts creditors, and hence the retired, and benefits debtors. In addition, it may help or hurt wage earners depending upon whether or not wages lag behind prices. All in all, the evidence suggests that in recent years inflation has helped the poor, thus making the distribution of income less unequal. But, this may not hold true for all inflations.

But regardless of what inflation does to the distribution of income among different income classes, it generates a substantial income redistribution *within* each income class, since some households are net borrowers and others net lenders. And this type of redistribution is surely deplorable. It is no more equitable than would be a tax on everyone who was born on an even-numbered day. To anyone genuinely concerned with equity, this redistribution must be a major, if not *the* major, loss from inflation.

Another loss from inflation is that it creates uncertainty and insecurity. Households can no longer plan confidently for the distant future since they do not know what their fixed dollar assets will then be worth in real terms. More generally, people have been taught the virtue of saving for a rainy day. But such prudent behavior is punished rather than rewarded by unanticipated inflation. This is likely to cause people to lose faith in the government and in the equity and reasonableness of social conditions in general. While this effect of inflation cannot be quantified, it may well be a major, perhaps even *the* major, disadvantage of inflation. Thus in the 1979 *Economic Report of the President,* President Carter wrote:

> The corrosive effects of inflation eat away at the ties that bind us together as a people. One of the major tasks of a democratic government is to maintain conditions in which its citizens have a sense of command over their own destiny. During an inflation individuals watch in frustration as the value of last week's pay increase or last month's larger social security check is steadily eroded over the remainder of the year by a process that is beyond their individual control. All of us have to plan for the future. . . . The future is uncertain enough in any event, and the outcome of our plans is never fully within our own control. When the value of the measuring rod with which we do our planning—the purchasing power of the dollar—is subject to large and unpredictable shrinkage, one more element of command over our own future slips away. It is small wonder that trust in government and in social institutions is simultaneously eroded.[2]

[2] Executive Office of the President, *Economic Report of the President* (Washington, D.C.: 1979), p. 7.

Economic growth. We defer the foreign-exchange-rate goal of the Federal Reserve until Part Six, since it needs extensive background discussion, and turn instead to economic growth. The actual economic growth rate can be decomposed into the growth rate of potential output, and the change in the relation between potential and actual output. We discuss here only the former, since actual output can be subsumed under the high-employment goal already discussed.

As everyone knows, there is much dispute about the desirability of a high rate of economic growth. However, the majority of Americans, nearly all policymakers, and certainly the Federal Reserve, do believe that a high rate of economic growth is desirable. In fact, there is now much concern that our current rate of growth is low relative to its trend in the postwar period, and relative to that in other countries. This lower growth rate is due to many factors, most of which are beyond the Federal Reserve's control, but the Federal Reserve can influence one important determinant of the economic growth rate: investment. A higher rate of investment not only means more capital per worker, but is also an important way in which technological progress comes about, since innovations are often embodied in new equipment. For example, the invention of a new machine tool does not increase productivity until firms invest by installing it. One way of raising investment is to keep the real interest rate fairly low. But this is inherently expansionary, and to prevent inflation such a policy would have to be accompanied by a restrictive fiscal policy, that is, by a large government surplus. This depends, of course, on Congress and the administration, and is beyond the Fed's control. And, to raise total investment, the surplus would have to be achieved either by raising taxes that impinge primarily on consumption, or by cutting government expenditures on items other than those that are government investment, as are, for example, road building or expenditures for research and development.

Another way the Federal Reserve can probably raise the rate of investment is by controlling the rate of inflation since the uncertainty created by an unpredictable rate of inflation lowers investment.

Prevention of widespread bank failures and financial panics. The prevention of bank failures and panics is in a way not a separate goal, since the main loss resulting from large-scale bank failures is likely to be a depression with very high unemployment. American economic history prior to 1934 shows a number of examples of massive bank failures that resulted in financial panics and depressions. The primary duty of any central bank is to prevent this from recurring. This certainly does not mean that the Federal Reserve has to be concerned about every single bank failure, or even about the failure of several banks at the same time. These cases can safely be left to the FDIC. But if somehow banks holding, say, 5 or 10 percent of total bank deposits were in danger of not being able to meet depositors' withdrawals, then it would be the Federal Reserve's job to step in and, through massive open-market operations, provide the banking system with enough reserves (and hence access to currency) to meet the depositors' demands.

Although the prevention of financial panics and massive bank failures is the Fed's most basic duty, it is a duty that is not frequently discussed because most of the time it does not call for any action. But this does not mean that it is unimportant. When it uses a strongly restrictive policy the Fed has to worry that it does not press this policy far enough to bring about massive bank failures.

Interest-rate stability. It is less clear why the Federal Reserve makes interest-rate stability one of its goals. Part of the answer is that this was one of the purposes for which the Federal Reserve was originally set up, but this is surely only a minor part of the story. Another part is a wish to protect the money market. Rising interest rates not only hurt thrift institutions, but they also hurt security dealers who make capital losses on their security holdings as interest rates rise and security prices fall. Moreover, there is a matter of equity that applies not only to security dealers, but to all holders of long-term assets. If interest rates fluctuate sharply, those who happen to have to sell a long-term asset, such as a house, at the time when interest rates are high make a capital loss. Another reason for Federal Reserve concern about interest-rate fluctuations is surely that the Federal Reserve gets blamed whenever interest rates rise. But in any case, since October 1978 the Fed has put much less emphasis on this goal than it previously did.

Sharing the burden of a restrictive policy. The final goal of the Federal Reserve is to avoid placing an excessive burden on any particular sector of the economy when it undertakes a restrictive policy. Monetary policy does not have a proportional impact on all industries; some are hurt much more than others. Academic economists sometimes argue that this is consistent with optimal resource allocation, and is therefore as it should be. But the Federal Reserve, subject as it is to potential congressional punishment, may feel it has to moderate a restrictive policy to protect a much affected, but powerful sector, such as the construction industry. More generally, residential construction is an industry with many friends in Congress, and further, rightly or wrongly, it is public policy to give this industry special aid, since good housing is an important social goal.

Conflict among Goals

Thus the Federal Reserve has many different goals, and its task is greatly complicated by the fact that there are numerous conflicts among them. Hence, it has to estimate the trade-offs and to decide the extent to which it will sacrifice one goal to attain the other.

High employment and price stability. To what extent do the high-employment and price-stability goals conflict? One possible conflict is that the

Federal Reserve might define high employment as a situation in which un-employment is below the natural rate. If so, as we discussed in chapter 19, not only would there be continual inflation, but the inflation would accelerate. There is less agreement among economists on whether the em-ployment goal and the inflation goal also conflict when unemployment is high and above the natural rate. Keynesian economists, such as Franco Modigliani, have argued that an expansionary policy then raises primarily output and has very little effect on prices. But monetarists argue that an expansionary monetary policy raises prices significantly even at times of substantial unemployment.

Another potential conflict between high employment and price sta-bility arises if we start from a situation in which inflation is already going on. Since firms and workers expect the inflation to keep going, they continue to raise their wages and prices. Unless the Fed can somehow change ex-pectations, the only way it can lower the inflation rate is to adopt a restric-tive policy that will create unemployment and excess capacity.

Economic growth. Since so far we are dealing with a closed economy, we leave conflicts between exchange-rate stability and the other goals until Part Six, and turn now to the relation of the economic growth goals to the price-stability and high-employment goals. Since inflation that is not fully anticipated reduces the economic growth rate there is no conflict between high economic growth and the price-stability goal in the long run. But in the short run there may be a conflict because, as we just mentioned, to eliminate or reduce an existing inflation generally requires that unemploy-ment and excess capacity increase. And the more excess capacity firms have, the less is the incentive to invest.

Bank failures and financial panics. The prevention of widespread bank failures does not clash with the employment goal, but it can, at times, conflict with the price-stability goal, and hence in this way also with the economic growth goal. For example, in 1966 the Federal Reserve called a halt to the severely restrictive policy it had adopted to fight inflation because it was afraid that a financial panic might occur. Admittedly this situation arises only rarely. Beyond this, bank regulation, by inhibiting banks in financial innovations, also has some, though presumably small, deleterious effects on economic growth.

Interest-rate stability and reducing special burdens. The relation between price stability and interest-rate stability is very different in the long run and the short run. In the long run there is no conflict between the two: the lower the rate of inflation, the lower is the nominal interest rate, and similarly, the more erratic the inflation rate the more erratic is the nominal interest rate. But the short run presents a very different picture. Suppose that aggregate demand increases because investment has become more prof-itable. As firms try to invest more the rate of interest starts to rise. The only way the Federal Reserve can postpone this rise (it cannot prevent it permanently) is to allow the quantity of money to increase at a faster rate.

But this is obviously inflationary. A similar short-run conflict arises if an inflation is already underway. To stop the inflation the Federal Reserve would have to cut the money growth rate, which would result in temporarily higher interest rates, and in attacks on the Federal Reserve.

Interest-rate stability has little direct effect on the rate of economic growth. But insofar as it changes the inflation rate and the capacity utilization rate it does affect economic growth indirectly in the ways we just discussed. Its effect on the possibility of massive bank failures is at most very indirect.

The final goal is minimizing the special burden that monetary policy imposes on particular sectors of the economy. Here too, one must distinguish between the long run and the short run. In the long run it is an expansionary policy that, by generating inflation, creates special burdens for particular sectors of the economy because many of our institutions are predicated on more or less stable prices. For example, the problem that thrift institutions face given their long-term assets and short-term liabilities, is mainly due to the inflation-induced rise in nominal interest rates. Thus, in the long run, the moderately restrictive monetary policy that is needed to curb inflation is consistent with minimizing distortions. But in the short run such a restrictive policy raises interest rates, and thus hurts sectors like residential construction.

What Should the Fed Do?

This whole problem of conflicts among goals would not arise if the Fed had as many separate tools as it has targets and constraints. But this is not the case. All its major tools operate by changing bank reserves and interest rates, so that in this sense it has but a single tool. Hence it frequently faces a dilemma; some of its goals suggest that it should increase bank reserves, and others that it should reduce them.

One possible solution would be to give the Fed only a single goal, or at least a predominant goal. *If* this is to be done, this should *perhaps* be price stability, since a consistent attempt to reduce unemployment would probably result in only a small reduction in unemployment and a high inflation rate. In the long run the Phillips curve is vertical. At best the Federal Reserve could reduce cyclical unemployment only.

But if we start from a situation in which a substantial inflation is already going on, a policy to stabilize prices would probably result in much unemployment. Besides, an overriding price-stability goal would prevent the Federal Reserve from taking expansionary action at those times when unemployment is very high, but a supply shock, such as a rising cost of oil imports, is raising prices. Most economists therefore believe that the Federal Reserve should deal with the conflict among its goals in an ad hoc manner, flexibly balancing the gain with respect to one goal against the loss with respect to another goal.

This raises the obvious question, what does the Fed actually do? How much importance does it attach to each of the above goals? Unfortunately, this is difficult to determine. The Fed does not issue statements revealing its trade-offs between various goals, nor does it tell us which one it considers the most important. Instead, it tends to deemphasize the conflict between its goals, and sometimes suggests that the achievement of any goal is necessary to attain the others. Such an unwillingness to reveal its hard choices is not surprising. If the Fed were to say that it is relinquishing one goal for the sake of the others, the proponents of this goal would react angrily and might join a coalition that would trim its independence. An attempt to be all things to all people is not unique to the Federal Reserve —other government agencies do it too (and even individuals have been known to do it!), though the Fed does it to a greater extent than, say, the Council of Economic Advisers.

The Fed's reluctance to spell out its goals has another great advantage for it. It makes it very hard to evaluate its actions since, when accused of failing with respect to one goal, the Fed can frequently point to another goal that, perhaps for reasons having little to do with monetary policy, has been attained. The exasperating task involved in evaluating monetary policy is well exemplified by the following comment of Senator Proxmire to former Federal Reserve Chairman Martin:

> I have the greatest respect for your ability, and I think that you are an outstanding and competent person, and everybody agrees with that, but the fact is, that when you try to come down and discuss this in meaningful specific terms, it is like nailing a custard pie to the wall. . . . And frankly, Mr. Martin, without specific goals, criteria, guidelines, it is impossible to exercise any Congressional oversight over you, and I think you know it.[3]

The problem of determining the Fed's trade-offs between its goals is complicated not only by its reluctance to reveal its trade-offs, but also by the fact that its trade-offs probably vary from time to time. Given the great power and influence of the chairman of the Board of Governors, goals may change when a new chairman takes over. In addition, the Fed is influenced by public attitudes, and, like the Supreme Court, it follows election returns. Moreover, the relative importance of goals is likely to vary along with economic conditions. For example, if the inflation rate suddenly accelerates, the Fed is likely to pay it more attention than the unemployment rate. But after several years have passed, the Fed will find this higher inflation rate less worrisome.

Monetary Policy and Fiscal Policy

As might be expected, the goals of monetary and fiscal policy overlap. This is not surprising since monetary and fiscal policy are both macroeconomic

---

[3] Cited in John Culbertson, *Full Employment of Stagnation?* (New York: McGraw-Hill, 1964), pp. 154–55.

stabilization tools. But it does raise the question of how to coordinate them, specifically whether one can coordinate them to ameliorate the problem that the Fed has too many and conflicting goals. Or, on the contrary, does fiscal policy interfere with monetary policy?

Coordination of Fiscal and Monetary Policy

An obvious way in which fiscal policy can support monetary policy is by taking over part of the general stabilization task, so that monetary policy can be used in a more moderate manner. If the government raises taxes or cuts its expenditures when aggregate demand is excessive, then this reduces the severity of the restrictive monetary policy that is required to prevent unacceptable inflation. But fiscal policy cannot help monetary policy in one important way. It cannot remove the conflict that exists in the short run between price stability and high employment. Both fiscal and monetary policies operate by changing aggregate demand, while the price stability–unemployment conflict is inherent in the way product markets and labor markets react.

Can monetary and fiscal policy be made to share the burden in a way that uses the comparative advantages of each? One possibility is to make use of a *possible* difference in their timing. In the United States fiscal policy changes are often slow to come about. Unless there is widespread agreement in Congress, changing taxes and government expenditures can take a long time. On the other hand, the Federal Reserve can change monetary policy fairly rapidly. However, what matters is not just how long it takes to change policy, but also the lag until the change in policy has its impact on income. When one takes account of this lag it is not clear that monetary policy is necessarily faster acting than fiscal policy.

Another possibility is to use fiscal policy to moderate the loss that a restrictive monetary policy imposes on some particular sectors. Thus, during periods of sharply rising interest rates, one tool of fiscal policy—lending by government credit agencies—has been used to provide additional funds to thrift institutions. But, on the whole, the idea of employing fiscal and monetary policies as a team founders on the fact that government tax and expenditure policies usually are not employed as countercyclical tools. Rather, government expenditure goes up when there is a perceived need for additional government services. Tax rates are raised primarily because government expenditures are going up, or are cut because the public is fed up with high taxes. Countercyclical considerations play some, but only a quite limited role in actual fiscal policy.

The Government Budget Constraint

Fiscal and monetary policies are inevitably related in one way. This is that the government, like everyone else, has a budget constraint. The Treasury must finance its expenditures either from its revenues or by borrowing from someone. But the government, unlike other sectors of the economy, has an apparent "out." It can borrow from itself, that is, from the Federal Reserve. As the Treasury sells securities to the public, the Federal Reserve can, at the same time, buy securities from the public, so that the public's holdings of government securities do not increase. In effect, the Federal Reserve "lends" to the Treasury. But this "out" has a nasty side to it. As the Fed buys government securities it provides banks with additional reserves, so that the money stock increases. This process is called *monetizing* the debt, and is, of course, inflationary.

Does the Federal Reserve follow a consistent policy of monetizing a specific proportion of the increase in the public debt such as buying, say, one-quarter of the new securities sold by the Treasury? No, it does not. But it does monetize debt in an unsystematic way. As the Treasury sells securities the interest rate tends to rise, and the Federal Reserve then adopts an expansionary policy—that is, it buys government securities in its open-market operations—to keep interest rates from rising in the short run. However, the extent to which the Fed monetizes the debt in this way varies from time to time and may now be smaller than it used to be.

But although the Federal Reserve does not *systematically* monetize increases in the public debt, it is clear that large Treasury deficits can make it hard for the Federal Reserve to control inflation. If it holds down the growth rate of the money stock, then the Treasury's security sales, as well as the rise in income that results from the increase in the government's deficit, raise interest rates. As interest rates rise the Federal Reserve comes in for much criticism and consequently is tempted to adopt a more expansionary policy.

It is therefore not surprising that Federal Reserve chairmen like to lecture both Congress and the administration on the need for fiscal prudence. These lectures also have the advantage of giving the impression that the Fed is a staunch foe of inflation, even though it may at the same time be allowing the money stock to grow at much too fast a clip.

Summary

The Federal Reserve has many goals: high employment, price stability, exchange-rate stability, high economic growth, the prevention of widespread bank failures, interest-rate stability, and a fair distribution of the burden of restrictive monetary policy. There are some difficulties in defining high employment, and in measuring the actual rate of unemployment. (Similarly, it is not clear how much of an increase in the price indexes is consistent with reasonable price stability.)

There are numerous conflicts among the Fed's goals. Although high employment and price stability are consistent in the long run, in the short run employment can be raised if the Fed is willing to accept some inflation. Moreover, once an inflation is going on, reducing it requires an increase in unemployment. Economic growth is consistent with price stability, but here, too, the reduction of an inflation requires a temporary fall in the economic growth rate. The avoidance of widespread bank failures is consistent with the high-employment goal, but insofar as it may require the Fed to suspend a restrictive policy it may conflict with the price-stability goal. Interest-rate stabilization frequently clashes with the price-stability and employment goals. The Fed's concern with the distribution of the burden of a restrictive policy also may interfere with the price-stability goal. Given these conflicts a few economists would have the Fed use only a single primary goal, price stability. However, the Fed generally argues that there is little conflict among its goals and that it can try to attain them all.

The goals of monetary policy and fiscal policy overlap substantially. The more effective fiscal policy is, the less is the task that monetary policy has to do. One possible way of combining monetary and fiscal policy is to rely on the fact that the Federal Reserve can change monetary policy faster than Congress changes fiscal policy. But when the lag between the change in policy and the change in nominal income is taken into account, it is not clear that monetary policy is really the faster of the two. Fiscal policy can be used to ameliorate the burdens that a restrictive monetary policy imposes on certain sectors of the economy.

The government has a budget constraint so that a deficit has to be financed by selling securities or by creating money. The Federal Reserve can monetize the debt by buying securities from the public. The Fed does this at times in order to prevent the deficit from raising interest rates, even though such a policy can be inflationary.

QUESTIONS AND EXERCISES

1. What are the goals of Federal Reserve policy? Either argue that one of them should not be treated as a serious goal, or argue that there is an additional goal that should be included.
2. Why does the Federal Reserve have an interest-rate stabilization goal? Do you think it is important?
3. Describe the conflict between the full-employment goal and the price-stabilization goal.
4. Describe the problems an inadequate fiscal policy can create for the Federal Reserve. Do you think fiscal policy is currently helping or hindering monetary policy?
5. Read through the current *Economic Report of the President* and prepare a statement of the trade-offs between various goals that are either explicit or implicit in it. Do you agree with these trade-offs?

FURTHER READING

ABRAMS, RICHARD; FROYEN, RICHARD; and WAUD, ROGER. "Monetary Policy Reaction Functions, Consistent Expectations and the Burns' Era." *Journal of Money, Credit and Banking* 12 (February 1980): 30–42. This is one of a series of articles that tries to estimate by regression analysis how the Fed reacts to unemployment, inflation, and foreign-exchange market pressures.

BACH, G. L. *Making Monetary and Fiscal Policy*. Washington, D.C.: Brookings Institution, 1971, pp. 3–25. A good discussion of the Fed's goals with emphasis on their evolution.

FISCHER, STANLEY, and MODIGLIANI, FRANCO. "Towards an Understanding of the Real Effects and Costs of Inflation." *Weltwirtschaftliches Archiv* 114, 4 (1978): 810–33. A useful summary of the losses from inflation.

JOHNSON, HARRY. *Essays in Monetary Economics*. London: George Allen, 1967, ch. 6. Although dealing directly with Canadian conditions, it contains many insightful points relevant to the United States.

MAISEL, SHERMAN. *Managing the Dollar*. New York: W. W. Norton, 1973. Provides an excellent "feel" for the pressures under which the Fed operates.

22

Tools of
Monetary Policy

In this chapter we take up the specific tools the Federal Reserve uses to reach the goals set out in the previous chapter. These tools can be divided into two groups: **general controls** that *affect the whole economy,* and the so-called **selective controls** that are *designed to reinforce, or ameliorate, the impact of general monetary policy in specific areas of the economy,* such as the stock market. This distinction between general and selective controls is, however, not watertight; selective controls also have some effects on the rest of the economy.

Open-Market Operations

Open-market operations are now by far the most important tool of monetary policy, a fact that would have greatly surprised the framers of the Federal Reserve Act. The original idea of the Federal Reserve was that, like the Bank of England, it would use discounting, that is, lending to member banks, as its main tool. But, more or less by accident, a much more efficient tool was discovered: open-market operations. In the early years of the Federal Reserve, the Federal Reserve banks bought government securities to provide themselves with earnings, with no realization of the effects of this on bank reserves. They soon discovered that their purchases or sales of securities had a powerful effect on bank reserves and on the money market. In 1923 they therefore agreed to carry them out with "primary regard to the accommodation of commerce and business." [1]

The present organization for open-market operations has already been discussed in chapter 7. The FOMC sends a Directive to the account manager (or "Desk") at the New York Federal Reserve Bank who undertakes the actual purchases and sales of securities. He deals, not with the general public, but with a small number of security dealers, some of which are banks and some of which are specialized wholesalers of government se-

[1] Statement by Federal Reserve Board, quoted in W. Randolph Burgess, *The Reserve Banks and the Money Market* (New York: Harper and Row, 1946), p. 241. This book provides a very good survey of pre–World War II Federal Reserve functioning.

curities. The Desk is in continual contact with them, asking them for bids or offers on securities. It therefore knows the price and the interest rate on these securities at all times, and has a very precise knowledge of money-market conditions, of what the Federal Reserve calls "the feel of the market." The Desk can adjust its open-market operations to ever-changing conditions, perhaps buying or selling several times during the day. The Federal Reserve does not force anyone to buy or sell securities; it buys or sells at the prices the dealers quote to it.

Operations of the Trade Desk

The "Go-Around"

The time is just before noon on the Tuesday before Thanksgiving Day. The place is the eighth floor trading room of the Federal Reserve Bank of New York. The Manager of the Federal Reserve System's Open Market Account has made his decision. He tells his second in command to buy about $500 million in United States Treasury bills for immediate delivery.

The decision made, the officer-in-charge turns to the ten officers and securities traders who sit before telephone consoles linking them to more than 30 primary dealers in U.S. Government securities. "We're going in to ask for offerings of all bills for cash," he says. Each person is quickly assigned two to four dealers to call.

Joan, a New York Federal Reserve trader, presses a button on her telephone console, sounding a buzzer at the corresponding console of a Government securities dealer.

"Jack," Joan says, "we are looking for offerings of all bills for cash delivery."

Jack replies, "I'll be back in a minute." The salesmen of his firm quickly contact customers to see if they wish to make offerings. Jack consults the partner in charge about how aggressive he should be in offering the firm's own holdings.

Ten minutes later Jack calls back. "Joan, I can offer you for cash $5 million of January 5 bills to yield 5.85 percent—$10 million of January 26 bills at 5.90—$20 million of March 23 bills at 6.05—and $30 million of May 30 bills at 6.14."

Joan says, "Can I have those offerings firm for a few minutes?"

"Sure."

Within minutes the "go-around" is completed. The traders have recorded the offerings obtained from their calls on special preprinted strips. The officer-in-charge arrays the individual dealer offerings on an inclined board atop a stand-up counter. A tally shows that dealers have offered $1.8 billion of bills for cash sale—that is, with delivery and payment that very day.

The officer then begins circling with a red pencil the offerings that provide the best—that is the highest—rate of return for each issue. The large quotation board facing the open end of the U-shaped trading desk tells him the yields on Treasury bills as they were in the market just before the "go-around" began. An associate keeps a running total of the amounts being bought. When the desired amount has been circled, the individual strips are returned to the traders, who quickly telephone the dealer firms.

"Jack, we'll take the $5 million of January 5 bills at 5.85 and the $30 million of May 30 bills at 6.14 both for cash; no, thanks, on the others," Joan says.

Forty-five minutes after the initial decision, the calls have been completed, and $523 million in Treasury bills purchased. Only the paper work remains. The traders write up tickets, which provide the basic authority for the Bank's government bond department to receive and pay for the specific Treasury bills bought. The banks that handle the dealers' deliveries—the clearing banks—will authorize deductions of the securities from the book entry list of their holdings at the Federal Reserve. In return, they will receive credit to the reserve accounts the banks maintain at the New York Reserve Bank.

The Federal Reserve credits to the dealers' banks immediately adds over $500 million to the reserves of the U.S. banking system.

SOURCE: Paul Meek, Open Market Operations (New York: Federal Reserve Bank of New York, 1978), pp. 1–2.

The Fed is authorized to deal in its open-market operations in U.S. Treasury securities, securities of government agencies such as GNMA (Ginnie May), certain state and local government securities, bankers' acceptances, and so on. But in practice the great bulk of open-market operations is in Treasury securities. And further, most of the transactions are in Treasury bills. This is so because the Federal Reserve wants to minimize the extent to which it changes security prices in its open-market operations. Since the market for Treasury bills is very large it can buy or sell a substantial volume without changing their price very much. By contrast, if the Fed were to sell an equal volume of, say, twenty-year government securities, their price would drop substantially. This would create unwarranted capital losses for many holders. Specifically, government-security dealers, who hold a large volume of securities relative to their capital, could be seriously hurt. And the Fed is afraid that as a result they might cease to "make a market" in such securities, that is, that they would cease to hold them, but would act merely as brokers who bring buyers and sellers together. This would reduce the efficiency of the capital market. Hence, while the Federal Reserve does deal from time to time in longer-term securities, it conducts most of its open-market operations in Treasury bills.

Actually, most open-market operations are not really sales or purchases in the usual sense of the words. The great bulk of "purchases" are done under repurchase agreements, often called **repos,** that is, under an *agreement with the "seller" that he will buy the securities back again at a fixed price at a certain date.* Similarly, most of the Fed's security sales are done under so-called **reverse repos,** more formally known as matched sale-purchase transactions, with the *Fed pledging itself to buy these securities back at a fixed price at a particular time.* The reason why the Fed uses such repos and reverse repos is that most open-market purchases or sales are intended to affect bank reserves only very temporarily. By using repos and reverse repos the Fed lets the market know that these transactions will soon be reversed.

These reversals result from the fact that most open-market operations are "defensive" rather than "dynamic." Dynamic operations are those in which the Fed wants to change the level of bank reserves from their previous level. Defensive operations, by contrast, are those in which the Federal Reserve, to keep bank reserves constant, buys or sells securities to offset the effects on bank reserves of the market factors (discussed in chapter 10). Fluctuations in market factors generate very large—but very temporary—changes in reserves. To stabilize the money market and the supply of money, the Federal Reserve tries to offset these changes, except insofar as they happen to change the federal funds rate and bank reserves in the direction the Federal Reserve wants. To do this the Fed expends considerable effort in predicting the probable behavior of market factors. In addition, the Fed tries to gauge the *overall* impact of market factors by obtaining the "feel" of the money market in its contacts with government security dealers and something that frequently triggers open-market operations is changes in the federal funds rate as market factors supply or withdraw reserves.

Defensive operations account for the great bulk of open-market operations. For example, in 1977, the net growth that occurred in the Federal Reserve's open-market portfolio, that is, dynamic operations, was only about one percent of total open-market operations.

The effect of open-market operations on bank reserves has already been demonstrated in chapter 10 by means of T accounts. But to repeat, if a bank sells $100 of securities to the Federal Reserve, its T account changes as follows:

Assets		*Liabilities*	
reserves with F.R.	$100	deposits	0
securities held	–$100		

If a customer of the bank, instead of the bank itself, sells the securities to the Federal Reserve, the T account entries after he or she deposits the funds are:

Assets		*Liabilities*	
reserves with F.R.	+$100	deposits	+$100
securities held	0		

As you can see, in both cases bank reserves increase, so that additional deposits can now be created. And open-market operations also change the federal funds rate. Obviously, if the Federal Reserve buys securities, this raises security prices and lowers interest rates.

Advantages of Open-Market Operations

Open-market operations are the prime tool of monetary policy for several reasons. First, the Federal Reserve can buy or sell enough government securities to set the size of the reserve base as it pleases; there is more than enough ammunition. This tool is always strong enough to do the job. Second, open-market operations occur at the initiative of the Federal Reserve, unlike member bank borrowing where the Fed can only encourage or discourage borrowing but has no precise control of the volume involved. Third, open-market operations can be carried out in small steps, very small ones if need be. This allows the Federal Reserve to make exact adjustments in the reserve base. Fourth, open-market operations enable the Federal Reserve to adjust the reserve base on a continuous basis as the federal funds rate changes, and as it receives new information about the impact of market factors on reserves. Because of its ability to move in large or small steps the Federal Reserve really does have fingertip control over the reserve base. Fifth, and finally, open-market operations are easily reversed. The Federal Reserve can buy at 10:00 A.M. and sell at 10:05 A.M., and since the federal funds rate could change at any time and the Desk's assessment of money-market conditions is continually subject to revision, this ability to change course is highly prized by the Federal Reserve. None of the other tools are as flexible.

The Discount Mechanism

The discount mechanism is a device by which member banks have been able to borrow from the Fed.[2] Under a law passed in 1980 this borrowing privilege was extended to nonmember banks, as well as to thrift institutions that have transaction accounts and hence keep reserves with the Fed. It serves several functions. One is to fulfill the Federal Reserve's lender-of-last-resort function, particularly in those cases where only a few banks experience a liquidity crisis. If many depository institutions are short of liquidity then the discount mechanism has to be supplemented by extensive open-market purchases, but even then it is important in channeling funds to those institutions that are particularly vulnerable. Widespread bank failures have not been a problem since 1933, but could possibly become a problem again in the future. Second, the discount mechanism provides a way in

[2] Discounting is a process of deducting the interest due from the face value of the borrower's promissory note. For example, if someone borrows by discounting, he or she will receive in exchange for his or her promise to pay, say, $10,000 next week, not the full $10,000, but only $9,990, the $10 interest being subtracted in advance. Banks normally borrow from the Federal Reserve by discounting their own promissory notes (using government securities as collateral), but they can, under certain conditions, instead discount a second time certain promissory notes they have discounted for their customers, hence the term *rediscounting* is sometimes used.

which the Fed can bail out a particular institution that is in difficulty, the prime example being the Federal Reserve's loan of $1.7 billion to the Franklin National Bank, as discussed in chapter 3. Third, the existence of the discount mechanism allows the Federal Reserve to undertake more restrictive open-market operations than it otherwise could because it provides a safety valve. A bank that loses too many reserves because its customers are buying more securities can temporarily restore its reserves by borrowing from the Federal Reserve, thus obtaining the breathing space needed to adjust its portfolio.

Fourth, by changing the discount rate, the Fed can encourage or discourage borrowing, and this is one way it has of changing the reserves available to the whole banking system.

Since depository institutions can *at times* borrow from the Fed at less than the prevailing market rate of interest, it is necessary to limit the amount of discounting they can do. For a long time the Federal Reserve did this by scrutinizing in detail the reason for a bank's borrowing, and the amount of borrowing the bank had done in the past. But this turned out to be very complex, and has now been replaced by a more standardized approach, which has reduced, but not eliminated, the Federal Reserve's scrutiny of institutions that borrow frequently.

There are several categories of borrowing. First, there is the **basic borrowing privilege.** Under this rubric *institutions can borrow up to a certain percentage of their required reserves,* and this percentage is higher for small ones than for large ones. Such loans are available with very little fuss, though the Federal Reserve does check that the institution is not borrowing to make a profit by borrowing at the discount rate to purchase higher yielding assets, such as Treasury bills. A bank simply calls the Fed and announces that it wants to borrow. In many cases the bank already has a promissory note as well as collateral on file with the Fed, so that the transaction can be completed over the telephone. The length of time for which it can borrow under its basic borrowing privilege is, however, limited. For large institutions these loans mature on the next business day, for medium-sized ones they mature at the end of the current weekly reserve period (that is, the coming Wednesday), and for small ones at the end of the following weekly reserve period.

A second category is the **seasonal borrowing privilege.** Certain *institutions,* for example, banks in resort areas, *experience heavy seasonal fluctuations in deposits or loan demand, and hence in their need for reserves.* Such banks, particularly the small and medium-sized ones, are allowed to borrow an extra amount at those times.

Third, there is **other adjustment credit.** This is a *provision for emergency borrowing,* and it is rarely used. It can be used in case of a natural disaster, for instance, a flood, or by a bank or thrift institution facing a serious internal problem, maybe the loss of some large accounts. In addition, this category is available for use in case we should experience another financial panic. In such an emergency the Federal Reserve could make loans secured by government securities (or securities guaranteed by federal agencies) to any individual, partnerships, and corporations.

The Discount Rate

Although we always speak of the "discount rate," there are actually several rates depending upon the collateral offered by the borrower. In addition, as a result of the Franklin National Bank experience, the Federal Reserve added a proviso that allows it to charge an unusually high discount rate should such a case occur again.

The Federal Reserve can vary the interest rate it charges borrowing institutions. Thus it can induce banks and thrift institutions to increase or to reduce their borrowing, and can in this way change bank reserves.[3] But the volume of reserves involved is small compared to the change that results from open-market operations.

The inducement to borrow can, and does, vary even if the Fed keeps the discount rate unchanged. If the federal funds and the Treasury bill rates rise, say, from 8 percent to 8.5 percent, and the discount rate stays put at 8 percent, then banks and thrift institutions have a greater incentive to borrow. Hence, a discount-rate policy that was restrictive before can become expansionary if other interest rates rise. To keep its discount policy on an even keel the Fed would therefore have to change the discount rate frequently. But this creates a problem. Many people interpret a rise in the discount rate as a restrictive policy, even if it is merely a response to rising interest rates on the open market. They argue that by increasing the discount rate the Federal Reserve has validated the rise in interest rates by showing that it thinks interest rates will stay high. And a restrictive monetary policy has many critics. Hence, the Federal Reserve is sometimes under considerable political pressure not to raise the discount rate. There have been occasions when a president has criticized the Fed for raising the discount rate and Congress has held hearings on the matter.

Reductions in the discount rate have less political fallout, though foreign central bankers and others might interpret a cut in the discount rate as a policy that will cause the dollar to decline on the foreign-exchange market. Beyond this, the Federal Reserve is reluctant to lower the discount rate because it knows the criticism that will follow if it has to raise it again later on. Thus, the Fed has much less freedom to change the discount rate than may appear at first.

Hence, it is not surprising that, as shown in figure 22.1, when other short-term interest rates rose sharply the discount rate was often not raised equally, so that there was a greater incentive to borrow. However, the Fed

---

[3] In terms of the money multiplier applicable to unborrowed reserves, the borrowing ratio (*b*) changes rather than unborrowed reserves changing.

Figure 22.1   Relation of Discount Rate to Federal Funds Rate and Member
Bank Borrowing

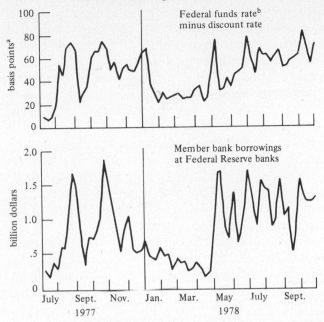

ᵃOne basis point is one-hundredth of one percent.
ᵇWeekly averages of daily effective federal funds rate.

SOURCE: Elijah Brewer, "Some Insights on Member Bank Borrowing," *Economic Perspectives* (Federal Reserve Bank of Chicago) 2 (November–December 1978): 17.

can offset the resulting increase in reserves by undertaking additional open-market sales. Since, by and large, changes in the amount of discounting that takes place are offset by the Fed's open-market operations (unless it wants reserves to change) the main effect of having a discount rate that is too low relative to open-market interest rates is that banks make a profit at the Fed's expense by borrowing from it and lending at a higher rate.

Figure 22.1 shows that member bank borrowing from the Fed does increase when the discount rate falls below the federal funds rate. Although banks and thrift institutions are supposed to borrow from the Federal Reserve only for "need" rather than to make a profit, this distinction is far from clear-cut. Suppose that high interest rates tempt a bank to reduce its excess reserves to zero, and that an unexpected outflow of deposits then forces the bank to have to borrow to meet its reserve requirement. Is this bank borrowing for need or for profit? In any case, one would expect banks to try to take advantage of a chance to borrow from the Fed at a low rate and lend at a higher rate regardless of what the Fed thinks of this. The question is whether the Fed can bring enough pressure to bear to keep such borrowing low. Some economists believe that when banks have had large borrowings outstanding for some time they tend to reduce them, presumably due to Fed pressure. This theory, known as the *reluctance theory* of borrowing, is questioned by other economists. In any case, it is far from clear that the thrift institutions, which were given access to the discount window in 1980, will be as susceptible to Fed pressure as member banks are, and the Fed may have to change its policy and keep the discount rate at, or above other short-term rates to discourage borrowing. At present (mid-1980) it is too early to tell whether this will happen.

Whether or not banks are under effective pressure to repay borrowings from the Federal Reserve is an important issue. If they are, then *unborrowed* reserves, rather than total reserves, may be the best measure of the reserves that banks have available to expand the money stock because banks are then not likely to expand deposits on the basis of borrowed reserves. But if banks feel under little pressure to repay, then total reserves is a better measure.

In addition to its effect on borrowing, and hence on bank reserves, the money stock, and on interest rates, a change in the discount rate also affects people's expectations. Not only the financial community, but also the general public "read all about it" in the newspapers. Thus, in November 1978, when President Carter wanted to stop the fall of the dollar on the foreign-exchange market by indicating to the world that the United States was ready to adopt a firm antiinflation policy, he announced that he had asked the Federal Reserve to raise the discount rate.

In general, when the Fed raises the discount rate the public *may* interpret this as a sign that the Federal Reserve is acting to curb excessive expansion and feel that there is now less reason to fear inflation. It may therefore reduce such inflationary activities as buying ahead to beat price increases or demanding higher wages to offset expected inflation. By contrast, when the Federal Reserve cuts the discount rate this may be interpreted as a sign that the Fed is now taking action to moderate an economic downturn. However, the public *may* also react in just the opposite way, and treat a rise in the discount rate as a sign that the Federal Reserve shares its prediction that inflation is becoming a more serious problem. Unfortunately, the public may also take the change in the discount rate as an indication of the Fed's predictions even in those cases where the Fed changes the discount rate only because market rates have changed. All in all, it is far from clear that the announcement effect of a change in the discount rate is helpful on the whole. In any case, it is probably not very important. The general public probably does not pay much attention to the discount rate, and financial specialists can easily predict changes in the discount rate so that when these changes actually do occur they do not convey any new information.[4]

The change in the discount rate is not the only tool of monetary policy that has an announcement effect. Changes in reserve requirements are also reported in the newspapers. Moreover, the financial and business specialists

[4] See Raymond Lombra and Raymond Torto, "Discount Rate Changes and the Announcement Effects," *Quarterly Journal of Economics* 91 (February 1977): 171–76.

whose decisions have the important effects are sophisticated enough to know how to interpret open-market operations and changes in the federal funds rate.

Many economists believe that the announcement effect of changes in the discount rate should be eliminated by tying the discount rate to a short-term interest rate, making it, say, the Treasury bill rate plus one-eighth of one percent. Then, nobody could read anything into a discount-rate change. Such an automatic system would also avoid the previously discussed problem that the Federal Reserve is sometimes unwilling to raise the discount rate even though banks are borrowing more than it wants. But the Federal Reserve is reluctant to adopt such an automatic policy and to give up its discretion in changing the discount rate, in part because any single interest rate, such as the Treasury bill rate, may get out of line with some of the other interest rates that banks also look at when they decide how much discounting to do.

Reserve-Requirement Changes

We described the reserve-requirements system in chapter 3. Now we will look at changes in reserve requirements. Congress has given the Federal Reserve permission to vary the reserve requirement within broad limits. Raising the reserve requirement affects the money stock in two ways. First, previously excess reserves of banks are now transformed into required reserves. Second, the reserve ratio is one of the components of the denominator in the money multiplier. Hence, a rise in the reserve ratio lowers the money multiplier, and thus lowers the deposit expansion that banks can undertake on the basis of their remaining excess reserves. Given the wide range within which the Federal Reserve can change reserve requirements the Federal Reserve has a *potentially* powerful tool here. But despite its strength, the Federal Reserve uses the reserve-requirement tool relatively infrequently. For example, the reserve requirements against demand deposits that were in effect March 1980 were set in December 1976, and the last change before that had been in February 1975. But due to the shift of deposits between large and small banks the reserve requirement against the *average* dollar of deposits changes over time, even though the reserve requirement ratios are constant.

Why is the Federal Reserve so reluctant to change requirements? One answer the Federal Reserve gives is that changes in the reserve requirement are a blunt tool, much inferior to open-market operations. Small changes in the reserve-requirement ratio have a powerful—often too powerful—effect on the excess reserves available to the banking system and on the money multiplier. (However, it is far from clear why the Fed cannot change the requirement by, say, one-tenth of one percent.) A second reason is that the Fed may have been afraid in the past that if it raised reserve requirements, member banks might be induced to leave the Federal Reserve System. But now that all banks have to meet the Fed's reserve requirement, this is no longer a factor.

Reserve Requirements: Some Controversies and Reform Proposals

The prevailing reserve-requirement system has been subjected to numerous criticisms and proposals for reform.

Elimination of Reserve Requirements

The most radical suggestion has been to do away with the reserve requirement altogether. Reserve requirements no longer serve the function of protecting depositors to any significant extent. An obvious counter-argument is that reserve requirements are absolutely necessary for monetary policy, that if there were no reserve requirements banks could create as many deposits as they wanted. Thus, using the simple deposit multiplier, where deposits are equal to one divided by the reserve ratio, it might seem that with a zero-reserve requirement there would be no determinate volume of deposits. But this is obviously wrong. After developing the simple deposit multiplier we developed more complex multipliers in which the legal reserve requirement is only one of several terms in the denominator. In particular these multipliers include a term for the banks' excess reserves. Surely, even if there were no legal reserve requirements banks would still want to hold some reserves to meet a deposit outflow. As long as this is true a legally imposed reserve requirement is not really *necessary*. The reserve ratio that banks hold for their own purposes could serve as the fulcrum of monetary policy instead.

Granted that a system without legal reserve requirements *could* work, would it work better than a system with legal reserve requirements? This depends in large part on how predictable a voluntary reserve ratio would be. If banks, on their own, want to keep a stable ratio of reserves to deposits, then the abolition of the *legal* reserve requirement would not hinder monetary policy. And the same would hold if the voluntary reserve ratio, while varying from time to time, does so in a predictable way. The Fed could then simply offset any changes in the reserve ratio of banks by open-market operations.

The true argument for a legal reserve ratio is therefore, not that it is necessary, but rather, that by setting a floor below which reserves cannot fall, it makes the actual reserve ratio more predictable, and hence facilitates monetary policy. Unfortunately, we have no data on how predictable the reserve ratio would be in the absence of a legal reserve requirement, and hence we do not know to what *extent* the existence of a legal reserve requirement actually stabilizes the total reserve ratio.

If there were no legal reserve ratio banks would probably keep a lower reserve ratio than they do now. What would be the effect of this? Lower reserve holdings have an effect that, at first, seems farfetched: they reduce Treasury receipts. If banks hold a lower reserve ratio, then, to keep the money stock unchanged, the Federal Reserve has to sell securities to bring the reserve base down sufficiently to offset the higher value of the money multiplier. If the Fed sells securities the interest on these securities is now received by their buyers rather than by the Fed, and thus the Federal Reserve's payments to the Treasury decline.

It is not clear whether this is desirable, in part, because there is no way of knowing what particular government expenditures, if any, would be cut to offset the loss in government revenues, or what taxes, if any, would be raised, or whether the deficit would increase instead. One thing is clear, however: the present reserve-requirements system does function as a tax on bank deposits. Every time a member bank creates a deposit it—in effect—has to make an interest-free loan to the government, because this is what the reserve requirement amounts to. If a bank has to keep, say, 10 percent more of its deposits in a non-interest-earning reserve account than it otherwise would, and the rate of interest is, say, 6 percent, then the legal reserve requirements impose an annual cost of 0.6 percent of deposits on the bank. Presumably this cost is passed on, at least in part, to depositors. As a result, depositors maintain smaller deposits than they otherwise would. In this way the reserve requirement, like other excise taxes, distorts resource allocation.[5]

If the legal reserve requirement is to be kept, the implicit tax on bank deposits that it imposes could still be avoided by paying banks interest on their reserve balances. In 1977 the Federal Reserve asked Congress for permission to pay interest on reserve balances as a way of keeping member banks from leaving the system but Congress refused because it objected to the loss in Treasury revenue that would have resulted.

One Hundred Percent Reserves

At the opposite extreme from eliminating the legal reserve requirement entirely is a proposal to raise the reserve requirement to 100 percent, thus abolishing deposit creation by the banking system. This 100 percent reserve plan would eliminate commercial banks as we know them, and replace them by two types of institutions: one would be a type of bank that accepts deposits and transfers them by check, but cannot make any loans—its income would come entirely from service charges. The second type of bank would be an institution that accepts longer-term savings and makes loans. It would pay interest to its depositors, but their deposits would not be available on demand. To prevent a radical reduction in the money stock at the time when the scheme is inaugurated, additional re-

---

[5] Note, however, that there is an offsetting factor for household deposits. The services received from holding deposits are not reached by the income tax, and this tax favoritism offsets, at least in part, the indirect excise tax on deposit holdings.

serves would have to be provided, perhaps by having the Fed buy securities and loans held by banks.

A major advantage of the 100 percent reserve proposal is that it would abolish multiple-deposit creation and, hence, give the Fed more precise control over the money stock. Each dollar of reserves would now result in one dollar, and in no more than one dollar, of money. There would not be the slippage existing under the present system where, at times, banks can add to the money stock by utilizing excess reserves and, at other times, can reduce the money stock by holding more excess reserves. Moreover, changes in currency holdings of the public would no longer change the potential money stock. At present, if the public decides to hold more currency there occurs a *multiple* decline in bank deposits, so that the total money stock (deposits plus currency) falls.[6] The second advantage of 100 percent reserves is that it would eliminate bank failures except for some possible cases of fraud. This would also result in fewer government regulations over banks being needed.

The most obvious disadvantage of the 100 percent reserve plan is the trouble and dislocation involved in setting it up. The banking system would have to be split into two parts, bank personnel and bank customers would have to be reeducated, and much uncertainty and confusion would result. Those who believe that even moderate fluctuations in the money supply have a powerful effect on income *may* consider these once-and-for-all costs as unimportant when compared to the gains resulting from 100 percent reserve banking, but others are unlikely to consider the changeover worthwhile.

Reserves against Time Deposits

Leaving aside this radical proposal, another proposal would exempt all time deposits from any legal reserve requirement, while still another one goes in the opposite direction, and would apply the same reserve requirement to time deposits as to demand deposits. The reason we control the money stock is that it affects aggregate demand. The required reserve ratio on various liquid assets should therefore reflect the impact of these items on aggregate demand. For example, if an additional dollar of time deposits raises aggregate demand only by as much as 50 cents of demand deposits

---

[6] However the money stock could be immunized against the impact of currency flows by a much simpler reform, that is, by excluding vault cash from reserves, but deducting it from the volume of deposits against which banks have to keep reserves. A deposit of a dollar of currency would then not increase reserves, but it would allow banks with their existing reserves to issue another dollar of deposits since their deposits subject to the reserve requirement would then be constant. Hence, a deposit of currency would leave the total money stock unchanged, merely substituting a dollar of deposits for a dollar of currency. See William Poole and Charles Lieberman, "Improving Monetary Control," *Brookings Papers on Economic Activity,* 1972:2, pp. 317–18.

does, then the reserve requirement against time deposits should be only half the reserve requirement against demand deposits.

But, as discussed in chapter 11, there is not a generally accepted definition of money that would allow us to say that a dollar of time deposits has, say, 50 percent of the moneyness—and impact on aggregate demand—that a dollar of demand deposits has. Hence, reform proposals that treat time deposits as though they have the same moneyness as demand deposits, or alternatively, as though they have no moneyness at all, are hard to evaluate.

The Lagged Reserve Requirement

As we described in chapter 4 the reserves that member banks have to keep are set as a percentage of their deposits two weeks earlier. This means that banks as a whole cannot do anything to reduce the reserves they need in the current week. If they reduce their deposits, say, by selling securities to depositors, this will not reduce their required reserves for two weeks. Hence, to allow banks to meet their reserve requirements the Fed may have to provide them with additional reserves, either by open-market purchases or by discounting. But if the Fed *has* to provide banks with any reserves they need, how can it exercise control over the reserve base, and hence the quantity of money? The Fed's answer is that if it forces banks to obtain the needed reserves by borrowing from it, then the banks feel under an obligation to repay these borrowings, and hence they proceed to contract their outstanding loans, so that deposits fall. But this works only if the banks *do* feel under strong pressure to repay their borrowings; otherwise the Fed is simply providing banks with the reserves they need to keep their deposits growing at any rate they desire. Unfortunately, it is far from clear whether banks actually feel all that strongly that they should repay their borrowings from the Federal Reserve.

Many economists would therefore like to see the lagged reserve requirement system abolished, and a return to the previous system under which a period's required reserves depend upon this same period's deposits. Then, in any week in which the banks are short of required reserves, they can simply reduce the amount of reserves they require by reducing the volume of outstanding deposits. (They can do this by not renewing outstanding loans, making fewer new loans, or by selling securities.) But the Federal Reserve believes that small banks find the lagged reserve requirement system much easier because they know at the start of the week what their required reserves for the week are, while with a contemporaneous reserve requirement they would have to estimate their deposits during the current week to know how many reserves they need. Small banks would find this hard to do since they lack the sophisticated technical staff of large banks.

If the discount rate were allowed to float with the Treasury bill rate, then the problem that lagged reserve requirements create for the Fed would be less severe. Banks would then no longer be tempted, as they are now, to meet their reserve requirement by borrowing from the Fed whenever open-market interest rates exceed the discount rate.

Are All Three Tools Needed?

Why have all three tools—open-market operations, discount-rate changes, and changes in reserve requirements—that we have discussed so far? Clearly, they are not all equally important. Open-market operations is by far the dominant one. It has the following advantages over discount-rate changes: it can bring about bigger changes in reserves, but also can be used to generate very small changes in reserves. Moreover, when the Fed changes the discount rate it does not know exactly by how much bank borrowing will change, but when it undertakes open-market operations it knows the change in reserves precisely. In addition, while the Federal Reserve can hardly change the discount rate several times each day, it can undertake open-market operations continually.

Similarly, reserve-requirement changes are a clumsy tool compared to open-market operations for much the same reason that discount-rate changes are. Hence, reserve requirements have been changed only infrequently.

It is therefore not so surprising that in 1978 the Fed did not oppose a congressional bill, which did not subsequently pass, that would have lowered the reserve requirement to 6 percent (thus helping to cure the Fed's membership problem) and, except for emergencies, would have allowed the Federal Reserve to vary the reserve requirement only between 5.5 and 6.5 percent.

However, the Fed did oppose a proposal in an earlier version of this bill that would have stripped it of its authority to change the discount rate by hooking it to an open-market interest rate. But, some economists, Milton Friedman, for example, believe that the Fed should have only a single tool, open-market operations.

Selective Controls

The tools discussed so far operate on aggregate demand by changing bank reserves and interest rates, and thus affect the whole economy. By contrast, "selective controls" have their initial impact on specific markets that are usually seen as relatively insulated from the effects of overall monetary policy. These controls are also designed to focus on trouble spots where demand may be excessive.

Stock-Market Credit

The Federal Reserve controls the use of credit to purchase listed stocks on the stock markets plus certain unlisted stocks. It has set the down payments, or *margin,* for stock purchases, limiting the percent of the price that may be borrowed. The Fed's regulations T, U, and G control credit for stock purchases extended respectively by brokers (and dealers), banks, and other lenders, while Regulation X closes certain loopholes, such as borrowing abroad, by controlling the borrower directly. The Fed varies the margin requirement from time to time, and can raise it up to 100 percent to control a speculative stock-market boom.

The reason the Federal Reserve was given this power in 1934 can be seen by looking back at the situation in the years 1927 through 1929. In these years prices were stable or gently falling, but there was a speculative boom in the stock market. The Fed was in a quandary. It had no power to affect the stock market directly. By raising the discount rate or by open-market operations it could make credit generally less available and, hence, could, to some extent, limit the purchase of stocks on credit. But with stock prices rising rapidly, it would probably have taken a *very* substantial boost in interest rates to have a significant effect on stock-market borrowing. And such a substantial rise in interest rates would have been too restrictive for the rest of the economy. If the Fed had had margin regulations available at that time it could have limited stock-market credit without such a restrictive effect on the rest of the economy.

As so often happens, the government locked the barn door after the horse was stolen. Since 1934 there has been no disastrous boom in the stock market and, although the margin requirement has been raised on occasion to 100 percent, it probably has not been an important factor in curbing excessive speculation. An empirical study of these regulations suggests that they have not succeeded in reducing fluctuation and risk in the stock market, or in limiting an "excessive" use of credit for security purchases.[7]

Consumer Credit

Potentially more important are selective controls over consumer credit. During World War II, as well as during the Korean War and briefly in 1948–49, the Fed set minimum down payments and maximum maturities on loans for consumer durable purchases—Regulation W. During World War II the Fed also controlled mortgage credit in a similar way. At present, neither type of control exists, but Congress has given the president the authority to ask the Federal Reserve to reimpose such controls.

[7] See Thomas Moore, "Stock Market Margin Requirements," *Journal of Political Economy* 74 (April 1966): 158–67.

Regulation Q

In recent years the Fed has used another regulation that is much more important than the margin-requirement regulations. This is Regulation Q, which sets ceilings on the interest rates member banks can pay on time deposits. We have already discussed "Reg Q" in chapters 5 and 7 in connection with its impact on thrift institutions and mortgage credit.

Moral Suasion

Another tool is **moral suasion.** This simply means that the *Fed uses its powers of persuasion to get banks, or the financial community in general, to behave differently.* Since the interests of the Federal Reserve frequently coincide with the long-run self-interest of financial institutions, this form of control may *in certain cases* be more effective than appears at first. For example, during an inflationary expansion, the Fed may urge lenders to be more cautious in their loan policies, and lenders *may* treat this as sound business advice from someone who can forecast business conditions better than they can. To be sure, sometimes banks and other institutions may feel that the stress is more on the "suasion" than on the "moral." For example, in 1965 when, in an attempt to reduce the balance of payments deficit, the Federal Reserve laid down guidelines to limit foreign lending, some banks, at least according to some reports, were afraid that if they ignored the guidelines, they might find it more difficult to borrow from the Fed. Admittedly, these fears may have been groundless; for an outsider it is hard to say. But in 1966 the Fed informed banks that discounting would be easier for banks that curbed their business loans and made more mortgage loans. The Federal Reserve's control over bank holding company activities, and its power to prohibit proposed mergers, has given it another *potential* threat over recalcitrant banks.[8]

Publicity and Advice

The Federal Reserve has many ways of making its opinions known to the general public. The chairman of the Board of Governors frequently testifies before congressional committees, and journalists pay attention to press releases by the Fed, and speeches by its officials, particularly the chairman's speeches. In addition, the Board of Governors publishes each month the *Federal Reserve Bulletin,* and the individual Federal Reserve banks publish *Reviews.* Given the high regard in which the business community and its journalists hold the Fed, it has no difficulty in getting its views and

---

[8] See Edward Kane, "The Central Bank As Big Brother," *Journal of Money, Credit and Banking* 5 (November 1973): 979–81.

opinions across to the general public. In these ways the Fed can affect business expectations, and hence actions. In addition, as discussed in chapter 7, the Federal Reserve also acts as an informal economic adviser to the administration.

Summary

Open-market operations are *the* tool of monetary policy; the others should be viewed as just supplementary tools. Open-market operations frequently are done under repurchase agreements or negative repurchase agreements, and are undertaken primarily in Treasury bills. They can be defensive to offset other factors changing bank reserves, or dynamic to bring about a desired change in reserves. The advantage of open-market operations as a tool of monetary policy is that they can be undertaken in large or small steps for the exact amount the Fed wants, and are easily reversible.

The Federal Reserve lends to banks and other institutions with transactions accounts under the basic borrowing privilege, the seasonal borrowing privilege, or as other adjustment credit. The Fed brings pressure to bear on institutions that borrow too much or too frequently. They are supposed to borrow for "need" rather than for profit. By varying the discount rate charged, the Fed can induce them to change the amount they borrow, and this changes bank reserves. Variations in the discount rate have an announcement effect. What actually measures the inducement that banks have to borrow is not the level of the discount rate but its relation to other interest rates. The Federal Reserve is sometimes under political pressure not to raise the discount rate and this allows banks to borrow at a subsidized rate.

The Fed can also change, within broad limits, the reserve requirement. Changing the reserve requirement changes both the volume of excess reserves and the money multiplier. In addition, it affects Treasury receipts.

Some economists have proposed eliminating the reserve requirement altogether. The main issue here is whether the reserve ratio that banks would then keep on their own volition would be stable. Other economists have advocated a system of 100 percent reserves. Other controversial issues about the reserve requirement are whether the reserve requirement should be the same for time and demand deposits, or whether all reserve requirements on time deposits should be abolished and whether the reserve requirement should be contemporaneous or lagged. Another potential reform is to abolish the Fed's powers to change the reserve requirement and to set the discount rate.

Apart from these general controls the Fed also has selective controls. One of these allows it to set margin requirements on stock purchases to curb excessive speculation. Another one is Regulation Q. In addition, the Fed can try to affect the behavior of individual banks through moral suasion, and the views of the general public through publicity. Finally, the Fed can influence the economy through the advice that it gives to the president and Congress.

All of this discussion of monetary policy tools is specific to the United States. In most other countries the central bank has to use different methods than in the United States. Probably in no other country are open-market operations the *dominant* tool of monetary policy, and in only very few countries are they even a major tool. Where broad, well-developed capital markets do not exist, large-scale open-market operations are not technically feasible. Moreover, in countries in which a few commercial banks dominate the banking industry—something that is the case not only in small countries, but also in Britain, for example—moral suasion can be a very potent and widely used tool. As a British banker once put it: ". . . we are in fairly constant touch with the Bank of England, and we listen with great care to what the Governor says to us at any time. He might give us a hint, and we should not be likely to ignore it." [9]

QUESTIONS AND EXERCISES

1. Write an essay describing the relative use the Federal Reserve has made of its various tools in the last three years. (Information on this is available in the Federal Reserve's Annual Reports.)
2. Using T accounts show why there would be no multiple-deposit creation with a 100 percent reserve system.
3. Discuss the relative advantages and disadvantages of two tools of monetary policy.
4. Write an essay supporting, or opposing, the removal of a legal reserve requirement.
5. Describe in your own words how a failure to raise time-deposit interest ceilings when other interest rates rise results in a lowering of excess reserves.
6. Write an essay either supporting, or criticizing, the floating discount rate.

FURTHER READING

General discussions

AHEARN, DANIEL. *Federal Reserve Policy Reappraised, 1951–59.* New York: Columbia University Press, 1963. Part two gives a scholarly and comprehensive discussion of the monetary policy tools.

ASCHHEIM, JOSEPH. *Techniques of Monetary Control.* Baltimore: Johns Hopkins Press, 1961. One of very few lengthy discussions of monetary policy tools.

FRIEDMAN, MILTON. *A Program for Monetary Stability.* New York: Fordham University Press, 1960. Chapter 2 is a stimulating and sparkling discussion of reforms.

[9] Cited in Brian Griffiths, "Two Monetary Inquiries in Great Britain," *Journal of Money, Credit and Banking* 6 (February 1974): 113.

SMITH, WARREN. "The Instruments of General Monetary Control." *National Banking Review* 1 (September 1963): 47–76. An excellent older survey highlighting some serious problems.

Specific tools

FEDERAL RESERVE BANK OF NEW YORK (Paul Meek). *Open Market Operations.* New York: Federal Reserve Bank of New York, 1969. A lively and authoritative description by the then number-two man at the Desk.

ROOSA, ROBERT. *Federal Reserve Operations in the Money and Government Security Markets.* New York: Federal Reserve Bank of New York, 1956. A fascinating description of the "nuts and bolts" of open-market operations by a former manager of the Desk.

SMITH, WARREN. "Reserve Requirements in the American Monetary System." In *Monetary Management,* edited by the Commission on Money and Credit, pp. 175–315. Englewood Cliffs, N.J.: Prentice-Hall, 1963. An excellent survey of the problem.

U.S., BOARD OF GOVERNORS, FEDERAL RESERVE SYSTEM. *Consumer Installment Credit.* Washington, D.C.: Board of Governors, Federal Reserve System, 1957. Volumes 1 and 2 are an exhaustive treatment.

U.S., BOARD OF GOVERNORS, FEDERAL RESERVE SYSTEM. *Reappraisal of the Federal Reserve Discount Mechanism.* Washington, D.C.: 1971. Volume 1, chapter 1, and volume 2, chapter 3, reprint two of the papers from the Federal Reserve study that led to reform of the discount mechanism. The former is the report of the Federal Reserve committee; the latter summarizes academic views on discounting.

23

The Federal Reserve in the Money Market

In the two previous chapters we have discussed the Federal Reserve's ultimate goals and also its tools. But these tools do not operate directly on the goal variables. Primarily, they change bank reserves and the short-term interest rate, and it is a long way from there to high employment and price stability. This problem is exacerbated by the fact that it takes a long time until changes in bank reserves and short-term interest rates affect nominal income, and hence employment and prices. Thus, if the Fed changes bank reserves in the wrong direction, or by the wrong amount, by the time it notices that income is moving inappropriately and hence reverses its policy, it is too late; the damage has been done.

Hence, the Fed interposes between its tools and its ultimate goals two sets of intermediate targets. The first set, called **targets,** *consists of variables,* such as the money stock or long-term interest rates, *that,* as we saw in Part Three, *have a direct effect on income, and hence on employment and prices.* But the Fed cannot reach even these targets directly with its tools. It determines directly and immediately, not the money stock, but only bank reserves. It therefore has another set of lower-level targets called **instruments** or **proximate targets** that *stand between its tools and its targets.* These are variables like the federal funds rate and bank reserves that it can affect directly. Figure 23.1 shows the relation between the Fed's goals, targets, short-run targets, and tools.

To illustrate, suppose that the Fed wants nominal income to grow by, say, 7 percent. What open-market operations should it undertake? It can use its econometric model (or informal estimates) to answer this question. But when it does so, the model will also tell it that these open-market operations will change the money stock, say, by 6 percent. Suppose now that it undertakes these open-market operations, and then observes that the money stock has risen, not by the predicted 6 percent, but, say, by 8 percent. Clearly, something has gone wrong, income will probably rise too much, and the Fed should now reverse its open-market operations until the money-stock growth is back at the 6 percent rate that the model says is consistent with the desired 7 percent growth rate of nominal income. After all, it is not open-market operations per se, but the resulting changes in

Figure 23.1   Relation between Federal Reserve Tools and Goals

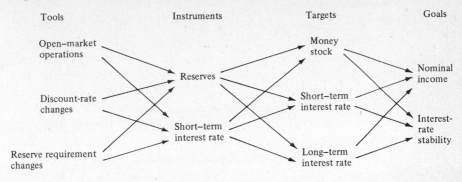

Note: The short-term interest rate appears as a long-run target as well as an instrument because it affects certain types of investment.

the money stock and interest rate that affect income. In doing so the Fed is using the money stock as its target and is setting its tools with a view to this target rather than focusing directly on its ultimate goal.

But while the money stock is something the Fed can influence more directly than nominal income, it is still some distance removed from its tools. Hence, in aiming at its money stock target the Fed uses instruments, such as bank reserves or the federal funds rate. Thus, the Fed will say to itself that it wants nominal income to grow by 7 percent, which requires a 6 percent growth of the money stock, and this 6 percent growth rate of the money stock, in turn, requires, say, a 7½ percent growth rate of bank reserves, or a 9 percent federal funds rate. Then, it can undertake open-market operations that directly change bank reserves or the federal funds rate by the necessary amounts.

By using such targets and instruments it can make midcourse corrections if the incoming data tell it that the economy is departing from the path charted out for it. By contrast, if the Fed were to aim directly at its nominal income target it would not be able to make such midcourse corrections because data on the way its policy is affecting income are available only with a much longer lag than are the money-stock data—it takes a long time until the effects on income occur. This does not *necessarily* mean that the use of targets and instruments is beyond criticism. Later on in this chapter we will discuss some alternatives.

Target Variables

The choice of a target, or intermediate target as it is sometimes called, is a crucial step in formulating monetary policy, since different target variables frequently tell the Fed to do very different things. For example, the interest-rate target may tell it to adopt an expansionary policy, while the money-stock target tells it to follow a restrictive policy. The selection of the proper targets is one of the most bitterly debated issues in monetary policy.

Criteria for Target Variables

To be a good target for monetary policy a variable, such as the interest rate, or the money stock, must meet three criteria: measurability, attainability, and relatedness to the goal variables.

The measurability criterion implies two things. First, accurate data must be available quickly. Second, the data must be readily interpretable in terms of our analytic concepts; that is, we must know what they mean. In chapter 11 we discussed the inaccuracy of our money stock data, and also the conceptual problems in deciding whether to use *M-1, M-2* or *M-3,* and, as we will discuss shortly, the interest rate presents similar problems.

The second criterion for a target variable is attainability. Unless the Federal Reserve has a reasonable chance of achieving, or at least approximating, its target, having the target does not do much good. Since the purpose of the target is to help bring about a particular level of income, using a target that it cannot attain means that the Fed does not do much to bring about the desired level of income. For example, suppose that the Federal Reserve would use as its target changing business expectations. This target is certainly related to its goals of price stability and high employment, but there is not very much that the Fed can do (apart from actually changing its policy) to affect expectations. Hence, changing expectations is not a useful target for the Fed. Unrealistic targets are not just unhelpful, but also make for sloppy policy; if a target is not reachable there seems to be little purpose in even trying very hard to reach it. (The use of unattainable targets does, however, provide a bureaucracy—or for that matter, all of us—with a wonderful excuse for failure and hence is a popular device.)

The third criterion, relatedness, is what using a target variable is all about. The only reason why the Federal Reserve uses a target is precisely because it believes that attaining the proper value for this target variable will result in it attaining, or at least coming close to, its ultimate goals. For example, suppose that the money stock had no effect on nominal income, why then should the Fed care whether it is growing at a 2 percent or a 20 percent rate?

Potential Targets

There are three leading contenders for the role of target. They are the money stock, interest rates, and bank credit. The Federal Reserve has to make a choice. Usually it cannot aim at all three, or even at two, of these targets precisely, though it can compromise between them. By using one of these variables as its target the Fed usually relinquishes control over the other two. Suppose, for example, that the Fed brings about a particular money supply. To make the public willing to hold exactly this amount of money requires a particular interest rate. And if the Fed prefers a different interest rate this is unfortunate; there is nothing it can do about it. If it wants a different interest rate it can reach this interest-rate target only by relinquishing its money-stock target, and giving the public the money stock it wants to hold at *that* interest rate. In the short run, until income, and hence the demand for money curve, have changed, the public's existing demand curve for money tells us the interest rate that corresponds to each particular quantity of money, and the Federal Reserve must settle for a combination of money stocks and interest rates that lies on this demand curve. A similar thing applies to bank credit. If the Fed selects a particular interest rate the quantity of bank credit outstanding at that interest rate depends upon the public's demand for bank credit, and not on the Federal Reserve's wishes. And a bank-credit target also implies a specific money stock. For example, if the Fed gives the banks enough reserves to induce them to increase outstanding bank credit by, say, 5 percent, this volume of bank reserves may result in the money stock growing by, say, a 4 percent rate.

Hence, the Fed must either choose to concentrate on only a single target variable, or else it must straddle by using a broad enough range for its targets, so that within this range two or more targets are consistent. This is illustrated in figure 23.2, where the ranges set for the interest-rate target and the money-stock target (shown by the rectangle $ABCD$) are broad enough so that they are consistent, even though the Fed's preferred target points, i_p and M_p, are inconsistent. And at times, as illustrated by the money demand curve M_2^d, even a broad range around the target points may not suffice to make two target ranges consistent. In such cases the Fed has to make a choice, or else broaden the range.

With this background let us now see how well the potential target variables meet the criteria.

Measurability. In chapter 10 we discussed the inaccuracies in the early estimates of the money stock, and it is these early estimates that the Federal Reserve has to work with. In addition, there is the conceptual problem of whether to focus on M-$1A$, M-$1B$, M-2, or M-3. This depends on which of these measures is more closely related to income, and which one the Fed can control better. Unfortunately, the empirical evidence does not give us unequivocal answers to these questions. And as table 11.1 demonstrated, the growth rates of M-1 and M-2, while showing some correlation, also show substantial differences. The fact the M-2 is growing at a faster rate than M-$1A$ or M-$1B$ is not bothersome. What matters is differences in the *changes* in their growth rates. Suppose that the growth rates of all three drop, say, by half. This would indicate a tightening of monetary policy despite the fact that M-2 is still growing faster than M-$1A$ and M-$1B$. But if the growth rate of M-2 rises while the growth rates of M-$1A$ and M-$1B$ fall, then it is hard to decide whether the "money stock" is rising or falling.

But however severe the measurement and conceptual problems are for the money stock, many—though certainly not all—economists believe, for reasons we have already briefly discussed in chapter 16, that they are just as bad, if not worse, for the interest rate. The term *the interest rate* as used

Figure 23.2   The Conflict of Money-Stock and Interest-Rate Targets

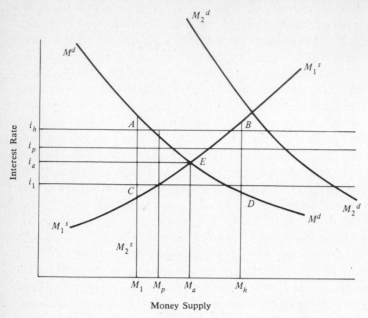

Money Supply

Legend: M^d = money demand curve

M^s = money supply curve

i_h = highest interest rate acceptable to the Federal Reserve

i_p = Federal Reserve's preferred interest rate

i_a = actual interest rate

i_1 = lowest interest rate acceptable to the Federal Reserve

M_1 = lowest money stock acceptable to the Federal Reserve

M_p = Federal Reserve's preferred money stock

M_a = actual money stock

M_h = highest money stock acceptable to the Federal Reserve

$ABCD$ = area within which both the interest rate and the money stock are acceptable to the Federal Reserve

in economic theory is a theoretical term referring to the weighted average of all the interest rates at which borrowing takes place. But the interest rates recorded by our data do not cover all of these rates. They include mainly the interest rates charged on public markets. For example, they do not cover the imputed interest rates that firms charge themselves on internally generated funds.

Second, some of the recorded rates are of doubtful accuracy. For example, while the interest rate on government securities is measured precisely, this is not true of interest rates charged on bank loans. Bank interest rates are badly measured because they fail to take into account certain costs of borrowing, such as the need to keep compensating balances, or the various restrictions that a bank imposes on the borrowing firm. More generally, the cost of borrowing—which is what affects investment decisions—contains much more than just the interest rate. The more a firm borrows now the smaller the additional amount it can borrow in the future if it suddenly needs funds. Moreover, the more it borrows the greater is the proportion of its earnings that it is required to pay to its lenders. A relatively small drop in its revenues may therefore cause a firm that has borrowed a great deal to go bankrupt.

Third, as discussed in chapter 4, banks and other lenders ration credit, so that for many borrowers the prevailing interest rate is of only limited relevance. Suppose, for example, that the interest rate is constant, but that credit becomes tighter, so that a firm that was previously a marginal borrower is now rationed out of the market. In one sense the interest rate for this firm has now become infinite, but this has no effect on the published interest rate data. Fourth, even if we had accurate data on interest rates charged on all borrowing, and if there were no capital rationing, we would still face the problem of how to combine the observed plethora of interest rates into a single weighted average that represents *the* interest rate. What weights are to be given, for example, to the Treasury bill rate, to the rate on twenty-year bonds, and to the five-year rate? The actually observed volume of borrowing at each rate does not provide us with a meaningful set of weights because in deciding how much importance to attach to the rise in any particular interest rate, we should also take into account the amount of borrowing that is choked off by this increase in the interest rate, and on this there are no data.

But the most serious difficulty results from the distinction between the nominal and the real interest rate. Obviously, our data record only the nominal rate. But what is relevant for most expenditure decisions is the *expected* real rate of interest. Hence, unless we know the price expectations of borrowers we do not know how to interpret a given nominal rate. For example, if the nominal rate is 9 percent, this is a high expected real rate (4 percent) if people think prices will rise at a 5 percent rate, but it is a low expected real rate (2 percent) if they think prices will rise at a 7 percent rate. Thus an entirely reasonable error in estimating the public's price expectations leads in this example to an error in estimating the expected real interest rate that is equal to 100 percent of the lower of the two rates. And very little is known about the public's price expectations, so that such an error is far from implausible.

The significance of having to estimate the expected real interest rate from data on the nominal interest rate varies from time to time. In a period when prices are stable, and have been stable for a long time, it is not very significant because then one can assume that the public expects prices to be stable, so that the nominal rate and the expected real rate coincide. But in a period of high and variable inflation rates such as the present, this is not so.

Measurement problems also plague the third major potential target, bank credit. Again, accurate final data are available only with a lag.

Attainability. The second criterion for a monetary target is attainability. There is no question that in the long run, say, over a period of a year or two, the Federal Reserve can reach or come close to its money-stock target. But the critical question is whether the Fed can do so in the short run. In a business-cycle context a year is a long time. The median contraction in postwar cycles has lasted only ten months.

What causes this problem is that a change in bank reserves does not have most of its effect immediately. Instead, this effect is distributed over a period of several months. Hence, the Fed must either be willing to wait some time for most of the change in the money stock to occur when it changes its policy, or else it must follow a policy of initially overshooting by undertaking a big change in the reserve base, so that the immediate effect of this change suffices to change the money stock by the desired amount. For example, suppose that the Fed wants to raise the money stock by $1 billion within the first month, but that in this time only 10 percent of the effect of an open-market operation on the money stock takes place. If so, the Fed will have to buy a volume of securities that would raise the money stock ultimately by $10 billion. Subsequently it will have to reverse itself sharply and adopt the opposite policy to offset the major part of the first policy when this first policy begins to have its main effects.[1] Since major changes in bank reserves tend to bring about large changes in the federal funds rate, the Federal Reserve does not like such erratic policies.

This brings us to a major issue in money-stock control. Many critics of the Federal Reserve, particularly monetarists, argue that the Fed could control the money stock much better *if* it were willing to let interest rates fluctuate more.

Going from the general to the specific, as was shown in table 10.4, over a period of a year changes in the money stock are dominated by changes in the base (that is, by bank reserves and currency), and the Fed can certainly control the base. Furthermore, it can predict—and offset—changes in the money multiplier. Thus James Pierce, a former high-ranking Fed economist, believes that over a period of a year, if it really wants to, the Fed can come within half a percentage point of hitting its money-stock target.[2] At the other extreme, it is also clear that the Fed cannot control the money stock accurately on a week-to-week basis. Not only do changes in the base take much longer than a week to have their substantial effects on the money stock, but, on a week-to-week basis, variations in the money multiplier are great enough to dominate changes in the base. Suppose that the monetary base is growing at an annual rate of, say, 6 percent. This means that week to week it is growing at an average rate of about 0.1 percent. Changes in the money multiplier can easily dominate such a small change in the base. Over a year, of course, the 6 percent change in the base

[1] Potentially there is a danger that the Fed would then have to undertake even larger changes in the next period to offset the lagged effects of this second change. In principle, this could lead to an explosive situation of bigger and bigger policies being required all the time. However, it seems that the economic system is such that this is not likely to become a danger.

[2] James Pierce, "Why the Fed Keeps Missing Its Monetary Targets," *Fortune,* 27 May 1978, p. 152.

is large relative to the net change in the money multiplier since positive and negative short-term variations in the money multiplier tend to wash out. Even on a monthly basis the Federal Reserve's ability to forecast and control changes in the money stock is only fair. Fortunately this does not matter because weekly changes in the money stock have no discernible effects on income, and even moderate month-to-month changes probably have only a very small effect.

The more relevant question is whether the Fed can control the money stock accurately over a longer period such as one or two calendar quarters. There is some dispute about this. The Fed sometimes argues that it has only quite limited control.[3] But many of its critics argue that it could control the money stock well, if only it would try hard enough. In terms of figure 23.1 the range of permissible fluctuations in the federal funds rate is too narrow, and in addition, the Fed could get better control over the money stock by changing its regulations, for example, by having simultaneous rather than lagged reserve requirements.

It may be useful, purely as an illustration, to look at one attempt to predict the money stock for 1970–72,[4] even though more accurate methods of forecasting may well have been developed by now. At that time the money stock (M_1) was growing at an annual rate of about 7.5 percent. Here are the forecast errors:

	Mean absolute error in forecasting the M_1 growth rate (annual growth rate data, seasonally adjusted, in percent)
monthly	3.36
quarterly	2.10
six-month periods	1.19

As you can see the errors decline very substantially as the period lengthens. One way of evaluating the significance of these errors is to ask how much effect such errors in money-stock control have on income. One study suggests that the above error of 1.19 percent in the money growth rate for six months has relatively little effect on income.[5] If this is correct—and some economists are skeptical—then it follows that the Fed can hit a money-stock target with tolerable accuracy.

[3] For example, former Chairman Burns stated "I do not think we have the power to achieve this or that rate of growth of the money supply . . . within a period of three months, or even six months." U.S., Congress, Senate, Committee on Banking, Housing, and Urban Affairs, *Hearings on S. Con. Res. 18,* 25, 26 February 1975, p. 47.

[4] Richard Davis, "Implementing Open Market Policy with Monetary Aggregate Objectives," Federal Reserve Bank of New York, *Monetary Aggregates and Monetary Policy* (New York: Federal Reserve Bank of New York, 1974), p. 16.

[5] See Gerald Corrigan, "Income Stabilization and Short-Run Variability in Money," *Monthly Review* (Federal Reserve Bank of New York) 55 (April 1973): 87–98.

Can the Fed attain any specific interest-rate target? At one time this was questioned on the argument that at a low enough interest rate the liquidity-preference curve is infinitely elastic. Few economists worry about this any more. But, a fall in the rate of interest generates a rise in income and prices that raises the interest rate again. Is this a serious limitation on the Federal Reserve's power? To the extent that it is an increase in real income that raises the interest rate back towards its previous level the Fed has nothing to worry about, because presumably it initially lowered the interest rate precisely to obtain this increase in real income. However, if the Phillips curve is vertical, and all the increase in nominal income stimulated by the lower interest rate is a rise in prices, then the Fed is obviously not achieving its purpose. But the problem is then not so much that the Fed has no power over the interest rate as it is that the Fed's target, a rise in output, is unattainable, at least by conventional macro policies.

But even if the Phillips curve is not vertical, there is another limitation on the Fed's ability to lower interest rates during a recession. This is that besides its income-stabilization goal it also has another goal, exchange-rate stability. As we will explain in Part Six, if interest rates fall this tends to reduce the value of the dollar on the foreign-exchange market.

So far, we have talked about the interest rate without specifying what interest rate we have in mind. But, as we discussed in the previous chapter, the Federal Reserve conducts its open-market operations primarily in short-term securities, so that its initial impact is on the short-term interest rate. The effects on the long-term or intermediate-term interest rates may be much attenuated and late to arrive. But most Keynesian economists believe that it is primarily the *long*-term rate of interest that affects investment in industrial plant and equipment, state and local government projects, and non-residential construction.[6] (Residential construction, however, is affected by both the long and the short rate.) In the Keynesian approach, which stresses the interest rate as the connection between changes in bank reserves and changes in nominal income, this loose link between the short-term rate and the long-term rate can be a serious limitation on the effectiveness of monetary policy.

Relatedness. The third criterion for a target is the target's relatedness to the Fed's higher level goals. What is important here is *not* by how *much* a given change in the target variable changes nominal income; if it has only a small effect on income, the Fed can simply change the target variable by a large amount. What is important is how *accurately* the Fed can predict by how much income changes when it changes its target setting.

[6] However, Professor Robert Hall has argued recently that it is the short-term interest rate that is relevant for investment decisions. In any one year a firm has to decide whether to invest this year or postpone the project until next year. Hence it compares the yield from investing this year with the cost of investing this year instead of next year, which is the one-year interest rate. See Robert Hall, "Investment, Interest Rates and Stabilization Policy," *Brookings Papers on Economic Activity,* 1977:1, pp. 61–103.

Does the money stock or the interest rate have a more predictable relation to income? This is a tough question. To see why, consider a situation where the interest rate is initially at the Fed's desired level but then suddenly rises. The Federal Reserve does not know the reason. But it must make a decision. Should it take the interest rate as its target, and keep it stable temporarily by increasing the money stock at a faster rate, or should it treat the money stock as its target, and keep it growing at the previously decided-upon rate, even though this means a higher interest rate?

The answer depends on why the interest rate is rising. With the supply of money growing at a constant rate, the unexpected rise in the interest rate must be due to a rise in the demand for money. And in terms of the Cambridge equation, $M = kY_n$, this rise in the demand for money must in turn be due either to a rise in k (the proportion of its income the public wants to hold in the form of money), or else to a rise in Y_n, nominal income.

Suppose first that a rise in k is responsible. In this case the Fed should use an interest-rate target, thus keeping the interest rate constant. With the demand for money per dollar of income having increased, to prevent income from declining, the Fed must meet the increased demand for money by increasing the supply by the same amount. Otherwise the interest rate rises and causes income to fall. Thus in this case where the increase in the interest rate is due to a rise in the Cambridge k the Fed should use the interest rate as its target.

But in the alternative case where the unexpected rise in the interest rate is due to a rise in Y_n rather than in k, the Fed should use a money-stock target. Since it does not want the rise in nominal income (for if it did, it would already have adopted a policy to change nominal income), it should keep the growth rate of money constant, and allow the interest rate to rise. This rise in the interest rate is desirable because it inhibits expenditures. In other words, when expenditure incentives, such as the profitability of investment, rise and income increases, the resulting rise in the interest rate acts as an automatic stabilizer that moderates the increase in income. If the Fed uses an interest-rate target in this case, where the rise in the interest rate is due to an increase in income, the Fed acts in a *de*stabilizing manner. By preventing the rise in the interest rate it removes an important automatic stabilizer. In other words, with an interest-rate target the Fed generates the money to finance an increase in nominal income that it does not want.

This principle can be illustrated with *IS–LM* diagrams.[7] In (A) of figure

---

[7] Our previous discussion in terms of income and the Cambridge k can be translated into *IS–LM* as follows. An increase in expenditure incentives shifts the *IS* curve. This curve tells what income will be, given the interest rate, while an increase in expenditure incentives means that at each interest rate firms or consumers want to spend more. The *LM* curve is drawn to equilibrate the money market by selecting those combinations of interest rates and incomes that equate the supply and demand for money. If people now want to hold more money, the curve shifts outward since it now takes a higher interest rate, or lower income, to make them demand no more money than is available. A problem with using a simple *IS–LM* diagram is that this

Figure 23.3   Comparison of Money-Stock and Interest-Rate Targets

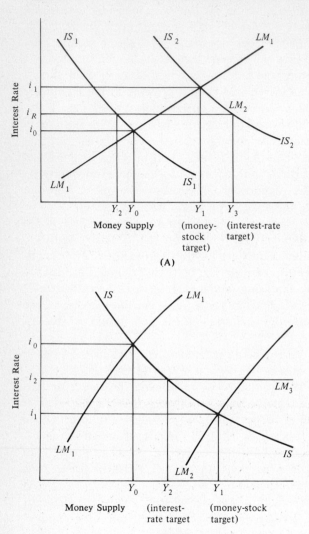

(A)

(B)

23.3, the *IS* curve shifts around anywhere between IS_1 and IS_2. If the Fed uses a money-stock target, it generates a fixed supply of money and lets the interest rate increase as a rise in income raises the demand for money. Hence, the *LM* curve slopes upward in the usual way. As a rise, say, in the profitability of investment, or in government expenditures, shifts the *IS* curve from IS_1 to IS_2, income increases from Y_0 to Y_1. By contrast, assume that the Fed uses an interest-rate target. It then keeps the interest rate fixed

assumes that prices are stable, which is not necessarily the case here. Fortunately, the results illustrated here with the *IS–LM* diagram can be reached also in algebraic ways that do not require price stability.

at the desired level by meeting changes in the demand for money with corresponding changes in the supply, so that the *LM* curve becomes a horizontal line, LM_2. As the *IS* curve shifts from IS_1 to IS_2 income now rises from Y_2 to Y_3, that is, by more than before.

In 23.3 (B) the *IS* curve is stable, but the demand for money fluctuates instead, so that the *LM* curve varies between LM_1 and LM_2. Income then varies between Y_0 and Y_1. Suppose, however, that the Fed now uses an interest-rate target, that is, it varies the supply of money enough to keep the interest rate fixed all the time at i_2. This changes the *LM* curve to LM_3, so that income stays at Y_2.

Thus we have the following rule: if the change in the interest rate is due to a change in the Cambridge k the Fed should follow an interest-rate target, but if the change in the interest rate is the result of a change in income as expenditure incentives change, in other words, a shift of the *IS* curve, then the Fed should use a money-stock target instead. And now here is the problem! *When the interest rate changes, the Federal Reserve does not know whether this is due to changes in the Cambridge* k *or in expenditure incentives.* All it observes is that the interest rate is, say, rising, and it has to decide whether or not to prevent this rise by increasing the money stock.[8] Whatever decision it makes, under one set of circumstances it will be the wrong decision, and will destabilize the economy.

This is a horrible situation. It would not be so bad if the Fed would know whether unexpected changes in the interest rate are *usually due to a* change in the Cambridge k or to a change in expenditure incentives. It could then do that which would usually yield the right result. But the Fed does not really know which is the usual case and which is the unusual one. This is a problem about which economists disagree. Monetarists believe that the Cambridge k is stabler and more predictable than expenditure incentives, and hence support a money-stock target, but Keynesian theory can be interpreted to favor either a money-stock or interest-rate target.[9] But it can be shown that if unexpected shifts in the *IS* and the *LM* curves are equally likely, then the money stock is a better target than is the interest rate.[10] Hence, unless there is some halfway reliable evidence that the unex-

[8] There is an additional complication. The above conclusions depend critically on the *IS* curve sloping downward. If, instead, it should have a positive slope the conclusions just obtained would be reversed. And one cannot be certain that the *IS* curve does not have a positive slope. See David Geitman, "Optimal Choice of Monetary Policy," *Quarterly Journal of Economics* 85 (November 1971) 712–15.

[9] Although we have discussed only the problem of choosing between a money-stock target and an interest-rate target, a similar analysis can be developed for the bank-credit–interest-rate targets choice.

[10] The argument is complex, but comes down to the following. First, assume that the Fed wants to minimize the square of the deviations of actual income from the desired income level. Second, assume that when the interest rate changes the Fed does not know at all whether the *IS* or *LM* curve has shifted. In this situation, the Fed should adopt a policy that is intermediate between what it would do if it were certain that the *IS* curve has shifted, or else, that the *LM* curve has shifted. But, it

pected changes in the interest rate are more likely to be due to a shift in the *LM* curve, the Fed should adopt a money-stock target.

In Conclusion

To summarize, on the first criterion, measurability, both the money stock and the interest rate perform very badly, though many (but by no means all) economists believe that the interest rate does worse, at least in a period of high and variable inflation. Similarly, the target variables have some, though lesser, problem on the second criterion, controllability. And their relative performance on the third criterion, relationship to the income goal, is much disputed.

Before leaving the targets issues there is one more important, practical consideration. We have talked about the Fed choosing an interest-rate target consistent with its desired income level. But the Fed is also concerned with keeping interest rates, and hence the money market, stable. With an interest-rate target the Fed is therefore continually tempted to keep the level of its target unchanged, even though income is changing in an undesired way. On the other hand, with a money-stock target the Federal Reserve would quite clearly be required to let interest rates change. Hence, a money-stock target is less subject to abuse; it does not lend itself to the temptation of overemphasizing a day-to-day concern (interest-rate stability) at the expense of the longer range, but much more important, task.

All in all, the selection of a target variable for monetary policy involves controversies on several different levels. First, there are narrow technical disagreements about the measurability of the variables, and the extent to which they can be controlled. Second, there are disputes about basic macroeconomic theory. Are fluctuations in income due more to fluctuations in the expenditure incentives, so that by using a stable money growth rate as its target the Fed could stabilize income, or are income fluctuations due more to variations in the Cambridge *k* that the Fed should offset? More specifically, does economic analysis tell us that there is a particular monetary variable, such as *M-1B* or *M-2,* that has a stable relation to income? Third, a disagreement about goals also enters the debate. Is the Fed justified in making interest-rate stability into an important goal? If so, then this would support using an interest-rate target.

---

turns out that the money-stock target is just such an intermediate policy. To see this, assume that the Fed knew for certain that the *IS* curve has shifted outward. Should it then adopt a policy of keeping the money stock constant? No, it shouldn't. While this policy would be better than keeping the interest rate constant, the Fed could do better still. It could *reduce* the money stock, thus offsetting the rise in income produced by the shift in the *IS* curve. Keeping the money stock constant is therefore already an in-between policy, and hence is the appropriate policy if shifts in the two curves are equally likely. For a rigorous analysis see Steven LeRoy and David Lindsey, "Determining the Monetary Instrument: A Diagrammatic Exposition," *American Economic Review* 68 (December 1978): 929–34.

Instruments

The targets discussed so far, the money stock and the long-term interest rates, are still some distance removed from the Federal Reserve's tools. The Fed does not directly set the money supply; this is done by banks when they create deposits, and by the public when it draws currency out of banks. And, since the Fed does not undertake many open-market operations in long-term securities, it does not have much direct effect on long-term interest rates. Only the short-term interest rate is directly and immediately determined (in the short run) by the Fed's open-market operations. Hence, to some extent the problems that the Fed faces in controlling nominal income apply also to its control over its target variables. It therefore uses instrument variables (or proximate targets), which stand in the same relation to the targets themselves as the targets stand to the goals. The criteria for these proximate targets are similar to those for the targets: measurability, attainability, and relatedness (now to the targets themselves rather than to the ultimate goals).

The Instrument Variables

The Federal Reserve can use as its instrument variable any of the several measures of bank reserves and related concepts discussed in chapter 10. One of these is the total reserves of member banks. Another is unborrowed reserves (sometimes called *owned reserves*). Suppose that banks are reluctant to make loans and buy securities, and thus to create deposits, when they are indebted to the Federal Reserve. If so, then unborrowed reserves are a better guide to the deposits that banks will create than are total reserves, some of which the banks may have to use to repay their debts to the Fed. But whether banks really are all that reluctant to expand deposits when they are in debt to the Fed is still an unsettled issue. A third measure is the base, that is, the sum of member bank reserves and currency held by the public. While total reserves and unborrowed reserves ignore currency holdings of the public, and thus one part of the money supply, the base errs in the opposite direction and counts a dollar of currency as equivalent to a dollar of reserves. This gives too much weight to currency since a dollar of reserves held by the banks generates several dollars of money, while a dollar of currency held by the public is, of course, only one dollar of money. Another measure is the **adjusted base** also called the **extended base,** which makes allowance for changes in reserve requirements.

A different instrument or proximate target is the short-term interest rate. This is also a target variable because it does affect some types of investment. And since one of the Federal Reserve's goals is interest-rate stability, it is a goal variable as well. But this does not prevent it from being a proximate target too, since the Fed can affect it directly in its open-market operations, and it, in turn affects the money stock, long-term interest rates and bank credit.

Another instrument is called **money-market conditions.** It is a rather nebulous amalgam of a number of variables that gauge supply and demand in the money market, such as the federal funds rate, the Treasury bill rate, the outstanding volume of member bank borrowing (which indicates the pressure on banks to repay their borrowings from the Fed), free reserves (that is, excess reserves minus borrowed reserves), as well as the Federal Reserve's general and rather subjective evaluation of the money market, sometimes called "color, tone, and feel." This proximate target played an important role in the Federal Reserve's thinking in the 1950s and early 1960s and then faded away.

Evaluation of Instruments

Total reserves and unborrowed reserves pass the measurability test with flying colors. The Fed can at any time read off its own books the reserves that member banks keep with it and the amount of their borrowings. And it can easily estimate the other part of bank reserves, vault cash, from the reports that banks file with it. Similarly, the Fed can readily estimate the reserve base and the extended base by estimating the currency holdings of the public. All of these variables also meet the attainability criterion very well since the Fed can use open-market operations to change bank reserves by any desired amount.

The relatedness criterion presents a more serious problem. We have already discussed it indirectly when we took up how well the Fed can control the quantity of money. If the money multiplier is constant, or otherwise closely predictable, the Federal Reserve can control the quantity of money precisely by changing bank reserves. But is the money multiplier so predictable? As discussed in chapter 10, it does vary, and not all of its variation can be predicted.

The reserve measures and the base are related not only to the money stock target, but also to the interest rate target. If the Fed provides the banks with more reserves, then banks buy securities, particularly short-term securities in the first instance, and this reduces short-term interest rates.

Is the short-term interest rate also a good instrument? It meets the measurability criterion very well since it can be observed at any time in the money market. It is not necessary to infer the expected real rate from the observed nominal rate since it is the nominal interest rate that determines the value of the target variables. And since the important short-term rates, the federal funds rate and the Treasury bill rate, are set in markets where there is virtually no rationing, another problem that bedevils the use of the interest rate as a target does not apply to its use as an instrument. The problem of combining several interest rates does not arise either; the Fed can simply use the federal funds rate.

Similarly, the Fed can control short-term interest rates in the short run (and it is the short run that matters for the proximate target problem) through open-market operations. It simply buys or sells securities until their price and yield correspond to what it wants.

But the relatedness to the targets needs more discussion. With respect to one target, the short-term interest rate, the relation is, of course, that of one-to-one. But the long-term interest-rate target is more elusive, because, as we pointed out in chapter 6, the term-structure relationship that links short- and long-term interest rates has considerable play.

The short-term interest rate can also be used to attain the money-stock target. The stock of money, like the stock of other assets, depends upon both supply and demand. And instead of focusing on the supply relationship by using a reserve measure, the short-term interest rate can be used to affect the money stock via the demand for money. Since banks have some excess reserves, and feel obligated to meet the loan demands of their good customers, when the short-term interest rate falls, and the demand for money therefore increases, banks create more money. Indeed, the Fed claims, though some economists dispute this, that the stock of money can be determined just as well or even better from an equation for the demand for money—which includes the interest rate as one of the variables—as it can be from the volume of bank reserves. By setting the short-term interest rate the Fed can therefore control the amount of money demanded, and hence the stock of money in existence.

The money-market-conditions instrument has a measurement problem since it is subjective. The Federal Reserve can control it well. But, in any case, this instrument has a fatal disease; money-market conditions do not have a consistent—and hence usable—relation to any of the target variables.

Alternative Approaches

The targets and instrument approach just discussed is used both by the Fed and by many academic economists. But some economists have rejected it. For example, two economists then at the St. Louis Federal Reserve Bank, Leonall Andersen and Denis Karnovsky, have argued that the Fed can achieve more accurate control over income by using a single variable, the monetary base, than by using separate target and instrument variables. The usual procedure of going from, say, the base to the money stock, and then from the money stock to income, introduces two errors: an error in the equation estimating the money stock from the base, and a second error in the equation linking the money stock to income. Andersen and Karnovsky have presented data showing that the error in the single equation linking the base directly to income is as small or smaller than the error in the equation linking the money stock to income.[11] Hence, the total error in estimat-

[11] Why this is the case has not yet been determined. See Leonall Andersen and Denis Karnovsky, "Some Considerations in the Use of Monetary Aggregates for the Implementation of Monetary Policy," *Review* (Federal Reserve Bank of St. Louis) 59 (September 1977): 2–7.

ing income is greater if the money stock is interposed as a target since we then have the additional error involved in going from the base to the money stock. However, some work by Carl Gams of the Kansas City Federal Reserve Bank challenges the findings that the error in the equation linking the base to income is no greater than the error linking the money stock to income.[12]

A more basic criticism of the instruments and targets approach has been presented by Professor Benjamin Friedman of Harvard University.[13] We began this chapter by discussing the case where the Fed observes that the money stock differs from what its econometric model or informal estimates predicted, and therefore adjusts the money stock to keep it on target. But, Friedman asks, why does the money stock differ from the predicted one? Obviously something has gone wrong in one of the equations of the model. This is useful information since it is likely to affect also the model's prediction of the relation between the money stock and income. This information should not be discarded as it is by saying, oh, well, we will just bring the money stock to the level we originally planned for it. Moreover, the money stock and the interest rate are not the only variables that affect income. Hence he suggests that the Fed should not use the money stock or the interest rate as its only target, but should instead use all the available information to predict how income is changing, and use this information in deciding on open-market operations.

Along similar lines, a number of economists (including Benjamin Friedman) have tried to extend the traditional analysis by focusing on the fact that when the Fed observes an unexpected rise in the interest rate or in the money stock it is being told by the data that one of its equations (or informal forecasts) is wrong. And this error may well be due to shifts in *both* the *IS* and *LM* curves rather than in just one of them, so that the simple rule we developed in figure 23.3 is not applicable. Hence, there is no easy way the Fed can respond. But the Federal Reserve is not the only one who faces this problem of being off-target. Electrical engineers face it too and have designed optimal mechanisms for bringing a variable back to its target. (The familiar furnace thermostat is an example of such a mechanism.) They have developed a branch of mathematics called "control theory" that can be used to decide how a mechanism should respond to information that it is off-target. This control theory has been applied to the problem of selecting a monetary policy target. Unfortunately, it requires some quite complex mathematics, and therefore having looked it firmly in the face we will pass on.

[12] "Federal Reserve Intermediate Targets: Money or Monetary Base?" *Economic Review* (Federal Reserve Bank of Kansas City) 65 (January 1980): 3–15.
[13] Benjamin Friedman, "The Inefficiency of Short-Run Monetary Targets for Monetary Policy," *Brookings Papers on Economic Activity*, 1977:2, pp. 293–335.

Indicators

A problem that is related to targets and instruments is the choice of an indicator of monetary policy. The Fed must know more than what target to aim at; it must also know what its current policy is so that it can decide in what way, if any, it should change it. Similarly, economists outside the Federal Reserve want to know its current policy. This may seem like a trivial problem; surely the Fed knows what policy it is pursuing. But this is not the case, because the point at issue is the *impact* of the policy, not the Federal Reserve's intentions. It is true that the Fed knows what its discount rate is and what open-market operations it is undertaking. But this is not sufficient. For example, if we know that the discount rate is, say, 5 percent, is this an easy or a restrictive policy? This depends in part on how free banks feel to borrow. Similarly, suppose that the Fed is buying $100 million of securities. Is this an easy policy? The answer to this question is far from obvious. Suppose that banks want to hold $150 million more excess reserves because interest rates are falling. If the Fed supplies only $100 million of additional reserves, the money stock will fall. Hence, what may seem like an easy money policy when one looks at what the Fed is doing with its tools may actually be a tight policy when one looks at the way the target variable is changing.

Thus we cannot determine whether monetary policy is tight or easy simply by looking at the operation of the Fed's tools. Instead, we have to find some *variable that measures the impact of these tool settings on the economy*. Such a variable is called an **indicator.**

The criteria for an indicator are more or less similar to those for the instruments and targets. Reliable and quick data on the indicator must be available. The indicator must be something under the Federal Reserve's control because it is supposed to tell what the Fed is doing. In fact, to be a good indicator the variable must not only be under the Fed's control, but must be affected only, or almost only, by the Fed's actions, because it should indicate only what the Fed is doing. Third, an indicator should have a predictable relation to a target variable, otherwise why care what it indicates?

The reserve measures and the base are good indicators because they are related to the targets, reliable data on them are quickly available, and the Federal Reserve—and nobody else—controls them. (Is the Fed really the only one determining total reserves and the base; can't the banks increase total reserves and the base by borrowing from the Fed? Not really, because the Fed can, offset, through open-market operations, any change in bank borrowing.)

The short-term interest rate, however, is a much more questionable indicator, because a rise or fall in it may be the result of changes in the demand for credit by the private sector rather than due to any action by the Federal Reserve. For example, when interest rates fall during a recession this does not necessarily mean that the Fed has adopted an expansionary policy. Since the demand for credit drops during a recession, interest rates decline if the Fed does nothing at all, or possibly even if it adopts a restrictive policy. All the same, many noneconomists, and even some economists, use the interest rate—and the nominal interest rate at that—as their indicator of monetary policy. Hence, at a time when the nominal prime rate is, say, 12 percent they may complain that monetary policy is restrictive, even though the after-tax real prime rate may be *minus* 3 percent, and the money growth rate may be high.

The Federal Reserve's Policy Procedures

How does the Fed actually conduct its policy? What targets, instruments, and indicators does it actually use? To get some perspective on this question it is useful to back up, and look first at the Fed's previous procedures.

The 1950s and 1960s

In the 1950s and early 1960s the Fed relied more on intuitive judgment than on economic analysis. William McChesney Martin, who was then chairman, believed that the informed judgment of market participants, even though not always well articulated, was superior to abstract economic analysis, that central banking is an "art" and not a "science." The Fed did not think that the quantity of money was central and instead emphasized short-term nominal interest rates, credit conditions, and bank credit. It did not see itself as determining the long-term interest rate, but rather as generating sufficient credit to finance "sound" expansions, while curbing inflationary and unsustainable rates of expansion. Its policy was expressed in phrases like "leaning against the wind." This preference for vague, intuitive notions over quantifiable magnitudes was quite explicit, with several Governors arguing that not enough is known to quantify the targets of monetary policy. Hence, the Directive that the FOMC sent to the account manager in New York would order him to change, for example, from a policy of "ease" to one of "active ease."

In formulating its Directive to the account manager the Fed used, without distinguishing between their employment as targets, instruments, and indicators, free reserves, the short-term interest rate and money-market conditions. The emphasis on free reserves, that is, excess reserves minus borrowed reserves, money-market conditions, and the short-term interest rate had some definite advantages for the Fed. A major aim of the Fed at the time was to keep interest rates from fluctuating too much. Essentially what the Federal Reserve did was to accommodate the demand for reserves. As the demand increased, and interest rates rose, it would provide additional reserves, primarily through open-market purchases. This tended to make its policy procyclical rather than countercyclical because the demand for credit, and hence the banks' demand for reserves, rises in the expansion and falls in the recession, often stabilizing interest rates.

This procyclical policy was due, in part, to the Fed's use of a nefarious target, free reserves. The Fed believed that banks want to repay all their borrowing from the Fed, and then use most of the excess reserves they have left over to extend loans and purchase securities. Hence, the Fed thought that it could control deposit creation, and thus bank credit and the money stock by controlling the volume of free reserves. But the assumption that banks want to keep only a fixed amount of free reserves is invalid. Free reserves are an inventory that banks keep, and their desired inventory of free reserves depends on the opportunity cost of holding these reserves (for example, the federal funds rate, or the Treasury bill rate) and the benefit of holding excess reserves, such as avoiding having to borrow at the Fed if there is a deposit outflow.

To see the damage a free-reserves target can do, assume that the Fed wants to prevent excessive ease by reducing the free reserves that banks have, say, from $100 million to $50 million. It therefore undertakes open-market sales of $50 million. But, given prevailing interest rates, banks *want* to keep $100 million of free reserves. They therefore reduce their loans and security holdings, and thus deposits, and hence the money supply falls. The Fed now sees that free reserves are still $100 million, so it undertakes another open-market sale of $50 million, to which the banks respond again by cutting their deposits and hence the money stock, to hold on to their $100 million of excess reserves. This process goes on until either the Fed finally gives in, or else interest rates change enough to make the banks want to hold only $50 million rather than $100 million of excess reserves. But either of these could take a long time, and in the meantime the money supply keeps on shrinking. By using a totally inappropriate target the Fed loses control of the money supply.

What made this policy particularly bad is that during a recession as interest rates fell banks wanted to hold more free reserves. The Fed, using free reserves as an indicator as well as a target, then interpreted the rise in excess reserves as showing that its policy was easy, when in fact the growth rate of the money stock was falling. And out of fear of credit conditions being too easy, the Fed reduced the growth rate of bank reserves, so that its policy was procyclical.

Its use of the short-term interest rate enhanced this confusion. During a recession interest rates fall as the demand for credit decreases. But the Fed interpreted this decline as showing that it was following an expansionary policy. With interest rates falling, sometimes substantially, the Fed concluded that its policy was too easy and reduced the growth rate of bank reserves.

As a result of a great deal of criticism by academic economists, particularly Brunner and Meltzer, by 1966 the Federal Reserve started to change its policy procedures. Not surprisingly, this has taken the form of an evolutionary series of steps rather than a once-and-for-all radical change.

Thus, in 1966 the FOMC added a so-called proviso clause to its Directive. This directed the account manager to carry out the free reserves and money-market conditions instructions *provided* they did not conflict with the growth rate specified in the Directive for some aggregate, usually bank credit. In case of conflict the account manager was to disregard the instructions about money-market conditions and free reserves. But this was only a minor step because this proviso clause came into operation only infrequently and to a small extent. However, the Fed then undertook a substantial review of its Directive, and in 1970 changed it by giving more emphasis to aggregates, which brings us to the current procedures.

The 1970s

The procedure that evolved by the late 1970s operated as follows: at FOMC meetings staff economists presented several economic forecasts *based on different assumptions about the growth rate of the money stock.* The staff's forecasts were based on a combination of the Fed's econometric model and informal, subjective forecasts. The various Federal Reserve banks also contributed to these forecasts. The FOMC then selected as its goal the forecast it preferred, and thus its long-run targets for the money growth rate during the next twelve months. However, it did not use a single-valued target, but set a fairly wide range for M_1, M_2, and M_3. For example, it might select as its longer-run targets growth rates of 4–6 percent for M_1, 6½–9 percent for M_2 and 8–10½ percent for M_3.

But the account manager had to decide on open-market operations on a day-to-day basis. Hence, to give him more guidance, the FOMC also set two-month targets for M_1 and M_2. In addition—and it is a very important addition—the FOMC also had a range for the federal funds rate. The account manager then tried to keep the federal funds rate around the midpoint of the range unless M_1, M_2, and M_3 were growing at rates inconsistent with their ranges. If so, he could change the federal funds rate within its range to bring the monetary growth rates back into their permitted ranges. Usually the federal funds rate range was set as a quite narrow band, for example, 9½ to 8¼ percent, while the band for the money growth rates was much broader, for example, 4–8 percent for M_1 and 6–10 percent for M_2. It was frequently not feasible to keep both the federal funds rate and the growth rate of the money stock within their ranges because they were inconsistent. In this case the account manager asked the FOMC for new instructions.

Can this procedure be described as one of using the money stock as a target, and the federal funds rate as an instrument variable? Not really. If the federal funds rate had been just an instrument variable then the account manager would probably not have been told to keep it within a certain narrow range, but would have been allowed to set it at a level needed to generate the desired growth rates of M_1 and M_2. Moreover, the FOMC would then not have set such broad ranges for M_1 and M_2, and such a narrow range for the federal funds rate. And most importantly, when it proved impossible to attain both the federal funds rate target and the money growth targets at the same time, then in most cases it would have been the federal funds rate target that was abandoned. But this was not the case. The Fed announced monetary growth rate targets first in 1975. In the following forty-seven months, the federal funds rate fell outside its target range on only five occasions, while the M_1 growth rate fell outside its target range close to 50 percent of the time.[14] Thus the Fed treated the federal funds rate, *not* just as an instrumental variable, but also as a target variable, and at least in the short run as a considerably more important target variable than the money growth rates.

Starting in 1975 Congress entered the scene and the chairman of the Board of Governors is now required to come before congressional committees four times a year to reveal the money growth rate targets (but not the federal funds rate target) and to answer questions, both about the targets and about past growth rates. In addition, the Fed has to provide Congress with a detailed report on its policy twice a year.

However, for several reasons, there is less to this than meets the eye. One is that the Fed in justifying past growth rates can select which variables it wants to discuss. It can use bank credit, or any of the Ms from *M-1A* to *M-3*. Given such a wide choice of variables, it is likely that at least one of them will happen to be growing at a rate that can easily be justified, and the Fed can focus on this one.

Second, the Fed presents Congress with growth rates for the next twelve months, and does not indicate the intended quarterly growth rates. So suppose that *M-2* has grown at a 10 percent rate while the Fed told Congress three months ago that it wants *M-2* to grow at a 6 percent rate. The Fed can claim that this 10 percent rate is not inconsistent with its annual target since it expects a much slower growth rate for the remaining nine months.

Third, the growth-rate targets are stated as wide ranges. For example, the Fed may state a 7–10 percent growth rate for M_2 despite the fact that a 7 percent growth rate may be consistent with a, say, 4 percent inflation rate, and a 10 percent growth rate with a 7 percent inflation rate.

The changes that the Fed made in its operating procedures in the 1970s did not satisfy its critics; they saw the Fed as still focusing primarily on interest rates. And what became more and more apparent was that the Fed was using the federal funds rate not just as a tool to attain the appropriate level of the money stock and of income, but that the Fed also tried to stabilize the federal funds rate. Using the federal funds rate as an instrument would at times require allowing it to rise or fall substantially. But the Fed was reluctant to do this. When interest rates rise, money-market dealers who hold a heavy inventory of securities can make large losses on

---

[14] Lawrence Roos, "Monetary Targets—Their Contribution to Policy Formation," *Review* (Federal Reserve Bank of St. Louis) 61 (May 1979): 13.

it. Many economists accused the Fed of being too concerned about these losses, and about the lessened efficiency of the money market that would result if dealers were afraid to carry large inventories. Moreover, these economists argued, any attempt to keep interest rates stable will frequently be fruitless. If the Fed prevents a rise in the federal funds rate for several months, and if the conditions that require the rise persist, then the Fed will eventually have to allow a very sharp and abrupt rise in the federal funds rate to bring it to its proper level.[15]

The Fed's critics believed that protection of money-market dealers may not have been the only reason for the Fed's reluctance to allow interest rates to rise. A rise in interest rates often results in much criticism from Congress and the general public.

The Fed replied to these criticisms in several ways. It denied that it allowed considerations of interest-rate stability to interfere with its stabilization goal. At the same time it stressed the benefits that result from protecting the money market from being whiplashed by the erratic changes in interest rates, which it, rightly or wrongly, believed would occur if it tried to keep the money stock close to its target at all times. As discussed previously, due to the lag in the response of money to changes in reserves, an attempt to reach the money-stock target rapidly would require large fluctuations in the interest rate. And as former Governor Maisel has put it:

> . . . sharp interest rate changes may disrupt economic decisions. Swings in the money supply or bank credit can destabilize the behavior of borrowers and lenders. Decision units rely to a great extent on the interest rate structure as a source of information about what is happening in credit markets and to the economy.[16]

Besides, the Federal Reserve argued, little would be gained by trying to keep the money growth rate very close to its target. The money data are subject to large errors. Hence, if the Fed allows interest rates to rise rapidly

[15] Another criticism of the Federal Reserve's procedures is that the money growth rate has usually fallen, rather than risen, during recessions, so that the Fed has behaved procyclically. But this is not *necessarily* bad. It is *not* true that to stabilize the economy one should raise income in the recession and lower it in the expansion. During the first part of the recession income is still above its normal level, and during the first part of the expansion it is still below its normal level. Hence, to stabilize income around its trend, monetary policy *should* lower income during the early stages of the recession. Thus, instead of seeing whether the money growth rate behaves pro- or anti-cyclically, one should compare it to some indicator, such as the unemployment rate, that tells us whether aggregate demand is insufficient or excessive. And if one compares changes in the growth rate of either M_1 or M_2 to cyclical changes in unemployment, then the money growth rate is seen to respond fairly well to unemployment. Does this mean that the Federal Reserve is actually stabilizing the economy? Not necessarily, because changes in the money growth rate affect aggregate demand with a lag, so that monetary policy could very easily be destabilizing after all. But whether or not it is destabilizing cannot be determined unless one knows the lag in the effect of monetary policy. The fact that the money growth rate usually behaves procyclically is not acceptable evidence.

[16] Sherman Maisel, *Managing the Dollar* (New York: W. W. Norton, 1973), p. 237.

because the money stock seems to be rising too much, then a few months later when more reliable data become available, it may turn out that the rise in the federal funds rate was unnecessary because the money stock was not growing as much as the previous data had indicated.

Beyond this, the Federal Reserve argued that its econometric model shows that if the money stock is moderately off its target for one or two calendar quarters, this has only a small effect on nominal income. However, monetarists question the reliability of the Federal Reserve's model, and, besides, with GNP being as large as it is, the social loss from having GNP off its target by, say, one-half percent for two quarters represents a lot of income, and may well outweigh the social loss that would result from greater interest-rate fluctuations.

Current Procedures

This debate, one of the main debates going on at the time among monetary economists, was terminated by events. In the second half of 1979 the money stock was growing at a much faster rate than was called for by the Fed's monetary target. At the same time the consumer price index was rising at double-digit rates, and the dollar fell substantially on the foreign-exchange market. On 6 October 1979, the Fed therefore announced a strong anti-inflation program, one component of which was the decision to control the money growth rate much more firmly. This required that the federal funds rate be allowed to fluctuate much more.

With the target range for the federal funds rate now being widened to four percentage points, it looked for a time as though the Fed had in large part abandoned its previous concern about interest-rate stabilization, and was using the bands around the federal funds rate only as a safety net. But at this time (July 1980) it seems that the Fed may be going back part of the way towards its old policy of interest-rate stabilization. In the first six months of the 1980 recession it allowed the growth rate of *M-1B* to be a mere 2.1 percent, at least partly because it did not want interest rates to fall further.

Summary

This chapter dealt with the way the Federal Reserve aligns its tools to its ultimate targets. It cannot observe the effect of its policy on income until a long time has passed, and these effects are hard to isolate since income is also influenced by many other factors. Hence, it uses as its target some variables that are closer to its reach. It can try to attain one target accurately, or approximate several targets, but usually it is impossible to attain several targets accurately at the same time. The criteria for a good target variable are the quick availability of reliable data, the ability of the Fed to attain this target, and the relatedness of the target variable to the Fed's ultimate goals. The main targets are the money growth rate and the short-term interest rate, though bank credit has been used too. But meaningful and reliable data are not available for any of them. A particular problem is the absence of data on the expected real rate of interest. While Federal Reserve control over the short-term interest rate is good in the short run, this is not so in the long run. In the short run the Fed cannot set the money growth rate accurately. If the unexpected fluctuations in the interest rate are mainly due to shifts in the *IS* curve, then the Fed should use a money-stock target, while if the unexpected changes in the interest rate mainly result from shifts in the *LM* curve, then the Fed should use an interest-rate target.

But the money-stock and the long-term interest-rate targets are still removed some distance from the Fed's tools. Hence, it uses proximate targets (also called instruments). The criteria for these instruments are the same as for the targets themselves. Both bank reserves or the base, as well as short-term interest rates, can be used as instruments. This system of using both targets and instruments is, however, not accepted by all economists; some have advocated instead the use of the sophisticated tools of control theory, or a policy of aiming directly at income, or else using the reserve base in place of a money-stock or interest-rate target.

In addition to using targets and instruments the Fed also has a need to know what its current policy is, and this need can be satisfied by using some of the instruments as indicators. In the 1950s and early 1960s the Fed did not distinguish between indicators, instruments, and targets, and focused on short-term interest rates, free reserves, and money-market conditions.

In the 1960s and 1970s the Fed shifted in the direction of putting more emphasis on the money growth rate. But, at the same time, it also had the conflicting objective of keeping the federal funds rate stable. Congressional oversight did not suffice to bring the money growth rate sufficiently to center stage. In late 1979, when the money growth rate was much higher than the Fed intended, it changed its techniques and now lets the federal funds rate fluctuate more.

QUESTIONS AND EXERCISES

1. To what extent is the money stock a good target? To what extent is the interest rate?
2. Using the data provided in the *Economic Report of the President* make a judgment about whether the Federal Reserve actually does offset borrowing and currency flows.
3. What are the criteria for targets and indicators? Explain in your own words.
4. Discuss: "Given the uncertainties about targets and indicators the Federal Reserve is just as likely to act in a destabilizing as in a stabilizing way."
5. Compare the Directives in recent issues of the *Federal Reserve Bulletin* with the data (also in the *Federal Reserve Bulletin*) on the *actual* changes that

occurred in the money stock and the federal funds rate. Is it still true that the Fed is putting little emphasis on its interest-rate target?

6. Explain in your own words why the Fed should use an interest-rate target if the observed change in the interest rate is due to a change in the amount of money demanded per dollar of income, and a money-stock target if it is due to a rise in income.

FURTHER READING

BURGER, ALBERT. *The Money Supply Process.* Belmont, Calif.: Wadsworth Publishing Co., 1971. Chapter 8 gives a clear discussion of the targets, proximate targets, and indicators approach.

DAVIS, RICHARD. "Short-Run Targets for Open Market Operations." In *Open Market Policies and Operating Procedures—Staff Studies,* edited by the Board of Governors, Federal Reserve System. Washington, D.C.: 1971. A good discussion of Federal Reserve tactics, though somewhat difficult.

FEDERAL RESERVE BANK OF BOSTON. *Controlling Monetary Aggregates.* Vols. 1 and 2. Boston, Mass.: 1972, 1973. Two collections of very useful papers.

FEDERAL RESERVE BANK OF NEW YORK. *Monetary Aggregates and Monetary Policy.* New York: 1974. This too is a very useful collection of papers. Particularly useful is the introductory chapter by Richard Davis, and the chapters by Gerald Corrigan and John Ciccolo.

FEDERAL RESERVE BANK OF ST. LOUIS. *Review.* Each year the February or March issue of the *Review* contains articles on the previous year's FOMC decisions and discusses changes in the Fed's procedures.

KEIR, PETER, and WALLICH, HENRY. "The Role of Operating Guides in U.S. Monetary Policy." *Federal Reserve Bulletin* 65 (September 1979): 679–91. An excellent survey of the development of Federal Reserve targets and indicators.

MAISEL, SHERMAN. *Managing the Dollar.* New York: W. W. Norton, 1973. An insider's view of the targets and instruments problem.

POOLE, WILLIAM. "Benefits and Costs of Stable Money Growth." *Carnegie-Mellon Conference Series on Public Policy* 3: 15–50. Supplement to *Journal of Monetary Economics,* 1976. An excellent, though somewhat difficult paper.

————. "The Making of Monetary Policy: Description and Analysis." In *New England Economic Review* (Federal Reserve Bank of Boston), March/April 1975, pp. 21–30. This journal also carries a reply by Paul Meek. Both articles provide good descriptions of Federal Reserve procedures in the 1970s.

24

The Transmission
of Monetary Policy

The previous chapter showed how the Fed operates in the money market to change the short-term interest rate or the money stock. In this chapter we carry the story further by seeing how these money market changes then affect aggregate demand, and hence real income. To a considerable extent this was already generally discussed in Part Three, so now we will focus on some specific issues.

Strength of Monetary Policy

One of these issues is the strength of monetary policy. From the 1930s until well into the 1950s most economists believed that changes in the stock of money and in interest rates had little effect on nominal income, so that monetary policy was weak and much less important than fiscal policy. For many years the question of whether monetary policy was strong or weak was the central issue in the debate about monetary policy. This debate has faded away as it came to be realized that monetary policy can have very powerful effects on the economy. One reason for this is that new empirical evidence came to light that contradicted earlier views. It had once been believed that the interest elasticity of the demand for money was very high, and the interest elasticity of investment was close to zero, in other words, that the *LM* curve was very flat and the *IS* curve very steep. Many new empirical studies, using more refined statistical techniques, showed, however, that investment does respond to the interest rate, and that the interest elasticity of demand for money is not great. Second, quantity theorists, such as Milton Friedman, argued persuasively that the quantity of money, and hence monetary policy, is important. Third, when interest rates rose in 1966 and 1969, the effects on residential construction were plain to the naked eye.

Fourth, economists came to realize that one must make a sharp distinction between the effect of monetary policy per se, and the effect of a particular change in the money stock or in the interest rate. Suppose, for example, that a $1-billion increase in the money stock raises income by only 5 percent of the desired amount. Does this necessarily mean that monetary policy is too weak? Of course not. The Fed can generate a $20-billion increase in the money stock to get the full effect on income it wants.

But one should beware of pushing this argument too far. While it is true that the Fed can always adopt a policy strong enough to brake a boom, there are substantial costs to doing so. First, since the Fed does not know exactly how strong a policy is required, it may go too far and adopt one that is so strong that it not only brakes the boom, but throws the economy into a severe recession. What makes this possibility so dangerous is that by abruptly changing its policy the Fed may frighten businessmen into a massive cutback. Second, a sharply restrictive policy may cause bankruptcies of firms that are overextended and now find it hard to borrow. In chapter 27 we will discuss how such a danger forced the Fed to moderate its policy in 1969. Third, as we will take up in the next chapter, a strongly restrictive policy does not affect every industry equally, but imposes larger, albeit temporary, burdens on some segments of the economy than on others. Hence the question is not *just* whether there exists a monetary policy strong enough to stop a boom, but it is also useful to ask whether a *moderately* restrictive policy can succeed in curbing an excessive expansion.

A related question is whether, once the economy is in a severe recession, monetary policy can pull it out again. Suppose that the Fed undertakes extensive open-market purchases and provides banks with a large volume of excess reserves. Will banks use these reserves to increase loans and security purchases, and hence the money stock? Monetarists answer yes, and point out that, as discussed in chapter 9, in the postwar period excess reserves have been very low and stable. But *some* Keynesians reject this reasoning, and argue that excess reserves have been low in the postwar period only because there was no extremely severe recession. In such a recession, they argue, banks would not have enough loan demand from credit-worthy borrowers, and would not want to buy securities because interest rates are too low. (Recall the discussion of speculative liquidity preference in chapter 12.) Whether this argument is right or (as the authors believe) wrong is something that with luck will not be put to a test. In a moderate or normal recession, however, the existing evidence strongly suggests that the Fed can generate an increase in the money stock, and that velocity is stable enough for this, in turn, to raise nominal income.

What emerges from all of this is that the Fed can curb even an exceedingly powerful expansion by stepping on the brake sharply, and that monetary policy is also strong enough to combat a normal recession, though (as will be discussed in chapter 26) it may take a long time to do so. There is still some disagreement about the extent to which a *moderately* restrictive policy can curb a strong expansion, and on whether monetary policy could pull the economy out of an extraordinary downturn, such as the Great Depression of the 1930s. But there is little disagreement that in both of these cases monetary policy could, at least, help.

Real Income and Prices

So far we have talked about monetary policy curbing an expansion or pulling the economy out of a recession, which essentially amounts to changing nominal income. But can monetary policy also affect the breakdown of changes in nominal income between changes in real income and changes in prices? Suppose, for example, that you are told that in an inflationary boom monetary policy can cut the growth rate of nominal income, say, from 15 percent per annum to 5 percent. You might think that this is desirable until you are told further that prices will continue to rise at the previous 12 percent rate, but that output will fall by 7 percent.

The main tools of the Fed act upon bank reserves and short-term interest rates, and hence affect aggregate demand rather than its breakdown between output and prices. It is the slope of the Phillips curve that determines this breakdown. But the Fed is not powerless in this respect. In the long run it can strongly influence the extent to which firms respond to an increase in demand by raising prices rather than output. If the Fed previously followed a policy that kept the price level stable, for example, a policy of stimulating aggregate demand only moderately and temporarily during a recession, then the public will expect that prices will remain stable in the future, and will respond to the expansion in aggregate demand mainly by raising output. But if it has learned that the Fed responds to a recession so massively that prices quickly start to rise, then as soon as it knows that the money stock is increasing, say, by 10 percent more than before, it will raise prices and wages at a 10 percent faster rate and not by increasing output. Thus it is *not* true that the Fed can influence only nominal income, and not the breakdown of changes in nominal income between output and prices, but almost the only way it can do so is by the reputation its previous policies have earned it. Insofar as the public is gullible, two minor tools, moral suasion and publicity, might also affect the extent to which wages and prices rather than output respond. But, all in all, the Fed's deeds count for more than its words.

The Transmission Channels

So much for the issue of the strength of monetary policy. Now we turn to the *ways* in which monetary policy affects nominal income and tell this story twice: once from the monetarist, or quantity theory, approach and once from the Keynesian one. This does not mean that these two approaches are everywhere in conflict. At many points it is just a matter of differences in formulating essentially the same point, or of differences in emphasis, rather than always representing substantial empirical differences.

The Monetarist Transmission Process

Having discussed the quantity theory in detail in chapters 16 and 17, we can describe this transmission process quickly. Quantity theorists point out that when, under the stimulus of increased reserves, banks create more money, they do so by buying securities or making loans. As they buy securities those people who have been induced by the higher prices of securities to sell them to the banks, temporarily hold excessive money balances. They henceforth proceed to spend them. Similarly, those who obtain bank loans obviously do so for the sake of increasing expenditures. Thus, an increase in the money stock results in an increase in expenditures either on securities or on goods by those who initially receive the newly created money. And as they spend their excess money balances, the recipients find themselves with excess balances, and *they* proceed to spend them. The public is holding more money than it wants to hold at the prevailing levels of income and interest rates. To induce the public to hold all the newly created money, interest rates decline but only temporarily (as lenders try to find customers for the increased supply of money) and income rises (as expenditures increase). As a first approximation, as interest rates rise back to their previous level, income must rise proportionately to the increase in the money supply. Thus, monetary policy has a very powerful effect on income.

The Keynesian Approach

This approach spells out the impact of changes in the quantity of money in much greater detail, and hence needs more discussion.

Suppose the Fed undertakes open-market purchases. This lowers short-term interest rates both directly, and indirectly as banks use their additional reserves to buy securities and to make loans. Although it is initially short-term interest rates and interest rates on bank loans that are affected, eventually all interest rates decline. One effect of this decline in interest rates is that stock prices rise.

Investment now increases for two reasons. First, to maximize profits firms borrow to invest until the cost of borrowed funds equals the marginal efficiency of investment, so that with a lower cost of borrowing they now undertake investment projects that were not worthwhile before. Second, the increase in stock prices means that the public is now willing to pay a higher price for corporations, and it becomes profitable to start new ones and expand existing ones. For example, suppose that it costs $100 million to construct a new plant, and that the public is willing to pay $110 million for the stock of a corporation that owns such a plant. It is now profitable to start new firms that possess such plants, or to add these plants to existing firms. A firm can sell stock for $110 million, spend $100 million of it to build the plant, and have $10 million left over. Thus, both the direct effects of a lower interest rate and its indirect effects via stock prices stimulate investment.

Two relations are central in determining by how much the Federal Reserve can stimulate investment. One is the extent to which it can reduce the interest rate, that is, shift the *LM* curve, and the second is the topic to which we now turn, the extent to which changes in the interest rate affect investment, that is, the slope of the *IS* curve.

Interest Rates, Credit Conditions, and Expenditures

In chapter 14 we showed why a decline in interest rates induces firms to invest more. This discussion assumed a perfect capital market in which firms can borrow as much as they want to invest. We will now extend this analysis by dropping this assumption and consider how a change in the interest rate affects investment by changing the availability of funds.

In chapter 4 we discussed capital rationing and how some firms are unable to obtain bank loans. If banks now obtain additional reserves they are more willing to make loans to some of these potential customers. These previously unsatisfied borrowers have a number of investment projects that they thought worth undertaking even at the previous higher interest rate, and they are even more eager to undertake these projects now that the interest rate has fallen.

Moreover, when interest rates fall another imperfection in the capital market is reduced. Some financial institutions are "locked in." They bought securities some time ago at a high price, and since then security prices have fallen. Their managers do not want to admit that they made a mistake in buying these securities, by selling them at a loss; instead they hold onto them. But once interest rates fall and security prices rise again, banks and other financial institutions can now sell these securities without taking a loss. Hence they sell them and make loans with the proceeds from these sales. This means that business borrowers get loans, and when they spend them, aggregate demand increases. But how about the buyers of the securities? As they buy them they have to reduce other expenditures. But they are not likely to reduce other expenditures dollar for dollar. Securities, particularly short-term government securities, are very liquid. Hence, a firm that buys government securities can satisfy part of its demand for liquidity in this way and can now run down its money holdings to some extent. Thus, the decline in expenditures by the purchasers of securities is less than the increase in expenditures by those who now get loans from banks and other financial institutions, so that there is a net increase in aggregate demand.

Finally, there is another consideration that is, in part, the result of imperfect capital markets. This is that, although we have talked of the interest rate as the cost of borrowing, this is an oversimplification. As we discussed in the previous chapters, there are many other costs and burdens to borrowing apart from having to pay interest. This is important because looking just at the interest rate may give a misleading idea about how much the cost of borrowing changes. For example, the interest rate can rise from, say, 8 percent to 10 percent during the course of a year. It may seem that even with a relatively low interest elasticity of investment such a 25 percent increase in the interest rate should lower investment substantially. But when one adds all the other costs of borrowing, the total cost of borrowing may have risen for the typical firm, not from 8 percent to 10 percent, but from, say, 18 percent to 20 percent, which is only an 11 percent increase. Thus, in this way, unlike the two previous ways just discussed, imperfections in the capital markets weaken monetary policy.

Financial intermediaries and residential construction. Market imperfections are also important in the impact of monetary policy on residential construction. As we discussed previously, when interest rates rise relative to the fixed Regulation Q ceilings, disintermediation takes place, fewer mortgage loans become available, and residential construction drops. To what extent the observed drop in residential construction as interest rates rise is due to disintermediation is a disputed issue, which we will discuss in the following chapter. But disintermediation must surely play some role in the sharp cutback of residential construction that occurs as interest rates increase. Whatever the reason for it, there can be little doubt that residential construction is one type of investment strongly affected by interest rates.

The fact that monetary policy now gets some of its punch from the disintermediation that occurs as open-market interest rates rise above the Regulation Q ceiling is ironic because before Regulation Q was made effective in 1966 some economists had worried that the thrift institutions would greatly weaken monetary policy. Their argument was that as interest rates rise people switch their deposits out of commercial banks into thrift institutions. Since the funds deposited in thrift institutions are promptly lent out, and after being spent, land up again as deposits in banks, the public's bank deposits are not reduced by the initial transfer into thrift institutions. But deposits in thrift institutions have increased, and hence M-2 and M-3 have gone up. Insofar as expenditure depends on M-2 or M-3, rather than just on M-1, here is one way in which a rise in interest rates *increases,* rather than reduces, aggregate demand. Conversely, if interest rates fall, M-2 and M-3 fall and the expansionary policy is now partially offset. As Regulation Q is phased out this *may* become a problem again, but currently it is not a problem.

Thrift institutions have substantially increased their share of total deposits in financial intermediaries. In 1954 they held 28 percent of total deposits and in 1979, 46 percent. This led some economists to worry that in controlling bank deposits the Federal Reserve was controlling a smaller and smaller proportion of M-3 each year. But this assumes that the Federal

Reserve's controls don't reach thrift institutions indirectly, and this is a questionable assumption.[1]

A number of economists have also been concerned about the activities of what may be called amateur financial institutions, that is, the extension of trade credit by nonfinancial firms. (Trade credit is the credit that a firm, say a wholesaler, extends to another firm, say a retailer, by shipping goods with payments to be made only in the future, perhaps in thirty or ninety days.) They have argued that if firms extend more credit to their customer firms this can, at least partially, offset the effect of a restrictive monetary policy. However, the empirical evidence suggests that, at least as far as manufacturing firms are concerned, trade credit does *not* expand when the Federal Reserve reduces the growth rate of the money stock.[2]

Consumption. Monetary policy affects consumption as well as investment. This is important because, while gross private domestic investment accounts for about 15 percent of GNP, consumer purchases account for about 64 percent. Hence, a small interest elasticity of consumption could well be much more important than a relatively large interest elasticity of investment.

There are several reasons why one would expect consumption to respond to interest rates. First, about 16 percent of total consumption consists of consumer durables. And purchases of consumer durables, being investment by the household, should be affected by changes in the interest rate, that is, in the cost of holding them. Consumers *may* not pay much attention to the interest rate per se, but the lower the interest rate, the lower are the required payments to which consumers certainly pay attention. Second, a decline in interest rates is accompanied by a relaxation of credit rationing, and households who previously could not get loans to purchase durables can now do so. For example, consumer finance companies find it easier and cheaper to borrow when interest rates are low, and hence, they are then more eager to find customers. Some empirical evidence suggests that consumer durable purchases do respond significantly to monetary policy.[3]

A third way in which interest rates affect consumer purchases is through changes in household wealth. As discussed in chapter 14, if wealth increases, so does consumption. And if interest rates fall the prices of stocks and bonds held by households—and hence household wealth—all increase

---

[1] See Jacques Melitz and George Martin, "Financial Intermediaries, Money Definition and Monetary Control," *Journal of Money, Credit and Banking* 3 (August 1971): 693–701.

[2] M. I. Nadiri, "The Determinants of Trade Credit in the U.S. Total Manufacturing Sector," *Econometrica* 37 (July 1969): 408–23; Paul Junk, "Monetary Policy and the Extension of Trade Credit," *Southern Economic Journal* 30 (January 1964): 274–77.

[3] See, for instance, Michael Hamburger, "Interest Rates and the Demand for Consumer Durables," *American Economic Review* 57 (June 1966): 1131–53, and Frederic Mishkin, "Illiquidity, Consumer Durable Expenditure and Monetary Policy," *American Economic Review* 66 (September 1976): 642–54.

so that consumption should rise. Fourth, if stock and bond prices rise, households are not only wealthier, they are also more liquid, since stocks and bonds are relatively liquid compared to the other assets owned by households. Moreover a rise in the value of any of its assets raises a household's liquidity in the sense of raising its ratio of net worth to liabilities. And if households become more liquid they are more ready to trade some of their liquid assets for such illiquid assets as consumer durables. Finally, *if* the supply curve of savings has a positive slope, then when interest rates are low households have less incentive to save, and hence they consume more.

Portfolio Equilibrium

We will now recapitulate the above analysis in a somewhat different way by using an explicit portfolio approach similar to that used by many monetarists. Such an approach, which differs more in style than in substance from the previous discussion, focuses neither on firms as investors nor on households as consumers, but looks at the menu of assets and liabilities that people own and want. Everyone has a portfolio of assets and liabilities and tries to keep the (monetary plus imputed) yields of all its assets equal at the margin. Now suppose that the quantity of money increases, so that at least some portfolios now include more money. Given, for the usual reasons, declining marginal utility, the yield on money is now less than before, and therefore also less than the yield on other assets. Hence, portfolio holders now exchange money for other assets. What assets they buy depends upon the cross-elasticity of demand, which, in turn, depends on the similarity between assets. For example, money and Treasury bills, being similar, are close substitutes (have a high cross-elasticity of demand). Not only are they both very safe assets, but the type of risks to which they are subject are similar. They are both subject to inflation risk, but not to significant default risk. Similarly, there is no significant fall in their values if interest rates rise. Hence, those who initially hold excess money balances use them to buy mainly securities, like Treasury bills. But the sellers of Treasury bills now receive these excess money balances and they buy mainly assets that are not too dissimilar to Treasury bills, for example, commercial paper and three-year government securities. The sellers of these items, in turn, then buy others, and eventually the increased demand for assets spreads (in principle) to all assets in the economy, until in the new equilibrium the (monetary plus imputed) yields on all assets are again equal. Among the assets whose prices are raised in this way are common stocks, and thus the value of corporations. And if the value of existing corporations exceeds the cost of creating new ones, new capital will be created, that is, investment will take place. Moreover, as yields on various assets such as money, stocks, and bonds decline, the imputed yield on consumer durables rises relatively to these other yields, so that households now purchase new consumer durables.

Monetary Policy and Stock Prices

To see how changes in monetary policy affect stock prices we will deal first with a situation in which there is not much fear of inflation. Assume that the Federal Reserve adopts an expansionary policy and the growth rate of money rises. The way stock prices are affected can be formulated in three ways. The first is to say that the public now holds more money in its portfolio, and since its money holdings were previously in equilibrium it now holds excessive money, and tries to exchange some of it for other assets including corporate stock. Another way of putting this is to look at relative yields and notice that as people get more money the yield on money falls at the margin, so that it is now less than the expected yield (adjusted for risk) on stock. So people can now increase their (nominal plus imputed) incomes by buying stock. As they buy stock they bid stock prices up so that at the new price the expected (risk-adjusted) yield on a dollar invested in stock is no greater than the marginal yield on a dollar held as money. A third way of putting it is to say that the present value of a stock, and hence its price, is equal to expected streams of future yields discounted at the interest rate. An increase in the quantity of money temporarily lowers the interest rate, and hence increases the present value of the expected future earnings on the stock, and thus its price.

Knowing this can you go out and make money on the stock market? Unfortunately not. The trouble is that other people have this information also. So when you rush down to your broker you find that there are already other people there who want to buy stock too, and worse still, that potential sellers who know what is happening are demanding a higher price. Information that everyone else has too is of no use to you in the stock market.[4] Only if you know something (something right, that is) that others don't, can you cash in on it. Suppose, for example, you discover that in every month in which there is a full moon on a Thursday, the Fed raises the money growth rate. Then, until others discover this too, you can predict stock prices in time to buy stocks before they go up. But it is very difficult to predict what the Fed will do, though many smart people will try.

Just to complicate things, there is the problem that in an inflationary period it is possible for the stock market to act "perversely." Many people know by now that an increase in the money growth rate is inflationary. And for reasons that are still somewhat obscure, inflation drives stock prices down. Hence, at a time when people are highly sensitized to inflation, perhaps you should sell, rather than buy stock, when your study of geese entrails tells you that the money growth rate is rising.

---

[4] This is an implication of the "random walk" theory of stock prices. For very clear discussions of this theory, see Burton Malkiel, *A Random Walk Down Wall Street,* New York: W. W. Norton, 1975; and Neil Berkman, "A Primer on Random Walks in the Stock Market," *New England Economic Review* (Federal Reserve Bank of Boston) September/October 1978, pp. 32–50. The latter contains a formal model of how money affects stock prices.

The MPS Model

Having taken up how monetary policy affects all the sectors of the economy, except imports and exports, which we leave aside for the moment, the time has come to put these various effects together. One way to do so is in an econometric model. In chapter 17 we discussed the monetarist St. Louis model, and now we will see how monetary policy functions in one large Keynesian model.

Although there are many such models that could be used, we will employ the Federal Reserve's MPS model. The main architect of the model is Professor Franco Modigliani of M.I.T., but economists in other universities, notably the University of Pennsylvania, have also played an important role in its development. The acronym MPS stands for M.I.T., the University of Pennsylvania, and the Social Science Research Council, which contributed to its financing. This large model, while essentially Keynesian, has a much more detailed monetary sector than most other models since it was built for the Federal Reserve's use. The Fed uses this model in two ways. One is to forecast income, prices, unemployment, and so on, with it. In forecasting, the Fed combines the predictions obtained from this model with judgmental forecasts, that is, forecasts made in an informal manner by experts familiar with developments in various sectors of the economy. The Fed also uses the MPS model to simulate how its policies affect the economy. For example, it may use the model to predict what income would be if unborrowed reserves rose by $1 billion and to compare the results to what income would be if there were no change in unborrowed reserves.

Do not treat this model as though it were *the* model of the economy. Some other models, that predict approximately as well, have different monetary sectors, and hence describe the impact of monetary policies differently. For example, the St. Louis model predicts just as well, if not better, than the MPS model, but is based on a very different theory. Moreover, the MPS model is constantly being revised, and the latest versions are not publicly available. Hence, treat it more as an illustration than as the last word.

In this model monetary policy affects income in three ways. One channel is the wealth effect; as interest rates rise, bond and stock prices fall, households feel poorer and respond by cutting consumption. This wealth effect is very important in the model, and at some times accounts for roughly half the *direct* impact (that is, the impact excluding the indirect multiplier and accelerator effects) of monetary policy as measured by the model. The second channel is the effect of changes in interest rates on the demand for capital, that is, a cost of capital channel. This applies not only to industrial plant and equipment, but also to consumer durables, to residential construction, and to nonresidential construction both by the private sector and by state and local governments. The third effect, called the

Figure 24.1   First-Round Effects of Monetary Policy in the MPS Model

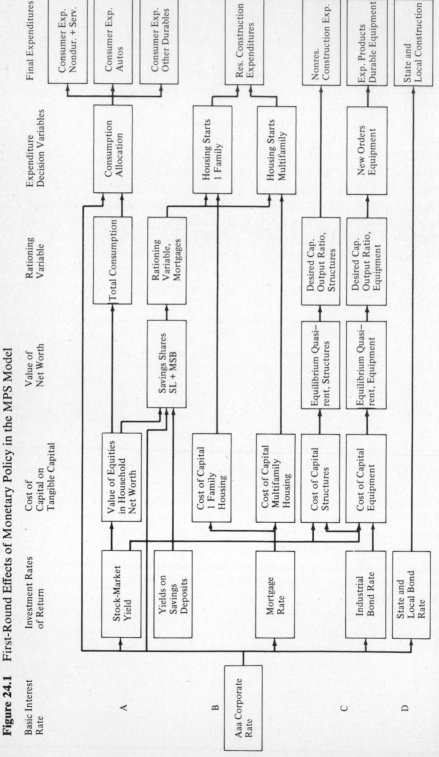

Note: This is the 1969 version of the model.
SOURCE: *Federal Reserve Bulletin,* June 1969, p. 484.

credit availability channel, operates through credit rationing; as policy becomes more restrictive, more potential borrowers are unable to obtain mortgage loans.

Figure 24.1 shows the flow chart of the MPS model for the first-round effects of monetary policy. Since it deals only with the first round it excludes the various feedbacks, such as the effects of rising income on interest rates, consumption, and investment. To include these would make the figure much too complex. We start out by assuming a rise in the Aaa bond rate; that is, the interest rate paid on the highest-quality corporate bonds, perhaps because the Fed has changed its policy. Part A shows the wealth-consumption channel. This has already been discussed, and the only thing that may need explanation is that the model does not stop with the change in consumption, but breaks it down into its major components. It also shows the effect of the rise in the interest rate on the distribution of consumption between durables and nondurables. This is a cost of capital effect.

Part B deals with the impact of monetary policy on mortgage lending by thrift institutions. The rise in the corporate bond rate causes deposits to flow out of thrift institutions into bonds and stock. (To be sure, the rise in the mortgage rate, discussed below, induces the thrift institutions to raise their deposit rates, insofar as they are below the Regulation Q ceiling. But deposit rates do not rise enough to prevent a deposit outflow.) Hence thrift institutions now have to reduce their mortgage lending, and do so, in part, by rationing credit. This is the credit availability channel. As a result, in part C, housing starts and residential construction decline.

Part B also shows the direct cost effect of the rise in the Aaa bond rate. Since bonds and mortgages are substitutes in the portfolios of lenders, a rise in the bond rate raises the mortgage rate. This increase in the cost of borrowing lowers the discounted yields of houses, so that housing starts and residential construction again fall.

Part C shows the effects on industrial plant and equipment and on private nonresidential construction. A rise in the yields on stocks, bonds, and mortgages raises the yield that firms must expect to obtain on investment in industrial plants to make them willing to undertake such investment. As this rate—the so-called equilibrium quasi-rent—rises the desired stock of capital per dollar of output is reduced. Hence new orders for equipment fall, and investment declines. Finally, as part D shows, the rise in the corporate bond rate raises the interest rate on state and local securities, and this discourages state and local construction expenditures. The version of the model shown in figure 24.1 does not include an effect on inventory investment. A later version of the model has such an effect as well as a liquidity effect on consumption, and a Phillips curve that becomes vertical in the long run. Hence, the MPS model shows monetary policy as affecting many components of aggregate demand.

To quantify these relationships, figure 24.2, taken from a somewhat later version of the MPS model, shows how several GNP components

Figure 24.2   Response of Components of GNP to a $2-Billion Decrease in
                   Demand Deposits

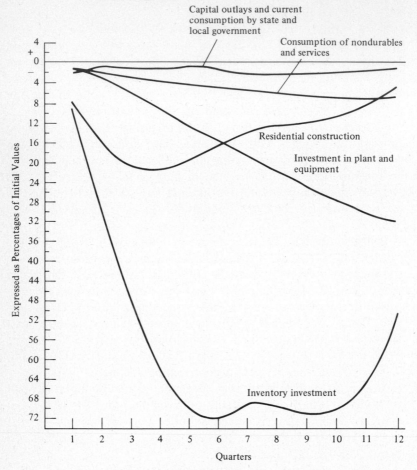

SOURCE: Franco Modigliani, "The Channels of Monetary Policy in the Federal Reserve–M.I.T.–
University of Pennsylvania Econometric Model of the United States," in *Modelling the
Economy,* ed. G. A. Renton (London: Heinemann Educational Publishers, 1975), p. 264.

respond to a $2 billion decrease in demand deposits. These predictions,
which cover all the effects, and not just the first-round effects, come from a
circa 1972 version of the model and therefore are somewhat outdated. Not
only has the model been revised since then, but the values of the variables
at the time of the prediction affect the predicted percentage changes.
Figure 24.2 shows that as a result of the drop in demand deposits various
components of GNP drop, some by a substantial percentage. But after
about three years, real residential construction, nondurable consumption,
and state and local government expenditures are again close to their initial
levels.

   But once again, remember, different models yield different predictions.
Figure 24.3 shows the impact of monetary policy as measured by several

Figure 24.3   Impact of a Maintained $1-Billion Increase in Unborrowed
Reserves upon Real GNP

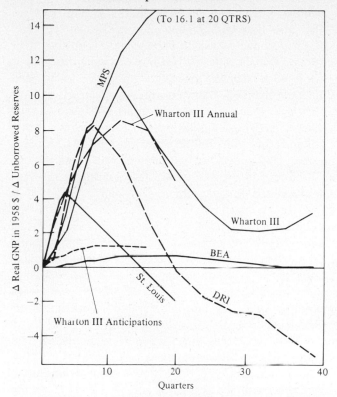

Note: In later versions of the MPS model real GNP turns down again. For the St. Louis model
data relate to a $1-billion increase in M_1 instead of unborrowed reserves. Data are gener-
ated by dynamic simulations.

SOURCE: Carl Christ, "Judging the Performance of Econometric Models of the U.S. Economy," *International Economic Review* 16 (February 1975): 71.

other models, and demonstrates that other models show significantly different results from the MPS model. (The fact that the St. Louis model here
shows the smallest effect is misleading because for this model the assumed
increase is $1 billion of M_1 rather than $1 billion of unborrowed reserves,
as it is for the other models.) In this particular version of the MPS model
the effect on nominal GNP increases for at least five years and is not shown
as falling off again. But in subsequent versions of this model, the effect of
monetary policy on nominal income eventually does fall off again.

International Trade Effects

So far we have dealt only with a closed economy. But if exchange rates
are flexible, monetary policy affects income also through its impact on foreign-
exchange rates. Suppose that, to reduce inflationary pressure, the United
States adopts a restrictive monetary policy so that interest rates in the

U.S. rise temporarily. Since, in the first instance, we can take interest rates in the rest of the world as constant, foreigners now have an incentive to buy U.S. securities. But to do so they must demand dollars on the foreign-exchange market. At the same time with higher interest rates in the U.S., Americans have less of an incentive to buy foreign securities, so that their demand for foreign currency (which is needed to buy foreign securities) is reduced. Hence, on the foreign-exchange market, with more dollars and less foreign currency being demanded, the value of the dollar rises. Foreigners therefore find that U.S. goods cost more in terms of their own currency, and they buy fewer U.S. goods. Similarly, with foreign goods being cheaper in terms of dollars (since the dollar buys more British pounds, German marks, and so on) U.S. imports increase. For both of these reasons the demand for goods produced in the U.S. falls. This reinforces the previously discussed domestic effects that a tight money policy has in constraining demand.

What has been presented so far is the traditional explanation. But in recent years another approach, which emphasizes the supply and demand for money, has been developed. Suppose that the Fed adopts a restrictive policy. The decline in the growth rate of money results in the supply of money being less than the demand for money. Hence, Americans *try* to increase their money holdings by selling more goods and securities to foreigners, and by buying less from them. But this succeeds in raising the dollar holdings of Americans only to the extent that foreigners relinquish dollars they hold, and this is rather minor. However, there is a more important—albeit indirect—effect. As Americans sell more goods and securities to foreigners, and buy less from them, the supply of foreign currency on the foreign-exchange market increases, and the demand for it falls. Hence, the price of foreign currency in terms of dollars falls; that is, the dollar rises. And as the dollar rises relative to foreign currencies, the price *in terms of dollars* of internationally traded goods falls. For example, suppose that the dollar rises by 15 percent relative to other currencies so that it is worth now, say, 2.3 German marks instead of 2 marks. If a pound of leather sold for, say, $3 before, it must now sell for less. For if it did not, it would sell in Germany for 6.9 marks ($3 × 2.3) instead of the previous 6 marks. But the German leather market was in equilibrium at 6 marks per pound. Hence at 6.9 marks there would be an excess supply of leather, and the price of leather would fall. It would have to settle somewhere between 6.0 and 6.9 marks. Precisely where it would settle depends upon the relative importance in the leather market of the U.S. and foreign countries (in this example exemplified by Germany). If it settles at, say, 6.3 marks, its price in the U.S. would be $2.74 (6.3 ÷ 2.3) compared to the previous price of $3. And not only goods that are traded internationally, like leather and wheat, but also goods not traded internationally, like houses, are affected because there is a chain of substitution linking all goods and services. As the price of leather falls this puts downward pressure on the prices of goods like plastic that compete with it, and the fall in the price of plastic in turn tends to lower the prices of those goods that compete with it. Furthermore, as import prices, and hence the cost of living, fall, wage demands are reduced. Thus the rise of the dollar on the foreign-exchange market helps the Fed in curbing inflation.

There is, however, another international-finance effect of monetary policy that tends to weaken it. This is that as the interest rate rises in the United States the increased purchases of U.S. securities by foreigners (and by Americans who would otherwise have bought foreign securities) works to moderate the rise in the interest rate. This, in turn, reduces the impact of the Federal Reserve's restrictive policy on investment and consumption. However, in a system of flexible exchange rates this offset is more or less limited. Since exchange rates fluctuate, foreigners take a risk in buying securities denominated in dollars rather than in their own currencies, and this limits capital inflows. This will be discussed further in Part Six.

Expectational Effects

So far, this discussion of the way monetary policy affects the economy has been rather mechanistic. It is high time to allow for the fact that people do not just react to events that have already occurred, but also respond to what they expect to happen. If one leaves room for expectations, there is yet another way in which monetary policy can affect prices, and hence nominal income.

Assume that at a time of full employment the Federal Reserve substantially increases the reserve base. Not only will this initially reduce interest rates, and hence stimulate expenditures, but people, particularly well-informed decision makers, will realize what is going on. They will expect aggregate demand to increase. More specifically, with the economy already operating at full employment they will expect wages and prices to rise. But if prices are expected to rise isn't it rational for people to try to protect themselves against this by buying ahead now, by withholding goods from the market to sell them in the future, and by raising wages and prices right away? Hence, an increase in the growth rate of the base can lead to an immediate increase in prices. This is, of course, much more likely to happen at a time when high and variable inflation rates have conditioned people to watch the growth rate of the base, than at a time when people have had little or no experience with inflation.

At the cost of some unrealism one can carry this example to an interesting conclusion. Assume that everyone knows that an increase in the base is inflationary, and, also, that all contracts have escalator clauses, and that laws and regulations do not inhibit a rapid adaption to inflation (for example, tax laws are fully indexed, and all outside money somehow is indexed too). If so, an increase in the growth rate of the base will result immediately in a rise in nominal interest rates as the higher rate of inflation is embodied in the inflation premium that is included in the nominal interest rate. Hence neither investment nor output rise, but the inflation rate responds instantly and fully to the higher growth rate of the base.

Admittedly the assumptions that people can predict accurately the impact of the higher growth rate of the base on prices, and that long-term contracts, tax laws, and so on, are indexed are extreme. But this example does warn us to watch for the way in which monetary policy affects expectations. Suppose, for example, that Congress would suddenly direct the Federal Reserve to aim at keeping unemployment to 3 percent, or to bring the Treasury bill rate down to 3 percent. Given the way people are already sensitized to inflation this would probably bring about an immediate and very substantial increase in the inflation rate. Conversely, if Congress were to pass a law that the Fed should make price stability its only goal, the inflation rate would start to decline even before the Fed takes any action at all.

Summary

This chapter started with a discussion of how strong monetary policy is. It pointed out that if a given dose of monetary policy is not strong enough the Fed can simply apply a bigger dosage. However, there are constraints on increasing the dosage, and there is some dispute about whether monetary policy could pull the economy out of a major depression, and also on whether it can moderate an expansion without throwing the economy into a recession. Moreover, while monetary policy can bring about changes in aggregate demand, it can affect the distribution of these changes between real income and prices only by having followed certain policies in the past that now determine the public's expectations.

Most of the chapter dealt with channels by which monetary policy affects aggregate demand. We first looked briefly at the monetarist approach, and then took up the Keynesian approach, which looks at changes in the interest rate and at the interest elasticity of investment and consumption and at credit rationing. From there we turned to a discussion of thrift institutions and residential construction, and pointed out that residential construction responds very strongly to changes in interest rates. We reviewed briefly an older argument that the thrift institutions can frustrate monetary policy. We then took up the ways in which monetary policy affects consumption, the cost of, and availability of, credit to purchase durables, the change in wealth and liquidity, and possibly a change in the wish to save.

We then recapitulated the previous story in terms of a portfolio-balance approach, and examined how monetary policy works in the MPS model, and also its impact on foreign trade. We concluded by seeing how changing expectations can cause Fed actions to be reflected quickly and directly in price changes.

QUESTIONS AND EXERCISES

1. Do you think monetary policy has had much influence on the behavior of income over the last ten years? To answer this question look at data presented in the *Economic Report of the President*. Document your conclusion by references to these, or other, data.
2. Compare and contrast the monetarist and the Keynesian approaches to the impact of monetary policy on income. Explain why this impact seems stronger in the monetarist than in the Keynesian approach.
3. Describe the ways in which an expansionary monetary policy increases consumption.
4. Discuss the portfolio effect and the locking-in effect of rising interest rates.
5. Discuss: "The strength of monetary policy is an irrelevant issue."
6. Describe the impact of monetary policy in the MPS model.
7. "With exchange rates being flexible, the Fed's power to combat a recession is increased." Discuss.

FURTHER READING

DE LEEUW, F., and GRAMLICH, E. "The Channels of Monetary Policy." *Journal of Finance* 24 (May 1969): 265–90. This is an exposition of how monetary policy works in the MPS model.

FISHER, R. G., and SHEPPARD, D. K. "Interrelations between Real and Monetary Variables: Some Evidence from Recent U.S. Empirical Studies." In *Issues in Monetary Economics,* edited by Harry G. Johnson and A. R. Nobay, pp. 179–259. New York: Oxford University Press, 1974. A detailed survey of the empirical evidence on the strength of monetary policy.

LAIDLER, DAVID. "Money and Money Income: An Essay on the Transmission Mechanism," *Journal of Monetary Economics* 4 (April 1978): 151–93. An excellent survey, particularly strong on the expectational aspects.

MISHKIN, FREDERIC. "Monetary Policy and Liquidity: Simulation Results." *Economic Inquiry* 16 (January 1978): 16–36. An interesting analysis of the importance of changes in household liquidity.

25

Monetary Policy
and Resource Allocation

The previous chapter discussed the strength of monetary policy only from a macroeconomic viewpoint. But one should go beyond this, and look also at the *micro*economic aspects of monetary policy. Is the change in income that is brought about by a restrictive policy distributed over the economy in an acceptable way? For example, if all the reduction in income resulting from a tight money policy would be concentrated on, say, retired families, then perhaps monetary policy should not be used as a stabilization tool. What matters is not only aggregate income, but also the distribution of this aggregate income among different groups and sectors.

Monetary Policy and Interest Rates

Complaints about the distorting effects of monetary policy, and about the undue burden it imposes on some sectors, are mainly complaints about the impact of high and rising interest rates. A first reaction might be to dismiss them all by pointing out that monetary policy cannot keep interest rates low. As previously explained, if the Federal Reserve increases the growth rate of the money stock, the immediate effect is, to be sure, that interest rates fall, but after some time the nominal interest rate rises again. As figure 25.1 demonstrates, a high money growth rate leads to a high, not a low nominal interest rate. Does this mean that the numerous complaints about the resource allocation effects of monetary policy should simply be dismissed? No, they should not, for several reasons.

To start with, although a high growth rate of the money stock does not succeed in the long run in reducing the nominal before-tax interest rate, it does succeed for a long time (though presumably not permanently) in reducing the *real* after-tax interest rate, albeit at the cost of inflation.

Moreover, there are several ways in which it may be possible to hold down even the nominal interest rate. First, although the Fed on its own cannot do so, a combination of fiscal and monetary policy could. Suppose

Figure 25.1 Effect of High Money Growth Rates on Nominal Interest Rates
1967–78

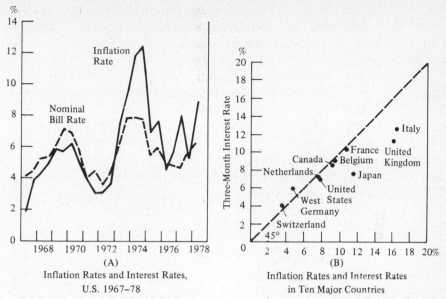

(A)
Inflation Rates and Interest Rates,
U.S. 1967–78

(B)
Inflation Rates and Interest Rates
in Ten Major Countries

Note: Data in (B) are annual averages 1973–April 1978, except for Switzerland where they start in 1976. The inflation rate is measured by the consumer price index.

SOURCE: Federal Reserve Bank of Minneapolis, *Quarterly Review,* Fall 1978, p. 3.

that the Fed increases the money growth rate, and that at the same time the federal government runs a large enough budget surplus to prevent nominal income from rising. This combination of monetary and fiscal policy would succeed in holding down the nominal interest rate. The reason is that the budget surplus means that one sector that before was usually a borrower is now no longer borrowing, but is reducing its outstanding debt. Hence, the basic supply and demand factors that determine the interest rates have changed.

Second, many of the problems created by a restrictive monetary policy result, not from a high interest rate as such, but from a rapidly *rising* interest rate, in part because our institutions can adapt to permanently high interest rates but they cannot adapt quickly enough if interest rates suddenly rise sharply. One can make a good case that rapidly rising interest rates are usually the result of the Federal Reserve, after having allowed the money stock to increase at too high a rate, having stepped abruptly on the brake because of the resulting inflation. If the Fed would keep the money growth rate stabler, and avoid stop-go policies, the authors believe (though the Federal Reserve disagrees) there would be fewer steep and abrupt increases in the interest rate.

Third, even if there would be no way in which conventional monetary policy could completely prevent occasional steep increases in interest rates, there is an unconventional monetary policy that could at least reduce their magnitude. This is a system of credit allocation that holds down interest rates by removing some potential borrowers from the market. Thus, it would be wrong to dismiss complaints about high and rising interest rates by saying that they are almost like an Act of God over which the government had no control.

But this does not mean that all the criticism that is directed at the Federal Reserve when interest rates rise is justified. As will be shown shortly, some of it is questionable.

We will now take up the burdens and dislocations that monetary policy is accused of imposing on the economy, and then will examine one of the ameliorating devices, credit allocation. Then in chapter 28, we discuss whether the Fed should follow a stable money growth rate.

The Criteria

To judge whether a restrictive monetary policy seriously distorts resource allocation one needs to decide on first what the desirable allocation of resources is. If a restrictive monetary policy is to be effective in reducing aggregate demand, then obviously some sectors of the economy have to relinquish resources. How does one decide which sectors this should be?

One possible criterion, very popular among noneconomists is that a restrictive policy should cut back on the use of resources in each sector roughly proportionately; for example, if real aggregate demand is to be cut by one percent, then each sector should give up one percent of the resources it is currently using. But this criterion has a fatal defect. One should take resources from where their utility is least, and this will generally *not* occur if one takes resources proportionately from each sector. By analogy, if a household decides to cut its expenditures by 10 percent, it will not cut *every* expenditure by 10 percent; it will usually cut its vacation travel more than its expenditure on bread. Hence, the proportionality criterion is useless because it lacks any significance in terms of economic welfare.

Fortunately there is another criterion, one clearly relevant for economic welfare, *if* two big assumptions are made. The first is that a competitive market brings about the best allocation of resources that can be achieved. Since the distribution of income is included in the term *allocation of resources,* this is a strong condition. It can be relaxed by excluding the distribution of income and assuming instead that monetary policy has no significant effect on the distribution of income. The second assumption is that our economic system closely resembles a competitive market. *If* one makes both of these assumptions, then one should allow the market mechanism to decide what resources each sector and each family should relinquish when aggregate demand has to be reduced to avoid inflation. Simply let the interest rate rise. Each sector then decides what resources to give up by comparing the marginal productivity of its resources with the new, higher rate of interest. The interest rate is, after all, a price, and as a price rises, those who have the least use for a resource are the ones who relinquish it. Suppose, for example, that the use of oil has to be reduced. If this is done by allowing the price of oil to rise, then people cut back on their use of oil until the marginal benefit of oil to them is equal to its new higher price. And this implies that the marginal productivity of oil is everywhere equal. Similarly, why not use a rising interest rate to reallocate resources in this way?

This principle that monetary policy should affect the allocation of resources in the way determined by a competitive market seems to imply that one does not have to worry about the allocational effects of monetary policy, that rising interest rates will withdraw resources from sectors where they are least useful. In fact, proponents of monetary policy sometimes argue that one of the great advantages of monetary policy is precisely that it leaves the allocation of resources to the market rather than to political forces, that it is "neutral." By contrast, fiscal policy is generally *not* neutral; particular taxes are raised, or particular government expenditures are cut. Fiscal policy does not have the "untouched-by-human-hands" aspect of monetary policy.

But neutrality is not necessarily a "good thing," because the two assumptions made above need not hold. First, it is *not* true that even a fully competitive market gives us an optimal allocation of resources and incomes. For example, it does not take account of externalities, and also the distribution of income that occurs in a competitive market need not correspond to someone's notion of what is fair and appropriate. Second, our economy does not consist only of perfectly competitive markets, and wages and prices are not very flexible.

Hence there are two types of criticisms of the incidence of monetary policy. One type focuses on the fact that markets, specifically the credit market, are not perfectly competitive, and asserts that monetary policy is not neutral because of this. Certain sectors have to relinquish resources, not because they are unwilling to pay the competitive price for these resources, but because credit is rationed. The other type of criticism is in a way more basic. It states that the social costs and benefits of certain activities differ from the private costs and benefits that the market uses as its signals. Hence, a neutral monetary policy that relies on the market to reallocate resources yields undesirable results. Instead of relying on the market, one should see to it that "socially desirable" investment is cut back less by a restrictive monetary policy than is other investment.

In discussing both of these types of criticisms of the incidence of monetary policy we will focus on the effects of a restrictive policy because it is this type of policy that evokes these criticisms. It is only natural that there is much more criticism of Federal Reserve policy when certain sectors are being squeezed than there is when an expansionary monetary policy increases the resources available to all sectors.

Consumption and Investment

The two broadest private sectors are consumption and investment. As discussed in the previous chapter, there is now considerable evidence that monetary policy affects consumption as well as investment. But it probably affects investment *relatively* more. Private consumption is very roughly four times as large as gross private domestic investment. But it is most unlikely that a restrictive monetary policy reduces consumption by four times as much as investment. Hence, a restrictive monetary policy appears to reduce capital formation relative to consumption. But one has to be careful about the alternative. If the alternative to a restrictive monetary policy is to cut government expenditures, or to raise the personal income tax, this is true. But if the alternative is to let inflation continue unchecked, then it is not necessarily true in the longer run, since inflation also discourages investment.

A number of economists have criticized restrictive monetary policy for discouraging investment and have instead advocated the use of restrictive fiscal policy. In particular, they are concerned about a tendency to use a restrictive monetary policy to curb excessive demand, with little reduction in government expenditures taking place, and to use an expansionary fiscal policy whenever demand is deficient. Such a policy reduces capital formation relative to one that uses either fiscal policy or monetary policy in both cases. This criticism of the one-sided use of monetary policy differs from the other criticisms of restrictive monetary policy because it is based neither on the argument that a competitive market does not produce socially desirable results nor on the argument that our markets are not properly competitive, since it deals essentially with the way the government is using fiscal policy.

Residential Construction

Figure 25.2 shows that residential construction as a percent of gross private domestic investment usually declines when the Treasury bill rate rises. This impression is reinforced by econometric studies that show residential construction to be very sensitive to rising interest rates. (This does not mean that the *stock* of housing is equally sensitive. Suppose, for example, that the housing stock is growing at a 10 percent rate, and that net investment in housing is reduced by 10 percent. The housing stock at the end of the year is then only one percent smaller than it otherwise would have been.) But as a result of this sensitivity of residential construction, as well as the great political power of the construction industry, it is hardly surprising that the Fed is much criticized for causing periodic depressions in the residential construction industry. Furthermore, it is likely that, out of concern for

Figure 25.2   Percentage Distribution of Private Domestic Investment and
Interest Rates
1963–78

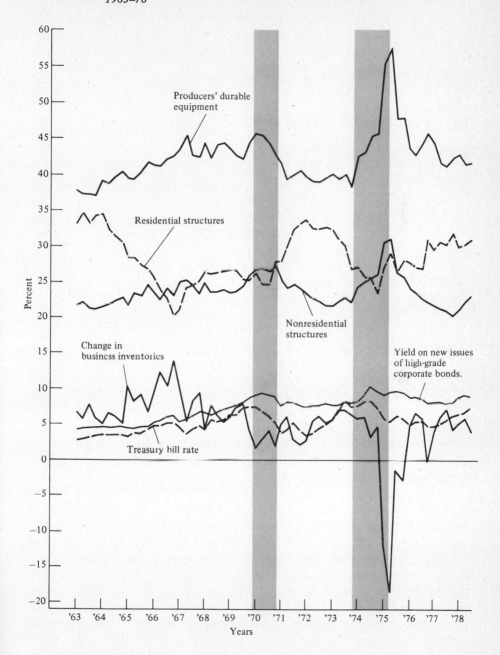

SOURCE: U.S., Department of Commerce, *Survey of Current Business, National Income and Product Accounts of the United States, Business Conditions Indicators,* various issues.

residential construction, the Fed at times adopts less restrictive policies than it otherwise would.

How serious a problem is created by this strong impact of rising interest rates on residential construction? At first glance it may seem obvious that the strong response of residential construction to rising interest rates means that monetary policy is not neutral, that residential construction bears a disproportionate part of the burden of a restrictive policy. But actually this is far from obvious.

First, this argument goes too far because it confuses a restrictive policy with high and rising nominal interest rates. Ultimately, it is an expansionary policy, in the sense of a high money growth rate that raises interest rates. Hence, the Fed should be blamed for high interest rates only when it previously has allowed the money stock to grow too fast, or when it suddenly reduces the money growth rate sharply but not at those times when interest rates rise despite an adequate or even a high money growth rate. To say that at those times the Fed could, all the same, hold interest rates down by allowing the money supply to grow faster is correct for the short run, but retribution follows in the long run.

Second, as previously pointed out neutrality does not mean proportionality. Even with perfectly competitive markets one would expect residential construction to decline more than most other types of investment because houses have a much longer life. As discussed in chapter 14, the longer the life of an investment project—that is, the longer the series of future yields that have to be discounted at the current interest rate to obtain its present value—the more responsive should this type of investment be to changes in the interest rate. Thus, the fact that residential construction declines much more than machinery investment as interest rates rise is entirely consistent with monetary policy being neutral, that is, with rising interest rates taking resources away from those sectors that are least willing to pay the new, higher cost of using them. (But it is a bit harder to explain in this way why residential construction drops more than nonresidential construction as interest rates rise since nonresidential construction is also long-term investment.)

But while figure 25.2 therefore cannot be used to show that monetary policy is not neutral in its impact on housing, there is another reason for thinking that its impact is actually excessive and not neutral. This is that the mortgage market is constrained by many government policies. First, there are the policies that lead to disintermediation as interest rates rise, that is, the Regulation Q ceiling, and the constraints on the asset choices and liability of thrift institutions. Second, the prohibition of interest payments on the demand deposits of business firms probably causes commercial banks to reduce their mortgage lending when credit becomes tight. Not being allowed to pay explicit interest they pay implicit interest by giving business firms first place in the queue for credit.

Third, the interest-rate ceilings on mortgages guaranteed or insured by the government (that is, by the Federal Housing Administration or the

Veterans Administration) are not sufficiently flexible. If the equilibrium mortgage rate rises above the ceiling rate set by the FHA and VA, then lenders have an incentive to make other loans rather than mortgage loans.[1]

As a result of all of these factors there is credit rationing in the mortgage market, and some borrowers who are perfectly willing to pay the higher interest rate are rationed out of the market. Thus investment funds are not allocated to those willing to pay the most for them, and hence resources are allocated inefficiently.

In addition to these results of government regulations, residential construction may also be discriminated against because it is more heavily financed by borrowed funds than is industrial plant and equipment investment, which is financed to a considerable extent by plowed-back profits. Hence, at least to some extent, business investment is partially sheltered from market forces; to increase the size of the firm, and hence the prestige of its officers, a firm *may* plow funds back into its own investment projects, even though these funds could earn more if lent on the market. (To some extent at least, the plow-back of corporate earnings is probably the result of a government regulation too, the personal income tax.)

All of these factors suggest that residential construction is cut back by rising interest rates more than is warranted by its long life. This raises two questions. First, how great is this discrimination against residential construction? There is much disagreement on this issue. While some economists attribute much, or most, of the cutback in residential construction as interest rates rise to this discrimination, others have challenged this view. Thus, in one simulation of the Federal Reserve's econometric model it turned out that the credit availability effect plus the wealth effect (via the change in security prices) accounted only for about 20 percent of the total impact on residential construction.[2] (Other simulations, and certainly other econometric models may, of course, show different results.) Similarly, Allan Meltzer has argued that credit availability is much less important than the interest rate in determining the volume of residential construction.[3]

Second, should monetary policy be blamed for this discrimination, since most of it is due to government regulations? Since both rising interest rates *and* these regulations are needed to generate discrimination against residential construction, it is to some extent arbitrary which of these one blames. Those who believe that the government restrictions are needed

[1] However, to a considerable extent lenders are able to avoid the ceilings by charging "points"; that is, they discount the borrower's note as well as charge interest on it. For example, a borrower may sign a promissory note for a $50,000 mortgage at, say, 8 percent interest and the lender gives him only, say, $45,000 for this promissory note, so that in effect the interest rate is greater than 8 percent.

[2] John Kalchbrenner, "Theoretical and Empirical Specifications of the Housing Sector," in *Ways to Moderate Fluctuations in Housing Construction,* ed. Board of Governors, Federal Reserve System (Washington, D.C.: 1972), pp. 259–63.

[3] Allan Meltzer, "Credit Availability and Economic Decisions," in *Government Credit Allocation,* ed. Karl Brunner (San Francisco: Institute for Contemporary Studies, 1975), pp. 123–50.

but that rapidly rising interest rates could somehow be avoided, treat the regulations as a "given" and put the blame on rising interest rates, while those who believe that interest rates have to rise sharply at times to curb inflation, and that many of the government regulations are not needed, put the blame on these regulations.

But how serious a problem is this discrimination? Clearly it is now less severe than it was a few years ago. First, as we discussed in chapter 8, thrift institutions can now compete much better with open-market securities when interest rates rise since they can issue six-month and four-year certificates with floating rates tied to U.S. Treasury securities of similar maturities. And the Regulation Q ceiling is being phased out, so that by 1986 it will no longer be around to generate disintermediation. Second the FHA and VA interest-rate ceilings are now allowed to rise more frequently. Moreover, as was discussed in chapter 8, the federal government has now eliminated numerous state usury laws that inhibited residential construction when interest rates rose.

So far we have discussed the impact on residential construction only in terms of the neutrality criterion. But many people who are concerned about the cutback in residential construction as interest rates rise would not be satisfied with monetary policy being neutral. This is because—rightly or wrongly—they consider housing to be a specially meritorious good that should be stimulated, rather than cut back by government policies. One reason for this belief is a concern about slums. However, maintaining low interest rates is hardly an efficient way to eliminate slums; it is more efficient as a way to subsidize middle-class households. Another reason is a belief that home ownership turns people into better citizens. A third is that there are aesthetic benefits from good housing beyond those received by the homeowner. *If* these arguments are compelling, and many do not find them so, then there could be substantial underinvestment in housing. If this is the case we should use stabilization policies that foster rather than retard residential construction.

To be sure, one might answer that countercyclical monetary policy is a two-way street, that, though residential construction is reduced at certain times by restrictive policies, at other times it is stimulated by expansionary policies. But those who wish to protect residential construction can reply that monetary policy should, on the average, be more expansionary than it is now; and that fiscal policy rather than monetary policy should be used to restrain aggregate demand when it is excessive. Moreover, they argue— though some other economists challenge this—that the large fluctuations experienced by the residential construction industry reduces its efficiency. They inhibit the use of more capital-intensive methods of production, and, in addition, during a decline in residential construction many firms fail, and construction teams are dispersed.

But if residential construction is to be aided, monetary policy is not the only way to do it. It can be, and is, subsidized through tax benefits and low interest loans from government credit agencies, as well as through construction paid for by the government. As figure 8.2 illustrated, when rising interest rates reduce residential construction there are massive inflows of funds from federal lending agencies. *If* residential construction is to be given special aid these methods are vastly superior to trying for as long as possible to hold down interest rates at the cost of accelerating inflation.

One unfortunate impact of rising interest rates on the housing sector is that it is not only the construction of new houses that is reduced when interest rates rise. The sale of the existing houses falls roughly proportionately. This is so because those households that have low-interest-rate mortgages have an implicit capital gain that they cannot always "sell" to the buyers of their houses. If a low-interest-mortgage loan has to be repaid when the house is sold, the lender gains at the expense of the buyer and seller. This acts like an excise tax on the sale of houses. This interference with the sale of existing houses distorts the allocation of resources while curbing aggregate demand only in two minor ways. Someone who buys a house, whether new or old, is likely to buy home furnishings too, and hence to increase consumption. Second, the seller of the old house might consume some of his or her capital gain. But this problem of interference with the market for used houses *might* be on a way to solution. The California Supreme Court ruled in 1978 that the lender must allow a buyer to assume an existing mortgage unless the buyer is a greater credit risk than is the seller. If similar rulings were issued in other states it would greatly ameliorate this problem, but it would increase the extent to which financial institutions are locked into relatively low-interest-rate mortgages when interest rates rise.

Impact on Governments

Some economists have been concerned that a restrictive monetary policy has an unduly large impact on investment projects by state and local governments, such as schools and highways. They have argued either that monetary policy is not neutral but hits state and local government investment particularly hard, or else, that this type of investment is especially meritorious because it has large external benefits, and should therefore be sheltered from the impact of tight money.

However, the empirical evidence shows that the impact of monetary policy on state and local government investment is quite moderate.[4] And as

[4] For a survey of the evidence see Paul F. McGouldrick, "The Effect of Credit Conditions on State and Local Bond Sales and Capital Outlays since World War II," in U.S. Congress, Joint Economic Committee, Subcommittee on Economic Progress, *State and Local Public Facility Needs and Financing,* 86th Cong., 2d sess., 1966, vol. 2, pp. 299–321. Subsequent studies by McGouldrick published in the *Federal Reserve Bulletin* reinforce this conclusion. Even if it were the case that state and local investment is reduced substantially by rising interest rates, this would be consistent with efficient resource allocation because state and local government investment is frequently very long-term investment.

more and more states raise their constitutional ceiling on the maximum interest rate they can pay, this problem is fading away. Moreover, if such investment has large external benefits, then it can be fostered directly by more federal grants-in-aid and revenue sharing. There is no reason why monetary policy should be used for this purpose.

Rising interest rates have a substantial impact on the federal government too since it is by far the largest debtor in the economy. For the fiscal year 1980 net interest paid by the federal government (after subtracting interest received by its trust funds) is estimated to account for 8.7 percent of total projected federal outlays. Hence, the federal government faces a temptation to try to avoid a rise in interest rates, even if such a rise is needed to stabilize aggregate demand. Fortunately, this is now recognized as a most questionable policy. Besides, since usually the rise in the nominal interest rate merely reflects a higher inflation rate, the *real* interest rate paid by the federal government is not excessive; in real terms it is, in effect, repaying some of the outstanding debt.

Small and New Firms

So far we have dealt only with the distribution of the burden of a restrictive policy between various broad sectors. But there are many complaints that within the business sector a restrictive monetary policy discriminates against small and new firms in favor of large and well-established ones. Is this true? At first glance it seems implausible because one might expect that a profit-maximizing bank will lend to those firms, regardless of size, who promise to pay the highest net return. But the credit market is not a perfect one. When money becomes tight, open-market interest rates, for example, bond rates, rise right away to equilibrate supply and demand. But negotiated rates, such as interest rates on bank loans, are somewhat sluggish, due to information costs, and in some states, due to usury laws. Hence, when money becomes tight this part of the credit market does not clear as well as before, and the degree of credit rationing increases. To the extent that lenders rely on credit rationing rather than on rising interest rates to allocate credit, it is the riskiest firms that are denied credit. Since small firms tend to be riskier than large firms, banks have an incentive to discriminate against small firms. But with modern techniques of liability management, credit rationing is probably becoming less important. Even in a tight period large and medium banks can now obtain additional funds, albeit at a high cost. A borrower willing to pay a correspondingly higher interest rate may now be able to get the loan, whereas previously the bank would have said no.

On the other hand, even if each individual lender does not discriminate against small firms as money becomes tight, the overall result can still be discrimination against small firms. This is so because a large firm usually has customer relationships with several banks. Hence, if any one bank cannot lend to it, it can go to one of its other banks that is still able to make loans. But the small firm frequently cannot do this because it has a customer relationship with only a single bank.[5] In addition, if banks generally are reducing their loans, large firms have the alternative of tapping the capital market by floating securities; small firms depend much more on bank credit. Moreover, the damage that a given degree of credit stringency does to a firm may be sufficient to wipe out a small firm, while a large firm can absorb the loss.

But, a mere listing of ways in which a restrictive monetary policy may result in discrimination against small firms is not sufficient to establish that *substantial* discrimination actually exists. It may exist but be relatively minor. Only empirical evidence can establish whether it is a *significant* problem. Unfortunately, while several studies have attempted to answer this question, their results are frequently conflicting. In their detailed survey of these studies Deane Carson and Ira Scott conclude that: "a review of the literature on the discriminatory impact of monetary policy on smaller enterprises leaves one with the impression that definitive answers have eluded the profession." [6]

Beyond the possible discrimination against small firms, there may be specially severe discrimination against newly founded firms. Some economists argue, though others disagree, that in a period when credit is tight, banks are unwilling to take on new loan customers, so that people who want to start new firms often cannot get credit.

Impact on the Financial Market

The very first sector to experience the impact of monetary policy is, of course, the financial market. What disrupts the financial market is not *high* interest rates, but rapidly *rising* interest rates. Financial institutions are both borrowers and lenders and, if interest rates are high, they both earn more, and pay out more. But if there is an unexpected rapid rise in nominal interest rates, then serious problems may develop.[7] And rapid run-ups of nominal

[5] Actually, there is some empirical evidence that contradicts this statement since a survey taken in 1966 showed that small firms turned down by one bank just about as frequently received a loan from another bank as did larger firms. But this study was based on a very small sample.

[6] Deane Carson and Ira O. Scott, "Differential Effects of Monetary Policy on Small Business," in *The Vital Majority,* ed. U.S., Small Business Administration, (Washington, D.C.: 1973), p. 200.

[7] It is the nominal interest rate rather than the real interest rate that is relevant for financial institutions since both their assets and liabilities are denominated primarily in nominal terms. Suppose, for example, that the inflation rate rises from 10 to 15 percent. A bank's net worth is in good part unaffected by this since the real value of both its debts and its liabilities declines. By contrast, a manufacturing firm, which is a net borrower, gains because the real value of its assets is constant while the real value of its debt declines.

interest rates do occur from time to time, as the Federal Reserve, after allowing the money stock to grow too rapidly for some time, suddenly steps on the brakes. In chapter 27 we will look at one of these episodes, the 1966 credit crunch, in some detail. If the Fed would not step on the brakes, but would allow the money stock to continue to grow at a high rate, nominal interest rates would eventually rise even higher as inflationary expectations become embedded in nominal interest rates. But the rise would probably be more gradual.

When nominal interest rates rise rapidly financial institutions face several problems. One of these is the much discussed problem of disintermediation as thrift institutions are prevented by Regulation Q from raising interest rates enough to compete with interest rates paid on the open market. Another problem is that a rise in interest rates causes a sharp decline in long-term security prices. Hence, a number of both financial and nonfinancial firms all of a sudden may find that the value of the assets they hold has declined substantially. Not only does this reduce their liquidity, and perhaps even threaten their solvency directly, but also they are now no longer good credit risks. Such firms may have counted on continual borrowing, for example, by renewing their outstanding commercial paper, and now find themselves unable to do so. They may now be in serious jeopardy and so may their major creditors, and these creditors, in turn, may find themselves unable to borrow. Moreover, as various firms experience difficulties, lenders become fearful in general and try to build up their own liquidity by sharply reducing their lending. And this in turn endangers firms that planned to borrow. In addition, other firms now find their markets evaporating as endangered firms cut back on their purchases (or payment of bills) to conserve liquidity. As a result, firms will cut back sharply on their investment spending, and a recession develops. If it were not for deposit insurance and the Federal Reserve's ability to act as a lender of last resort, there might be numerous bank failures too!

Of course, such a drama need not happen, and, in the postwar period, has *not* happened. But it is a potential danger if the Fed tries to make up for a previously excessive money growth rate by suddenly cutting this growth rate back very sharply. The Fed has to be ready, as it was in 1966 and 1970, to terminate a strongly restrictive policy if it threatens to bring on a financial panic. Moreover, even if there is no danger of financial panic, still *some* firms find the value of their assets declining enough that they are in trouble and find it difficult to borrow. This is a social loss even if only a few firms are affected.

Beyond the immediate danger of a financial panic there is another problem. This is that as interest rates rise firms find ways of economizing on cash balances. And once interest rates decline they do not unlearn these cash-economizing techniques. Hence, over time, as various periods of high interest rates succeed each other, the liquidity of firms declines along with their cash holdings, and thus the economy becomes more and more prone to a financial panic. Fortunately occasional close brushes with failure may make firms more cautious.

Income Distribution

We have left until last what may seem one of the most obvious effects of a restrictive monetary policy: that by increasing the real interest rate the distribution of income becomes more unequal. This argument is much too simple.

First, a seemingly high interest rate may be only a nominal rate and not the real rate that is relevant for the distribution of income. An 11 percent rate when the inflation rate is 10 percent does not unduly foster property income. Second, the old stereotype of the rich lending to the poor is inaccurate. Low-income groups hold a disproportionate share of their assets in the form of loans to financial institutions (that is, deposits), while the upper-income groups tend to hold more corporate stock.

Third, and most fundamentally, one should not look at the rise in the interest rate in isolation, but should ask what is the alternative. If it is to allow an inflation to continue and even accelerate, then one should ask further how low-income groups are affected by inflation. There is some evidence that in recent years inflation raised their share of national income, though it is far from clear that this is true for all, or most, inflations. Hence, if one goes on the evidence of the last few years, and the alternative to a restrictive monetary policy is to allow further inflation, then in the short run the imposition of a restrictive monetary policy makes the distribution of income less equal. But, eventually, the real interest rate will have to rise if the inflation is to be kept from continually accelerating. If instead of inflation the alternative to a restrictive monetary policy is a more restrictive fiscal policy then it all depends on what type of fiscal policy is instituted.

All in all, trying to keep the real interest rate low is hardly an efficient way of achieving greater income equality. Increasing the progressivity of the tax system could do this much more efficiently. And even if, for some strange reason, it were decided to reduce income inequality by keeping the real interest rate low, this would still allow the use of a restrictive monetary policy occasionally. What most people are concerned with is the distribution of income over many years, and not necessarily in every year. Hence, we could keep interest rates low on the average, and still allow them to rise to a high level, relative to this average, occasionally.

But one should look beyond the question of income inequality and look also at distributional effects *within* various income classes. Rising nominal interest rates, by lowering security prices, hurt sellers of securities and benefit buyers. For example, in the 1972–74 period, the capital value of long-term government securities (including, of course, those that were held, as well as those sold) fell by $1.5 billion (15.6 percent) and the value of long-term corporate bonds by $15.2 billion (16.1 percent).[8] Moreover, rising interest rates make it harder to sell houses and reduce their prices. Hence, interest-rate changes can bring about a significant redistribution of wealth within each income class. Those who have to sell assets in years when interest rates are high lose. This is hard to justify on equity grounds. Equity considerations therefore suggest that public policy should try to keep interest rates relatively stable; and that if an erratic growth rate of the money stock causes interest rates to fluctuate it generates inequities.

Credit Allocation

As we have just seen, a sharp rise in interest rates has some deleterious effects on the allocation of resources. At the same time, a restrictive policy may be needed to curb inflation. Can this dilemma be avoided? One solution sometimes advocated is to use a system of government credit allocation.

In a system of credit allocation, such as that used extensively in France, the government determines how much credit various sectors should receive. If everything goes well this prevents the burden of a restrictive monetary policy from falling disproportionately on some sectors, such as residential construction, but if things turn out badly, credit allocation becomes a device whereby politically powerful sectors increase their share of total credit, and reduce the interest rates they pay, at the expense of other sectors.

Credit allocation could take several forms. It could operate on a permanent basis, or only when interest rates are unusually high. In the former case its purpose would be to allocate more credit to those sectors where investment has large external benefits, while in the latter case its main purpose would be to offset the discriminatory effects of a restrictive monetary policy. One way credit allocation could be implemented is by setting floors on certain types of loans or ceilings on others. For example, banks could be told that they must increase their mortgage loans by, say, at least 10 percent or can increase their business loans by, say, at most 5 percent per year. Alternatively, instead of setting rigid floors and ceilings, member banks could be given an incentive to make more of the "right" types of loans. This could be done by giving them a credit against their reserve requirements on the basis of the increase in, say, their mortgage loans, or by imposing an additional reserve requirement if their business loans increase too much. In March 1980 the Federal Reserve adopted such a policy by imposing a 15 percent reserve requirement for increases in the outstanding volume of certain types of consumer loans made by all significant consumer

---

[8] The figure for corporate bonds is for marketable bonds with a ten-year-and-over maturity held by private investors. See Ervin Miller, *Microeconomic Effects of Monetary Policy* (London: Martin Robertson, 1978), p. 24.

lenders. In addition, to slow the flow of funds out of banks and thrift institutions, it also imposed a 15 percent reserve requirement on increases in the assets of money-market funds, but these requirements were then eliminated after a few months.

The case for credit allocation takes two forms. One is to argue that certain types of investment have large external benefits and hence deserve a government subsidy. By requiring banks and other lenders to make more loans to these sectors, the cost of credit to them is reduced, and their investment is stimulated without any expenditure of government funds. The second form the argument can take is to say that the discriminatory effects of tight money are so severe that we have to offset them with another policy, credit allocation. Admittedly, while credit allocation would, in part, abrogate the market mechanism, credit rationing by banks and other lenders already does so too. And if we are to have credit allocation it should be done by the government, which takes social usefulness into account, rather than by bankers just concerned with private profits.

But there exists a cogent case against credit allocation. To start with, it is not at all clear that governmental decisions about where credit should flow would necessarily be superior to the decisions of the private market. In principle, they should be since the government can take into account any externalities that the private market ignores (though it is far from clear that the externalities that could be taken into account by credit allocation are all that large). But in practice, various pressure groups may succeed in obtaining undeserved preference for their credit demands. In effect, with credit allocation, the distribution of political power may well determine access to credit. More specifically, credit allocation is actually just one more proposal for subsidizing residential construction since in most credit-allocation schemes this industry would be the primary beneficiary of easy credit. And as far as temporary credit allocation to offset the discriminatory effects of tight money is concerned, since we really do not know how large these effects are, we might try to offset too much, and distort the allocation of resources in the opposite direction.

Furthermore, while a system of credit allocation could work in the short run, eventually it would become ineffective. If banks or other financial intermediaries were forced to make less profitable loans, they would reduce the interest rate they pay on deposits. Depositors would then switch to other intermediaries. If necessary, new types of uncontrolled intermediaries would spring up. Moreover, borrowers can also confound a system of credit allocation. For example, a family buying a house can take out a larger mortgage, and use its own funds thus freed to buy securities. *In the long run* one cannot control the allocation of credit by controlling the portfolio choices of financial intermediaries. Britain, which made heavy use of controls over bank lending as a tool of monetary policy in the 1950s and 1960s, found that this device became less and less effective with the passage of time and with the growth of nonbank financial intermediaries.

Moreover, credit allocation reduces the efficiency of the financial system. New institutions may spring up that are viable merely because they can avoid this regulation, though they are otherwise less efficient than existing institutions. Efficiency is also reduced by a decline in intermediation below its optimal level. If financial intermediaries cannot invest the saver's funds in the most profitable way, savers and ultimate borrowers both have an incentive not to use financial intermediaries and to undertake direct finance.

Summary

In this chapter we have examined some serious charges that have been raised against monetary policy. Since the charges involve high and rising interest rates we first discussed whether the Fed should be held responsible for them. Then we discussed what criteria should be used to evaluate the impact of monetary policy on various sectors. After rejecting proportionality, we looked at two criteria, neutrality and social value.

We discussed the effect of monetary policy on the choice between investment and consumption, and then turned to its impact on various types of investment. This impact is very strong on residential construction, both because houses are long-lived assets and also because of market imperfections and certain government regulations, such as Regulation Q and interest-rate ceilings set by the FHA, and VA. We also took up the tendency of banks to give preference to their business borrowers. We then discussed whether small firms and new firms face discrimination when credit becomes tight. We looked at the impact of monetary policy on financial markets, and saw that this may require the Fed occasionally to break a restrictive policy. We also dealt with the effect of rising interest rates on the distribution of income.

One problem that complicates this discussion throughout is that of deciding what the alternative to restrictive monetary policy is. If the alternative to a restrictive policy is to continue an unduly expansionary policy, then nominal interest rates will, in any case, rise eventually. On the other hand, if the alternative is a restrictive fiscal policy, then interest rates can be kept down. We concluded by taking up the main arguments for and against the proposal to avoid the undesirable effects of a restrictive monetary policy on resource allocation by imposing government credit allocation.

QUESTIONS AND EXERCISES

1. To evaluate the seriousness of the impact of monetary policy on particular sectors one needs some criterion of what this impact should be. Describe what you consider to be the right criterion and defend it.

2. "The argument that monetary policy distorts resource allocation is invalid. If a restrictive monetary policy has a disproportionate impact on one sector, then so does an expansionary policy. Since these two policies alternate, disproportionate impacts cancel out after some time, and therefore create no problem." Discuss.
3. Discuss the impact of monetary policy on residential construction.
4. Do you believe that residential construction should be protected from the impact of a tight money policy? Why or why not? If yes, then how?
5. Discuss the effect of monetary policy on the distribution of income.

FURTHER READING

General

U.S., CONGRESS, JOINT ECONOMIC COMMITTEE. *Staff Report on Employment, Growth and Price Levels*. 86th Cong., 1st sess., 1959, pp. 363–93. A strong criticism of the discriminatory impact of monetary policy.

SCHLESINGER, JAMES. "Monetary Policy and Its Critics." *Journal of Political Economy* 68 (December 1960): 601–16. A strong defense of monetary policy.

Residential construction

BOWSHER, NORMAN, and KALISH, LIONEL. "Does Slower Monetary Expansion Discriminate against Housing?" *Review* (Federal Reserve Bank of St. Louis) 50 (June 1968): 5–12. Presents cogent arguments that a slower monetary growth rate does not hurt housing unduly.

U.S., BOARD OF GOVERNORS, FEDERAL RESERVE SYSTEM. *Ways to Moderate Fluctuations in Housing Construction*. Washington, D.C., 1972. A wide-ranging and informative collection of essays by Federal Reserve economists.

Small business and state and local governments

CARSON, DEANE, and SCOTT, IRA O. "Differential Effects of Monetary Policy on Small Business." In *The Vital Majority*, edited by U.S., Small Business Administration, pp. 197–237. Washington, D.C., 1973. A very useful survey and discussion of various empirical studies.

U.S., CONGRESS, JOINT ECONOMIC COMMITTEE. "The Effect of Credit Conditions on State and Local Bond Sales and Capital Outlays since World War II." in U.S., Congress, Joint Economic Committee, Subcommittee on Economic Progress, *State and Local Public Facility Needs and Financing*, 86th Cong., 2d sess., 1966, vol. 2, pp. 229–31. Presents a very useful survey of previous empirical studies and also new results.

Monetary policy and financial markets

MINSKY, HYMAN. "Central Banking and Money Market Changes," *Quarterly Journal of Economics* 71 (May 1957): 171–87. Describes how rising interest rates lead to financial innovations.

————. "Financial Instability Revisited: The Economics of Disaster." In *Reappraisal of the Federal Reserve Discount Mechanism*, edited by Board of Governors, Federal Reserve System, Washington, D.C., 1972. Cogent arguments that there is a real danger of financial panics.

Credit allocation

BRUNNER, KARL, ed. *Government Credit Allocation.* San Francisco: Institute for Contemporary Studies, 1974. A series of essays by critics of credit allocation.

KAMINOW, IRA, and O'BRIEN, JAMES, eds. *Studies in Selective Credit Policies.* Federal Reserve Bank of Philadelphia, 1975. Chapters one and four give a good survey of the issues.

26

Can Countercyclical
Monetary Policy Succeed?

The old-fashioned, traditional functions of monetary policy were to maintain the gold, or silver, standard and to prevent financial panics. When in the early 1920s Keynes advocated using monetary policy to stabilize the domestic economy on a continuous basis, this was a radical proposal. Since then this idea has become respectable and generally accepted by the public. But this conventional wisdom has now been challenged by a number of economists, mainly monetarists, who have argued that it is a vain hope; that in attempting to stabilize the economy, monetary policy is more likely to generate further instability and inflation. In this chapter we take up the reasons why they think so, and in chapter 28 we examine their preferred alternative of keeping the growth rate of the money stock constant regardless of the stage of the business cycle.

The belief that a monetary policy that tries to be countercyclical will actually worsen economic fluctuations and inflation is based on any, or all of four grounds. First, there is the problem of choosing the correct target, which we discussed in chapter 23. As explained there, if the Federal Reserve uses an interest-rate target when it is the *IS* curve that is shifting, then the Fed will cause income to fluctuate more.[1] The second reason why countercyclical, or discretionary, monetary policy could enhance economic fluctuations is that it takes time for monetary policy to affect income. Thus, the Fed may adopt an expansionary policy in a recession, and this policy may raise income only after a long time when the recession is over, and aggregate demand is excessive. Third, the public's reactions to the Fed's policy may cause it to be destabilizing. Finally, due to political pressures, the Fed may follow a policy that is highly inflationary and destabilizing. We will now take up each of these potential problems in turn except for the already discussed targets problem. Although the discussion will deal only with monetary policy, the same problems also apply to that great rival of monetary policy, fiscal policy.

---

[1] However, if it uses a money-stock target when that target is inappropriate because it is the Cambridge *k* rather than the *IS* curve that varies, then it will not seriously worsen the fluctuations of income; it will simply not reduce them.

The Problem of Lags

This problem arises with respect to a policy that tries to reduce the fluctuations of income around its trend rather than with a policy that tries to raise, or lower, the trend of income. But before we discuss the problem that lags create for such a countercyclical policy it is necessary to clarify what this term means. Do not think of the lag as the time that elapses from the date the Fed adopts a certain policy, and a specific date on which income changes, because not all the change in income will occur at one particular time. Some of the change in income will occur quite soon, but it may take a much longer time until the full effect is reached. We are dealing here, not with a point-input-point-output situation, but with a "distributed" lag, so that, instead of saying that it takes monetary policy, say, fifteen months to change income, we should say that, say, 30 percent of the effect is reached after four months, 60 percent after twelve months, 90 percent after fifteen months, and 100 percent after twenty-four months. This is the type of situation that was shown in figure 24.3, which compared the impact of monetary policy shown by several econometric models.

If monetary policy would have all of its effect on income immediately, the Federal Reserve's task would be greatly simplified. Once it becomes aware that the economy is in a recession it could simply adopt an expansionary policy, and, conversely, if demand is too high it would adopt a restrictive policy. By looking at the current level of income it could make sure that its policy is just strong enough to keep nominal income close to the right level. Admittedly, the fact that accurate data on current income are not available right away would create a problem, but this would be relatively minor.

Unfortunately, this is not the way monetary policy works; once the Fed changes its policy it takes quite a long time for its main effects on income to show up. And when they do, economic conditions *may* have changed so that an expansionary policy initiated in the recession raises income when income is already too high, or a restrictive policy adopted during the previous boom lowers income during the subsequent recession. When the Fed then reverses itself and adopts a new policy, the effects of this new policy may again come at the wrong time. We may therefore get the stabilizer's nightmare shown in figure 26.1 in which monetary policy increases the amplitude of the business cycle. This possibility has to be taken seriously because in the postwar period business cycles have been rather short. In the years 1945–75, the median length of a recession was only ten months, and the median length of an expansion was thirty-nine months.

A Formal Model

Milton Friedman has developed a model that highlights the importance of the proper timing of countercyclical monetary and fiscal policy. Assume

Figure 26.1   Effects of Badly Timed Stabilization Policy

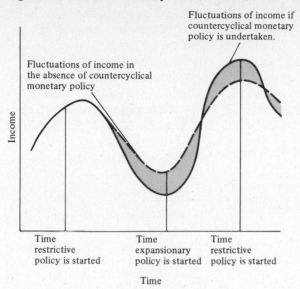

that the trend of aggregate demand is just right, and that we want to minimize the fluctuations around this trend. *A convenient way of measuring fluctuations is a statistical measure* called the **variance.** (To obtain this variance the difference is taken between each observation and the mean and squared. Then the average of these squared differences is taken.) Since the variance involves the *squared* deviations from the mean, treating the minimization of the variance as the goal of stabilization policy implies that we are trying to minimize, not the differences of aggregate demand from the desired level, but instead are trying to minimize the *squares* of these differences. In turn, this implies that we are more than proportionally concerned about a few large differences than about more frequent small ones. For example, compare two policies. Policy A generates the following series of deviations from the mean: 0, 4, 0; while policy B results in deviations: 2, 2, 1. If our criterion is to minimize the absolute deviations, policy A is superior to policy B. But if we are trying to minimize the square of the deviations, policy B (with a sum of 9) is better. Specifically, we are using what is called a quadratic utility function, such as $U = f(P^2, U^2)$ where P is the excess of the actual inflation rate over the desired inflation rate, and U the excess of the actual unemployment rate over the full-employment rate. (Since both inflation and unemployment lower utility, f denotes a negative function.) This use of a quadratic utility function involves a value judgment, which not everyone may wish to accept. Another implicit value judgment is involved in the treatment of a dollar of excessive income as being exactly as undesirable as a dollar of shortfall in income.

But, all the same, let us assume that we *do* want to minimize the variance of nominal income. Changes in the propensity to consume, the marginal efficiency of investment, and in liquidity preference will in the absence of stabilization policy, cause income to vary. We will designate the variance of income that is due to these "private sector" fluctuations and is independent of policy by $\sigma_x{}^2$. Stabilization policy then consists of generating changes in income that offset these independent fluctuations. Since the average level of aggregate demand is just right, these policy-induced changes are sometimes positive and sometimes negative and have a mean of zero. Their variance around this mean of zero we will call $\sigma_y{}^2$. The total variance of income, designated by $\sigma_z{}^2$, will be the result of both these original fluctuations of income and of the policy-induced fluctuations. A theorem in statistics tells us that this is:

$$\sigma_z{}^2 = \sigma_x{}^2 + \sigma_y{}^2 + 2R\sigma_x\sigma_y,$$

where R is the coefficient of correlation between the original variance of income, $\sigma_x{}^2$, and the variance induced by the stabilization policy, $\sigma_y{}^2$.[2]

Applying this formula for the sum of two variances to the problem at hand we can see how important the correlation is between the original variations in income and the variations induced by monetary policy—that is, the timing of policy. If a policy is badly timed—R being positive—so that it raises nominal income when nominal income is already above its mean, and lowers income when it is below its mean, then we have the case of the stabilizer's nightmare.

If this obvious point were all that the above equation shows we would not have bothered to introduce it. But it also shows two other, not so obvious things. One is that it does not suffice for the policy to be "neutral" in its timing, that is, to be right half the time. If it is, $R = 0$, the last term in the previous equation drops out, and the variance of income is equal to $\sigma_x{}^2 + \sigma_y{}^2$, which is, of course, greater than $\sigma_x{}^2$. Hence, if the Fed's timing is half-right it is *de*stabilizing income. This suggests that there is a genuine danger that stabilization policy may actually be destabilizing. Second, by algebraic manipulation one can obtain the maximum effective size of the stabilization policy's impact on income for each R. This is $\sigma_y{}^2 = (R\sigma_x)^2$. Any policy that *tries* to do more than this will actually do less. For example, assume that the Federal Reserve adopts a policy powerful enough to offset all the fluctuation in income; that is, that it sets $\sigma_y = \sigma_x$. If the correlation coefficient is -0.5 such a policy will not succeed in reducing the net fluctua-

---

[2] The correlation coefficient can best be explained by considering the regression equation $y = a + bx + u$ in which a is a constant, b measures the "gearing ratio" of x and y, and u is a randomly distributed variable. The computer is then kindly requested to select those values of a and b that allow x to explain most of the squared variation in y, that is to minimize the square of u. If u is zero, then x and y are perfectly correlated; that is, since we know the constant, a, once we are given x we know what y has to be. In this case the correlation coefficient is unity (or minus unity if b is negative). Now suppose that there is no relation at all between x and y: assume, for example, that x is your age and y the last digit of your driver's license. In this case knowledge of x would not allow you to predict y at all. In the above equation, the value of y would be determined entirely by u, b being zero. In this case the correlation coefficient is zero. The square of the correlation coefficient tells you that proportion of y "explained" by x.

tion of income at all.[3] And if the correlation coefficient were, say, −0.4, it would actually *in*crease income fluctuation.[4] Too much can be even worse than nothing at all.

This way of looking at policy therefore has much to teach us. It shows the great importance of the timing of the impact of the policy since it is this that determines R. It warns us that it does not take very great errors in timing to be destabilizing, and it shows that one must beware of adopting a policy that is too strong. But remember that it has two limitations. First, it applies only to what is strictly a *stabilization* policy, that is, to a policy that tries to even out fluctuations in nominal income. Policy may be more concerned with changing the average level of income. For example, a policy that causes the unemployment rate to fluctuate between, say, 4 and 6 percent would be better than one that causes the unemployment rate to lie between 10 and 10¼ percent, even though the latter unemployment rate is stabler. Second, it requires a quadratic utility function with equal weights for positive and negative deviations.

But despite these qualifications, R, the coefficient of correlation between the original fluctuations in income and the fluctuations induced by policy, is obviously critical for a stabilization policy. To avoid destabilizing actions the Fed must ensure that R is negative, and large enough for the size of the policy being used. This requires that it forecast sufficiently well (1) the future level of income in the absence of policy, and (2) the effect of its policy on income *in each period,* say each calendar quarter. It is not sufficient for the Fed to know the total impact of its policy. To calculate σ_y^2 it must also know how this total impact is distributed over time—the distributed lag of monetary policy.

Problems Created by the Lag

If monetary policy would have most of its effect on income almost immediately, the prediction of "future" income would not create a problem for the Fed. Since income changes very little over a short span of time, such as a calendar quarter, the Fed could use as its estimate of income, when the policy becomes effective, the income level prevailing currently (or rather at the time to which the available statistics relate) with perhaps a small adjustment for the growth trend. But, obviously, this does not work if monetary policy takes a long time to affect income. Assume that most of the effect occurs only after two years. In two years the economy may well be in a different business-cycle stage. Hence, if the Fed selects its policy on the basis of what income is currently, the correlation between the original income fluctuations (σ_x^2) and the income fluctuations caused

---

[3] If $\sigma_x^2 = \sigma_y^2$ and $R = \frac{1}{2}$, then the expression $\sigma_x^2 + \sigma_y^2 + 2R\sigma_x\sigma_y$ reduces to σ_x^2, which is the original fluctuation of income in the absence of stabilization policy. If the correlation coefficient is −0.5, the maximum by which policy could reduce the variation of income is 25 percent; any policy more powerful than that would be less effective.

[4] In this case the variance of income would be $2\sigma_x^2 - .8\sigma_x^2 = 1.2\sigma_x^2$ compared to σ_x^2 in the absence of policy.

by policy ($\sigma_y{}^2$) is likely to be around zero, and monetary policy will destabilize the economy. If monetary policy has a long lag—as much of the empirical evidence suggests—then the Fed has to use an explicit forecast of income. Since obviously the Fed's forecasts are not without errors, this provides a limitation on the effectiveness with which the Fed can stabilize income.

Another way in which the length of the lag is important is the leeway the Fed has to offset errors it has made. Suppose that it expected income to decline and adopted an expansionary policy; nominal income then turns out to be much higher than expected. If the lag is short, the Fed can quickly reverse itself, and offset the effect of its previous action, but it cannot if the lag is long.

In principle, the Fed could avoid this problem by adopting corrective policy that is much stronger than the initial policy it is trying to offset. For example, assume that only 20 percent of the impact on income occurs in the first quarter, and that after one year monetary policy has 80 percent of its full effect. The Federal Reserve could then fully offset within a quarter a policy action that it took a year ago, *if* it were willing to adopt an offsetting policy that is four times as strong as the original policy. But such large policy changes have costs; in particular, they lead to violent swings in interest rates. There is also the *possibility* that a continual policy of a quick offset via stronger and stronger offsetting policies would cause an explosive increase in the size of policies. However, this possibility does not appear likely.

And there is still a third problem. To use stabilization policy effectively, the Fed must know, not only the total size of the effect its policy will have on income, but it must know also how this effect is distributed over time. As we saw before, it has to know $\sigma_y{}^2$, the variance of income resulting from its policy actions *in each period* (say, a quarter), as well as *R,* the correlation of this variance with the initial variance of income. Thus it has to make an estimate of the distributed lag. This would be a difficult econometric problem even if the lag were fairly constant. But the problem is much worse if the lag is highly variable. Thus suppose that the Fed's staff were to tell the FOMC that the lag is, *on the average,* one year, but that in one-third of the cases, it is only three months, and in another third it is two years. In deciding whether to adopt an expansionary, or a restrictive, policy the FOMC would then not know whether to orient its policy towards the income level it expects to prevail in three months, in a year, or in two years. What the FOMC must consider is not the average lag, but the lag for the particular action it is contemplating. Hence, knowledge of the average lag may not be sufficient. It is sufficient only if most of the lags cluster closely around the average. If the Fed uses the average lag from its econometric model this *could* make its policy destabilizing in the majority of cases, even if the model estimates the average lag correctly. However, this is not so if the Fed avoids all explicit forecasting and simply bases its actions on the current level of income. Rather sur-

Table 26.1   Mean Absolute Errors in Eight Forecasts[a]

| | Rate of growth of: | | | Change in |
Year	Nominal GNP	Real GNP	Price level[b]	unemployment rate
1971	1.3	.4	2.8	.4
1972	.9	.3	4.1	.2
1973	1.9	.8	3.7	.2
1974	.6	2.8	1.4	.2
1975	1.0	.8	8.1	1.1
1976	.7	.4	1.6	.2
MEAN	1.1	.9	3.6	.4

a. Forecasts made by Council of Economic Advisers, Chase Econometric Associates, Inc., Data Resources Inc., General Electric, Manufacturers Hanover Bank, University of Michigan, Wharton, and by a survey of forecasters undertaken by the National Bureau of Economic Research and the American Statistical Association.

b. Implicit price deflator for GNP.

SOURCE: Stephen K. McNees, "An Assessment of the Council of Economic Advisers' Forecast for 1977," *New England Economic Review* (Federal Reserve Bank of Boston), March/April 1977, p. 6.

prisingly, in this case it can be shown that the more variable the lag, the greater the probability that monetary policy will be stabilizing.[5]

Thus the existence of a significant lag in the effect of monetary policy creates three problems for the Fed. It must forecast income, even if only by saying that income will not change, it cannot offset past errors quickly, and it must estimate the effect of its policies in each period.

Hence, to evaluate whether the Fed has reliable enough information to be an effective stabilizer we would have to know how accurate its forecast of income is and how well it predicts the effect of its policy in each period. Neither can be known precisely since the Fed does not publish its forecasts. However, since, by and large, the major forecasters do about equally well, some idea of the Fed's forecasting error can be obtained by looking at the mean errors made by eight other forecasts. These are shown in table 26.1. But, unfortunately, no material is available that shows how well the Fed can predict the second item, the effects of its policies on GNP.

Empirical Estimates of the Lag

It is convenient to divide the lag of monetary policy into two parts. There is first the *inside lag,* that is, *the lag from the time the need for action arises until the Federal Reserve takes action.* This lag can be divided into

[5] The authors apologize for saying "it can be shown" without actually showing it. The proof is complex and mathematical, and we know of no intuitive explanation. See Haskel Benishay, "A Framework for the Evaluation of Short-Term Fiscal and Monetary Policy," *Journal of Money, Credit and Banking* 4 (November 1972): 779–810.

two further components: (1) the lag from the time the need arises until the Fed recognizes that a new policy is needed, and (2) the lag between the time the Fed recognizes it and the time it takes action. This is a distributed lag since the Fed is unlikely to undertake all its action at one time. Usually it will undertake its new open-market policy in a series of steps spread out over several months because it is uncertain whether the new policy is really the appropriate one, and hence wants to move slowly. Then there is the *outside lag.* This is *the distributed lag from the time of the Fed's action until income changes.* Obviously, an increase in the money stock and a decrease in interest rates do not raise income immediately. As far as investment is concerned, firms have to make a decision to invest, they have to draw up plans, place orders, and so on. Turning to consumption, it takes some time until interest rates on consumer credit decline and until households respond to the rise in security prices that results from lower interest rates.

The inside lag can, but need not, be very short; it depends upon the extent to which the Federal Reserve is willing to take action on a forecast as opposed to waiting until conditions have actually changed. It also depends upon whether the Fed is willing to take much of the required action in one fell swoop, or spreads its action out over many months, either because it wants to avoid a rapid change in interest rates, or because it is not sure of itself. Thus if it is willing to undertake much of its open-market purchases before a business downturn actually occurs, its inside lag will be negative. The inside lag therefore depends upon the Fed itself and hence depends on who the chairman of the Board of Governors is.

The outside lag is more objective and less subject to Fed control. Many academic economists have tried to estimate it. Some have used econometric models, and we showed some of their results in figure 24.3, while others have regressed income on money, or have measured the lag between turning points in the money growth rate and business-cycle turning points. Several economists have measured the length of time it takes firms to invest, while still others have (following the analysis described in chapter 16) looked at the length of time it takes interest rates to snap back after changes in the money growth rate. Unfortunately, little agreement has been reached, though most, but not all, of these studies show that it takes *at least* two quarters for monetary policy to reach half of its ultimate effect.[6] Beyond this, the range of estimates is large with the big econometric models usually showing long lags. A major reason for the long lags shown by econometric models is that most of them use a term-structure equation that shows a very slow adaption of long-term interest rates to the changes that the Fed brings about in short-term rates. However these term-structure equations with their long lags are now suspect. But the other

[6] A complication here is that it is quite possible that the effect of monetary policy does not build up smoothly to a peak, but rises to a certain level, and then declines again to a lower level or cycles around some level.

methods of measuring the lag in monetary policy are also open to serious criticism. This wide range of estimates is disturbing and suggests that some skepticism is in order about the accuracy of all of them. Moreover, although very little empirical work has been done on the extent to which the lag of monetary policy varies from case to case, the limited amount of information that is available suggests that the lag is highly variable. If correct, this is most disturbing.

Policy Tools: A Further Consideration

We are now in a position to return to the discussion of the tools of monetary policy, and take up briefly a sophisticated problem that we could not discuss before. Suppose several tools are available, such as open-market operations, discount-rate changes, and reserve-requirement changes or, alternatively, fiscal policy and monetary policy, all of which are strong enough to change income by the required amount. Which one should be used? One possible answer is the strongest. But a moment's reflection will show that unless there is a cost from using a tool too much or too often, there is no reason for choosing the strongest. Instead of the strength, one should look at the predictability of the impact of each tool, and use the one that predicts best; (if one is willing to accept a quadratic utility function) this is the tool with the lowest variance. Moreover, we are generally better off using several of the tools at the same time. This is so because if their variances are not perfectly correlated, then an averaging-out process ensures that the variance of the impact is less for several tools jointly than it is for any single tool. The exact mixture in which our tools should be used depends upon their relative variances and upon the correlation of their variances.

Rational Expectations

The lag in the effect of monetary policy is not the only factor that may cause countercyclical policy to be ineffective. Rational expectations may do this too. Firms do not act to maximize *actual* profits, they act to maximize *expected* profits. Hence, to predict how firms will act one has to find some way of determining what profits they *expect* to earn from various possible alternatives. There are several ways of doing this. One is to assume that they form their expectations by looking only at the present and past behavior of the variable they want to predict. For example, if prices have been rising, they will expect them to rise in the future too. A useful specification of this approach is the error-learning model, in which a firm makes a forecast for one period ahead, and then, at the end of the period, looks at the errors in its forecast and adjusts its prediction for the second period accordingly. For example, if you predict that prices will rise at an 8 percent annual rate this month, but they actually rise at a 6 percent rate, it is reasonable for you to adjust your prediction for the next month down to, say, 7 percent.[7]

But such a backward-looking method of prediction is not always the best possible one. Suppose, for example, that at the end of the month you hear that Congress has ordered the Fed to bring the Treasury bill rate down from, say, 10 percent to 5 percent and to keep it there. Surely, you should use this piece of information in predicting what will happen to prices in the future. Since there has been an important change in the economy it would not be rational to predict future prices merely by projecting the past behavior of prices into the future. When discussing the term structure of interest rates in chapter 6, we mentioned rational expectations, and also made use of this approach in chapter 24, to explain why you cannot make a killing in the stock market merely because you know that stock prices rise when the money growth rate does. But rational expectations are much more important than these examples suggest; they *may* make counter-cyclical stabilization policy both unnecessary and impossible. To see why it is useful to look first at the meaning of rational expectations in more detail.

What are Rational Expectations?

According to the rational-expectations approach, people forecast in a fully rational way, given all the information available to them. This is quite different from just projecting the past behavior of a series, such as interest rates, into the future as is done in the error-learning model of expectations formation. In the error-learning model, when interest rates decline more than expected, people simply adjust their forecasts of future interest rates, but they do not ask why their previous forecast was wrong. Since they usually adjust their forecasts only part of the way each period, they tend to make systematic errors, for example, they overestimate for several periods. By contrast, in the rational-expectations approach people use all the information they can get at reasonable cost to make their forecasts. To do this they must have in their minds some model of the economy that allows them to interpret the incoming information. For example, using what they have learned from economics courses, they predict that inflation will speed up substantially if Congress orders the Fed to lower interest rates. But, how about those who have never taken an economics course? They too will have some information that will allow them to make a (correct or incorrect) judgment about how the inflation rate will be affected. Everyone, including someone who despises theories, has an implicit theory in his or her mind that is used to interpret incoming information.

Economics would be much further advanced if we knew these (largely

---

[7] Why not adjust your expectations down all the way to 6 percent? Well, you used quite a lot of information in deciding that prices will rise at an 8 percent rate. Do you really want to discard all of this information merely because you were wrong in one month?

inchoate) theories that people use. But we do not, so we have to make some assumptions. One possible assumption is that people's theories correspond fairly well to the economists' theories. This does not mean that everyone reasons the way economists do, but merely that their conclusions average out to what is shown by the economists' models. This is not as unrealistic as it sounds at first, because the most important decisions are made mainly by experienced managers who have reached their positions because they usually predict correctly. These managers can reach the same conclusions as economists without having the economists' theories in their toolbox. For example, someone may not know the theories that explain the term structure of interest rates, but may simply observe that long-term interest rates behave in a certain way when short-term rates change; birds can fly without having studied aerodynamics.

Moreover, assuming that expectations are rational is not the same thing as assuming that people have perfect foresight; economic models certainly do not. What it does mean is that, unlike in the error-learning model, people will not make *systematic* errors for any length of time. They will still make errors, but these errors will be random, and have a mean of zero. To illustrate, here is an example from everyday life. Suppose that without this being announced, trains are now running slower, so that the average trip takes ten minutes longer. On the first day almost everyone will arrive at work late. Someone using an error-learning model will leave the next day, say, six minutes earlier and be four minutes late. But someone operating according to rational expectations may remember that in previous years when the weather was like this, trains were usually ten minutes late, or else he or she may call the railroad to get a new timetable. Such a person will still not always be exactly on time; some days the train takes a bit longer, and some days it is faster. But this person will be late (or early) no more frequently than before.

This example assumes that people will act on the available information, and leave ten minutes earlier, and this assumption that people do *act* on their available information is an important assumption of rational-expectations theory. Specifically, the theory assumes that if workers realize that the demand curve for their services has shifted downward they will be ready to accept wage cuts. Many Keynesians, on the other hand, assume that workers are unwilling to accept money wage cuts.

Rational Expectations and Unemployment

Assume that people act rationally in the sense just described, and consider a labor market in which workers and employers set wages for the following week at the level that they think will clear the market. Since they lack perfect knowledge this wage will sometimes be too high, so that unemployment occurs, and sometimes too low, so that there is an unsatisfied demand for labor. Now assume that aggregate demand falls suddenly so that extensive unemployment develops. At first workers and employers may think that this unemployment is merely a random event just as likely to be followed next week by an unsatisfied demand for labor as by a recurrence of unemployment. But after some time they will realize by looking at all the available information that the unemployment they are observing is not just the previously experienced random unemployment, but is more persistent and widespread. Hence, after a few weeks they will negotiate lower wages. As wages fall, so do prices, and the resulting real balance effect restores employment to its equilibrium level.

This picture of a self-equilibrating economy was rejected by Keynes. He maintained that since workers are reluctant to accept money wage cuts, unemployment could persist for a long time. Hence, if aggregate demand falls, why go through this lengthy and painful process of reducing wages and other costs, why not instead raise aggregate demand back to its previous level by expansionary fiscal and monetary policy.[8] And it is this reasoning that underlies the widespread support for countercyclical policies.

But in recent years a number of economists have challenged this. They interpret unemployment very differently and argue that it is due, not to any stickiness of money wages, but to the fact that it takes time for workers and employers to realize that aggregate demand has fallen permanently and that money wages should fall too. As soon as one makes unemployment the result of ignorance rather than of an unwillingness to accept lower money wages, the traditional justification for countercyclical stabilization policy becomes suspect. Ignorance is not confined to the labor market; the government has its share too. Assume that the government is exactly as well informed as those who set wages. In this case by the time the government realizes what has happened and raises aggregate demand, wages are being cut and the real balance effect brings about full employment in any case. Hence expansionary policy is not needed. If one assumes that money-wage stickiness is due entirely to lack of information, rather than to a reluctance to take a wage cut, then only if the government is better informed than the private market will stabilization policy be useful. And there is no reason to assume that this is the case.

It is therefore an important issue whether money wages are flexible and fall when it is realized that aggregate demand has fallen, or whether they are sticky. Many economists rationalize wage stickiness in several ways. One way is to say that a person's wage affects his or her self-respect so that workers are willing to risk unemployment rather than take a wage cut, or, more questionably, to try to argue that unions keep wages up.[9] An-

[8] Keynes was not the only one who advocated raising aggregate demand in the 1930s. Economists who then constituted the "Chicago School" advocated that the government should increase the quantity of money, and put it into circulation by using it to pay for public works.

[9] Prior to the 1930s, when only a small proportion of the U.S. labor force was unionized, money wages also did not fall during recessions, they just stopped rising. See Clarence Long, "The Illusion of Wage Rigidity: Long and Short Cycles in Wages and Labor," *Review of Economics and Statistics* 42 (May 1960): 140–51.

other way is to point out that workers do not set wages on their own; in nonunionized firms—which employ about three-quarters of the labor force —wages are set by the employer subject to a minimum wage floor, and in unionized industries they are set by employers and workers jointly. And, it may well be the employers rather than workers who are unwilling to cut wages during a recession. There is a theory, known as the implicit-contract theory that argues that the employer makes an implicit contract with the employee along the following lines: "I cannot supervise you all the time, and I expect you to work efficiently even when I am not watching you. In return for this, I will not try to take advantage of every slight decline in your equilibrium wage: for example, even if I could hire an unemployed worker in your stead at, say, 10 percent less than I am paying you, I will neither fire you nor ask you to take a 10 percent wage cut." If such mutual loyalty arrangements are common, then many wages will not fall even after it becomes apparent that aggregate demand has fallen.

Wage rigidity may therefore furnish a justification for stabilization policy. But in the previous section of this chapter we raised the question whether, given its lags, stabilization policy can be effective. Can these two arguments be combined? Yes, to some extent they can since they both concern lags. Suppose that aggregate demand drops. If money-wage cuts and the resulting real balance effect occur quicker than the effect of the expansionary monetary policy does, then monetary policy should not be used in this case. But if money wages are very slow to respond, then unemployment *may* continue for a long enough time for monetary policy to do some good.

The Impact of Stabilization Policy

If the rational-expectation theorists are correct, countercyclical policy not only does no good, it does positive harm because it is inflationary. To see why, consider first an economy with rational expectations and high employment. The government now undertakes a long-run expansionary policy. The traditional story is that firms react to the increase in aggregate demand for their products initially by raising their output and raise their prices only with a lag. This is so primarily because firms do not know whether this increase in demand is permanent or just temporary, as it so often is, and they want to avoid frequent price changes. But, say the rational-expectations theorists, this story is wrong. Entrepreneurs read newspapers, and, hence, when demand increases, *in this case,* they realize that it is because of an expansionary policy and that the higher demand will persist. Hence, they raise prices right away instead of raising output.

This example has the government raising aggregate demand during a period of high employment, which is hardly an example of a good stabilization policy; so now assume instead that it raises aggregate demand only during a recession, but does so very consistently. If so, whenever a recession occurs firms know that the government will raise aggregate demand, and hence they raise their prices. Or more realistically, they refrain from doing what they otherwise would have done during the recession, cutting prices. Before World War II prices fell in recessions. In the postwar period they fell by less and less in successive recessions, and then started to rise in recessions. In part, this is due to the spread of multiyear labor contracts that spread wage increases out among years of expansions and recessions, but, in part, it *may* be the result of a spreading realization that the government will adopt expansionary policies that make price reductions less necessary.

Suppose, for example, that the government were to announce that every time unemployment exceeds, say, 6 percent, it will raise the money growth rate by 3 percentage points. Both firms and unions would then take an unemployment rate of over 6 percent as an indication that they should raise their wages and prices. Carrying this approach a bit further, rational expectations theorists have argued that an *expected* increase in the money growth rate only raises prices and does not raise output even temporarily, and that output rises temporarily only in response to an *unexpected* increase in the money growth rate. Hence, the only way the Federal Reserve can raise output and employment would be if it could adopt expansionary policies that are unexpected. But sooner or later the public will figure out any consistent Federal Reserve policy; and even if the Fed could somehow fool the public in the long run, it is far from clear that it should do so since this would cause people to make wrong decisions.

But while rational expectations weaken or eliminate the standard argument for stabilization policy, they enhance the efficacy of one type of stabilization policy. This is a policy to end or reduce inflation by cutting aggregate demand. The usual story is that if a restrictive monetary or fiscal policy cuts aggregate demand the initial result is a much greater fall in output than in the inflation rate. Firms and unions do not realize that the government is serious about ending inflation. They continue to expect inflation, and therefore raise their wages and prices. Only after a long time of substantial unemployment will the inflation rate decline substantially. Rational-expectations theory suggests such a period of high unemployment is not necessary; the government should let the public know that it really will cut aggregate demand sufficiently to bring the inflation rate down. If this is done, then prices and wages will adjust relatively quickly.

But what is needed is not just a statement by the government that it is "against inflation"—such talk is cheap. The government would have to show that it means what it says, perhaps by a dramatic gesture, such as amending the 1946 Employment Act to put price stability ahead of high employment, or by directing the Fed to concentrate on price stability, or even by a constitutional amendment.

But such measures would be strongly opposed by organized labor and others who cherish high employment. They would not be convinced that such a policy would succeed. They could reply that while the rational-expectations theory sounds plausible, it may not work, and people's jobs are too important to be experimented with. Moreover, by making such a commitment, the government would have to give up its flexibility. It would then be costly for it to change the antiinflation policy even if it does not seem to work. The cost is that if the government changes its mind, and, for example, changes the directive given to the Federal Reserve, then later on if it wants to change expectations again by a similar method it will not be believed.

But even if therefore the government does not want to abandon the employment goal completely, rational-expectations theory still has an important lesson: this is that if the Fed adopts a restrictive policy and intends to stick with it the public should be told. In general, one does not have to accept rational-expectations theory completely to conclude that expectations do matter, and that monetary policies will have different effects depending on what expectations they generate. For example, some of the variation in the lag with which changes in the money stock affect income *may* be due to differences in the extent to which the public realizes what is happening.

Predicting the Effects of Policies

The rational-expectations approach has another important implication for policy. This is that government policy may quite unintentionally change the way the public reacts to events. For example, take a policy that cuts personal income taxes during a recession and raises them again during the following expansion. To find out how big a tax cut is needed the government's economists may calculate the marginal propensity to consume from past data on consumption and disposable income, or they may look at how consumption changed every time taxes were cut previously. But they may be in for a disappointment. When income taxes are now cut as a counter-cyclical policy, the public *may* raise its consumption very little. It knows that, unlike in the past, income taxes will from now on be raised again in the future when the economy expands. And since it sets its consumption on the basis of its long-run disposable income, it reacts very differently to a tax cut than before.

Thus, the adoption of a new policy has made outdate and inapplicable the information obtained from past experience. This implies that it is very dangerous to use the information obtained from econometric models, single regression equations, or economic history in general, to predict the effects of a new policy that may change people's expectations. Hence, rational-expectations theorists argue, we know very little about the effects that economic policies have, and this too makes it very questionable that stabilization policy can succeed.

Political Problems

The technical problems created by long and variable lags and by rational expectations are not the only difficulties that confront discretionary monetary policy. Political difficulties too may prevent effective policy. The political assumption underlying economic policy is that the electorate knows what is best for it and that the technicians who operate the government carry out policies that will achieve these ends. Now obviously this is an idealization, and the real question is not whether this political assumption mirrors reality exactly, but whether it is close enough to reality, so that stabilization policy does more good than harm. Although economists generally assume that this is the case, some economists, particularly monetarists, are challenging it. Unfortunately, this discussion is still in its very early stages, and little evidence has been presented by either side, so that we can only give a rather impressionistic sketch of the problem.[10]

Several things can go wrong in a process that has the public decide on its desired goal, which the technicians in government then carry out. One is that the public may not know its own interests. A second is that special-interest groups may be able to substitute their wishes for those of the majority, and a third problem is that the majority may override the legitimate interests of a minority. And finally the bureaucracy may be unresponsive to the public's interests.

The public may at times mistake its own interests in the goals it indirectly sets for monetary policy through its elected representatives. This does not require that the public is ignorant or stupid, but merely that any one person has so little influence on monetary policy that it is not worth his or her while to devote even a trivial amount of time to it. Consequently, the public may sometimes support policies that are clearly wrong. More specifically, the public *may* have a short memory about recent economic policy. This creates a danger of the political business cycle. As discussed in chapter 7, the administration may pressure the Federal Reserve into undertaking an expansionary policy that has its benefits (higher employment and lower interest rates) before the election, but its costs only after the election. Whether this has actually occurred in the United States is an open question. One reason why it is so difficult to answer this question is that a political business cycle may be operative only in years of presidential elections. And since 1953, when monetary policy was freed from its constraint of supporting government security prices, we have had, as of 1980, only seven presidential elections. This is a very small sample for statistical analysis. Moreover, the theory of the political business cycle need not apply

---

[10] Although the political problems of monetary policy have received little discussion, those of fiscal policy have been discussed more. See, for instance, James Buchanan and Richard Wagner, *Democracy in Deficit* (New York: Academic Press, 1977), and the symposium on this book in the *Journal of Monetary Economics* 4 (August 1978): 567–636.

to every election. It might be valid, say, only for close elections or for those in which an incumbent president seeks a second term. If so, the available sample is still smaller.

A second possibility is that monetary policy may be used to hide the true costs of government programs. The government may undertake a popular expenditure program, perhaps one that will redistribute income toward a particular group, and run a deficit as a result. If this occurs at a time of high employment, the resources used by the government must be withdrawn from the private sector. If the money growth rate is kept constant, then the government obtains these resources by selling securities to the public, and this raises interest rates. This rise in interest rates makes the private sector willing to give up some current resources since it raises the cost of using resources currently rather than in the future. But rising interest rates are unpopular, and hence there is pressure on the Fed to generate a sufficiently large increase in the money stock to hold interest rates down temporarily. The public is thereby fooled into believing that it has obtained a desirable government program at zero cost since it attributes the then resulting inflation to big business or big labor.

Another variant of this approach has the Fed act as a scapegoat for politicians. The public demands that we achieve the goals of very little unemployment, price stability, and low and stable nominal interest rates. But these goals are incompatible, and hence the politicians need an "out." As Professor Kane of Ohio State University has put it:

> The Fed is a political institution designed by politicians to serve politicians. . . . Fed officials are expected to let Congressmen and Senators blame them for whatever financial or economic developments their constituents back home dislike. In exchange for playing economic-policy scapegoat, Fed officials are offered unusually long terms in office and substantial budgetary autonomy. . . . The Fed has allowed elected politicians to make it responsible for a series of impossible economic-policy tasks, with the implicit understanding that, when the Fed fails, how loud these politicians and their successors will bark (and whether or not they will also bite) depends on the quality of Fed efforts to get along.[11]

Further, by not being vigilant about monetary policy the public may allow special-interest groups to exert excessive influence on monetary policy.

One of these potential interest groups is composed of the Fed's own officials, and we discussed the Federal Reserve's self-interests in chapter 7. A second special-interest group consists of bankers and financial institutions in general. Some economists attribute the Fed's previous emphasis on interest-rate stabilization, and its permissive attitudes toward risk taking by banks, and toward the fudging of the line between money and near-moneys, to both the Fed's self-interest, and to the pressures on it from banks and other financial institutions.

[11] Edward J. Kane, "Politics and Fed Policymaking: The More Things Change the More They Remain the Same," *Journal of Monetary Economics* 6 (April 1980): 209.

Moreover, as we discussed in the previous chapter, rising interest rates have particularly strong effects on certain industries, such as residential construction. These industries can be expected to pressure the Fed, both directly and through Congress, or by arousing public opinion, into adopting a more expansionary policy that would postpone the rise in nominal interest rates. The costs of adopting a too expansionary policy are diffused over the general economy, while the short-run benefits from such a policy are much more concentrated. Hence, those who gain from such a policy organize to pressure the Fed, while those who lose from it do not. This is the same situation as arises with respect to tariffs and other import restrictions.

The last potential problem with government policy is that the majority might override the legitimate interests of the minority. This may not be a problem with monetary policy except insofar as the Fed *might* show too little concern about unemployment because it is a problem that directly affects only a minority of the electorate.

How serious are all of these factors that prevent monetary policy from serving the public welfare? This is a hard question to answer. Obviously, they cause *some* loss of welfare, but the majority of economists believe, rightly or wrongly, that they do not prevent monetary policy from having some net beneficial effect on the economy.

Summary

This chapter dealt with three difficulties that may prevent monetary policy from stabilizing the economy. The first is that monetary policy affects aggregate demand with a distributed lag. Hence, it may be badly timed and therefore increase the fluctuations of income. This possibility can be explored in a model that looks at instability as the sum of two variances: the variance of income in the absence of policy, and the variance added by government policy. This shows that it would not take so very much of an error in timing for monetary policy to be destabilizing, and that a policy can be too strong as well as too weak. More specifically, the existence of a lag in the impact of monetary policy creates several problems: the Fed must forecast income, it must be able to predict the impact of its policy at various times, and it may not be able to reverse readily a mistaken policy. This raises the question of how accurately the Fed can predict income as well as the impact of its policies, and we presented some information on the errors made by forecasters. But no information is available on how well the Fed predicts the effect of its actions. We then looked at some empirical aspects of the lag, and differentiated between the inside lag and outside lag, and mentioned some of the techniques that have been used to measure the outside lag.

A second problem arises if the public's expectations are rational. We pointed out that this requires the public to use all the readily available information, and to interpret it in a reasonable way, but that it does not require perfect foresight, that random errors are still possible. We showed that if the public acts rationally, then stabilization policy will be effective only if the government has better information, or its policy affects the economy quicker than the public is willing to act. This raises the question of wage stickiness, and we discussed some reasons why wages might be sticky. Rational-expectations theory also suggests that if the government reacts to a recession by a predictable expansionary policy, this policy will have its main effects on prices rather than on output; that only unexpected increases in the money growth rate will raise output temporarily. Moreover, rational-expectations theory tells us that the adoption of a new policy changes the way the public acts, and this makes it very hard to predict what effects this policy will have.

The last set of issues discussed are the political problems that may subvert stabilization policy. One is the political business cycle, another is the use of an expansionary monetary policy to hide a rise in the government's use of resources, and a third is an undue effect on policy by special-interest groups.

QUESTIONS AND EXERCISES

1. "The problem with monetary policy is not, as was once thought, that it is too weak, but that it is too strong." Explain.
2. Explain why monetary policy is destabilizing if the correlation coefficient between σ_x^2 and σ_y^2 is zero or positive.
3. Discuss the problem that the lag in the effect of monetary policy creates for the Federal Reserve.
4. Why does a variable lag create a more serious problem than a stable one? What factors could account for it being variable?
5. Read one of the empirical studies trying to measure the lag. (The items by Hamburger and Uselton in Further Reading have references to these studies.) Write a critique of it.
6. Explain in your own words the rational-expectations criticism of stabilization policy.
7. "If expectations are rational, an expansionary monetary policy will raise only prices and not output." Discuss.
8. Is it sometimes more reasonable to use an error-learning model than rational expectations? If so, under what conditions? How do you form your own expectations?
9. What are the political problems that may hinder effective stabilization policy? Do they apply to fiscal policy as well as to monetary policy?

FURTHER READING

BARRO, ROBERT. "Unanticipated Money Growth and Unemployment in the United States." *American Economic Review* 67 (March 1977): 101–15. A very good example of the rational-expectations approach.

BRAINARD, WILLIAM. "Uncertainty and the Effectiveness of Monetary Policy." *American Economic Review* 57 (May 1967): 411–25. An excellent discussion of how to use various policy tools that have different degrees of predictability.

FRIEDMAN, MILTON. "The Effects of a Full Employment Policy on Economic Stability: A Formal Analysis." In his *Essays in Positive Economics.* Chicago: University of Chicago Press, 1953. This is a classic.

HAMBURGER, MICHAEL. "The Lag in the Effect of Monetary Policy: A Survey of Recent Literature." *Monthly Review* (Federal Reserve Bank of New York) 53 (December 1971): 289–98. An excellent survey of several empirical studies.

HAVRILESKY, THOMAS. "A Theory of Monetary Instability." In *The Political Economy of Policymaking: Essays in Honor of Will E. Mason,* edited by M. Dooley, H. Kaufman, and R. Lombra, pp. 59–88. Beverly Hills: Sage Publications, 1978. An interesting attempt to explain Fed actions.

KANE, EDWARD. "Politics and Fed Policy-Making: The More Things Change the More They Remain the Same." *Journal of Monetary Economics* 6 (April 1980): 199–211.

SARGENT, THOMAS, and NEIL, WALLACE. *Rational Expectations and the Theory of Economic Policy,* pts. 1 and 2, *Studies in Monetary Economics,* nos. 2 and 3. Minneapolis, Minn.: Federal Reserve Bank of Minneapolis, 1975 and 1976. A clear discussion of some complex material.

TOBIN, JAMES. "How Dead Is Keynes?" *Economic Inquiry* 15 (October 1977): 459–68. A very good defense of Keynesian economics against the rational-expectations criticism.

TUFTE, EDWARD. *Political Control of the Economy.* Princeton: Princeton University Press, 1978. A discussion of the political business cycle by a political scientist.

USELTON, GENE. *Lags in the Effects of Monetary Policy.* New York: Marcel Dekker, 1974. Chapter two is a useful survey. Both this, and the article by Hamburger above, contain references to the numerous empirical studies the reader may wish to consult.

27

The Record of
Monetary Policy

Having looked at the ways in which monetary policy affects the economy and at the problems it faces, we are almost ready to evaluate counter-cyclical monetary policy. But before doing so it is useful to take an historical perspective and see how monetary policy has actually been conducted in the past. To be sure, some might say that past errors in the conduct of monetary policy are irrelevant because we have learned from the past, and are unlikely to repeat these errors. But this view is too optimistic for two reasons. First, the errors that were made need not have been due wholly, or even largely, to a lack of knowledge; they could have resulted from political pressures on the Fed, from its own bureaucratic instincts, or from its having so many conflicting goals. If so, the fact that the Fed now knows more about monetary policy than it did when it made mistakes is no guarantee that in similar circumstances it will not repeat them. Second, even if the Fed does not repeat the same mistakes, opportunities to make new mistakes arise all the time. Hence, knowledge of how well it has avoided mistakes in the past provides some indication of how likely it is to make mistakes in the future.

In taking up the history of monetary policy we are therefore motivated primarily by a wish to evaluate the Fed's performance rather than to study monetary history for its own sake. While history is certainly worth studying for its own sake, the history of monetary policy, taken out of the context of the society in which it functions, is hardly the most life-enhancing type of history.

Since we are concerned with evaluating Federal Reserve performance rather than with monetary history for its own sake, we will stress critical episodes rather than try to cover all of the more than sixty years of Fed history in a balanced manner.

The Early Years

When the Federal Reserve System was inaugurated in 1913 one of its major goals, perhaps *the* major goal, was the maintenance of the gold standard, which at the time was generally considered the foundation of sound money. We will discuss the gold standard in Part Six. Here it suffices to note that under the gold-standard "rules of the game" the Federal Reserve should let the quantity of money be determined by the country's gold stock. A gold inflow is supposed to increase the quantity of money, and a gold outflow to decrease it. (Previously, in chapter 10, we discussed the mechanics by which a gold flow changes bank reserves.) This gold standard was to some extent written into the 1913 Federal Reserve Act by requiring the Fed to maintain a gold reserve of 40 percent against Federal Reserve notes (that is, against its currency) and 35 percent against its deposits.

Although it also had some belief in the quantity theory, a second guiding idea of the Fed was the real-bills doctrine. According to this theory what matters is the quality rather than the quantity of money; as long as deposits are created as a result of short-term self-liquidating loans that finance real (as opposed to financial) activities, deposit creation cannot be inflationary. This too was written into the Federal Reserve Act by the provisions governing discounting. (And discounting was then the only major mechanism of monetary policy.) Member banks could borrow from the Fed only by rediscounting **eligible paper,** that is those *promissory notes they had discounted for their customers that met the requirements of the real-bills doctrine,* or by discounting their own promissory notes backed by government securities. The theory was that this would provide an "elastic" currency that would allow the money supply to expand when the demand for money for real transactions increased. At that time banks would discount more eligible promissory notes for their customers, and could then rediscount this eligible paper with the Fed.

Another guiding idea was the wish to avoid financial panics. It was widely believed that recessions were often the result of financial panics that were, in turn, caused by excessive speculation. Hence, one of the tasks of the Federal Reserve was to limit speculation. In addition, the provision of an elastic currency would also help to prevent financial panics, as would the Fed's supervision of member banks, and the centralization of member bank reserves in the Federal Reserve banks. The law of large numbers makes centralized reserves a more effective barrier against failure than are reserves kept individually by each bank.

Another goal of the Fed was to stabilize interest rates. It was to eliminate, or at least reduce, the pronounced seasonal swings in interest rates that occurred before 1914, and to avoid the sharp interest-rate increases that would accompany periods of financial stringency and panics.

All in all, the initial goals of the Fed were those that seemed reasonable to a small-town merchant in 1913, rather than those that an economist would now set for a central bank. Full employment had not yet been "invented"—there were not even any unemployment statistics. Although in the 1920s there were several attempts to add a price-stabilization goal to the Federal Reserve Act, these attempts failed. But, while we now set other goals for the Fed, these 1913 goals have not completely disappeared. We no longer have the gold standard, but the Fed still has as one of its goals the maintenance of the exchange rate of the dollar. The Federal Reserve is still opposed to excessive speculation—a dislike of speculation being one of the few Puritan ideas not challenged in the turmoil of the 1960s. And, of course, the Fed is still concerned about interest rate fluctuations. And even the real-bills doctrine lives on in occasional admonitions to banks to avoid "unproductive" loans.

But in its early years the Fed had little chance to aim at these goals. Shortly after it got its organizational problems under control, World War I broke out. Belligerents increased their purchases in the U.S., which resulted in a large gold inflow. The Fed could not offset the impact of this gold inflow on bank reserves since it did not yet have enough securities to sell.

In April 1917 the United States entered the war. It has been said that in every war, truth is the first casualty. It might be added that sound ideas on finance are the second. During the war the Fed became subservient to the Treasury Department since it lacked the political influence needed to do otherwise. Its policy was therefore dominated by the Treasury's goal of raising funds. Two-thirds of the government's wartime expenditures were financed by borrowing (in World War II it was only about half). The Treasury wanted to borrow at below-market interest rates and to rely on patriotic appeals to sell its securities. But to provide a material incentive too, individuals could borrow from banks to buy government securities at an interest rate equal to the rate they received on these securities, that is at no net interest cost. Banks could borrow from the Fed on their promissory notes secured by Treasury certificates at an interest rate below what the banks earned on these Treasury certificates. Hence, they had an incentive to borrow, and at that time there was not yet a tradition against borrowing from the Fed. With these incentives it is not surprising that the Treasury could sell its securities, but it is also not surprising that this was highly inflationary. And with this policy continuing after the war, so did the inflation. In the postwar expansion, March 1919 through January 1920, the wholesale price index rose by about 50 percent, and the GNP deflator by about 10 percent.

Although the Federal Reserve was concerned about the inflation, it was more or less willing to go along with the Treasury's inflationary policy until late 1919. Then in January 1920 it raised the discount rate applicable to commercial-paper borrowing (as opposed to borrowing secured by Treasury securities) from 4½ percent to 6 percent. This is the sharpest jump in the discount rate that has ever occurred. In June 1920 this discount rate was raised to 7 percent where it stayed despite the recession until May 1921. The reason for this highly restrictive policy was the Fed's concern about the inflation and about the decline in the Federal Reserve banks' gold reserve ratio. The Treasury, far from opposing the restrictive policy, favored it because it too was concerned about the gold-reserve ratio.

The month, January 1920, in which the Fed shifted to such a highly restrictive policy was also the month of the upper turning point of the business cycle. The ensuing recession started mildly, but then turned into one of the deepest recessions in American history, though fortunately it was short-lived. Real GNP declined by 12 percent and, due to a sharp price decline, nominal GNP fell by 31 percent. Clearly the Fed is not to blame for *initiating* this recession since the upper turning point occurred before the restrictive policy could have become effective. However, Milton Friedman and Anna Schwartz have blamed the Fed for the subsequent severity of the recession. Other economists have explained the downturn by such factors as the breaking of a speculative boom, the occurrence of supply ceilings, the decline in exports and in the deficit, and by a dynamic instability of the economy resulting from the peculiar combination of monetary and fiscal policies that were undertaken.

It is obvious that, at the very least, the adoption of a severely restrictive policy just when the economy turned down was not what was needed. And the continuation of this policy despite a major recession was hardly a proud moment for monetary policy. As Professor Wicker (of Indiana University) has said:

> The Federal Reserve System maintained the same high rate schedule throughout one of the sharpest deflation periods in U.S. cyclical experience. By June 1921 wholesale prices had fallen 56 percent of the level attained in May 1920, and the money supply had declined 9 percent. Unemployment at its peak exceeded 10 percent of the civilian labor force. In retrospect, judging by present standards, no other period in Federal Reserve history furnishes a better example of mistaken monetary policy.[1]

What were the reasons for this blunder? One reason was the fall in the Fed's gold reserve ratio. But this was probably more a public justification for the policy than its main reason since the Fed had the legal power to suspend the reserve requirement. Instead, the main reason was probably the inadequacy of the Fed's underlying monetary theory. Thus, it did not understand that once high interest rates have succeeded in breaking the boom they should be lowered again to ameliorate the ensuing recession, and not be kept at a high level that would continue to exert deflationary pressures. This is so particularly when sharply falling prices raise very substantially the expected real interest rate corresponding to a given nominal rate.

Moreover, the Fed held to the pernicious real-bills doctrine. It believed that it should provide additional reserves only temporarily for seasonal needs or to prevent panics, and did not realize that it should provide additional reserves to take care of secular growth. It therefore wished, in accordance with the real-bills theory, to eliminate the money creation that had resulted during the war from discounting notes secured by government securities. It also wanted to reduce the seeming excessive liquidity of bank

---

[1] Elmus Wicker, *Federal Reserve Monetary Policy 1917–1933* (New York: Random House, 1966), p. 47.

portfolios that resulted from banks holding large amounts of government securities. In addition, the Fed believed that a deflation was desirable to offset the previous inflation, and it feared that an easy money policy would lead to excessive speculation. In general, the Fed did not think that it should manage the money stock with a view to cyclical factors and to secular growth in the demand for money. Rather it saw its function as increasing reserves only temporarily to stabilize interest rates on a seasonal basis and during potential panics.

Other Events in the 1920s

In the 1920s Federal Reserve policy was influenced by several considerations. One was the gold standard, though there is still considerable dispute about how important this really was in determining Fed policy. European countries, particularly Britain, were trying to return to the gold standard. To ensure that Britain had enough gold for this, the Federal Reserve wanted low interest rates in New York so that gold would not flow from London to New York. Later on, the Fed was concerned with preventing a gold outflow that could drive the United States off the gold standard. However, at the same time, the Fed was also paying attention to domestic conditions, and in particular, there was now some emphasis on the quantity of credit rather than just on the quality of credit. There was some attempt at countercyclical monetary policy, and the Fed began to pay attention to the level of output as well as to prices.

The great stock-market boom of 1928–29 placed the Federal Reserve (which, at that time, did not have the power to set margin requirements) in a difficult position. It wanted to raise the discount rate to stop the boom, but this would have raised interest rates to business when business conditions did not call for higher rates. Moreover, it would have stimulated a gold flow from London to New York, thus hurting British stabilization policy. Hence, the Fed decided to try indirect pressures, that is, moral suasion and the denial of discounts to banks making excessive loans for security purchases. The New York Bank, which, unlike the Board, actually had to carry out this policy, was strongly opposed to it because it thought that denial of discounts was an interference with the privileges of member banks. It wanted to raise the discount rate instead. Finally, in August 1929 the discount rate *was* raised. But by then the stock-market boom was so strong that the relatively small increase in the price of credit did little to curb it, while it did hurt ordinary business borrowing. Had the Fed raised the discount rate earlier, instead of relying on indirect pressures and moral suasion, it might have succeeded in stopping the stock-market boom before it gathered steam. Not surprisingly, the Fed has been heavily criticized for this policy. Thus Milton Friedman and Anna Schwartz wrote of the Federal Reserve System's actions:

The issues involved in that dispute have recurred several times in the System's history. Whenever the System has felt that external circumstances limit the extent to which it can push quantitative measures of monetary restraint, it has resorted to qualitative measures. It has done so partly in the hope of thereby escaping the external constraints, partly—even though it knew or strongly suspected that this hope was largely in vain—in order to demonstrate to itself and others that it was taking some action to meet clear and pressing problems. This was the story not only in 1929 but also . . . in 1919 when supposed Treasury needs imposed the external constraint. It was to be so again . . . in World War II and in the postwar period up to 1951. . . . And in all three episodes, any hopes placed in direct pressure and "moral suasion" were doomed to disappointment.[2]

The Great Depression

The Great Depression is by far the most serious and dramatic episode in our economic history. Its correct interpretation is important, not only for evaluating the Federal Reserve's record, but also for an understanding of how the economy reacts to monetary policy. At the time, and since then, many economists have argued that the 1930s demonstrated that, at least during a major depression, monetary policy is ineffective. It was the experience of the Great Depression, as well as the publication of Keynes's masterpiece in 1936, that swung economists away from the quantity theory toward the income-expenditure approach. On the other hand, monetarists point to the Great Depression as showing exactly the opposite: the immense damage a perverse monetary policy can do, and hence, the great power of monetary policy. It is therefore not surprising that of all the historical episodes discussed in this chapter only the Great Depression is still the subject of an extended debate among economists. We will therefore discuss this episode at much greater length than any of the others.

Before turning to the rival explanations here are some facts about the depression. The upper turning point was reached in August 1929, that is, a few months prior to the stock-market crash. The recession continued until March 1933 when an upswing started. This upswing reached a submerged peak, a peak that still had very substantial unemployment, in May 1937. The following recession reached its trough in June 1938. The ensuing expansion carried us into and through World War II. In the period 1929–33, net national product fell by more than one-half when measured in current prices; real net national product fell by more than one-third as did the wholesale price index. Table 27.1 shows the appalling unemployment rates as well as the GNP deflator. Note, incidentally, that despite very high unemployment, prices rose after 1933. Contrary to the impression given by many commentators, "stagflation" is not a new development of the 1970s.

---

[2] Milton Friedman and Anna Schwartz, *A Monetary History of the United States* (Princeton: Princeton Unversity Press, 1963), p. 266. Similarly, Wicker (*Federal Reserve Monetary Policy,* p. 143) refers to this episode as showing the Fed's "errors of knowledge . . . about how monetary policy works."

Table 27.1   Unemployment, Prices, and Money
1929–41

Year	Unemployment as percent of nonfarm employees	GNP deflator (1958 = 100)	Per capita nominal money stock as percent of 1929[a]	
			M_1	M_2
1929	5.3%	50.6	100.0%	100.0%
1930	14.2	49.3	95.6	97.6
1931	25.2	44.8	89.5	91.1
1932	36.3	40.2	76.2	73.2
1933	37.6	39.3	71.2	63.5
1934	32.6	42.2	77.5	69.4
1935	30.2	42.6	92.1	79.3
1936	25.4	42.7	107.5	89.8
1937	21.3	44.5	110.4	93.0
1938	27.9	43.9	104.5	90.1
1939	25.2	43.2	115.8	96.6
1940	21.3	43.9	136.4	109.0
1941	14.4	47.2	158.1	121.8

a. Money-stock data are for June of each year.

SOURCE: Stanley Lebergott, *Manpower in Economic Growth* (New York: McGraw-Hill, 1964), p. 512 (used with permission of McGraw-Hill Book Co.); U.S. Bureau of the Census, *Historical Statistics of the United States* (1976 ed.), p. 224; Milton Friedman and Anna Schwartz, *A Monetary History of the United States* (Princeton: Princeton University Press, 1963), pp. 712–16.

To some extent, price increases in the 1930s can be attributed to a government program that tried to raise wages and prices.

Turning to the monetary data, from August 1929 to March 1933 nominal M_1 fell by one-quarter, and nominal M_2 fell by more than one-third. This decline in the stock of money was the accompaniment of widespread bank failures, failures which occurred in three waves, one in October 1930, one in October 1931, and the final one, which led to the bank holiday when all banks were closed for a time, in March 1933.

Figure 27.1 shows the immediate determinants of the money stock. It shows that the decline in the money stock was not due to a decline in the reserve base, but resulted from a fall in the deposit-reserve ratio and in the deposit-currency ratio. Not surprisingly, as many banks failed, the surviving banks tried to ensure their own safety by holding more reserves, while the public tried to avoid losses by withdrawing deposits.

The discount rate fell radically in this period. It was reduced from a level of 5 to 6 percent in various Federal Reserve banks in the fall of 1929 to a level of 1½ to 3 percent in September 1931. As figure 27.2 shows other short-term rates declined sharply, too. However, in this period the rate on long-term government securities did not decline as much, and the rate on Baa corporate bonds, that is, bonds of "lower medium grade"

Figure 27.1   The Stock of Money and Its Proximate Determinants, Monthly
1929–March 1933

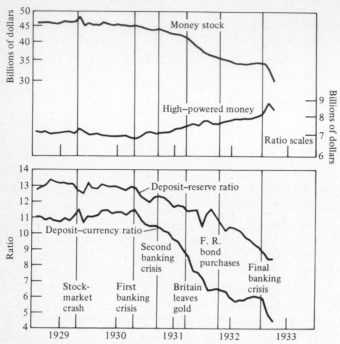

SOURCE: Milton Friedman and Anna Schwartz, *A Monetary History of the United States*
(Princeton: Princeton University Press, 1963), p. 333.

Figure 27.2   Selected Interest Rates
1927–39

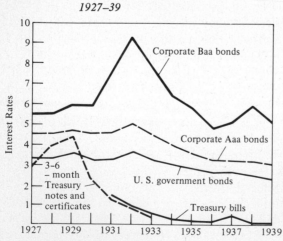

SOURCE: Thomas Mayer, *Monetary Policy in the United States* (New York: Random House,
1968), p. 219.

quality, actually rose substantially in the early part of the period, then fell, and in 1939 was not far from its 1928 level. Moreover, note that the price declines that occurred in the early 1930s meant that for these years the real rate of interest was substantially greater than the nominal rate of interest shown in figure 27.2. For subsequent years the real rate of interest was less than the money rate. But since the price level was lower in 1939 than in 1929, for the decade as a whole, the real rate exceeded the nominal rate of interest.

Federal Reserve Policy

Where was the Fed while all of this was going on? For many years after the depression it was widely believed that, on the whole, it behaved well. Right after the stock-market crash it cut the discount rate, and as figure 27.2 shows, the discount rate was kept low during most of the depression. To be sure, it was raised in 1931 when there was a gold outflow as fears developed that the United States would follow Britain off the gold standard. Perhaps this discount-rate increase could, and should, have been avoided. Apart from this, the Fed made a serious mistake in raising reserve requirements in 1936 and 1937, but it certainly cannot be blamed for the depression. This resulted from a massive collapse in the marginal efficiency of investment, and monetary policy is almost powerless in such a situation. The Fed kept the discount rate, and other short-term rates low, but business had little incentive to borrow. The Fed made reserves available, but banks simply held them as excess reserves. And even if they had not, the liquidity-preference curve was so flat at the extraordinarily low Treasury bill rates of much less than one percent that it would not have been feasible to reduce rates any further. You cannot push on a piece of string.

Although some economists—for example, Warburton and Mints—had challenged this view of monetary policy earlier, it was the prevailing orthodoxy until the 1960s, when it was powerfully challenged by Friedman and Schwartz and by Wicker. Although the Friedman-Schwartz book presents a strongly monetarist interpretation, many Keynesians have to a considerable extent accepted its interpretation of Federal Reserve policy. Given their monetarist outlook, Friedman and Schwartz placed much more emphasis on what was happening to the reserve base and the quantity of money than on interest rates.

But even as far as interest rates are concerned, they pointed out that while the discount rate and the commercial-paper rate were low during most of the depression, this was not true for the interest rates that are more important for business borrowers, for instance, the Baa bond rate shown in figure 27.2. The public, fearing further financial crises, bid up the prices of highly liquid securities such as commercial paper, thus creating an unusually large gap between interest rates on highly liquid securities and on less liquid and safe ones. Moreover, in the first part of the depression, with prices falling, the expected real rate of interest was presumably much higher than the nominal rate. Also, the discount rate, while low by historical standards, was not low relative to open-market rates, thus providing little incentive to discount. In addition, the low discount rate may not have had much significance because, as Warburton had pointed out earlier, it was accompanied by a very restrictive policy of discount administration—"the Federal Reserve authorities had discouraged rediscounting almost to the point of prohibition. . . ." [3]

But the main focus of the reinterpretation of Federal Reserve policy is not on interest rates, but on the Fed's open-market operations, or lack thereof. The Fed did not undertake large-scale open-market purchases until 1932. In fact, until then it was offsetting the expansionary impact on the reserve base that would have occurred naturally from the large gold inflow that took place as Europeans became afraid that their currencies would be devalued. Friedman and Schwartz described the policy as:

> . . . one of monetary "tightness" not "ease." During a period of severe economic contraction extending over more than a year, the System was content to let its discounts decline by nearly twice its net purchases of government securities, and to let its total credit outstanding decline by almost three times the increase in the gold stock. . . . The System's holdings of government securities plus bills bought was nearly $200 million lower at the end of July 1930 than they were at the end of December 1929.[4]

In 1932 the Fed finally undertook large-scale open-market purchases. Friedman and Schwartz suggested that the reason for this was political. Congress was considering expansionary legislation, such as a bill to pay a bonus to World War I veterans, and the Federal Reserve thought that an activist policy could reduce support for such proposals. After Congress adjourned in July these open-market purchases ceased.

Why did the Federal Reserve not adopt a more expansionary policy? Friedman and Schwartz and Wicker have suggested several reasons. One was the Fed's choice of the wrong indicators, that is its almost exclusive focus on certain interest rates (such as the discount rate), on excess reserves, and on the availability of credit, and its disregard of the decline in the quantity of money. A second reason was the Fed's failure to understand the nature of excess reserves. Although some of its officials realized that banks wanted to hold more excess reserves because the successive waves of bank failures had made banks afraid of further runs on them, the Federal Reserve persisted in thinking of excess reserves as *unwanted* reserves, that is, as reserves that banks held only because they had too few customers for loans, and had little incentive to buy securities at the prevailing low interest rates. Given the Fed's underestimate of the volume of reserves that banks wanted to hold it is not surprising that it treated the fact that banks held more reserves than they were legally required to,

---

[3] Clark Warburton, *Depression, Inflation and Monetary Policy, Selected Papers, 1945–53* (Baltimore: Johns Hopkins University Press, 1966), p. 340.

[4] Friedman and Schwartz, *Monetary History of the United States*, p. 375.

as evidence that nothing would be gained by giving banks even more reserves by open-market purchases. Hence, already in 1932, when in retrospect the pileup of excess reserves had not yet started, one Fed official wrote:

> There is another reason why you may not be able to go as fast as you might like to go, and that is this: That you run the risk, if you go too fast, of flooding the market or the banks with excess reserves faster than they can use them, or faster than is wise for them to use them. The proper and orderly operation of the open market, I think, is to create a volume of excess reserves gradually, gradually increasing them, and keeping it up constantly, and not have periods when you have got excess reserves one week and none another week.[5]

Moreover, the Fed did not consider itself under any great obligation to prevent bank failures by providing banks with the additional reserves to meet deposit withdrawals. It believed that these failures resulted in large part from the purchase of unsound earning assets, and hence were the fault of the banks. Besides, failures were concentrated among nonmember banks, who the Fed believed were not its responsibility. In addition, the failing banks tended to be small banks, and the Fed may perhaps have been influenced by the belief that there were too many small banks in any case. All in all, Wicker concludes that by 1932 "it was becoming increasingly clear that System officials did not recognize any strong obligation to maintain the solvency of the banking system." [6]

Perhaps two things should be said in defense of this dismal record. First, the advice the Fed obtained from the writings of academic economists was not good either, and, second, by no means did all Federal Reserve officials agree with the prevailing policy. The New York Federal Reserve Bank generally advocated much more expansionary policies, but it did not prevail. Friedman and Schwartz argued that a major factor accounting for the bad monetary policy was the shift of power from the New York Federal Reserve Bank to the Board of Governors, and also the illness, and subsequent death, of the New York Bank's outstanding president, Benjamin Strong, who Friedman and Schwartz believe would have carried through the right policy. However, Wicker is skeptical on both these points.

Effects of Federal Reserve Policy

How much difference would it have made had the Federal Reserve aggressively undertaken substantial open-market operations and been able to prevent bank failures in this way? There already was an unusually severe depression in 1930 before there were any large-scale bank failures. This part of the depression is not really explained well by the Friedman-Schwartz analysis. But the economy had suffered such depressions in 1908, 1914–15, and 1921, and each time had recovered within a reasonable time.

[5] Cited in Wicker, *Federal Reserve Monetary Policy*, p. 179.
[6] Ibid., p. 173.

What was unique about the Great Depression was not only its depth, but also the tardiness of the recovery. Can these characteristics be attributed to the waves of bank failures, and could the Federal Reserve have prevented these failures?

The answer to the first of these questions depends in large part upon how important the quantity of money is. It also depends upon whether there were other factors at work that caused this depression to be so severe and prolonged. And the answer to the second question, whether the Fed could have prevented the bank failures, depends upon whether banks were basically sound or whether they held too many bad assets.

On the first question, the importance of money, we have little to add at this point, having discussed this at length in chapters 12–18. But one does not have to be an out-and-out monetarist to accept a monetary interpretation of the 1930s. Between 1929 and 1931, M_1 fell by about one-quarter and M_2 by about one-third. Modern Keynesians too consider such a decline to be a disaster. To be sure, the fall in the money supply was not the only thing that happened, velocity also fell, but Friedman and Schwartz argue that this decline was not an independent factor causing the depression, but was induced by the fall in income. Hence, they say that the fall in velocity was the result of permitting banks to fail. Keynesians, on the other hand, usually do not accept Friedman's theory of velocity that underlies the calculation that velocity dropped just because of the decline in income; they stress instead the effect of low interest rates on velocity.

Yet regardless of the details of the relative movements of velocity and of money, it is clear that there was a quite extraordinary fall in the money stock. Thus, even if it turns out that there were many other factors at work that could have caused a depression, it seems highly plausible to attribute much of its persistence and severity to the great fall in the money stock.

But critics of the monetary explanation frequently argue that the drop in the money stock was only an intermediate cause and not the real (or interesting) cause. In their view, bank failures resulted from banks having acquired unsound assets, and hence could not have been prevented by expansionary Federal Reserve policy. Friedman and Schwartz, on the other hand, argue that the massive bank failures would not have occurred if the Fed had undertaken large-scale open-market purchases. In their view, any deterioration in the quality of bank assets that might have occurred in the 1920s was minor:

> If deterioration of credit quality or bad banking was the trigger, which it may to some extent have been, the damaging bullet it discharged was the inability of the banking system to acquire additional high-powered money to meet the resulting demands of depositors for currency, without a multiple contraction of deposits.[7]

[7] Friedman and Schwartz, *Monetary History of the United States,* p. 356.

Friedman and Schwartz do not merely blame the Federal Reserve for dereliction of duty, they go further and suggest that most of the bank failures would not have occurred had the Fed not existed. Prior to 1913, when massive bank failures threatened, banks would all agree to suspend currency payments for a time, while still clearing checks among themselves by paying each other in clearinghouse certificates. The public could then still use its deposits to make payments from one account to another. And banks that were temporarily short of currency and other liquid assets did not fail. But the existence of the Federal Reserve with its discount mechanism reduced the interest of strong banks in initiating—as they had usually done in the past—such a suspension of currency payments.

But how can Friedman and Schwartz blame the Fed in view of the fact that, as is shown in figure 27.3, after 1934 member banks had large excess reserves, though in no year did they amount to as much as 10 percent of deposits? Their answer is, as already mentioned, that these reserves were not "excess" reserves in an economic sense, as distinct from a legal sense. They believe that bank failures had frightened the surviving banks enough for them to want to keep a large volume of "excess" reserves. In terms of a liquidity-preference analysis, which relates bank hold-

Figure 27.3   Member Bank Excess Reserves as a Percent of Member Bank Deposits
1929–39

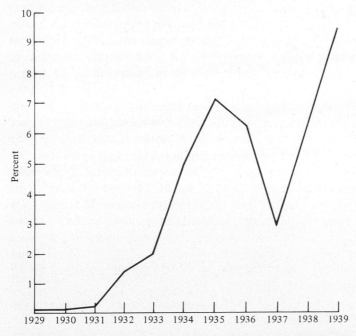

SOURCE: Thomas Mayer, *Monetary Policy in the United States* (New York: Random House, 1968), p. 220.

ings of excess reserves to the interest rate, the Federal Reserve's view was that banks were holding so many excess reserves because they had moved down the liquidity-preference curve as interest rates fell, whereas in the Friedman-Schwartz view the liquidity-preference curve had shifted outward. Hence, if the Fed had provided the banks with additional reserves, reserves beyond the level banks wanted to hold as a precaution, they would have used these reserves to expand their earning assets. Friedman and Schwartz's prime evidence for this is the way banks reacted in 1936–37 when the Fed doubled reserve requirements. The Federal Reserve did this to reduce excess reserves because it was afraid that the banks could suddenly use all these reserves to create more loans with inflationary consequences. It did not think that the reduction in excess reserves would have any *current* effect since it would still leave banks with substantial excess reserves. But instead, banks sold securities on a large scale to restore their excess reserves, thus suggesting that they were holding such a large volume of excess reserves because they wanted to, not because they could not find any outlets for their funds. However, some economists believe that the Friedman-Schwartz interpretation of the excess reserves is weak because, if banks held these reserves because they were afraid of failure, why did they wait so long to start to accumulate these reserves, and why did they hold them so long after the FDIC was set up and large-scale failures were a thing of the past?

An Alternative View

In 1976, the Friedman-Schwartz interpretation of the Great Depression was challenged by Professor Peter Temin of M.I.T., who raised many important issues. One of these is whether the observed decline in the money stock was the result of a shift in the supply curve of money, as Friedman and Schwartz claim, or the result of a shift in the demand curve for money. Suppose that the depression was actually caused by a collapse of the marginal efficiency of investment or an exogenous drop in consumption. As income declined the demand for money declined too, and so did interest rates. And a fall in interest rates can reduce the money stock by inducing banks to hold more excess reserves, and to borrow less from the Fed, and perhaps also by raising the currency-deposit ratio. Someone might then observe the reduction in the money supply, and the fall in income, and conclude that the decline in the money supply caused income to fall, whereas actually the story is just the other way around. And Temin argued that Friedman and Schwartz failed to show that the decline in the money stock was the cause rather than the effect.

In Temin's view there is no evidence that money was tight, at least in the earlier part of the depression. The per capita *real* money stock was slightly higher in 1931 than in 1929, though it did fall after that. Hence he argues that since into 1931 prices fell enough to offset the decline in the nominal money stock, it was the decline in velocity, rather than a decline in the nominal money stock, that was responsible for falling output. Furthermore, interest rates on highly liquid securities were low, which again suggests that there was no shortage of money. (However, Friedman and Schwartz explain the decline in these interest rates by a rise in the demand for highly liquid securities, which raised their prices and lowered their yields, because the public was afraid to hold less-liquid assets. In particular, banks bid up the price of commercial paper because it could be discounted with the Fed. And, as figure 27.2 shows, the yield on less-liquid and safe securities was *not* low.)

Moreover, Temin criticizes Friedman and Schwartz for not explaining the causes of bank failures sufficiently. Temin argues that part of the decline in the stock of money should be attributed to falling prices of farm products and to the agricultural distress that caused rural banks to fail. Many bank failures, Temin argues, were ultimately due to a real factor, the relative decline of agricultural prices, rather than to a monetary factor, such as Federal Reserve policy.

In addition to the rural banks, a large New York bank, the Bank of the United States, failed. Temin argues that, contrary to the Friedman-Schwartz view, this failure was due to fraud and illegal activities by the bank's management, so that the Federal Reserve could not have prevented this failure. And all of these bank failures then frightened depositors into runs on other banks. When these banks tried to meet deposit withdrawals by selling bonds, bond prices fell. This then forced other banks to write down the prices at which they carried these bonds on their books, which, in turn, impaired the capital position of many of these banks, and forced them to close.

An important issue arises here. Friedman and Schwartz blame the Fed for the depression because it was passive, and did not move aggressively through open-market operations to provide banks with the reserves they needed. They take some bank failures as a given and focus on the behavior of the Fed that allowed these failures to spread to other banks. By contrast, Temin takes the inaction of the Fed as his given and treats as the cause of the decline in the money stock those factors that initially caused some banks to fail. Hence, to a considerable extent, the protagonists are talking past each other since they are discussing different questions. Temin's work does not really vindicate the Federal Reserve.

Beyond the question of what caused bank failures, Temin accuses Friedman and Schwartz of overemphasizing what the Fed did, or rather did not do, and underemphasizing what the private sector did. Thus, Friedman and Schwartz wrote that the discount rate, while falling, was still too high because market rates were falling even faster, and they blame the resulting decline in discounting on the Fed. Temin, on the other hand, puts the blame for the decline in discounting on the falling market rates. In his view the changes in the money stock that occurred were not *caused* by the Fed merely because the Fed could have prevented them.

Temin believes that changes in the supply of money played only a subsidiary role. Thus he points to Friedman and Schwartz's concession that the first banking crisis (1930) left no pronounced imprint on the major economic indicators. In his view, the initial downturn resulted from an unexplainable drop in the consumption function (which, incidentally, is an explanation that does not fit well into Keynesian theory either), and he believes that the unique severity of the depression resulted from a whole series of factors. The most dramatic, though by no means the largest, was the stock-market crash, which, by reducing wealth, reduced consumption and caused people to reduce their financial leverage.[8] Agricultural developments (a bad harvest in the United States and a good harvest in Europe) played a role. Then there was the large unexplained fall in consumption.[9] And in the fall of 1930 when no recovery appeared, businessmen lost confidence. Then in 1931, there was an international financial crisis triggered by the failure of an Austrian bank. This endangered German banks that had lent to it and caused Germany to impose exchange controls, which limited foreign payments by Germans. And the British pound came under pressure because British banks had made large loans to German banks. This brings Temin up to 1931. "After that time the story becomes so complex and the interactions so numerous that it is no longer possible to envisage separate movements in different parts of the world." [10]

All in all, Temin has presented the monetary explanation of the Great Depression with a sharp challenge. But this is not the place to argue its pros and cons; we must hurry on to the next episode.

War Finance and Interest-Rate Pegging

During World War II, like during World War I, the overriding goal of the Federal Reserve was to finance the war, that is, to ensure that the government could borrow at low interest rates the difference between its intended expenditures and its tax receipts. And, although the monetary policy followed during World War I had hardly been beyond criticism, the policy used in World War II did not differ as much from it in substance as it did in detail. However, the postwar policies differed sharply. After World War II the Fed did not adopt a restrictive policy, and no major depression occurred.

[8] Frederic Mishkin ("The Household Balance Sheet and the Great Depression," *Journal of Economic History* 38 [December 1978]: 918–37) has argued that the stock-market decline, as well as the falling price level, reduced consumption substantially by decreasing the value of household assets, while raising the real value of household debts. Insofar as the fall in the price level, and also the failure of stock prices to recover, were due to bank failures, this is consistent with the Friedman-Schwartz conclusion.

[9] But Temin's evidence for an unexplained drop in consumption is very much open to question. See Thomas Mayer, "Consumption in the Great Depression," *Journal of Political Economy* 86 (February 1978): 139–47.

[10] Peter Temin, *Did Monetary Forces Cause the Great Depression?* (New York: W. W. Norton, 1976), p. 173.

Pegged Rates

Comparing the war periods, one difference was that despite the greater reliance on taxation during World War II, the much greater scale of the war effort meant that the deficits were much larger than in World War I. During 1942–45 these deficits amounted to nearly 30 percent of GNP, truly an immense financing burden. Another difference was that the government decided right at the start of the war to prevent any rise in interest rates, whereas during World War I a limited increase in interest rates had been permitted. The policy adopted was to "peg" interest rates by having the Federal Reserve stand ready to buy all government securities offered to it at least at par, that is, at 100 percent of face value. The level at which interest rates were pegged was the then prevailing low level of the Great Depression, ranging from ⅜ of one percent on Treasury bills to 2½ percent on long-term securities, though after the war the bill rate was allowed to rise to over one percent. The decision to maintain the currently prevailing level of interest rates was an obvious one at the time. It would not only allow the deficit to be financed cheaply, but would, most economists believed, be appropriate for the postwar period when, according to a generally prevailing view, the economy would again be depressed. It should have been obvious, but it was not, that a policy of pegging short-term interest rates much lower than long-term rates would generate trouble. If the Federal Reserve stands ready to buy long-term bonds at par, long-term bonds are in effect as liquid as short-term securities, so that everyone has an incentive to sell ⅜ of one percent Treasury bills to the Federal Reserve and hold 2½ percent bonds instead. And, eventually, the Federal Reserve did end up holding nearly all the Treasury bills in existence.

During the war there was little dispute about monetary policy, and even in the early postwar years the Fed accepted interest-rate pegging with few complaints. This was so despite the fact that this policy had an obvious inflationary potential, since it eliminated the Federal Reserve's control over the stock of money. The Fed had to provide reserves to any bank that offered it government securities in exchange. Monetary policy was therefore completely passive in the sense of being unable to curb an expansion of the money stock.

Why was such a policy more or less acceptable to the Fed? One reason was the slowness with which the persistence of the postwar inflation was recognized. Almost everyone expected a depression after the war, and it took some time for people to realize that the problem was excessive, rather than insufficient, aggregate demand. Another reason was the low repute of monetary policy, that is, the widespread belief that the Great Depression had demonstrated the unimportance of the quantity of money, and that the country should therefore rely on fiscal policy rather than on monetary policy. This belief was, of course, connected with the victory of Keynesian theory and the eclipse of the quantity theory. Still another important reason for the widespread acceptance of pegging was that, although this policy could not have prevented a vast growth of the nominal money stock *if* the public had actually demanded more money, in fact, the money stock was *not* growing rapidly; M_1 averaged trivially *less* in 1949 than in 1947. And for much of the pegging period, market forces kept the bond rate below the 2½ percent ceiling. Velocity was increasing rapidly so that even at the low interest rates that prevailed, the demand for money was low. The pegging policy meant that had the demand for money increased rapidly the money supply could have exploded, but it never did. All the same, as time went by, the Fed became more and more uneasy about its lack of control.

The Debate

And with the outbreak of the Korean War in 1950, the Federal Reserve's restiveness turned into open opposition. As long as pegging was taking place it was the Treasury and not the Fed that was, in effect, conducting monetary policy since the Fed was bound to support the Treasury's decisions about interest rates. Now with renewed war, accompanied by inflation (the consumer price index rose by 11 percent between June 1950 and December 1951), the Fed wanted to reclaim monetary policy. A great debate took place. The Treasury argued that a small rise in interest rates would be insufficient to restrain aggregate demand significantly, while a large increase could throw the economy into a recession. The Fed replied that somewhere between too little and too large there must be "just right," which was open to the rejoinder that nobody knows where this "just right" level of interest rates is.

The Treasury pointed out that a rise in interest rates would, given the large size of the public debt, raise government expenditures significantly, but the Federal Reserve's supporters replied that the Treasury gets back in higher taxes approximately half of its interest payments. Apart from these technical issues there were also some broader ones. President Truman had populist suspicions of high finance and wanted interest rates to remain low in the belief that this would help the average citizen. And the Treasury held the bizarre notion that if government bond prices fell below par this would reduce confidence in the United States government. Besides, there was the danger that the Korean War would turn into World War III, with massive financing needs that the Treasury did not want to meet at high interest rates. This does not mean that the Treasury and administration were oblivious to inflation; rather, instead of monetary policy, they wanted to rely on fiscal policy and price controls (price controls were then in effect). The Fed has less faith in price controls. In addition, the Treasury believed that a major decline in government security prices could have some terrible (though rather vague) effects on economic stability, a fear that subsequently turned out to be groundless.

In its dispute with the Treasury the Federal Reserve had substantial support among academic economists, and, what is much more important, also in Congress. It therefore felt powerful enough to challenge the Treasury.

In August 1950 it allowed some short-term securities to fall slightly below par. A major row occurred, but was resolved in March 1951 by an agreement known as the "Accord" under which short-term interest rates were allowed to rise moderately and long-term rates very slightly. The Fed was relieved of the burden of complete pegging, but, de facto, agreed to prevent government securities from falling much below par. This Accord lasted only until after the 1952 election when the incoming Eisenhower administration restored the Fed's full freedom.

The Mid- and Late-1950s

After receiving its freedom the Federal Reserve followed a restrictive policy in terms of maintaining a low growth rate for the money stock. From 1952–53 to 1959–60, M_1 grew only at a 1.9 percent rate per annum and M_2 at a 3.2 percent rate. But since velocity was rising, GNP grew at a faster rate, and the price level rose at an average rate of 1.4 percent. About half of the total price rise in the period occurred in the short span, 1957–59. From June 1957 to June 1958 the consumer price index rose 2.9 percent, which was considered an unacceptable inflation rate at the time. Since unemployment was not abnormally low in 1957 by the standards of those days, this led to a rather inconclusive debate about cost-push inflation. This debate was intensified in 1958 when, despite a 6.8 percent unemployment rate, a very high rate for those days, prices continued to rise.

The Fed was much criticized at the time for following a too restrictive policy, and many economists thought that the administration's fiscal policy was also too restrictive. By hindsight one possible interpretation of this policy is that the Fed was "drying out" the economy and eliminating the inflationary expectations that had developed during the post–World War II and Korean War inflations. If so, this is a fascinating experiment deserving of much discussion. However, it will not get this discussion because we know much too little about how expectations changed, or even whether the Fed was actually trying to change them. But certainly one *possible* explanation of the fact that during the long expansion of the 1960s there was very little inflation until 1965, is that the Fed set the stage in the 1950s by creating the expectation that prices would be stable.

Another characteristic of Fed policy in this period was a change, albeit small, in its targets. It started to place *some,* though still quite limited, emphasis on the growth rate of the money stock, rather than looking *just* at credit conditions and interest rates. Countercyclical monetary policy, "leaning against the wind" as a favorite Fed phrase puts it, received more emphasis too. But, as we discussed in chapter 23, this policy was mistakenly undertaken by using money-market conditions and free reserves as its indicators and targets. This prevented the Fed from having the desired effects on the money stock and on income, so that its policy was actually not countercyclical.

Bills Only

One big dispute brewing at the time concerned the type of securities the Fed should use in its open-market operations. Under the "bills-only" policy (or "bills preferably" as the Board of Governors preferred calling it), the Fed decided to confine its open-market operations at normal times to Treasury bills. The benefits claimed for this are, first, that it lets the market determine the structure of interest rates; that by not dealing in securities of various maturities, the Fed leaves the determination of the term structure of interest rates to the market, and deals only in those securities, Treasury bills, that are closest to money. Most of its open-market operations are defensive ones that merely try to offset the effects of operating factors (such as float) on reserves, and hence the Fed does not want them to affect relative interest rates. Second, such a policy protects government security dealers who can incur large losses (relative to their capital) if the Fed in its open-market operations causes a fall in the prices of longer-term securities they hold in their inventories. The Fed was afraid that unless it adopted the bills-only policy, government security dealers would leave the market or cease holding large inventories. In addition, an issue of the distribution of power within the Fed was also involved. Under the previous policy of dealing in securities of various maturities the Federal Reserve Bank of New York (which strongly opposed bills only) had considerable leeway in deciding what securities to deal in. Under bills only it lost this power.

Critics of the bills-only policy were angry at the Fed for placing so much emphasis on the welfare of government security dealers. They argued that by operating only in bills the Fed's open-market operations would have only little—and long-delayed—effects on the long-term interest rate, and hence on investment. From a monetarist standpoint, on the other hand, the bills-only policy was unimportant since what matters is the volume of bank reserves, and not whether open-market operations make credit more available in the long-term, or short-term, security markets. In any case, as will be explained below, the bills-only policy was abandoned in 1961. However, most, though not all, open-market operations are still conducted in short-term securities.

The Last Two Decades

The following decade, which witnessed the longest expansion in United States history (February 1961–December 1969), saw a number of important developments for monetary policy. (The relevant data are shown in the endpaper inside the front cover.) Since these events occurred primarily in the second half of the decade, it is this period that we will now discuss.

The Second Half of the 1960s

One important development was an increasingly severe balance-of-payments problem. The dollar was overvalued and large balance-of-payments deficits were the norm. It should have been clear, but for a long time was not, that unless the United States was willing to curb the growth rate of the money stock—and accept the unemployment that would result in the short, and perhaps not so short, run—the dollar would *have* to be devalued. But instead of taking such a drastic step, various palliatives were tried. One was to abandon the bills-only policy. With the economy in a recession the Fed wanted to follow an expansionary policy. But if it had bought a large volume of Treasury bills, it would have forced short-term interest rates down, and with short-term interest rates lower in the United States than in other countries there would have been a capital outflow that would have worsened the balance-of-payments deficit. But since international capital flows respond more to differences in the short-term rates than in long-term rates the Fed still felt free to try to lower long-term rates. It therefore bought longer-term securities rather than Treasury bills. This policy has sometimes been described as "operation twist," that is, a conscious attempt to twist the interest-rate term structure. But apparently it was more an attempt by the Fed to avoid lowering short-term interest rates. Not much twisting was actually done, and there is no evidence that it had any effect.

Exchange control was tried too in a modest way; a special tax was levied on interest earnings on foreign securities to eliminate the gains from buying foreign securities with a higher yield than domestic ones. And there were restraints on large-scale capital exports by banks and other firms.

Moreover, it is likely that, had it not been for the balance-of-payments problem, the Federal Reserve would have followed a more expansionary policy. But it is hard to know whether balance-of-payments considerations really were important in making monetary policy. While qualitative evidence suggests that they played some role, much of the statistical evidence does not.

In the 1960s there also occurred a major internal change in the Fed; a change that was informal, and does not show up in any law or regulation. This is its increased professionalization. For the first time since 1936 there was a professional economist on the Board of Governors, and eventually economists became a majority on the Board and also among Reserve bank presidents. Moreover, there occurred a great improvement in the professional quality of the staff of the Fed's research departments, and research started to deal less with the details of banking and to focus more on macroeconomic analysis. Thus, in the MPS model, which we discussed in chapter 24, the Board of Governors now has one of the country's major macroeconomic models, while the St. Louis Federal Reserve Bank is a leading center of monetarist thought. And formal forecasts are now presented at

FOMC meetings, which was not the case in the 1950s. One can only speculate about the reasons for this increased professionalization. One reason may have been that the Fed wanted to react to the criticism it received from Keynesians as well as monetarists, both by seeing whether this criticism was actually justified, and by marshaling evidence in defense of its policies. This required a strong research staff. Second, economics became much more quantitative during the 1960s as the econometrics revolution took hold, and this made economists more useful to the Fed. Third, the public's esteem for economists rose, so that it became natural to appoint economists to the Board, and to spend more money on economic research. (Economics became much more professional also in other government agencies in the 1960s.)

A second—again informal—change was the rise of monetarist influence in the Federal Reserve. There was a shift in its targets from money-market conditions to at least somewhat greater emphasis on monetary targets, a development we discussed in chapter 23.

In mid-1966 Regulation Q became important. Although the Board of Governors had set a ceiling on time-deposit interest rates since the 1930s, this ceiling had not been very effective since the Fed generally raised it when interest rates rose high enough for it to become constrictive. But in 1966 not only was the ceiling not raised, but for certain types of time deposits it was actually lowered. This made it hard for banks to sell certificates of deposit (CDs). At the same time a ceiling was imposed on interest rates paid by federally insured nonmember banks, savings and loan associations, and mutual savings banks.

Another very important development was that, as the endpaper figure shows, the growth rate of the money stock increased substantially in the second half of the decade, particularly in 1967 and 1968. The reason for this was the large deficits that resulted from the Vietnam War and the "Great Society" programs. In principle, a large deficit does not have to result in a high money growth rate. But unless the Fed "monetizes" the debt by buying government securities, the increased flow of government securities into the market raises interest rates and crowds out private expenditures. Both of these are highly unpopular, and hence, whenever there is a large deficit and nominal income rises, the Fed is under pressure to increase the growth rate of the money stock in the rather questionable belief that it will limit the rise in interest rates. This rapid growth of the U.S. money stock in the late 1960s proved to be inflationary, as did the deficit itself.

This period also saw two examples of sharply restrictive policies. The first of these, sometimes called "the crunch," occurred in 1966. As former Fed Governor Maisel explained it:

> The 1966 experience was a rude awakening. The degree of inflationary demand from the expanding Vietnam War was greater than United States monetary policy had attempted to cope with since 1920. The decision to fight inflation vigorously caused high costs elsewhere. A choice became necessary. It appeared that there was a limit to what traditional monetary pol-

icy could do. . . . In 1966 it became apparent that the Federal Reserve could not neglect the side-effects of decreased money and credit, and higher interest rates. Three of these side-effects reached critical dimensions with relation to (a) the composition of demand and output, (b) the maintenance of viable financial markets, (c) the protection against large-scale failures of financial institutions.[11]

The Fed's response to the gathering inflationary pressure was strong, even brutal. The growth rate of M_1 had been 4.6 percent in both 1964 and 1965; in the second half of 1966 it was cut to zero. As the endpaper shows, interest rates rose sharply. In addition banks gave preference to their steady business customers and cut back on their mortgage loans.[12] Moreover, the net flow of funds into savings and loan associations fell to one-quarter of the previous year's level. A sharp drop in residential construction occurred that was widely blamed on tight money. Signs of financial strains appeared. There was a danger of widespread failures of savings and loan associations. Moreover, the restrictive Regulation Q ceiling prevented banks from "buying" deposits as they had been able to do previously. Rightly or wrongly, the Council of Economic Advisers concluded that in August 1966 "monetary policy was probably as tight as it could get without risking financial disorder."[13]

By October 1966 it was apparent that an economic slowdown was more likely than a continuation of the excessive expansion, and monetary policy was eased. Though a slowdown did occur in 1967 it was not severe enough to be a full-blown recession. The Fed, after stepping heavily on the brake, had released it in time. And it had learned from this episode not to prevent banks from buying reserves through CDs. Hence, Regulation Q was eventually removed from large CDs, and large banks—if willing to pay the price —were able to obtain the reserves and deposits held by other banks.

The economy expanded in 1968, and a number of economists thought that the Fed should adopt a less expansionary policy because of the rise in prices. But Congress had finally raised taxes in 1968 and the Fed was afraid of "overkill," and hence allowed the money stock to rise rapidly.

1969 to 1980

As the endpaper shows, the Fed became very restrictive again in 1969 and tried to break the inflation, even at the cost of risking a recession. In December 1969 there was a downturn with a trough in November 1970.

[11] Sherman Maisel, *Managing the Dollar* (New York: W. W. Norton, 1973), pp. 63–64.

[12] For a few months in 1966 the Fed used moral suasion to get banks to allocate more funds to the mortgage market, and to give banks a material incentive as well, it announced that those banks that held down their business loans would be allowed to borrow from the Fed for somewhat longer periods than other banks. This use of the discount window to affect the allocation of bank credit was a sharp break with the discount policy generally followed in the postwar period.

[13] *Economic Report of the President, 1967* (Washington, D.C.: 1967), p. 60.

This cycle too was accompanied by severe financial strains, and if the Fed had not acted promptly as a lender of last resort there could well have been a financial panic. The money market was very tight, which is hardly surprising given the Fed's restrictive policy, and the United States incursion into Cambodia had created great political tensions. By June 1970 stock prices had declined by more than 20 percent below their 1969 average.

In that month the Penn Central Transportation Company, one of the country's major corporations, filed for bankruptcy. Shock waves spread throughout the financial market. Penn Central's credit rating had been high enough for it to have issued commercial paper. Lenders were now asking themselves who would be next, and were worried about the safety of commercial paper issued by other firms. There were rumors that Chrysler Corporation would not be able to sell new issues of commercial paper to replace the maturing ones, that is be able to "roll over" its commercial paper. And this would have made lenders afraid to buy the commercial paper of some other firms. Firms issuing commercial paper frequently arrange bank lines of credit as a back-up measure. There was now a danger that if firms were unable to roll over their commercial paper, banks would suddenly have to find the wherewithal to increase their business loans substantially, and they might not be able to honor all their lines of credit. The volume of commercial paper outstanding had risen substantially in the 1960s, probably, in part, because the Regulation Q interest-rate ceiling drove lenders into the commercial-paper market.

Fortunately, the Fed stepped in promptly, and did what a central bank is supposed to do. It calmed the money market by announcing that the discount window was wide open for banks that had to make loans to firms unable to roll over their commercial paper. In addition, it suspended the Regulation Q ceiling for certain large CDs, so that banks would be able to "buy" funds readily. In August 1970 it also lowered reserve requirements. All in all, the Fed emerged as the hero of this episode; however, a cynic might suggest that had it not been for its sharply restrictive policy in 1969, which itself was the consequence of its prior too expansionary policy, the market could have handled the Penn Central failure, so that there would have been no emergency that required heroic action.

In the early 1970s another event occurred that was just as dramatic as the incipient panic of 1970, and was to have a much longer-lasting effect. This was the collapse of the fixed exchange-rate system. As time passed the United States balance-of-payments deficits grew rapidly. Foreign central banks were forced to buy an immense volume of dollars to prevent the dollar from declining relative to their currencies. This raised the reserves of commercial banks in their own countries. Since they were unable, or unwilling, to offset this increase, a worldwide inflation occurred. There was also a great speculative capital outflow from the United States to take advantage of any future devaluation of the dollar.

Finally, the fixed exchange-rate system broke down. On 15 August 1971, President Nixon announced that the dollar was no longer convertible into gold by foreign central banks and government agencies (for private holders it was already inconvertible). The dollar, no longer having a fixed gold value, could now float relative to other currencies. The purpose of this step (and of a temporary import surcharge that was imposed) was to force other countries to agree to a devaluation of the dollar, which they did in December 1971. But this devaluation was insufficient. There was a widespread expectation that the dollar would be devalued again, and hence there was a great speculative outflow of short-term capital. And the dollar *was* devalued again in February 1973. But even this did not prove sufficient, and it became apparent that the era of fixed exchange rates was over. For a fixed exchange-rate system to work, the United States, and other major economic powers, would have had to allow balance-of-payments considerations to have precedence over the domestic aims of monetary policy. The United States for one was not willing to do this. All of this will be discussed in more detail in Part Six.

In 1971 President Nixon also imposed wage and price controls. These controls may well have helped to reduce the inflation rate temporarily, but resulted in numerous distortions. To some (substantial?) extent price controls hid rather than reduced the inflation rate since firms can respond to price controls by reducing the quality of their products. After the removal of controls in April 1974, prices rose rapidly; the consumer price index rose by over 12 percent that year. The removal of price controls was not the only cause: oil prices had been raised by the OPEC cartel, and other raw material prices had risen due to poor harvests in much of the world and to the coincidence of booms in many major industrial countries. Whether or not price and wage controls had any long-run effects on prices, or merely hid and delayed price increases until controls were removed, is a question on which economists still disagree. Controls probably encouraged the Federal Reserve to generate a rapid growth of the money stock since it hoped that these controls would limit the inflationary dangers of such an expansionary policy. With unemployment having risen substantially, the Fed had an obvious incentive to adopt an easy policy, though some cynics suggested that its expansionary policy resulted also from a concern about the outcome of the 1972 election.

Turning to banks, as we discussed in chapter 4, during the 1960s banks had expanded rapidly as they discovered liability management. We described also how in the 1970s the roof fell in on such "go-go" banking when several large banks failed, particularly the United States National Bank of San Diego in 1973 and the Franklin National Bank in 1974. In addition, many banks were absorbing unusually large losses on loans they had made to Real Estate Investment Trusts (REITs).

The collapse of Franklin National and United States National, as well as of a German bank, Bankhaus Herrstatt, which had been very active in the foreign-exchange market (and at its collapse owed large sums to American banks), generated much fear. For example, a two-tier CD market developed so that the very largest banks sold their CDs at a lower rate than other banks, reflecting in good part a belief that the FDIC would not allow a really large bank to fail. More important was that, in general, lenders tightened their credit standards so that many borrowers with lesser credit ratings could not sell securities and had to use stand-by lines of credit at their banks. Not only did this increased demand for bank loans result in a sharply rising prime rate, which reached 12 percent in July 1974, but, also some potential borrowers were simply refused credit. Fortunately, during the summer, as it appeared that no disaster would occur, the market settled down again, and thus a possible panic was avoided.

While this was going on in the financial sphere, what was the rest of the economy doing? The endpaper shows the dismal answer. The most severe recession since the 1930s occurred in 1974–75, with the unemployment rate reaching 8.5 percent in 1975. At the same time the inflation rate remained high, the consumer price index rising by 7 percent in 1975. The term *stagflation* entered the public's vocabulary.

Due to the high inflation rate the Fed adopted a very restrictive policy in the second half of 1974. This policy was much criticized. The inflation rate had risen in 1973–74 in part because of "supply shocks" and the Fed seemed intent to partially offset these shocks by putting downward pressure on other prices. Keynesians objected that while monetary policy should perhaps be used to fight demand-pull inflation, it should not be used to fight that part of the inflation that resulted from such obvious cost-push factors as bad harvests and the rise in oil prices. Specifically, they opposed adopting a sharply restrictive policy in the midst of a recession. Monetarists also objected to changing the money growth rate so rapidly. The Fed caught it from both sides.

Defending the Dollar

Not only was the inflation rate high in the recovery from the 1974–75 recession, but it was accelerating as the Fed then allowed the money stock to grow at a high rate. Largely as a result of this, in late 1978 the dollar fell rapidly on the foreign-exchange market, and there was a danger that some foreign central banks, as well as private holders, would now dump their dollar holdings, thus accelerating the dollar's fall. In response, on 1 November 1978, President Carter followed up his earlier call for "voluntary" wage and price ceilings with a series of measures. He announced that the United States would borrow $30 billion dollars of foreign currencies it could use to support the dollar in the foreign exchange market. More fundamentally, President Carter asked the Federal Reserve to impose a special reserve requirement on large CDs, and to raise the discount rate by a full percentage point, an unusually large increase. For a president, particularly a Democratic president, publicly to ask the Fed to raise interest rates was an extraordinary step with a symbolic significance that far transcends the importance of the increase in the discount rate.

But what matters are not dramatic gestures, but the consistency with which they are followed up. The initial follow-up was strong; between October 1978 and March 1979 the *M-1B* annualized growth rate fell to 6.5 percent from the 9.7 percent it had been in the July–September 1978 period.

However, it did not last long. In the second quarter of 1979 the money growth rate started to rise sharply and stayed very high for the rest of the year. It seemed that the Fed had lost control over it. This, by itself, might not have caused a radical change in policy, but two other events occurred. First, the inflation rate accelerated with the consumer price index rising at double-digit rates. Second, as a result of this rise in the inflation rate and in the money growth rate, foreigners lost confidence in the dollar and the dollar fell sharply (by 5½ percent between mid-June and early October) in the foreign-exchange market. The policy changes of the previous November had bought less than a year's respite, and the dollar now was back on square one.

One can make a reasonable case that the Fed faced disaster. It seemed unable to control the money stock. A rapid rise in the prices of gold (by $100 an ounce between late August and early October) and of certain raw materials suggested that the high inflation rate was generating a belief that the only safe thing to do was to dump dollars and buy commodities. Obviously, if such a belief spreads it results in much more inflation. In addition, there was a danger that the dollar would plummet on the foreign-exchange market as foreigners saw that the Fed's action of November 1978 had failed. Foreign central banks held a large volume of dollars they could dump on the market to cut their losses.

In October 1979 the Fed therefore took another dramatic step. Despite the fact that it was widely believed that the economy had already entered a recession the Fed adopted a highly restrictive policy. It raised the discount rate by another percentage point to 12 percent, and it imposed an 8 percent reserve requirement on increases in certain managed liabilities of banks, such as borrowings of Eurodollars, funds obtained through repurchase agreements, federal funds borrowed from nonmember banks, and large CDs with maturities of less than a year. (These are *marginal* reserve requirements that apply only to increases in these liabilities above their previous level.) And what will probably prove to be much more important in the long run, the Fed announced that it would try to get a better grip on the money stock by allowing the federal funds rate to fluctuate much more.

The October 1979 policy initiative succeeded in stopping the threatened collapse of the dollar on the foreign-exchange market. In addition, the Fed succeeded in bringing the money growth rate down, though subsequently it was still high relative to the midpoint of the Fed's target ranges. Nominal interest rates rose sharply. The Treasury bill rate, which had been 8.68 percent in September 1979, rose by March 1980 to 15.53 percent, and the prime rate, which had averaged 12.90 percent in September 1979, was 20 percent in April 1980 at many banks. However, with prices also rising rapidly these extraordinary nominal rates represented much lower real interest rates. Unlike in 1966 and 1969 the Fed did not produce a "credit crunch" by restricting the availability of funds. Although some banks did respond by rationing credit more severely, rationing by price rather than by availability was more prominent than it had usually been during restrictive policies.

Despite its success in the foreign-exchange market, domestically the October 1979 program failed. Financial markets did not believe that the Fed would succeed in controlling inflation. Had they anticipated that the Fed would succeed, long-term bond prices would have risen, and long-term interest rates would have fallen along with the anticipated inflation premium that is contained in interest rates. But instead, bond prices fell!

And, at least in the short run, the market was right. In three months, December 1979–February 1980, the inflation rate as measured by the consumer price index spurted at an annual rate of 17 percent. Credit markets became demoralized. Given the danger that the inflation rate was getting completely out of control, and that interest rates would therefore zoom in the future, how could market participants determine what interest rates to set on new bonds? They couldn't. As a result the long-term bond market as well as the mortgage market in large part suspended operation for a time, and even short-term markets, such as the commercial-paper market, ceased to function properly. Some major banks were reported to have difficulties at that time in selling large CDs. And the high interest rates threatened thrift institutions, particularly mutual savings banks, with losses as customers shifted out of relatively low interest time deposits into money-market certificates, which have interest rates linked to the Treasury bill rate.

By March 1980 the October 1979 policy was in shambles domestically. Relief from inflation and high interest rates had been hoped for as a result of a widely anticipated recession, which finally started in January 1980. Strange as it may seem many people were actually hoping for a recession. It is reported that when Federal Reserve Chairman Volcker was asked whether monetary and fiscal tightening would result in a recession, he replied, "yes, and the sooner the better." [13]

It was clear that something had to be done, and on 14 March 1980 President Carter announced a multifaceted program to break inflationary expectations. In response to the widely accepted view that the inflation was in considerable part due to federal deficits he revised the fiscal year 1981 budget he had just recently sent to Congress to eliminate the deficit it showed, and even made some very small cuts in the ongoing fiscal year 1980 budget. But the ongoing recession will in all probability result in a large deficit all the same.

The Fed's role in the new program was both to tighten conventional monetary policy, and to operate a newly instituted credit-allocation program. In its 6 October 1978 policy initiative the Fed had imposed a special

---

[13] Clyde Farnsworth, "Washington Watch," *New York Times,* 17 March 1980, p. D2.

reserve requirement on increases above a certain base in a bank's acquisition of managed liabilities, such as Eurodollars and large CDs with a maturity of less than one year. These reserve requirements were now tightened substantially, and under the president's authority to invoke credit allocation, they were extended to large nonmember banks. The Fed also imposed a 3 percentage point surcharge on top of the discount rate charged large banks that borrow frequently, the prevailing 13 percent discount rate being very low compared to other short-term interest rates.

The unconventional part of the program was the imposition of a fairly mild form of credit allocation. Banks as a whole were told to let their loans expand by no more than 9 percent, with banks that were growing slowly in any case, or had low capital and liquidity ratios, staying well below this ceiling. This part of the program is "voluntary," but banks must surely have been afraid that the Fed is implying the old army saying, "you don't have to, but you'll be sorry if you don't." Since large and medium banks frequently come to the Fed for permission to undertake mergers or to start holding-company affiliates, the Fed is not exactly powerless.

To cut consumer spending, which was running at a very high rate, the Fed, under its credit allocation powers, also imposed a 15 percent reserve requirement on unsecured consumer loans, such as credit-card borrowing and charge-account borrowing. This reserve requirement applied not only to banks, but also to other financial institutions, as well as to retailers. Finally, a 15 percent reserve requirement was also imposed on increases in the assets of money-market funds. This was done to reduce the shift of deposits out of banks and thrift institutions into money-market funds. The purpose was to protect not only banks and thrift institutions, but also mortgage borrowers and small businesses that borrow from small banks and thrift institutions. Since the money-market funds buy the CDs and bankers' acceptances primarily of large banks, they tend to drain funds away from small banks towards large banks.

But these new March 1980 policies were soon phased out as the economy went into a recession. Despite the Fed's October 1979 commitment to focus on the money growth rate rather than the federal funds rate, in the first six months of the recession which started in January 1980 the Fed kept the money growth rate low, which suggests that it is still willing to let the money stock behave procyclically in order to control the federal funds rate.

How Much Has the Fed Learned?

This excursion into history shows that the Federal Reserve has learned some things from past experience. It has definitely learned to be a lender of last resort, and to take aggressive action to avoid financial panics. Were it faced today with a sharp decline in the money stock, such as occurred in the 1930s, it would surely undertake massive open-market operations.

Similarly, if it were to adopt a sharply restrictive policy in the same month as a really major cyclical downturn, as happened in 1920, it would probably reverse its policy more rapidly unless the ongoing inflation rate was very high. How much it has learned from the bond-pegging episode is harder to say because the exigencies of wartime finance leave few options. But should a similar situation arise again it is unlikely that it would try to peg as lopsided a term structure as it did during World War II.

Thus, it is clear that the Fed has learned to avoid many of its past mistakes, but this does not necessarily mean that its policy has improved; it may be making new mistakes now.

Moreover, one could argue that while the Fed has learned to counter potential deflations by acting as a lender of last resort in a crisis, it has in recent years become much too soft on inflation. Many economists blame much of the inflation of the late 1960s and the 1970s on the Fed's too expansionary policy. And they strongly object to the erratic changes in the money growth rate that have occurred.

In any case, the really important question is not whether the Fed has learned anything from its experience, but whether it has learned enough to be able to operate an effective countercyclical policy. In our view the historical record does not provide a clear-cut answer to this question.

Summary

In this chapter we have looked at past monetary policy. After discussing the Fed's initial ideas we showed how it financed World War I, and then dealt with its role in the 1920–21 recession. After a brief glance at the rest of the 1920s we turned to the Great Depression. We discussed at some length the Friedman-Schwartz interpretation, which blames the Federal Reserve for the extraordinary magnitude of this depression, and then took up Temin's criticism of this interpretation.

We then dealt with the bond-pegging episode of World War II and the immediate postwar years. From there we turned to the Fed's rather restrictive policy of the 1950s, and then discussed its bills-only policy. We then took up several events that occurred in the 1960s: various attempts to maintain the fixed-exchange-rate system, the increased professionalization of the Fed and its shift of emphasis towards aggregates, the firm application of the Regulation Q ceiling, the sharp increase—and then decrease—in the growth rate of the money stock, and the resulting "crunch."

The 1970s started out with a dramatic episode as the Penn Central failure threatened to unloosen a financial panic. More important was the collapse of the fixed exchange rate system in 1973. Wage and price controls, accompanied by a high monetary growth rate, were tried for a time, but a substantial inflation occurred. Three dramatic attempts to rescue the dollar on the foreign-exchange market and to reduce the inflation rate occurred in the October 1978–March 1980 period. All in all, this historical study shows that the Fed has now learned that it must prevent financial panics, but while avoiding the mistakes it made in the prewar period, it may have made other major ones.

QUESTIONS AND EXERCISES

1. Use the description of monetary policy in recent issues of the *Economic Report of the President* and the Federal Reserve *Annual Report* to bring the discussion of this chapter up to date.
2. "In the Great Depression the Federal Reserve did all it could reasonably have been expected to do." Discuss.
3. "Prior to World War II the Federal Reserve usually did the wrong thing." Discuss.
4. "There has been little real improvement in the conduct of monetary policy. What looks like improvement is merely that the Fed, instead of being too soft on unemployment, as it used to be, is now too soft on inflation." Discuss.
5. What do you think has been the Fed's biggest mistake in the postwar period?
6. For what action does the Fed deserve the most credit in the postwar period?
7. Discuss the ways in which World Wars I and II were financed.
8. What were the ideas with which the Fed started out? To what extent, if any, were they responsible for the Fed's actions in 1920?
9. Take one issue in the dispute between the rival interpretations of the Great Depression given by Friedman and Schwartz and by Temin and write an essay on it.
10. What do you think is the most effective argument used by (1) Friedman and Schwartz and (2) Temin in their discussions of the Great Depression?

FURTHER READING

BRUNNER, KARL, ed. *Contemporary Views of the Great Depression.* Amsterdam: Martinus Nejhoff, 1981. A series of important articles on the Great Depression.

FRIEDMAN, MILTON and SCHWARTZ, ANNA. *A Monetary History of the United States.* Princeton: Princeton University Press, 1963. A classic. The chapter on the Great Depression has been published separately as *The Great Contraction.*

MAISEL, SHERMAN. *Managing the Dollar.* New York: W. W. Norton 1973. An important source for the history of the Fed in the 1960s.

MAYER, THOMAS. "Money in the Great Depression." *Explorations in Economic History* 15 (April 1978): 127–45. A critique of Temin's criticism of Friedman and Schwartz.

PIERCE, JAMES. "The Political Economy of Arthur Burns." *Journal of Finance* 24 (May 1979): 485–96. A very good survey of monetary policy in the 1970s.

POOLE, WILLIAM. "Burnsian Monetary Policy: Eight Years of Progress?" *Journal of Finance* 24 (May 1979): 473–84. Another very good survey of monetary policy in the 1970s.

TEMIN, PETER. *Did Monetary Forces Cause the Great Depression?* New York: W. W. Norton, 1976. A major response to Friedman and Schwartz by a leading economic historian.

TOBIN, JAMES. "The Monetary Interpretation of History." *American Economic Review* 55 (June 1965). A response to Friedman and Schwartz by a leading monetary theorist.

U.S., EXECUTIVE OFFICE OF THE PRESIDENT. *Economic Report of the President,* Washington, D.C. Each issue carries a history of monetary policy in the previous year.

WICKER, ELMUS. *Federal Reserve Monetary Policy 1917–1933.* New York: Random House, 1966. A very thorough piece of historical research.

28

Alternative
Monetary Policies

Chapter 26 dealt with some very serious criticisms of discretionary monetary policy while chapter 27 suggested that it is far from obvious that the Fed has been a stabilizing influence in the past. This leads naturally to the question of what is the alternative. This chapter discusses the main alternative, a fixed money growth rate, as well as some other monetary policy stances that are popular.

Rules Versus Discretion

A number of economists, of whom Milton Friedman is the most prominent, have advocated that instead of trying to counteract the business cycle, the Federal Reserve should ensure that the money stock grows at a constant rate. To the supporters of this stable growth-rate rule, keeping the money stock growing at *some* stable rate is much more important than the particular rate that is chosen.[1] They believe that a stable growth-rate rule would result in a relatively stable rate of change of the price level. Whether this rate is positive, zero, or negative is not as important as that it be stable—and hence predictable. As was discussed in chapter 21 the unfavorable results of inflation are largely due to its being unanticipated. If everyone knows with certainty that inflation will proceed at a, say, 10 percent rate, all incomes would be adjusted for it, and institutions, such as tax laws, could be adapted, so that most of the disadvantages of inflation would then disappear.

Before looking at the specific arguments for, and against, the rule, there are several characteristics of the rule that should be kept firmly in mind. First, it is a second-best policy. Friedman and other supporters of the rule do

---

[1] Some versions of the rule choose a zero growth rate, that is, a constant *stock* of money, and others would allow the money stock to rise at the same rate as the population, but not rise with increased productivity. Increased productivity would then show up as falling prices. This continually increasing purchasing power would mean that the public is earning an imputed yield from holding currency, and hence would have no incentive to spend valuable resources to economize on its currency holding.

not claim that it would give us perfection. They believe that even with a monetary growth-rate rule the country would still experience some fluctuations in output. But, they argue, these fluctuations would be less severe than the ones now experienced, since currently the net destabilizing effects of monetary policy are added to the fluctuations that are inherent in the economy. They therefore advocate the use of a monetary growth-rate rule as the best that can be done under present conditions.

Second, since the main argument for a stable growth rate is that at the present stage of our knowledge about monetary policy we can do no better, it follows that one might advocate the rule as a temporary device until more is learned about monetary policy. And indeed, Friedman has suggested that eventually the United States may want to return to discretionary monetary policy.

Third, the adoption of the rule is not necessarily a matter of all or nothing. One might adopt the rule in a partial form by, for example, telling the Federal Reserve to adhere to a given monetary growth rate, except insofar as it has to act as a lender of last resort. Or, instead of imposing a precise money growth rate, one might tell the Fed to keep the growth rate within certain bounds. Thus in 1967 the Joint Economic Committee of the U.S. Congress recommended that the Federal Reserve normally keep the growth rate of M_1 in a 3–5 percent range (later amended to a 2–6 percent range), except insofar as very special conditions require otherwise.

The Case for a Monetary Rule

The main argument for a monetary rule is that, for reasons discussed in chapter 26, discretionary monetary policy is more likely to destabilize than to stabilize the economy. Thus, the leading proponent of a rule, Milton Friedman, has stressed that the lags in the effect of monetary policy are highly variable, so that even if the Fed knew the average lag, it would not be able to conduct a stabilizing monetary policy. To be sure, this argument is vulnerable to the rejoinder that even if the Fed knows very little about the lag, so that the correlation coefficient (R) between the initial fluctuations in income and the policy-induced changes in income is very close to zero, as long as it is negative, there exists some small policy that will stabilize income to some limited extent. Only if our ignorance is so great that R is zero or positive will a *very small* policy do more harm than good.

Adherents of the rule can reply that although the Fed could in principle stabilize the economy to a very small extent *if* it would conduct its policy solely to this end, in actuality it is constantly being distracted from its stabilization task by other claims on it, so that its policy is often wrong. One example is the bond-pegging episode after World War II, another is the reluctance to let interest rates rise out of fear of what this would do to residential construction. Friedman therefore believes that the Fed has often followed a policy that is perverse from a stabilization viewpoint. A leading Keynesian, Abba Lerner, once likened stabilization policy to a steering wheel that is needed to keep the economic car on the road. Reviewing the history of monetary policy Friedman replied:

> In light of experience, the most urgent need is not to have some everpresent back-seat driver who is going to be continually correcting the driver's steering, but to get off the road the man who has been giving the car a shove from one side to the other all the time and making it difficult for the actual driver to keep it on the straight and narrow path. . . . I am tempted to paraphrase what Colin Clark once wrote about the case for free trade. Like other academicians, I am accustomed to being met with the refrain, "It's all right in theory but it won't work in practice." Aside from the questionable logic of the remark in general, in this instance almost the reverse of what is intended is true. There is little to be said in theory for the rule that the money supply should grow at a constant rate. The case for it is entirely that it would work in practice. . . .[2]

More generally, in a debate with Franco Modigliani, a leading Keynesian supporter of discretionary policy, Friedman stated:

> My major difference of opinion with Franco is in two respects: First, with his assumption that he knows how to accommodate [changes in the need for money] (or that I do, for that matter, or that anybody does); and second with the assumption that if in fact you adopt a policy of accommodation, Franco Modigliani will be twisting the dials. . . . Once you adopt a policy of accommodating to changes, there will be all sorts of changes that he and I know should not be accommodated, with respect to which there will be enormous pressure to accommodate. And he and I will not be able to control that. . . . The real argument for a steady rate of monetary growth is at least as much political as it is economic; that it is a way of having a constitutional provision to set monetary policy which is not open to this kind of political objection.[3]

Beyond the problem of lags and political pressures there is also, as discussed in chapter 26 the more fundamental and basic rational-expectations case against discretionary policy. In a more positive vein, another argument for the monetary rule is that it would generate confidence. If businessmen know that the money stock will increase at a given rate, they know what to expect and can confidently plan ahead, instead of having to watch continuously for changes in monetary policy. Finally, the rule has also been advocated on the broader philosophical ground that it is desirable to reduce government interference by replacing the "rule of men" by the "rule of law."

The Case against the Rule

But these arguments favoring a monetary rule have been accepted only by a minority of economists. First, many economists doubt that the lag

[2] U.S., Congress, Joint Economic Committee, *Employment, Growth and Price Levels, Hearings* (Washington, D.C.: 1959), p. 615; Milton Friedman, *A Program for Monetary Stability* (New York: Fordham University Press, 1960), p. 98.

[3] Milton Friedman and Franco Modigliani, "The Monetarist Controversy: A Seminar Discussion," *Economic Review* (Federal Reserve Bank of San Francisco) supplement, Spring 1977, pp. 17–18.

of monetary policy is really so long and variable that countercyclical policy is likely to be destabilizing. It is generally agreed that the lag makes countercyclical policy less effective, but does it reduce its effectiveness to zero? This is a tough, technical question. Second, many economists, while disappointed with the Fed's past policies, are not disillusioned, and believe that in the future it will conduct a more successful stabilization policy. Third, the rational-expectations case against countercyclical policy is probably accepted by only a distinct minority of economists because of its assumption of a high degree of wage and price flexibility.

The monetary growth-rate rule is also criticized for ignoring the occurrence of major supply shocks to the economy. For example, in 1973 when the oil cartel and poor harvests raised oil and food prices, the Fed had the *choice* of validating these price increases by raising the monetary growth rate, or keeping the monetary growth rate constant, so that the increased prices of food and oil would exert downward pressure on prices in other sectors. Under a rule the Fed would not have had this choice.[4]

Moreover, are the proponents of the rule right in asserting that a stable money growth rate would generate a stable trend of prices? Are the growth rates of velocity and output really that stable? If not, there would be some fluctuations in prices. A related argument is that if the rule is set to aim at price stability, and if velocity then grows at a rate lower than expected or potential output at a faster rate, high employment would require falling prices. Would firms be willing to cut prices rather than output? To be sure, eventually firms would become accustomed to cutting their prices every year, but it may take many years of unemployment and excess capacity to overcome downward price inflexibility, and to make workers accept money-wage cuts. On the other hand, if the rule results in inflation because velocity is growing faster or output less, eventually the inflation will be fully anticipated, and hence do little damage. But it takes time until expectations adjust, and until all contracts have expired, or have been renegotiated to take account of the inflation. Hence, if the rule results in inflation, even at a steady rate, it would do serious harm for a time.

This raises a nasty problem. Suppose one decides to adopt a monetary rule. How does one get there? Does one incorporate the existing inflation rate into the rule by setting the monetary growth rate accordingly, or does one bring the inflation rate down first at the cost of unemployment?

Another problem with the rule is the danger of evasion. After the Civil War when a tax was imposed on state bank notes, banks turned to checks. If

---

[4] Rather surprisingly the Fed responded to the rise in food and oil prices by adopting a restrictive policy in the second half of 1974. This suggests that it did not use its freedom from a restrictive monetary growth rate very effectively. However, one study found that the results of this policy were better than those that would have followed from adherence to a monetary rule. But it could not take into account that the adoption of a rule would have changed the public's expectations, and hence its behavior. See Roger Crane, Arthur Havenner, and James Barry, "Fixed Rules vs. Activism in the Conduct of Monetary Policy," *American Economic Review* 68 (December 1978): 769–83.

the growth rate of money is limited, near-monies may take over more and more of the work of money, so that the monetary growth-rate rule would become irrelevant. But with respect to the deposit component of the money stock this would not be much of a problem once Regulation Q is repealed, if the Fed would pay interest on required reserves. Deposits would then pay an interest rate that (after taking account of free services) does not differ much from the interest paid on highly liquid securities. There would still be a temptation to find substitutes for currency since it does not pay interest, but if the inflation rate is low, so that the interest rate is also low, this would probably not be an insuperable problem. A more serious problem might perhaps be that the Fed could evade a monetary growth-rate rule if it wants to. It could let the money stock grow faster by fostering the development of items like automatic transfer accounts, overnight repurchase agreements, and other devices described in chapter 11. Many economists object to a monetary rule because it seems too rigid. But it could also be criticized for being too loose.

In addition, there is the fact that a monetary rule would require the Federal Reserve to ignore all targets other than the money stock. For example, it could not act to moderate swings in the exchange rate and in interest rates. While many economists would welcome this, others believe that the goals the Fed would have to relinquish to adopt a rule are important goals.

And the argument that the rule would reduce government interference has drawn the response that this interference is not so terrible. Then, there is the question of the political feasibility of adherence to a rule. If the rule is adopted, wouldn't it be abandoned as soon as interest rates fluctuate sharply, or the unemployment rate rises substantially? Furthermore, the late Jacob Viner has argued that:

> In the economic field important rules affecting important social issues have in fact been extremely scarce, and to the extent that they have had a substantial degree of durability this has been largely explicable either by the fact that they evolved into taboos, or ends in themselves, and were thus removed from the area of open discussion and rational appraisal, or by the tolerance of widespread evasion. The most conspicuous instances of economic rules with a substantial degree of durability were the prohibition of lending at interest and the maintenance of fixed monetary standards in terms of precious metals. The most enthusiastic advocate of rules can derive little comfort from the availability of these historical precedents.[5]

Some Possible Compromises

Given these arguments for, and against, the monetary growth-rate rule, it is not surprising that some economists have looked for a compromise position. One compromise has already been mentioned, giving the Fed, not

[5] Jacob Viner, "The Necessity and Desirable Range of Discretion to Be Allowed to a Monetary Authority," in *In Search of a Monetary Constitution,* ed. Leland Yeager (Cambridge: Harvard University Press, 1962), p. 248.

a single-valued target, but a range, say, 4–6 percent for *M-1B,* and perhaps allowing it to move outside this range under special circumstances. Such a rule, and for that matter even the fixed rule, would not require new legislation or formal announcement. The Fed could simply adopt a money-stock target and stick with it.

Another possible compromise is to adjust the monetary growth rate each quarter to offset the changes in velocity and in potential output in the most recent quarter, or quarters, for which data are available. This would prevent the drift in the price level that would result if the long-term trends in velocity or potential output differ from what was assumed in setting up the rule.

Still another compromise is known by the inelegant name of "semi-rules." These are rules, not for a constant monetary growth rate, but for a constant reaction to changes in income. For example, the Fed could announce as its policy an equation that relates the growth rate of the money stock to the rate of change of income in the recent past. Some studies using both an earlier version of the MPS model and the St. Louis model have shown that, *if* either of these models is a correct description of the economy, there exists such a semirule that would have performed better than a constant monetary growth rate.[6] But these studies have two great weaknesses. First, by assuming that the lag of monetary policy in each individual case is equal to the average lag, they assume away a good part of the case for the monetary rule, and, second, as discussed in chapter 26, the adoption of a rule would change the public's expectations, and thus the way it acts. Hence, even if the MPS model or the St. Louis model were absolutely true descriptions of how the economy functioned at the time they were constructed, they would *perhaps* be misleading guides to how the economy would function once a monetary rule were in effect.

All in all, the issue of whether the Fed should continue using discretionary monetary policy, a growth-rate rule, or a semirule is far from settled.

The Monetarist Position

Support of a monetary growth-rate rule is a major characteristic of monetarism. Franco Modigliani has stated that this is *the* basic issue dividing monetarists and Keynesians, since nowadays Keynesians agree that money is a highly important variable.[7] However, this may go a bit too far. There are probably some economists who support a monetary rule, but do not consider themselves monetarists, and besides, Keynesians generally still attribute *less* importance to changes in the money stock than do monetarists.

[6] See J. Phillip Cooper, *Development of the Monetary Sector, Prediction and Policy Analysis in the FRB-MIT-Penn Model* (Lexington, Ky.: Lexington Books, 1974), ch. 4.

[7] Franco Modigliani, "The Monetarist Controversy; or, Should We Forsake Stabilization Policy?" *American Economic Review* 67 (March 1977): 1–19.

Moreover, there is much more to monetarism than just a preference for a stable money growth rate. In chapter 17 we discussed briefly six attributes that characterize monetarist theory: changes in the money supply are the dominant factor driving money income, a particular view of the transmission process, the stability of the private sector, the irrelevance for the determination of nominal income of the allocation of demand among various sectors, focus on the price level as a whole rather than on individual prices, and a preference for small models.

In discussing monetary policy we have, so far, looked at three other monetarist propositions: use of the money stock rather than the interest rate as the proper target of monetary policy (together with the belief that the Federal Reserve can control the money stock), the use of some measure of reserves rather than the short-term interest rate as the indicator of monetary policy, and support of a monetary growth-rate rule. Three remaining policy propositions serve to round out a set of twelve propositions that constitute a description of monetarism. One is that there is no useful trade-off between unemployment and inflation since the Phillips curve is in real terms. Probably most Keynesians agree that *ultimately* there exists little or no trade-off between unemployment and inflation, but believe that there is such a trade-off for a long enough time to be usable for stabilization policy. Second, monetarists are more strongly opposed to unanticipated inflation than are Keynesians, and are *relatively* less concerned with unemployment. Finally, monetarists usually favor free-market processes, and oppose government intervention, more than Keynesians do. These characteristics of monetarism can generally be related to the monetarist's tendency to take a long-run point of view and to put less emphasis on immediate effects.

All of these monetarist propositions are connected. For example, if most of the historically observed fluctuations in nominal income are due to changes in the money growth rate rather than to variations in velocity, then a stable money growth rate seems a "good thing." (One proviso, however: suppose that velocity has been fairly stable in the past only because the Federal Reserve met changes in the demand for money by changing the money supply correspondingly, so that interest rates, and hence velocity, did not change. If so, adoption of a stable money growth-rate rule need not reduce income fluctuations, because it will make velocity more variable in the future.)

Moreover, if, in the absence of fluctuations in the money growth rate, the private sector is stable then countercyclical monetary policy is not needed. Similarly, someone who wants a stable monetary growth rate obviously wants the Federal Reserve to use a money-stock target. In addition, if one looks at the price level as a whole, then, as discussed in chapter 16, cost-push inflation seems less of a danger, and hence there is less need for the Federal Reserve to adopt the policy of increasing the money stock to maintain high employment despite rising prices. Besides, if there is no usable trade-off between unemployment and inflation, then there is one less thing that stabilization policy could potentially do. A monetary growth-rate rule also eliminates the danger that the Federal Reserve will shift to an inflationary policy, and it gets rid of one type of government interference.

But this does not mean that one can accept the monetary growth-rate rule only if one accepts all the other monetarist propositions too. Suppose, for example, that there are long and unpredictable lags in the effects of monetary policy, or that there is irresistible political pressure on the Fed, or else, that the rational-expectations criticism of discretionary policy is correct. If any of these conditions prevail, then the monetary growth-rate rule would be preferable to discretionary policy.[8]

The Countercyclical Policy Position

Only a minority of economists support a monetary growth-rate rule. The majority believe that stabilization policy can succeed. This does not mean that they brush aside the difficulties created by lags, political pressures, and rational expectations. They believe that these factors may create difficulties that do reduce the effectiveness of stabilization policy, but do not eliminate its effectiveness altogether. While in their view stabilization policy will be misdirected from time to time, on the average, it will do *some* good. And this, they believe, is fortunate because the private sector generates considerable fluctuations that the government has to offset. This does not mean that, in the absence of stabilization policy, we would again experience a depression as severe as that of the 1930s—this was clearly a unique event in U.S. economic history. It also does not mean that there is no mechanism that eventually eliminates large-scale unemployment or stops an inflation. Eventually, the real balance effect restores high employment or stops an inflation, but "eventually" can be an intolerably long time. Hence, monetary or fiscal policy is needed. While some economists would put more stress on monetary policy, others prefer to rely more on fiscal policy. We will now present both cases.[9]

The Case for Monetary Policy

Monetary policy has a substantial advantage over fiscal policy. This is that it can be changed much faster since this does not require congressional action. Moreover, monetary policy has the advantage of being controlled by the experts at the Fed rather than by politicians. Furthermore, one can

---

[8] A leading Keynesian, W. A. Phillips (of Phillips curve fame), concluded that due to lags stabilization policy "may well cause cyclical fluctuations rather than eliminate them" ("Stabilization Policy and the Time Form of Lagged Responses," *Economic Journal* 67 [June 1957]: 276).

[9] We do not present a criticism of them, as we do of the other viewpoints, in part because chapter 24 already contains a criticism of stabilization policy, and in part because the case *for* monetary policy is the case *against* fiscal policy and vice versa.

argue that fiscal policy usually cannot be used in a countercyclical way but follows its own imperatives. Thus, government expenditures are raised at certain times, not because aggregate demand is deficient, but because of an international crisis, or out of a desire to help certain disadvantaged people. These people are not likely to approve of postponing aid to them for a year or two until aggregate demand is deficient. Similarly, at a time when taxpayers are angry about high taxes, neither the administration nor Congress is likely to support a tax increase just because the Council of Economic Advisers predicts that aggregate demand will be excessive next year. This sort of thing is much less of a problem for monetary policy, though as complaints about high interest rates show, monetary policy is not wholly immune.

It is, of course, true that monetary policy creates some distortions in resource allocation. But these distortions are much smaller than is frequently claimed. The sharp impact of a restrictive monetary policy on residential construction is not as much of a distortion as it seems because to a considerable extent it reflects the market's reasonable response to rising interest rates. And increased lending by government credit agencies, as well as institutional reforms can ameliorate it. Moreover, since Congress is frequently unwilling to raise taxes or cut government expenditures, the alternative to a restrictive monetary policy is often inflation. And inflation too distorts the allocation of resources.

The Case for Fiscal Policy

On the other hand, the case is sometimes made for relying primarily on fiscal policy, and using monetary policy mainly in a supportive role. Such a view is natural if one thinks that monetary policy is very weak, as was widely believed from the mid-1930s until the mid-1950s. But one may prefer fiscal policy to monetary policy even if monetary policy is strong because of the effects that a restrictive monetary policy has on resource allocation. According to this argument, residential construction, an industry with a high social priority, is badly hurt, and, in addition, rising interest rates impose arbitrary capital losses on some families and firms. By contrast, the burden of fiscal policy can be allocated in accordance with the government's wishes. Suppose, for example, that as demand becomes excessive, the government wants most of the necessary cutback in spending to occur in industrial plant and equipment investment. It can accomplish this by repealing the investment tax credit. Or, if consumer durable expenditures are to be cut back instead, excise taxes can be used. Obviously, the extent to which one is favorably impressed by such arguments depends in large part on one's attitude towards economic planning.

To be sure, *at present,* fiscal policy has a long inside lag since it requires congressional action. But it is not true that Congress is *always* slow to change taxes. If there is widespread agreement about the need for tax changes, Congress can act quickly. It has passed many tax bills with little delay. And it is also not true that Congress will not raise taxes in an election year. Moreover, for tax changes, and for certain types of government expenditures, the outside lag *may* be short.

Besides, a long inside lag is not written in the stars, or for that matter in the Constitution. Congress could give the president authority to change tax rates, and to increase, or reduce, government expenditures as economic conditions change. If this is done, so the argument runs, and more generally, if the public is educated about the great importance of using fiscal policy as a stabilization tool, then the political problems that currently hinder fiscal policy will disappear. Fiscal policy can then be used as our main stabilization tool.

Monetary policy could then be relegated to the supportive role of keeping interest rates stable. Thus, if government expenditures are raised, or taxes lowered, interest rates tend to rise. It is then the Fed's task to prevent this increase in interest rates by raising the supply of money, so that rising interest rates do not partially offset the expansionary fiscal policy.

The Easy-Money Position

This is a populist position that has much support among the general public and in Congress. It is also supported by some economists, particularly those who reject "orthodox theory," such as Professor Kenneth Galbraith. It comes in various degrees of strength. For the sake of contrast with the foregoing we will summarize a strong version.

Proponents of the easy-money position usually argue that the current inflation is not due to excess demand, but results from cost-push factors, such as increasing industrial concentration, or the unwillingness of low-income groups to put up any longer with the existing distribution of income. Consequently, a restrictive monetary policy is a most inappropriate way to fight inflation. It would create a totally unacceptable amount of unemployment without bringing the inflation under control. In fact, it would make the inflation worse because firms pass on in higher prices any increases in their costs, and higher interest rates certainly raise costs.

Consequently, the government should make sure that aggregate demand is always sufficient for full employment. In other words, the Fed should decide what interest rate is low enough to generate full employment, and then provide sufficient reserves to keep it at that level. (This is a policy prescription similar to that of the real-bills doctrine discussed in the previous chapter.) Inflation should then be combated, not by the immoral policy of creating massive unemployment, but by incomes policy—wage and price guidelines, or outright controls—perhaps in combination with a policy to redistribute income so that low-income groups no longer feel it necessary to demand inflationary wage increases.

If aggregate demand is to be reduced this should be done through fiscal policy rather than monetary policy, since a restrictive monetary policy distorts resource allocation. Specifically, it discourages such socially useful investment as low- and middle-income housing, while allowing large corporations to carry out some investment projects that do little to enhance public welfare. Moreover, rising interest rates hurt the poor and help the rich.

Adherents to the easy-money position frequently want to reduce or eliminate the Federal Reserve's independence. They look on the Fed as having a deflationary bias since it is controlled by financial interests, such as banks, that profit from high interest rates.

Orthodox economists reject this easy-money position. They think that inflations are largely demand-pull, or at least contain large demand-pull elements, and that incomes policies are incapable of holding back inflation for any length of time. Furthermore, they believe that an attempt to hold interest rates below their equilibrium level would lead to ever-accelerating inflation, that easy-money proponents confuse nominal and real interest rates, and that rising interest rates do *not* contribute to inflation.[10]

Summary

This chapter tried to summarize some of the material covered in Part Five by looking at various policy prescriptions. The first one is to adopt a monetary growth-rate rule. This is an obvious response to the difficulties created for discretionary monetary policy by long and unpredictable lags, by political pressures on the Federal Reserve, and by rational expectations. We looked also at a number of criticisms that have been made of this monetary rule, such as its inability to deal with major supply shocks and the difficulty of anticipating how velocity and productivity will change in the future. But one does not have either to reject a monetary rule absolutely or accept a rigid one; various compromises, such as keeping the money growth rate normally between narrow limits, or adjusting the money growth rate in accordance with previous changes in velocity or productivity, are possible. In addition, the Fed could adopt a rule that sets, not a fixed money growth rate, but a fixed reaction to income changes.

This discussion led to a consideration of the monetarist policy prescription, which centers around a money growth-rate rule, though one can advocate this rule without being a monetarist. We saw how this growth-rate rule fits in with several other major monetarist propositions. We then discussed

[10] Even if one grants for the sake of argument that prices are entirely cost determined, and ignores the fact that a rise in some prices exerts downward pressure on other prices, there is the fact that interest rates are a very small component of total costs in most industries, and that it is hard to see why firms should pass on in the prices of their current output the higher costs incurred in financing new investment, i.e., future output. A rise in borrowing costs, unlike a rise in wage costs, affects various firms differently, depending upon how much borrowing they do. Hence, it is difficult for oligopolists to agree to pass it on in higher prices. For an orthodox model that rejects the possibility that firms raise prices to compensate for higher interest rates, see George Horwich, "Tight Money, Monetary Restraint and the Price Level," *Journal of Finance* 21 (March 1966): 15–33.

briefly the rival policy prescription that monetary or fiscal policies should be used to stabilize the economy. We then turned to the choice between monetary and fiscal policies. This choice centers essentially on two problems. One is whether it is realistic to expect Congress and the administration to change government expenditures and taxes in the required way, and to do so on time, and the other is whether one prefers the resource distribution effects of fiscal policy or of monetary policy.

The final position taken up is the easy-money approach. This approach advocates keeping the interest rate low even if it leads to a rapid expansion of the money stock, and then offsetting the inflationary consequences by incomes policy, and perhaps by fiscal policy. It strongly opposes the use of monetary policy as a weapon against inflation, both because it would be ineffective, and because it would lead to massive unemployment, as well as undesirable effects on the allocation of resources and the distribution of income.

QUESTIONS AND EXERCISES

1. Write an essay defending the easy-money position.
2. Write an essay criticizing the easy-money position.
3. Consider the monetary policies that have been followed over the last ten years. Do you think they are superior to what would have resulted from a rule?
4. List the major arguments for a monetary rule. Which do you find most persuasive?
5. List the arguments against a monetary rule. Which do you find most persuasive?
6. Formulate your own position on the issue of policy.

FURTHER READING

BRONFENBRENNER, MARTIN. "Monetary Rules: A New Look." *Journal of Law & Economics* 8 (October 1965): 173–94. An excellent discussion of the rules debate.

CONFERENCE ON ECONOMIC PROGRESS. *Tight Money and Rising Interest Rates.* Washington, D.C.: Conference on Economic Progress, 1966. A fervent statement of the easy-money position.

FRANKEL, S. H. *Two Philosophies of Money.* New York: St. Martin's Press, 1966. This very short book takes up a basic issue about monetary policy that is generally ignored.

FRIEDMAN, MILTON. *A Program for Monetary Stability.* New York: Fordham University Press, 1959. A classic statement of the rules position.

LERNER, ABBA. "Review of Milton Friedman's *A Program for Monetary Stability.*" *Journal of the American Statistical Association* 57 (March 1962: 211–20. An outstanding criticism of the monetary growth-rate rule.

MILLER, ERVIN. *Microeconomic Effects of Monetary Policy.* London: Martin Robertson, 1978. Another fervent statement of the easy-money position (but watch for the distinction between nominal and real rates).

MODIGLIANI, FRANCO. "The Monetarist Controversy; or, Should We Forsake Stabilization Policy?" *American Economic Review* 67 (March 1977): 1–19. An excellent criticism of monetarist policy prescriptions.

MODIGLIANI, FRANCO, and FRIEDMAN, MILTON. "The Monetarist Controversy." *Economic Review* (Federal Reserve Bank of San Francisco) supplement, Spring 1977. An extremely stimulating debate.

SELDEN, RICHARD. "Stable Money Growth." In *In Search of a Monetary Constitution,* edited by Leland Yeager, pp. 322–55. Cambridge: Harvard University Press, 1962. A very good survey of the rules debate.

Part Five Appendix

Debt Management

In Part Five we discussed the Federal Reserve's monetary policy. But the Treasury has some monetary powers too, such as switching its cash balances between commercial banks and the Fed. However, much more important than that is one of its powers that is in between monetary and fiscal policy, that is, debt management. Debt management refers to the Treasury's policy about the *composition* of the national debt. Quite apart from the size of the debt, which is determined by the interaction of outlays and revenues, the Treasury has to decide in what types of securities the debt should be. Since a large part of the debt is continually becoming due and being refinanced by issuing new securities, the Treasury can, in principle, bring about fairly substantial changes in the maturity of the public's holding of government securities. Since such debt management is in between fiscal and monetary policy, we will discuss it only briefly.

There are three distinct policies for managing the debt, though, of course, the Treasury can decide to adopt a bit of each. First, there is countercyclical policy. Under this policy the Treasury switches the maturity composition of the debt during the business cycle. When aggregate demand threatens to be excessive it refunds those securities that become due by issuing long-term securities, and when aggregate demand seems insufficient, it does the opposite by replacing long-term debt as it becomes due with short-term securities.

The effect of these changes in the average maturity of the debt on expenditures can be described in two ways. One is to say that an increase in the supply of short-term securities relative to long-term securities lowers the long-term interest rate and raises the short-term rate. Since private investment depends more on the long-term interest rate than on the short-term rate, the net effect of this is to raise investment. Another way of putting it is to look at quantities rather than interest rates, and to say that an increase in the public's holdings of short-term securities relative to its holdings of long-term securities increases its liquidity. Since expenditures depend, in part, upon overall liquidity, such an increase in liquidity should raise aggregate demand during the recession. And, conversely, debt management can be used to reduce demand when it is excessive.

Shortly after World War II, when economists first considered how the great wartime growth of the national debt would affect stabilization policies, such countercyclical debt management was widely thought of as a very helpful addition to our armory. But since then, disillusionment has set in. First, statistical studies that have tried to estimate the effect on expenditures of differences in the maturity distribution of the debt have come up with mixed results. The empirical evidence is far from clear that countercyclical debt management has any *significant* effects. Second, if the Treasury shifts the debt into long-term securities during the late stages of an expansion, it is in effect issuing long-term securities at a time when interest rates are high, thus locking itself into paying high interest rates for a long time. One may well argue that this is trivial compared to the importance of the stabilization objective, particularly since the Treasury receives a substantial proportion of higher interest back via taxes. Moreover, how does anyone really know whether interest rates are high? An efficient market ensures that the interest rate is set at the level that is neither "high" nor "low" relative to the available information. But the Treasury tends not to see it this way. In addition, if the Treasury issues long-term securities during the late stages of an expansion when interest rates are high, it is criticized for competing with corporations trying to issue their own securities. This is a strange argument since the very purpose of the policy is to reduce investment, but the Treasury does not like to be criticized. More legitimately, one might ask whether countercyclical debt management can do anything that could not be done just as well—or badly—by monetary policy. Hence, it is not surprising that countercyclical debt management is no longer treated as an important stabilization tool. In addition, at present the Treasury is very severely limited in the volume of long-term securities it can sell. Congress has set a completely unrealistic interest-rate ceiling of 4.5 percent for long-term securities, from which it has exempted only a small proportion of the national debt.

But the Treasury has to make a decision about what types of securities to issue, and if it rejects countercyclical debt management what other policies are there? One is interest minimization. The Treasury, like any other borrower, could issue those securities that bear the lowest interest rate. But, can such a policy be implemented? On the surface it may seem that if long-term securities carry a, say, 6 percent interest rate, and short-term securities a 5 percent rate, it is cheaper to finance by issuing short-term securities. But is this right? The expectations theory of the term structure discussed in chapter 6 suggests that over the long run it costs the same to finance the deficit via long-term and short-term securities. And the empirical evidence suggests that, while there exists a liquidity premium that makes the yield on short-term securities lower than on long-term securities even in the long run, this premium is not very large. Moreover, there is a subtle point here. There is a liquidity premium because the holding of long-term securities discourages expenditures more than does the holding of short-term securities. Now consider why the government borrows rather than just printing money. It is because borrowing discourages private expenditures, and hence is less inflationary than printing money. But if the issue of short-term securities discourages expenditures less than the issuing of long-term securities, then much of the gain from the lower interest rates on short-term securities is offset.

A third possibility is to place much of the debt into long-term securities, and keep it there regardless of economic conditions and relative interest rates, thus giving up on both the stabilization and the interest-minimization objectives. This makes consumption more responsive to interest rate changes since the longer the average maturity of the public's security holdings is, the greater is the change in the market value of the public's securities, and hence in its wealth, as interest rates change.

But the trouble with shifting the debt into long-term securities is that this is hard to accomplish. During a recession, it is unwise to do so because a reduction in the public's liquidity may reduce expenditures. But, if the Treasury tries to sell long-term bonds during an expansion, business complains about the Treasury competing with it in the market, and unfortunately the Treasury tends to heed these complaints. It is therefore not surprising that despite some attempts to lengthen the debt, the average maturity of the marketable debt has been falling fairly steadily in the postwar period. It was nine years and two months in fiscal year 1948, five years and three months in fiscal 1958, and in fiscal 1979 was 3 years and 7 months.

All in all, in the view of many economists debt management can be described as "the big engine that couldn't."

PART SIX

••

International Money and Finance

When monetary policy is analyzed in a world of more than one hundred national currencies—an open economy—the primary question is whether the major conclusions about its effectiveness in a one-currency nation—a closed economy—are seriously changed, and if so, how. A related question is how changes in U.S. monetary policy affect the exchange rate and the U.S. balance-of-payments surplus or deficit.

Changes in U.S. monetary policy may have two effects on the foreign-exchange value of the U.S. dollar and the U.S. payments balance. One is immediate and direct and operates through the relationship between investor demand for financial assets denominated in the U.S. dollar and for comparable assets denominated in the mark, the yen, the Swiss franc, and various other foreign currencies. The second effect is delayed and indirect, and operates through the impacts of changes in consumption and investment spending in the United States on the demand of U.S. residents for foreign goods and securities.

One issue in the analysis of the effectiveness of monetary policy in an international context involves the substitutability between domestic securities and foreign securities: the more perfect the substitutability, the smaller the impact of a given change in monetary policy on consumption and investment spending and the larger the immediate impact of a given change in monetary policy on imports of foreign securities. The less perfect the substitutability between domestic bonds and foreign bonds, the greater the impact of a given change in U.S. monetary policy on interest rates on dollar securities and consumption and investment spending. As U.S. income increases, U.S. commodity imports increase; at the same time, some domestic goods will be diverted to the U.S. markets from export markets. The increase in U.S. income leads to increased demand for securities, and more foreign bonds

651

may be imported and fewer domestic bonds exported as U.S. income increases.

To the extent investor views about the substitutability between domestic and foreign securities vary with whether foreign currencies are pegged to the U.S. dollar or instead float, the impact of a given change in U.S. monetary policy on domestic income depends on the exchange-rate system. If the monetary authorities abroad peg their currencies to the dollar, then the increased investor confidence that the exchange rates will not change greatly is likely to strengthen investor views about the close substitutability between dollar securities and comparable securities denominated in other currencies. In contrast, the less investors believe in their ability to predict future exchange rates, perhaps because the price of the dollar in terms of foreign currencies moves freely in response to changes in supply and demand, the smaller is the substitutability between domestic and foreign securities. Consequently, a given change in U.S. monetary policy is likely to have a larger impact on domestic interest rates and domestic incomes under a floating-exchange-rate regime than under a pegged-exchange-rate regime.

Changes in the exchange-rate regimes as the international payments arrangements have evolved in the last century are discussed in chapter 29. During the gold standard of the nineteenth century and under the Bretton Woods system of the 1945–70 period, exchange rates were fixed. During the decade of the 1970s, the currencies of major countries have not been pegged; they have floated freely. The pattern of evolution in the arrangements of international payments is discussed in this chapter.

The organization of the foreign-exchange market and the relation between spot-exchange rates and forward-exchange rates are considered in chapter 30 along with the determinants of the level of the exchange rate, and the various explanations for the large movements in exchange rates. This chapter concludes with a brief discussion of the central concepts of balance-of-payments accounting.

The structure of the banking system in an international context, with special attention to the growth of the Eurodollar market and its impact on the effectiveness of national monetary policies, is analyzed in chapter 31. The rapid growth of international banking and the expansion of banks headquartered in the major countries in the foreign markets are examined.

Chapter 32 evaluates several of the major continuing policy issues in international money and banking, including the choice of exchange-rate systems and the changes in the organization of the foreign-exchange market, and the future monetary roles of gold and the dollar as the system continues to evolve.

29

The Evolution of
the International
Payments System

The international monetary system provides a framework for financial payments so that residents of one country can make payments to residents of other countries. Such payments are necessary because importers in one country must pay exporters in other countries; either the importers must first acquire the currency of the country in which exporters live, or the exporters must, after being paid in the importer's currency, exchange it for their own.

The business and financial needs of industry and trade are served by the minimization of the costs and inconvenience of international transactions relative to domestic transactions. These costs, while generally small, have varied with changes in the international financial system. Over the last century, the international monetary system has evolved from primary reliance on gold to primary reliance on national monies to meet the demand for international reserves assets, and from pegged exchange rates to floating exchange rates. The changes in these arrangements for international payments have not been accidental, but instead are responses to economic disturbances, both monetary and structural, and to changes in political relationships among major countries.

As the institutional basis for organizing the foreign-exchange market and for producing international reserve assets has changed, so has the name given to the international financial system. Before World War I, the term *the gold standard* was applied to international financial arrangements; after World War I *the gold-exchange standard* described the mechanism. A treaty-based system known as the Bretton Woods system developed after World War II and functioned until the early 1970s. With the breakdown of the Bretton Woods arrangement in the 1971–73 period, arrangements for payments among countries have become more varied and eclectic, and no comprehensive term has been accepted as descriptive of the system.

In the most general sense, the international financial system includes the set of institutional arrangements for the organization of the foreign-exchange market, and especially the commitments of national central banks

653

about their participation in the foreign-exchange-market intervention and the assets they hold as international reserves.

The term *standard* used in the nineteenth century suggests a measure or unit of account, like a yard or a liter. National monies at that time had values that were stated in terms of gold. Changes in the volume of gold available as money had a major impact on the world commodity price level. In contrast, the term *system* has been used since World War II to imply a set of arrangements for organizing the foreign-exchange market and for producing international reserves.

This chapter first describes the three international financial systems that prevailed over nearly a hundred years. Then attention is given to the economic and political factors that may explain the evolution of the institutional features of the system, especially the rise of the United States as a dominant economic power.

The Gold Standard

The nineteenth century is frequently described as the gold-standard era, although more detailed analysis suggests that for most countries the term is more appropriately applied to the years 1880–1913 (some countries had been on the gold standard earlier). A country "joined" the gold standard when its national legislation required that its major banks and financial institutions redeem or repurchase their monetary liabilities at a fixed price, the mint parity, that indicated the value of the national currency unit in terms of a specified amount of gold. Thus at the beginning of January 1879, the United States went back on the gold standard, having abandoned it in 1863, and U.S. commercial banks were once again obliged to convert their monetary liabilities into gold at the parity of $20.67 per ounce.

The mint parities of major countries are shown in Table 29.1. Thus,

Table 29.1   Parities of Major Currencies under the Gold Standard

Country	Unit	Weight[a]	Fine-ness[b]	Value of one pure ounce	Dollar parity
United States (1879)	1 dollar	1.672	.900	$20.67	—
Great Britain (1816)	1 pound	7.988	.917	3/17/10½	$4.86
France (1878)	1 franc	.3226	.900	FF107.1	$ .193
Germany (1871)	1 mark	.398	.900	DM86.8	$ .238
Italy (1878)	1 lira	.3226	.900	IL107.1	$ .193
Netherlands (1875)	1 florin	.672	.900	DF51.4	$ .402

a. Weight of standard coin in grams.
b. Fineness of standard coin = proportion pure gold.
SOURCE: M. L. Muhleman, *Monetary Systems of the World* (New York: Charles H. Nicoll, 1894).

the British Act of Parliament of 1816 obliged the Bank of England to buy gold at three pounds, seventeen shillings, nine pence per ounce and to sell gold at the price of three pounds, seventeen shillings, ten and one-half pence per ounce: the gold was .916⅔ fine or pure. Some countries pegged their currencies to silver as well as to gold, and so they were on a bimetallic standard; monetary institutions in these countries were obliged to buy and sell gold and silver on demand at the respective parities. Managing a bimetallic system proved difficult because of the need to maintain the implicit fixed-price relationship between the mint parity for gold and the mint parity for silver. From time to time, when large new discoveries of silver or gold were made, changes in one mint parity were necessary.

Adherence to the gold standard did not involve participation in an international treaty or agreement at an international conference. Rather the choice was decentralized, and individual countries pegged their currencies to gold at somewhat different times. For most, adherence to the gold standard meant that managing a bimetallic system was too difficult.

A major by-product of commitments of individual countries to peg was a system of pegged exchange rates. Thus, given the willingness of the Bank of England to buy and sell one ounce of gold at 77 shillings and 10 pence and the willingness of the U.S. Treasury to buy and sell one ounce of gold at the parity of $20.67, the dollar price of one pound sterling could be calculated as $4.865 (once an adjustment was made for the somewhat greater purity of the British gold coin).[1]

Some central banks bought and sold gold at their mint parities. Most central banks, however, bought gold at prices fractionally below their mint parities and sold gold at prices fractionally above their mint prices. These *small differences between the mint parities and the gold buying and selling prices* were called **handling charges,** and were intended to compensate the national central banks for their costs in buying and selling gold. In addition, some central banks varied their gold selling prices modestly, increasing these prices when the demands for gold were substantial so as to discourage demand; these countries were said to be on the "limping gold standard."

Gold and International Reserves

A key aspect of the gold standard was that central banks held a large part of their international reserves in the form of gold. Some central banks, especially the Bank of England, held virtually all their assets in the form of gold, while others held a large proportion of their assets in gold and the rest in assets such as government securities denominated in the pound sterling, French francs, and their own currencies. Differences among central

---

[1] Thus if an ounce of gold equals both 77 shillings 10 pence times $\frac{.916}{.900}$ (the adjustment for differences in the proportion of pure gold in the several coins) and $20.67, then 20 shillings, or one pound, equals $4.865.

banks in the proportion of gold in their international reserves reflected differences in their business needs. One reason these banks outside Great Britain held such a large proportion of their assets in sterling was that they received sterling after selling sterling-denominated debt in London; London was then the world's principal financial center. Similarly, they received French francs after selling franc-denominated debt in Paris. Moreover, these countries were obliged to acquire these currencies to repay debts denominated in these currencies. Similarly, foreign banks were obliged to hold sterling deposits or franc deposits to make payments in London and in Paris.

Gold and Payments Imbalances

A second feature of the gold standard was that gold might flow from the countries with payments deficits—broadly, those whose imports of goods, services, and securities exceeded their exports of goods, services, and securities—to countries with payments surpluses. Gold flows were supposed to settle payments imbalances. One of the paradoxes of the gold standard was that relatively little gold was actually transferred among countries to finance payments imbalances. Shipments of gold between New York and London incurred costs of freight and insurance as well as the forgone interest on the wealth invested in gold between the date the payer acquired the gold in one country and the date the payee received gold in the second country. Consequently, traders and investors sought less costly methods to make international payments.

As an alternative to the gold transactions, a market developed in bills of exchange, which were a type of checks. These bills were issued by importers or buyers, and were IOUs indicating that payment for the purchase would be made in thirty, sixty, or ninety days. Thus, a U.S. importer with a payment to make in London might, as an alternative to shipping gold, buy a sterling-denominated bill of exchange in New York from a U.S. exporter who previously had received this sterling bill from a London importer of U.S. wheat. The U.S. wheat exporter wanted dollars, not sterling; he might sell the sterling bill in London, and buy gold to ship to the United States, or he could sell the bill of exchange to a U.S. importer and avoid the costs and inconvenience of the gold shipment. The U.S. importer would pay for the sterling bill in dollars, and so the U.S. wheat exporter would receive dollars and avoid the costs of the gold shipment.

Because the costs of shipping the bill of exchange to London were much lower than the costs of shipping the gold to London, the U.S. importer would pay a higher dollar price for the bill of exchange than for the amount of gold that would generate the same volume of sterling payments. The ability to make the London payment by shipping gold set an upper limit to the dollar cost of the sterling bills. Similarly, the ability to make a payment from London to New York by shipping gold set a lower limit to the dollar price that the U.S. exporter would accept for his sterling bills; if the dollar price were lower, the exporter would instead ship gold.

"Rules of the Game"

The third feature of the gold standard was the concept of "rules of the game"—the idea that countries with balance-of-payments surpluses would follow expansive monetary policies because the gold inflows would lead to an increase in the monetary liabilities of the central bank in the form of currency and various types of deposits. Conversely, the countries with balance-of-payments deficits and gold outflows would follow contractive monetary policies: the money supplies in these countries would decline. Commodity price levels would rise in the countries with the payments surpluses and fall in the countries with the payments deficits. Because of this change in international competitiveness, the imports of the first group of countries would rise, and their exports would fall; in contrast, the imports of the second group of countries would fall and their exports would rise. The change in national price levels would continue until balance-of-payments equilibrium was achieved. Hence international payments imbalances would be automatically self-correcting without the need for discretionary monetary policies.

This adjustment process appeared to be automatic, guided by an invisible hand. The evidence that countries followed the rules of the game is mixed. Yet countries, once they accepted gold parities, were able to maintain these parities, and so there was apparently some mechanism in the system for restoring payments equilibrium once disturbances occurred that led to imbalances.

One important aspect of the operation of the "rules of the game" should be noted: in order to maintain the fixity of one price, their gold parities, countries had to accept variations in their national price levels. Increases in these price levels occurred when a country had a payments surplus and decreases in these prices occurred when a country had a payments deficit. Without such variations in national price levels, maintaining the gold parities would have been difficult.

Gold and Commodity Prices

The fourth feature of the gold standard was the promise of commodity price-level stability in the long run. If on a worldwide basis monetary gold stocks were increasing rapidly, either because of new gold discoveries or because of new and lower cost techniques for gold ore refining, then central banks in many countries might experience gold inflows simultaneously, and the money supplies would rise in many countries at the same time. At the new and higher commodity price levels, gold mining would be more costly, the level of gold production would decline, and a damper or brake would be placed on further upward pressure of the commodity price levels.

Conversely, if the demand for gold increased relative to the supply, the commodity price levels would fall because less gold would be available for monetary purposes. At the lower price level, more gold would be mined, and eventually the decline in the commodity price level would be checked. So just as national price levels moved relative to each other to restore balance-of-payments equilibrium, so changes in the world price level would prove self-limiting. Thus, price-level stability would be achieved in the long run, if not in the short run, over a period of several decades.

The U.S. and British commodity price levels for the 1800–1950 period are shown in figure 29.1. The commodity price levels at the outbreak of

Figure 29.1   The U.S. and British Wholesale Price Indexes
          1800–1950

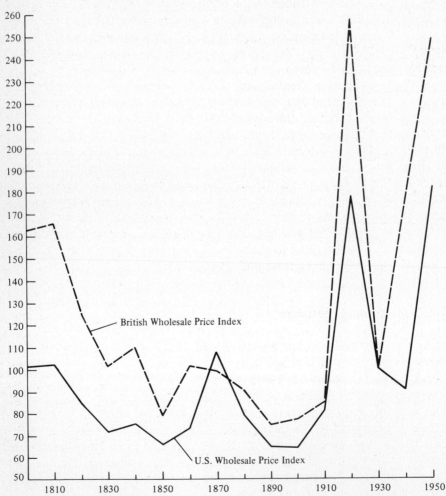

SOURCE: U.S. Department of Commerce, *Historical Statistics of the United States* (Washington, D.C., 1961), pp. 115–16; B. R. Mitchell, with the collaboration of Phyllis Dean, *Abstract of British Historical Statistics* (Cambridge: Cambridge University Press, 1962), pp. 465–78.

World War I are not very different from the price levels a century earlier. The average annual change in the price levels was small, certainly less than one percent. And there are very few years, except those at the times of major wars, in which the annual change in the price level exceeded three percent.

The attractions of the gold standard were inherent in its anonymous, automatic, self-correcting properties. Balance-of-payments adjustments could be made easily and without much fuss. Moreover, in the long run, this system promised price-level stability, even though price levels were not stable on a year-to-year basis. Perhaps the most important cause of its attractiveness was the tremendous economic growth in the international economy during the half-century before World War I, which may have been helped by national commitments to the gold standard.

The gold standard ended at the outbreak of World War I when many central banks ceased converting their liabilities into gold on demand, partly because wartime inflationary finance meant that the demand for gold would increase sharply. Yet central banks continued to maintain their pre-1913 gold parities even though they no longer were willing to deal in gold. They retained a commitment to adhere once again to their gold-standard parities when the war was over. Since increases in the money supplies were substantial, the required decreases in commodity price levels would have had to be large. Some countries, the neutrals as well as Great Britain, managed to return to their prewar parities but at considerable cost in terms of high levels of unemployment, since the needed changes in commodity price levels required deflationary monetary policies. Others eventually gave up, and adopted new parities (in effect, they increased the price of gold in terms of their currencies). In retrospect, it appears that it would have been easier and less costly to reestablish the gold standard if countries had been willing to increase the price of gold in terms of their currencies to match the increase in the price levels.

The Gold-Exchange Standard

The gold-exchange standard was developed in the early 1920s in response to an anticipated gold shortage due to reduction in the supply of gold and an increase in the demand. The anticipated reduction in the supply would result from the combination of the increase in world price levels and the concomitant increase in costs of gold production together with the fixed selling price for gold. The increase in demand would result both from an increase in the number of central banks in Central Europe due to the breakup of the Austro-Hungarian Empire and an increase in the demand for gold for monetary uses because of the increase in the world price level during and after World War I.

The possible shortage of gold was extensively discussed at two conferences sponsored by the League of Nations concerned with postwar economic stabilization, one in Brussels in 1920 and one in Genoa in 1922. Because central banks were reluctant to raise the price of gold in terms of their currencies, they sought to economize on the use of gold. The use of gold coins for private payments was discouraged; monetary gold holdings would be concentrated in central banks. Moreover, a practice that had been evident before World War I received formal recognition and approval: some central banks—especially in the "newly created" countries in Central Europe—would hold their reserves in the form of foreign exchange, such as bank deposits, Treasury bills, and bankers' acceptances, denominated in sterling, the dollar, and the currencies of other major countries instead of gold.

The intent of the gold-exchange standard was to modify only the composition of international reserves; most central banks were still supposed to follow the "rules of the game" for balance-of-payments adjustment. Countries would still maintain parities for their currencies in terms of gold. Yet there was a change: if the United States or Great Britain incurred payments deficits and the countries with the payments surpluses acquired reserves denominated in dollars or in sterling, the United States and Great Britain would not follow the rules of the game; only the countries with the payments surpluses would do so. The automatic adjustment tendencies of the gold standard were maintained, but in a somewhat more asymmetric way than before World War I.

The rationale for the development of the gold-exchange standard was that it would provide a stable framework in which national currencies would again exchange at their mint parities. Yet exchange rates were not pegged during most of the period between the two world wars. In May 1925 Great Britain pegged sterling to gold at the 1913 parity; before that, sterling, along with most of the other European currencies, floated in terms of the dollar and gold. In September 1931 Great Britain decided that maintaining the gold parity was too costly in terms of its domestic employment, so sterling was allowed to float until World War II with the difference that the British authorities intervened much more extensively in the foreign-exchange market. The 1930s was a decade of sharp changes in parities, which followed a dominolike pattern: the U.S. dollar was devalued in 1933–34, and the French franc and the Dutch guilder in 1936. The alignment of the exchange rates at the end of the 1930s was not very different from that at the end of the 1920s. The sequence of exchange-rate changes led to the "beggar-thy-neighbor" charge—countries devalued to increase their exports and employment in their export industries so as to import jobs from their trading partners. Because of the sequence of devaluations, the monetary price of gold was 75 percent higher.

The growth of international reserves denominated in sterling, the dollar, and other major currencies during the 1930s was reasonably small. At the end of the 1920s, holdings of foreign exchange accounted for 20 percent of international reserves. At the end of the 1930s this ratio was lower, because of the effective worldwide increase in the price of gold.

In the 1940s, in contrast, the foreign-exchange component amounted to 30 percent of international reserves; most of the reserves involved claims on the United States and Great Britain. Their wartime imports were financed "on-the-cuff"; thus the neutral countries in Latin America, Asia, and elsewhere added greatly to their holdings of liquid assets denominated in the U.S. dollar and sterling.

The monetary instability in the interwar period was reflected in the combination of movements in exchange rates, large unemployment, and the growth of ad hoc restrictions on international payments. This instability is sometimes associated with the tension between Great Britain, whose economic power was declining, and the United States, whose economic position was getting stronger; monetary and financial power was shifting to the United States. One aspect of this tension was that interest rates the United States felt appropriate for its domestic economy attracted funds from London, and so the British had to counter by raising sterling interest rates. In the early 1930s, there was a conflict about the appropriate value for the dollar-sterling exchange rate. The value preferred by the U.S. authorities would have increased the competitiveness of U.S. goods and reduced the competitiveness of British goods.

This shift in the balance of power from Great Britain to the United States was almost inevitable given the differences in economic size and long-term growth rates. Whether this shift could have been accommodated without the instability that actually occurred is conjectural. A number of major policy errors were committed. Even without any shift in relative economic positions, these errors would have led to some instability. One error was the unwillingness to adjust exchange parities to reflect the changes in the post–World War I price levels. The second error was the unwillingness of many countries to raise the monetary gold price to correspond with the increase in the world price level. At the lower price of gold, there was a severe shortage of international reserves. Much of the instability in the 1930s reflected the efforts of countries to earn reserves from each other.

The Bretton Woods System

Early in World War II, the United States and Great Britain took the initiative in development of economic institutions to deal with anticipated problems of the postwar period—and to avoid a repetition of monetary and trade disturbances of the interwar period. Thus, the International Bank for Reconstruction and Development (the IBRD or World Bank) was established to facilitate the postwar recovery in Western Europe; once this task was completed at the end of the 1940s, the bank focused on extending financial assistance to the developing countries. Plans for the International Trade Organization (ITO) were developed to provide a framework for reducing tariffs, for establishing commodity arrangements to limit variations in prices of basic raw materials, and to coordinate antitrust policies. The ITO never came into existence. However, the first article in its charter led to the General Agreement on Trade and Tariffs (GATT), which has been the dominant agency promoting a reduction of tariffs and other trade barriers. The third institution, the International Monetary Fund (IMF), was established to enhance stability in international payments in several ways: by providing rules for changes in exchange parities, and for exchange controls on international payments, and by acquiring a pool of national currencies that individual countries might borrow from to help finance their payments deficits.

The International Monetary Fund

The IMF, which is the institutional embodiment of the Bretton Woods system, is based on an international treaty; the system took its name from the resort in New Hampshire where the treaty was signed. Hence, this system differs sharply from both the gold standard and the gold-exchange standard in its legal aspects as the earlier systems had no international legal basis. Moreover, the Bretton Woods system was to be managed by a set of international civil servants, responsible to the board of governors from its members (usually their secretaries of the treasury or ministers of finance) and a full-time board of executive directors, essentially ambassadors from its member countries.

Each member country of the IMF was required to state a parity for its currency in terms of gold or in terms of the U.S. dollar. Most subsequent changes of the exchange parities required consultation with, or approval by the Fund.

When the Fund was established, its capital was projected to be the equivalent of $10 billion in U.S. dollars. Countries joining the IMF were obliged to subscribe to its capital; the amount of each country's capital subscription was based on a formula that included its share of world imports and its gold holdings. One-fourth of the payment of each country's capital subscription was made in gold and the remaining three-fourths in its own currency in the form of a non-interest-bearing demand note. Whenever a member country had a payments deficit, it could borrow one of these currencies from the pool held by the Fund, with the amount it might borrow geared to the size of its share in the Fund's capital or quota. About one-quarter of its quota was automatically available, and the rest was available on a discretionary basis, subject to the approval of the Fund managers. To finance these drawings, the Fund would cash part of the non-interest-bearing demand notes. For example, in 1956, at the time of the Suez crisis in the Middle East, Great Britain borrowed nearly $2 billion from the Fund. In the Fund's terminology, Great Britain "drew" or bought dollars from the Fund with sterling, with the consequence that the Fund's holdings of non-interest-bearing dollar deposits declined while its holdings of sterling increased. The Fund obtained the dollars by cashing part of its non-interest-bearing demand note at the U.S. Treasury. Great Britain paid interest to the Fund, with the interest rate based on the size of the borrowing in relation to its quota, and the length of the period of the loan. When Great Britain repaid the loan, it repurchased its sterling with dollars or some other currency acceptable to the Fund. The gold held by the Fund could be sold to a member to obtain its currency.

Three other features of the Bretton Woods system merit attention. One was its position on exchange controls, various types of licenses, special tariffs, and other devices to limit foreign payments; the Fund rules sought to eliminate the use of exchange controls on payments for goods and services like shipping and tourism, although members were to be allowed to retain such restrictions during the postwar reconstruction period. Members could maintain restrictions on transactions in securities, such as stocks and bonds, for an indefinite period.

The Fund rules also provided that the IMF might declare a currency "scarce in the Fund" if the amount of that currency some members wished to borrow exceeded the Fund's holdings of that currency. IMF members would then be entitled to apply discretionary exchange controls on their payments to that country, which might force an appreciation of that country's currency. The scarce-currency clause was never invoked, even though some currencies were scarce in the Fund.

Special Drawing Rights

The Fund's Articles of Agreement provided that the ability of a member to borrow would not be conditional on its approval of the member's economic and social policies. Over the years, however, the Fund management has taken the view that credit should be extended if there is a reasonable prospect that the member country could resolve its balance-of-payments problems. By 1980 the capital of the Fund was the equivalent of $50 billion, with the increase a result of increases in quotas. Two important institutional innovations, one in the early 1960s and the second in the late 1960s, complemented the increases in IMF quotas as a way to increase the funds available to the IMF or the supply of international reserves. To alleviate a possible shortage of currencies in the Fund, the General Arrangements To Borrow was attached to the Fund structure in 1963; this agreement formalized the terms on which the Fund could borrow the currencies of member countries, so the Fund would have more funds to lend to member countries with payments deficits.

A major modification in the late 1960s involved the establishment of Special Drawing Rights (SDRs), a new international reserve asset. Ten billion dollars of SDRs were produced in three years, through a form of international open-market operation; each member country received newly produced SDRs in proportion to its share of total IMF quotas. Each member country could then use SDRs to buy foreign currencies from other members or from the Fund. For example, if Great Britain had a payments deficit, it might sell some of its holdings of SDRs to the U.S. Treasury to get the dollars to use to support sterling in the foreign-exchange market, or instead it might sell SDRs to the Fund to get dollars or marks or some other national currency. In addition, SDRs began to develop some characteristics of a unit-of-account, and some countries began to state the parities for their currencies in terms of SDRs, just as, at earlier dates, they had stated their parities in terms of gold and then the U.S. dollar.

During the 1950s and 1960s, international trade and payments grew rapidly, and exchange controls adopted by countries in Western Europe in the 1940s on international payments were reduced. For the major industrial countries, the increase in national incomes was very large, so that the contrast between the post–World War I and post–World War II eras was sharp.

One interpretation was that this boom in national incomes and international trade reflected the success of the Fund structure, and especially the orderly arrangement both for changes in exchange rates and the reduction in exchange controls. Indeed, one of the surprising features of the 1950–70 period was the infrequency of changes in exchange parities of major currencies. Thus sterling was devalued once, the French franc was devalued twice, while the German mark was revalued twice and the Dutch guilder once; the parities for the Japanese yen, the Swiss franc, the Italian lira, and the Belgian franc were not changed. A possible explanation of the stability was that the United States provided a stable framework for the growth of national incomes abroad by maintaining a relatively stable price level. According to this view, the growth of the international economy reflected the underlying economic stability of the major countries.

The irony of the IMF system was that the IMF rules were established to avoid too frequent changes in parities; the problem, however, was that changes in parities were infrequent, and, alternative means of adjustment such as deflating or inflating income were considered too expensive to national objectives. Payments imbalances were extended because there were no longer any "rules of the game" for balance-of-payments adjustment: countries were committed to their domestic full-employment policies. There was no agreement or understanding about whether the countries with the payments deficits or those with the payments surpluses should take the initiative to reduce extended payments imbalances. The reluctance to change parities reflected that the countries with deficits believed that devaluations would be viewed as evidence of the failure of economic policies, while the surplus countries believed that the persistent imbalances reflected the inflationary policies of the deficit countries.

The Fund's successes and failures are closely linked to the successes and failures of U.S. economic policy. When the U.S. inflation rate was low, the Bretton Woods system worked. The United States incurred small but persistent payments deficits. Until the late 1960s, deficits largely reflected the demand of other countries to increase their holdings of gold and other international reserve assets, rather than the overvaluation of the U.S. dollar.

As U.S. economic policies became less successful—as the U.S. inflation rate increased in the late 1960s—the U.S. payments deficit became larger than could be readily explained by the demand of other countries for payments surpluses and international reserves. The Fund was virtually powerless to effect a change in the alignment of exchange rates of the major countries, either by inducing a revaluation of the currencies of the surplus countries or a devaluation of the U.S. dollar. As long as international payments imbalances were those of smaller industrial countries, the Fund had been useful in inducing the return to payments equilibrium. But when the imbalances invaded the largest industrial countries, the Fund mechanisms proved ineffective. With the increase in the inflation rates in the major countries in the 1970s, a move to floating exchange rates became inevitable because countries could no longer successfully maintain their parities. The Fund rules on exchange parities became obsolete. And with the explosion in the growth of international reserves in the 1970s, the SDR mechanism seemed irrelevant in meeting the need for international reserves, and the amount of reserves produced by the International Monetary Fund relative to the total of international reserves declined.

In the early 1970s, the Fund charter was modified to accommodate the adoption of floating exchange rates by the major industrial countries—these practices were, in fact, in violation of treaty commitments. The purpose of the modification was to attempt to develop a set of rules affecting exchange-market-intervention practices to reduce the likelihood of competitive intervention practices that were costly to the interests of their trading partners.

The Switch to Floating Exchange Rates

When the Bretton Woods system was established, the U.S. international economic position seemed supreme. There was considerable concern about a perpetual dollar shortage—that Europe's desire to spend dollars would exceed its ability to earn dollars at *any* exchange rate, so that Western Europe would have a persistent payments deficit. Even though the 1949 devaluations immediately led to a deficit in the U.S. payments balance and a surplus in that of Western Europe, the concern with a dollar shortage remained for much of a decade.

The story of the U.S. payments balance from 1950 to the present can be segmented into three stages. In the first, which runs from 1950 to the mid-1960s, the annual U.S. payments deficits remained small, and largely reflected the desire of other countries to add to their holdings of gold and dollars; their demand for these assets was the cause of the U.S. deficit. During this period, U.S. price-level performance was more impressive than that of any other industrial country. From the mid-1960s on, the U.S. inflation rate began to increase, and to exceed that in other industrial countries; several years later, the U.S. payments deficits began to increase above the levels that could be readily explained by the foreign demand for gold and dollar assets. In a three-year period, 1969–71, the cumulative U.S. payments deficit reached $40 billion, partly as a consequence of a decline in U.S. competitiveness in an array of manufactured products and increasingly in response to speculation about a devaluation of the dollar or a revaluation of other currencies. In the fall of 1969, the German mark was revalued; in the spring of 1970, the Canadian authorities ceased pegging their currency, and the Canadian dollar immediately appreciated by nearly ten percent. For the next fifteen months, the pressures for changes in parities became increasingly intense.

The Smithsonian Agreement

In August 1971 the U.S. Treasury formally suspended gold sales to foreign official institutions, and the U.S. government adopted a tariff surcharge of ten percent to induce other industrial countries to revalue their currencies; the premise was that the surcharge then would be dropped. Negotiations with the Europeans and the Japanese formalized this bargain; at the end of 1971, in the context of the Smithsonian Agreement of 1972, the dollar price of gold was increased to $38, the dollar was effectively devalued by about 12 percent, and the tariff surcharge was withdrawn. The new system of pegged exchange rates lasted little more than a year, and there was renewed speculation against the dollar. Because of the inability of national monetary authorities to adopt policies that would have made the new system of pegged exchange rates viable, floating rates again became inevitable, as in the immediate post–World War I period.

The move to floating rates reflected that there was no viable alternative mechanism to accommodate the changes in the international economy. One change was the more rapid inflation in the United States than in some of its major trading partners. Whereas greater success in achieving price stability had increased the foreign demand for dollar assets in the 1920s, 1950s, and early 1960s, the failure to maintain a low inflation rate in the United States in the 1970s led to a reduction in this demand. Moreover, the foreign demand might have fallen because the United States seemed to have lost its dominant lead in world manufactures. Finally, the sharp increase in the world price of petroleum and the large payments surpluses of OPEC nations led to sharp changes in money flows; movements in exchange rates were necessary to accommodate to the sharp changes in payment surpluses and deficits.

In the context of the floating-rate system, the dollar was weaker than would have been predicted on the basis of the increase in the U.S. price level relative to foreign price level. Moreover, the cyclical movements in exchange rates were also larger than would have been predicted on the basis of changes in national price levels.

Investors—both central banks and private institutions—began to develop alternatives to the dollar as investment currency. The problem was partly circular. Investors moved out of dollar assets because the dollar was weak in the foreign-exchange market, however, the weakness of the dollar in the exchange market reflected that the foreign demand for dollar assets had declined as foreign official institutions were diversifying the currency denomination of their assets from dollar assets.

Analogies with the decline of U.S. economic power in the 1970s, the breakup of Bretton Woods, and the weakness of the dollar were made to the decline of British economic power in the 1920s, the breakdown of the gold standard, and the continued weakness of sterling. One factor common to both experiences was the reluctance to increase the monetary price of gold to compensate for the worldwide inflation during and after both world wars. One shortcoming to this analogy is that the dominant U.S. economic position in the 1940s and 1950s was bound to be temporary, and last only as long as Germany and Japan were still recovering from the economic decline associated with the war. Hence, part of the decline in the international economic position was almost certainly inevitable. In this sense, the ability of the United States to provide a framework for global monetary stability also declined.

The historical evidence suggests that the system will again move back to a system of pegged exchange rates, for such a system has been maintained for nearly ninety years of the last century. Yet such a move seems unlikely until there is considerable similarity in the inflation rates among the major countries. The institutional basis of the new system of pegged exchange rates, and the roles of gold, SDRs, and the dollar and mark as reserve currencies still have to be defined.

Summary

An international financial system is identified by several major features, including the organization of the foreign-exchange market, and especially with whether the monetary authorities in the major countries peg their currencies to an international asset, or instead permit the foreign-exchange values of their currencies to vary in response to changes in demand or supply. A second identifying characteristic is the asset traded among countries to finance payments imbalances. A third key feature of any system is the approach toward adjustments to reduce payments imbalances adopted both by countries with payments surpluses as well as by those with payments deficits.

The history of the international financial system in the last one hundred years can be segmented into three major periods, each with its somewhat distinctive name. The period from 1880 to the outbreak of World War I in 1914 is identified with the gold standard. The gold-exchange standard is the applicable term for the period between World War I and World War II, and especially to that interval from 1926 to 1931 when each of the major countries had a fixed parity for its currency in terms of gold. After World War II to the early 1970s, the Bretton Woods system is used to describe the system of international payments. No general term has been applied to the payments arrangements in the last decade after the collapse of the Bretton Woods system.

The identifying characteristic of the gold standard was that each national currency had a parity stated in terms of gold. International reserves were held primarily in the form of gold; payments imbalances were ultimately financed by shipment of gold from countries with payments deficits to those with payments surplus. The attraction of the gold standard was that adjustments to payments imbalances to restore equilibrium would occur automatically. As gold flowed from the country with a balance-of-payments deficit, its money supply would fall, and prices and incomes would decline, enhancing the international competitiveness of goods produced within that country. Conversely, prices and incomes would rise in the country with the payments surplus, for its money supply would rise as its gold holdings increased.

The rationale for the adoption of the gold exchange in the interwar period was to reduce the demand for gold: some countries began to hold short-term liquid financial assets denominated in dollars and sterling as part of their international reserves. These countries would then acquire these assets when they had a payments surplus and sell these assets when they had a payments deficit.

The key change incorporated in the Bretton Woods system was a set of treaty-based rules stipulating the procedures for changes in exchange parities as a means of balance-of-payments adjustment to reduce payments imbalance. This system also established a pool of national currencies; a member country might borrow these currencies to help finance its payments deficit.

The changes in the dominant features of the international financial system over the last century partly reflect the greater reluctance of authorities within each country to permit domestic price levels to rise or fall to reduce payments imbalances. Moreover, there is also much greater attention to discretionary financial management and less of a willingness to permit adjustment to occur in response to automatic forces. The Bretton Woods system of adjustable exchange parities broke down in the early 1970s because this system was not readily compatible with the significant differences in inflation rates among major countries.

QUESTIONS AND EXERCISES

1. Describe the major differences between the key features of the gold standard and of the Bretton Woods system of adjustable parities.
2. List the major alternative ways a country might achieve equilibrium in its payments balance when a disturbance has led to a payments deficit or a payments surplus.

3. Why did the gold standard break down at the beginning of World War I? Why did the Bretton Woods system of adjustable parities break down in the early 1970s?

FURTHER READING

ALIBER, ROBERT Z. *The International Money Game*. 3d ed. New York: Basic Books, 1979. A romp through the major issues in international finance.

COOMBS, CHARLES. *The Arena of International Finance*. New York: John Wiley and Sons, 1976. A central banker's brief for pegged exchange rates.

MAYER, MARTIN. *The Fate of the Dollar*. New York: Times Books, 1980. A journalist's view of international monetary developments.

SOLOMON, ROBERT. *The International Monetary System, 1945–1976*. New York: Harper & Row, 1977. A comprehensive blow-by-blow account of negotiations.

TEW, BRIAN. *The Evolution of the International Monetary System, 1947–77*. London: Hutchison, 1977. A succinct analysis of the Bretton Woods system and its breakdown.

TRIFFIN, ROBERT. *Gold and the Dollar Crisis.* / New Haven: Yale University Press, 1961. A classic on the U.S. international financial dilemma.

YEAGER, LELAND B. *International Monetary Relations*. New York: Harper & Row, 1966. An excellent text with comprehensive historical treatment.

30

The Organization of
the Foreign-Exchange Market

Trade and payments across national borders require that one of the parties to the transaction contract to pay or receive funds in a foreign currency. At some stage, one party must convert domestic money into foreign money. Moreover, knowledgeable investors based in each country are aware of the opportunities of buying assets or selling debts denominated in foreign currencies when the anticipated returns are higher abroad or when the interest costs are lower. These investors also must use the foreign-exchange market whenever they invest or borrow abroad.

There are two unique features of any international financial system: the exchange rate and the payments balance. In a world with only one currency, there would not be an exchange rate nor would there be a payments balance. The **exchange rate,** which is the *price of foreign monies in terms of domestic money,* is determined in the foreign-exchange market. The payments balance, which is frequently viewed as a measure of "how well" a country is doing, is one entry in the **balance of payments,** which is the *accounting record of all international transactions.* The payments balance is the value of the transactions of the central bank or monetary authority in liquid assets, such as gold, U.S. Treasury bills, bank deposits, and claims on the International Monetary Fund.

At any moment, the exchange rate provides a basis for comparing prices of domestic goods, services, and securities with comparable goods, services, and securities available in other countries. Few individuals or investors use the foreign-exchange market because they want to hold foreign monies; rather they buy foreign exchange as a necessary intermediate transaction before they can buy a foreign good or security or sell a debt denominated in a foreign currency. Merchants in each country seek to take advantage of any significant difference between the prices of domestic goods and comparable foreign goods; the exchange rates permit them to compare the price of Chevrolets with the price of Datsuns and Fiats. Similarly, producers in each country use the exchange rate to determine whether they have a competitive advantage in foreign markets and to judge whether their production costs are below those of firms producing similar goods abroad.

If imports of goods, services, and securities exceed exports of goods, services, and securities during any time period, the country has a deficit for its payments balance that must be financed by selling liquid assets or borrowing abroad. Under a floating-exchange-rate regime, the exchange rate would change to restore equilibrium; under a fixed- (or pegged-) rate regime, the equilibrium is restored by changes in national price levels induced by changes in national money supplies that result from deficits or surpluses in the payments imbalances.

The terms on which national currencies trade with each other determine the significance of the segmentation of the world into separate currency areas. The foreign-exchange market is the market in which national monies, primarily in the form of demand deposits, are traded. If the exchange rates were fixed and known with certainty, then the differences among national monies would be a trivial matter (except for differences in political risk), of little more significance than the difference between $50 bills and $100 bills, or between the notes issued by the Federal Reserve Bank of San Francisco and the Federal Reserve Bank of New York. Individuals and investors would be indifferent about the currency mix of their assets and liabilities. Changes in the consumer price level in one country would fully correspond to the changes in similar price levels in other countries. National money supplies would be readily summed into a world money supply. Just as within one country a variety of financial assets—such as currency and demand deposits—are aggregated to determine the national money supply, the analysis of the monetary policy would involve evaluation of the impacts of changes in the global money supply on world income and employment.

If exchange rates move freely, and at the same time, the exchange rates for all future dates were known with certainty, individuals and investors would still be indifferent about the currency mix of their assets and liabilities. In this world, the differences in interest rates on similar assets denominated in different currencies would fully reflect anticipated changes in exchange rates. These differences in interest rates would compensate investors for forthcoming changes in exchange rates.

The assumption of the perfect substitutability between assets denominated in different currencies is too extreme. Substantial uncertainty about future exchange rates characterizes the foreign-exchange market. Even if countries pledge to maintain fixed or pegged exchange rates (for instance, when £1 was set equal to $2.80 in the 1950s and 1960s), the parities could still be altered. Because of the uncertainty about future exchange rates, traders and investors are concerned with the currencies in which they denominate their assets and liabilities. The case with which traders and investors can alter their holdings of assets and liabilities denominated in different currencies complicates the management of national monetary policies, and has an impact on both the supply of domestic money and the demand for domestic money. Hence the critical question is the significance of the factors that segment the dollar currency area from the currency areas for the mark, the yen, and other currencies.

The Market for Foreign Exchange

Although each of the financial centers in the major countries is sometimes said to have its own foreign-exchange market, the markets for foreign exchange in London, New York, Frankfurt, and Tokyo are geographic extensions of one, worldwide market. The banks in each financial center are linked by telephone and telex to each other and to the major banks in other centers. The units traded are demand deposits; the basic unit in dollar-sterling trading is a sterling deposit of £100,000 while the basic unit in dollar-mark trading is DM200,000. At any moment, the prices or exchange rates for one currency in terms of another are virtually the same in every center, with the differences in prices quoted for comparable large transactions significantly smaller than one-tenth of one percent, and frequently no more than several one-hundredths of one percent.

The foreign-exchange market is the largest market in the world in terms of the volume of transactions; on some days, the volume of trading may reach $100 billion, many times larger than the volume of international trade and investment. That the volume of foreign-exchange trading is many times larger than the volume of international trade and investment reflects that a distinction should be made between transactions that involve only banks and those that involve banks, individuals, and firms involved in international trade and investment.

The foreign-exchange market is extremely competitive; there are many participants, none of whom is large relative to the market. Prices—exchange rates—change continuously, and the change can be as small as one one-hundredth of one percent. The major international commercial banks act as both dealers and brokers. In their dealer role, banks maintain a net long or short position in a currency, and seek to profit from an anticipated change in the exchange rate. (A long position means their holdings of assets denominated in one currency exceeds their liabilities denominated in this same currency.) In their broker function, banks compete to obtain buy and sell orders from commercial customers, such as the multinational oil companies, both to profit from the spread between the rates at which they buy foreign exchange from some customers and the rates at which they sell foreign exchange to other customers, and to sell other types of banking services to these customers. If a large U.S. multinational firm wishes to buy $150 million of marks to make a payment in Frankfurt, the bank that offers marks at the lowest price is most likely to get the business; almost immediately, the bank will seek to buy an equivalent amount of marks to minimize its risk of loss from any subsequent appreciation of the mark.

In their transactions with their customers, banks quote both the price at which they will buy and the price at which they will sell, usually in the form of 1.8380–90 marks per dollar, for a standard volume, say, $100,000; the small price difference reimburses the banks for their costs incurred in their foreign-exchange transactions. If an investor or trader wants to buy dollars, the bank will buy marks at the rate of 1.8390, so 183,900 marks is needed to buy $100,000. If the investor or traders wants to buy marks, the bank will buy dollars at the rate of 1.8380, or $100,000 will buy 183,800 marks. The bid-ask spread of 100 marks, or about $60, is six one-hundredths of one percent of the dollar value of the transactions. The size of the bid-ask spread differs by currency and by the bank providing the quotation. The major international banks are likely to quote a smaller bid-ask spread than those in provincial centers, where the competition may be less extensive. The rates quoted also indicate whether the bank wants to increase or reduce its position in a currency; if a bank owns more marks than it thinks optimal, it will set its quotes low enough to discourage sellers of marks and encourage buyers of marks.

Foreign-exchange brokers are used in some centers to bring buyers and sellers together in an anonymous fashion; the brokers relay the exchange rates quoted by particular banks to various customers. Most commercial customers do not use brokers; instead they may "shop" the banks for the most attractive rate quotations. Commercial banks frequently deal with each other through brokers, and central banks deal with commercial banks through brokers. Brokers generally are paid a flat percentage fee, generally no more than one thirty-second of one percent.

Organization of the Foreign-Exchange Market

The pattern of the organization of the foreign-exchange market follows the pattern of trade financing. More international trade transactions are denominated or invoiced in the U.S. dollar than in any other currency. Thus, in U.S.–Canadian trade, Canadian exporters to the United States quote a price in U.S. dollars and receive payment in U.S. dollars. Similarly Canadian importers agree to pay U.S. dollars for their purchases of U.S. goods. The Canadian importers and exporters prefer to undertake their foreign-exchange transactions close to home—in Canada rather than the United States—so relatively more U.S.–Canadian dollar transactions occur in Toronto than in New York. Both for convenience and to reduce indirect transaction costs, importers and exporters with the need to undertake foreign-exchange transactions prefer to deal with banks closer to their home offices rather than with banks in distant foreign centers. Because the volume of foreign-exchange transactions in each currency pair is so much larger in the centers outside the United States, the markets may be modestly more competitive and the rates quoted by banks to commercial customers somewhat more favorable than the rates quoted in the United States. Hence, the paradox is that because such a large volume of international trade and financial transactions is denominated in the U.S. dollar, most foreign-exchange transactions involving the U.S. dollar occur outside the United States.[1]

The principal center for mark-dollar transactions is Frankfurt; New York is the secondary center. Similarly, Tokyo is the principal center for yen-dollar transactions and London for sterling-dollar transactions. Banks in each center specialize in trading the domestic currency against the U.S. dollar. New York is a secondary center in all foreign currencies. Table

Table 30.1   Distribution of Banks and Traders
in Foreign Exchange

North America

	Number of banks with foreign-exchange department	Number of traders
New York	62	397
Toronto	7	55
Chicago	10	52
San Francisco	8	27
Los Angeles	8	27

Western Europe

	Number of banks with foreign-exchange department	Number of traders
London	192	1008
Luxembourg	45	196
Paris	55	280
Zurich	27	147
Frankfurt	41	219
Milan	32	163
Brussels	27	132

Asia and Middle East

	Number of banks with foreign-exchange department	Number of traders
Tokyo	23	102
Singapore	27	87
Hong Kong	20	60
Bahrain	20	40

SOURCE: *Foreign Exchange and Bullion Dealers Directory, 1978,* Hambros Bank, London.

[1] Paradoxically, prior to World War I much more of U.S. trade was denominated in foreign currencies, so relatively more of the foreign-exchange transactions associated with U.S. trade occurred in New York.

30.1 shows the distribution of banks and foreign-exchange traders. Paris is a tertiary center for trading in the dollar relative to all currencies other than the French franc, while Zurich is a tertiary center for trading in the dollar relative to the mark, sterling, and the French franc.

The large banks are dealers in the currencies in which they specialize. Within most of the major financial centers—London, Frankfurt, New York —a large number of banks participate actively in the foreign-exchange market. Only a smaller number qualify as dealers, identified by the size of their inventories of foreign exchange. When banks are not dealers, they participate as brokers, buying and selling foreign currencies on the basis of exchange-rate quotations from dealers.

Once the rates for two currencies such as the mark and the yen are known in terms of the dollar, the price of the mark in terms of the yen, the so-called cross-rate, can be inferred. For example, on 31 December 1979 the yen-dollar rate was 239.70 yen per dollar, and the mark-dollar rate was 1.7315 marks per dollar, so the yen-mark rate was 138.43 yen per mark.

One consequence of the organization of the market along the lines of a series of currency pairs, each involving the U.S. dollar, is that the financial counterpart of many international trade transactions involves two foreign-exchange transactions. Assume, for example, that a German distributor of automobile parts buys Japanese-produced components. The banks in Frankfurt quote a yen-mark rate based on their rates for the dollar in terms of both the mark and the yen. The banks in Frankfurt are not likely to hold a significant amount of yen, so the bank supplying the yen to the Frankfurt importer undertakes two transactions: marks are used to buy dollars and dollars are then used to buy yen. Since the yen-dollar market is primarily in Tokyo, the bank may act as a dealer in the first transaction and as a broker in the second.

Trading in foreign exchange occurs on almost a continuous time basis, since the markets in various cities are located in different time zones. The Tokyo market closes for the day before the market in London opens.

The Relation between the Spot-Exchange and the Forward-Exchange Rates

Traders and investors who desire to alter the currency mix of their assets or liabilities can readily do so by *leading and lagging;* they increase their loans denominated in the dollar and reduce their loans denominated in another currency, say, the mark. Alternatively, they can increase their holdings of assets denominated in the mark and reduce their holdings of assets denominated in the dollar.

Foreign-exchange transactions are either **spot transactions,** which *involve an exchange of deposits two days after the date of the contract,* or **forward transactions,** which *involve an exchange of deposits at specified* *future dates.* Most foreign-exchange transactions are forward transactions. Traders and investors frequently prefer forward exchange contracts because they do not "tie up" scarce working capital; usually margin or down-payment requirements for established customers are modest. Forward contracts are generally available on maturities up to a year or longer in the major currencies. Some maturities are standardized—three months, six months, and one year—which reflects the standardization of terms of payment on commercial-trade transactions. Banks also offer maturities to match traders' needs; they can readily supply a thirty-nine-day forward contract or a seventy-eight-day forward contract. Transactions costs associated with forward-exchange contracts are modestly higher than those on spot-exchange contracts. Moreover, these costs are higher on distant forward maturities than on near forward maturities and higher on the more volatile currencies than on the less volatile currencies. The spot-exchange rates and forward-exchange rates for major currencies relative to the dollar are shown in table 30.2. If a currency is less expensive in the forward market

Table 30.2   Foreign-Exchange Rates
Closing market rates on 4 April 1980
(U.S. dollars per foreign currency unit)

	Spot rate	Forward rates			
		I MONTH	3 MONTHS	6 MONTHS	I2 MONTHS
Canadian dollar	.83835	.84035	.84445	.85060	.86530
English pound	2.1350	2.1390	2.1415	2.1475	2.1440
Belgian franc	.031646	.031716	.031817	.031969	.032000
French franc	.2205	.2218	.2237	.2257	.2265
German mark	.5076	.5121	.5194	.5291	.5411
Italian lira	.001101	.001102	.001102	.001100	.001989
Dutch guilder	.4654	.4688	.4746	.4812	.4874
Swiss franc	.53475	.5408	.55125	.5693	.58615
Japanese yen	.003867	.003886	.003910	.0039485	.0040145

SOURCE: Harris Trust and Savings Bank, *Weekly Review: International Money Markets and Foreign Exchange Rates* (Chicago, Harris Bank, 4 April 1980).

than in the spot market, the currency is at a forward discount. And if the currency is more expensive in the forward market, then the currency is at a forward premium.

The banks act as intermediaries between buyers and sellers in the forward-exchange market, just as they do in the spot-exchange market. A bank may have a long spot position with a short forward position in a particular currency to limit its exposure in the currency; if the currency appreciates, the value of the spot position increases and so, however, does the value of the short position. Or it may have a long position in some forward maturities and a short position in others.

One of the basic propositions in international finance is that the difference between the forward- and the spot-exchange rates, when expressed in percentage terms, equals the difference between domestic and foreign interest rates for assets with the same maturity as that on the forward contract. This equivalence results from the profit-maximizing behavior of individual investors. Those same investors who seek to profit from anticipated changes in exchange rates continually compare whether it will be more profitable to alter their position in foreign exchange by spot transactions or by forward transactions. They prefer the forward market if the currency is cheaper there than in the spot-exchange market. Other investors take advantage of profit opportunities by buying a currency in the financial center in which it is cheap and selling the same currency in the center in which it is expensive, after adjustment for any difference between the spot- and forward-exchange rates and the interest-rate differential. The first group of investors are sometimes called **speculators;** by definition, *they seek to profit from anticipated changes in exchange rates.* The second group of investors are known as **arbitragers;** *they seek to profit from deviations between the interest-rate differential and the interest equivalent of the spread between the forward- and spot-exchange rates.* Arbitragers avoid exchange risk—they forgo the loss from a possible appreciation of the mark even if it means they must forgo the gain from a possible depreciation of the mark.

For example, assume a U.S. firm has agreed to pay 10 million marks to buy some machinery in Germany. The actual payment will be made in three months—ninety days. The importer might buy marks in the spot market and invest his mark funds for ninety days in Frankfurt at the prevailing interest rate. At the maturity of the investment, he will pay the German seller of the machinery. If the importer can invest his funds in Frankfurt at 8 percent, and the spot-exchange rate is 2 marks per dollar, the importer would pay $4,902,000 to buy 9,804,000 marks, which could be invested at 8 percent for ninety days to yield 10 million marks. The cost of this transaction is the interest rate of 10 percent that the importer might earn on a comparable dollar investment for ninety days. Alternatively, the importer might buy the mark forward, and pay for the forward marks with the proceeds of the ninety-day dollar investment. If the mark is at a forward premium of 2 percent, the importer would pay $5,025,000 for ten million marks. If the importer had invested his $4,902,000 at a 10 percent annual rate for ninety days, he would have $5,025,000. In the real world, one form of payment may be slightly less expensive than the other, and the importer will normally prefer this form of payment. Some U.S. importers may decide to acquire marks immediately prior to the date when payment is due. A similar set of statements can be made about the German importers of U.S. products.

For both groups of importers, the financing pattern depends on the relationship between the spot- and forward-exchange rates, the interest rate on mark assets, and the interest rate on comparable dollar assets. The equivalent relationship between the money-market interest-rate differential and the difference between the spot- and forward-exchange rates is known as the interest-rate-parity theorem. The formal expression is

$$a \frac{(F - S)}{S} = \frac{1 + r_d}{1 + r_f}$$

where a is the factor to convert the percentage difference in the two exchange rates to an annualized rate of return (a is 4 if the forward-rate quotation is on a three-month contract), F the forward-exchange rate, S the spot-exchange rate, r_d the domestic interest rate, and r_f the foreign interest rate.

Empirical studies indicate that the differences between the forward-exchange rates inferred from the interest-rate differential and the observed forward rates are most always less than one percent, and frequently only several tenths of one percent. That there is any measurable deviation from interest-rate parity reflects either that investors encounter costs and incur risks in undertaking transactions to take advantage of the "apparent" riskless arbitrage profit opportunity, or that the securities available in the several centers are not perfect substitutes for each other.

Traders and investors prefer forward transactions to leading and lagging as a way to alter their exposure because of the greater convenience. But traders and investors lead and lag if the costs of acquiring foreign exchange in the forward market exceed the costs in the spot market—if the forward discount is significantly larger than the discount "predicted" by the interest-rate differential.

The Accuracy of Forward-Exchange Rates

One analytic issue involves the relationship between the values of the forward-exchange rates and the values for the spot-exchange rates on the dates when these forward contracts mature.[2] The key question is whether investors who buy and sell forward exchange contracts demand a risk premium. Each forward contract is not likely to "predict" accurately the spot-exchange rate on the dates when the forward contracts mature, because of the large number of unforeseen disturbances or shocks between the dates when traders and investors buy forward contracts and the dates when these same contracts mature. Those who argue that the forward-exchange rates are likely to be biased predictors of future spot-exchange rates—that is, that investors demand a risk premium for buying foreign exchange in the forward market—rely on the analogy of payment for risk-bearing in other markets. They assert that if investors are risk averse, then the *average* of the exchange rates on a set of forward mark contracts would be below

---

[2] The relationship between the forward-exchange rates (or the money-market-interest differential) and the spot-exchange rates when the forward contracts mature is identified as the Fisher proposition, or Fisher open, after Irving Fisher. Analysts frequently confuse the interest-rate-parity theorem with Fisher open: the former involves the efficiency of arbitrage in circumstances in which all values are known, while the latter involves investment decisions in an uncertain environment.

the *average* of the spot-exchange rates on the dates when these forward contracts mature, so that the sellers of forward marks would incur—on average—a loss. If these investors sought to avoid this loss by leading and lagging they might fail, for the difference between the interest rates on mark assets and the interest rates on dollar assets of comparable maturities would be large—on average—relative to changes in the exchange rate during the period when the assets denominated in the several currencies mature.

The response to this argument is that while some traders and investors are sellers of forward marks, others are buyers of forward marks. If the first group pays a risk premium, then the second group, who are also hedging their foreign-exchange positions, would receive a profit, which is the mirror of the cost incurred by the sellers. Empirically, no significant risk premium has been measured, either because the marginal investors are not risk averse or because the willingness of each group of importers to pay a risk premium is offsetting.

Uncertainty about future exchange rates can deter international trade and investment, even though traders and investors can hedge any commitments through forward contracts or through leading and lagging, and at no apparent cost. The explanation for this paradox is that the cost (or profit) from hedging will be known only at the conclusion of their investments—when the forward contracts mature, and the rates on these contracts can then be compared with the spot rates. The impact of the uncertainty about this cost in deterring trade and investment is an empirical issue on which there is scant evidence.

The Level of The Exchange Rate

The foreign-exchange market is one component of the international money market, which also includes the various national markets in bank deposits and money-market assets, such as Treasury bills, bankers' acceptances, and commercial paper. The unique aspect of the foreign-exchange market is that neither of the assets traded in a particular transaction, domestic demand deposits and foreign demand deposits, is unique to that market in the sense that gold is unique to the gold market and wheat to the wheat market. Instead, the demand deposits denominated in different currencies are acquired and held to facilitate payments, store value, and serve as a unit of account in the country of issue. Thus U.S. traders and investors buy marks so they can then acquire commodities or securities available in Germany.

Since all foreign-exchange transactions are intermediate to some other economic transaction, the basic question is how the exchange rate is determined and why exchange rates vary so extensively within a year or a few months, as evident in figure 30.1.

One response to the question is that the exchange rate is the price of

Figure 30.1   Spot-Exchange Rates
Dollar Prices of Foreign Currencies—Averages for Week Ending Wednesday

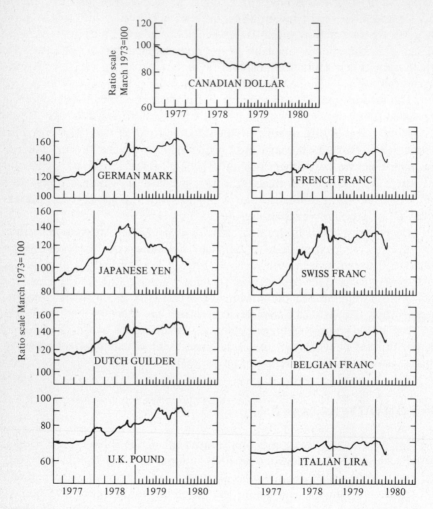

SOURCE: Board of Governors of the Federal Reserve System, *Selected Interest & Exchange Rates: Weekly Series of Charts* (Washington, 4 April 1980).

national monies that causes the prices of similar goods available in the several national markets to be more or less equal, or at least to differ by no more than transaction and transportation costs. The story is that if the prices of similar goods available in the several countries differ significantly at the prevailing exchange rate, traders would buy the goods in the countries in which they are cheap and ship them to the countries in which they are dear, and profit from the price differential. The prices of these goods would rise in the first country and fall in the second; at the same time, the foreign-exchange value of the first country's currency would increase. Arbitrage in commodities would continue until the difference in the prices of similar goods at the new exchange rate was no greater than transaction and transportation costs. In this case, then, the exchange rates move to reduce differences in the prices of comparable goods available in different countries.

This relationship between the prices of tradable goods and the exchange rate is the *purchasing-power-parity* (PPP) *theory*. At times the prices of similar goods available in the several countries are compared at the exchange rate in the absolute version of purchasing-power parity; usually, however, *changes* in the commodity price levels in the several countries are compared with changes in the exchange rate in the relative version of PPP.

During the 1970s, as in the 1920s, changes in the exchange rates in a month or a quarter or a year were 15 to 25 percent greater than the contemporary change in relative national price levels. Thus, during the summer of 1976, sterling became greatly undervalued when it appeared that the British government would not be able to limit wage increases. In six months, the sterling price of the dollar increased by nearly 25 percent (at an annual rate of 50 percent). Sterling goods became greatly undervalued; Parisians flew to London for Saturday shopping. Then sterling subsequently appreciated, so that by the end of 1977, exchange rates were back to the early 1976 levels. Similarly in 1977 and the first ten months of 1978, the dollar became substantially undervalued; after a dramatic commitment by the U.S. administration to save the dollar (in October 1978, as was discussed in chapter 27), the dollar appreciated sharply. Yet for an extended period, U.S. goods remained undervalued. The statement, then, that the exchange rate moves to reflect changes in national price levels is not consistent with much recent data.

Transactions in commodities are only one of the reasons firms and investors participate in the foreign-exchange market. The demand and supply of foreign exchange also is affected by investment or security transactions, as funds are moved between currencies to profit from the differences in interest rates on comparable assets denominated in different currencies, or from anticipated changes in exchange rates. From the investors' point of view, the spot-exchange rate is "just right" when, given the interest rates on domestic securities and the anticipated rate of change of the exchange rate, comparable foreign securities are no more and no less attractive.

Thus $r_d = r_w + \left(\frac{\dot{E}}{E}\right)*$, where r_d is the interest rate on domestic financial assets of the same maturity, r_w the interest rate on comparable foreign financial assets, $\left(\frac{\dot{E}}{E}\right)*$ the anticipated rate of change of the exchange rate during the interval until the maturity of the two securities. This statement is the *Fisher proposition*.[3] As new information about possible changes in government policy becomes available and investors alter their demand for assets denominated in the several currencies, the spot-exchange rate

[3] This statement is named after Irving Fisher, who was an outstanding American economist in the early decades of the twentieth century.

may change. If the new information about the trade accounts, inflation rates, national monetary policies, or election campaigns leads investors to conclude that the mark-denominated assets will prove a less attractive investment than dollar-denominated investments, they will sell mark assets and the mark will depreciate in the exchange market. The mark will continue to depreciate until the return on the mark assets adjusted for the anticipated change in the exchange rate equals the return on dollar assets.

The anticipated rate of change of the exchange rate, $\left(\frac{\dot{E}}{E}\right)^*$, depends both on investors' estimates of where the spot-exchange rate will be at various future dates, and the current spot-exchange rate. In equilibrium, the anticipated rate of change of the exchange rate must be equal to the money-market interest differential. If investors believe there is a disequilibrium— that $r_d \neq r_w + \left(\frac{\dot{E}}{E}\right)^*$—then in the move to equilibrium, the adjustment may occur in the current spot-exchange rate, the anticipated spot-exchange rate, or either of the two money-market interest rates. The anticipated spot-exchange rate, however, is not likely to adjust greatly, since it reflects investor estimates of the exchange rate consistent with the domestic and foreign price levels expected to prevail in the future. Some adjustments may occur in the two interest rates as investors shift funds from one money market to another; however, the volume of funds shifted may be small relative to the size of the two money markets. Consequently, much of the adjustment may occur in the current spot-exchange rate, with the consequence that the changes in the current spot-exchange rate may be much greater than the changes that would be predicted from the contemporary changes in the several national price levels.

Analyzing Exchange-Rate Disturbances

Two different types of disturbances that affect the foreign-exchange market—nonmonetary and monetary—should be distinguished. Assume investors believe that mark-denominated assets will decline in value at a time when interest rates on mark assets and dollar assets remain the same because the German and U.S. monetary policies are unchanged; increased "bearishness" does not lead to any increase in interest rates on mark assets. In this case, the value for the mark in the spot-exchange market will move to the level of the anticipated spot-exchange rate, perhaps abruptly. Alternatively, assume that the Bundesbank follows a more contractive monetary policy, and interest rates on mark assets increase, at least for a short while. However, the anticipated spot-exchange rate is unaffected. Then investors would acquire mark-denominated assets because of the higher interest rate, so the mark would appreciate. As long as interest rates on mark assets are higher than those on dollar assets, the only factor that can equalize the return to investors from holding dollar assets and mark assets is the subsequent depreciation of the mark. The paradox is that in response to the initial increase in interest rates on mark assets, there is a sudden unanticipated appreciation of the mark, so the mark may then subsequently gradually depreciate, with the anticipated rate of depreciation equal to the excess of interest rates on mark assets over those on dollar assets.

Price movements in other financial markets, in the stock and the bonds market and in the wheat, soybeans, and gold markets, also are large, and comparable to those in the foreign-exchange market. The spot prices in any speculative market are the discounted values of anticipated future values. In the foreign-exchange market, the discount factor is the difference between the money-market interest rates on similar securities denominated in different currencies. For example, if interest rates on dollar Treasury bills are 10 percent and interest rates on mark Treasury bills are 8 percent, the discount rate is 2 percent a year. If the anticipated values are unchanged, then during each week and each month the exchange rates should change by the amount of the interest-rate differential. Thus if the interest rates on dollar assets are two percentage points higher than interest rates on mark-denominated assets, the appropriate inference is that traders and investors believe that the mark will appreciate at the rate of 2 percent a year, or 0.166 percent a month, 0.038 percent a week, or 0.0055 percent a day. Even a weak currency—one that might depreciate at a rate of 20 percent a year—would depreciate at an average daily rate of 0.0624 percent. But this cannot be the whole story. Since the changes in exchange rates on a daily and weekly basis are many times larger than these values, they must reflect sharp movements in anticipated exchange rates. Occasionally, the spot-exchange rate may change because the interest-rate differential changes; the changes in the interest-rate differentials, however, are too infrequent and too small to explain the large swings in exchange rates.

A variety of factors affects anticipations of future exchange rates, including investor estimates of inflation rates or money-supply growth rates. Thus traders and investors may extrapolate recent changes in domestic and foreign price levels to obtain estimates of future national price levels, which serve as a basis for their anticipations of exchange rates in the future. Hence, anticipations of future exchange rates are based on the purchasing-power-parity concept. Alternatively changes in money-supply growth rates may be used to generate estimates of the national price levels in the several countries, which in turn lead to estimates of the future exchange rates; in this case the forecast of future price levels is based on money-supply growth rates rather than on the extrapolation of current price levels.

Some analysts believe that the mark appreciates when U.S. monetary policy becomes more expansive or German monetary policy becomes more contractive. When the interest-rate differential changes, the exchange rate may change sharply, even if anticipated spot-exchange rates remain unchanged. If investors focus on spot-exchange rates anticipated in several years, then the change in exchange rates may be substantially larger, in percentage terms, than the change in the interest-rate differential. For example, assume U.S. monetary policy becomes more expansive and interest rates on dollar assets fall by one percentage point. If investors expect U.S. interest rates to remain at this level for two years, then the dollar might depreciate by two percent in the spot-exchange market to equalize the anticipated returns on short-term mark and dollar investments.

Central Bank Intervention in the Foreign-Exchange Market

For most of the last one hundred years, as we have seen, the currencies of the major countries have been pegged to each other, initially because each currency had a mint parity that was the price of a standard unit of gold. After World War II, many foreign countries expressed the parities for foreign currencies in terms of the U.S. dollar. Under a pegged-rate arrangement, central banks committed themselves to limit the range of movement in the price of their currencies around their parities. These limits were narrow under the gold standard, usually set by the costs of gold shipments. In the post–World War II period, these limits were set by central banks, usually about one percent either side of parity. Within these limits, the exchange rates were free to float, although many monetary authorities intervened within these limits to smooth the hour-to-hour, day-to-day exchange-rate movement. At the limits, a central bank was obliged to intervene so its currency would not move more than one percent away from its parity.

Intervention involved purchases or sales of the national money against a foreign money, most frequently the U.S. dollar. A central bank was obliged to prevent its currency from depreciating below its lower support limit. The central bank would buy its own currency from commercial banks operating in the exchange market and sell them dollars in exchange. These transactions were effectively an open-market sale using dollar demand deposits rather than domestic bonds. Such transactions reduced the central bank's domestic liabilities in the hands of the public. The ability of a foreign central bank to prevent its currency from depreciating depended upon its holdings of dollars, together with dollars that might be obtained by borrowing. Even if a national monetary authority had the foreign exchange necessary for intervention, its need to support its currency in the exchange market might be inconsistent with its efforts to undertake a more expansive monetary policy to achieve its domestic economic objectives.

Similarly, if a country's currency was strong, its central bank was obliged to sell more of its currency in the exchange market to limit its appreciation. In effect, the foreign central bank undertook an open-market purchase in dollars. Such open-market purchases might confound its desire to limit the expansion of its monetary liabilities. Thus Germany, with a strong currency in the 1960s and early 1970s, faced the choice between maintaining the exchange parity for the mark with the consequence of a more rapid than desired increase in the German money supply or limiting the growth in the reserves of the banking system in Germany at the cost of either revaluing the mark occasionally or permitting the mark to float. While the German central bank might have undertaken open-market sales in mark-denominated securities to counter or neutralize its open-market purchases in dollar securities, such transactions were not costless, for they raised interest rates on German securities more than was deemed desirable for domestic objectives. As German interest rates went up, investors would have shifted out of dollar-denominated securities into mark-denominated securities, intensifying the problem for the Bundesbank.

Thus the Bundesbank's transactions in the foreign-exchange market are shown in figure 30.2. The price of the dollar in terms of marks is measured

Figure 30.2   The Market For Foreign Exchange

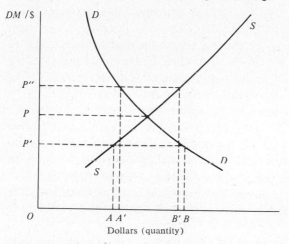

Dollars (quantity)

on the vertical axis, the volume of dollars demanded and supplied is measured on the horizontal axis. The demand of traders and investors for dollars is shown as *DD;* as the price of the dollar increases, the amount of dollars demanded declines. The supply of dollars by traders and investors is shown as *SS;* as the price of the dollar increases, the amount of dollars supplied increases. At *OP* the demand and supply of dollars are equal; *OP* is the rate that clears the exchange market without official intervention. If the Bundesbank had pegged the mark at *OP'*, the demand for dollars would have exceeded the supply. Each period the Bundesbank would have sold dollars equal to *AB* and Germany would have had a payments deficit. If instead, the Bundesbank had pegged the mark at *OP''*, and the Bundesbank would have bought dollars equal to *A'B'*, Germany would have had a payments surplus.

The maintenance of the exchange parity appeared to conflict with the achievement of domestic economic objectives. No such conflict was supposed to occur with floating exchange-rate systems, since the exchange rates would change to neutralize any payments imbalance. Hence monetary policy could be directed solely to attainment of domestic objectives; changes in the exchange rate would continuously insure that payments and receipts would be equal. Hence central banks would not have to undertake open-market operations in foreign exchange that might offset their open-market operations in domestic securities. However, authorities found that market forces sometimes caused the exchange rate to deviate from the level deemed appropriate for domestic objectives and so they again felt the need to intervene in the exchange market even at the cost of complicating attainment of their domestic objectives.

The Segmentation of National Money Markets

One of the key policy issues in international finance, known as optimum currency-area issue, involves whether there are any economic gains from maintaining independent national central banks, each with its own currency. Does the Bank of Canada have the capacity to cause interest rates in Canada to change and deviate significantly from U.S. interest rates? If the Bank of Canada attempts to follow a more expansive monetary policy, and buys bonds denominated in the Canadian dollar, it is possible that the sellers of Canadian bonds will buy U.S. bonds, so that the interest rates on Canadian bonds would remain virtually unchanged? If Canada is following a pegged exchange rate, is it possible for Canadian interest rates to differ significantly from U.S. interest rates? And if Canada is on a floating rate system, can changes in Canadian monetary policy affect any real variables, such as the level of employment, or will the impacts of these changes be limited to altering nominal values such as the Canadian price level and the exchange rate?

The scope for national monetary independence depends on how fully investors believe that assets that are alike in all attributes except for currency of denomination are close or near substitutes for each other. Transactions costs might deter investors from shifting funds among these assets. Exchange controls might deter these shifts. Such shifts might also be deterred by exchange-risk in the form of uncertainty about future exchange rates, or political risk in the form of uncertainty about future changes in exchange controls. Investors are likely to shift funds to profit from differences in interest rates only if they are compensated for these costs and for the associated risks. At most, the differential in interest rates on similar assets denominated in different currencies adjusted for any anticipated changes in exchange rates cannot exceed the sum of these costs and the payments demanded by investors for incurring the risks associated with the movements of funds across the borders between currency areas.

Transactions costs are small or even trivial, especially for the large international firms; transactions costs are smaller still for the major international banks. Transactions costs have two components—one involves those external to the firm, the actual costs incurred in buying and selling foreign exchange, and the second involves those internal to the firm and incurred in managing their foreign exchange or international monetary investments. Transactions costs to the commercial customers are measured by the bid-ask spread—the difference between the prices at which traders and investors could buy and sell a relatively large amount—$3 to $5 million—of a par-

ticular currency at any moment. The costs encountered by commercial customers in using the foreign-exchange market are substantially smaller than
those they would incur with transactions of equivalent value in most other
markets—the government securities market or the stock market. Depending
on the currency, the time, and the maturity of the forward contracts, the
cost of a foreign-exchange transaction of $1 million would be $100 to $500,
or in the order of one one-hundredth of one percent to one-twentieth of one
percent. Transactions costs are smaller, the less volatile the currency; thus,
bid-ask spreads in the Canadian dollar have generally been lower than the
bid-ask spread in sterling, the mark and other European currencies, and the
yen. Transactions costs on forward contracts with relatively distant forward
maturities—those longer than six months—have generally been larger than
those on shorter maturities; transactions costs on the spot transactions are
below those on forward transactions. That transactions costs are so small
reflects both the technical efficiency of payments, the virtually riskless character of the transactions, and the large size of the transactions.

Transactions costs on interbank transactions in the foreign-exchange
market are generally smaller than those on the transactions between banks
and customers—the transactions are larger and less risk is associated with
interbank transactions. The lower level of transactions costs encountered by
banks than by their commercial customers means that the banks have an
advantage in responding to any potential profit opportunities.

Measuring the payment demanded by investors for carrying exchange
risk and political risk is more difficult. One issue is whether firms are risk-
averse, and require payments for bearing these risks. It is sometimes argued
that firms are (or should be) risk-neutral and seek to maximize profits.
Even if firms are risk-averse, the cost they would incur in hedging their exposure to this risk is trivial in the long run (because forward rates are on
average unbiased "predictors" of future spot rates) if not in the short run.
Yet firms may nevertheless be deterred from the movement of funds internationally by the uncertainty about this cost.

National financial markets appear segmented to a greater extent than
can be readily explained by transactions costs, exchange risk, or political
risk. Segmentation provides some opportunity for national monetary independence under pegged exchange rates. If over time, traders and investors
become more knowledgeable about the returns and the risks and costs from
altering the currency mix of their assets and liabilities, so that the segmentation of national money markets declines, changes in monetary policies will
be less effective in altering real variables.

The Balance-of-Payments Accounts

The data on international transactions of a country are presented in its balance of payments of accounts, a record of payments and receipts, organized
by major type of transactions, between residents and nonresidents during a

particular period such as a quarter or a year. Table 30.3 summarizes U.S. international transactions for 1976, 1977, and 1978.

The system used in developing such accounts is based on the system of double-entry bookkeeping. All transactions represent changes of equal value and so for every import of a good, service, or security there must be a corresponding export of a good, service, or security—so the balance-of-payments accounts must necessarily balance. When U.S. residents import Scotch whiskey, they export dollars, usually in the form of demand deposits, in payment. The U.S. accounts then show an increase in U.S. exports of demand deposits. The British payments accounts, in contrast, show the export of the Scotch whiskey and the import of U.S. security (demand deposits).

The data for the entries in the balance-of-payments accounts are ob-

Table 30.3   U.S. International Transactions, 1976–1978
(Millions of dollars)

Item credits or debits	1976	1977	1978
1 Balance on current account	4,605	−14,092	−13,478
2 Merchandise trade balance	−9,306	−30,873	−33,770
3 Merchandise exports	114,745	120,816	142,052
4 Merchandise imports	−124,051	−151,689	−175,822
5 Military transactions, net	674	1,679	492
6 Investment income, net[c]	15,975	17,989	21,645
7 Other service transactions, net	2,260	1,783	3,241
8 Memo: Balance on goods and services	9,603	−9,423	−8,392
9 Remittances, pensions, and other transfers	−1,851	−1,895	−1,934
10 U.S. government grants (excluding military)	−3,146	−2,775	−3,152
12 Change in U.S. government assets, other than official reserve assets, net (increase, −)	−4,214	−3,693	−4,656
12 Change in U.S. official reserve assets (increase, −)	−2,558	−375	732
13 Gold	0	−118	−65
14 Special drawing rights (SDR)	−78	−121	1,249
15 Reserve position in International Monetary Fund	−2,212	−294	4,231
16 Foreign currencies	−268	158	−4,683
17 Change in U.S. private assets abroad (increase, −)[a]	−44,498	−31,725	−57,033
18 Bank-reported claims	−21,368	−11,427	−33,023
19 Nonbank-reported claims	−2,296	−1,940	−3,853
20 U.S. purchase of foreign securities, net	−8,885	−5,460	−3,487
21 U.S. direct investments abroad, net[c]	−11,949	−12,898	−16,670
22 Change in foreign official assets in the United states (increase, +)	17,573	36,656	33,758
23 U.S. Treasury securities	9,319	30,230	23,542
24 Other U.S. government obligations	573	2,308	656
25 Other U.S. government liabilities[b]	4,507	1,240	2,754
26 Other U.S. liabilities reported by U.S. banks	969	773	5,411
27 Other foreign official assets[c]	2,205	2,105	1,395

Table 30.3   (continued)

Item credits or debits	1976	1977	1978
28 Change in foreign private assets in the United States (increase, +)[a]	18,826	14,167	29,956
29 U.S. bank-reported liabilities	10,990	6,719	16,975
30 U.S. nonbank-reported liabilities	−578	473	1,640
31 Foreign private purchases of U.S. Treasury securities, net	2,783	534	2,180
32 Foreign purchases of other U.S. securities, net	1,284	2,713	2,867
33 Foreign direct investment in the United States, net[a]	4,347	3,728	6,294
34 Discrepancy	10,265	−937	10,722
MEMO: Changes in official assets			
35 U.S. official reserve assets (increase, −)	−2,558	−375	732
36 Foreign official assets in the United States (increase, +)	13,066	35,416	31,004

a. Includes reinvested earnings of incorporated affiliates.

b. Primarily associated with military sales contracts and other transactions arranged with or through foreign official agencies.

c. Consists of investments in U.S. corporate stocks and in debt securities of private corporations and state and local governments.

SOURCE: Board of Governors of the Federal Reserve System, *Federal Reserve Bulletin* (Washington, 4 April 1980).

tained in various ways. Data on commodity imports and exports are obtained from U.S. tariff collection authorities. Data on tourist expenditures are estimated by sampling travelers. Data on exports of securities are obtained from reports filed by banks and brokerage firms. Because the sum of all recorded receipts and the sum of all recorded payments in a time period are unlikely to be equal, there is a statistical discrepancy. The value for this entry is determined as a residual between recorded payments and recorded receipts (the difference between receipts and payments is added to the smaller figure so that the two are set equal to each other).

The millions of international transactions are summed into three major categories or groups. The trade balance (line 2) is the difference between the values of commodity exports and commodity imports, usually with imports valued at their landed price, so the value of imports exceeds that reported by the exporting countries by the amount of cargo insurance and freight (CIF) costs. A country has a trade surplus if the value of its commodity exports exceeds the value of its commodity imports. The current-account balance (line 1) includes all transactions in commodities, together with all international transactions in services such as transportation, tourism, royalties and license fees, film rentals, investment income, and private remittances such as Social Security payments, and various gifts, such as religious charity, UNICEF, and foreign aid. The characteristic of all international transactions not included in the current-account balance is that they involve transactions in foreign assets, ranging from equities and direct investment to non-interest-bearing demand deposits; transactions in monetary gold, government securities, and bonds are included in the capital-account balance. Lines 12 through 33 summarize various capital-account transactions.

The most important conceptual relationship in the balance-of-payments accounts is the relationship between the current-account balance and the capital-account balance; all international transactions are included in the calculation of one of these balances and no transaction is included in both. (Although purchases of foreign investments are in the capital-account balance and the dividends and interest on these investments are in the current account, these are separate transactions, even in time.) Because of the double-entry character, a surplus on the current account means a deficit on the capital account of the same arithmetic value. Thus if a country has a current-account surplus (its exports of goods and services exceed its imports of goods and services) it must necessarily—by definition—have a capital-account deficit, and so its imports of securities must exceed its exports of securities. The country's net international creditors position is increasing.

The last major group is the payments balance, at one time thought a measure of how well a country "was doing"; this balance is the sum of lines 35 and 36. Payments surpluses were considered indicative of a successful economic performance, and payments deficits of a less successful performance, perhaps because of the association of payments deficits and domestic inflation. Initially payments surpluses were associated with gold inflows, deficits with outflows. Subsequently transactions in other types of assets, including liquid assets denominated in the major currencies and claims on the International Monetary Fund, were included in the calculation of the payments balance.

At times, the entry payments balance was thought of as the sum of "financing transactions"; all international transactions were segmented either into an autonomous category or an induced category, and those items in the induced category were considered to be the payments balance. Because of the reliance on the concept of double-entry bookkeeping, the value for the entry on the autonomous payments necessarily equals the value for the entry for the induced payments, but with the opposite signs. So if a country's exports of goods, services, and long-term securities exceed its imports of goods, services, and long-term securities, so that there is a surplus on the autonomous account, there must be a deficit on the induced account—the country's imports of monetary gold and foreign-exchange reserves exceed its exports of monetary gold.

An alternative approach considers the payments balance as the sum of transactions in money—liquid assets including gold—by the monetary authorities. A country with a payments surplus imports monetary assets. In effect the country has a deficit in the money account—its imports of monetary assets exceed its exports of monetary assets. The shorthand approach is that a country's payments surplus or deficit should be measured by the change in its central bank's holdings of international money. If the central bank imports money, the country has a payments surplus.

Over the last twenty years, various agencies in the U.S. government have debated which transactions are to be included in the measurement of the payments balance, or, which transactions should be considered induced. Prior to 1964, changes in the foreign holdings of liquid dollar assets of foreign commercial banks and foreign private parties as well as of foreign central banks were included in the measurement of the U.S. payments balance. In the 1960s, the U.S. authorities took the view that only transactions of foreign monetary authorities should be included. The decision to exclude changes in liquid dollar holdings of foreign commercial banks and foreign private parties at a time when they were adding to their holdings of liquid dollar assets led to a reduction in the measured U.S. payments deficit. The United States was exporting money because these foreign groups had a secular demand for dollar assets. Then, with the move to the floating exchange-rate system, the U.S. authorities downplayed the significance of the payments balance as a concept.

Summary

A market in national monies is a necessity in a world of national currencies; this market is the foreign-exchange market. The assets traded in this market are demand deposits denominated in the different currencies. Individuals who wish to buy goods or securities in a foreign country must first obtain that country's currency in the foreign-exchange market. If these individuals pay in their own currency, then the sellers of the goods or securities use the foreign-exchange market to convert receipts into their own currency.

The costs and risks encountered by participants in the foreign-exchange market are important to the question of whether conclusions about the management of monetary policy in a one-currency world differ significantly in a world of several currencies. The higher the costs and the risks encountered by those who deal in foreign exchange, the larger the segmentation of national financial markets, the smaller the difference. If these costs and risks are small, then changes in the monetary policy within one country may have a significant impact on capital flows, and a modest impact on domestic interest rates and investment and consumption spending.

Most foreign-exchange transactions entail trades involving the U.S. dollar and individual foreign currencies. The exchange rate between any two foreign currencies can be inferred as the ratio of the price of the U.S. dollar in terms of each of their currencies. More of the trading in each foreign currency pair occurs in the foreign financial centers than in the United States, primarily because much of the foreign trade of the United States is denominated in the U.S. dollar, and the foreign exporters and importers are much more likely to be involved with foreign-exchange transactions than are U.S. exporters and importers.

Most foreign-exchange transactions involve forward transactions, which are commitments to exchange demand deposits at specified future dates, rather than spot transactions, which are commitments to trade these deposits within the next several days. The forward-exchange rates for any given pair of currencies at any moment almost always differ from the spot-exchange rates; moreover, at any moment the rates on forward contracts of different maturities differ. The spot-exchange rates are systematically related to forward-exchange rates for different maturities by the difference in interest rates on comparable assets denominated in the several currencies. This relationship is known as the interest-rate-parity theorem. Thus, if interest rates on sterling assets exceed interest rates on comparable dollar assets by one percent a year, the appropriate inference is that the sterling will be at a forward discount of one percent a year.

The exchange rates are prices that equalize the demand and supply of foreign exchange. In recent years, exchange rates have moved sharply, more sharply than is suggested by the change in the relationship between domestic price level and foreign price level. Exchange rates do not accurately reflect the relationship between the domestic price level and foreign price levels. Rather, exchange rates change so that the anticipated rates of return from holding domestic securities and foreign securities are the same after adjustment for any anticipated change in the exchange rate. Thus if interest rates on sterling assets are one percent higher than interest rates on comparable assets denominated in the dollar, it can be inferred that investors anticipate that sterling will depreciate at one percent a year. Sharp changes in exchange rates occur whenever anticipated spot-exchange rates or the interest-rate differentials change sharply.

Transaction costs in foreign-exchange markets are low. Yet there appears considerable scope for monetary independence because national money markets are segmented by uncertainty about changes in exchange rates and in exchange controls.

The balance-of-payments accounts record the payments and receipts between domestic residents and foreign residents. The accounts are based on double-entry bookkeeping; all transactions involve exchanges of equal value. The millions of transactions included in the accounts are organized into several major groups; thus the difference between commodity exports and commodity imports is the trade balance. The balance of trade in goods and services is known as the current-account balance. The capital-account balance indicates the net volume of trade in securities.

QUESTIONS AND EXERCISES

1. Discuss why the costs and risks associated with the transactions in the foreign-exchange market are important for the effective operation of monetary policy in an open economy.

2. Why is volume of dollar-sterling foreign-exchange transactions in London larger than the volume in New York?

3. Describe how the values for exchange rates for forward-exchange contracts for various maturities are related to the spot-exchange rate. What are the consequences of an increase in the interest-rate differential on the relationship between the spot-exchange rate and the forward-exchange rates?

4. Describe the determinants of the level of the spot-exchange rate. If interest rates on sterling-denominated assets fall, why might the price of the dollar in terms of sterling increase? Why might the sterling price of the dollar increase even if the interest-rate differential remains unchanged?

FURTHER READING

ALIBER, ROBERT Z. *Exchange Risk and Corporate International Finance*. New York: Halsted Press, 1979. A systematic guide for analysis of exchange-rate movements.

FEDERAL RESERVE BANK OF BOSTON. *Managed Exchange Rate Flexibility: The Recent Experience*. Boston: Federal Reserve Bank, 1978. A conference volume with numerous essays analyzing the movement of exchange rates in the 1970s.

FRIEDMAN, MILTON. "The Case for Fluctuating Exchange Rates." In his *Essays in Positive Economics*. Chicago: University of Chicago Press, 1953. A classic statement of the case for floating exchange rates.

INTERNATIONAL MONETARY FUND. *Annual Report*. Washington, D.C.: yearly. This report discusses annual developments in the foreign-exchange markets.

KUBARYCH, ROGER. *The New York Foreign Exchange Market*. New York: Federal Reserve Bank, 1979. A comprehensive description of the institutional aspects of the foreign-exchange markets in the United States.

31

International Banking and National Monetary Policies

Traditionally studies in international finance implicitly assumed that the banking structure in each country was self-contained. In the last several decades, commercial banking has become internationalized in two important, distinct, but related ways: branch systems of U.S. banks have been extended into the domestic markets abroad, and branches of U.S. banks in other countries have been established to compete with domestic banks for dollar deposits. The key concern is how these changes in the structure of banking affect the management of monetary policy in the major countries.

The Internationalization of Commercial Banking

The commercial banking systems of the major industrial countries have become internationalized in the last decade and banks headquartered in New York, Chicago, Tokyo, Frankfurt, Zurich, and Toronto have begun to compete aggressively in each other's domestic markets. United States banks have nearly one thousand branches and subsidiaries in Western Europe, Asia, and Latin America. Banks headquartered in Western Europe and Japan have set up over three hundred banking offices in New York, Chicago, San Francisco, and Los Angeles, and account for 15 percent of U.S. banking assets.

One consequence of the internationalization of commercial banking is that there is now more extensive competition in the major international centers due to the presence of foreign banks that are seeking to increase their shares of markets for loans and deposits. Banking in Great Britain is dominated by four major banks (National Westminster, Barclays, Midland, and Lloyds) and twenty major non-British banks compete for the sterling deposits and loans of major and modest customers. Similarly, the three big German banks (Deutsche, Dresdener, and Commerz) have encountered increased competition for loan and deposit business from forty or fifty branches of foreign banks in Frankfurt, Düsseldorf, and Hamburg.

The Eurodollar Market

The surge in international banking competition has been facilitated by the growth of the external currency market, sometimes called the Eurodollar or offshore banking market. A **Eurodollar** is a *dollar-denominated deposit issued by a banking office located outside the United States,* while a Euromark deposit is a mark-denominated deposit issued by a banking office located in Luxembourg, London, or any other center outside Germany. These offshore offices engage in an intermediation function virtually identical with that of the domestic banks, with the difference being that they sell deposits and buy loans denominated in a currency other than that of the country in which they are located. Thus the London offices of U.S. and German banks sell deposits and buy loans denominated in dollars, marks, Swiss francs, and perhaps ten currencies other than sterling. While the volume of their dollar transactions in London is five to ten times larger than the volume of their sterling transactions, their sterling transactions are sizable. Foreign banks with U.S. branches obtain a substantial part of their funds by selling dollar deposits in London and other offshore centers.

Offshore banking occurs in "monetary havens" such as London, Luxembourg, Singapore, Panama, and the Cayman Islands. Banking is less extensively regulated in these centers than elsewhere. One analogy is tax havens, political jurisdictions to which income is transferred because tax rates are lower than elsewhere. Investors hold offshore dollar deposits because the additional income more than compensates for the additional costs and inconveniences and risks. The additional risk arises because exchange controls may restrict the repatriation of funds from offshore centers.

Banks that operate in an international environment sometimes encounter two sets of regulatory authorities, those in the country in which they are headquartered and those in the countries in which their foreign branches and subsidiaries are located.[1] For example, foreign banks find it extremely difficult, if not impossible, to set up branches in Norway, Mexico, and Canada; in each of these countries, the markets for loans and deposits have been reserved for domestic banks. In a few cases, however, the offices of foreign banks may have a regulatory advantage over domestic banks.

International Banking and Domestic Monetary Policy

The internationalization of banking and the growth of the offshore dollar market raises important questions for the management of U.S. monetary policy. Should offshore dollar deposits be included in the calculation of the U.S. money supply? If so, should the dollar deposits of the offshore offices of U.S. banks be distinguished from dollar deposits of offshore offices of non–U.S. banks? Should the dollar deposits of U.S. offices of foreign banks

---

[1] A subsidiary is a legally incorporated firm that is owned by the parent bank. A branch is an unicorporated extension of the parent bank.

be included in the calculation of the U.S. money supply, just as if they were U.S. banks? Should the nondollar deposits of the offshore offices of U.S. banks be included in the measurement of the U.S. money supply? Similarly, should the Federal Reserve regulate only the domestic offices of U.S. banks, or should regulation of the offshore offices of U.S. banks be identical with the regulation of domestic offices?

From the point of view of monetary analysis, the critical question is whether the money supply should be measured to include the volume of bank deposits produced within a country (say, the United States or Germany) regardless of currency, the volume of bank deposits denominated in a particular currency (say, the U.S. dollar of the German mark) regardless of the country in which the deposits are produced, or the volume of deposits produced by banks headquartered in particular countries (say, U.S. banks or German banks) regardless of currency and location of the country in which the deposits are produced. The most appropriate answer will be determined in terms of the ability of each of these alternative approaches to the measurement of the money supply to explain changes in the level of income within a country. The narrowest definition of the money supply involves dollar liabilities of U.S.-owned banks produced only by their U.S. offices. This measurement might be expanded in the ownership dimension to include the dollar liabilities produced by the U.S. offices of non–U.S. owned banks, or in the geographic dimension to include the dollar liabilities produced by the foreign offices of U.S. banks, or in the currency dimension to include the nondollar liabilities of U.S. banks.

One view is that the most relevant measure for the U.S. monetary policy includes the total of dollar-denominated bank liabilities regardless of whether dollar deposits are produced by U.S. banks or by foreign banks and regardless of whether the deposits are produced in the United States or abroad. The rationale is that the borders among currency areas—between the dollar area and the mark area, for example—are significantly higher than the borders between the domestic and external segments of a particular currency area, which in turn are probably higher than the distinctions between domestic and foreign-owned banks producing similar types of bank deposits. There is general agreement that the liabilities of foreign-owned banks operating in the United States should be included in the measurement of U.S. money supply. Households and firms generally view their deposits in foreign-owned banks in the United States as close substitutes for their deposits in U.S. banks; otherwise the branches and subsidiaries of foreign banks would be at a significant competitive disadvantage in selling deposits. However, there is less agreement that offshore deposits denominated in U.S. dollars should be considered part of the U.S. money supply, even though offshore dollars can ultimately only be spent in the United States.

The first issue discussed in this chapter involves the structural differences among countries in the character of banking regulations and the significance of these differences for the management of monetary policy. The second issue involves the relation of the offshore dollar deposits to domestic dollar deposits, and the relation of offshore German mark deposits to domestic German mark deposits, and the monetary implications of the development of offshore markets. Special attention is given to the implications of the growth of offshore dollar deposits for the management of U.S. monetary policy.

The Structure of International Banking

The traditional approach to the analysis of the structure of international banks examines the shares of each national market for loans and deposits held by foreign-owned banks. If data were available, it would be useful to examine the extent to which residents in each country acquire deposits from foreign banks and sell loans to them; as the costs incurred by residents of any country in acquiring deposits abroad or obtaining loans abroad declines, the size of the market in which banks located in a particular center and the number of competing firms in this market area increases, while the number of market areas declines.

The growth of international banking is important because foreign-owned banks may have readier access to external funds than domestic banks, and so they may be able to sidestep changes in domestic monetary policy, more so than domestic banks can. For example, if the Bank of England pursues a more contractive monetary policy, so that British banks find it difficult to extend sterling loans, U.S. and other foreign banks with ready access to nonsterling funds may sell these funds for sterling and buy more sterling loans. Alternately, borrowers in London may go to banks in Paris, Frankfurt, and New York to offset their reduction in domestic opportunities to borrow.

One of the striking differences in the comparisons of the domestic banking systems in the major countries is in the size distribution of banks. Another is in the form and extent of bank regulation. Although the largest banks in terms of assets are in the United States, the number of banks in the United States is much larger than the number in any other country. In most other countries, three, four, or five banks, each with hundreds of branches, account for 60 or 70 percent of bank deposits and loans.

That U.S. banks are both very large and yet much more numerous than in other countries reflects two factors—one is that the total bank deposits are much larger in the United States than elsewhere because the U.S. economy is much larger. The second is the concern in the United States with maintaining competition in banking, which has led to regulations against expansion of bank branches across state lines (the McFadden Act of 1927), and, in many cases, across political jurisdictions within states, or even across the boundaries between zip-code areas. Paradoxically, the large size of major U.S. banks may have contributed to the mergers among foreign banks so they would not be at a size disadvantage relative to the U.S. banks in meeting the financial needs of large multinational firms. Thus, in Great Britain in the early 1970s, the National Provincial Bank merged with Westminster Bank while Lloyds merged with British and Overseas Bank. In the Netherlands, Amsterdam Bank and Rotterdam Bank merged.

Most of the foreign offices of U.S. banks are branches; they are not incorporated in the country in which they are located. In a few cases, however, the parents have set up subsidiaries, which have a separate legal status abroad. Frequently, host countries require that foreign-owned banks have minority domestic ownership so that the subsidiary form is essential. The distinction between branch and subsidiary is important for determining U.S. corporate income tax liability, for the income of offshore branches is included in U.S. income in the year in which the income is earned, while income of the foreign subsidiaries is subject to U.S. taxation only when the subsidiaries pay dividends to their U.S. parents. Conceivably the subsidiary could close with a loss to its shareholders while the parent remained in business; a branch could not fail independently of the failure of the parent.

Competition and Regulation

The rapid growth of foreign banks in the United States in the 1970s focused attention on bank regulation, and especially on whether foreign banks had competitive advantages in the United States relative to U.S. banks because of regulatory oversights. Moreover, the rapid growth of foreign banks in the United States led to the concern whether the regulations applied by foreign authorities to the activities of U.S. banks within their jurisdictions are more restrictive than the comparable regulations applied to the activities of foreign banks within the United States by various U.S. authorities, that is, whether there was reciprocity in banking. A key feature of banking regulation within the United States is the multiplicity of regulatory authorities, which was extensively discussed in chapter 3. The regulatory dilemma is that if U.S. regulation of foreign banks seeks to follow the principle of reciprocity, then the severity of regulations applied to U.S. offices of banks headquartered abroad may vary, depending on the country in which the bank is headquartered.

The growth of offshore banking has facilitated the growth of international banking in several important ways. Branches of U.S. banks established in London to do offshore deposit business, primarily in dollars, could easily compete for sterling deposits and loans at the same time. Similarly, branches established to do offshore banking business in Brussels could sell deposits and buy loans denominated in the Belgian franc. These Brussels branches could obtain funds to make loans by issuing Belgian franc deposits to Belgian residents or by borrowing Belgian francs from the major Belgian banks in the interbank market. Or these branches might have issued Belgian franc deposits in the offshore market, or issued deposits denominated in various foreign currencies in the offshore market and converted the funds to Belgian francs. Because transactions costs encountered by banks are very low, the costs of the currency swap would be insignificant. Similarly, foreign banks that wanted to develop a loan business could obtain the funds to buy dollar loans by obtaining dollar deposits in the offshore dollar market and by borrowing in the U.S. interbank market.

The major expansion of U.S. banks abroad occurred in the 1960s (although a few U.S. banks had established foreign branches in the 1920s and several in the latter part of the nineteenth century) for several reasons. One was to follow the foreign expansion of U.S. firms. A second was to avoid domestic limits on growth; this was especially true for U.S. banks headquartered in New York City. Finally, a large number of U.S. banks went abroad to participate in the offshore money market; many to avoid the loss of deposits to U.S. and foreign banks offering higher interest rates on dollar deposits than those available on domestic dollar deposits. The distribution of foreign offices of U.S. banks matches the pattern of U.S. foreign investment with two major exceptions: U.S. banks were underrepresented in those countries in which entry was restricted or prohibited, including Canada and Mexico, and overrepresented in London, Luxembourg, the Bahamas, and other monetary havens.

Foreign-owned banks also set up offices in London, Luxembourg, Singapore, and other monetary havens to participate in the offshore market for deposits denominated in the dollar, the mark, and the Swiss franc. Setting up branches abroad to engage in the offshore market was generally less costly or more profitable than setting up additional offices to compete for domestic business. The major expansion of foreign banks in the United States took place in the 1970s for several reasons. One major reason was to circumvent the domestic constraints on growth and to participate directly in the dominant international center of finance. Another was to participate in the financing of international trade between their own countries and the United States; because much of the trade was denominated in dollars, foreign banks may have been at a disadvantage in trade financing. A third was to serve the particular ethnic markets in the United States, both the expatriate business community and immigrants. Moreover, foreign investment was also increasing in the United States, and the German, Japanese, and British banks did not want to lose their customers to the U.S. banks.

Foreign banks contemplating entry in the U.S. faced a number of key decisions—one was whether to set up offices in New York or in other cities; a second was whether to enter by starting a new office or through purchase of a U.S. bank; a third was whether to set up a branch, a subsidiary, or an agency. Foreign banks had certain advantages in the United States. One was that although they were not allowed to branch across state lines they might place branches in one state and a subsidiary in another (or subsidiaries in several other states). A second was that their U.S. branches were not required to join the Federal Reserve, nor were they required to hold reserves. Capital ratios were below those of the U.S. banks; indeed the branches had no separate capital of their own.

The International Banking Act of 1978 (IBA) significantly reduced the competitive advantages previously available to foreign banks in the United States by treating them as if they were U.S. banks; the principle of "national treatment" was established. All foreign banks operating in the United States are to be treated as if they were U.S. banks, regardless of the treatment afforded U.S. banks in their home countries (the reciprocity principle has not been applied). While foreign banks might not join the Federal Reserve, they were required to hold reserves, providing they had deposits in excess of $1 billion, comparable to those held by the U.S. banks. The U.S. branches of foreign banks were provided with the option of federal licenses; previously they had only state licenses. Those branches of foreign banks that were involved in retail banking were required to participate in federal deposit insurance. Foreign banks could set up Edge Act corporations, and the powers of the Edge Act corporations of U.S. banks were expanded.[2] The U.S. offices of large foreign banks now are subject to the same supervisory and supervision requirements as comparable U.S. offices.

The impact of the IBA will slow the growth of foreign banks in the United States. Yet these banks are sufficiently numerous and large to increase significantly competition in banking, especially in the wholesale market, but also in the retail markets in New York and California. By subjecting foreign-owned banks to reserve requirements, the effectiveness of U.S. monetary control will be increased.

The Growth of Offshore Banking

The growth of offshore deposits has generated considerable controversy about their impact on the rate of world inflation, about the stability of the international financial system, and about the effectiveness of national monetary control. One assertion is that the growth of the offshore dollar deposits led to a surge in the rate of world inflation in the 1970s, largely because offshore banks have not been subject to reserve requirements and hence have been in a position to create a massive amount of credit on the basis of a modest increase in their reserves. A second concern is that the offshore banking system might collapse along the lines of the failure of banks in the Great Depression. One scenario has the closing of one or two poorly managed offshore banks due to losses on their loans to high-risk borrowers triggering the collapse of better managed banks from whom they had borrowed; the metaphor sometimes used is that of a collapsing "house of cards." The third concern is that the growth of the offshore market has reduced the

[2] Edge Act corporations are permitted by an amendment to the Federal Reserve Act that relaxes restrictions on U.S. banks engaged in financing international trade and investment.

segmentation among national financial markets, so there is less scope for independent national monetary policies. A variant of this argument is that the weakness of the dollar in the foreign exchange market has resulted from the monies "sloshing about" in the offshore market. Finally, there is concern that the effectiveness of monetary control has declined because the banks can circumvent domestic monetary tightness through their offshore activities.

The rapid growth of offshore deposits denominated in the U.S. dollar reflects investor response to the excess of interest rates on offshore deposits over the interest rates on comparable domestic deposits. Two factors explain this interest-rate differential. One is that offshore banks incur lower costs than domestic banks, largely because they are located in financial centers where they are not obliged to hold reserves against offshore deposits. Similar statements can be made about offshore deposits denominated in the mark. Reserve requirements are an implicit tax on deposits. The second factor is that offshore banks are not constrained by ceilings from paying interest rates higher than those they can pay on domestic deposits. Both factors reflect that banking is less extensively regulated in offshore financial centers than in domestic financial centers.

Offshore banks are virtually unregulated by the authorities of the countries in which they are located; thus, the British authorities recognize that dollar transactions in London are a matter of geographic convenience and believe these dollar, mark, and other foreign currency transactions have no more significance for the management of the British economy than if they had occurred in Luxembourg or New York. Great Britain benefits from exporting more banking services. Indeed, to the extent *dollar* banking services occur in London, the British have "poached" the banking activities that almost certainly would have occurred in New York or other U.S. cities. Employment in banking and related industries is higher in London and lower in the United States.

Competition for deposits among offshore banks means they pass on to investors or depositors most, if not all, of the cost savings realized by producing deposits in the offshore market. Fifty or eighty international banks, the dominant banks in each country, are important competitors in the London offshore market, while another two hundred banks from various countries also participate. Competition among different political jurisdictions such as Great Britain, Luxembourg, the Bahamas, and Singapore for offshore banking business causes each to be reluctant to apply any regulations on offshore banks, lest costs of the banks increase and they move to less extensively regulated offshore centers.

Interest Rates in Domestic and Offshore Banks

Once major international banks have established offices to produce and sell offshore deposits, large investors have a new set of investment alternatives. They can buy domestic deposits, or alternatively, they can buy offshore deposits denominated in the same currencies, even from the branches of the same banks from which they can buy domestic deposits. Interest rates on the offshore deposits are higher than those on comparable domestic deposits. If owners of domestic dollar deposits know about the higher interest rates available on offshore deposits, their continued demand for domestic deposits even at the cost of forgone interest income must be explained. They perceive additional risks associated with offshore deposits, especially that exchange controls might be applied to the repatriation of funds from the offshore market to the domestic market either by the country in which the deposit is located or by the United States. While the probability of these controls may seem slight, the additional interest income is also modest.

To the extent interest rates on offshore dollar deposits exceed those on comparable domestic deposits by the amount that reflects differences in costs of the two kinds of deposits (primarily those of reserve requirements), each U.S. bank is indifferent between selling an additional offshore deposit and selling an additional domestic deposit. In the absence of exchange controls, banks can use offshore deposits to finance domestic loans, just as they can use domestic deposits to finance offshore loans. There is no necessary link between where a deposit is generated and where a loan is acquired. Interest rates charged to a borrower on an offshore loan are comparable to the interest rates the same borrower would be charged on a domestic loan and banks have no financial incentive to charge customers lower interest rates on offshore loans than on domestic loans.

Once a bank has decided on the maximum interest rate it can pay on an offshore deposit denominated in U.S. dollars, the bank can readily determine the maximum interest rate it can pay on offshore deposits denominated in the mark, the Swiss franc, and other currencies, and still be no worse off than if it had sold an offshore dollar-denominated deposit. Thus the London branch of a U.S. bank may issue deposits denominated in the mark and then use the funds to purchase a dollar loan, after first buying dollars in the foreign-exchange market. To reduce or eliminate the exchange exposure that occurs if it sells liabilities denominated in the dollar, the bank would buy the Swiss franc in the forward market at the same time the bank sold the Swiss franc in the spot-exchange market. If banks sought to fully cover any possible exchange exposure (or to be compensated for carrying the exposure), differences in interest rates on offshore deposits denominated in various currencies would reflect the cost of covering the exchange risk, or the percentage difference between the forward-exchange rate and the spot-exchange rate.

Some U.S. banks have branches in London, Zurich, Luxembourg, and Paris. At any moment, the branches of a U.S. bank in these centers would offer virtually the same interest rate on a dollar-denominated deposit of a particular maturity. In general, there is no economic incentive for the London branch to offer a higher interest rate on a dollar deposit than the Zurich branch does, especially if the funds realized from issuing the deposits are to be used to finance a purchase of a loan in New York. If interest rates on offshore deposits sold by the branches of a given bank in different centers are the same, then the volume of deposits produced in each center will depend on investor appraisal of the differences in the risks associated with deposits in the various centers; relatively more deposits will be produced in centers in which the risk of exchange controls is lower. If investors believe the risk attached to London dollar deposits is increasing relative to the risk attached to Luxembourg dollar deposits, they would shift funds from London to Luxembourg. Nevertheless, the interest rates on London dollar deposits would not change significantly relative to that on Luxembourg dollar deposits.

Occasionally, branches of a bank in a particular center seek to sell offshore deposits there because they wish to buy loans in that country. If investors associate higher risk with offshore deposits available in a particular country because of greater likelihood of exchange controls, then the offshore offices located there must offer higher interest rates on deposits than the offices located in the principal offshore centers. For example, offshore offices in Milan, Italy, have had to pay modestly higher interest rates on dollar deposits than have the branches of the same banks in London to induce investors to acquire deposits in Milan; investors perceive larger risk is attached to offshore deposits in Italy. The banks that sell dollar deposits in Milan use the funds to buy dollar loans from Italian banks. If these banks offered the same rate on Milan dollar deposits as on London dollar deposits, they would sell a smaller volume of deposits, or perhaps not sell any at all.

Just as some offshore centers are judged riskier than others, so some offshore banks are judged safer than others. The riskier banks must pay higher interest rates to sell offshore deposits. The differences in the perception of risk reflect several factors, including the size of each bank, measures of its solvency such as its capital-deposit ratios, the country of domicile of its parent, and the total of offshore deposits sold by the bank relative to its total domestic deposits. Investors rank offshore banks into three or four major groups, with the result that there has been a "tiering" of offshore interest rates (an analogy is the rating of bonds issued by various firms and governments). The spread between the lowest interest rates paid by banks at any time and the highest interest rates paid by other banks has ranged from less than one-half percent to nearly two percent.

At each moment, investors have a large range of deposits available to them: they can choose between domestic deposits and offshore deposits denominated in the U.S. dollar, the mark, and the Swiss franc, and several other currencies. Moreover, they can choose among offshore deposits denominated in a particular currency in various offshore centers and among offshore deposits and domestic deposits offered by several hundred banks that differ in size and country of domicile. The much more rapid growth of offshore deposits than of domestic deposits reflects two factors. One is that the interest incentive to shift to offshore deposits has increased as interest rates have increased, since the tax implicit in non-interest-bearing reserves has increased, and the second is that the assessment of the risk associated with offshore deposits has decreased.[3]

The Monetary Implications of Offshore Deposits

The rapid growth of offshore deposits in the 1970s, at a time when the world inflation rate increased, led to the assertion that the growth of offshore deposits caused or at least intensified the inflation. The analysis of this proposition depends on whether the growth of offshore deposits has been in addition to the growth of domestic deposits or instead a substitute for the growth of domestic deposits. A related issue is whether the supply of reserves to the commercial banking system has been independent of the growth of offshore deposits and credit.

Two extreme views about the process of credit creation in the offshore deposits led to different conclusions about the inflationary implications of the growth of offshore deposits. One is that the offshore banking system is comparable to the domestic banking system, with the exception that the offshore system lacks a central bank. One implication of this view is that a modest increase in the reserves of the offshore banks leads to a substantial expansion of credit in the offshore banking system, because offshore banks are not required to hold reserves. Thus, the story is that once an individual shifts funds from a domestic bank to an offshore bank, the latter in turn lends to some other individual who buys goods or securities from someone who in turn deposits the receipts in another offshore bank, which in turn lends funds to someone who buys goods, and so on. Those who argue that the growth of offshore deposits has had a significant impact on the rate of world inflation generally share this view about a segmented offshore banking system.

The competing extreme view is that the offshore market is exclusively an interbank market, the international counterpart of the U.S. federal funds market. According to this view, no credit is created in the offshore system; rather, the market facilitates more efficient allocation of credit. Thus, banks in countries with balance-of-payments surpluses extend credit to banks in countries with balance-of-payments deficits. Extensive interbank transactions in the offshore market support this view.[4] But this view is in-

---

[3] The U.S. payments deficit may have contributed modestly to the growth of offshore deposits, to the extent that foreign central banks hold part of their dollar reserves in offshore banks. But such holdings are small. And offshore deposits denominated in the Swiss franc and the mark have increased, even though these currencies have had payments surpluses.

[4] One reason for the large volume of interbank transactions is that banks that are deemed less risky lend to riskier banks. A second is that banks seek to match maturi-

consistent with the data that show that a substantial proportion of liabilities of offshore banks are to private firms and investors, including central banks.

Offshore banks are not part of a segmented financial system but rather offices of major international banks located in centers where they are not obliged to hold reserves. There are virtually no important offshore banks that are not branches (or subsidiaries) of major international banks; the offshore offices of major international banks compete with the domestic offices of these same banks to sell deposits. If the domestic office of a U.S. bank sells an additional domestic deposit, its required reserve holdings increase; if the offshore office of the same bank sells an additional deposit, required reserves are unchanged. Banks mingle the reserves held against domestic deposits and against offshore deposits. By selling an additional offshore deposit, a bank is able to reduce the effective or economic level of reserves below the legal level required to be held against domestic deposits. Hence the ratio of non-interest-earning assets to the total assets of each bank decreases as it sells offshore deposits.

The more rapid growth of offshore deposits than of domestic deposits means that the effective reserve requirements applied to each bank has declined. So there may have been a larger than anticipated increase in the supply of dollar credit for a given increase in the supply of dollar reserves because of the increase in the money multiplier. To the extent that growth of offshore deposits has been unanticipated by the central bank, there has been a more rapid increase in the volume of credit than was anticipated. Estimating the impact of this unanticipated increase in the supply of credit on the U.S. inflation rate and on the world inflation rate is difficult, in part because this source of growth of credit may have been a substitute for some other source of credit that otherwise would have grown more rapidly.

Hence the growth of the offshore deposits has reduced the effectiveness of monetary control because the authorities can never be confident of the changes in the money supply associated with a given change in reserves of the banking system. The source of their uncertainty lies in the changes in the money multiplier as the volume of offshore deposits increases relative to the volume of domestic deposits. On a year-to-year basis, the trend is variable and appears unpredictable.

The growth of offshore deposits has probably decreased the significance of the barriers among currency areas, and complicated the management of monetary policy. Both investors and banks are more conscious of the returns associated with crossing currency borders. The growth of offshore deposits has increased the willingness of firms to estimate the costs and risks asso-

---

ties of their assets and liabilities to economize on the need for liquidity. A third is that some countries have an advantage in taking deposits while others have an advantage in making loans. A fourth is that there are limits on their willingness to acquire loans of individual borrowers, or loans of borrowers in a particular country or loans of borrowers in a particular industry. Once a bank's loans in each category are at its ceilings, it extends credit to banks less able to sell deposits to investors.

ciated with altering their currency exposures, although it has not reduced these costs or risks in any significant way. Thus, the segmentation of currency areas has declined, and so the scope for independent national monetary policies has also declined.

The concern that the failure of offshore banks might trigger the collapse of the banking system is greatly exaggerated because the major offshore banks are branches of the major international banks. Most offshore banks are unlikely to make riskier loans than their home offices. Offshore offices are unlikely to fail because their liabilities exceed their deposits while their head offices of the same banks remain open.

Reducing the Appeal of Offshore Banking

One impact of the growth of offshore banking is the proposal that free-banking zones be created in New York, Chicago, San Francisco, and other financial centers in the United States. Banks operating in these zones would not be obliged to hold reserves. Some of the offshore banking business now undertaken in London and elsewhere would shift to New York. Yet many holders of domestic deposits in Minneapolis and Salt Lake City and other U.S. cities would find it attractive to shift funds to the free-banking zones in New York, Chicago, and San Francisco. Their concern with exchange controls, which might have deterred them from acquiring dollar deposits in London or Zurich, is unlikely to deter them from acquiring dollar deposits in one of these free-banking zones. So the potential rush to acquire deposits in the free-banking zone would mean that each major metropolitan area in the United States would seek to establish its own free-banking zone. If, as seems unlikely, such zones were established, the increase in the demand for deposits produced by these banks would lead to a sharp decline in the volume of domestic deposits subject to reserves. The implication is that efforts of the Federal Reserve to maintain high reserve requirements on one class of deposits while virtually identical deposits are not subject to reserve requirements would be readily circumvented. While regulations might be adopted to limit shifts of funds to the banks in the free-banking zone, these regulations would be avoided. Thus, the implications of establishing free-banking zones in the United States only highlights the problems for monetary management in a world in which similar deposits are subject to different reserve requirements. As long as banks operating in the United States are subject to higher reserve requirements than are banks operating in London and other offshore centers, the reserve requirement creates an incentive to export the U.S. banking system.

A second proposal to reduce the incentive to export the U.S. banking system is that reserve requirements be applied to offshore deposits. Reserve requirements might be applied to all offshore deposits produced in a particular center. The almost certain response is that investors would shift funds to other offshore centers, which, in order to increase their share of offshore deposits, choose not to apply reserve requirements. Hence, if reserve requirements are applied to offshore deposits in London, owners of offshore deposits would shift their funds to Luxembourg, Paris, and Panama. Alternatively, reserve requirements might be applied by monetary authorities in each country to the offshore offices of banks headquartered in their jurisdictions; thus, the U.S. authorities could extend domestic reserve requirements to the offshore offices of U.S. banks. The German authorities might extend their own domestic reserve requirements to the offshore offices of German banks. Then owners of offshore deposits would shift their demand for offshore deposits produced by British, French, and Swiss banks. A third proposal is to pay market interest rates on reserves held by the central bank.

The regulatory problem is that the U.S. authorities must choose between reducing the incentive for investors to acquire offshore deposits or adjusting to the more rapid growth of offshore deposits than of domestic deposits. In a period of high interest rates and low-cost communications, banks and their customers have found it easy and profitable to circumvent the implicit tax on domestic deposits in the reserve requirements. The U.S. authorities must recognize that the structure of U.S. financial regulation cannot be independent of that elsewhere; they cannot maintain a level of reserve requirements significantly higher than that available abroad, inducing more of the banking business to go abroad.

Bank Regulation and Monetary Policy

One of the key questions is whether the idiosyncratic nature of banking regulation has a significant impact on the effectiveness of monetary policy. Several different comparisons of banking regulation are relevant. One involves the comparison of the regulation of the domestic transactions of U.S. banks with the regulation of their offshore transactions. The second involves the comparison between the regulation of the domestic activities of U.S. banks and the activities of foreign banks in the United States. The third involves the comparison of offshore activities of U.S. banks with the offshore activities of non–U.S. banks. The fourth involves the comparison between the domestic regulation of U.S. banks and the regulation of foreign banks in the countries in which they are headquartered.

The questions about whether U.S.-owned or foreign-owned banks provide banking services to U.S. residents should be distinguished from the broader questions about the effectiveness of monetary policy when national regulations differ. Differential regulation has an impact on the competitive position of different groups of banks, and on their growth rates. The question of the ownership of the institutions that provide banking services is independent of the monetary implications, with one exception: namely, to the extent foreign-owned banks may have easier access to funds at their home offices, they may be able to circumvent changes in monetary policy. The significance of this nonmarket source of funds is an empirical matter. On an a priori basis, the argument would appear to be much more significant for smaller countries than for the United States.

Currently, U.S. monetary control is weakened because of the differential in reserve requirements and the lack of a stable relationship between the growth of offshore dollar deposits and the growth of domestic deposits. In periods of monetary contraction, as interest rates rise and the effective interest cost of reserve requirements applied to U.S. banks increases, there would be a cyclical reduction in the share of U.S. banks in the dollar deposit markets. To reduce the disadvantage of U.S. banks, either domestic reserve requirements might be lowered to reduce or eliminate the financial incentives in favor of offshore deposits, or interest might be paid on required reserves. The argument for such adjustments demonstrates that the U.S. regulatory authorities cannot operate independently of foreign regulations; more severe regulation tends to lead to the export of the U.S. banking industry.

Summary

The last several decades have witnessed a remarkable growth in the internationalization of the commercial banking industry. Banks headquartered in New York, Chicago, and other major financial centers in the United States have established branches in London, Zurich, Frankfurt, Paris, and Tokyo to sell deposits and buy loans in competition with domestic banks in these centers. Similarly, the major banks based in Western Europe, Latin America, and Asia have established offices in New York and other U.S. financial centers to compete with the deposit and loan business of the U.S. firms. Moreover, virtually all the major international banks have set up offices in one or several of the offshore financial centers, primarily London, Luxembourg, Singapore, the Bahamas, the Cayman Islands, and Panama, where they buy deposits and sell loans denominated in a currency other than that of the country in which they are located. These two developments in the structure of the banking industry are closely related because banks that have expanded into the domestic markets abroad frequently have done so using funds realized from the sale of offshore deposits.

The major question raised by the changes in the institutional structure of banking is whether they complicate the management of U.S. monetary policy, and as well, the management of monetary policy in other countries. Thus is it possible that the U.S. branches of British, Swiss, and Japanese banks might be able to sidestep the contractive monetary measures adopted by the Federal Reserve by extending loans to U.S. borrowers using funds acquired from their home offices? Perhaps more importantly, to what extent has the growth of an offshore banking system and of offshore dollar deposits, more frequently known as the Eurobanking system, reduced the effectiveness of U.S. monetary control?

Virtually all offshore banks are branches (and in a few cases subsidiaries) of the major international banks. The offshore branches of U.S. banks account for a significant part of total offshore deposits. Offshore branches have one significant advantage over the domestic offices of the same bank: they are not subject to the reserve requirements that are applied to domestic banks. Thus offshore offices do not incur the cost of reserve requirements and can afford to pay higher interest rates on deposits than domestic offices and still remain competitive. Hence, at any one time investors can choose between domestic and offshore deposits denominated in the dollar and six or eight other currencies offered by the same bank; they can also choose among deposits denominated in different currencies and offered by different banks. These choices reflect risk and return calculations; a principal concern is whether the additional interest income is adequate compensation for the additional risks, especially the risk that exchange controls might delay or interfere with the repatriation of funds from the offshore center.

The growth of offshore dollar deposits has an impact on the U.S. financial system much like a reduction in the reserve requirement (or an increase in the fractional reserve-credit multiplier); the total volume of money and credit associated with a given volume of commercial bank reserves is larger. Since offshore deposits have grown several times more rapidly than domestic deposits but with considerable variation in the year-to-year-growth rate, the U.S. monetary authorities cannot be confident of the impact of the growth of the reserve base on the supplies of money and of credit because of the period-to-period variability in the growth of offshore deposits. Consequently the offshore banking system has led to the decline in the effectiveness of monetary control.

QUESTIONS AND EXERCISES

1. Discuss the conditions necessary for the growth of an external currency market. Why do interest rates on offshore deposits exceed those on comparable domestic deposits? What is the upper limit to this difference? If interest rates on external deposits are higher than those on domestic deposits denominated in the same currency and issued by those on domestic deposits, why does anyone continue to hold domestic deposits?

2. Why might the growth of an offshore market in dollar deposits weaken the effectiveness of monetary control of the Federal Reserve?

3. Is it possible or likely that a financial collapse or disaster might develop in the offshore banking system, and be independent of the domestic banking system?

4. Discuss the ways in which the growth of offshore dollar deposits has contributed to the growth of branches of foreign banks in the United States.

FURTHER READING

FIELEKE, NORMAN. *Key Issues in International Banking.* Boston: Federal Reserve Bank of Boston, 1977. A conference volume with good descriptive material.

LITTLE, JANE SNEDDON. *Eurodollars.* New York: Harper & Row, 1975. A descriptive survey of actors in the offshore money market.

U.S., CONGRESS, HOUSE, COMMITTEE ON BANKING, CURRENCY, AND HOUSING. *International Banking.* Washington: Government Printing Office, 1976. A comprehensive survey of international banking; background materials for the International Banking Act of 1979.

32

The Issues in International Finance

Over the next several decades, the monetary authorities in the major countries must remain concerned with changes in international financial arrangements. A dominant need is to reduce the range of movement in exchange rates, and the frequency and severity of the disturbances that countries import from their trading partners. The monetary authorities will seek to develop arrangements that will enhance the effectiveness of monetary policy without infringing on freer international trade and payments.

Toward a New International Monetary System

Since the breakdown of the Bretton Woods system of pegged exchange rates, the arrangements for organizing the foreign-exchange market and producing international money are seen as too haphazard to qualify as an international monetary system. To pass this hurdle, the arrangements must have more "order," or be more systematic, or be based on an international treaty. There are numerous proposals to modify existing arrangements to achieve greater "order." Some proposals seek to improve the operation of the floating exchange rates, while others favor a return to pegged exchange rates, either on a global or regional basis. There is a need to develop a set of arrangements that will constrain the behavior of national authorities in the foreign-exchange market so they will not export shocks to their neighbors. These constraints might be self-imposed, as under the gold standard or, more likely, they might be based on an international treaty, much like the Bretton Woods agreement. Proposals abound to alter the roles of assets that have been used as international reserves. One issue is whether gold should continue to be phased out of the international monetary system, or whether arrangements should be devised so gold again will be used as an important international reserve asset. A second issue involves the future international monetary roles of dollar assets, and whether the U.S. authorities should adopt measures to alter the international role of the dollar. The related issues include the international monetary roles of assets denominated in other currencies, such as the mark and perhaps the yen, and assets produced by the International Monetary Fund, such as SDRs. These arrangements must provide for an orderly growth in the volume of international reserves, and avoid the deflationary impacts like those of the 1920s or the inflationary impacts comparable to those of the 1970s.

A major concern is how the changes in these institutional frameworks would affect the management of monetary policy, both the need or demand for monetary independence in the major countries and the ability of the monetary authorities to follow policies appropriate for domestic objectives with minimal external constraints. The need or demand for monetary independence arises because the phases of the business cycle are not perfectly correlated across countries; even if they were, however, countries differ in the importance they attach to full employment, price stability, and rapid growth. Even if individual countries decide they wish to pursue greater monetary independence, there may be significant external constraints and the changes in monetary policy may have significant adverse impacts on the flows of capital or on exchange rates.

In modifying the international monetary arrangements, the objective is to develop arrangements so that countries can pursue their domestic objectives without forgoing the advantages of openness and specialization possible in the international economy.

Some of these proposals are much more ambitious than others in the extent to which they would modify current arrangements for the organization of the foreign-exchange market and the supply of international reserves. A new system implies a set of rules, perhaps based on an international treaty like the Bretton Woods agreement, that would lead to changes in the intervention practices of the participants in the foreign-exchange market. The participating countries would commit themselves to following particular practices about exchange-market intervention and international reserve holdings and refraining from adopting other actions. Adhering to many of these commitments is likely to have *no* significant cost; even without the treaty, the countries would have behaved as if they were following the commitments. To the extent adherence to the commitment has a cost in that one or several of the participating countries are obliged to pursue measures they would not have in the absence of the treaty, the key question is how long they will abide by the commitment, and forgo pursuing their own interests to satisfy an international obligation. So one issue is how far "in front" of the consensus the treaty can get; treaties that are expensive to domestic interests may, like the Smithsonian Agreement, soon fall by the wayside.

So a major question involves the significance of changes in economic policy and international arrangements. The relevant question is how long efforts of central banks to peg or manage exchange rates can cause the exchange rates to assume significantly different values than they otherwise would have. Intervention can have a greater impact on the exchange rate in the short run—a period of a few months or even a year—than over a more extended period. In the long run, exchange rates are determined by relative prices and incomes and expectations about relative prices and incomes.

The success in devising an international financial arrangement that will remain viable for some time depends on the relationship between the implied commitments and the prevailing set of monetary and even political relationships. An attempt to adopt a system of pegged exchange rates is not likely to be viable in an inflationary period; one characteristic of inflation is that rates of price increases differ sharply across countries and vary significantly from one year to the next, and so pegged rates are not viable in these circumstances. Similarly, proposals that require extensive centralization of authority are not likely to be viable if nationalist pressures become stronger.

If the new arrangements are to be viable, they must be consistent with the distribution of political and economic power. Thus, the gold standard succeeded during a period of British economic dominance, and broke down as U.S. economic power was increasing relative to British power. The Bretton Woods system flourished during a period when U.S. economic and political power was dominant. As the relative U.S. economic position declined with the resurgence of German and Japanese economies, the fragility of the Bretton Woods system became more apparent. The new set of arrangements must be consistent with a dispersion of economic power among at least three major economic centers—the United States, Germany and the European Community, and Japan.

Changes in institutional arrangements involve complicated interplay of interests of various countries. Few policymakers attempt to optimize or maximize a cosmopolitan or universal interest. Rather, in developing positions on these issues, each deals with a national variant on a familiar theme, "What's in it for me?" Implicitly, the policymakers in each country develop a cost-benefit analysis of the impacts of the adoption of each proposal on the well-being of their constituents and on the ability of their own government to realize its objectives. Relatively few national monetary authorities would agree to proposals that might advance the cosmopolitan interest if doing so has a major cost to their own constituents.

The source of international problems is that national interests diverge. Differences across nations are more extensive, usually, than the differences within nations. Moreover, within countries, there are usually established legal procedures, frequently based on a written constitution, for determining the public interest, whereas across nations procedures for determining the cosmopolitan interest are far less advanced. Developing solutions to the questions might be easier if national interests were more malleable or alterable. Because such interests change only slowly, the problem is how to devise a set of international arrangements that will best accommodate these divergent national interests.

This chapter first traces developments in international monetary arrangements in the last decade. Then attention is given to the modification of exchange market arrangements, the development of reserve arrangements, and the unified currency idea. Three issues are considered—the scope for mergers of national currencies and the optimum currency issue, the choice between pegged rates and floating rates, and the future roles of competing international monies, especially the role of gold, the dollar, and IMF monies.

International Monetary Developments in the 1970s

The 1970s was a decade of extensive change in international monetary arrangements, much more extensive than in any previous decade. The market price of gold, which had been $35 at the end of the 1960s, exceeded $600 a decade later. Efforts were made to demonetize gold, or to reduce its role in the international monetary system, and both the U.S. authorities and the International Monetary Fund sold gold to the private markets. The surge in the price of gold seemed inconsistent with the view that gold would no longer be used as an international money and central banks would then sell gold.

At the end of the 1960s, the IMF system of adjustable parities appeared under pressure, largely because the necessary changes in exchange parities to the increasing overvaluation of the dollar were long delayed. The system broke down once in August 1971, was patched and stumbled through 1972, only to break down again in early 1973, because the monetary authorities could no longer convince traders and investors that monetary policies consistent with a system of pegged exchange rates would be pursued. Yet the floating-rate system did not conform to the textbook model, in that the range of movement in exchange rates was much greater than the difference in national price levels. The resulting changes in real exchange rates appeared to have a modest impact in correcting trade and current-account imbalances. The authorities intervened extensively in the effort to dampen movement in the exchange rates; indeed, by some measures, especially purchases and sales of international reserves, intervention was more extensive than in the previous decade with pegged exchange rates. In the 1960s, one of the major concerns was the shortage of international reserves, which culminated in the establishment of the SDR arrangement and the production of $10 billion in SDRs. In the decade of the 1970s, total reserves minus gold had increased by nearly sevenfold, from $40 billion at the end of 1969 to $270 billion at the end of 1979; total reserves including gold had increased from $80 billion to nearly $600 billion if gold is valued at $300 an ounce.

Finally there was a very sharp change in the position of the dollar in international financial relationships, and an effort by the monetary authorities in many countries to diversify their portfolios to include relatively more assets denominated in currencies other than the dollar, especially the mark, the Swiss franc, and the yen.

The Impact of Inflation

The factor that relates all these changes in international financial relationships is the surge in the world inflation rate, from an annual average rate of 4.3 percent in the 1960s to one of 11.1 percent in the 1970s; the U.S. inflation rate increased from an average of 2.3 percent in the 1960s to 7.1 percent in the 1970s. Inflation rates were at their highest-ever levels at the end of the decade. While this inflation rate was intensified by the succession of increases in the price of crude petroleum promoted by OPEC in 1973–74 and then again in 1978–79, the world inflation rate was already at the double-digit level before the fourfold increase in 1973–74. Nevertheless in 1974 and again in 1979, the sharp increases in the price of oil caused the world inflation rate to be higher by two to three percentage points. In some countries, the impact was greater, because the oil price increase triggered increases in other prices, and expectations of future price increases.

If the stability in the world price level in the 1950s and the early 1960s was a result of stability in the U.S. price level, the subsequent U.S. inflation was a major factor in the increase in the world price level, in part because the United States is such a large part of the world economy. In the late 1960s, all other currencies were pegged to the U.S. dollar, and so increases in U.S. prices were quickly reflected in increases in prices of similar goods around the world. Before the system of pegged exchange rates broke down, the U.S. payments deficit surged, and the increase in international reserve holdings of other countries in the 1969–73 period led to a very rapid increase in their money supplies.

One element in the stability of the world economy in the 1950s and much of the 1960s was the stability of the U.S. price level; another was the willingness of the United States to accept persistent payments deficits. Many countries still have a "mercantilist" bias; they feel it is important to accumulate gold and other international reserve assets. Yet if the system lacks a means to produce an increment in reserves from new gold production, then the success of some countries in adding to their gold holdings means other countries must incur deficits and sell gold. And the United States accepted the deficits, which were partly financed by gold sales and partly by sales of dollar-denominated assets to foreign monetary authorities.

The system of adjustable parities was a casualty of the surge in inflation rates. Countries differed in the priority given to minimizing the inflation rate. Changes in monetary policy were more dramatic in some countries than in others; as expectations about inflation rates were revised, so were the anticipated exchange rates. Thus, when Germany pursued a sharply contractive monetary policy early in 1973, investors rushed to acquire mark-denominated assets both because interest rates were higher on these assets than on comparable assets denominated in other currencies and because they anticipated the mark would appreciate.

The amendments to the IMF treaty based on the Jamaica Agreement of 1976 permitted Fund members to follow any exchange-rate practices they wished; the rules were permissive rather than constraining. The Fund developed "guidelines for floating" and a multilateral surveillance mechanism, measures that did not constrain the members.

Partly to dampen the sharp movements in exchange rates in the late 1970s, the monetary authorities intervened extensively in the foreign-exchange market, and their reserve holdings increased sharply. A second factor behind the surge in reserves is the growth of OPEC demand for financial assets as they sought to diversify part of their wealth from natural or oil wealth to financial wealth. In addition, part of the increase in international reserves was an adjustment to the higher commodity price levels. The rules did not constrain the growth of reserves, and while there was a concern with the composition of reserves, there was no obvious way to increase the supply of reserve assets denominated in currencies other than the dollar.

In periods of inflation, the demand for gold increases because it functions as an inflation hedge. Those investors with the highest inflationary expectations set the price in this market. While gold was clearly undervalued at the end of the 1960s, since its price had remained constant since 1934 while the world price level had increased by a factor of four, the increase in the gold price in the 1970s suggests expectations of continued and accelerating inflation. From time to time, the rules concerning official transactions in gold have been changed. As a result of the Jamaica Agreement, it was agreed not to deal in gold at a price other than the official price; then the official price was abandoned. A few monetary authorities have raised the valuation attached to their holdings of gold; many monetary authorities consider gold an important component of their international reserves, and are not likely to demonetize gold. The experience with floating rates in the 1970s demonstrated that countries can have somewhat greater control over their price level than they could in a world with pegged rates. But no country was able to maintain an inflation rate as low as the average in the 1960s. While major changes in the institutional arrangements seem unlikely until the inflation rate is reduced, some modest changes might be developed to contribute to the reduction in the inflation rate.

Optional Currency Areas and Monetary Unions

One of the central issues in international finance involves the span of the use of particular currencies. Should each country have its own currency, which is the dominant tendency, or should countries merge their currencies, which is frequently contemplated as the monetary counterpart of integration in the European Community? Or would it be worthwhile for certain large countries, say China or Brazil, to develop two currencies for distinct regional areas?

In the nineteenth century, currency unification was extensive within

Germany, Japan, and Italy, in each case as part of the program of political unification—and in each case, among peoples who shared the same language and culture. Within Western Europe today, currency unification is sometimes viewed as a step towards political unification. But because the countries involved in the European Community have different languages and cultures, they may still retain sovereignty—although the significance of sovereignty may decline with the acceptance of a common currency.

Yet the dominant tendency in the last several decades has been an increase in the number of currencies. Thus the Irish pound, which had been firmly pegged to the British pound since Irish independence in 1922, now floats relative to the British pound. With the breakup of British, Dutch, French, and Portuguese empires and the establishment of new, independent countries, many new currencies were adopted. Initially these currencies were pegged to the currencies of their former metropoles. Over time, as the monetary policies in the new countries became more independent and more expansive, parities have been altered. Moreover, some countries have changed the currencies to which their own currencies are pegged; thus the Australian dollar, formerly pegged to sterling, is now pegged to the U.S. dollar.

At the more abstract level, the issues about unification of national currencies involve the attributes of countries whose currencies might be merged so as to maximize the economic welfare of the participating countries. The gains from currency unification involve the more efficient allocation of resources and capital on a worldwide basis, including the reduction in the costs of servicing the foreign-exchange market. If there were only one currency in the world, these costs would disappear. The United States might be viewed as a unified currency area, comprising twelve Federal Reserve districts and fifty states. Financial capital flows smoothly and efficiently from high saving–low growth areas to low saving–high growth areas; one indication of the almost frictionless movement is that interest rates on comparable securities are virtually the same. Payments can be made on a virtually costless basis from Maine to California by check. Internationally, the segmentation of Western Europe into currency areas incurs costs that would be avoided if the national currencies areas were merged into one European currency.

The costs of currency mergers are those associated with the loss of a central bank in one of the areas or countries, and so the ability to manage monetary policy to enhance employment and price-level objectives in the area, country, or region. If the Federal Reserve Bank of Boston were independent of the other units in the Federal Reserve System, it might pursue a more (or less) expansionary monetary policy than the other parts of the Federal Reserve in order to counter the surge in the unemployment rate in New England. The value of having a separate currency area centers on the advantages attached to altering the rate of monetary expansion. The significance of these costs of unification varies with the choice of countries involved, and with the similarity of their economic structures.

One logical proposition relevant to optimizing the number of currency areas is that there should be no more central banks than there are labor markets. If there were, some of the central banks would be redundant (as eleven of the regional Federal Reserve banks are), in that the unemployment rates in these labor markets would always be identical with those other labor markets. A labor market is defined as an area in which excess demand for labor and excess supply of labor of the same type cannot simultaneously exist. If labor is perfectly mobile between or among several labor markets, these several labor markets effectively are components of one larger labor market, in that the levels of money wages and the changes in these levels cannot differ significantly in geographic subsectors of this larger labor market. The explanation is straightforward; if the unemployed workers would move to the firms with excess demand for labor and competition among workers maintains reasonable uniformity of wages, no firm would pay a higher wage to attract labor than the prevailing market wage.

Hence the necessary condition for having separate national central banks is that there are segmented labor markets and that labor is not perfectly mobile between them. Economic welfare might be enhanced if the central banks in the area with high unemployment followed an expansive monetary policy while the central bank in the area with the inflation followed a more contractive policy. However, a second condition is that if financial capital is perfectly mobile between these currency areas, then an independent central bank would be redundant, for the central bank could not, by changes in its monetary policy, induce a change in its interest rates and money supply relative to world interest rates. In the case where capital mobility negates the efforts at monetary independence, central banks should merge to eliminate the costs of servicing the exchange market. Hence the *sufficient* condition for separate currency areas is that there are separate national banks, and national capital markets are partially segmented.

Even if both labor markets and capital markets are partially segmented, so that independent monetary policies are needed and feasible, the costs of maintaining separate national currencies may exceed the benefits. The tradeoff associated with the merger of currencies involves whether the welfare gains from the enhanced flow of goods and securities and the elimination of the costs of servicing the foreign-exchange market are larger or smaller than the welfare costs of higher unemployment because of a reduction in the number of central banks.

These general propositions must be made operational. It has been suggested that currencies be merged if the countries' economies are complementary, or if their trade patterns are similar, or if their business cycles are similar in timing and amplitude. The rationale is that the central banks in these countries would be following similar monetary policies. Small countries would have much to gain from mergers of their currencies with each other, or with the currency of a large country as a result of the increased flow of goods and financial capital. Large countries like the United

States have already realized the gains from flows of goods and capital between quite different areas. Canada and Mexico might gain from merging their currencies with the U.S. dollar because each would have much better (and cheaper) access to the U.S. financial market. In addition, currency unification has been suggested for countries that are physically congruent or share the same language. Proximity appears to be a dominant factor in the voice to merge currencies.

The European Community and Currency Unification

The historical experience suggests that currencies are merged to secure political objectives rather than economic objectives. Currency unification is seen as an important step toward political unification.

The most ambitious effort to merge national monies in recent years has been that of the European Community. This effort followed the Treaty of Rome (1957), which led to the elimination of tariffs on internal trade among members of the community, to the development of a common external tariff and a common agricultural policy, and to the harmonization of social security, welfare policy, and business taxes in the member countries. So it might seem natural for the member countries to harmonize or coordinate monetary policies, and to move toward a common community-wide money, a change that would eventually require mergers of their central banks.

The motives for currency unification in Western Europe differ. Certainly some view political unification as a desirable objective, and a merger of currencies would be a meaningful step in this objective. Some note the growth of intra-European trade; an increasing share of the trade of various European countries is with other European countries. Payments for this trade would be facilitated if there were only one currency—and if there were only one currency, then trade within Europe would be promoted relative to trade between Europe and other areas. Hence the move to a European currency would provide a modest amount of trade protection to European firms in competition with non-European firms. A third motive for currency unification is that the development of a European currency area might provide a larger center of monetary stability and better enable the European countries to insulate their economies from monetary shocks generated by the United States.

Once a decision has been reached to merge currencies, the authorities must decide on how to realize this objective. One approach is to harmonize monetary policies and then, if inflation rates are similar, to maintain the same foreign-exchange values for the two currencies. An alternative approach involves pegging these currencies in the exchange market, and then attempting to gain greater harmonization of monetary policies so as to reduce the likelihood of extended payments imbalances at the established parities.

The likelihood that countries outside Western Europe will merge their currencies in the near future is not overwhelming. Moreover, there may be substantial setbacks in efforts to achieve this objective. Nevertheless, the insights generated by the issue are applicable to two other questions. The first is if a country decides to peg its currency, how it should choose whether its interests are advanced by pegging to the U.S. dollar, the German mark, the Japanese yen, or some other currency. The second is whether a country's interests are better served by pegging its currency or permitting its currency to float.

When the monetary authorities in a country deliberate about the choice of a foreign currency to which they should peg their own currency, they want to maximize the benefits from pegging by increasing the ease with which external capital can be attracted while reducing the costs in the form of the constraint on national monetary independence.

The Choice between Floating and Pegged Exchange Rates

For most of the last century, the U.S. dollar has been a pegged currency. Prior to World War I, a system of pegged rates resulted because the dollar and other major currencies were pegged to gold. The pegs were maintained because central banks were supposed to follow the "rules of the game" for adjustment to payments imbalances, deflating when in deficit and inflating when in surplus.

The 1920s (really, 1919–26) was the first extensive period with floating currencies. At the outbreak of World War I, central banks stopped pegging their currencies at their mint parities; they embargoed gold exports and supported their currencies at levels five to fifteen percent below their prewar parities. Inflation was extensive and at different rates in various countries. Returning to the 1913 parities, while the dominant objective in most countries, was not immediately feasible at the end of the war because of the wartime inflation. Countries permitted their currencies to float, and some countries attempted to deflate so it would again be possible to peg to gold at their 1913 parities.

A few countries—Great Britain and the various neutrals, including Switzerland, the Netherlands, and the Scandinavian countries—succeeded in again pegging their currencies at their 1913 parities. The other Allies—France, Belgium, Italy, and Japan—eventually pegged their currencies in the late 1920s, after continued inflation and extended depreciation of their currencies at parities one-third to one-fourth of their previous parities. In effect gold was three to four times as expensive in terms of their currencies than before the war. The defeated belligerents—Germany, Austria, Hungary, and Russia—also pegged their currencies to gold after hyperinflations forced the adoption of new currencies.

The exchange-rate experience in the 1930s was substantially different from that of the 1920s. Great Britain permitted sterling to float in September 1931; a few countries—Ireland, Denmark, Sweden, and some Commonwealth countries—decided to peg to sterling and their currencies floated in terms of the dollar and other currencies pegged to gold. Then when President Roosevelt took office in early March 1933, he closed all U.S. banks, nationalized private U.S. gold holdings, and eliminated the gold parity for the dollar. For the next ten months, the dollar price of gold varied, for the most part increasing; the dollar was depreciating in terms of gold and most foreign currencies. Then at the end of January 1934, the dollar price of gold was again fixed, this time at $35 an ounce, so the effective increase in the dollar price of gold was 75 percent. Then speculative pressures developed against currencies that had not devalued, and, in mid-1936, three currencies, the French franc, the Belgian franc, and the Dutch guilder, were all devalued.

The interwar experience led to a number of assertions about the operation of floating exchange rates. One was that floating rates would disrupt international trade and investment; a second, that speculation would be destabilizing, both in the sense of a wider amplitude of exchange-rate movements and in the sense that speculators would cause the trend value of the exchange rate to follow a path different from that it would have followed in their absence. Thus, if speculators sold a weak currency, the price of foreign exchange would increase, and so would the price of imports. The domestic price level would increase more rapidly; in contrast, the domestic price level would increase less rapidly in those countries whose currencies were acquired by speculators. So speculation would be self-justifying. At a later stage, this self-justifying behavior led to what has been called "vicious and virtuous circles."

The proponents of floating exchange rates criticized these conclusions, but only after asserting that the primary advantage of floating exchange rates was that countries would be able to pursue or realize greater monetary independence. They claimed that countries would be able to follow monetary policies independent of the constraint on payments deficits because any tendency towards a payments imbalance would lead to a depreciation of their currencies. For example, if a country followed a more expansive monetary policy, one that would be associated with a larger payments deficit than it could readily finance under the pegged-exchange-rate system, its currency would depreciate under the floating-rate system. Similarly, no country would be obliged to purchase large amounts of foreign exchange and hence increase its own money supply to maintain its exchange parity; instead, its currency would appreciate and the monetary base would not be affected by external events. The profloaters argued that trade and investment would not be disturbed by uncertainty about exchange-rate movements because traders and investors would hedge their foreign-exchange commitments through forward-exchange contracts. Hence countries would have greater freedom to follow policies so their price levels would differ from those in other countries; similarly, they would have greater freedom to follow different employment objectives. They also argued that speculation would not be destabilizing, or that destabilizing speculators would soon go bankrupt because they would be betting against long-run trends.

A litany developed between the critics and the proponents of floating exchange rates. The critics argued that there were inadequate forward-exchange-market facilities in most currencies, and that, besides, hedging was not a costless activity. They also asserted that monetary independence was a chimera, and that countries would have much less control over their own price and income targets than the proponents promised. Moreover, the critics noted that the removal of the exchange parities would eliminate one of the last barriers to domestic inflation, so that the average level of inflation would be higher with a floating exchange-rate system than with a pegged-exchange-rate system.

Uncertainty and Independence under a Floating-Rate System

The resolution of the issue between the proponents and the critics of floating rates partly involves the nature and consequences of uncertainty under the floating-rate system. The greater monetary independence under a system of floating exchange rates than under a system of pegged exchange rates is possible only because the increased uncertainty about future exchange rates increases the segmentation of national money markets. Without an increase in segmentation, there is no scope for greater monetary independence. Yet the uncertainty that enhances monetary independence also deters trade and investment. True, trader and investor uncertainty about future exchange rates can be hedged through the purchase of forward contracts, and hedging may be costless to the extent that forward rates are unbiased predictors—on average—of future spot-exchange rates. Yet hedging is not riskless because forward rates individually are not very good predictors of the spot-exchange rates on the dates when the forward contracts mature. The "forecast" errors are substantial; the reason that the forward rate is an unbiased predictor of future spot rates is that two types of forecast errors are more or less offsetting—those that underpredict the appreciation of the foreign currency and those that underpredict the depreciation of the foreign currency.

The benefits of monetary independence with floating exchange rates cannot be attained without increased uncertainty, and the cost of this increased uncertainty is a reduced level of trade and investment—or, in a growing world economy, a reduction in the rate of growth of trade and investment. The economic significance of this cost and its value relative to the value of greater monetary independence remain important and unresolved empirical issues.

The critics of floating rates base their assertion that speculation would be destabilizing on the observation that changes in exchange rates have been much sharper than might be inferred from contemporaneous changes in the differences in national price levels. The proponents of floating rates respond that the period-to-period movement in the exchange rates follows a random walk, that there is no systematic or predictable movement, and hence the exchange market is efficient.[1] There are no "runs" in the time-series—periods when the direction or changes in exchange rates can be accurately predicted from past changes. But if the exchange-rate movement follows a trend, then the forces "driving" the exchange rate also may follow a trend. Alternatively the monetary authorities may have been "leaning against the wind"—and while intervening in the foreign-exchange market—retreating.

The efforts of national monetary authorities to follow independent monetary policies must inevitably lead to large movements in the spot-exchange rate since the current spot rate primarily reflects the anticipated future rates. Changes in monetary policy affect the anticipations of future exchange rates because of the impacts on the price-level developments and the interest rates at which these future exchange rates are discounted to the present. So a move toward a more expansive monetary policy would be associated with an anticipation of a more rapid increase in the domestic price level and a decline in the domestic interest rate; both factors would cause the currency to depreciate. The large swings in the exchange rates that are evident from hindsight reflect that the changes in monetary policy have been offsetting, either a domestic contractive policy is followed by a domestic expansive policy, or by contractive policies abroad.

If these swings in exchange rates induced by changes in monetary policy are substantial, then the authorities may be obliged to intervene in the exchange market to limit the swings in the exchange rate; a "would-be" clean float becomes a managed float. Assume the U.S. authorities follow a more expansive monetary policy. If other currencies appreciate extensively, then their monetary authorities may feel the need to sell their own currencies and buy dollars. The purchase of dollars leads to an increase in their money supplies. Unless these sales are offset when the currency movement is reversed, there is upward bias in the growth of the money supplies and the price-level movement. The authorities may have less control over their money supplies in the floating-rate period than in the pegged-rate period, because the private capital flows are so much larger.

Problems of Managing a Pegged-Rate System

The proponents of floating exchange rates can always point to the difficulties of managing a pegged-rate system. Changes in parities almost always occur after too great a delay because the authorities hope that divine providence will intervene so that almost certain change in a parity will not be necessary. A floating-rate system has the advantage of flexibility.

The move to floating exchange rates in the early 1970s did not occur

---

[1] A financial market is said to be efficient when there is an instantaneous adjustment of the market price of the asset to new information. If "good news" and "bad news" occur randomly, then the changes in the price of the asset should follow a random walk.

because the proponents of floating exchange rates won the arguments; rather, in a period of growing inflation and increased divergence in inflation rates, the authorities were unwilling to pay the domestic political costs of maintaining the pegged-rate system. Commitments to the pegged-exchange-rate system lacked credibility. Such a system might have been maintained if the foreign monetary authorities had been more willing to accept the U.S. inflation rate, at the cost of higher domestic inflation rates than they preferred. In the end, their inflation rates were not significantly lower than the U.S. rate. And their lower inflation rates may have largely reflected the domestic impacts of the initial appreciation of their currencies.

The evidence of the last one hundred years suggests the monetary system has a tendency to gravitate to pegged rates—as long as such a system is feasible. If inflation rates among major countries are similar and low (and they cannot be similar and high), a return to pegged rates seems likely. Countries will peg their currencies to that of a nearby and larger metropole, which is the pattern of the European monetary system. Hence the number of major countries with floating rates will decline, currency blocs will develop, and eventually pegging will reduce the exchange-rate movements between the major currency blocs.

A crawling-peg system has been proposed as an arrangement that combines the advantages of both a pegged- and a floating-rate system. On frequent occasions, perhaps as often as once or twice a month, the authorities would change their parities, usually no more than two or three percent. Because the changes in parities are frequent, no political trauma would be associated with these changes. Because the amount of the change is so small, few traders and investors would deem it worth their while to attempt to predict these changes, and profit from them. Between the time of changes in parities, the monetary authorities would peg the rate; however, because of the frequency of changes in the parity, the domestic monetary implications of pegging the rate would be slight.

The System of Reserve Assets

In the 1960s, the concern was that monetary authorities in many countries feared a shortage of international reserves. In the 1970s, there was an unplanned and unanticipated surge in reserves, especially if monetary gold holdings are valued to reflect the sharp increase in the market price. The surge in reserves contributed to the surge in the inflation rate; and so one of the major concerns is how the growth of reserves might be managed to limit any further inflationary impacts. A related question involves the components of reserves, and whether gold and liquid financial assets denominated in the dollar, the mark, the Swiss franc, and other currencies will continue to serve as reserves, along with SDRs.

The surprise in the 1970s has been the growth in the volume of reserve assets even during a period of floating exchange rates. Foreign central banks have acquired dollar assets to limit the appreciation of their currencies when private parties, both American and non-American, have "unloaded" their dollar holdings. Some foreign central banks may now hold more dollar assets than they prefer; if their currencies had appreciated less rapidly they would have acquired a smaller volume of reserves.

At the end of 1965, international reserves totaled $67 billion; when floating began in 1973, reserves totaled $150 billion. Determining the value of reserves at the end of the 1970s is complicated by the need to place a value on monetary gold holdings. If monetary gold is valued at $500 per ounce, reserves exceed $800 billion, and if, instead, gold is valued at $400 per ounce, reserves total above $700 billion. Even if gold is valued at $250 per ounce, international reserves amount to $600 billion or about five times the 1970 level. Even after an adjustment for the increase in commodity price levels, the increase in reserves has been substantial in real terms. The measurement of the change in the volume of reserves is complicated because of the uncertainty about the value that should be attached to monetary gold holdings; even if gold remains in monetary limbo, countries in deficit will be able to sell gold at or near its market price (or else borrow against their gold holdings) to obtain currencies to finance their payments deficits.

The reserve shortage anticipated in the mid-1960s has disappeared, partly because of the continuing U.S. deficits, partly because of a surge in the market price of gold. Far fewer countries are likely to be constrained in their choice of domestic monetary and fiscal policies by the difficulty in financing payments deficits.

A second concern of the 1960s was that the "system" then could not produce international reserves without forcing the United States to incur "payments deficits"; the United States was the major supplier of reserves, both in the form of gold and liquid dollar assets. During the fifteen-year period, 1950–65, U.S. gold sales were almost as large as new gold production. As foreign holdings of dollars increased and U.S. gold holdings declined, the ability of the United States to maintain the $35 parity of gold for an indefinite future appeared questionable. The conundrum was that to the extent the United States was successful in reducing its payments deficit, most other countries would no longer be able to increase their holdings of gold and other reserve assets at the desired rates. But unless the United States could reduce its payments deficit, the $35 parity could not be maintained. As U.S. gold holdings declined, numerous other countries became more reluctant holders of dollar assets; they could not readily sell dollar assets to buy gold without jeopardizing the U.S. ability to maintain the gold parity.

A third problem was the asymmetry between the apparent ease with which the United States financed its payments deficits and the difficulties other countries encountered in financing their payments deficits. Other countries "spent" owned reserves and reserves borrowed from international institutions; either they had first to acquire reserve assets before they could use these assets to finance payments deficits, or, if they borrowed from foreign official institutions to finance deficits, they had then to repay these loans. In contrast, the United States financed much of its deficits by "passive borrowing" to the extent other countries were willing to acquire dollar-denominated assets. Thus that part of the U.S. deficit not financed by gold sales could be financed "automatically." Such automatic financing led to the concern that there could be an "uncontrolled" growth of liquidity.

Gold As International Money

Gold's future monetary role is subject to two opposing forces. One is a continuation of the pressures for economic efficiency that led to the progressive decline in gold's monetary role in the last century—gold no longer is used as a domestic money, nor do any countries peg their currencies to gold. Gold seems a "barbarous relic." The U.S. and British authorities have sought to reduce the international monetary role of gold, "to remove it from the center of the market system." They have succeeded, for in the last decade since the price of gold has been variable, gold has rarely been traded among central banks. Yet central banks have hoarded gold, because its market price has been so much higher than the official price.

Gold has been an important monetary asset for centuries; investors and monetary institutions acquired gold because gold "promised" to hold its value better than competing assets. Gold kept its promises. Moreover, partly because of its underlying commodity value, gold maintained its value over a wider geographic span than any other monetary asset; gold had a credibility as a monetary asset that other assets lacked. More importantly, there was relative price stability in the century of the gold standard, if not on a year-to-year basis, then over the century. Whether price-level stability was a cause or a consequence is arguable. But the period since gold has been shifted from the center of the system is one of much more rapid inflation than experienced during the previous century.

The case for reducing the monetary role of gold further is that gold is not readily manageable. Once a generation, the monetary price of gold would have to be increased, otherwise there would be a cumulative reserve shortage. And investors would continually speculate about the timing and amount of these increases. Such increases, however, are likely to be necessary only if inflation continues; with a stable price, there is no evidence that the monetary price of gold must be raised.

The case for maintaining gold as a reserve asset has several elements—gold already is an important monetary asset, gold has a large constituency, and considering gold as an acceptable reserve asset would restore a balance to central bank portfolios, now overloaded with dollars. The importance attached to gold suggests that once again a monetary role will develop for gold, for the value of gold in reserves is so large that no substitute can readily be found. Several scenarios for enhancing the monetary role of gold are feasible. One is that central banks will develop arrangements so that countries in deficit will have greater confidence that they will be able to sell gold to other central banks to obtain the foreign exchange necessary to support their currencies in the exchange market. Alternatively, the United States and other countries might agree to a new monetary price for gold in terms of their currencies as part of a complex negotiation involving the roles of gold and other reserve assets.

The Dollar and Other Fiat Assets

A major concern in the evolution of the international financial system is the role of the dollar as a reserve asset. While holdings of dollars as reserves will be supplemented by holdings of assets denominated in marks, Swiss francs, and other currencies, perhaps the yen, and by reserve assets produced by an international institution, it seems highly unlikely that the dollar holdings will be phased out as an international reserve asset, or even decline significantly. The growth of reserves denominated in various national currencies represents many decisions of foreign central banks; almost always they begin to acquire the currencies of the countries with whom they have major trade and financial relations, provided those countries have a reasonable record for commodity price-level stability. Inevitably, only the currencies of a very few countries are acquired as reserves. Sterling was initially acquired before World War I by foreign borrowers who sold debt in London. Foreign dollar holdings increased during World War I.

Over the long run, the growth of assets denominated in these currencies is usually demand determined; the countries acquiring these reserve assets first decide on the volume of reserves they wish to acquire and then decide on the currency denomination of these assets. On several occasions, however, changes in the volume represent excess production, as with sterling during World War II, or during the 1969–71 period, when foreign central banks accumulated more dollar assets than they wished because of the reluctance to alter exchange parities; excess production occurs because countries with the payments surpluses are reluctant to revalue their currencies.

A key policy issue is whether U.S. interests are served by having the dollar used as an international reserve asset. The dollar became a reserve asset because monetary authorities around the world found it to their advantage to acquire dollar assets rather than other types of reserve assets; the development of the dollar as a reserve asset was not the result of a plan of the U.S. authorities. Indeed about all the U.S. authorities did to enhance the international role of the dollar was attempt to induce other countries not to buy gold (a possible substitute for dollar assets), and to eliminate interest-rate ceilings on U.S. time deposits held by foreign official institutions.

The United States gains several advantages from being an international banker. One is the seigniorage gain that involves the profits from the production of money—the difference between the cost of producing money and its purchasing power in terms of other assets. In a competitive banking system, such gains would be competed away in the form of higher interest rates on dollar deposits. But U.S. interest rates may be lower, not higher, because of the foreign demand for dollar assets, and so the United States was able to borrow from foreign central banks at lower interest rates.

A second advantage of being banker is the flexibility advantage that became apparent in the late 1960s. The U.S. payments deficit was financed by the willingness of others to add to their holdings of dollar assets. The U.S. payments deficit could be financed much more easily than the payments deficits of other countries to the extent that there was an "automatic" demand for dollar assets at the prevailing exchange rates.

In the 1960s, some analysts concluded that the use of the dollar as a reserve-asset currency was not in the U.S. interest. One criticism was that the United States had less control over its monetary policy because there was a greater constraint on changes in U.S. interest rates due to the concern of the Federal Reserve that shifts of funds to foreign financial centers by private parties would be larger because of the volume of central bank-owned dollars. To the extent that foreign official institutions were buyers of dollar assets rather than of gold, these shifts of private funds presented no problem; the constraint became apparent only if foreign official institutions might sell dollars and buy gold as U.S. interest rates fell. A second criticism was that the United States had less control over its exchange rate than did other countries; a U.S. devaluation would be more likely to be followed by comparable devaluations of other countries. The evidence of the early 1970s suggests that offsetting devaluations probably reflect the unwillingness of other countries to incur the adverse change in their international competitive position due to a U.S. devaluation, rather than the possible losses on their holdings of dollar assets. Finally, increases in U.S. exports of securities led to smaller U.S. exports of commodities, which was a cost to the producers of commodities if not to the U.S. economy.

Now that foreign holdings of dollar assets approach $200 billion, the question is whether changes in the demand for these assets can have a significant impact on the U.S. economy. For example, assume certain foreign holders of dollar assets decide to shift to reserve assets denominated in a foreign currency. The U.S. dollar would tend to depreciate in the foreign-exchange market. Moreover, their sale of these dollar assets will tend to raise the U.S. interest rates.

From time to time, especially when the dollar has been weak in the exchange market, there have been proposals for new arrangements to manage foreign dollar holdings. One proposal is that the United States extend exchange guarantees on foreign dollar holdings; if the dollar depreciated by more than a specified amount, the U.S. authorities would make a direct payment to some or all foreign official holders of dollars to compensate them for their exchange losses. Alternatively, some or all of foreign central bank holdings of dollar assets would be transferred to the International Monetary Fund; the Fund in turn would acquire these claims on the United States. The U.S. authorities would extend a maintenance-of-value guarantee on these dollar holdings of the Fund, and the Fund in turn would be able to extend a similar guarantee on its liabilities to foreign official institutions. A third proposal is that the U.S. authorities begin to support the dollar in the foreign-exchange market to limit the variations in the foreign-exchange value of the dollar; in this case, the U.S. authorities might draw on U.S. reserves and borrow foreign currencies from the International Monetary Fund and from foreign central banks.

The common feature of all these proposals is that the U.S. authorities incur the exchange risk on some or all U.S. liabilities held by foreign official institutions. The presumption is that the U.S. willingness to acquire the exchange exposure would limit variations in the foreign-exchange value of the dollar. Foreign central banks would be less reluctant to intervene in response to sharp movements in exchange rates that seem out of line with general underlying economic movements.

The Role of Multinational Monetary Institutions

One type of proposal to resolve the problems raised by use of assets denominated in major national currencies as reserve assets is to establish an international institution to produce reserve assets. Member countries holding reserves in the form of deposits in this institution would, when in payments deficits, transfer part of their deposits to the countries with the payment surpluses. This type of arrangement has a number of advantages; one is that reserves could be produced without the need for any particular currency to become overvalued. The seigniorage attached to the production of international money could be distributed to all countries. The rate of growth of international reserves could be managed deliberatedly; the overpopulation of reserves could be limited.

The movement toward an international reserve-providing institution has been slow, and for several reasons. High rates of national inflation negate the argument that the growth of international reserves can be managed to avoid inflationary or deflationary biases. Few countries can manage their growth of money to achieve price stability. Moreover, the ability to limit inflationary growth of international reserves will be smaller in the international context than in the domestic context for the decisions about the rate of growth of reserves appear likely to be dominated by the inflation-prone countries. Hence the countries with the strongest commitments to price stability would realize larger-than-desired payments surpluses from holding the liabilities of the international institution, and face the choice of either accepting a higher-than-desired inflation rate or else be continually revaluing their currencies. If, as seems not unlikely, reserves were produced at too rapid a rate, the surplus countries would be reluctant to acquire deposits in the new institution.

From the point of view of individual countries, the relevant question is whether the attainment of national objectives will be eased by the activities of an international reserve-providing institution. Thus the U.S. authorities would necessarily be concerned with the implications for the management of domestic monetary policy of U.S. participation in such an institution. If the United States tended to be in payments deficit, financing the deficit might be more difficult than under the current arrangement because foreign official institutions would no longer acquire dollar assets, and so monetary policy might have to be directed to reduce the deficit. If the United States is in payments surplus, it would be obliged to extend credit to countries with payments deficits; as a consequence, the U.S. authorities might face the choice between monetary expansion to reduce the U.S. payments surplus or monetary contraction to dampen or counter the expansive impacts of the large surplus.

National attitudes toward the idea of a central reserve-producing institution generally tend to reflect whether a country is more likely to incur payments deficits or payments surpluses. The countries with a greater tendency toward payments deficits generally favor the development of such an institution, since they believe financing their deficits in the future would be easier. Countries with a tendency toward payments surpluses are more skeptical since they would be obliged to extend credit to countries with the payments deficits.

Developing a new reserve-producing institution does not resolve the problems of accommodating the differences among countries in their inflation rates and their growth rates. Some countries would have payments surpluses, others would have payments deficits, and the problem under the new arrangement, as under previous arrangements, is which group of countries would take the initiative in adopting measures to reduce the payments imbalance. Countries would still have to take measures to minimize the domestic consequences of imported shocks.

Summary

The demise of the Bretton Woods system of adjustable parities in the early 1970s and the sharp movements in exchange rates for many of the major currencies subsequently has led to the concern about international monetary disorder. Those who share this view sometimes associate monetary order with a system based on an international treaty, although, as the gold standard indicated, monetary order can be achieved without any treaty. The developments in the system over the last century suggest that changes in international payments arrangements will be negotiated to reduce uncertainty incurred by those involved in international trade and payments. Such negotiations might involve three types of issues—the domain of currency areas, the organization of the foreign-exchange market, and the selection of assets to be used as international reserves.

Since many of the problems that arise in international finance would disappear if national currencies were merged into one international currency, a central question is whether there are net economic gains from the unification of national currency areas. One benefit from the merger of national currencies is that traders and investors would no longer incur costs associated with the use of the foreign-exchange markets; activities of foreign-exchange traders and the capital equipment now involved in the operation of the foreign-exchange market would be available for other uses. Perhaps more importantly, traders and investors would no longer be uncertain about changes in exchange rates and changes in exchange controls, with the consequence that investment funds might flow more readily to those countries with the highest investment returns. Yet there are costs to monetary unification, which result from the reduction in the number of independent central banks and the loss of opportunity in individual countries to manage monetary policy to achieve employment and price-level objectives. The magnitude of these losses depends on whether the characteristics of the labor markets in countries whose currencies might be merged are similar, especially in the phasing of the business cycles, and whether the countries agree on the priority for employment and price-level objectives.

The choice about whether national currencies should be pegged as they were under both the gold standard and the Bretton Woods system, or whether currencies should float partly depends on the monetary environment. If inflation rates and, especially, target rates of inflation differ significantly, then the ability of the monetary authorities to maintain pegged exchange rates is reduced, because investors will shift funds among currencies in anticipation of parity changes. The advantage of pegged rates is identical with that of the merger of currencies—the reduction in uncertainty about future changes in exchange rates and in exchange controls. The costs of pegged exchange rates are the constraint on monetary policy.

Should there be a move back toward pegged exchange rates, then the monetary authorities will again be concerned with the adequacy of international reserves, as they were through much of the 1960s. Yet two significant changes in the last decade reduce the likelihood of any reserve shortage. One is the sharp increase in the volume of foreign-owned liquid dollar assets from $16 billion at the end of the 1960s to $175 billion at the end of the 1970s. The second is the dramatic increase in the market price of gold, with the result that the value of official holdings was easily ten times higher at the end of the 1970s. The problem may be avoiding significant increases in the volume of reserves while effecting desired changes in the composition of reserves.

QUESTIONS AND EXERCISES

1. Discuss the costs and the benefits of the maintenance of the separate national currencies. Why might the major countries in Western Europe now think the time appropriate to merge their currencies?

2. Discuss the basic argument for floating exchange rates and the arguments for a system of adjustable parities. What conditions must be satisfied if the major countries are again to peg their currencies?

3. During the 1960s financial officials in the major countries were concerned with the shortage of international reserves. Discuss the conditions that might lead to the conclusion that the volume of international reserves is too small or too large.

4. Why has the relationship between the demand for reserves and the supply of reserves changed in the last decade?

FURTHER READING

MURPHY, J. CARTER. *The International Monetary System: Beyond the First Stages of Reform*. Washington: American Enterprise Institute for Public Policy Research, 1976. A liberal's approach to international monetary developments.

SCHMIDT, WILSON E. *The U.S. Balance of Payments and the Sinking Dollar*. New York: New York University Press, 1979. The title tells the story.

Index

ıllıllıllıllıllıllıllıllıllıllıllıllıllıllıllıllıllıllıllıllıllıllıllıllıllıllıllıllıllıllıllıllıllıllıllıll

acceleration principle, 349–51, 456
"Accord" (March 1951), 621
advertising, 310
  by banks, 96, 98, 116, 117, 124, 198
A/E (actual/extrapolated) ratio, 394
aggregate demand, 19–20, 31, 217, 343,
    363, 648
  in Brunner-Meltzer approach, 408, 422,
    423
  fiscal policy in reduction of, 644–45
  in monetarism vs. Keynesian theory,
    392–93, 398
  monetary policy and, 377–78, 485, 512–
    13, 546–63, 593–96, 620, 643
  quantity theory and, 380–82
  in real balance approach, 411, 414, 416
  in St. Louis approach, 418, 420
  shifts in investment demand and, 349–
    50
  uneven growth of, 374–78
aggregate-demand curves, 331–37, 422,
    423
  downward sloping, 333, 437
  prices and, 331–37, 370–71, 372–73,
    374, 436–37
aggregate supply, 335, 418
aggregate-supply curves, 422, 437–42
American Revolutionary War, inflation
    during, 433
American Stock Exchange, 148
Amsterdam Bank, 698
Andersen, Leonall, 535–36
  see also St. Louis approach to mone-
    tarism
Ando, Albert, 406–7
apartments:
  financing of, 106, 148
  investment in, 351–53
a priori definition of money, 256–57,
    258–59
arbitrage, 678, 680
  defined, 677
Asiadollars, 264
assets:
  of commercial banks, 35, 41, 44–47,
    72, 81–95, 99, 219–22, 224–25, 240–
    46, 503

demand for, vs. demand for money,
    298–303
diversification of, 26–29, 101
earning, 84–93, 189n
ideal, characteristics of, 72
liquidity of, see liquidity of assets
separation theorem and, 289–90
total, ratio of capital to, 45–47
see also balance sheets; portfolios; spe-
    cific kinds of assets
assets markets, 421
Austria, pegged currency in, 720
automated payment systems, 14–15, 56n,
    198, 207–8, 212, 259
automobiles, 140, 283, 308–9, 310
  demand for, 134, 135, 363, 375, 376,
    465

Bagehot, Walter, 173
Bahamas, banking in, 699, 702
balance of payments, 3, 186, 627, 651,
    691
  deficits, 66, 516, 623, 626, 656, 657,
    660, 664, 665–66, 704n, 705, 725–
    26, 728
  defined, 670
  in gold-exchange standard, 660
  gold standard and, 657, 659
  surpluses, 657, 660, 664, 665, 685,
    690–91, 704n, 705
balance-of-payments accounts, 652, 687–
    91
  defined, 687–88
  most important relationship in, 690
balance sheets:
  of commercial banks, 72–95, 219–22,
    224–25, 240–46, 503
  defined, 73
  of Federal Reserve, 239–46
  of households, 101, 102
  T accounts and, 219–22, 224–25, 240–
    46, 503
  of thrift institutions, 106–8, 200–202
banker's acceptances, 84, 93, 241
  defined, 80–81, 241
  in international finance, 660, 679
  as L, 263–64

bank failures, 30, 37, 44, 49–55, 173–74,
    396
  depressions and, 31, 33, 39, 54
  distribution of losses in, 49, 51, 52, 54,
    70, 210
  FDIC insurance against, *see* Federal
    Deposit Insurance Corporation
  holding companies and, 65
  in 1930s, 52, 53, 103, 174, 504, 609,
    612–16, 617–18
  in 1960s, 52–53
  in 1970s, 48, 53–54, 505, 506, 627
  prevention of, as monetary policy goal,
    487, 491–92, 493, 512
  in small vs. large banks, 45, 54, 97
  as too infrequent, 54–55, 70, 209–10
Bankhaus Herrstatt, 627
banknotes, 36, 37–38, 44
Bank of America, 73
Bank of California, 60
Bank of Canada, 686
Bank of England, 66, 174, 175, 485, 500,
    655, 697
Bank of North America, 36
Bank of the Commonwealth, failure of
    (1972), 54
Bank of the United States, failure of, 617
bankruptcy, etymology of, 35–36
banks and banking:
  central, *see* central banks; Federal Re-
    serve banks; Federal Reserve policy;
    Federal Reserve System
  international, *see* international finance;
    offshore banking
  savings, *see* savings banks
banks and banking, commercial, 1, 21,
    35–100
  assets of, 35, 41, 44–47, 72, 81–95, 99,
    219–22, 224–25, 240–46, 503
  branch, 32, 60–63, 64, 66, 69, 70, 73,
    98, 198, 210, 260
  capital of, 44–47, 54, 55, 70, 80, 81
  capital markets and, 64, 141–42, 143,
    148
  central banks compared to, 173, 174,
    189
  central reserve city, 38–39
  chartering of, 29, 35, 36–38, 40–41,
    69–70, 210, 211–12
  closing of, 218n
  commercial paper sold to, 140, 142
  concentration in, 58–64, 67
  correspondent, 38, 39, 43, 57, 58, 70,
    81, 83, 97
  country, 38, 39, 58, 84
  criteria for activities "closely related"
    to, 65n
  dealer and broker roles of, 672–73
  defined, 35
  elimination of, 511–12
  examination of, 41–42, 43, 66, 69–70,
    175, 180, 212
  financial reform and, 207–8, 210–12
  as firms, 41, 72–100, 217, 265
  free, 37, 69
  history of, 35–39
  internationalization of, 65–67, 197,
    652, 672–73, 676, 694–97
  liabilities of, 35, 72, 73–81, 95–98, 99,
    219–22, 224–25, 240–46, 503, 654,
    696
  management of, 35, 42, 51–52, 63–64,
    93–98, 112
  mergers of, 48, 49, 51, 63–64, 70, 175,
    180, 210
  minority, 69
  money stock created by, 3, 29, 31, 35,
    217–37, 408
  national, *see* national banks
  number of, in U.S., 58, 70
  problem, 42
  profit maximization by, 35, 46, 72, 86–
    87, 99, 173, 225–26, 230–31, 233n
  reserve city, 38–39
  reserves of, *see* reserves, bank
  savings deposits in, 12, 16, 111, 116,
    120
  social regulation of, 67–69, 70
  state, *see* state banks
  stock in, 44, 46, 52, 64
  thrift institutions compared to, 102,
    212, 259, 260
  trust departments of, 98, 99, 126, 155
  wholesale, 73
  wildcat, 37
  see also check clearing; checks and
    checking; demand deposits
Banks for Cooperatives, 129
Barclays (bank), 697
barter, 6–8, 15
basic borrowing privilege, defined, 505
"beggar-thy-neighbor" charge, 660
Belgium, international finance and, 664,
    699, 720, 721
bellwether interest rate, defined, 90
Biddle, Nicholas, 37
bills of exchange in gold standard, 656
bills-only policy, 622, 623
bimetallic standard, 655
Board of Governors (Federal Reserve
    Board), 43, 84, 177, 183, 193, 495,
    622, 624
  Congress and, 181, 182, 189, 541
  Federal Reserve banks supervised by,
    178, 180, 182, 613
  members and functions of, 57, 181–82,
    184, 516
  professionalization of (1960s), 623–24
bonds, 10, 101
  as bank capital, 44, 47
  in Brunner-Meltzer approach, 407–9
  corporate, 27–29, 103, 107–8, 109, 126,
    136, 145, 146–47, 154–55, 157–58,
    609–11
  foreign, 146, 651–52
  interest rates and, 54, 85, 118, 147,

150–52, 160–63, 165–66, 407–8, 609–11, 630
as *L,* 263–64
long-term capital market for, 138, 145, 146–47, 150–52, 154–56, 157–58
municipal, 108, 126, 145, 146, 147, 154, 155, 156–57
perpetual, 152
in real balance approach, 415–17
Treasury, 145, 147, 150
Boston Five Cent Savings Bank, 103
Bretton Woods system (1945–70), 652, 653, 661–65, 711, 713
decline of, 664–65, 711, 713
legal basis of, 662, 711, 712
see also International Monetary Fund
British and Overseas Bank, 698
broad-money multiplier, 229
Brunner-Meltzer approach to monetarism, 384, 404, 407, 409, 421–23, 539
multiple-assets problem in, 299, 302–3
transmission process in, 397, 407–9, 421–23
Brussels conference (1920), 660
budget constraint, government, 423, 496–97
Bundesbank, 461, 485, 682, 684–86
Bureau of Printing and Engraving, U.S., 217
Bureau of the Mint, U.S., 217
Burns, Arthur F., 184, 527*n*
business cycles:
currency mergers and, 718
length of, 526
political, 192, 598–99
short-run problems of, 287, 307, 308, 312, 374–78
see also depressions; inflation; recessions

Cagan, Phillip, 395–96
California, 69, 116, 178
branch banking and, 60, 63
foreign banks in, 66, 700
Supreme Court in, 573
call loans, defined, 84, 92
Cambridge equation, 287, 382, 384
target variables and, 529–32
Canada, 666, 673, 686, 687, 719
foreign banks in, 695, 699
capital, 44–47, 80, 81, 314
defined, 44, 47
Federal Reserve, 245–46
formation, *see* investment
IMF, 662, 663
physical, 27–29, 87, 391
ratios, 45–46, 47, 54, 55, 70, 700
capital-account balance, 690
capital consumption allowances, *see* depreciation
capital gains, 108, 129, 137, 148, 188, 292, 352, 362

capitalism, Great Depression and, 307, 399
capital-market-model approach, 299, 302, 303
capital markets, 1, 16, 58, 64, 133–72, 303
functions of, 133, 140–45, 166
interaction of, 133, 140, 143–45, 154–66, 197
long-term, 133, 138, 145–66
long-term, specialization and competition in, 154–57
long-term, valuation in, 150–54
monetary policy weakened by imperfections in, 550–51
New York Bank and, 178, 182*n,* 183
short-term, 133, 138–45, 147, 150, 154–66
transfer of funds in, 133, 137, 140–43, 166
types of, 138
Carson, Deane, 575
Carson, Keith, 407
Carter, Jimmy, 181, 490, 508, 628, 630
CDs, *see* certificates of deposit
central banks, 173–96, 242*n,* 243*n,* 457, 485–86, 673, 714
British, 66, 174, 175, 485, 500, 655, 697
dollar holdings of, 626, 724–25
in foreign-exchange market intervention, 242*n,* 653–54, 684–86
future of gold and, 726–27
gold-exchange standard and, 659–60
gold standard and, 655–56, 659
offshore banking and, 705
optimum currency areas and, 717, 718
pegged-rate system and, 684, 712–13
profile of, 173–77
West German, 461, 485, 682, 684–86
see also Federal Reserve banks; Federal Reserve policy; Federal Reserve System
certificates of deposit, 12*n,* 96, 126, 136, 229, 284, 625, 626, 628, 630
interest rates and, 77, 78, 86, 97, 120, 129, 141, 143–45, 198, 200, 291, 624
maturity of, 77–78, 629
short-term capital market for, 138, 140, 141, 143, 144
term, 109, 119–21, 123–24, 129, 150, 202–3, 208
two-tier market for, 627–28
check clearing, 20, 27, 55–58, 84, 266
Federal Reserve System in, 39, 56–58, 70, 180, 189
innovations in, 14–15
in National Banking System, 38, 39
as service to firms, 73, 74, 75
checks and checking, 4, 11–12, 35, 38, 111
certified, 76
as credit money, 14

checks and checking (*continued*)
  officer's, 76
  overdraft privileges for, 92, 264
  traveler's, 257
Chemical Bank, 91
Chicago, banking in, 60, 73, 178
Chicago approach to monetarism, 379,
    383, 384–97, 404, 407
  evidence as "mere correlations" in,
    392, 393–97, 407
  fiscal policy in, 392–93
  interest-rate behavior in, 387–89
  nominal income predicted by, 389–91
  political views as factor in, 384, 393
  transmission mechanism in, 391–92,
    397
Christ, Carl, 408
Chrysler Corporation, 626
circuit velocity of money, 283–84
Citibank, 90
Civil War, U.S., 218*n*, 433, 638
  national banks and, 37, 207
Clark, Colin, 637
clearinghouse certificates, 39, 615
clearinghouses, 14, 57, 70
  defined, 56
clipping of coins, 12
coal, 283, 308–9
coins, 12, 217–18, 435
  as bank assets, 81
  shortages of, 218*n*
Commerce Department, U.S., 186
commercial banks, *see* banks and bank-
    ing, commercial
commercial loan theory, 94, 604, 605,
    606, 644
commercial paper, 65, 90, 97, 126, 129,
    198, 200, 208
  defined, 84
  in Great Depression, 611, 617
  issued by firms, 136, 139–40, 141, 626
  as *L*, 263–64
  short-term market for, 138, 139–40,
    141, 142, 143, 144–45, 157–58
Commerz (bank), 694
commodities, *see* goods and services
commodity money, full-bodied, 12, 13, 17
Community Redevelopment Act (1975),
    68
Community Reinvestment Act, 68–69
competition, 90, 147, 149, 176
  effect of deposit insurance on, 51, 52,
    55*n*
  "excessive," 438
  financial reform and, 75, 197, 199,
    205–6, 209–10, 211, 212
  government regulation of, 29–30, 32,
    41, 59–64, 116–24, 198, 199, 436,
    470
  in international finance, 657, 665, 666,
    672, 694–95, 696, 697, 698–700, 702
  in long-term capital markets, 154–57
  market, resource allocation and, 566–
    67

thrift institutions and, 108–9, 111–13,
    116–24, 198, 199, 205–6
Comptroller of the Currency, 37, 39, 41,
    42, 46, 55, 70, 80, 212
computers, 65, 264
  in check clearing, 14, 56*n*
  in evolution of money, 14–15
Conference of Federal Reserve Bank
    Presidents, 183
Congress, U.S., 129, 515, 612
  banks chartered by, 36, 37
  Board of Governors and, 181, 182, 189,
    541
  Federal Reserve independence and,
    189–91, 193
  financial reform and, 206, 207, 208,
    211, 259
  fiscal policy set by, 265, 345, 377, 486,
    489, 491, 496, 497, 625, 630, 643–
    44
  interest-rate policies and, 147, 187, 506,
    511, 649
  Joint Economic Committee of, 636
  reserve requirements set by, 83–84, 509
consolidation component, defined, 262
Constitution, U.S., 36
construction industry, 31, 106, 119, 310,
    492, 528, 600
  disintermediation as factor in, 551, 570
  financial reform and, 199–200, 202,
    204, 206
  government in subsidizing of, 32, 204,
    579
  investment in, 341, 351–55, 370, 551
  market imperfections as factor in, 551
  resource allocation and, 568–73
consumer ignorance, banks and, 30, 33
consumer information:
  on credit, 67
  on risk taking, 30–31, 33
consumer price index, 395–96
  as indicator of inflation, 154, 445, 465,
    466–67, 469, 621, 627, 628
consumption, 94, 651–52
  function, defined, 319, 371
  Great Depression and, 618
  in Keynesian theory, 304, 310, 318–23,
    331, 357–63, 367–76, 382, 392, 399,
    552–53, 555, 557
  monetarism and, 304, 385–86, 391–92,
    393, 401, 413, 414, 416–17
  MPC and, *see* marginal propensity to
    consume
  nonmonetary sources of instability and,
    374, 375–76
  resource allocation and, 568
  short-run variations in, 362–63
control theory, 536
corporations, *see* firms
"cost-push" factors in inflation, 399, 434,
    468–71, 472, 621, 628, 644
costs, 524–25, 550–51
  cargo insurance and freight (CIF), 689
  of consumer loans, 92

of credit money, 13
currency unification and, 717
of gold standard, 656–57
information, 7, 21, 22, 155
of interest ceilings, 123–24
investment, 342–44, 346, 348, 351–54
labor, 312, 443–45, 465
maintenance, 342, 343, 344, 348, 352, 354
of mortgages, 21–22, 148, 154–55, 201
of offshore banking, 695, 699, 701, 702
replacement, 154, 342, 343, 344, 346
of savings deposits, 112–16
transactions, *see* transaction costs
see also marginal cost
Council of Economic Advisers, 186, 495, 625, 643
countercyclical policy, 485, 636, 637–38, 642–44
in debt management, 648–49
stability vs. instability of, 485, 583–602
crawling-peg system, 724
credit, 3, 22, 65
bank, as target variable, 522, 523, 525
consumer, selective control over, 515
consumer protection and, 67–68
creation, in offshore banking, 701, 704–5
crunch, 456, 457, 468, 630
discrimination in granting of, 67, 68–69, 70, 86, 87, 182, 198, 574–75
lines of, 87–89, 99, 209, 264, 626, 628
against residential construction, 571–72
revolving, 87
stock-market, 515
trade, 552
see also loans; mortgages
credit allocation, 566, 574, 578–80, 630–31
pros and cons of, 579–80
credit cards, 92, 209, 264, 265, 631
credit money, 12–14, 17
defined, 12–13
credit rationing, 99, 118–19, 149, 391, 525, 557, 571, 574, 579, 630
defined, 85
reasons for, 85–86
credit unions, 12, 83, 101
financial reform and, 75, 207, 208, 209
insurance of, 55
near-money and, 16, 17
"crowding out" effect, 392–93
currency, 11–14, 37, 489
as bank asset, 81
definitions of money and, 4, 11–12, 16, 257, 265–66
demand deposits converted to, 219–20, 226–27
elastic, real-bills doctrine and, 604
in increase vs. decrease of reserves, 243, 248
insurance and withdrawal of, 13, 176, 180, 217–18

long or short position in, 672, 676
optimum areas for, 686, 716–20
ratio (k), 229, 231, 234–35, 250, 609
"scarce in the Fund" clause for, 663
see also foreign-exchange rates; M_1; M_2; *M-2*; *M-3*
currency blocs, 724
currency market, external, *see* offshore banking
current-account balance, 689–90, 714

debt management, 485
debt markets, 303
debts, 13, 20, 87, 135
fixed value of money and, 10, 11, 17
government, monetizing of, 497, 624
government, payment of, 29
government, wealth and, 167–69
deficits, 66, 133–37, 166
balance of payments, 66, 516, 623, 626, 656, 657, 660, 664, 665–66, 704n, 705, 725–26, 728
defined, 134
of federal government, 66, 133–34, 140, 142, 316, 337, 377, 405, 408, 409, 422–23
financing of, 134–37, 140–43
demand:
aggregate, *see* aggregate demand
for automobiles, 134, 135, 363, 375, 376, 465
empirical studies of theories of, 291–94
for foreign goods and securities, 651
investment, *see* investment demand
transactions, 279–82, 284–86, 287, 291, 300, 382n
see also elasticity of demand; supply and demand
demand curves, 298–99, 331–37, 391
for money, 523
see also aggregate-demand curves
demand-deposit multiplier, 222–23, 226–29
demand deposits, 35, 36, 102, 136
as bank liabilities, 73–76, 81, 96
contraction of, 223–28
correspondent banks and, 58
creation of, 215, 217, 218–23, 225–28, 512
defined, 259n
definitions of money and, 4, 10, 11–12, 16, 257, 259–64, 265
erosion of distinctiveness of, 212, 259–64, 293
in foreign-exchange market, 671, 672, 679
interest rates and, 58, 73–75, 96, 141, 198, 199, 210, 231, 293–94
NOW accounts as, 75, 96, 198
see also check clearing; checks and checking; M_1; M_2
demand for money, *see* money demand

Denmark, international finance and, 720–21
deposit assumption, defined, 51
Deposit Insurance National Bank, 49n
Depository Institutions Deregulation Committee, 208
deposits:
  Eurodollars as, 264–65, 268
  Euromark, 695
  freezing of, 218n
  goldsmiths', 14, 36
  insurance of, see Federal Deposit Insurance Corporation
  legal tender and, 13
  nature of, 218–19
  offshore, 652, 695–97, 699, 701–7
  Treasury, 244, 248
  see also checks and checking; demand deposits; savings deposits; time deposits
depreciation, 87, 311, 312, 316, 345–46, 347, 352, 370, 443, 490, 683–84
Depression, Great, 31, 94, 95, 97, 207, 307, 374, 375, 548
  Federal Reserve policy in, 608–18
  Keynes's explanation of, 287–88, 308, 383, 608, 619
  monetarism and, 385n, 399, 608, 611–18
  quantity theory and, 383, 608, 619
  Temin's analysis of, 616–18
depressions, 39, 278
  bank failures and, 31, 33, 39, 54, 609
  government regulation and, 31, 33, 479–80
Deutsche (bank), 694
Dime Savings Bank, 103
discount mechanism, 500, 504–6, 604
discount rate, 182, 203n, 248, 344, 348, 352, 506–9, 514, 605, 607, 628
  defined, 180
  in Great Depression, 609–11, 612, 615, 617
discretionary policy, see countercyclical policy
discrimination:
  against consumers, 67, 68–69, 70, 198
  in granting credit, 67, 68–69, 70, 86, 87, 182, 198, 574–75
  in pricing, 120, 123–24, 202–5
disintermediation, 118, 197, 198, 199, 202, 204, 551, 580
Dolby, R. G. A., 272
dollars, Australian, 717
dollars, Canadian, 666, 686, 687
dollars, U.S., 628–31
  devaluations of, 626–27, 664, 666, 681, 728
  foreign-exchange value of, 651, 666–67
  future role of, 711, 714, 727–29
  shortage of, 665
Dresdener (bank), 694

easy-money position, 644–45
econometric models, 302, 389n, 392, 398, 401
  of Federal Reserve, 406–7, 520, 543, 555–59, 571, 623, 640
  long lags shown by, 590–91
  in Modigliani-Ando study, 406–7
  predictive validity of, 420
economic growth, as monetary policy goal, 487, 491, 493, 494
Economic Report of the President, 490
economics, physical sciences compared to, 273
economies of scale, 7, 32, 59, 101, 284
Edge Act subsidiaries, 61, 700
education:
  employment and, 473, 474
  GNP and, 313, 314
efficiency, 21, 278–79, 502
  in banking, 41, 54, 63–64, 209–10
  employment levels and, 487n, 488
  of financial markets, 723n
  inflation and, 433, 470
  marginal, of investment, 382, 385–86, 405, 410, 412, 414, 419, 549, 611
  of resource allocation, 75, 121, 314, 580
elasticity of demand, 290–91, 292, 294, 553
  income, 390–91
  interest, 386, 387, 388, 401, 427–28
  for mortgages, 92
elasticity of supply, deposits and, 112, 113
electronic funds transfer (EFT) systems, 197, 212
eligible paper, 604
empirical definition of money, 257–59
empirical studies of demand theories, 291–94
employment, 278, 307, 314, 701
  high, as monetary policy goal, 487–89, 491, 492–93
  part-time, 474, 475, 488
  see also unemployment
employment, full, 173, 177, 186, 412, 604, 664
  easy-money position on, 644
  equilibrium and, 410, 413–15
  inflation and, 472, 480–81
Employment Act (1946), 596
equilibrium, 19, 67, 320–29, 682
  balance-of-payments, 657, 671
  circular flow, 316–17, 327, 334
  GNP, 320–22, 323–25, 327, 334
  goods-market, 318–19, 421–23
  income, 303, 321–22, 323–31, 350, 367–71
  inflation, 436–37, 455–56, 457–59
  portfolio, 553, 554
  price, 7, 149, 334–35, 337, 367, 371–73, 374, 388, 436, 455

quantity theory and, 380, 381, 382
real balance approach and, 413–15, 416
requirements of, 318, 380
see also IS-LM curves
equity capital, 44, 47
escalator clauses, 449, 479, 561
Eurodollar market, see offshore banking
Eurodollars, 82, 97, 230, 264–65, 629, 631
defined, 66, 695
as L, 263–64
Euromark deposits, 695
European-American Bank, 48
European Community, 713
currency unification and, 716, 717, 719–20
exchange:
equation of, 281, 283
money as medium of, 5, 6–8, 10–11, 16, 17, 257, 279–86
see also foreign-exchange markets; foreign-exchange rates; trade
exchange controls, 175, 618, 623, 662, 663, 664, 686
offshore banking and, 695, 702, 706
expectation theory, 158–66, 257, 349, 369, 508
error-learning model of, 592, 593
inflation, 346–47, 418, 434, 442, 450–54, 456, 459–60, 479, 480, 489–90, 491, 493, 596, 621, 715
monetarism and, 387, 391, 408, 411, 418
monetary policy and, 508, 561–62
nonmonetary instability and, 374, 375
price, 411, 442, 450–54, 456, 480, 525
timing and, 162–63
see also rational expectations
Export-Import Bank, 241
export markets, 651
exports, 277, 310, 311, 412, 657
in balance-of-payments accounts, 688, 689
"beggar-thy-neighbor" charge and, 660

Farm Credit agencies, 118, 129–30
FDIC, see Federal Deposit Insurance Corporation
Federal Advisory Council, 183
federal credit agencies, 101, 118, 129–30, 204, 572
capital markets and, 142, 145
Federal Deposit Insurance Corporation (FDIC), 42, 46, 103, 267, 628
deposits insured by, 23, 31n, 40, 45, 48–55, 70, 81–82, 174, 209, 210, 211, 212
establishment of (1934), 23, 48, 52, 616
insurance ceiling of, 31, 43, 45, 49, 51–52, 174, 209

interest rates set by, 59–60, 77, 78, 117
membership requirements of, 40, 49, 67, 210
premium income of, 49, 52, 55
size of membership of, 48, 70
federal funds, 78–80, 82, 93, 97
short-term market for, 138, 140, 142, 143
federal funds rate, 79, 233–34, 503, 509, 543, 629
as instrument, 520, 521, 534, 540–41
federal government:
assets issued by, 29, 175–76
credit money regulated by, 13–14
deficits of, 66, 133–34, 140, 142, 316, 337, 377, 405, 408, 409, 422–23
foreign loans made by, 54
securities of, see securities, government
in short-term market, 142
see also specific branches, departments, and organizations
Federal Home Loan Bank (FHLB), 107, 142
Board (FHLBB), 106, 117, 130, 148–49
Federal Housing Administration (FHA), 91, 570–71
Federal Intermediate Credit Banks, 129
Federal Land Banks, 129
Federal National Mortgage Association (FNMA), 130, 142, 149
Federal Open Market Committee (FOMC), 180, 182–83, 188, 193, 500–502, 588
Directive, 500–501, 538, 540
procedure used by (1970s), 540–41
professionalization of, 624
Federal Reserve Act (1913), 39, 177, 500, 604
revisions of, 177, 181, 700n
Federal Reserve banks, 43, 139, 177–81, 183, 242n, 244, 609
Board of Governors in supervision of, 178, 180, 182
in check clearing, 56–58, 180, 189
currency issued by, 13, 189, 218
directors of, 178–80, 188–89
finances of, 188–89
Reviews of, 516
Federal Reserve Board, see Board of Governors
Federal Reserve Bulletin, 188, 516
Federal Reserve policy, 267, 303, 485–560
alternatives to, 635–47
borrowing categories in, 505–6
countercyclical, 485, 583–602, 636, 637–38, 642–44
criticism of, 539, 541–42, 564–66, 567, 624, 628, 635
current procedures in, 543

Federal Reserve policy (*continued*)
  econometric model and, 406–7, 520,
    543, 555–59, 571, 623, 640
  evaluation of powers of, 494–95
  expectational effects and, 561–62
  goals of, 481, 485, 487–99
  in Great Depression, 608–18
  history of, 485, 603–34
  indicators of, 537–38
  inflation and, *see* inflation
  international trade effects of, 559–61
  lags in, 525, 584–91, 636, 637–38
  in money market, 79, 485, 492, 500,
    503, 520–45
  money supply and, 17, 215, 229–30,
    256, 257, 260–64, 296, 301, 377,
    396, 459
  in open-market operations, *see* Federal
    Open Market Committee; open-mar-
    ket operations
  in 1950s, 538–40, 620–22
  in 1960s, 47, 538–40, 622–25
  in 1970s and 1980s, 540–43, 625–31
  political problems and, 192, 486, 598–
    600, 612, 637
  procyclical (1950s and 1960s), 538–39
  rational expectations and, 591–97, 637,
    638
  regulatory duties as distraction from,
    193, 212
  resource allocation and, 485, 564–82
  restrictive, distribution of burdens of,
    487, 492, 493–94, 547, 564–82
  strength of, 546–48, 643
  targets and instruments approach in,
    256, 520–35
  tools of, 182–83, 485, 500–545, 591
  transmission of, 546–63
  Treasury in relation to, 245, 485, 605,
    620–21
  war finance of, 605, 618–21
  see also Regulation Q; monetary policy
Federal Reserve System, 64, 92, 173–
    96, 212, 250–52
  advantages vs. disadvantages of mem-
    bership in, 43, 82–83
  as bureaucracy, 187–88, 192
  in check clearing, 39, 56–58, 70, 180,
    189
  constituency of, 185–86
  distribution of power within, 184–85
  establishment of, 39, 175, 177, 603–7
  federal funds and, 78–79
  finances of, 188–89
  formal structure of, 177–83
  inadequacies of, 39, 46–47, 119, 192,
    278
  independence of, 181, 189–93, 645
  informal structure of, 184–88
  interest rates and, *see* interest rates;
    Regulation Q
  in international banking, 66, 175, 178,
    559–61, 696, 700, 728
  as lender of last resort, 174, 504, 626

professionalization of, 623–24
regulatory functions of, *see* member
    banks; Regulation Q; reserve re-
    quirements
risks classified by, 45
size of bank reserves and, 238, 239–42,
    245–46, 248
transition process in, 43, 82–84, 209
see also Board of Governors; Federal
    Reserve banks; Federal Open Mar-
    ket Committee
Federal Savings and Loan Insurance
    Corporation (FSLIC), 55, 106
FHA (Federal Housing Administration),
    91, 570–71
FHLB, *see* Federal Home Loan Bank
finance, international, *see* international
    finance
finance companies, 61, 142
  commercial paper issued by, 139–40
financial institutions, 1, 3, 19–214
  description vs. analysis of, 3–4
  as intermediaries, 20–24, 29, 33, 101–
    32, 141, 302, 551–52, 579–80
  overview of, 19–34
  regulation of, *see* financial regulation
  role of, 20–24, 33
financial markets:
  monetary policy's impact on, 575–77
  see also specific markets
financial reform, 1, 33, 197–214
  of bank regulatory structure, 210–12
  competition and, 75, 197, 199, 205–6,
    209–10, 211, 212
  of interest-rate ceilings, 121–24, 197–
    205, 207–9, 572, 639
  problems and difficulties of, 206–7
  technological change as factor in, 197,
    212
financial regulation, 35, 36–43
  of credit money, 13–14
  efficiency of firms and, 54, 63–64
  FDIC and, *see* Federal Deposit Insur-
    ance Corporation
  Federal Reserve and, *see* Federal Re-
    serve policy; Federal Reserve Sys-
    tem; Regulation Q; Board of Gover-
    nors; Federal Reserve banks
  of international banking, 66–67, 695,
    697, 698–700, 701, 706–8, 712, 714,
    716
  National Banking System and, 37–39,
    69
  offshore banking and, 695, 701, 706–8
  reasons for, 1, 29–33, 39, 41–42, 48,
    67
  social, of bank loans, 67–69, 70
firms, 59, 67, 103
  banks as, 41, 72–100, 217, 265
  banks distinguished from other, 265
  bank services provided to, 73–75, 86–
    87, 98
  borrowing relationships of, 44, 73, 86,
    91, 96–97, 98, 524–25

CDs purchased by, 77–78, 136
commercial paper issued by, 136, 139–40, 141, 626
deficits of, 134, 135–37, 140, 141, 142–43
easy-money position and, 644
failures of, 51, 54, 121, 124, 525, 547, 576–77
holding companies as, 59n, 64–65, 70, 80
international finance and, 66, 653, 672, 681, 686, 687, 696, 698
investments of, 341–48, 465, 672
in monitoring of banks, 51–52
profits of, in GNP, 311–12, 549
transactions demand and, 280–81, 282, 285
value added for, 309–10
see also bonds; stocks
First Bank of the United States, 36
First Pennsylvania Bank, 36, 54
fiscal policy, 192
  aggregate demand and, 644–45
  Congress in setting of, 265, 345, 377, 486, 489, 491, 496, 497, 625, 630, 643–44
  inflation and, 434, 436, 448, 455, 456, 459, 467, 479–81
  Keynesian theory and, 322, 327–29, 349, 374, 375, 377–78, 397, 404, 409, 430–31
  lag of, 643–44
  monetarism and, 383–84, 392–93, 397, 404–7, 409, 430–31
  monetary policy compared to, 486, 487, 495–97, 546, 564–65, 567, 619, 642–44
Fisher proposition, 678n, 681
fixed exchange rates, see pegged exchange rates
Flannery, Mark, 212
float, in increase of reserves, 241–42, 246, 248
floating exchange rates, 652, 653, 660, 665–67, 720–24
  equilibrium under, 671
  in 1970s, 627, 666–67, 685, 714, 716, 723–24, 725
  uncertainty and independence under, 722–23
Florida, 116
  land boom in (1920s), 375, 400
FNMA (Federal National Mortgage Association), 130, 142, 149
FOMC, see Federal Open Market Committee
forecasting, 584–97, 623–24
  lags in, 584–91
  rational expectations and, 591–97
foreign-exchange markets, 506, 665
  central bank intervention in, 242n, 559–61, 684–86
  organization of, 652, 670–93
  as system, 654

volume of transactions in, 672
foreign-exchange rates, 3, 486, 675–84
  analyzing disturbances in, 682–84
  anticipated rate of change of, 681–82, 683
  cross-rate, 675
  defined, 670
  determinants of level of, 652, 679–84
  floating, see floating exchange rates
  forward, 652, 675–79, 722
  future, uncertainty of, 671–72, 679, 682–84, 686, 722–23
  in long vs. short run, 712–13
  monetary policy and, 487, 491, 559–61
  pegged, see pegged exchange rates
  spot, 652, 675–79, 681–82, 683, 722
forward-exchange rates, 722
  accuracy of, 678–79
  spot-exchange rates in relation to, 652, 675–79
forward transactions:
  advantages of, 676
  defined, 675–76
franc, Belgian, 664, 699, 721
franc, French, 655, 656, 675
  devaluations of, 660, 664, 721
franc, Swiss, 664, 714
France, 578
  international finance and, 655, 656, 660, 664, 675, 720, 721
Franklin National Bank, failure of (1974), 48, 54, 505, 506, 627
free-banking zones, offshore banking and, 706–7
Friedman, Benjamin, 536
Friedman, Milton, 258–59, 284, 379, 405, 451, 514, 606, 607–8, 611–18
  growth-rate rule advocated by, 635–37
  lag model of, 584–87
  monetarism of, see Chicago approach to monetarism
FSLIC (Federal Savings and Loan Insurance Corporation), 55, 106

Galbraith, Kenneth, 644
Gams, Carl, 536
General Agreement on Trade and Tariffs (GATT), 662
general controls, 500–514
  defined, 500
General Motors Acceptance Corporation, 140
General Theory of Employment, Interest and Money, The (Keynes), 308, 379
Genoa conference (1922), 660
geometric average, construction of, 160n
Germany (nineteenth century), currency unification in, 717
Germany, West, 664, 666, 667, 713
  barter used in, 7–8
  central bank of, 461, 485, 682, 684–86
  dominant banks in, 694

Germany Weimar, pegged currency in,
    720
GNMA (Government National Mortgage
    Association), 149, 502
GNP, *see* Gross National Product
gold, 11, 36, 277–78
    as commodity money, 12, 13
    exchange standard, 653, 659–61
    future role of, 714, 726–27
    in increase of bank reserves, 242–43
    inflow vs. outflow of, 604, 605
Goldfeld, Stephen, 292
Goldfeld equation, 300
gold standard (1880–1913), 14, 192,
    607, 611, 652, 653, 654–59, 667,
    684
    automatic adjustment process in, 657,
        659, 660
    commodity prices and, 657–59
    establishment of Federal Reserve and,
        603–4, 605
    international reserves held under, 655–
        56
    "limping," 655
    payments imbalances and, 656–57
    "rules of the game" in, 604, 657
goods and services, 19–20, 260
    exchange of, 4, 6–9, 13, 670, 680–81
    exchange controls and, 663
    foreign, demand for, 651
    gold standard and prices of, 657–59
    purchasing power and, 10, 275, 276–
        77, 322
    see also Gross National Product; out-
        put
goods markets, 418, 472
    equilibrium in, 318–19, 421–23
    IS curves and, 325–26
    in real balance approach, 411, 413
Government National Mortgage Associ-
    ation (GNMA), 149, 502
Great Britain, 8, 11, 66, 579, 618, 720
    banking activities "poached" by, 701
    central bank of, 66, 174, 175, 485,
        500, 655, 697
    decline in economic power of, 661,
        667, 713
    dominant banks in, 694
    gold-exchange standard of, 660, 661
    goldsmiths' deposits in, 14, 36
    gold standard of, 607, 611, 655, 656,
        659
    IMF and, 662–63
    overdraft system in, 92, 264
    wages in, 445, 681
Great Depression, *see* Depression, Great
Gross National Product (GNP), 20, 291,
    308–31, 349
    consumer expenditures in, 358, 552
    defined, 308
    distribution of, 311–12
    equilibrium, 320–22, 323–25, 327, 334

as final product, 311, 312
fiscal policy in changing of, 322, 375
gap, in St. Louis approach, 418, 419
growth rates of, 313, 374, 376
inflation and, 436, 444–45, 455, 457,
    458, 459, 466, 467
inventory investments in, 356, 400
monetarism and, 303, 398, 418, 419
money demand and, 285–86, 300–302,
    303
nonfarm deflator, 444–45
real, 281, 327, 436, 454–55, 457, 606
real, price and quantity adjustments
    and, 318–23
real, relation of potential output to,
    317, 334, 373, 436, 457
real, vs. nominal, 312–13
total, 310–11
velocity of money and, 283, 284
guilder, Dutch, 664
    devaluations of, 660, 721

Hamilton, Alexander, 36
handling charges, defined, 655
Harris Trust Company, 73
hedging:
    defined, 25
    in foreign exchange, 679, 722
    against inflation, 10, 153–54, 716
Herfendahl index, 59
Hester, Donald, 207
Higgins, Byron, 394
holding companies, 64–65, 70, 80
Holding Company Act, 64
Hong Kong and Shanghai Banking Corp.,
    210
households, 198, 490, 552–53, 696
    financial intermediaries used by, 21–
        22, 23, 101–31
    NOW accounts held by, 75, 210
    portfolio decisions of, 20, 24–29, 104–
        5
    in short-term market, 140, 142
    surpluses and deficits of, 134, 140
    transactions demand and, 279–80,
        281–82, 285–86
House of Representatives, U.S., Commit-
    tee on Banking, Currency and Hous-
    ing of, 207
housing,   *see*   construction   industry;
    mortgages; redlining
Hungary, pegged currency in, 720
Hunt Commission, 207

IBA (International Banking Act), 700
IBRD (International Bank of Recon-
    struction and Development), 661
Illinois, banking in, 60, 73, 82, 178
IMF, *see* International Monetary Fund

implicit-contract theory, 595
imports, 277, 310, 311, 395, 445, 657, 721
  in balance-of-payments accounts, 688, 689
  income increases and, 651–52
  "on-the-cuff" financing of, 661
income, 5, 652
  aggregate demand and, 19–20
  in Brunner-Meltzer approach, 422–23
  demand for money and, 283–84, 287, 291, 294–98, 301
  determination, see monetary theory
  disposable, 312, 319, 321, 322, 357, 358, 363
  distribution, 311–12, 490, 566, 577–78, 599, 644
  effects of money supply on, 5, 215, 230, 256, 257, 265, 271, 294–98
  equilibrium, 303, 321–22, 323–31, 350, 367–71
  Federal Reserve policy and, 520–36, 547–59
  imports affected by, 651–52
  lags in monetary policy and, 584–91, 595
  life-cycle theory and, 359–63
  measures of money and, 256, 257, 258
  money as, 5, 17, 277
  in money-supply theory, 230, 231
  MPS model and, 555–59
  national, see national income
  "permanent," 284
  St. Louis approach and, 404–7, 418, 555, 559
  variance of, 585–87, 588
income elasticity of demand, 390–91
income-expenditure theory, see Keynesian theory
income velocity of money, 283–84
indicators, 537–38
inflation, 4, 94, 313, 314, 373, 383, 433–83, 605
  aggregate demand and, 337, 434, 436–37, 439–41, 442, 454–59, 467–68
  aggregate supply and, 434, 437–42
  Bretton Woods system and, 664–65
  case studies in start of, 465–67
  causes of, 3, 14, 36, 401, 409, 434, 435–37
  common-stock prices and, 153–54
  cost-push, 399, 434, 468–71, 472, 621, 628, 644
  easy-money position on, 644–45
  equilibrium, 436–37, 455–56, 457–59
  expectations about, 346–47, 418, 434, 442, 450–54, 456, 459–60, 479, 480, 489–90, 491, 493, 596, 621, 715
  Federal Reserve in curbing of, 186, 191–92, 301, 302, 459–60, 480–81, 489–91, 494, 495, 508, 559–61, 630
  Federal Reserve as engine of, 186, 393,

409, 456, 467–68, 480–81, 493–94, 497, 508
  financial reform and, 197, 201, 208
  hedges against, 10, 153–54, 716
  inherited, 458–59, 468, 480, 481
  interest rates and, 25, 164, 191, 201, 301, 302, 387–88, 460–61, 559–61, 574, 644, 645
  international finance and, 664–65, 701, 704–5, 715–16, 724
  IS-LM curves in analysis of, 437, 456, 459, 460–61
  long-term structural change and, 477–80
  monetarism and, 397, 398–99, 409, 411, 418, 430–31, 437, 459–60, 467–68
  monetary growth-rate rule and, 635, 638
  money supply and, 3, 7, 14, 36, 218, 277, 278, 296, 301, 456–57, 459–61, 468
  NAIRU and, 430, 451–53, 455, 457, 458, 468, 471, 481
  offshore banking and, 701, 704–5
  persistence of, 471–72
  recent record of, 375, 435–37, 464–83, 701, 715–16
  stabilization policy and, 479–80
  theory of, 433–34, 435–63
  unemployment and, 314, 430, 434, 443, 445–49, 466, 468, 470–81, 489
instruments, 533–35
  criteria for, 533, 534
  defined, 520
  evaluation of, 534–35
insurance, 20, 29, 286
  of credit unions, 55
  federal vs. private control of, 31, 33
  health, 469–70
  of savings and loan associations, 22, 52, 55
  of savings banks, 103
  see also Federal Deposit Insurance Corporation
insurance companies, 85, 158, 161, 310
  life, 101, 124–25, 126, 146, 155
  marine, fire, and casualty, 126
  mortgages financed by, 107, 125, 148, 149
Interdistrict Settlement Fund, 57
interest elasticity of demand, 386, 387, 388, 401, 427–28, 546
interest elasticity of expenditure, 428
interest elasticity of investment, 546
interest-rate ceilings, 29, 67
  of Board of Governors, 624
  FDIC and, 59–60, 77, 78, 117
  of FHA and VA, 570–71, 572
  see also Regulation Q
interest-rate-parity theorem, 678
interest-rate risk, 25–26, 27, 33

interest rates, 21, 81, 82, 89–91, 111–24,
    652, 677–78
  behavior of, Chicago approach and,
    387–89
  bonds and, 54, 85, 118, 147, 150–52,
    160–63, 165–66, 407–8, 609–11, 630
  CDs and, 77, 78, 86, 97, 120, 129, 141,
    143–45, 198, 200, 291, 624
  changes in, and capital markets, 133,
    143–45, 157–66
  competition and, 59–60, 116–19, 293
  demand deposits and, 58, 73–75, 96,
    141, 198, 199, 210, 231, 293–94
  demand for money and, 275, 284–86,
    287–91, 292, 293–98, 300–303, 327
  discounting and, see discount mecha-
    nism; discount rate
  federal funds and, 78–79, 143
  Federal Reserve in reduction of fluctu-
    ations in, 39, 176, 268, 604
  in Great Depression, 609–12, 615, 616–
    17, 619
  inflation and, 25, 164, 191, 201, 301,
    302, 387–88, 460–61, 559–61, 574,
    644, 645
  Keynesian theory and, 303, 304, 308,
    318, 323–31, 347–51, 352–53, 360–
    61, 367–69, 370, 371, 388–89, 391,
    392, 408, 415, 420, 528
  monetarism and, 381–82, 386–89, 391,
    392, 393, 406, 413, 418, 419, 420
  money-market view of, 300–301
  mortgages and, 32, 91, 114–16, 121,
    123, 149–50, 200–206, 354–55, 456
  offshore banking and, 701, 702–4
  "operation twist" and, 623
  pegged, 618–21
  penalties and, 77, 120, 260
  real rate of, 347, 389
  as rental price of money, 275
  residential construction affected by
    rises in, 569–73
  resource allocation and, 566–67, 569–
    78
  for savings deposits, in unregulated
    market, 111–17
  short-term, as indicators, 537–38
  short-term, as instruments, 521, 533–
    35
  stability of, as monetary policy goal,
    256, 487, 492, 493–94
  as target variables, 520–21, 522–25,
    528–32, 583
  Treasury bills and, 109, 143–45, 200,
    201, 290, 291, 300, 355, 506, 509,
    534, 629
Internal Revenue Service, 126
International Banking Act (IBA; 1978),
    700
International Bank of Reconstruction and
    Development (IBRD; World Bank),
    661

international finance, 651–732
  defined, 4
  Edge Act subsidiaries and, 61, 700
  new international monetary system re-
    quired in, 711–14
  1970s developments in, 714–16
  optimum currency areas as issue in,
    714, 716–20
  political factors in, 653, 654, 661, 713,
    719
  role of central banks in, 66, 175, 176,
    178, 684–86
  role of multinational monetary institu-
    tions in, 729–30
  structure of banking in, 652, 697–700
  U.S. economic power and, 654, 661,
    665, 666–67, 713, 715
International Monetary Fund (IMF),
    245, 662–65, 670, 690, 712, 714
  dollar holdings of, 728–29
  General Arrangements To Borrow of
    (1963), 663
  Jamaica Agreement and, 715–16
  successes and failures, as linked to
    U.S., 664–65
international payments system, evolu-
    tion of, 652, 653–79
international trade effects of monetary
    policy, 559–61
International Trade Organization (ITO),
    661–62
inventory cycles, 376, 400
inventory investment, 318, 355, 356–57,
    376, 400, 456, 465
investment, 341–57, 370, 401
  demand, 318, 336, 347–51, 370
  determinants of, 323, 341–57, 399,
    491
  evaluation of, 342–47
  inflation expectations and, 346–47,
    456, 489–90, 491
  interest rates and, 323–25, 347–48,
    550–52
  inventory, 318, 355, 356–57, 376
  in long run, 341, 343
  marginal efficiency of, 382, 385–86,
    405, 410, 412, 414, 419, 549, 611
  new products and, 343, 344, 399, 491
  nonmonetary sources of instability and,
    375–76
  opportunity, sources of, 342–43
  plant and equipment, 341, 342, 343,
    344, 346, 409, 456, 571
  in residential construction, 341, 351–
    55, 370
  resource allocation and, 568
  shifts in, 349–51
  tax rates and, 345–46, 349
investment demand, 318, 336, 347–51,
    370
investment-saving equilibrium curves, see
    IS curves

investment tax credits, 346, 370
Ireland, international finance and, 717, 720–21
IC curves, 323–31, 332–35, 355, 375, 392, 407, 409, 427–28, 546
  in analysis of inflation, 437, 456, 459, 460–61
  defined, 325
  factors causing shifts in, 369–70, 372
  investment demand and, 350
  position and slope of, 325
  target variables and, 529–32, 536, 583
  wealth and, 367–71
Italy, international finance and, 664, 703, 717, 720
Italy, Renaissance, banking in, 35–36
ITO (International Trade Organization), 661–62

Jackson, Andrew, 37
Jaffee, Dwight, 212
Jamaica Agreement (1976), 715–16
Japan, 341, 358
  international finance and, 664, 666, 667, 672, 674, 675, 713, 717
Jordan, Jerry, see St. Louis approach to monetarism
Justice Department, U.S., 64

Kane, Edward J., 599
Karnovsky, Denis, 535–36
Keran, Michael, 405–6
Keynes, John Maynard, 282, 287–90, 308, 383
Keynesian investment multiplier, 223, 321–23, 325, 328, 369, 392, 399, 400
Keynesian-monetarist dispute, 383–84, 425–31
  Chicago approach and, 385–86, 388–89, 391–93, 396
  economic theory in, 397–99
  growth-rate rule in, 637–39, 640–42
  interest elasticities in IS-LM model and, 427–28
  policy differences in, 430–31
  recent models in, 428–30
  stability issue in, 385, 397, 398–401, 419–20
Keynesian theory, 271, 307–78
  in analysis of short run, 272–73, 308, 319, 343, 349, 358, 362–63, 367, 374–78, 426
  circular flow in, 314–17, 318, 327, 334
  criticisms of, 308, 379, 383, 407–8
  defined, 303–4
  Great Depression and, 287–88, 308, 383, 608, 619
  interest rates and, see interest rates
  investment and consumption in, 304, 310, 318–78, 382, 392, 399, 549–54
  key variables in, 412
  monetary instability in, 374, 385, 397, 398–400
  monetary policy and, see monetary policy
  price adjustments in, 317–18, 331–37
  quantity adjustments in, 317–23
  quantity theory vs., 272–73, 379, 382
  relative importance of variables in, 425–26
  simple model of, 307–40
  as synthesis, 379
  transmission process in, 391–92, 407, 420, 549–59
  wealth and, 319, 358, 360–61, 362, 367–71, 552–53, 555, 557
Korean War, 395, 620–21
  economic instability and, 375, 377
  Federal Reserve in, 620–21
  inflation and, 465, 467, 480, 621
Kuznets, Simon, 308

L (measure of liquid assets), 263–64
labor, 6, 20, 596
  changing composition of, 474–75
  costs, 312, 443–45, 465
  productivity of, 312, 314, 343, 470–71
  shortages, 314, 473–74
  surpluses, 473–74, 475–76
  see also employment; unemployment; wages
Labor Department, U.S., 186
labor markets, 314, 411, 718
  defined, 718
  inflation and, 434, 438–41, 443, 445, 448–49, 454, 464, 472–79
  labor unions, 186, 436, 438, 445, 449, 465–66, 480
  Phillips curve and, 472, 473, 478–79
  rational expectations and, 594–95, 596–97
lagging (in foreign-exchange markets), 675, 678, 679
lags (in monetary policy), 584–91, 595, 636, 637–38
  defined, 584
  empirical estimates of, 589–91
  formal model of, 584–87
  inside, 589–90, 643–44
  outside, 590
  problems created by, 587–89
Lance, Bert, 58
leading, 675, 678, 679
League of Nations, 659–60
legal tender, defined, 13
lender of last resort, central bank as, 173–74, 504, 626
Lerner, Abba, 636–37
less-developed countries, 54, 485
liabilities:
  of central banks, 175, 189, 245–46

liabilities (*continued*)
  of commercial banks, 35, 72, 73–81,
    95–98, 99, 219–22, 224–25, 240–46,
    503, 654, 696
  of offshore banks, 705
  of thrift institutions, 200, 205
  see also balance sheets; *specific kinds
    of liabilities*
life-cycle theory, 358–63, 367
  limitations of, 361–62, 369
liquidity of assets, 16–17, 27–29, 137,
    145, 257
  in banking, 51, 72, 81, 84, 92, 93–94,
    99, 259–60
  financial intermediation and, 23–24, 33,
    101, 109
  L as measure of, 263–64
lira, Italian, 664
Lloyds (bank), 694, 698
LM curves, 294–96, 297–98, 392, 407,
    409, 427–28, 546
  in analysis of inflation, 437, 456, 459,
    461
  defined, 296
  IS curves compared to, 326–27
  Keynesian theory and, 303, 304, 325–
    31, 332–35, 350, 367, 370–72
  monetarism and, 385, 393n
  target variables and, 529–32, 536
loan production offices, 61
loans, 54, 58, 66, 87, 91, 99, 103, 208
  amortization of, 67, 87, 91, 92
  as bank assets, 81, 84–93, 99
  bank examiners and, 41–42
  business, 32, 73, 85–91, 93–95, 96, 99,
    102, 205, 209n, 212
  call, 84, 92
  collateral for, 21, 89, 92, 96, 99
  compensating balance requirements
    and, 89, 99
  credit-card, 92, 631
  FDIC and, 48, 49, 52, 54
  of federal credit agencies, 129–30
  federal funds as, 78, 93
  Federal Reserve and, 39, 48, 97, 180,
    189, 209, 241, 248, 504–9, 604
  holding companies and, 65, 80
  IMF and, 662–63
  maturity of, 87, 91, 99
  real-estate, *see* mortgages
  short-term market for, 138, 140
  short- vs. long-term, 23, 87, 91–92, 93–
    94
  social regulation of, 67–69
  student, 93
Luxembourg, international finance and,
    695, 699, 702

M_1 (currency and demand deposits), 11–
    12, 17, 27–29, 98, 257, 258–60
  A, 229, 260, 290, 294
  average supply of (1978), 283
  B, 230, 260, 290, 629, 640
  creation of, 217–30, 232
  data available for, 258, 266
  demand for, 291, 292
  FOMC targets for, 540–41
  in Great Depression, 31, 609, 614
  growth rates of, 266, 269, 620, 625,
    636
M_2 (currency and all commercial bank
    deposits), 12, 17, 258–60
  creation of, 217–29, 232
  data available for, 258, 266
  FOMC targets for, 540–41
  in Great Depression, 31, 609, 614
M-2 (1980 definition), 12, 230, 260–63,
    551
  demand for, 290–91, 292
M-3, 230, 239, 262–63, 265, 291, 540,
    551
McFadden Act (1927), 697
Maine, branch banking in, 60
Maisel, Sherman, 184, 191, 542, 624–25
marginal cost, 232–33, 272
  of risk taking, 30
  of savings deposits, 112–13, 114
marginal money multiplier, 250–51
marginal propensity to consume (MPC),
    382, 385–86, 419
  defined, 322
  real balance approach and, 410–11,
    412, 413, 414
marginal revenue, 233, 272
marginal utility, 21, 75
  equilibrium and, 19, 553
marginal yield, 21
  bank capital and, 44, 45
Marine Midland Bank, 210
mark, German, 664, 666, 672, 675, 684,
    697, 712, 714
market (operating) factors, 248, 503
Marshall, Alfred, 287
Martin, William McChesney, 191, 495,
    538
Massachusetts, banking in, 75, 103
Medicaid/Medicare, 312, 469, 470
Meiselman, David, 405
Meltzer, Allan, 571
  see also Brunner-Meltzer approach to
    monetarism
member banks, 70
  defined, 40, 48n
  examination of, 42, 175, 180
  FDIC and, 40, 42, 48, 70
  Federal Reserve banks influenced by,
    178, 188, 193
  in Great Depression, 612–16
  loans made by, 39, 48, 97, 180, 189,
    209, 241, 248, 504–9, 604
  see also Regulation Q; reserve require-
    ments
mercantilism, 277–78, 715
Merrill Lynch Pierce Fenner & Smith,
    265

Mexico, 54
  international finance and, 695, 699, 719
Michigan, free banking in, 37
Midland (bank), 694
minority groups:
  in banking, 180
  credit discrimination and, 68–69, 70
mint parity, 654
Modigliani, Franco, 406–7, 493, 555, 637, 640
monetarism, 271, 303, 384–401, 404–24
  Brunner-Meltzer approach to, see Brunner-Meltzer approach to monetarism
  Chicago approach to, 379, 383, 384–97, 404, 407
  criticisms of, 406–7
  defined, 304
  interest rates and, 386–89, 391, 392, 393, 406, 413, 418, 419, 420
  monetary policy and, see monetary policy
  quantity theory related to, 380
  real balance approach to, see real balance approach to monetarism
  research strategy in, 398
  St. Louis approach to, see St. Louis approach to monetarism
  wealth effects and, 369
  see also Keynesian-monetarist dispute; quantity theory
monetary base, 535
  defined, 405
  St. Louis approach and, 405–7
monetary growth-rate rule, 635–42
  case against, 637–39
  case for, 636–37
  characteristics of, 635–36
  compromise position to, 639–40
monetary havens, 695, 699
monetary policy, 4, 35, 218, 349, 485–650
  defined, 3
  fiscal policy compared to, 486, 487, 495–97, 546, 564–65, 567, 619, 642–44
  gold standard and, 657
  importance of money measurement to, 256, 257, 266
  importance of timing of, 584–87
  international finance and, 559–61, 651–52, 657, 695–97, 707–8, 712
  international finance as complication in, 671–72
  Keynesian theory and, 308, 329–31, 367, 370, 374, 375, 377–78, 389, 397, 409, 493, 528, 547, 549–59, 583, 624, 628
  monetarism and, 379, 404–7, 409, 430–31, 526, 539, 547, 549, 598, 608, 611–18, 624, 628
  monetarism on growth-rate rule as, 635–37, 640–42

neutrality of, 567, 570, 572
  offshore banking and, 695–97, 707–8
  role of Treasury in, 245, 485, 648–50
  see also Federal Reserve policy
monetary theory, 4, 256, 271–431
  criteria for selection of, 271–74, 420
  defined, 3
  Keynesian, see Keynesian-monetarist dispute; Keynesian theory
  monetarist, see Keynesian-monetarist dispute; monetarism
  quantity, see quantity theory
money, 3–18, 27–29
  creation of, 3, 4, 29, 31, 35, 175–76, 215, 217–37, 408
  definitions of, 4–12, 16–17, 256–66, 276–77
  economic impact of, 277–79
  erosion of distinctiveness of, 198, 259–64
  functions of, 1, 5–11, 16, 17, 279
  future evolution of, 14–15
  as investment, 286–90, 291
  liquidity of, 16–17
  measurement of, 215, 229–30, 256–70, 273n
  as medium of exchange, 5, 6–8, 10–11, 16, 17, 257, 279–86
  narrow, 16, 17, 98, 228–29
  nature of, 1, 13–14, 257
  near-money and, 16–17, 32, 639
  popular and technical definitions of, 4–5
  price or value of, 275
  real vs. nominal, 276–77, 296–98, 331–34
  representative full-bodied, 12, 13, 17
  specific definition of, 11–12
  as standard of value, 5, 8–9, 11, 17, 257
  as stock, 5
  as store of value, 4–5, 9–11, 16, 17, 257, 286–90
  substitutes for, 264–65, 553
  types of, 12–13, 17
  velocity of, 282–84, 287, 614, 616–17
  see also M_1; M_2; M-$1A$; M-$1B$; M-2; M-3
money demand, 275–306
  demand for assets vs., 298–303
  empirical studies of, 291–94
  in Great Depression, 616
  interest rates and, 275, 284–86, 287–91, 292, 293–98, 300–303, 327
  monetarism and, 384–86, 408, 411, 415, 419
  in quantity theory, 380–82
  recent instability in, 292–93, 374
  in short run, 292–93, 300–301, 307
  speculative, see liquidity preference theory of demand
  as stable number vs. stable function, 384–85

money demand for (*continued*)
  target variables and, 523, 528, 529
  transactions, 279–82, 284–86, 291
money illusion, 410
money-market and term-structure approach, 299, 300–302
money-market certificates, *see* certificates of deposit
money-market conditions, 534, 535, 538, 540, 621, 624
money-market funds, 197–99, 230, 260, 290, 293, 631
money-market interest-rate differential, 677–78, 682, 683
money markets, 1, 39, 200, 303, 326, 385
  Federal Reserve in, 79, 485, 492, 500, 503, 520–45
  "Federal Reserve data" in analysis of, 238–48
  international, *see* foreign-exchange markets
  national, segmentation of, 686–87, 701
  in real balance approach, 411–12
money multipliers, 228–35, 238, 250–52, 397, 526–27
  leakages of, 230–31, 233, 235
  reserve ratio and, 509, 510
  stability of, 233–35, 250–51
money supply, 5, 29, 31, 82, 173, 215–70, 277
  for credit vs. commodity money, 13–14
  defined, 696
  difficulties in measuring of, 215, 695–96
  expenditures influenced by, summarized, 370
  Federal Reserve and, 12, 215, 229–30, 256, 257, 260–64, 296, 301, 377, 396, 459
  gold standard and, 657–58, 659
  in Great Depression, 609, 614, 616–18, 619
  growth rates of, 3, 173, 215, 250–52, 266–69, 278, 459, 527, 554, 564–65, 620, 621, 623, 624, 625, 629, 631, 636
  Keynesian theory and, 303–4, 308, 327, 329–32, 335, 336, 337, 350–51, 358, 367–70, 374, 375, 382, 391, 398
  monetarism and, 303, 383–84, 385, 387–88, 389–97, 398, 399, 408–9, 410, 411–13, 415–17, 418, 419
  new measures of, 229–30
  offshore banking in calculation of, 695–96
  one hundred percent reserves and, 513
  prediction of, for 1970–72, 527
  in quantity theory, 380–82
  recessions and, 3, 45, 266, 277, 301, 394, 547
  reserves vs. money multiplier in changing of, 233, 238, 250–52

  as target, 520–21, 522–23, 526–27, 529–33, 535, 536, 540
  unemployment and, 3, 14, 217
  unreliability of data on, 266–69
money-supply theory, 230–31, 232–33
monopoly, 314
  banking and, 36, 59, 61–63
moral suasion, defined, 516
Morgan, J. P., 152
Morgan Guarantee, 90
mortgage "banks," 148
mortgages, 15, 21–22, 31, 91, 155, 354–55
  costs of, 21–22, 148, 154–55, 201
  countercyclical lending pattern for, 91–92
  federal government and, 32, 33, 94, 121, 130, 148–49, 570–71
  FNMA and, 130, 142, 149
  illiquidity of, 22, 91
  insurance companies in financing of, 107, 125, 148, 149
  interest rates and, 32, 91, 114–16, 121, 123, 149–50, 200–206, 354–55, 456
  long-term market for, 138, 145, 148–50, 154–55, 157
  national market for, 148, 149
  net vs. gross amount of, 135
  thrift institutions and, 102, 103, 106–8, 109, 114–16, 118–19, 120–21, 122, 123, 199, 200–206, 209
  variable-interest-rate (VIM or VRM), 200–201, 202
MPC, *see* marginal propensity to consume
mutual funds, 128–29, 155, 212, 260, 293
mutual savings banks, *see* savings banks

NAIRU, *see* nonaccelerating inflation rate of unemployment
narrow-money multiplier, 228–29
National Banking Act, 37, 207
National Banking System, 37–39, 69, 177
national banks, 36–43, 210, 211–12
  branches of, 60–61
  capital of, 80, 86
  defined, 40
  as member banks, 40, 41, 43, 70
National Bureau of Economic Research, 308, 383
National Credit Union Administration (NCUA), 55
National Currency Act (1863), 37
national income, 271, 281, 296, 367–78
  distribution of, 311–12
  as double-entry system, 308, 310–11
  post-World War II boom in, 664
  structure of, 308–13
  see also income; GNP; output
National Monetary Commission, 39
National Provincial Bank, 698
"national treatment," principle of, 700
National Westminster Bank, 694, 698

NCUA (National Credit Union Administration), 55
near-money, 16–17, 32, 639
negotiable certificates of deposit, see certificates of deposit
negotiable orders of withdrawal, see NOW accounts
negotiated markets, defined, 138
neoclassical economics, 307, 308
Netherlands, international finance and, 660, 664, 698, 720, 721
New View of money creation, 231–33, 234
New York (city), 69, 134
  as foreign-exchange market, 672, 674, 675
New York (state), 67, 103
  foreign banks in, 66, 700
  NOW accounts in, 198, 259
New York Federal Reserve Bank, 177, 178, 182, 183, 500–502, 607, 613, 622
New York Stock Exchange Index, 128, 147, 148
New York Times, 296
Nixon, Richard M., 207, 626–27
nonaccelerating inflation rate of unemployment (NAIRU), 430, 451–53, 455, 457, 458, 468, 471, 481
nonprofit organizations, 75, 84, 210, 309
Norman, Sir Montague, 188
Norway, international finance and, 695
NOW accounts, 75, 96, 124, 198, 205, 206, 208, 209, 210, 231, 257, 259, 260, 290

offshore banking, 652, 695, 700–7
  controversial elements in, 700, 704–6
  domestic monetary policy and, 695–97
  growth of, 695, 700–4
  as interbank market, 704
  international banking facilitated by, 699
  monetary implications of, 704–6
  reducing appeal of, 706–7
  tiering of, 703
oil prices, rises in, 398, 400, 454, 466–67, 627, 628, 638, 715
oligopoly, banking and, 61–63
OPEC (Organization of Petroleum Exporting Countries), 466, 627, 715, 716
open-market operations, 140, 142, 408, 485–86, 500–504, 509
  advantages of, 504, 514
  bank reserves and, 239, 246, 248, 408, 491–92, 500–504, 509
  bills-only policy and, 622, 623
  defined, 182
  discounting and, 507
  dynamic vs. defensive, 503
  in Great Depression, 612, 613, 614, 617
  international, 663, 684–85
  see also Federal Open Market Committee
open markets, 138
operating (market) factors, 248, 503
"operation twist," 623
other adjustment credit, 505–6
output, 277, 278, 283, 287, 307–40, 400–401
  acceleration principle and, 349–51
  inflation and, 436–37, 439, 440, 442, 443, 455, 456
  investment in expansion of, 343
  measurement of, 308–10, 318
  monetary growth-rate rule and, 636, 638
  potential, 313–14, 317, 372, 374, 436
  potential, growth of, 341, 349, 377, 491
  potential, price levels and, 334–37, 351, 373
  potential, in St. Louis approach, 418–20
  short-run fluctuations in, 308, 367, 374–78
  see also Gross National Product; income

Patinkin, Don, see real balance approach to monetarism
Patman, Wright, 186
payments balance, 690–91
pegged exchange rates, 652, 653, 660, 666, 667, 714, 716, 720–24
  Bretton Woods system of, 661–65, 711
  central banks under, 684, 712–13
  collapse of (1970), 626–27
  decline of colonialism and, 717
  equilibrium under, 671
  gold standard and, 654–59
  problems in managing of, 723–24
  selection of currency for, 720
Penn Central, 10, 144, 626
pension funds, 98, 101, 107, 149, 155, 312, 469
  as bond market, 124, 146, 155
  growth of, 124, 125–26, 127
  life-cycle theory and, 359–60, 362, 363
Petty, William, 281
Phillips, A. W., 445
Phillips curves, 445–48, 450–54, 457, 458, 470–71, 528, 548
  defined, 445–46
  structural shifts in, 464, 472–77, 480–81
  trade unions and, 472, 473, 478–79
Pierce, James, 526
Pigou, A. C., 287
portfolios, 1, 19–20, 52–53, 286–90, 553
  balance of, 24–29, 33
  defined, 19
  of thrift institutions, 106–8, 118, 122, 155
Postal Service, U.S., 241

pound, British, 618, 672, 675, 681, 717, 727
 gold-exchange standard and, 660, 661
 gold standard and, 655–56
pound, Irish, 717
precautionary balances, 281–82, 284, 286, 287
present value, 291
 of future dividends, 152–53, 154
 of interest on bonds, 150–52
 investment considerations and, 342, 343–44, 345, 347, 348, 351–53, 391
press, Federal Reserve and, 186, 508–9
price controls, 7–8, 154, 620
 in 1970s, 184, 466, 470, 627, 628
 in World War II, 314, 465
prices and pricing, 20, 31, 443
 adjustments in, Keynesian theory and, 317–18, 331–37, 389
 aggregate-demand curves and, 331–37, 370–71, 372–73, 374, 436–37
 Brunner-Meltzer approach and, 407, 422, 423
 Chicago approach and, 386, 388–89, 390, 392, 395
 discriminatory, 120, 123–24, 202–5
 disequilibrium, inflation and, 436, 438–40, 489
 equilibrium, 7, 149, 334–35, 337, 367, 371–73, 374, 388, 436, 455
 exchange rate as, 679–81
 flexibility of, Keynesian theory and, 382, 388–89, 398
 gold-exchange standard and, 661
 gold standard and, 656–59
 in Great Depression, 608–11, 612, 616
 inflation and, 10, 153–54, 434, 437–45, 447–59, 464, 465–67, 471, 480–81, 489–90, 493, 713, 715
 labor costs and, 443–45
 monetary growth-rate rule and, 635
 money demand and, 275, 276–77, 283, 287, 296–98, 303, 374
 money supply as factor in, 215, 217, 303
 oil, 398, 400, 454, 466–67, 627, 628, 638, 715
 PPP theory and, 681
 quantity theory and, 380, 381–82
 real balance approach and, 410–17
 real vs. nominal money and, 276–77
 St. Louis approach and, 418, 419, 420
 stability of, as monetary policy goal, 173, 177, 487, 489–90, 492–93
primary markets, 138
prime rate, 90–91
private placements, 147
production, 94, 489
 in short run, 278, 319
 see also Gross National Product; output
product markets, see goods markets
profit maximization, 65, 121, 174, 677

in commercial banking, 35, 46, 72, 86–87, 99, 173, 225–26, 230–31, 233n
profits, 309, 310–12, 490, 591
 net, 311, 312
promissory notes, 84, 91, 139, 175, 605
 eligible paper, 604
 see also commercial paper
Proxmire, William, 495
public, nonbank:
 currency held by, 217–18, 243
 defined, 217
 size of bank reserves and, 238, 243
public interest:
 Federal Reserve banks as representatives of, 178–80, 188–89
 monetary policy and, 598–600
publicity and advice, as monetary policy tool, 516–17
purchasing-power-parity (PPP) theory, 681

quadratic utility function, 585
quantity theory, 271, 379–97, 546, 608, 619
 in analysis of long run, 272–73, 385n
 basic principles of, 380–82
 as counterrevolution, 379, 384
 criticism of, 383, 386–87, 392, 393–97, 407
 defined, 380
 Keynesian theory vs., 272–73, 379, 382
 recent developments of, 383–84
 relation of monetarism to, 380
 transmission process in, 549
 see also monetarism
quotas, 436, 470
 of IMF, 662–63

railroads, investment demand variations and, 375, 400
"random walk" theory of stock prices, 554n
rational expectations, theory of, 163–64, 591–97, 637, 638
 defined, 592–93
 impact of stabilization policy and, 595–97
 prediction of policy effects and, 597
 unemployment and, 593–95, 596–97
real balance approach, 404, 409–17
 assumptions of, 410–11, 415
 theorems established by, 410
 workings of model in, 412–15
real balance effects, 361, 369, 370, 642
real bills doctrine, 94, 604, 605, 606, 644
real estate, 5, 20, 106, 149
 liquidity of, 16, 22
 see also construction industry; mortgages
Real Estate Investment Trusts (REITs), 627
recessions, 134, 154, 307, 355, 477

fall of interest rates during, 537–39
monetarism in analysis of, 394, 396, 460, 547
money supply in, 3, 45, 266, 277, 301, 394, 547
role of inventory cycles in, 376
strength of monetary policy in combating of, 547–48
after World War I, 605–6, 608
since World War II, 376–77, 394, 454, 465–67, 596, 628, 630, 631
redlining, 68–69, 70
regression analysis, 273, 395, 404–7
regulation, *see* financial regulation
Regulation Q (Federal Reserve), 59–60, 68, 111, 264, 625, 626
alternative policies to, 124, 199–205
bank competition and, 116–24, 198, 199
costs of, 123–24
disadvantages of, 197–98
July 1979 ceilings and, 78, 79
mortgage market and, 121, 123, 551, 570
net earnings affected by, 121, 122
reform of, 75, 121–24, 197–205, 207–9, 572, 639
risk of failures and, 121–22
as selective control, 515, 516
regulations T, U, and G (Federal Reserve), stock-market credit and, 515
Regulation W, consumer credit and, 515
REITs (Real Estate Investment Trusts), 627
reluctance theory of borrowing, 507–8
rents, 10, 310–11, 312, 351–53
repurchase agreements (RPs; repos), 74–75, 80, 82, 93, 260
defined, 97, 240
reverse, 502–3
reserve base, 248–52, 561–62
adjusted or extended, 248–49, 533, 534
defined, 533
in Great Depression, 609, 611
as indicator, 537
as instrument, 533, 534
reserve requirements, 39, 43, 81–84, 94, 209, 509–14
changes in, 267, 508, 509–10, 578–79
controversies and reform proposals for, 510–14
elimination of, 510–11
in Federal Reserve Act, 604
for foreign banks, 700, 707
in Great Depression, 611, 616
lagged, 513–14
marginal, 629
offshore banking and, 701, 702, 705–7
one hundred percent, 219, 511–12
for time deposits, 83, 84, 239, 512–13
transaction accounts and, 82, 83–84, 239

reserves, bank, 33, 43, 45, 66, 173, 175, 215, 238–55
Brunner-Meltzer approach and, 408, 409
central banks in creation of, 176–77, 238, 239–42, 246
centralized, 604
changes in (1976–78), 247–48
in deposit contraction, 223–28
in deposit creation, 215, 218–23, 225–28
excess, 225–26, 227, 230–31, 235, 249, 534, 535, 538, 539, 547, 611, 612–13, 615–16
factors in decrease of, 238, 239, 243–48, 253
factors in increase of, 238, 239–43, 246–48, 253
free, 249, 534, 538–40
as indicators, 537
as instruments, 520, 521, 522, 533, 534, 535
as leakage from deposit creation process, 225–28
measures of, 238, 248–49
open-market operations and, 239, 246, 248, 408, 491–92, 500–504, 509
primary, as assets, 81–84, 99
pyramiding of, 38–39, 177
ratio of, 219–20, 222–23, 226, 230, 509, 510–11, 605, 606, 609
secondary, 84–85, 96, 99
unborrowed, 249, 533, 534
reserves, international, 654, 661, 665, 711–12, 714, 716, 724–30
determining value of, 725
dollar as, 727–29
future of gold in, 726–27
gold-exchange standard and, 660–61
gold standard and, 655–56
international institution as provider of, 729–30
system of, 724–26
resource allocation, 86, 166, 511, 643, 645
criteria for, 566–67
currency unification and, 717
efficiency of, 75, 121, 314, 580
monetary policy and, 485, 546–63
retirement savings, *see* pension funds
risks, 27–29, 41, 45–46
borrower's avoidance of, 24–26, 33
credit rationing and, 85–86
default, 25, 27, 29, 33
exchange, 677, 678–79, 686, 687, 722
holding companies and, 65
interest-rate, 25–26, 27, 33
in long-term market, 146, 165–66
money as investment and, 287–88, 289–90
in offshore banking, 703–4
pooling of, in financial intermediation, 24

risks (*continued*)
  purchasing-power, 25, 27
  "selling" rights to, 55
  in short-term market, 144–45
  of unregulated banking, 29–31, 33, 211
Robertson, D. H., 282
Rockefeller, David, 42
Rome, Treaty of (1957), 719
Roosevelt, Franklin Delano, 721
Rotterdam Bank, 698
RPs, *see* repurchase agreements
"rules of the game," 604, 657, 660, 664, 720
Rural Electrification Administration, 129

St. Louis approach to monetarism, 383–84, 398, 404–7, 418–20, 555, 559, 640
  exogenous variables in, 418
  predictive validity of, 420
St. Louis Federal Reserve Bank, 623
San Diego National Bank, failure of (1973), 51, 54, 627
saving:
  life cycle approach to, 358–63, 367
  see also IS curves
savings and loan associations, 15, 21, 75, 101, 102–7, 198, 624, 625
  financial reform and, 197, 200–203, 205, 207, 208–9
  government regulation of, 1, 31–33, 83, 116–17
  insurance of, 22, 52, 55
  mortgages made by, 106–7, 115–16, 118, 119, 148, 149, 155, 200–202
  near-money and, 16, 17
  origins of, 102–3
savings banks, 12, 21, 52, 75, 83, 101, 148, 198, 624
  commercial banks vs., 35
  financial reform and, 203, 209n
  near-money and, 16, 17
  origins of, 102–3
  portfolios of, 107–8, 155
  savings and loan associations compared to, 103–6, 107
savings deposits, 109–16, 284, 290
  characteristics of, as assets, 27–29
  in commercial banks, 12, 16, 111, 116, 120
  defined, 76–77
  erosion of distinctiveness of, 212, 259–64, 293
  money demand and, 300–301
  as near-money, 16–17
  passbook accounts, 77, 95–96, 119–20, 200
  see also certificates of deposit; M_2; *M-2*; Regulation Q
Schwartz, Anna, 383, 394–96, 606, 607–8, 611–18
Scott, Ira, 575

SDRs (special drawing rights certificates), 243, 245, 663–65, 712, 714
seasonal borrowing privilege, 505
SEC (Securities and Exchange Commission), 146–47
secondary markets:
  defined, 138
  for long-term securities, 147, 148
  for short-term securities, 139, 140, 141
Second Bank of the United States, 36–37
securities, 58, 81, 92, 178, 182–83, 189
  as bank assets, 84–85
  bank examiners and, 41–42
  debt management and, 648–50
  fixed-income, 98, 128
  long-term market for, 145–66
  quantity theory and, 381–82
  RPs for, 74–75, 93
  short-term market for, 133, 138–45, 147, 150, 154–66, 265, 284
  substitutability between foreign securities and, 651–52, 681
  see also bonds; certificates of deposit; commercial paper; Federal Open Market Committee; open-market operations
securities, government, 27–29, 45, 83, 103, 175, 176, 485, 619, 624
  increased bank holdings of, 52–53, 94, 96–97
  increase of reserves and, 239–41, 246, 248, 500–504
  as L, 263–64
  monetizing of debt and, 497
  as near-money, 16, 17
  of savings and loan associations, 106, 107
  see also Treasury bills
Securities and Exchange Commission (SEC), 146–47
selective controls, 500, 514–16
semi-rules, 640
Senate, U.S., 181, 189
separation theorem, 289–90, 299
share draft accounts, 75
Shaw, George Bernard, 152
Shultz, George, 186
silver, 11, 13, 277–78, 655
Singapore, 264
  as monetary haven, 695, 699, 702
single-house market, investment in, 352, 354
six-month certificates, 109, 120, 129, 150, 202–3, 208
Smithsonian Agreement (1972), 666–67, 712
social classes:
  easy-money position and, 644, 645
  income distribution by, 490, 644
  insurance requirements and, 124
  saving patterns and, 95–96, 103, 362
  types of money and, 11

social security, 311, 312, 322, 469, 719
Social Security System, 126, 362
Solow, Robert, 426
Soviet Union, 466, 720
special drawing rights certificates (SDRs), 243, 245, 663–65, 712, 714
special interest groups, monetary policy influenced by, 598, 599
specialization, 91, 712
  in long-term capital markets, 154–57
speculation, 94, 162, 375, 400
  defined, 677
  Federal Reserve opposition to, 604, 605, 607
  international finance and, 677, 721–22
  in stocks, 92, 375, 400, 515, 607
speculative demand for money, see liquidity preference theory of demand
spot-exchange rates, 681–82, 683, 722
  forward-exchange rates in relation to, 652, 675–79
spot transactions, 675
stagflation, 436, 608, 628
Standard & Poors index, 128
state banks, 86
  banknotes issued by, 36, 37
  branches of, 60–61, 64
  chartering of, 29, 36, 37–38, 40–41, 69, 70, 103, 210, 211–12
  defined, 40
  growth of, 36, 39
  as member banks, 40, 43, 70
  reserves of, 43, 82–83
state governments, 265, 311
  financial institutions examined by, 42, 106
  resource allocation and, 573–74
  savings and loan associations chartered by, 106, 201, 208
  surpluses and deficits in, 134, 135, 140, 141
  welfare programs of, 477
statistical techniques in economics, 273, 302, 389, 395, 404–7, 488, 585–87, 649
stock-market crash (1929), 608, 611, 618
stock-market credit, 515
  see also Regulations G, T, U
stock, 10, 17, 27–29, 101, 108, 126, 407–8
  in banks, 44, 46, 52, 64
  cyclical, 289
  in deficit financing, 136–37
  dividends on, 137, 147–48, 152–53, 189, 282, 292, 309, 311, 312
  of Federal Reserve banks, 188, 189, 193
  investment value of, 152–53
  long-term market for, 138, 145, 147–48, 152–54, 155
  monetary policy and prices of, 554

money as, 5
  mutual funds and, 128–29, 155, 212, 260, 293
  speculation in, 92, 375, 400, 515, 607
Strong, Benjamin, 613
Suez crisis (1956), IMF and, 662–63
supply, aggregate, see aggregate supply
supply, elasticity, see elasticity of supply
supply and demand, 94, 374, 652
  for apartments, 352–53
  barter and, 7–8
  for gold, 655, 658, 659
  in labor markets, 411–12, 473–74, 475–76, 487n, 718
  mortgages and, 91–92, 149, 355
  term structure and, 165–66
supply curves:
  aggregate, 422, 437–42
  savings deposits and, 114
supply of money, see money supply
supply shocks (1973–74), 628
Supreme Court, U.S., 208, 219, 266, 495
surpluses, 140–43, 189, 285
  balance-of-payments, 657, 660, 664, 665, 685, 690–91, 704n, 705
  defined, 134
  labor, 473–74, 475–76
  trade, defined, 689
sweating (of coins), defined, 12
Sweden, 8
  international finance and, 720–21
Switzerland:
  international finance and, 664, 714, 720
  monetary policy in, 485–86
syndicates, defined, 146

targets and instruments approach, 520–36
  alternatives to, 535–36
targets and target variables, 520–32, 583, 624
  attainability criterion for, 522, 525–28
  criteria for, 522, 523–32
  defined, 520
  indicators relation to, 537
  measurability criterion for, 522, 523–25, 532
  potential, 522–32
  proximate, see instruments
  relatedness criterion for, 522, 528–32
tariffs, 436, 470, 661, 663, 666, 719
  GATT and, 662
tax credits, 346, 370
taxes, 29, 37, 106, 134, 184, 496, 719
  advantages, 87, 108, 126, 154, 155, 345, 362
  corporate income, 154, 309, 311, 312, 345–46, 370, 443
  evasion of, 8, 488
  excise, 311, 442–43, 469, 643
  inflation and, 465, 466, 469, 489, 635
  investment affected by, 345–46, 349

taxes (*continued*)
  in Keynesian theory, 310–11, 322, 335,
    337, 383, 392
  personal income, 94, 108, 137, 154,
    201*n*, 203*n*, 311, 322
  property, 282, 286, 291, 311, 351–52,
    442–43, 469
  reserve requirements as, 82, 701
  sales, 311, 442–43
  social security, 312
  see also fiscal policy
technological change, 307, 313, 314, 336,
    341, 374
  financial reform and, 197, 212
  gold standard and, 657
  as investment consideration, 342–43,
    344, 399
  nonmonetary instability and, 374, 375
Temin, Peter, 616–18
term structure, 157–66, 301–2, 303
thrift institutions, 101–16, 149, 239, 267,
    631
  accounting conventions applied to, 122
  commercial banks compared to, 102,
    212, 259, 260
  competition of, 108–9, 111–13, 116–
    24, 198, 199, 205–6
  deposit growth in, 109–11
  deposit-rate rise and, 113–16
  deposit rates set by, 111–13
  discounting by, 508
  disintermediation and, *see* disinter-
    mediation
  evolution of, 102–6
  financial reform and, 199–206, 207,
    208–9, 212
  investment portfolios of, 106–8
  monetary policy weakened by, 551–52
  mortgages and, *see* mortgages
  see also credit unions; savings and loan
    associations; savings banks
time-deposit ratio (t), 231, 235, 250
time deposits, 27–29, 35, 76–78, 99, 284,
    300–301
  CDs, *see* certificates of deposit
  defined, 259*n*
  definitions of money and, 12, 16, 17,
    257
  demand deposits converted to, 227–28
  interest rates on, *see* Regulation Q
  reserve requirements for, 83, 84, 239,
    512–13
  see also M-2; savings deposits
Tobin, James, 288–90, 331, 409
trade, 278
  balance, 689, 714
  in mercantilism, 277–78, 715
  see also exchange; foreign-exchange
    markets; foreign-exchange rates
trade acceptances, 80
trade credit, 552
trade surplus, 689
transactions accounts, 257

reserve requirements and, 82, 83–84,
    239
  see also NOW accounts
transactions costs, 16, 19, 97
  in financial intermediation, 21, 22
  international, 653, 673, 676, 678, 680,
    686–87, 699
  money and, 9–10, 11, 17
transactions demand, 279–82, 284–86,
    287, 291, 300, 382*n*
transactions velocity of money, defined,
    283
transmission process, 546–63
  in Brunner-Meltzer approach, 397,
    407–9, 421–23
  in Chicago approach, 391–92, 397
  defined, 391
  in Keynesian theory, 391–92, 407, 420,
    549–59
  in quantity theory, 549
Treasury, U.S., 106, 265
  bonds sold by, 145, 147, 150
  Comptroller of the Currency in, 37, 39,
    41, 42, 46, 55, 70, 80, 212
  FDIC and, 52
  federal credit agencies and, 129–30
  Federal Reserve and, 82, 176, 189, 191,
    245, 485, 496–97, 605, 620–21
  gold sales suspended by (1971), 666
  monetary policy and, 245, 485, 648–50
  size of bank reserves and, 238, 241,
    242–43, 245, 246–47, 248
  as supplier of currency, 13, 217–18
Treasury bills, 97, 108, 117, 118, 126,
    129, 136, 284, 374, 502
  bills-only policy and, 622, 623
  interest rates and, 109, 143–45, 200,
    201, 290, 291, 300, 355, 506, 509,
    534, 629
  in international finance, 660, 670, 679
  short-term market for, 138, 139, 140,
    142–43, 144–45
  six-month certificates and, 109, 120,
    202, 203
trust funds, 49, 98, 126, 155, 209
truth-in-lending regulations, 67, 209

unemployment, 3, 51, 485, 661
  frictional, 473, 474, 475, 480, 487–88
  in Great Depression, 608–9
  inflation and, 314, 430, 434, 443, 445–
    59, 466, 468, 470–81, 489
  Keynesian theory and, 307, 313–14,
    322, 363, 397, 399, 401, 415, 430,
    431
  monetarism and, 397, 399, 401, 414,
    415, 418, 419, 430
  money supply and, 3, 14, 217
  nonaccelerating inflation rate of
    (NAIRU), 430, 451–53, 455, 457,
    458, 468, 471, 481
  Phillips curves and, 445–48, 450–54,
    458, 472–77, 478–79

rational expectations and, 593–95, 596–97
structural, 473, 474
temporary layoffs and, 474, 475, 477
youth, 474, 475–76
unemployment compensation, 472, 476–77, 488
unions, see labor unions
United Nations, 245
United States:
  balance of payments and, 66, 486, 516, 623, 626, 651, 660, 665–66, 691, 704n, 725–26, 728
  decline in economic power of, 666–67, 713
  as international banker, 727–29
  rise in economic power of, 654, 661, 665, 713, 715
  as unified currency area, 717, 718–19
usury laws, 67, 70, 209, 572

VA (Veterans Administration), 91, 571
valuation:
  in long-term markets, 150–54
  of wealth, 166–70
value added, 309, 311, 312, 318
variance, 585–87, 588
vault cash, 81
  see also coins; currency
Veterans Administration (VA), 91, 571
"vicious and virtuous circles," 721
Vietnam War, 117, 624
  economic instability and, 375, 377
  inflation and, 466, 468, 469
Viner, Jacob, 639
Volcker, Paul, 630

wage-price spirals, 434, 443–54, 468, 471
  checking of, 457
wages, 126, 310–11, 312, 399, 438
  controls on, 314, 627, 628
  determination of, 445
  inflation and, 434, 435, 438–39, 440, 442–54, 464, 465–67, 469, 470–80
  minimum, 472, 475–76, 477, 595

monetarism and, 410, 411, 414, 415, 418, 423
rational expectations and, 594–95
real vs. money, 448–50
Wales, barter used in, 8n
Wall Street Journal, 238–39
Warburton, Clark, 383, 611, 612
wealth, 231
  defined, 291
  Keynesian theory and, 319, 358, 360–61, 362, 367–71, 552–53, 555, 557
  monetarism and, 369, 410, 411, 413, 414, 416–17
  money as, 4–5, 9–11, 16, 17, 257, 277, 286–90
  money demand and, 286–90, 291–92
  real vs. nominal, 169–70
  valuation of, 166–70
welfare, 312, 472, 477, 719
West Germany, see Germany, West
Wicker, Elmus, 606, 611, 612–13
Wilson, Woodrow, 39, 177
women:
  in banking, 69, 180
  credit discrimination and, 68, 69, 70
  in labor force, 474, 475, 476
  welfare payments and, 477
World Bank, 661
World War I, 433
  Federal Reserve in, 605, 618, 619
  international finance and, 659, 727
World War II, 135, 314, 375, 727
  Federal Reserve in, 605, 618–20
  government securities and, 53, 94
  world economy after, 218, 383, 435–37, 464, 465

yen, Japanese, 664, 712, 714
yield, 155–66
  as characteristic of assets, 27–29, 72
  explicit, 10, 17, 232
  holding-period, 161–62
  implicit, 10n, 232
  portfolio equilibrium and, 553, 554
  term structure and, 157–66
  see also interest rates; marginal yield